Library of
Davidson College

MEMOIRS

OF THE

AMERICAN ACADEMY IN ROME

Volume XXXIX

AMERICAN ACADEMY IN ROME
1994

COSA:
THE LAMPS

COSA:
THE LAMPS

BY

CLEO RICKMAN FITCH AND NORMA WYNICK GOLDMAN

DRAWINGS BY

CLEO RICKMAN FITCH

PUBLISHED FOR THE AMERICAN ACADEMY IN ROME
by
The University of Michigan Press
Ann Arbor, Michigan
1994

Copyright © 1994 American Academy in Rome
All rights reserved
Published in the United States of America by
The University of Michigan Press
Manufactured in the United States of America
⊗ Printed on acid-free paper

1997 1996 1995 1994   4 3 2 1

A CIP catalogue record for this book is available from the British Library.

Library of Congress Cataloging-in-Publication Data

Fitch, Cleo Rickman.
    Cosa, the lamps / by Cleo Rickman Fitch and Norma Wynick Goldman ; drawings by Cleo Rickman Fitch.
       p.   cm. — (Memoirs of the American Academy in Rome ; v. 39)
    Includes bibliographical references.
    ISBN 0-472-10518-3 (alk. paper)
    1. Lamps, Roman—Italy—Cosa—Catalogs. 2. Pottery, Roman—Italy—Cosa—Expertising—Catalogs. I. Goldman, Norma, 1922–
II. Title. III. Series.
DG12.A575 vol. 39
[NK 4680]
700 s—dc20   93-48547
[738.3′82′09375]   CIP

Dedicated to Frank Edward Brown and James Marston Fitch
without whose support and encouragement
this book would never have been written.

THE COSA PUBLICATIONS

Cosa I, History and Topography, by Frank E. Brown, *MAAR* 20 (1951) 5–113
La Centuriazione di Cosa, by Ferdinando Castagnoli, *MAAR* 24 (1956) 149–65
Cosa: Black-Glaze Pottery, by Doris Mae Taylor, *MAAR* 25 (1957) 65–193
Cosa II, The Temples of the Arx, by Frank E. Brown, Emeline Hill Richardson, and L. Richardson, jr, MAAR 26 (1960)
The Roman Thin Walled Pottery from Cosa (1948–54), by Maria Teresa Marabini Moevs, *MAAR* 32 (1973)
Cosa: The Utilitarian Pottery, by Stephen L. Dyson, *MAAR* 33 (1976)
Cosa: The Coins, by T. V. Buttrey, *MAAR* 34 (1980) 11–153
Italo-Megarian Ware at Cosa, by Maria Teresa Marabini Moevs, *MAAR* 34 (1980) 161–227
Aco in Northern Etruria: The Workshop of Cusonius at Cosa, by Maria Teresa Marabini Moevs, *MAAR* 34 (1980) 231–80
Cosa IV: The Houses, by Vincent J. Bruno and Russell T. Scott, *MAAR* 38 (1993)

The following studies of archaeological material from the excavations at Cosa are in progress and will be published in due course: *Cosa III: The Buildings of the Forum* by Frank Edward Brown, Emeline Hill Richardson, and L. Richardson, jr, *Inscriptions on Stone and Brick-Stamps* by Edward Jan Bace, *The Sculpture and Furniture in Stone* by Jacquelyn Collins-Clinton, *The Glass* by David Grose, *The Arretine Pottery, The Italic and Gaulish Sigillata* by Maria Teresa Marabini Moevs, *Black-Glaze Pottery Studies* by Ann Reynolds Scott, *The Storage Ware* by Elizabeth Lyding Will, and supplementary studies of the Arx by Russell T. Scott, Elizabeth Fentress, Michelle Hobart, and Teresa Clay.

FROM OTHER PUBLISHERS:

A Late Antique Shrine of Liber Pater at Cosa, by Jacquelyn Collins-Clinton (Etudes préliminaires aux religions orientales dans l'empire romain, edited by M. J. Vermaseren, volume 64), Leiden (E. J. Brill) 1977
Cosa, The Making of a Roman Town, by Frank E. Brown (Jerome Lectures, 13th series), Ann Arbor, Michigan (The University of Michigan Press) 1980
The Roman Port and Fishery of Cosa, by Anna Marguerite McCann, Joanne Bourgeois, Elaine K. Gazda, John Peter Oleson, and Elizabeth Lyding Will, Princeton, New Jersey (Princeton University Press) 1987

TABLE OF CONTENTS

List of Illustrations	xiii
Preface	xvii
Introduction	3
Chronology	9

THE CATALOGUE

WHEELMADE LAMPS

Introduction to Wheelmade Lamps (Catalogue Numbers 1–182)	19
1. Truncated-Cone Type Lamps (Catalogue Numbers 1–45)	23
2. Doughnut Type Lamps (Catalogue Numbers 46–132)	27
3. Central-Tube Type Lamps (Catalogue Numbers 133–143)	35
4. Watch Type Lamps (Catalogue Numbers 144–150)	37
5. Esquiline Type Lamps (Catalogue Numbers 151–182)	39

MOLDMADE LAMPS

Introduction to Moldmade Lamps (Catalogue Numbers 183–1089)	45
6. Imported Delphiniform Lamps (Catalogue Numbers 183–204)	47
a. Lamps with Radiating Grooves (Catalogue Numbers 183–187)	49
b. Lamps Decorated with Looped Vines with Flowers Between the Loops (Catalogue Numbers 188–191)	49
c. Lamps with Concentric Bead-and-Reel Moldings Alternating with Bands of Stemmed Leaves and Buds and Leaves and Flowers (Catalogue Numbers 192–198)	50
d. Lamp Decorated with a Garland Tied with a Ribbon (Catalogue Number 199)	51
e. Fragments of Delphiniform Lamps with No Decoration Preserved (Catalogue Numbers 200–204)	51
7. Late Roman Republican Lamps with Hellenistic Features (Catalogue Numbers 205–323)	53
a. Lamps with One Ear, Cup-Shaped Oil Reservoir and Roman Nozzle (Catalogue Numbers 205–219)	53

      b. Lamps with One Ear and Roman Nozzle, (*Warzenlampen*) (Raised-Dots Lamps)
         (Catalogue Numbers 220–270)   55
      c. Lamps with Circular Raised Nozzles (Catalogue Numbers 271–278)   64
      d. Lamps with Nozzles Ending in a Triangle (Catalogue Numbers 279, 280)   68
      e. Lamps with Swallowtail Ears (Catalogue Numbers 281–303)   69
      f. Lamps with a Biconical Body and Roman Nozzle (Catalogue Numbers 304–307)   73
      g. Lamps with a Wide Decorated Discus and a Roman Nozzle
         but without Ears (Catalogue Numbers 308–316)   74
      h. Lamps with Evolving or Proto-Volutes   76
      i. Miscellaneous Late Republican Lamps (Catalogue Numbers 317–323)   76
8. Birds'-Heads Lamps (*Vogelkopflampen*) (Catalogue Numbers 324–344)   79
9. Triangular Nozzle Lamps (Catalogue Numbers 345–511)   84
      a. Group A1: Triangular Nozzle Lamps with Narrow Nozzle, Widespread,
         Narrow Volutes, and a Channel (Catalogue Numbers 345–376)   86
      b. Group A2: Triangular Nozzle Lamps with Narrow Nozzle and Widespread,
         Narrow Volutes, without a Channel (Catalogue Numbers 377–451)   89
      c. Group B1: Triangular Nozzle Lamps with Wide Nozzle, Thick, Short
         Volutes, and a Channel (Catalogue Numbers 452–454)   99
      d. Group B2: Triangular Nozzle Lamps with Wide Nozzle and Thick, Short
         Volutes, without a Channel (Catalogue Numbers 455–493)   99
      e. Group C: Triangular Nozzle Lamps with Very Wide Nozzle and Thick, Short
         Volutes (Catalogue Numbers 494–511)   104
10. Lamps with a Long, Slender, Voluted Nozzle with a Rounded End, and
    Decorated Discus (Catalogue Numbers 512–521)   109
11. Lamps with Pouter Pigeon Voluted Nozzles (Catalogue Numbers 522–598)   111
      a. Pouter Pigeon Lamps with a Bead Molding for Rim Outer Border
         (Catalogue Numbers 522–524)   113
      b. Pouter Pigeon Lamps with a Flat Band or Fillet for Rim Outer Border
         (Catalogue Numbers 525–541)   115
      c. Pouter Pigeon Lamps with Narrow Beveled Shoulders (Catalogue Numbers 542–558)   118
      d. Probable Pouter Pigeon Lamps (Catalogue Numbers 559–598)   119
12. Decorated Discus Fragments from Lamps with Triangular, Rounded, or
    Pouter Pigeon Nozzles (Catalogue Numbers 599–652)   124
13. Lamps with Simple Volutes with Only One Scroll (Catalogue Numbers 653–662)   130
14. Lamps with Volutes in New Positions (Catalogue Numbers 663–670)   133
15. Lamps with Long, Voluted Nozzles and Heat Shields (Catalogue Numbers 671–735)   135
      a. Lamps with Two or More Nozzles and a Heat Shield (Catalogue Numbers 671–693)   137
      b. Lamps with One Nozzle and a Heat Shield (Catalogue Numbers 694–705)   141
      c. Triangular Heat Shields (Catalogue Numbers 706–732)   144
      d. Lunate Heat Shields   147
      e. Heat Shields without Known Parallels at Cosa (Catalogue Numbers 733–735)   148
16. Fat Lamps, or Lamps with Short, Rounded, Unvoluted Nozzles (Catalogue Numbers 736–983)   149
      a. Shoulders Decorated with a Band of Ovules (Catalogue Numbers 736–772)   151
      b. Decorated Disci and Plain Shoulders (Catalogue Numbers 773–814)   154
      c. Undecorated Disci and Shoulders (Catalogue Numbers 815–823)   160

d. Shoulders Decorated with Toothed Leaves Obliquely Set (Catalogue Number 824)	161
e. Shoulders Decorated with Lanceolate Leaves with Double Outlines Obliquely Set (Catalogue Numbers 825, 826)	162
f. Shoulders Decorated with Lanceolate Leaves Obliquely Set (Catalogue Number 827)	162
g. Shoulders Decorated with a Band of Hearts, Points Outward (Catalogue Numbers 828, 829)	163
h. Shoulders Decorated with a Band of Hearts, Points Inward (Catalogue Number 830)	163
i. Shoulders Decorated with Raised Dots (Catalogue Numbers 830A–847)	164
j. Shoulders Decorated with Looped Vines, with Grapes and Leaves Within Loops (Catalogue Numbers 848–861)	166
k. Shoulder Decorated with a Wreath of Olive Leaves and Olives, with a Circular Boss around the Central Filling Hole (Catalogue Numbers 862–865)	168
l. Shoulder Decorated with a Wreath of Olive Leaves in Clusters of Three (Catalogue Number 866)	168
m. Shoulder Decorated with a Band of Radiating Grooves Terminating in Small Circular Punches (Catalogue Numbers 867, 868)	169
n. Shoulder Decorated with a Band of Rectangles and Raised Dots (Catalogue Number 869)	170
o. Shoulder Decorated with Olives and Olive Leaves Bound in Threes, with Discus Relief (Catalogue Numbers 870–899)	170
p. Shoulder Decorated with Alternating Bunches of Grapes and Leaves, Cut from Vine (Catalogue Numbers 900–906)	173
q. Shoulder Decorated with a Band of Lotus Buds and Palmettes (Catalogue Number 907)	174
r. Shoulder Decorated with Looped Vines with Grapes or a Leaf in Alternate Loops Enclosed by Thread Moldings (Catalogue Number 908)	175
s. Shoulder Decorated with a Crude Zigzag Design (Catalogue Number 909)	175
t. Disci Unassociated with Other Elements (Catalogue Numbers 910–932)	176
u. Plain Shoulder and Discus with a Vitreous Green Glaze (Catalogue Number 933)	178
v. Fragments of Bases with Signatures (Catalogue Numbers 934–983)	178
17. Deep-Bodied Lamp with a Right-Angled Nozzle (Catalogue Number 984)	184
18. Plastic Lamps (Catalogue Numbers 985–986)	185
19. Lamps with "Inchworm Ears" and a Channel (Catalogue Numbers 987–998)	187
20. Lamp with Ovoid Discus and Base (Catalogue Number 999)	191
21. Wall Lamps (Catalogue Numbers 1000–1002)	192
22. Factory Lamps (*Firmalampen*) (Catalogue Numbers 1003–1041)	194
a. Factory Lamps from North Italy (Catalogue Numbers 1003–1014)	196
b. Roman Copies of Factory Lamps from Central Italy (Catalogue Numbers 1015–1039)	197
c. Factory Lamps with a Short Nozzle (*Kurzform*) (Catalogue Numbers 1040, 1041)	201
23. Pinecone Lamps (Catalogue Numbers 1042–1053)	202
24. Fat Globular (*Kugelform*) Lamps (Catalogue Numbers 1054–1063)	205
25. North African Lamps (Catalogue Numbers 1064–1077)	207
26. Roman Copies of North African Lamps (Catalogue Numbers 1078–1089)	214
27. THREE FOREIGN LAMPS	**218**
a. Athenian Lamp by Ariston (Catalogue Number 1090)	218
b. Corinthian Lamp by Loukios (Catalogue Number 1091)	219
c. Split-Handled Lamp, Probably from Cnidus (Catalogue Number 1092)	220

28. Iron Lamp (Catalogue Number 1093) 222

29. The Cosan Lantern (Catalogue Number 1094) 223

Note on the Cosan Lamp Marks and Signatures 225
Plates I–IX 235
Concordance 245
Glossary 252
Abbreviations and Selected Bibliography 256

LIST OF ILLUSTRATIONS

FIGURES

Figure 1. Map of Italy, showing location of Cosa	2
Figure 2. Plan of Cosa, after F. E. Brown	4
Figure 3. The development of the oil lamp	6
Figure 4. Chart of the Cosan molded lamp sequence	10
Figure 5. Chart of the Cosan molded lamp sequence (cont.)	11
Figure 6. North corner of the Forum between 25/20 B.C. and A.D. 40/45, after F. E. Brown	15
Figure 7. Truncated-Cone Type Lamps, scale 1:2	23
Figure 8. Doughnut Type Lamps, scale 1:2	27
Figure 9. Central-Tube Type Lamps, scale 1:2	35
Figure 10. Watch Type Lamps, scale 1:2	37
Figure 11. Esquiline Type Lamps, scale 1:2	39
Figure 12. Molded lamp construction	44
Figure 13. Delphiniform Lamps, imported, scale 1:2	48
Figure 14. Delphiniform Lamps, imported, scale 1:2	48
Figure 15. Delphiniform Lamps, imported, scale 1:2	48
Figure 16. Delphiniform Lamps, imported, scale 1:2	48
Figure 17. Delphiniform Lamps, imported, scale 1:2	48
Figure 18. Delphiniform Lamps, imported, scale 1:2	48
Figure 19. Lamps with one ear, cup-shaped oil reservoir, and Roman nozzle, scale 1:2	52
Figure 20. Lamps with one ear, cup-shaped oil reservoir, and Roman nozzle, scale 1:2	52
Figure 21. Lamps with one ear, cup-shaped oil reservoir, and Roman nozzle, scale 1:2	52
Figure 22. Lamps with one ear, cup-shaped oil reservoir, and Roman nozzle, scale 1:2	52
Figures 23–26. Lamps with one ear and Roman nozzle: *Warzenlampen* (Raised-Dots Lamps), scale 1:2	56
Figures 27–30. Lamps with one ear and Roman nozzle: *Warzenlampen* (Raised-Dots Lamps), different designs, scale 1:2	57
Figure 31. Lamps with circular raised nozzles, scale 1:2	65

Figure 32. Lamps with circular raised nozzles, scale 1:2 — 65
Figure 33. Lamps with circular raised nozzles, scale 1:2 — 65
Figure 34. Lamps with circular raised nozzles, scale 1:2 — 65
Figure 35. Lamps with circular raised nozzles, scale 1:2 — 66
Figure 36. Lamps with circular raised nozzles, scale 1:2 — 66
Figure 37. Lamps with circular raised nozzles, scale 1:2 — 66
Figure 38. Lamps with nozzles ending in a triangle, scale 1:2 — 68
Figure 39. Lamps with nozzles ending in a triangle, scale 1:2 — 68
Figure 40. Lamps with swallowtail ears, scale 1:2 — 70
Figure 41. Lamps with swallowtail ears, scale 1:2 — 70
Figure 42. Lamps with swallowtail ears, scale 1:2 — 70
Figure 43. Lamps with swallowtail ears, scale 1:2 — 71
Figure 44. Lamps with swallowtail ears, scale 1:2 — 71
Figure 45. Lamps with a biconical body and Roman nozzle, scale 1:2 — 74
Figure 46. Lamps with a biconical body and Roman nozzle, scale 1:2 — 74
Figure 47. Lamps with a biconical body and Roman nozzle, scale 1:2 — 74
Figure 48. Lamps with a wide, decorated discus and a Roman nozzle without ears, scale 1:2 — 75
Figure 49. Lamps with a wide, decorated discus and a Roman nozzle without ears, scale 1:2 — 75
Figure 50. Lamps with evolving or proto-volutes, scale 1:2 — 77
Figure 51. Lamps with evolving or proto-volutes, scale 1:2 — 77
Figure 52. Lamps with evolving or proto-volutes, scale 1:2 — 77
Figure 53. Birds'-heads Lamps (*Vogelkopflampen*), full scale — 80
Figure 54. Triangular Nozzle Lamps A1 and rim profiles, full scale — 85
Figure 55. Triangular Nozzle Lamps A2 and rim profiles, full scale — 90
Figure 56. Additional rim profiles of Triangular Nozzle Lamps A2, full scale — 91
Figure 57. Variant form of Triangular Nozzle Lamp A2, full scale — 97
Figure 58. Triangular Nozzle Lamps B1 and rim profiles, full scale — 98
Figure 59. Triangular Nozzle Lamps B2 and rim profiles, full scale — 100
Figure 60. Variant form of Triangular Nozzle Lamp B2, full scale — 101
Figure 61. Triangular Nozzle Lamps C and rim profiles, full scale — 105
Figure 62. Lamps with a long, slender, voluted nozzle with a rounded end, and decorated discus, full scale — 108
Figure 63. Lamps with Pouter Pigeon voluted nozzles and rim profiles, full scale — 112
Figure 64 Additional Pouter Pigeon Lamp, full scale — 113
Figure 65. Additional Pouter Pigeon Lamp, scale 1:2 — 114
Figure 66. Additional Pouter Pigeon Lamp, full scale — 117
Figure 67. Lamp with simple volutes with only one scroll, scale 1:2 — 131
Figure 68. Lamp with simple volutes with only one scroll, scale 1:2 — 131
Figure 69. Lamps with volutes in new positions, scale 1:2 — 133
Figure 70. Lamps with a long, voluted nozzle and a heat shield showing the two parts before joining in the mold — 136
Figure 71. Lamp with seven long, voluted nozzles and a heat shield, scale 1:2 — 138
Figure 72. Lamp with two long, voluted nozzles and a heat shield, with rim profiles, full scale — 139
Figure 73. Lamps with one long, voluted nozzle and a heat shield, with rim profiles, full scale — 142
Figure 74. Triangular heat shields, scale 1:2 — 145
Figure 75. Triangular heat shields, scale 1:2 — 146

Figure 76. Lunate heat shields, scale 1:2 — 147
Figure 77. Heat shields without known parallels at Cosa, scale 1:2 — 148
Figure 78. Fat Lamps: Nozzle classification, reduced — 150
Figure 79. Fat Lamps: a. Shoulders decorated with a band of ovules, scale 1:2 — 151
Figure 80. Fat Lamps: b. Decorated discus and plain shoulder, scale 1:2 — 155
Figure 81. Fat Lamps: b. Decorated discus and plain shoulder, scale 1:2 — 155
Figure 82. Fat Lamps: b. Decorated discus and plain shoulder, scale 1:2 — 155
Figure 83. Fat Lamps: c. Undecorated discus and shoulder, scale 1:2 — 161
Figure 84. Fat Lamps: d. Shoulders decorated with toothed leaves obliquely set, scale 1:2 — 161
Figure 85. Fat Lamps: e. Shoulders decorated with lanceolate leaves with double outlines obliquely set, scale 1:2 — 162
Figure 86. Fat Lamps: f. Shoulders decorated with lanceolate leaves obliquely set, scale 1:2 — 162
Figure 87. Fat Lamps: g. Shoulders decorated with a band of hearts, points outward, scale 1:2 — 163
Figure 88. Fat Lamps: h. Shoulders decorated with a band of hearts, points inward, scale 1:2 — 163
Figure 89. Fat Lamps: i. Shoulders decorated with raised dots, scale 1:2 — 164
Figure 90. Fat Lamps: i. Shoulders decorated with raised dots separated from the discus by a bead-and-reel molding, scale 1:2 — 165
Figure 91. Fat Lamps: j. Shoulders decorated with looped vines, with grapes and leaves within loops, scale 1:2 — 167
Figure 92. Fat Lamps: k. Shoulder decorated with a wreath of olive leaves and olives; with a circular boss around the central filling hole, scale 1:2 — 168
Figure 93. Fat Lamps: l. Shoulder decorated with a wreath of olive leaves in clusters of three, scale 1:2 — 169
Figure 94. Fat Lamps: m. Shoulder decorated with a band of radiating grooves, scale 1:2 — 169
Figure 95. Fat Lamps: n. Shoulder decorated with a band of rectangles and raised dots, scale 1:2 — 170
Figure 96. Fat Lamps: o. Shoulder decorated with olives and olive leaves bound in threes, with discus relief, scale 1:2 — 170
Figure 97. Fat Lamps: p. Shoulder decorated with alternating cut bunches of grapes and leaves, scale 1:2 — 174
Figure 98. Fat Lamps: q. Shoulder decorated with a band of lotus buds and palmettes, scale 1:2 — 175
Figure 99. Fat Lamps: r. Shoulder decorated with looped vines with grapes or a leaf in alternate loops enclosed by a thread moldings, scale 1:2 — 175
Figure 100. Fat Lamp: s. Shoulder decorated with a crude zigzag design, scale 1:2 — 176
Figure 101. Fat Lamp: t. Plain shoulder and discus with a vitreous green glaze, scale 1:2 — 178
Figure 102. Deep-bodied lamp with a right-angled nozzle, scale 1:2 — 184
Figure 103. Plastic lamp in the form of a bull's head, scale 1:2 — 185
Figure 104. Plastic lamp in the form of a barbarian's head, full scale — 186
Figure 105. Lamps with "inchworm ears" and a channel from the discus toward the wick hole — 188
Figure 106. Lamp with ovoid discus and base, scale 1:2 — 190
Figure 107. Wall Lamps, scale 1:2 — 192
Figure 108. Factory Lamps from north Italy, scale 1:2 — 196
Figure 109. Roman copies of Factory Lamps from central Italy, scale 1:2 — 198
Figure 110. Factory Lamps with a short nozzle (*Kurzform*), scale 1:2 — 201
Figure 111. Pinecone Lamps, scale 1:2 — 203
Figure 112. Fat Globular Lamps, scale 1:2 — 205
Figure 113. Fat Globular Lamps, scale 1:2 — 206
Figure 114. North African Lamps, scale 1:2 — 208

Figure 115. North African Lamps, scale 1:2 — 208
Figure 116. North African Lamps, scale 1:2 — 208
Figure 117. North African Lamps, scale 1:2 — 208
Figure 118. North African Lamps, scale 1:2 — 209
Figure 119. North African Lamps, scale 1:2 — 209
Figure 120. North African Lamps, scale 1:2 — 209
Figure 121. North African Lamps, scale 1:2 — 209
Figure 122. North African Lamps, scale 1:2 — 210
Figure 123. North African Lamps, scale 1:2 — 210
Figure 124. North African Lamps, scale 1:2 — 210
Figure 125. Roman copies of North African Lamps, scale 1:2 — 215
Figure 126. Roman copies of North African Lamps, scale 1:2 — 215
Figure 127. Roman copies of North African Lamps, scale 1:2 — 215
Figure 128. Roman copies of North African Lamps, scale 1:2 — 215
Figure 129. Roman copies of North African Lamps, scale 1:2 — 216
Figure 130. Roman copies of North African Lamps, scale 1:2 — 216
Figure 131. Athenian Lamp by Ariston, scale 1:2 — 218
Figure 132. Corinthian Lamp by Loukios, scale 1:2 — 219
Figure 133. Split-handled lamp probably from Cnidus, scale 1:2 — 220
Figure 134. The Cosan Lantern, scale 1:2 — 224
Figure 135. Inscriptions and marks made before and after firing, full scale — 226
Figure 136. Marks from Roman Republican wheelmade and moldmade lamps, full scale — 227
Figure 137. Incised and stamped marks, late Republican, full scale — 228
Figure 138. Marks and makers' signatures in relief, full scale — 229
Figure 139. Makers' names and initials, full scale — 230
Figure 140. Makers' names and initials, full scale — 231
Figure 141. Makers' signatures with a bull's eye centered above and below, full scale — 232
Figure 142. Marks and makers' signatures on imported or foreign lamps, full scale — 233

PLATES

Plate I. Geometric designs — 236
Plate II. Myths, gods, goddesses, and heroes — 237
Plate III. Minor divinities — 238
Plate IV. New Year's greetings; hunchback dwarf; maenad; horse and rider; fisherman — 239
Plate V. Gladiators; Parthian stringing his bow — 240
Plate VI. Marine life; charioteers — 241
Plate VII. Wreaths and plants; erotic symplegmata — 242
Plate VIII. Animals and birds — 243
Plate IX. Lamp with seven nozzles — 244

PREFACE

Any study of an excavation's small finds, such as lamps, must naturally be viewed in perspective, as part of the larger picture of the whole town, a picture that has gradually been emerging at Cosa as the various volumes on different aspects of the site have been published. The earliest work on the history and topography of the site was written by Frank E. Brown (*Cosa I*); it was followed by the publication of the temples of the Arx of Cosa by Brown and his colleagues, Emeline Hill Richardson and L. Richardson, jr (*Cosa II*), the buildings of the forum (*Cosa III*) by Frank E. Brown, Emeline Hill Richardson, and L. Richardson, jr, and the houses (*Cosa IV*) by Vincent J. Bruno and Russell T. Scott. In addition, the publications of Maria Teresa Marabini Moevs on Roman thin-walled pottery, the workshop of Cusonius at Cosa, and Italo-Megarian ware complemented the work of Stephen L. Dyson on the utilitarian pottery and that of T. V. Buttrey on the coins, all of these studies appearing as parts of the Memoirs of the American Academy in Rome (20, 26, 32, 33, 34, 37, 38). Jacquelyn Collins-Clinton has published the Shrine of Liber Pater and Anna Marguerite McCann, Joanne Bourgeois, Elaine K. Gazda, John Peter Oleson, and Elizabeth Lyding Will the port and fishery of Cosa. These studies, as well as the book on Cosa by Brown, *Cosa: The Making of a Roman Town*, have produced a background against which to project the publication of the Cosan lamps.

A study and catalogue of the Cosan lamps must also be viewed as part of the total picture of lamp production in the Mediterranean basin, and again we must acknowledge the pioneering work of the cataloguers who have established the basic typology and dating systems for ancient lamps in their studies, either at particular archaeological sites or in museum collections. For the former one must cite as examples Siegfried Loeschcke at Vindonissa and Haltern; Oscar Broneer at Corinth and Isthmia; Philippe Bruneau at Delos; Jean Deneauve at Carthage; and Annalise Leibundgut at sites in Switzerland. For the latter one must acknowledge the comprehensive work of Donald Bailey at the British Museum; Heinz Menzel in Mainz; Gerald Heres in Berlin; and Karin Goethert-Polaschek in Trier. Because the same lamp types appear at most sites and in most museums throughout Europe and the Mediterranean world, we must go beyond the town walls and the cases and storerooms of the museums to see reflected the larger picture of trade and commerce in the Mediterranean. The lamps certainly indicate patterns of provincial regionalism, but factors of expanding industry, pirating and plagiarism of forms, and tourism also affect the picture.

The Cosan lamps have been recovered from houses, shops, streets, temples, public buildings, the Arx, and a dump along the town wall. Their fragility, however, argues against the likelihood of their being found whole in houses, in shops, or along streets, especially when their findspots indicate the reuse of materials as fill. Thus most of them have been recovered as fragments.

Only a few experts would be able to identify the

Cosan lamps on the basis of photographs of the shards alone. The problem of identification was met by making drawings of the tops, side views, and cross sections through the oil reservoirs, reconstructing the missing parts from other fragments of the same types from Cosa or from *comparanda* in other publications. It is from *comparanda* that we can accurately reconstruct some of the Cosan lamps, which must be re-created on the drawing board rather than photographed. The few whole lamps and the large lamp fragments were photographed first by the late Johannes Felbermeyer in the early years of the Cosan excavations and more recently by the late Barbara Bini. We are indebted to both of them for the sensitivity and expertise of their work.

In the preparation of this manuscript, we thank the following for their patience, good judgment, advice, editing skills, and moral support: first our husbands, James Marston Fitch and Bernard M. Goldman. We should like to acknowledge the early work of Eric C. Baade, who in 1953 catalogued the lamps from Atrium Building I and provided an initial organization of them. We also thank our friends Charles Babcock, Lionel Casson, David D. F. Grose, Anne Laidlaw, Helen F. North, James Packer, Russell T. Scott, Elizabeth L. Will and Judith Perlzweig Blinder for their criticism and advice in reading portions of the manuscript. We also thank our secretaries, Deanna Merritt, Karen Jenkins, Eleni Mareskas, Orletta Ekpene, and Anika Terrell for their careful typing of the computer printout of the manuscript, and we especially thank the Office of the Vice President for Research represented by Garrett T. Heberlein and Daniel Graf of Research and Sponsored Programs of Wayne State University for the grant that has enabled us to complete the computer typing of the final manuscript. Thanks must go to the Word Processing Center, under the capable direction of David Nelson, for the speed and efficiency of its production of the computer printout.

The authors wish to thank Lawrence Richardson for his valuable assistance in the final editing of the manuscript. Without his immaculate scholarship and tireless scrutiny, it would not have reached its final form as a worthy contribution to the Cosa series.

Most of all we are deeply grateful to the late Frank E. Brown for his unfailing encouragement, for sharing with us his sense of history and his comprehensive knowledge of the site, and for his sound advice.

Cleo Rickman Fitch
New York City

Norma Wynick Goldman
Wayne State University

COSA:
THE LAMPS

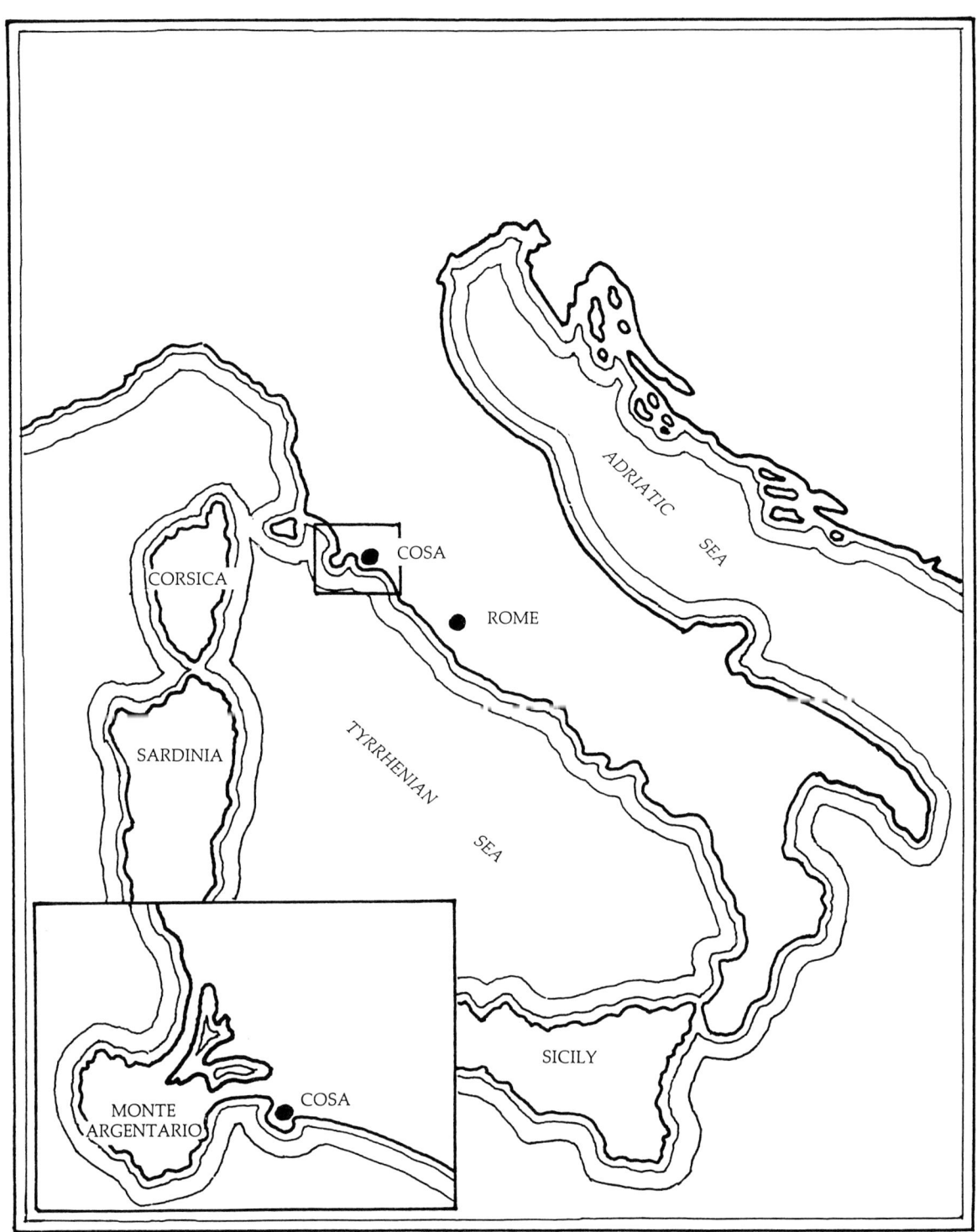

Figure 1. Map of Italy, showing location of Cosa

INTRODUCTION

The lamps in this catalogue were recovered during eighteen seasons of excavation and research from 1948 to 1954 and from 1965 to 1975 by the American Academy in Rome at the site of the Latin colony of Cosa, ninety miles northwest of Rome just off the Via Aurelia, the ancient coast road (Fig. 1). Eight seasons of excavation were under the direction of Professor Brown.[1] Two excavation seasons were directed by Professor L. Richardson, jr,[2] and Professor Russell T. Scott was Field Director of the excavation for the 1972 season.[3]

The lamps of Cosa provide evidence of the types of lamps produced in Italy between 273 B.C. and A.D. 416, and document the history of the lamp industry through the most important years of ancient Rome. During the almost seven centuries of the existence of this harbor town with its agricultural community and fish hatchery, the need for illumination after dark or in places with little natural light is eloquently reflected in the lamps and the hundreds of lamp fragments recovered. The lamps of Cosa were excavated from houses in the residential part of the town, from public buildings and shops around the Forum (its civic center), and from temples, both on the Arx and in the Forum, all sites within the walls of the town (Fig. 2). (No tombs have been excavated at Cosa.) These lamps, both domestic and imported, are probably representative of the full repertoire of lamps to be found in a typical Italian town during these centuries. Because of the coastal setting of the town with its harbor facilities below the promontory, the imported lamps at times reflect trade with other centers in the Mediterranean world. More important, however, the lamps indicate the dependence of the colony on the region around the mother city, Rome, since most of the lamps were probably not made locally but were produced in central Italy, possibly in or near Rome itself.

The history of lamps in the Mediterranean world goes back to a primitive form of lamp used in late Paleolithic times, as is shown by a wick lamp discovered in the cave at Lascaux in France.[4] Oil-burning lamps have

---

1. The late Frank E. Brown, formerly Thatcher Professor of Latin and Master of Jonathan Edwards College at Yale University, excavated at Dura Europus in Syria and was in charge of the Classical School at the American Academy in Rome from 1947 to 1952 and from 1963 to 1976. He was the Academy's first Mellon Professor and served as Director of the Academy from 1965 to 1969. Professor Brown was Director of excavations at Cosa from 1948 to 1952 and from 1963 to 1967, and was in charge of post excavation research until 1986.

2. L. Richardson, jr, is James B. Duke Professor of Latin Emeritus at Duke University in North Carolina. He was director of excavations at Cosa from 1953 to 1954.

3. Russell T. Scott, Professor of Latin at Bryn Mawr College, was field director of the Cosa excavations from 1968 to 1972.

4. B. and G. Delluc, "L'éclairage," in J. Allain, ed., *Lascaux Inconnu*, Gallia Préhistorique 2d Supplement (Paris, 1977), 121–39. S. A. de Beaune and R. White, "Ice Age Lamps," *Scientific American* 266.3 (March 1993), 108–13.

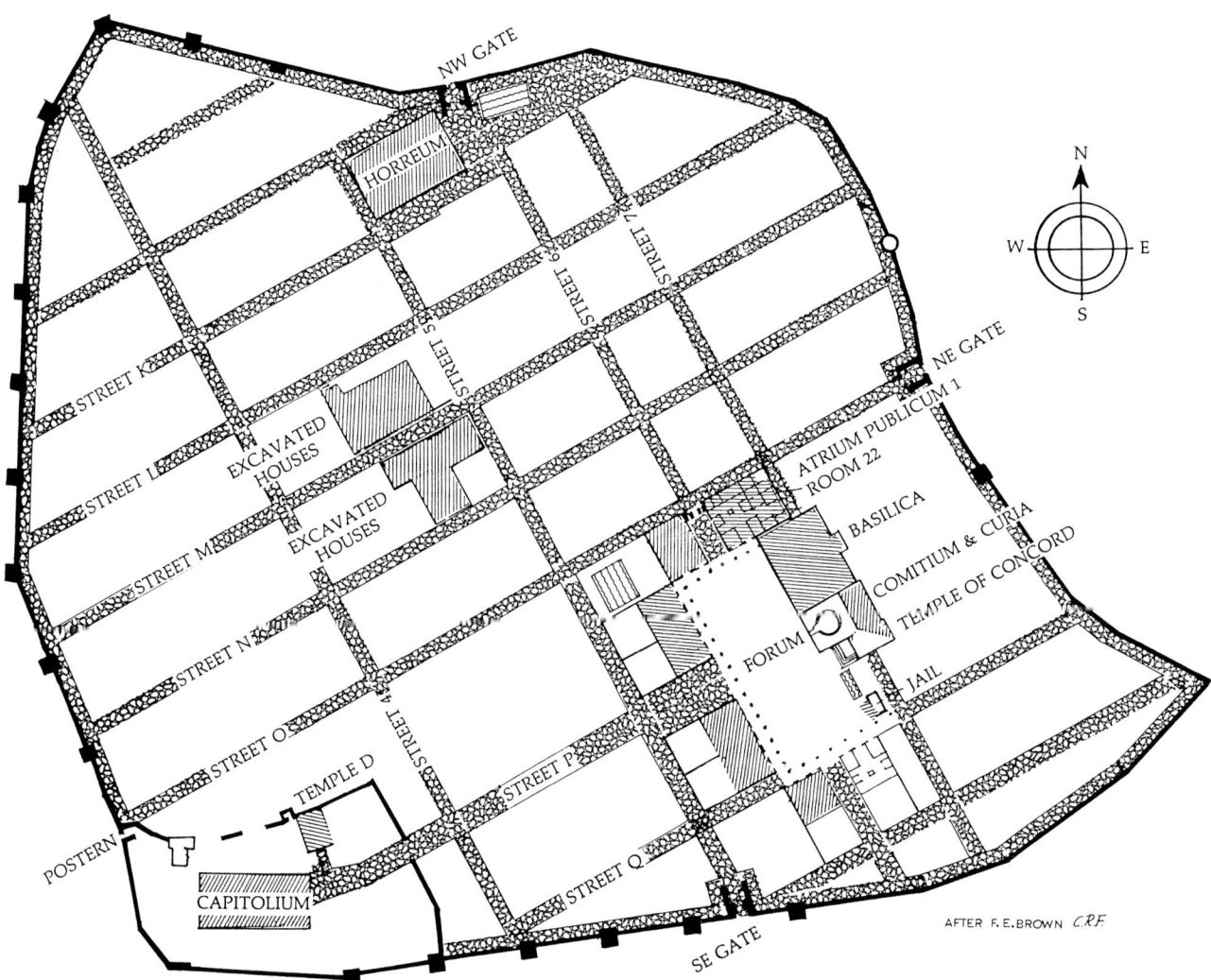

Figure 2. Plan of Cosa

been found in ancient Egyptian tombs[5] and at sites in the ancient Palestinian littoral.[6] Lamps have been found at Minoan sites in Crete[7] and at Mycenaean ones in Greece.[8] After a hiatus of several centuries, lamps were reintroduced to Greece from Asia Minor in the seventh century B.C.[9] Some of these lamps from the East may have been exported to the Greek cities of southern Italy and Sicily, as well as to Etruscan cities. The earliest Roman lamps published so far date from the fourth century B.C.,[10] although the surviving example of the famous fifth-century Etruscan bronze multilight lamp of Cortona indicates that highly developed lamps were known and used in Etruria at a much earlier date.[11]

Despite its apparent simplicity, the oil lamp of antiquity was a remarkable invention (Fig. 3). It began as a simple wheelmade or handmade shallow bowl containing oil with a wick floating on its surface. Then some imaginative potter pinched the edge of the bowl while the clay was still soft to create a small lip on which one end of the wick could be lifted out of the oil. The next development seems to have been to turn the rim of the bowl inward to help prevent oil spillage. Then, by degrees, the rim was pulled further inward until only a filling hole remained, and the lip was bridged. A plastic handle might be attached either horizontally or vertically.

Next was the addition of a hand-formed nozzle with a hole in the top near the tip. The hole was connected to the oil reservoir by a channel through which a wick inserted in the nozzle extended to the oil through a hole in the wall of the reservoir. After the clay dried, the lamp was often glazed or coated with a slip and fired, although some lamps were neither glazed nor slipped. The Greeks favored a rounded nozzle on their lamps; the Romans, on their early wheelmade lamps, developed their own spatulate nozzle form, which differed from the Greek type, as well as from that of their western Asian predecessors. With few exceptions, all Roman lamps, both wheelmade and moldmade, until the appearance of the voluted nozzle, had these distinctive spatulate nozzles with a slightly convex end. Where the ends meet the curve of the nozzle sides are flukes or points.

Until about 150–120 B.C. the lamps at Cosa were made on the wheel. These are divided into five basic types: Truncated-Cone, Doughnut, Central Tube, Watch or "Kitchen," and Esquiline. The only Cosan lamps that used the rounded Greek nozzle belong to the Watch type or "Kitchen" lamp. The constraining factor of wheelmade lamp production, however, was that each lamp had to be shaped individually.

In the third century B.C. some potter in western Asia developed the technique of making lamps in molds,[12] thus creating the possibility for new forms and for relief decoration. It also made possible mass production of lamps, since part of the process could be handled by semiskilled workers, who could easily reproduce the hollow lamps from two-piece molds or matrices taken from the patrix or prototype (a solid original) or from another lamp.

---

5. G. Soteriades, "Proistorika Angeia Chaironeias kai Elateias," *Ephemeris Archaiologike* (Athens, 1908), 81, fig. 10.; W. M. Flinders Petrie, *Abydos*, Part I (London, 1902), small bowls in stone, alabaster, and pottery, possibly lamps, pls. 27 no. 18 and 28 no. 199:1–5.

6. Rosenthal/Sivan 1978, 9–15, 75–77.

7. P. Warren, *Minoan Stone Vases* (Cambridge, 1969), 49–60, plates and drawings in Section 24; S. A. Xanthoudides, "Ek Kretes," *Ephemeris Archaiologike* (Athens, 1906), 149; S. A. Xanthoudides, "Guide to the Candia Museum," in M. Elliade, *Crete Past and Present* (London, 1933), 178; S. A. Xanthoudides, *Vaulted Tombs of Mesara* (Liverpool, 1924), pls. 31, 37; D. G. Hogarth, "Excavations at Zacro," *BSA* 7 (1900–1901), 128, fig. 41; L. Pernier, "Il Palazzo di Phaestos," *MonAnt* 14 (1904), 482, fig. 88; R. C. Bosanquet, "Excavations at Petras," *BSA* 8 (1901–1902), 285, fig. 4.

8. A. Furumark, *The Mycenaean Pottery* (Stockholm, 1941), 78 and fns. 1–4; E. Coche de la Ferté, *Essai de classification de la céramique mycenienne d'Enkomi* (Paris, 1951), pl. 5 no. 3; R. M. Burrows and P. N. Ure, "Kothons and Vases of Allied Types: The Lamp Theory," *JHS* 31 (1911), 88–99, figs. 16–19. Anne Blasingham is preparing a study of Mycenaean lamps.

9. Broneer 1930, 5 n. 3, maintains that torches were used in the Homeric world. Homer speaks of a golden lamp held by Pallas Athena to light the work of Odysseus and Telemachus in clearing the hall of weapons, *Odyssey* 19.39–42, although most of the lighting references indicate torchlight.

10. Dressel 1880, 267; *Roma medio repubblicana, Aspetti culturali di Roma e del Lazio nei secoli IV e III A.C.* SPQR Assessorato Antichità, Belle Arti e Problemi della Cultura (Rome, 1973), 221–337 and pl. 49.

11. See E. del Monte, "Le lampadarie de bronze du Musée de Cortona," in F. Lenormant, *Les principes d'art et la décoration des monnais*, abstract without publication data, 227–28, for a detailed description of the Cortona lamp, with an excellent drawing.

12. Broneer 1930, 7.

Figure 3. The development of the oil lamp

The first moldmade lamps appear at Cosa about 150 B.C. and have been discovered in large numbers in contexts dated from 120 to 70 B.C. Most of these lamps are probably from central Italy, possibly from Rome itself or nearby. The fabric is thick; they have the traditional Roman spatulate nozzle, and the designs or reliefs are rather crude, except for some belonging to the Raised-Dots category. Some of these Raised-Dots Lamps were probably made by a potter using a bronze lamp as a patrix. The workmanship and designs of bronze craftsmen were very advanced compared with those of potters; witness the granulation on the finest Cosan example of the Raised-Dots Lamps (235), which duplicates in clay the decoration of the bronze original. Distinctive moldmade lamps of excellent quality in this period are the fine Delphiniform (dolphin-shaped) Lamps, which were probably imported from Sicily. An outstanding lamp found in the area of the Capitolium is a foreign example from the workshop of the Athenian potter Ariston, signed ARISTONO. He and his workshop disappeared after the sack of Athens by Sulla in 86 B.C.[13] His lamp might have been brought back by a soldier as loot and offered in a temple, or it may have been a votive offering of a traveler who had visited Athens before 86 B.C. These examples of imported lamps found at Cosa may be considered a small indication of the wealth of material brought to Rome from other cultures that were annexed by the emerging center of power.

Most of the early Roman moldmade lamps found at Cosa have Hellenistic features borrowed from Greece and Asia Minor: lamps with a raised circular nozzle and/or lamps with one or two ears. These forms were eventually discarded, but they inspired experimentation. The Roman potters created a new type in which the wide discus and rim covered the entire top of the oil reservoir, a forerunner of the fine Picture Lamps. They also began to experiment with a decorative device to mark the separation of the discus from the nozzle, a step that led to the voluted nozzle. One example of this experimentation was the Birds'-heads Lamp with its slender addorsed birds' heads decorating the nozzle.

The elegant Roman Picture Lamps with their voluted nozzles, which appeared during the early Augustan period and continued through Neronian times, marked the high point of lamp development. The first Roman Picture Lamps were found in material from the resettlement of Cosa from 25 to 20 B.C. These lamps were of excellent quality made from finely levigated clay that allowed for an extremely thin fabric. There were two types, distinguished by the ends of the delicate nozzles—triangular and rounded. The rims were a complex series of rings, which would make it difficult to extract the lamp top from the mold. This seems to have led eventually to a simplfied and less breakable version of Picture Lamp developed during the Julio-Claudian period. The relief decoration on both types of Picture Lamps includes a vast repertoire of images from classical mythology, gods and goddesses, genre scenes, gladiators,[14] erotic scenes, heroes, real or imaginary animals, sea creatures, Victory figures with New Year's greetings, and hunting scenes.

A development of the Picture Lamps just prior to the mid-first century A.D. was the "Pouter Pigeon Lamp" with its shorter, strengthened nozzle and with a handle formed in the mold. This lamp type was followed by lamps with a long, wide nozzle and an ornate heat shield, a baroque phase of lamp production. Next appeared lamps showing experimentation with the location of the volutes on the nozzle, followed by the "Fat Lamps," which were sturdy, less liable to break, and easy to extract from the mold because of their rounded shoulders and their short, unvoluted nozzle set into the shoulder.

Mass production of lamps started with the introduction of the mold. However, in the last quarter of the first century A.D. there was introduced a plain, simple form of lamp, appropriately named the "Factory Lamp," which semiskilled labor could produce, except for making the patrix. The Factory Lamp was easy and inexpensive to make, pack, and transport, and it continued to be a dominant type for more than two centuries.[15] Matrices could also have been made directly from a bronze prototype by semiskilled labor.

Very few so-called "Plastic Lamps" have been found at Cosa. These are modeled in various shapes: human figures, animals, parts of the body, and other natural forms. For a short time, some of the potteries

---

13. Bruneau, 45.
14. Gladiators were a popular subject on Cosan lamps. Cosa had no amphitheater, but gladiatorial games were probably staged in the Forum.
15. Three debased copies of the Factory Lamp were found at Cosa in contexts dating as late as the early fifth century A.D.

that made Factory Lamps also produced an ornate model in the form of a pinecone resting on its side, with each scale of the cone in relief. Since it would have been difficult and time-consuming to make these lamps, they must have been expensive, although once the original lamp had been made in some exotic shape, it could become a patrix and molds could be taken from it.

By the end of the second century A.D. the creative period of Roman lamp making was over. Thereafter few new types were introduced, and most of these were merely variations on previous designs. From the last faint attempt at a revival of Cosa around the middle of the fourth century to the end of the town in the early fifth century, the majority of the lamps were crude, strong types with elongated bodies imported from North Africa or Roman copies of the North African lamps. Rome itself was no longer the center of, and the inspiration for, lamp production; the provinces had taken over the industry.

Siegfried Loeschcke at Vindonissa[16] and Oscar Broneer at Corinth[17] have pioneered in the field of lamp study with their basic classification of types and rim profiles. Each used lamps from a particular site, and naturally the typology developed was limited to the types that appeared there. However, a number of rim profiles that occur at Cosa are unknown at these sites; thus there are many additions to the Loeschcke and Broneer rim profiles in this catalogue. Drawings at the beginning of each chapter illustrate the complete repertoire of rims within each type: for example, there are thirty-eight rim profiles within the Cosan Triangular Nozzle Lamps in Group IB alone. Wherever applicable, however, we have also listed the Loeschcke and Broneer classification.

Many previous cataloguers of lamps from archaeological sites and in museums[18] have established typologies and chronologies that are extremely useful in dating the lamps of Cosa. Because these catalogues are essential to any consideration of lamps, we also precede the description of each lamp type with the correlative classifications assigned by most other writers.

The order in which all the Cosan lamps are listed, both wheelmade and moldmade, is by chronology and type, and within each type the lamps are listed chronologically. Dimensions are given in meters following the abbreviations P.L. for Preserved Length, P.H. for Preserved Height, and P.W. for Preserved Width. Where the word is written out in full, the Length, Height, or Width is intact and the measurement is for the complete dimension. Since only one Cosan lamp has a vitreous glaze, we have used the word "slip" instead of "glaze" in the catalogue. In describing lamps, this catalogue conventionally considers a view from above looking down on the lamp as if set on a flat surface with the nozzle pointing down and the handle (if any) at the top. The position of nozzle and handle thus determines left and right in describing the discus scene or the ears or lugs. When there are useful *comparanda,* they are given immediately following the individual lamps, along with the particular references for each. A discussion of the potters' marks and signatures, along with the drawings, appears at the end of the catalogue.

---

16. Loeschcke 1919.
17. Broneer 1930, Broneer 1977.
18. Bailey, *Catalogue of Lamps in the British Museum,* 3 vols. (London, 1975, 1980, 1988), is particularly important, since it is a comprehensive and well-illustrated study of the collection of lamps in a major museum.

CHRONOLOGY

Ancient lamps served several purposes: they lighted domestic, commercial, religious, and public buildings; they were votive offerings at temples and shrines; they were buried with the dead to light their way to the next world. (At Cosa, however, the lamps come from only the first two contexts, buildings excavated within the town walls; none is from a tomb.)

In 273 B.C., when Cosa was founded, lamps were standard household furnishings. Yet for ordinary families they were used mostly in emergencies, since the fuel—olive oil—was also an important food, only the poorest quality of oil being used for the lamps. Like peasants everywhere, even today, most families went to bed at sunset and rose at dawn. No doubt in the houses of the wealthy there were many lamps with many nozzles, some of precious metal, to keep the dark at bay. At Cosa, however, only clay lamps have been found to date, with the exception of one iron lamp.[1]

Terra-cotta lamps help to date levels at newly excavated sites, although not so precisely as do coins. In the excavated areas listed in this chronology, hundreds of terra-cotta lamps have been found. They represent an almost unbroken chronological sequence from the early third century B.C. to the early fifth century A.D., constituting a cross section of the international lamp-making industry. Inevitably, this sequence was interrupted in times of unrest: during the Punic Wars; during the Gallic invasion, which was finally turned back at Telamon within sight of Cosa in 227 B.C.; after 70 B.C. with the sack of Cosa, perhaps by pirates; and during the civil wars. When peace was finally restored and Cosa was partially resettled in the Augustan period, the lamp sequence recommenced and continued, although in diminishing quantity, until about A.D. 225, when the town was almost deserted. However, people continued to climb the hill to the temples to worship the old gods and to come to meetings in the Forum; and there may have been a few shops and a tavern for travelers. Then, around the middle of the fourth century A.D., a small village grew up around the northwest end of the Forum. Life on the site revived in a small way and continued for the next fifty years, attested also by the lamps found in the Shrine of Liber Pater at the southeast end of the Forum.[2]

Thus the sequence of lamps covers a period from around 270 B.C. to the early fifth century A.D., (Figs. 4, 5). The final ancient reference to the site was made by the poet Namatianus, who spent a night at Portus Herculis across the bay from Cosa. In 416 he reported that a pestilence of mice (perhaps rats that had brought the

---

1. The iron lamp was found in the storeroom (Room 22), Level II of Atrium Building I.

2. Collins-Clinton 1977, 3–7, 14–15, 59–71.

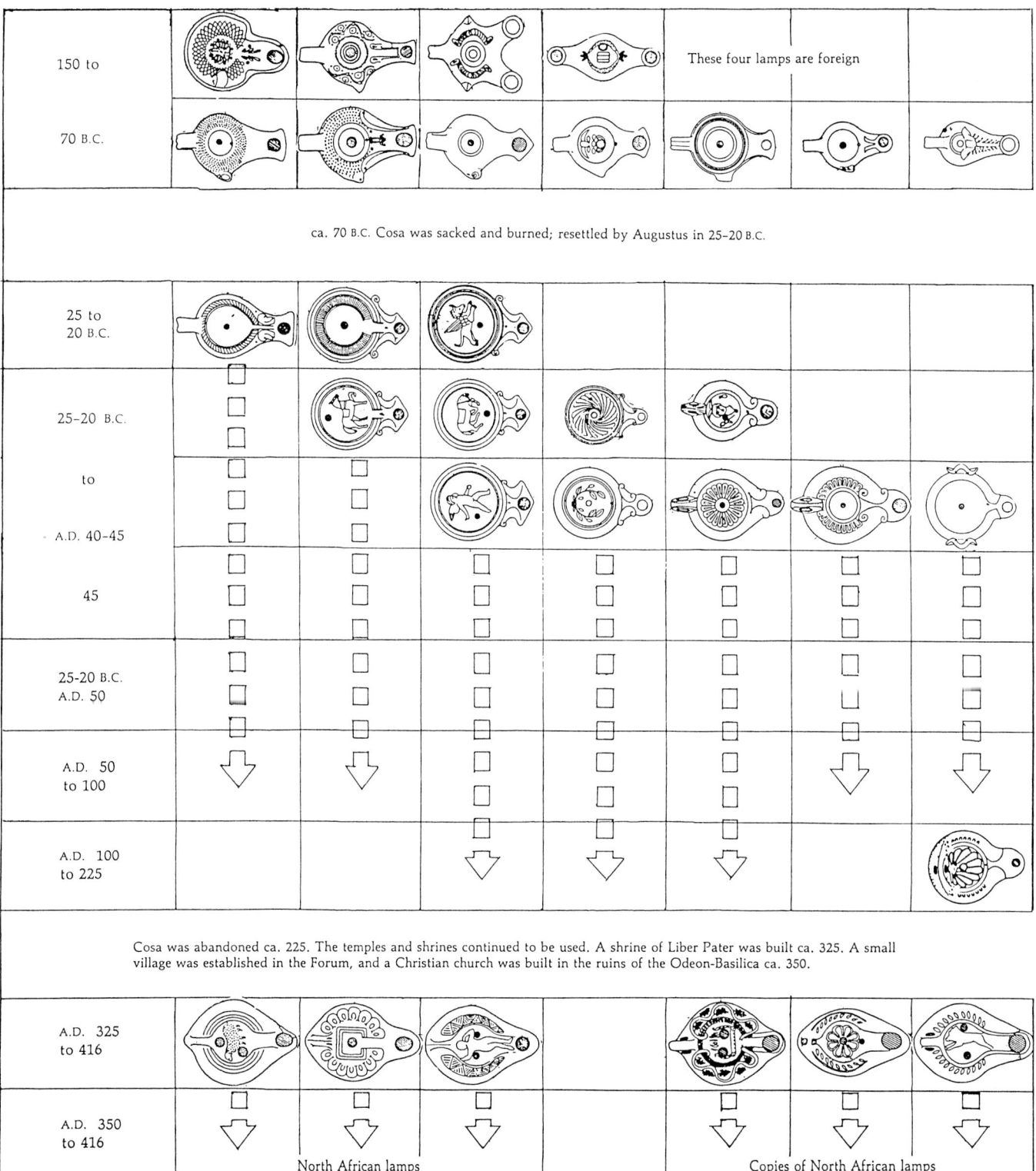

Figures 4, 5. Chart of the Cosan molded lamp sequence

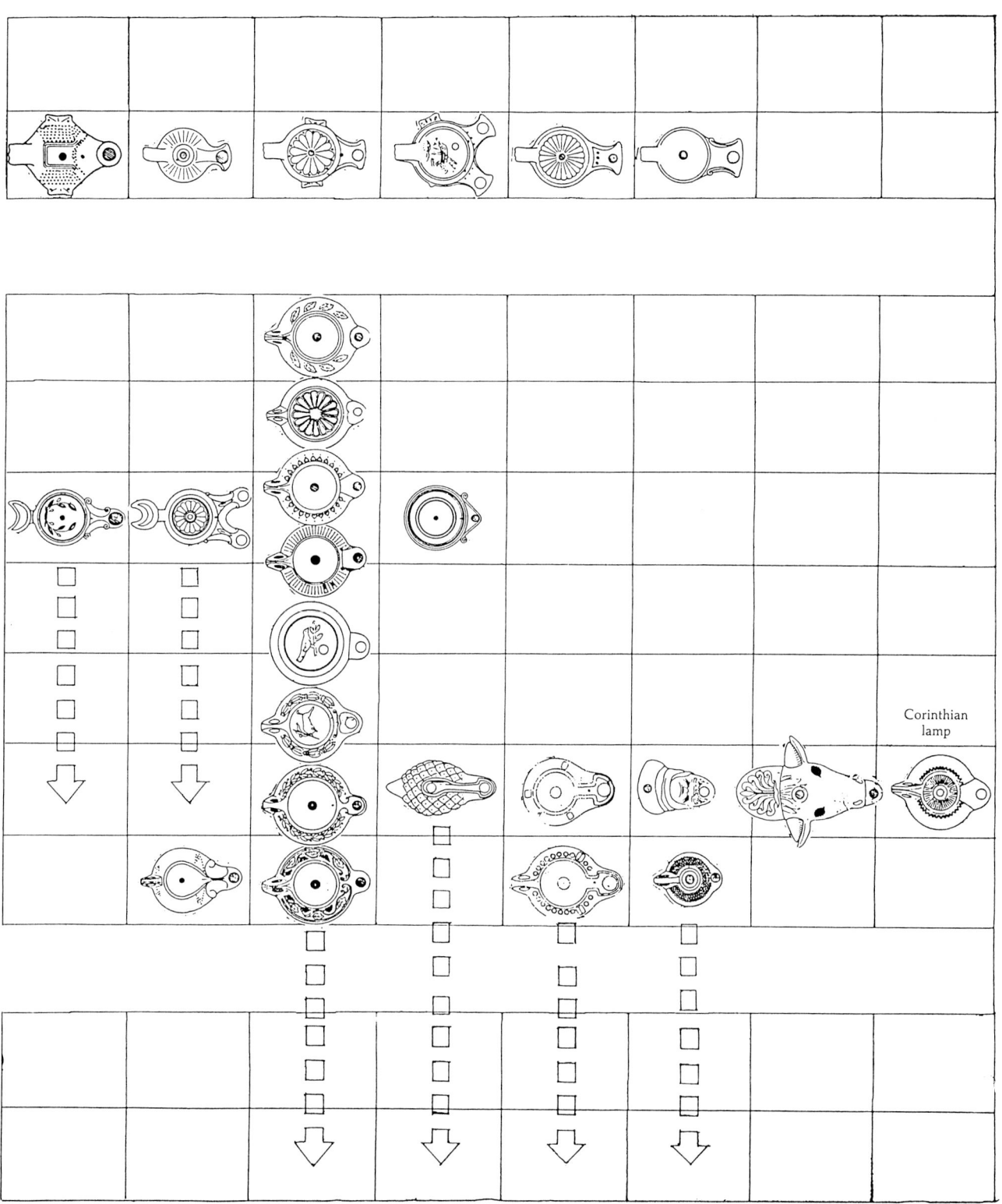

bubonic plague) had caused the abandonment of Cosa.³

The chronology lists events significant for the history of Cosa and the lamps from the excavations.

273 B.C.
Cosa founded.

270–240 B.C.
The sounding under the pavement of the inner circle of the Comitium yielded material including two lamps.⁴

225–200 B.C.
Lamps were found in a small, undisturbed area of the bedding for an unpaved street (a continuation of Street 6), which entered the Forum at the center of the southeast side.⁵ Two coins were found in this bedding: 1. a *sextantal triens* (C68.213) of the early third century B.C.; 2. a *semilibral semuncia* (C68.214) of before 215 B.C.⁶ Pottery found in the same context corroborates the dating.⁷

200–175 B.C.
Lamps were found in the sealed material from a pit under Room 12 in the House of Salvius (later incorporated into the House of the Birds), which went out of use ca. 175 B.C.⁸

A hall was added to either side of the Curia. Temple B was constructed.⁹

200–150 B.C.
Lamps were found in material in Room 16 of Atrium Building I below a mortar throw from the construction of the Basilica, dated by both a stamped amphora handle made in Rhodes between 220 and 180 B.C. and by Black Glaze Ware and Domestic and Coarse Wares.¹⁰

197 B.C.
Due to the loss of many Cosans in the Second Punic War, a thousand new colonists from Rome were enrolled.¹¹ A period of prosperity and building activity followed.

197–180 B.C.
Eight Atrium Buildings were built around three sides of the Forum. In the portico in front of Atrium Building I on the Forum side, a sounding was cut through the earth ramp leading up to the shop in Room 5. Lamps found in the lowest level above bedrock are contemporary with or soon after the construction of the building. A sidewalk subsequently supplanted the ramp.¹²

185–170 B.C.
Lamps were found in the gray deposit at the bottom and in crevices of rock that acted as drainage for the cesspit under Room 13 in Atrium Building I. This cesspit, closed when the sewer was installed under Street 6, was reopened ca. 25–20 B.C. The material in it is dated 185–170 B.C. by two examples of Italo-Megarian Ware and some Black Glaze Ware dated between the late third and the middle of the second century B.C.¹³

180–175 B.C.
Porticos were constructed around three sides of the Forum. The streets were paved, and sewers were installed, projects taking several years to complete.¹⁴ Lamps were found in all these areas.

---

3. Claudius Rutilius Namatianus, *De Reditu Suo* 1.285–290.
cernimus antiquas nullo custode ruinas,
et desolatae moenia foeda Cosae
ridiculam cladis pudet inter seria causam
promere sed risum dissimulare piget.
Dicuntur ciues quondam migrare coacti
muribus infestos deseruisse Lares.

We see the ancient ruins with no one watching over them, and the overgrown walls of abandoned Cosa. I am embarrassed to relate the absurd explanation of the disaster amid serious things, but it is difficult to conceal a smile. People say that the townsfolk finally had to emigrate and had to abandon their household Lares because they had been infested by mice.
4. Richardson 1957, 49–51.
5. *Cosa III*.
6. Buttrey, 40 no. 30. Information about coins in the present study is from this monograph on the Cosan coins.
7. Dyson 1976, 39.
8. *Cosa IV* 1993.
9. *Cosa III*.
10. Dating of amphora handle by Will, confirmed by V. Grace; for Black Glaze Ware, see Taylor, 91–94, 106; for Domestic and Coarse Wares, see Dyson 1976, 51.
11. Brown 1977, 32–33.
12. Brown 1977, 37.
13. Taylor, 105–7; Moevs 1980, 171–72.
14. Brown 1977, 39–40 for portico dating, 42 and fig. 50 for sewers.

175–150 B.C.
Lamps were found in material under the floors of the cellae of the Capitolium, predating its construction.[15]

175–70 B.C.
Corroborative evidence for the destruction in 70–60 B.C. comes from a group of twelve houses in grid squares V-D and VI-E that were destroyed and/or abandoned at that time. Two of these built or remodeled shortly before 70–60 B.C. are particularly noteworthy: the so-called House of the Skeleton and the House of the Treasure of Quintus Fulvius.[16] A hoard of 2,004 *denarii* was found in a jar under the floor of the pantry in the second house, probably buried by someone who was killed or enslaved in the attack. Almost every issue of *denarii* from 110 down to 72–71 B.C. is included in this hoard, which supplies a secure terminal date for the lamps from this house.[17] Two cisterns, one under Room 5 in the House of the Treasure and the other now under the courtyard of the antiquarium complex, also contained debris, including lamps, from this destruction.

Before 150 B.C.
The Basilica was built on the Forum.[18] Material, including lamps, was found in Room 16 of Atrium Building I under a mortar throw from the construction of the Basilica. This area was an open courtyard before 25–20 B.C. Lamps found in Levels V and IV on either side of the Basilica tribune and in the soundings in the aisles must also be dated before its construction.[19]

150 B.C.
The Basilica was constructed about 150 B.C.

150–70 B.C.
Lamps were found in material excavated from Level IV of the Basilica exterior, NE Sectors 1, 2, and 3, and Level III of the Basilica exterior, NE Sectors 4, 5, and 6.[20]

In Atrium Building I, in the cesspit in Room 15, an Esquiline Type Lamp was found.[21] One of the largest deposits of broken lamps was found around the Capitolium in debris from the disaster of ca. 70 B.C., debris probably collected from areas throughout the town.[22] The coin of latest date found in the fill was a *denarius* dating from 84 B.C. struck by M. Fonteius (CB.1819).[23]

Lamps of this period were also found in a cistern below the retaining wall of the forecourt of the Capitolium near the Via Sacra.

100–25/20 B.C.
During the recolonization of 25/20 B.C. an area outside the town walls between Towers 8 and 9 was used as a dump for debris from the disaster of 70 B.C. Broken pottery and lamps found in this dump date from two periods: before 70 B.C., and the cleanup of 25/20 B.C. Three coins were found: a *quinarius* of M. Porcius Cato dated 93–91 B.C., a bronze of Panormus dated to the first century B.C., and a halved uncial *as* dated ca. 20 B.C.[24] with Thin Walled Ware and Red Glaze Ware, including Arretine, dated from 110/100 to 40/30 B.C.[25]

119–70 B.C.
Four lamps and other artifacts including six uncial *asses* were found in 1967 in a dolium set in the floor of Room 21 of a Republican house destroyed in 70 B.C. Two *asses* are dated from 119–91 B.C. (C66.341 and C66.342).[26]

89–70 B.C.
The fill used to level the garden area adjacent to the portico of the House of the Skeleton is contemporary with the construction of the house.[27] Very few lamps were found in the house, but several came from the garden fill. The construction of the house is dated by a coin sealed below the floor: a *quadrans* struck in 90/89 B.C. (C70.448).[28]

---

15. Brown 1977, 38–39.
16. Brown 1977, 67; *Cosa IV*; Bruno, 1970, 233–41 for a description of the House of the Skeleton and the House of Fulvius.
17. Buttrey, 81–88 and Catalogue, 91–147.
18. Brown 1977, 38–39.
19. Basilica dating from newly minted coin of 157/156 B.C., Buttrey, 42; Brown 1977, 58; and *Cosa III*.
20. *Cosa III*.
21. *Cosa III*.
22. Brown 1977, 73–74.
23. Buttrey, 41–42.
24. Buttrey, 42.
25. Moevs 1972, 22–24; Dyson 1976, 87–88; Taylor, 133–35.
26. Buttrey, 42; *Cosa IV*.
27. Bruno *Cosa IV* 1993.
28. Buttrey, 42.

Before 70 B.C.

The settling tank of one of two cisterns in the Forum fish market was not used after 70 B.C.; all material found here, including lamps, is dated from before this time.[29]

The material, including lamps, found in Atrium Building IV, Level II, is dated by a coin: a *denarius* issued by L. Rutilius Flaccus in 77/75 B.C. (C69.319).[30]

70–60 B.C.

Cosa was captured and sacked, probably by pirates.[31] It was partially reoccupied in the Augustan period.

25/20 B.C.

Lamps were found in Level II in Rooms 16 and 11, and in Level III in Room 21 in Atrium Building I. These rooms were damaged by fire during the conversion of part of the building into a private dwelling.[32] The damaged area was leveled and covered over by a new floor sealing in pottery and glass fragments between the two levels.[33] According to Moevs, the *terminus ante quem* of Thin Walled Ware found here is the end of the third quarter of the first century B.C. An *as* (CE.720) dating between 43 and 25 B.C. was found in the same context.[34]

Two of the Republican houses destroyed in the disaster of 70 B.C. were rebuilt as a single house, the so-called House of the Birds.[35] Lamps were found here.

25 B.C.–A.D. 45

The Basilica collapsed around A.D. 40/45 (see plan, Fig. 6). Six rooms in the adjacent house (formerly Atrium Building I) and the storeroom of the hardware and pottery shop (Room 22) were buried by parts of the fallen Basilica roof and party wall between it and the house. There is evidence of a tidying up in all the rooms except Room 22, which was found by the excavators still filled with the debris of building material forming a sealed deposit. Underneath were goods that could have been for sale in the shop, including one hundred seventy identifiable lamps. Many more were crushed beyond retrieval into several pounds of tiny unassignable shards. Since, however, the identifiable one hundred seventy belong to nine types, it seems safe to assume that they represent all the available types for sale in the shop at this time.

None of the one hundred seventy is complete, but all have enough remaining to make classification certain. They can be divided into nine types, whose classification by other students of lamps is given at the beginning of the chapter devoted to each type. There were thirty Triangular Nozzle Lamps, but only two Picture Lamps with a long slender nozzle with rounded end, indication that the type was rare. There were forty-six Pouter Pigeon Lamps with voluted nozzles each also having a relief on the discus, but with a short, wide nozzle and thick volutes, a direct descendant of the lamps with long, slender, voluted nozzles with a rounded end. Nine decorated disci lack identification as to nozzle type.

There were forty-one lamps with long, thick, voluted nozzles and heat shields; there was only one lamp with a single volute with scrolls only at the lower end near the wick hole. A new experimental type of lamp is represented by five examples, a lamp with wide decorated shoulders, a molded, pierced handle, a wide nozzle with volutes in new positions, and with flat scrolls near the center of the nozzle next to the discus, where they interrupt the shoulder decoration. There were four lamps with a wide discus that has a channel opening out toward the wick hole and two inchworm ears. There were twenty-three Fat Lamps with wide shoulders, a short, rounded, unvoluted nozzle set into the shoulder, and a molded, pierced handle.

This securely dated deposit and the earlier small sealed deposit of 25/20 B.C. also in Atrium Building I (Rooms 16, 11, and 21, Level III) cover the most important period of Roman lamp production, when lamps of the finest quality were produced.

The earliest Triangular Nozzle Lamps—A1 and A2 (with and without channels)—were found in the deposit of 25/20 B.C., as were two lamps of the B group. No Triangular Nozzle Lamp with a channel, either A or B, was found in the deposit sealed in A.D. 40/45. The channel seems to have gone out of date by that time. However, the Group A2 without a channel was still popular in A.D. 40/45, as was the B2 Lamp without a channel. The Triangular Nozzle Lamp with a very wide nozzle and with very broad volutes—Group C—had been introduced only shortly before A.D. 40/45, and few

---

29. *Cosa III.*
30. Buttrey, 42.
31. Brown 1977, 73–74.
32. *Cosa III.*
33. Moevs 1972, 24–25; D. F. Grose, *Cosa: The Glass*, forthcoming.
34. Buttrey, 43.
35. *Cosa IV* 1993, pp.185–87.

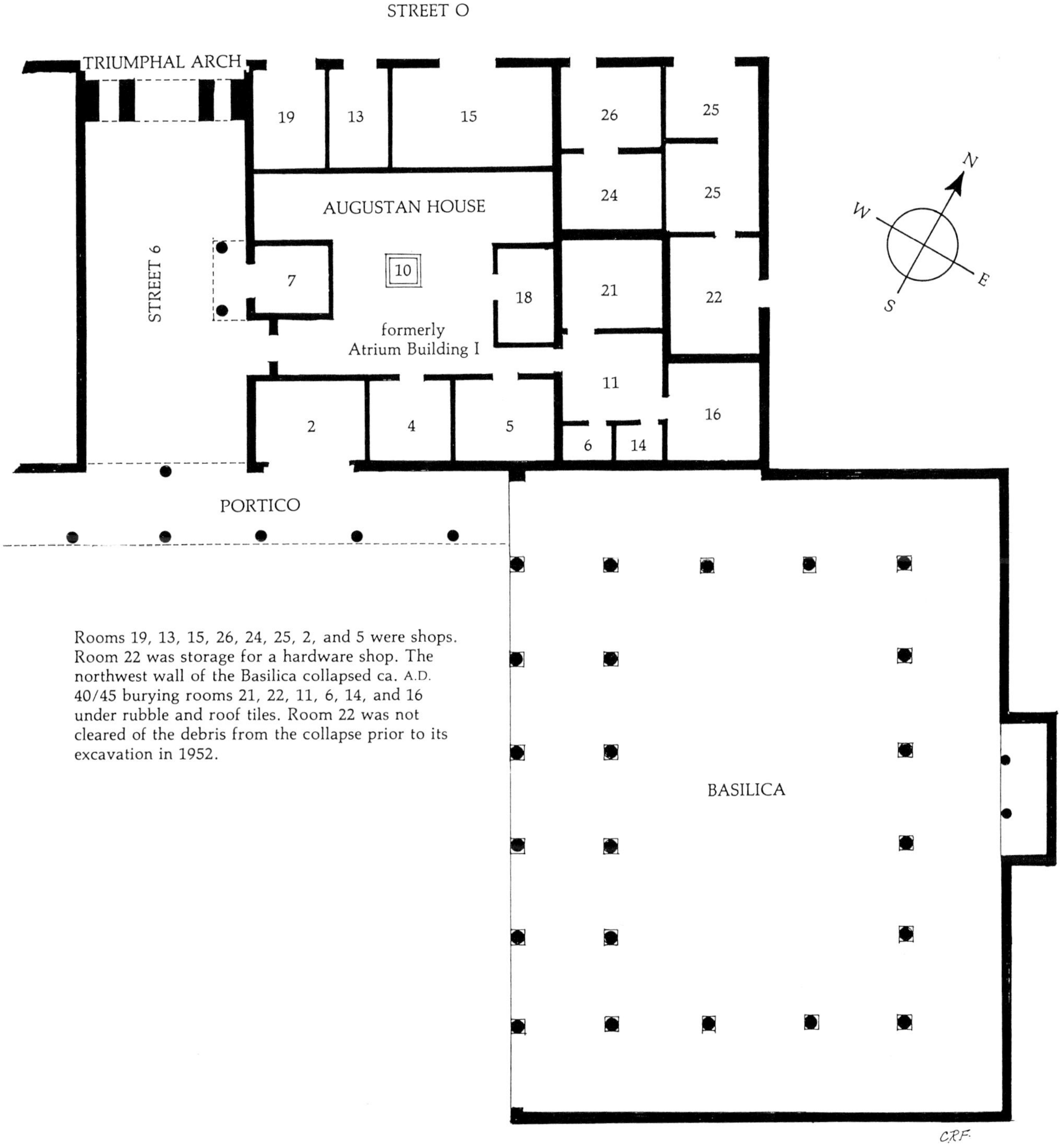

STREET O

TRIUMPHAL ARCH

19 | 13 | 15 | 26 | 25

AUGUSTAN HOUSE

24 | 25

STREET 6

7 | 10 | 18 | 21 | 22

formerly
Atrium Building I

11

2 | 4 | 5 | 6 | 14 | 16

PORTICO

BASILICA

Rooms 19, 13, 15, 26, 24, 25, 2, and 5 were shops. Room 22 was storage for a hardware shop. The northwest wall of the Basilica collapsed ca. A.D. 40/45 burying rooms 21, 22, 11, 6, 14, and 16 under rubble and roof tiles. Room 22 was not cleared of the debris from the collapse prior to its excavation in 1952.

C.R.F.

Figure 6. North corner of the Forum between 25/20 B.C. and A.D. 40/45, after Cosa III

of these were found. This type seems to have been in the process of being replaced by the more popular Pouter Pigeon Voluted Nozzle Lamp.

The early rim profiles of Roman Picture Lamps are very varied, but all have narrow outer moldings level with or higher than the other moldings that make up the rim. The downward-sloping outer molding making a narrow shoulder first appears in the A.D. 40/45 deposit at Cosa. This shoulder made a molded handle possible, since there was now purchase for it. The handle made in the mold along with the rest of the lamp must have been invented only shortly before the collapse of the Basilica in A.D. 40/45. Until the molded handle was invented, the heat shield was not possible.

At the same time a new lamp type was introduced with a short, rounded, unvoluted nozzle set into a wide shoulder. The shoulder, decorated and undecorated, reduced the size of the discus, but there was still room for reliefs on some of the lamps, sometimes on the shoulder, sometimes on the discus, sometimes on both. This lamp is referred to as the Fat Lamp (Loeschcke VIII). It became popular at once in Italy and in all the Mediterranean provinces, and it remained in production for more than three centuries. Indeed, a debased version of this lamp was found at Cosa in a context dated close to A.D. 416 (909).

Most of the material in this deposit is dated to the last few decades before the collapse of the Basilica, but some fragments of glass and pottery pressed into the earthen floor are from the first third of the first century A.D.[36] Two *asses* of the Divus Augustus Pater series were found in Room 22: one coin (CE.1201) was struck in A.D. 15/16 and the other (CE.440) in A.D. 34/37.[37] The dating is confirmed by forty-two out of forty-eight Arretine stamps found in the same context, some in *planta pedis*, a type thought to have been introduced at the beginning of the reign of Tiberius. One of the remaining stamps (CE.1796) is that of the potter Perennius, active at Arezzo between A.D. 20 and 40.[38] Thus the date for the lamps and other material should be no later than A.D. 45/50.

25 B.C.–A.D. 50
Lamps have been found in material from the Basilica exterior, NW Sectors 1 and 2, Level II, and the Basilica exterior, NE Sectors 1, 2, and 3, Level III, and Sectors 4, 5, and 6, Level II.

After A.D. 50
An Odeon was constructed in the ruins of the Basilica by Nero before his accession to the principate but after his adoption by Claudius.

A.D. 50–100
Lamps were found in Level I of Rooms 6, 11, 14, 16, 21, and 22 and in Level IV of Room 25 of Atrium Building I; material from Level II of the Basilica exterior, NE Sectors 1, 2, and 3, and Level I of the Basilica exterior, NE Sectors 4, 5, and 6 and the Basilica exterior, North Level I also included lamps. Lamps were also found in a Mithraeum installed in the southeast basement room of the Curia sometime in the last half of the first century A.D.[39]

25 B.C.–A.D. 200
Lamps were found in the material from Atrium Building III, Level I. Lamps are included in the material from Atrium Building I, Room 25A and B, Levels II and III, which were in continuous use from 25/20 B.C. until the end of the second or early third century A.D. No more precise dating is possible. There were, in fact, few inhabitants within the walls of Cosa after the end of the second century.[40]

Early fourth century
A shrine of Liber Pater was constructed in the southeast entryway to the Forum.[41]

Mid-fourth century
A Christian church was constructed within the ruins of the Basilica/Odeon; some shops in Atrium Building I were refurbished. Two of the basement rooms in the Curia were cleared out, roofed over, and used either as

---

36. Grose, *Cosa: The Glass*, forthcoming; Grose 1983, photograph at top left is glass from Room 22, Level II; Moevs 1972, 27–28.
37. Buttrey, 48.
38. Moevs 1972, 25, 27–28; Dyson 1976, 115.

39. *Cosa III*.
40. *Cosa III*.
41. Collins-Clinton 1977, 15–16.

a dwelling or a barn. There is evidence of continued use of the third room as a Mithraeum.[42]

A.D. 410–416

The Shrine of Liber Pater was deliberately wrecked. According to Collins-Clinton, it existed for decades after the Edicts of Theodosius of 391 and 392 outlawing paganism.[43] The dating of the destruction is based on the evidence of 109 coins found there: the earliest is a *follis* of Licinius II minted in 317 (C68.178); and the latest is a coin of Honorius minted between 410 and 423 (C68.33).[44] Most of the coins were concentrated in one spot, perhaps from a collection box or basket. An unusually large number of lamps suggests that the cult met at night. The Mithraeum in the Curia was probably also wrecked at the same time.

Early fifth century

The abandonment of Cosa is mentioned by Claudius Rutilius Namatianus, who spent a night at Portus Herculis across the bay from Cosa in 416. The people there told him that Cosa had been deserted because of a pestilence of mice.[45]

---

42. *Cosa III.*
43. Collins-Clinton 1977, 1; C. Pharr, *The Theodosian Code*, Princeton, 1952, 472 ff. There is no solid evidence that the edicts directly affected the destruction of the Shrine of Liber Pater, however.
44. Collins-Clinton 1977, 15–16. Buttrey 1980, 522–55.
45. See note 3.

INTRODUCTION TO WHEELMADE LAMPS

(Catalogue Numbers 1–182)

More than two hundred fifty wheelmade lamps have been found at Cosa, most of them fragmentary; one hundred eighty-five are described in this catalogue. From the foundation of the colony to the middle of the second century B.C. only wheelmade lamps were in use at Cosa. Then moldmade lamps gradually began to replace them, and after ca. 25/20 B.C. few wheelmade lamps were still in use.

1. Assigning provenance or location of the workshops by clay color, a practice begun by Fritz Fremersdorf in 1942 in his investigation of the manufacture of lamps and still accepted by such reliable lamp cataloguers as Karin Goethert-Polaschek ("Zur Frage der Lokalisierung der Werkstätten," 184–89) is now being replaced by a more scientific analysis of the clay of the lamp and the clay from various beds in Italy. Samples of both are subjected to neutron activation and compared for composition. The following summary of the method has been provided by Shirley Schwartz of the University of Evansville.

At present it is possible to study the chemical data from a pot [or lamp] and to fingerprint precisely its unique geological content through neutron activation and electron microprobe analyses. A small amount of clay drilled from the core of a pot is subjected to neutron activation in the nuclear reactor and the resulting chemical data read by a computerized recording program. These data are then submitted to various statistical analyses (cluster and multivariate) in order to distinguish chemically derived compositional groupings. The results permit the identification of statistically valid chemically distinct groups of pot samples. Samples from different workshops are dispersed and distinguished in the charted groups. Thin slivers (sections) are cut from the pot and "read" geologically, using an electron microscope in order to determine coarse constituents. Both methods provide independent means of confirmation of a proposed attribution and permit comparison with archaeologically excavated ceramics.

In January 1992, a symposium was held at the American Academy in Rome entitled "Production and Distribution in the Roman Economy: The Evidence of *Instrumentum Domesticum*."

Dr. Theodore Peña of the State University of New York at Albany and the Smithsonian Institution presented a paper entitled "Procedures and Problems in the Analysis of Ceramic Composition and the Study of Pottery Assemblages," in which he discussed the analysis of ceramic material through the application of Neutron Activation Analysis, giving two examples from Italy as illustration. Dr. Peña has been working on clay beds in Italy to establish provenance for clays of different composition that have appeared at various Italian archaeological sites. In the same symposium, Dr. Gerwulf Schneider of the Freie Universität in Berlin presented his

The Cosan wheelmade lamps fall into five distinct types: Truncated-Cone, Doughnut, Central-Tube, Watch (Kitchen), and Esquiline. The evidence of the clay suggests that central Italy was the source for most of these lamps, perhaps Rome itself.[1] The examples of the Esquiline Type in general, however, and a single example of the Watch Type are made from clays that are different. Despite the name, most of the Esquiline Type

Lamps found at Cosa were probably made locally.

Potteries must have been a beehive of activity. First the clay had to be dug and carted to the workshop, where it was prepared into a working body by removal of impurities; then master potters and their apprentices shaped and decorated ceramic wares in all their variety, including lamps; carriers took the ware to and from the drying racks and the kilns; the kilns had to be loaded, and wood had to be cut and hauled to the kilns or other fuel procured for the firing. A kiln was attended during firing; after the desired temperature was attained and maintained for a suitable length of time, the kiln was allowed to cool. When the kiln was opened, the ware was removed, priced, and displayed for sale.

Lamps made on a wheel took a great deal of time and energy. First, the body or oil reservoir was thrown, leaving a filling hole on top for the oil. The potter usually formed each small lamp "off the hump" of a large, centered mass of clay, and it was removed from the hump by a taut string, much the way cheese is cut today. Any finishing of the base (the trimming away of excess clay or the shaping of a base or foot) was done when the clay was firm enough to be tooled. It was then left to dry until it was firm enough to be handled and not pushed out of shape when other parts were attached.

While the body was drying, the potter modeled a solid nozzle by hand, trimmed and smoothed it to the desired shape with a tool or with the fingers, and attached or "luted" it to the body. When it was firm, the nozzle was pierced with a sharp circular tool from the end of the top down through its length to the bottom of the oil reservoir to make the wick hole, so that when inserted in the fired lamp, the wick would reach the oil supply. The handle was made from a narrow strip of clay of uniform width and thickness. Usually the potter ran a finger or two down the center lengthwise to create a fluted effect. The resulting strip was then cut to the proper length and bent into a loop, partially dried, and then luted on to the oil reservoir in two places. There is no evidence for "pulled" handles, which are more appropriate for larger vessels, such as pitchers.

If a slip was to be added, the dried lamp was grasped by the base and dipped quickly into a slip composed of lamp clay slaked with water, often containing a colorant. Because of the expense of firing, there was seldom a biscuit or first firing; the lamp was slipped "green" or unfired, and both the lamp and its slip fired in a single process. The slipping was often so careless that the bottom and even the lower side wall of the oil reservoir were not covered by the slip and the fingerprints of a sloppy workman frequently appear. When the slip was dry, the lamps were taken to the kiln, loaded among the variety of objects made in that particular pottery, and fired. Since it was difficult to regulate the fire, the results were seldom perfect; consequently, lamps are often mottled from uneven firing.[2]

With very few exceptions (e.g., the Watch Type) all early Roman lamps, both wheelmade and moldmade, have spatulate nozzles with flukelike corners, a form that remained in vogue until the introduction of the voluted nozzle in the early Augustan period. These early spatulate nozzles are broad and deep, with a flat top level with the top of the oil reservoir. The underside of the nozzle is a swelling curve from the base of the oil reservoir to the nozzle tip. The sides of the nozzle at

---

work in discovering ceramic provenance in a paper entitled "Conclusions Concerning the Production and Distribution of *Firmalampen* and *terra sigillata* from Analyses of X-ray Fluorescence." Dr. Schneider has generously offered to run some of the Cosan lamp material through his X-ray analysis, a project for future cooperation between the Cosan lamp project and this emerging technology. The papers of the symposium are to be published under the editorship of Professor William Harris of Columbia University, who organized the symposium.

Much work remains to be done in both fields before a combination of the method of Fremersdorf and these modern methods combine to give a precise location for the clays from which the lamps were made. There is also the possibility that clay was imported from one region to another, and that a "clay body" was made from several kinds of clay, the modern method of making a desirable clay—clays being combined for their properties of malleability, resistance to shrinkage and cracking, and resultant color.

2. It was difficult to control the heat in the kiln, and one side of a lamp could be subjected to more heat than the other, giving a variation in color. No kiln has as yet been found at Cosa. A number of kilns have been excavated at different sites in the Mediterranean world, including one at Pompeii, published by Giuseppina Cerulli-Irelli (Cerulli-Irelli 1977, 53–72), showing how the pieces could have been loaded and how the kiln was fired. The excavations at Morgantina in Sicily under the direction of Malcolm Bell of the University of Virginia have discovered several kilns, including a large walk-in kiln, as yet unpublished.

first narrow almost imperceptibly from the oil reservoir, then splay, and join the straight or convex end in blunt points. The Watch Type, on the other hand, has a very broad, short, and rounded nozzle extending only slightly beyond the oil reservoir; unlike that of its Greek prototype, the nozzle is an integral part of the lamp. These small utilitarian lamps, found throughout the Greek and Roman world, are sometimes called "Kitchen Lamps." Whatever the lamp's shape, it was by the nozzle that the wick, inserted to convey the oil from the reservoir, was held in place so that it could be safely lit.

Two of these wheelmade lamps that are complete, a Truncated-Cone Type and a Central-Tube Type, have been tested for performance. They burned with a tall flame that ended in a blue point, a flame brighter than that of a candle, with little or no smoking. On a filling of good olive oil, the flame lasted for about two and a half hours. The wicks used were braided in a four-ply plait from eight strands pulled from a fisherman's wick made of multiple strands of soft, absorbent cotton encased in loose netting. (Such wicks are used in lanterns that hang from the prows of Mediterranean fishing boats today to attract fish at night.) Wicks in antiquity were made from fibers of flax, wool, oakum, mullein, cotton, or any other absorbent, long-strand material that would take the oil by capillary action from the reservoir to the flame at the wick hole. The oil used at Cosa was olive oil, but in the East other oils, such as sesame, flaxseed, and castor, were also used.

The height of the flame and degree of smoking seem to depend on the size of the filling and wick holes. Larger openings admit more oxygen into the reservoir above the oil bowl and into the nozzle around the wick. Both lamps that were lit at Cosa, and all other wheelmade lamps found there, have ample filling and wick holes. We have experimented with several molded lamps in our possession that have small openings, and these burn with a smaller flame and have a tendency to smoke. Much depends on the height of the wick, which can be regulated to prevent smoking. The small pierced holes that appear on almost all Roman moldmade lamps near the juncture of the rim and the nozzle were perhaps for additional oxygen. These are usually referred to as air holes.

The Esquiline and Truncated-Cone Type Lamps found at Cosa are both forms descending from an earlier Roman clay lamp shape found in burials on the Esquiline Hill in Rome. The Roman version is dated to the fourth and the third centuries B.C.[3] The shape of the oil reservoir of these lamps from Rome varies from a cylinder to a truncated cone in which the walls slope inward from the base. Some Esquiline Lamps have a disk base; some do not. All the lamps from Rome have a black slip, with the exception of one that has vertical side walls and no base, features that connect it more closely with the Cosan Esquiline Type, which is usually unslipped.

The Cosan wheelmade lamps of the Esquiline Type fall into two distinct groups: lamps with a base supporting a Truncated-Cone-shaped oil reservoir, a type that developed into the separate Cosan Truncated-Cone Type; and lamps with a cylindrical oil reservoir without a base, the Cosan Esquiline Type. All Truncated-Cone Type Lamps have plastic strap handles, whereas only one example of the Esquiline Type Lamp has a handle. The Cosan Truncated-Cone Type Lamps have a black slip, whereas the Cosan Esquiline Type Lamps are unslipped with but two exceptions, which have a black slip. Forty-eight of the fifty Truncated-Cone Type Lamps have a disk base; two have none. Only one Cosan Esquiline Type Lamp has a base.

From the evidence of these lamps, it appears that by the time of Cosa the form of the Esquiline Lamps of Rome had become standardized with a truncated-cone-shaped body on a base, a plastic strap handle, and a black slip. The cylindrical body form had become obsolete. Later the cylindrical body form was revived, and this lamp, without a base or a handle, was either unslipped or had a self-slip. The Truncated-Cone Type Lamps appear first at Cosa in contexts dated from ca. 270 to 240 B.C.;[4] the Esquiline Type, found in the pottery

---

3. See the catalogue of the exhibition at the Antiquarium Comunale in the Capitoline Museums in 1973, entitled *Roma medio repubblicana, aspetti culturali di Roma e del Lazio nei secoli IV e III A.C.* SPQR Assessorato Antichitá, Belle Arti e Problemi della Cultura (Rome, 1973), 221–337 and pl. 49. Photographs of only three lamps are shown in the catalogue, but there were a number in the exhibition with both truncated cone and cylindrical bodies. These were from the cemetery on the Esquiline Hill referred to above.

4. Cf. 1 and 2 found under the paving in the inner circle of the Comitium.

dump, was not found in any context earlier than ca. 150 B.C.

For an experienced potter, the body of a simple wheelmade lamp is easy to make. Many could be thrown quickly off the hump of a large mass of centered clay, and the same form could be duplicated rapidly in large quantity in a single day. The attachments of nozzle and handle, naturally, would prolong the production, but the simplicity of the process and the need for such small household objects kept the tradition of wheelmade lamps alive for more than two hundred years at Cosa, until tastes changed and consumers demanded the new decorative moldmade "Picture Lamps."

1. TRUNCATED-CONE TYPE LAMPS
(Fig. 7)

(Catalogue Numbers 1–45)

Of the large number of Truncated-Cone Type Lamp fragments found at Cosa, forty-five have been catalogued. They were found in contexts dated 270–70 B.C., with one exception, 44, from a level dated 25/20 B.C.

The clay of these lamps is micaceous, grogged with white and black sand, buff in color with variations from cream to light brown, sometimes buff with a pink or orange tint, sometimes greenish or gray, colors characteristic of lamps made in or near Rome. Most have a black slip, with seven exceptions, where the slip is red. They were carelessly slipped, and usually the base is not covered by the slip or is only partially covered.

These lamps have been named for the shape of the oil reservoir, a truncated cone. They have a disk base, with two exceptions, and all have flat bottoms that are unfinished. There is a filling hole in the center of the small depressed discus, and a raised ridge encircles the discus. The nozzles are long, broad, and deep; the top of the nozzle is in a plane with the rim of the discus. The bottom of the nozzle rises from the bottom of the lamp, usually covering the base at the point of attachment. It is the usual Roman spatulate nozzle described in the Introduction to Wheelmade Lamps. The wick holes and filling holes are large. Most Truncated-Cone Type Lamps have handmade strap handles; the three exceptions have none. The handles have one or two shallow vertical grooves, like fluting.

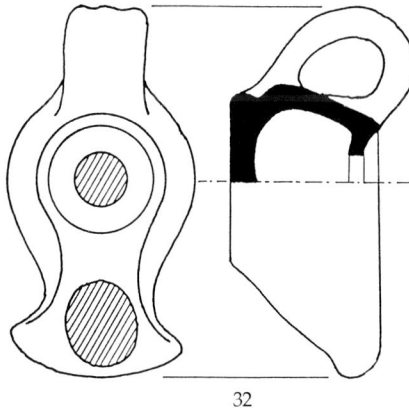

Figure 7. Truncated-Cone Type Lamps, scale 1:2

270–240 B.C.
1 CG.533 Center of Comitium, Sounding under pavement. Pinkish-buff clay, black slip. P.L. 0.065 m; Height 0.037 m; P.W. 0.054 m.
 Five joining fragments preserving the nozzle and parts of the base, side wall of the oil reservoir, and discus. Very worn.
2 CG.585 Center of Comitium, Sounding under pavement. Pinkish-buff clay, black slip. P.L. 0.024 m; P.H. 0.022 m; P.W. 0.014 m.
 Two joining fragments preserving parts of the base and the lower side wall of the oil reservoir. Very worn and chipped.

225–200 B.C.

3 C68.723 Forum SE, Street bedding (*statumen*). Orange-buff clay, black slip. P.L. 0.042 m; P.H. 0.038 m; P.W. 0.023 m.

   Fragment preserving parts of the top and side wall of the oil reservoir. Very worn and chipped; most of the slip missing.

4 C68.729 Forum SE, Street bedding (*statumen*). Buff clay, black slip. P.L. 0.038 m; P.H. 0.036 m; P.W. 0.025 m.

   Two joining fragments preserving parts of the base and the lower side wall of the oil reservoir. Worn and chipped.

200–150 B.C.

5 CEL.225 Atrium Building I, Room 16, Level IV, beneath the mortar throw from the construction of the Basilica. Reddish-buff clay, black slip. P.L. 0.059 m; Height 0.032 m; Width 0.061 m.

   Five joining fragments preserving parts of the top, side wall of the oil reservoir, base, and the start of the handle. Worn and scratched.

175–70 B.C.

6 C66.16 Republican houses, V-D west quadrant, Cesspit 1. Pinkish-buff clay, red slip. P.L. 0.080 m; Height 0.038 m; Width 0.054 m.

   Incomplete, the end of the nozzle and the handle broken away. Worn, encrusted. The discus is unusually wide, with a large air hole at the edge of the discus toward the nozzle.

7 C66.190 House of the Treasure, V-D south quadrant, Level 0. Orange-buff clay, black slip. P.L. 0.059 m; Height 0.038 m; Width 0.048 m.

   Incomplete, the handle and nozzle broken away. Chipped and worn.

8 C66.205 Republican houses, V-D west quadrant, Level I. Buff clay, black slip. P.L. 0.073 m; Height 0.039 m; Width 0.052 m.

   Incomplete, parts of the nozzle and handle broken away. Slip peeling in places. Encrusted and chipped. The discus is unusually wide, almost as wide as the base. The lip of the central filling hole is slightly raised. There is an air hole toward the nozzle, perhaps for drainage as well as air.

9 C66.216 Republican houses, V-D west quadrant. Cream clay, red slip. P.L. 0.075 m; Height 0.032 m; Width 0.052 m.

   Incomplete, the handle and the end of the nozzle broken away. Worn and chipped. An incised groove encircles the central filling hole.

10 C66.882 Republican houses, V-D north quadrant, Sounding 3, Levels I/III. Buff clay, black slip. P.L. 0.067 m; Height 0.036 m; P.W. 0.045 m.

   Fragment preserving the nozzle and parts of the side wall of the oil reservoir and base. Surface rubbed and chipped. Smoke-blackened around the wick hole. Encrusted. A graffito of three letters, *BIO*, was carefully incised after firing (see Fig. 135).

11 C68.591 Republican houses, V-D north quadrant, Room 4, cesspit. Buff clay, black slip. P.L. 0.086 m; Height 0.044 m; Width 0.058 m.

   Two joining fragments. The handle is broken away, and there is minor chipping of the left end of the nozzle. Worn, encrusted, with root marks. Smoke-blackened around the wick hole. The nozzle end is unusually wide.

175–150 B.C.

12 CA.722 Capitolium foundation, Area 4. Buff clay, grayish-black slip. P.L. 0.065 m; P.H. 0.031 m; P.W. 0.050 m.

   Fragment preserving parts of the top, including the filling hole, the side wall of the oil reservoir, and the handle. Worn and chipped.

Before 150 B.C.

13 CD.1201 Sounding under Basilica, NE Aisle I, Level III. Orange-buff clay, mottled black to red slip. P.L. 0.046 m; Height 0.029 m; P.W. 0.031 m.

   Fragment preserving parts of the base, side wall of the oil reservoir, and right side of the nozzle, including half of the wick hole. Chipped and worn, smoke-blackened around wick hole.

150–70 B.C.

14 CB.1692 Capitolium exterior, S, Level II. Pinkish-buff clay, black slip. P.L. 0.094 m; Height 0.037 m; Width 0.052 m.

   Incomplete, the handle, nozzle, and part of the base broken away. The filling hole has a slightly raised lip. A small drainage or air hole has been punched through the discus toward the nozzle. Worn.

15 CB.1725 Capitolium exterior, S, Pronaos, Level II. Orange-buff clay, black slip mottled to brown in places. P.L. 0.083 m; Height 0.038 m; Width 0.056 m.

   Incomplete, the end of the nozzle broken away. Chipped and worn.

16 CB.1729 Capitolium exterior, S, Pronaos, Level II. Grayish-buff clay, black slip. P.L. 0.062 m; P.H. 0.022 m; P.W. 0.053 m.

   Fragment preserving parts of the discus, upper side wall of the oil reservoir, and nozzle. Slip peeling and scratched. An unusual Truncated-Cone Type Lamp—a ridge around the discus opens out toward the wick hole, forming a channel.

17 CB.1835 Capitolium exterior, S, Pronaos, Level II. Buff clay, mottled black slip. P.L. 0.069 m; Height 0.043 m; P.W. 0.057 m.

   Fragment preserving the nozzle and parts of the discus, side wall of the oil reservoir, and base. Worn. The end of the nozzle is deformed and turns sharply down.

18 CB.1837 Capitolium exterior, S, Pronaos, Level II. Cream clay, black slip mottled to brown in places. P.L. 0.067 m; Height 0.039 m; Width 0.062 m.

   Incomplete, the handle and end of the nozzle broken away. Worn. A groove encircles the outer edge of the discus.

19 C65.29 Capitolium exterior, E trench, Level II. Pinkish-buff clay, black slip. P.L. 0.060 m; Height 0.040 m; P.W. 0.055 m.

   Fragment preserving the base and parts of the side wall of the oil reservoir and discus. Worn and encrusted.

20 C65.105 Capitolium exterior, E, SE trench, Level II. Orange-buff clay, red slip. P.L. 0.074 m; Height 0.043 m; Width 0.056 m.

   Incomplete, the end of the nozzle broken away. Slightly worn. No handle. The filling hole has a raised lip. The base is slightly concave. Restored; in the Museo Archeologico della Maremma at Grosseto.

21 C65.106 Capitolium exterior, E, SE trench, Level II. Yellow-buff clay, black slip. P.L. 0.065 m; Height 0.040 m; Width 0.055 m.

   Incomplete, the end of the nozzle and handle broken away. Worn and chipped.

22 C65.107 Capitolium exterior, E, SE trench, Level II. Pinkish-buff clay, black slip. P.L. 0.086 m; Height 0.049 m; Width 0.055 m.

   Incomplete, the handle broken away; minor chipping around the filling hole. Worn. The nozzle is unusually wide and heavy, with an unusually large wick hole.

23 C65.256 Capitolium exterior, NE cut, Level IV. Yellow-buff clay, red slip. P.L. 0.083 m; Height 0.041 m; Width 0.052 m.

   Incomplete, the handle broken away. Worn and chipped.

24 C65.290 Capitolium W, Barracks, Level II. Cream clay, thin black slip. P.L. 0.065 m; Height 0.045 m.

   Fragment preserving parts of the base, side wall of the oil reservoir, and discus. Worn.

25 C65.313 Capitolium W, Barracks, Level II. Pinkish-buff clay, black slip. P.L. 0.069 m; Height 0.045 m; Width 0.052 m.

   Incomplete; the nozzle and handle broken away. Worn and chipped.

26 C65.332 Capitolium exterior, S cut, Level III. Pinkish-buff clay, mottled brown to black slip. P.L. 0.090 m; Height 0.035 m; Width 0.050 m.

   Incomplete, the handle broken away; a chip missing from one fluke of the nozzle. Worn and scratched.

27 C65.333 Capitolium exterior, S cut, Level III. Grayish-buff clay, black slip. P.L. 0.074 m; Height 0.045 m; Width 0.058 m.

   Incomplete, the handle and end of the nozzle broken away. Worn.

28 C65.351 Capitolium exterior, W, Inside medieval enclosure, Level III. Pinkish-buff clay, red slip. P.L. 0.065 m; Height 0.039 m; Width 0.056 m.

   Incomplete, the handle and nozzle broken away. Worn and chipped.

29 C65.353 Capitolium exterior, E, Level III. Pinkish-buff clay, black slip. P.L. 0.062 m; Height 0.039 m; Width 0.055 m.

   Incomplete, the handle and nozzle broken away. The filling hole has a raised lip. Worn.

30 C65.402 Capitolium exterior, W trench, Level III. Grayish-buff clay, dull brown slip poorly applied. P.L. 0.086 m; Height 0.048 m; Width 0.062 m.

   Incomplete, the handle and part of the nozzle broken away. Scratched and worn.

31 C65.403 Capitolium exterior, W trench, Level III. Pinkish-buff clay, black slip. P.L. 0.066 m; Height 0.035 m; Width 0.049 m.

   Incomplete, parts of the nozzle, side wall of the oil reservoir, and a small part of the discus broken away. Worn. An unusual Truncated-Cone Type Lamp, handleless, with a ring base. There is a channel between discus and wick hole, within which is a rectangular opening, very carefully cut, 0.012 m by 0.007 m, about midway between the filling and wick holes.

32 (Fig. 7) C65.429 Capitolium exterior, W trench, Level III. Pinkish-buff clay, black slip. Length

0.093 m; Height 0.049 m; Width 0.049 m.

A complete lamp, except for a small chip from the nozzle. Slip slightly worn. Restored and now in the Museo Archeologico della Maremma at Grosseto.

33 C65.430 Capitolium exterior, W trench, Level III. Grayish-buff clay, black slip. P.L. 0.093 m; Height 0.033 m; Width 0.048 m.

Incomplete, the end of the nozzle and a chip from the top of the handle broken away. Worn and scratched. The end of the nozzle slopes downward. Two ridges extend along the top of the nozzle forming a channel that does not connect the discus and wick hole. The disk base tapers, thinner toward the nozzle.

34 C67.15 Capitolium exterior, W, Levels II/III. Dark buff clay, black slip. P.L. 0.084 m; Height 0.039 m; Width 0.057 m.

Incomplete, the handle and the end of the nozzle broken away. Slip slightly chipped, root marks.

35 C67.74 Capitolium exterior, W, Level III. Buff clay, black slip. P.L. 0.093 m; Height 0.046 m; Width 0.063 m.

Incomplete, part of the handle and left fluke of the nozzle broken away. The handle attached off center to the right. Worn.

36 C67.136 Capitolium exterior, W, Level III. Grayish-buff clay, black slip. P.L. 0.058 m; Height 0.036 m; Width 0.055 m.

Incomplete, the nozzle broken away. Slightly worn and scratched. An unusual Truncated-Cone Type Lamp without base or handle, and with a wider discus than usual.

This is closely related to two lamps found in a tomb on the Esquiline in Rome that are dated fourth/third century B.C. Cf. *Roma medio republicana, aspetti culturali di Roma e del Lazio nei secoli IV e III A.C.* (Rome, 1973), pl. 49.

37 C67.137 Capitolium exterior, E, Level III. Buff clay, black slip. P.L. 0.075 m; Height 0.043 m; Width 0.056 m.

Incomplete, the nozzle broken away. Worn and scratched.

38 C67.193 Capitolium exterior, E, Level III. Buff clay, black slip with a metallic luster. P.L. 0.070 m; Height 0.035 m; Width 0.050 m.

Incomplete, the end of the nozzle and part of the rim broken away. Chipped and worn.

39 C67.216 Capitolium exterior, E, Level III. Buff clay, black slip mottled to brown in places. P.L. 0.067 m; Height 0.040 m; Width 0.060 m.

Fragment preserving part of the base, side wall, and top of the oil reservoir. Worn, chipped, and encrusted.

40 C67.292 Capitolium exterior, E, Level III. Buff clay, thin, red slip. P.L. 0.080 m; Height 0.045 m; Width 0.053 m.

Incomplete, part of the handle and nozzle broken away. Worn and encrusted.

41 C67.537 Capitolium exterior, E, Levels I/II. Buff clay, thin, black slip. P.L. 0.080 m; Height 0.030 m; Width 0.045 m.

Incomplete, the handle broken away. Worn, encrusted, and chipped. Smoke-blackened around the wick hole. The nozzle is unusually wide.

89–70 B.C.

42 C69.172 House of the Skeleton, Sounding I, Level II. Buff clay, black slip. P.L. 0.087 m; Height 0.038 m; Width 0.053 m.

Incomplete, the handle broken away and minor chipping of the end of the nozzle and base. Slip worn and flaking. The large disk base is crudely formed.

43 C70.180 House of the Skeleton, Main garden trench near portico. Orange-buff clay, black slip. P.L. 0.083 m; Height 0.038 m; Width 0.055 m.

Incomplete, the handle and part of the end of the nozzle broken away. Worn; slip peeling. The central filling hole was punched twice, elongating it, and the end of the nozzle was pinched, making it almost triangular.

25/20 B.C.

44 CEL.235 Atrium Building I, Room 16, Level III. Reddish-buff clay, black slip with a metallic luster. P.L. 0.056 m; Height 0.034 m; Width 0.050 m.

Incomplete, parts of the discus, handle, and base broken away. Worn and scratched.

25/20 B.C.–A.D. 50

45 C68.633 House of the Skeleton, Perimeter trench SE of the garden (House of the Birds), Level 0-B (6.5 NE x 12.5 SE). Orange-buff clay, black slip. P.L. 0.087 m; Height 0.035 m; Width 0.049 m.

Four joining fragments making an incomplete lamp, the handle and right fluke of the nozzle broken away.

2. DOUGHNUT TYPE LAMPS

(Fig. 8)

(Catalogue Numbers 46–132)

More than one hundred examples of a wheelmade lamp termed the Doughnut Type, which appears to have been the most popular of all the wheelmade lamp types, have been found at Cosa. Eighty-six examples have been catalogued. Sixty-nine of the eighty-six come from contexts dated before 70 B.C. The remaining fifteen were found in material dated after the resettlement of Cosa in 25/20 B.C.

The clay of these lamps ranges from soft to medium hard; the color is buff, or a variation of buff with green, gray, pink, or orange tint. The lamps are carelessly slipped either black or red, usually with the base unslipped.

The bodies of the oil reservoirs of Doughnut Type Lamps are bun-shaped, flattened top and bottom. A large filling hole centered on the top makes them resemble a doughnut. With few exceptions, they have a wide disk base with a flat and unfinished bottom. The nozzles are broad, deep, and heavy, of the usual spatulate form. The top of the nozzle is on a plane with the top of the oil reservoir. The bottom of the nozzle rises from the bottom of the lamp, covering the base where it is attached. There is usually a large strap handle. The filling hole is usually encircled by a groove, and both the filling and wick holes are very large.

The earliest group of Doughnut Type Lamps consists of five from a context that is dated from 225 to 200 B.C. They were found in a small, undisturbed area of the bedding for a street that led from the center of the Forum on the southeast side, connecting the southeast part of the town with the Forum.

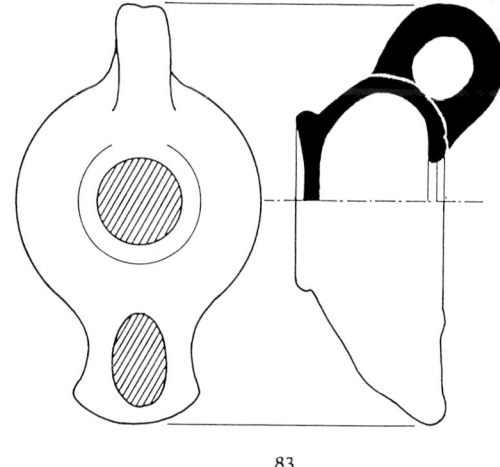

83

Figure 8. Doughnut Type Lamps, scale 1:2

225–200 B.C.

46 C68.273 Forum SE, Level I. Buff clay, mottled black slip. P.L. 0.064 m; Height 0.038 m; Width 0.058 m.

Five joining fragments preserving parts of the oil reservoir, base, and start of the nozzle. Worn, chipped, encrusted. Wide, high disk base. Center of floor raised inside; base slightly concave outside.

47 C68.720 Forum SE, Level I. Orange-buff clay, black slip. P.L. 0.088 m; Height 0.035 m; Width 0.069 m.

Three joining fragments preserving the base, nozzle, parts of the oil reservoir, and start of the handle. Worn and encrusted; slip peeled away in places.

48 C68.721 Forum SE, Level I. Buff clay, mottled black slip. P.L. 0.054 m; P.H. 0.044 m; P.W. 0.032 m.

Fragment preserving the handle and part of the side wall of the oil reservoir. Worn and encrusted. The handle is round in section.

49 C68.722 Forum SE, Level I. Buff clay, black slip. P.L. 0.065 m; P.H. 0.032 m; Width 0.063 m.

Two joining fragments of a lamp; the handle, nozzle, base, and parts of the lower side wall of the oil reservoir are broken away. Very worn and encrusted.

50 C68.735 Forum SE, Level I. Pinkish-buff clay, black slip. P.L. 0.033 m; P.H. 0.025 m; P.W. 0.033 m.

Fragment preserving the nozzle and part of the adjoining side wall of the oil reservoir. Encrusted, chipped; surface worn away in places.

200–150 B.C.

The fourteen lamps below were found under a mortar throw from the construction of the Basilica. Room 16 was a courtyard at that time, later occupied by an addition to Atrium Building I.

51 CE.1404 Atrium Building I, Room 16, Level IV. Buff clay, black slip. Length 0.111 m; Height 0.037 m; Width 0.060 m.

Five joining fragments preserving a complete lamp. Slip worn and slightly chipped. The nozzle is deformed. The large vertical strap handle has raised edges.

52 CE.1409 Atrium Building I, Room 16, Level IV. Reddish-buff clay, black slip. P.L. 0.099 m; Height 0.035 m; Width 0.069 m.

Incomplete lamp, the handle and end of the nozzle broken away. Slip rubbed and chipped.

53 CEL.93 Atrium Building I, Room 16, Level IV. Pinkish-buff clay, black slip. P.L. 0.101 m; P.H. 0.030 m; Width 0.064 m.

Two joining fragments preserving the base, lower side wall of the oil reservoir, bottom and side wall of the nozzle, and lower half of the handle. Slip rubbed. The handle is made from two rolls of clay joined but separated at the lower end (see 55 for a similar handle).

54 CEL.94 Atrium Building I, Room 16, Level IV. Buff clay, glossy black slip. P.L. 0.044 m; P.H. 0.032 m; P.W. 0.041 m.

Two fragments preserving parts of the base, side wall of the oil reservoir, and handle. Worn and chipped.

55 CEL.95 Atrium Building I, Room 16, Level IV. Greenish-cream clay, glossy black slip. P.L. 0.028 m; P.H. 0.033 m.

A complete handle, broken from the oil reservoir at the attachment. The handle is made of two rolls of clay, joined but separated at one end (see 53 for a similar handle).

56 CEL.96 Atrium Building I, Room 16, Level IV. Pinkish-buff clay, mottled brownish-red to black slip. P.L. 0.055 m; P.H. 0.034 m; P.W. 0.051 m.

Fragment preserving most of the nozzle and parts of the adjoining side wall of the oil reservoir. This does not have the usual groove around the filling hole.

57 CEL.98 Atrium Building I, Room 16, Level IV. Reddish-buff clay, mottled brownish-red to black slip. Length 0.108 m; Height 0.032 m; Width 0.054 m.

Two joining fragments; parts of the top and side wall of the oil reservoir are broken away. Worn and chipped.

58 CEL.99 Atrium Building I, Room 16, Level IV. Buff clay, mottled brownish-red to black slip. P.L. 0.087 m; Height 0.036 m; Width 0.066 m.

Four joining fragments; the end of the nozzle, part of the top and side wall of the oil reservoir, and a chip from the top of the handle are broken away. Worn and scratched. The disk base is poorly turned.

59 CEL.100 Atrium Building I, Room 16, Level IV. Buff clay, mottled brownish-red to black slip. P.L. 0.077 m; Height 0.031 m; Width 0.063 m.

Incomplete lamp; the handle and end of the nozzle are broken away. Glaze rubbed and chipped.

60 CEL.101 Atrium Building I, Room 16, Level IV. Reddish-buff clay, mottled brownish-red to black slip. P.L. 0.103 m; P.H. 0.027 m; Width 0.065 m.

Two joining fragments preserving parts of the top of the oil reservoir, the nozzle, and the start of the handle. Slip chipped and worn.

61 CEL.103 Atrium Building I, Room 16, Level IV. Cream clay, black slip. P.L. 0.029 m; P.H. 0.032 m; P.W. 0.025 m.

Fragment preserving part of the top and side

wall of the oil reservoir. Surface worn and flaked.

62 CEL.104 Atrium Building I, Room 16, Level IV. Buff clay, black slip. P.L. 0.031 m; P.H. 0.029 m; P.W. 0.032 m.

Two joining fragments preserving parts of the top and side wall of the oil reservoir and nozzle.

63 CEL.192 Atrium Building I, Room 16, Level IV. Reddish-buff clay, black slip. P.L. 0.082 m; Height 0.035 m; Width 0.069 m.

Incomplete, the handle and end of the nozzle broken away.

64 CEL.193 Atrium Building I, Room 16, Level IV. Buff clay, black slip. Length 0.111 m; Height 0.037 m; Width 0.061 m.

Five joining fragments preserving a complete lamp, except for minor chipping. Surface worn and chipped. The large vertical strap handle has raised edges.

197–180 B.C.

The three lamps below are from a sounding on the northwest side of the Forum in the packed soil of a dirt ramp or apron that led up to the door of one of the shops in Atrium Building I.

65 CD.1185 Basilica exterior, SW 1, Portico sounding, Level III. Orange-buff clay, black slip. P.L. 0.070 m; P.H. 0.030 m; P.W. 0.053 m.

Two joining fragments preserving parts of the top, side wall of the oil reservoir, and start of the handle. Chipped and worn.

66 CD.1186 Basilica exterior, SW 1, Portico sounding, Level III. Orange-buff clay, mottled black and red slip. P.L. 0.054 m; P.H. 0.027 m; P.W. 0.029 m.

Fragment preserving parts of the base and lower side wall of the oil reservoir. Chipped and worn.

67 CD.1187 Basilica exterior, SW 1, Portico sounding, Level III. Orange-buff clay, mottled black and red slip. P.L. 0.049 m; P.H. 0.011 m; P.W. 0.038 m.

Fragment preserving parts of the lower side wall of the oil reservoir and nozzle. Chipped and worn.

185–170 B.C.

The four lamps below came from the accumulation at the bottom of a cesspit containing material deposited before the sewers were installed along Street 6.

68 C72.70 Atrium Building I, Room 13, cesspit, gray deposit, Level II. Yellow-buff clay, mottled black to red slip. Length 0.101 m; Height 0.033 m; Width 0.058 m.

Four joining fragments making an almost complete lamp. Parts of the side wall and top of the oil reservoir are broken away. Worn, encrusted. The wick hole is punched off center and slightly deformed, and the handle bent to the right.

69 C72.71 Atrium Building I, Room 13, cesspit, gray deposit, Level II. Pinkish-buff clay, mottled black to red slip. P.L. 0.107 m; Height 0.034 m; Width 0.058 m.

Three joining fragments preserving most of a lamp. The base and handle are intact, and parts of the side wall, the top of the oil reservoir, and the nozzle are preserved. Worn, encrusted. The large vertical strap handle was bent to the right before firing.

70 C72.135A Atrium Building I, Room 13, cesspit, gray deposit, Level II. Pinkish-buff clay, red slip. P.L. 0.069 m; P.W. 0.065 m.

Two joining fragments preserving the nozzle, parts of the side wall, and top of the oil reservoir. Smoke-blackened around wick hole. Worn and encrusted.

71 C72.136A Atrium Building I, Room 13, cesspit, gray deposit, Level II. Buff clay, black slip. P.L. 0.060 m; P.H. 0.036 m; P.W. 0.056 m.

Fragment preserving the handle and parts of the top and side wall of the oil reservoir. Worn and encrusted.

175–150 B.C.

The five lamps below are from beneath the floors of two of the cellae of the Capitolium and must predate the construction of that building.

72 CB.476 Capitolium, Cella I W, Level: first meter. Dark buff clay, black slip mottled to brown in places. P.L. 0.059 m; P.H. 0.034 m; P.W. 0.023 m.

Fragment preserving parts of the top, side wall, and base of the oil reservoir. Worn and chipped. On the preserved part of the top is a fragmentary graffito of three roughly parallel grooves scratched after firing (see Fig. 135).

73 CB.540 Capitolium, Cella I W, Level: second meter. Grayish-buff clay, black slip. P.L. 0.076 m; P.H. 0.032 m; P.W. 0.036 m.

Fragment preserving parts of the base, side wall of the oil reservoir, and nozzle. Slip rubbed.

74 CB.556 Capitolium, Cella I W, Level: third meter. Buff clay, black slip. P.L. 0.053 m; P.H. 0.033 m; P.W. 0.048 m.

Fragment preserving most of the nozzle and parts of the top and side wall of the oil reservoir. Smoke-blackened around wick hole. Worn.

75 CB.606 Capitolium, Cella I E, Level: 0.50–1.50 m. Buff clay, black slip. Width of handle 0.026 m.

Fragment preserving most of a vertical strap handle with raised edges and part of the side wall of the oil reservoir. Worn and chipped.

76 CB.610 Capitolium, Cella I E, Level: 0.50–1.50 m. Buff clay, black slip. P.L. 0.078 m; P.H. 0.040 m; P.W. 0.037 m.

Fragment preserving the left half of the nozzle and parts of the top and side wall of the oil reservoir. The top of the lamp is unusual in that it continues convex instead of turning down toward the edge of the filling hole. Slip worn.

Before 150 B.C.
The five lamps below were found below the foundations of the Basilica.

77 CD.1196 Basilica exterior, NE 6, Level V. Orange-buff clay, black slip. P.L. 0.086 m; Height 0.035 m; Width 0.058 m.

Incomplete, the end of the nozzle broken away. Worn and chipped. Smoke-blackened around the wick hole. This lamp does not have the usual groove around the filling hole. Large vertical strap handle with three ribs.

78 CD.1198 Basilica exterior, NE 6, Level V. Orange-buff clay, mottled black to red slip. P.L. 0.079 m; P.H. 0.023 m; Width 0.064 m.

Four joining fragments preserving most of a lamp. The handle, end of the nozzle, and base are broken away. Worn and chipped.

79 CD.1199 Basilica, NE Aisle I, Level III. Buff clay, black slip, mottled red on the base. P.L. 0.082 m; P.H. 0.030 m; P.W. 0.068 m.

Fragment preserving the base, lower side wall of the oil reservoir, and parts of the nozzle. Worn, chipped, and pitted. An uneven groove separates the disk base from the oil reservoir.

80 CD.1200 Basilica, NE Aisle I, Level III. Buff clay, black slip. P.L. 0.048 m; P.H. 0.039 m; P.W. 0.036 m.

Fragment preserving a rather thick vertical strap handle with raised edges and parts of the top and side wall of the oil reservoir. Worn, chipped, and scratched.

81 CD.1202 Basilica, NE Aisle I, Level III. Orange-buff clay, red slip. P.L. 0.043 m; P.H. 0.033 m; P.W. 0.038 m.

Fragment preserving the nozzle and part of the side wall of the oil reservoir. Chipped, worn, smoke-blackened around the wick hole.

The three lamps below are all from a cesspit in a republican house. They are similar and were obviously made by a single potter who was careless in handling all three before they dried, since the ends of the nozzles and the handles were all pushed to the right.

82 C71.53 House of the Birds, Room 12, cesspit, Level II C. Buff clay, thin, mottled black slip. Length 0.110 m; Height 0.034 m; Width 0.055 m.

Three joining fragments preserving a lamp complete except for a chip broken from the base. Worn, smoke-blackened around wick hole.

83 (Fig. 8) C71.92 House of the Birds, Room 12, cesspit, Level II A & B. Orange-buff clay, black slip. Length 0.110 m; Height 0.035 m; Width 0.065 m.

Three joining fragments preserving a complete lamp. Slip rubbed and chipped. Smoke-blackened around the wick hole.

84 C71.218 House of the Birds, Room 12, cesspit, Level II A & B. Buff clay, black slip. Length 0.117 m; Height 0.032 m; Width 0.067 m.

Incomplete, part of the base and lower side wall of the oil reservoir broken away. Smoke-blackened around wick hole. Chipped, slip worn away in places.

175–70 B.C.
85 C66.167 House of Quintus Fulvius, V-D west, Level I. Buff clay grogged with brown clay, red slip mottled to black. P.L. 0.087 m; Height 0.036 m; P.W. 0.049 m.

Fragment preserving the base and part of the top with groove around opening, the side wall of the oil reservoir, and parts of the looped vertical handle and triangular nozzle. Worn and encrusted. Smoke-blackened around wick hole. Broneer Type 17.

86 C66.226 House of Quintus Fulvius, V-D west, Cesspit 3. Buff clay, red slip. Length 0.107 m; Height 0.042 m; P.W. 0.052 m.

Three joining fragments forming most of a lamp, parts of the top and side wall of the oil reservoir broken away. Slip worn. The top of the nozzle is lower than the top of the oil reservoir. The large vertical handle is almost round in section.

87 C66.349 V-D north, Sounding I, between Rooms 14 & 15, Level I. Buff clay, red slip mottled to black in places. P.L. 0.076 m; Height 0.036 m; Width 0.057 m.

Incomplete, the nozzle and part of the handle broken away. Worn, surface peeling in places. This lamp lacks the usual groove around the filling hole.

88 C68.592 House of the Birds, Room 4, cesspit. Buff clay, black slip. P.L. 0.080 m; Height 0.038 m; Width 0.057 m.

Incomplete, the handle and parts of the top and side wall of the oil reservoir broken away. Very worn.

89 C68.708 House of the Birds, Room 4, cesspit sediment. Buff clay, black slip. P.L. 0.100 m; Height 0.036 m; Width 0.058 m.

Two joining fragments forming a lamp complete except for minor chipping of the handle. Very worn, encrusted.

150–70 B.C.

The group of lamps below is from contexts containing debris of the destruction of ca. 70 B.C.

90 CB.1679 Capitolium exterior, S, Level II. Buff clay, black slip, mottled to brown in places. Length 0.089 m; Height 0.030 m; Width 0.049 m.

A complete lamp. Surface rubbed. Vertical strap handle with raised edges.

91 CB.1836 Capitolium exterior, S, Pronaos, Level II. Buff clay, black slip, mottled to brown in places. Length 0.102 m; Height 0.039 m; Width 0.063 m.

Incomplete, the top of the nozzle and parts of the side wall of the oil reservoir broken away. Worn and scratched. Large vertical handle of semicircular section. Disk base. The floor of the oil reservoir is swirled up to a point. The filling hole lacks the usual encircling groove.

92 CB.1865 Cistern below the wall of the Arx (VI-G, "rock crevice"). Pinkish-buff clay, black slip. Length 0.117 m; Height 0.041 m; Width 0.056 m.

Almost complete Doughnut Type Lamp. Surface worn and chipped. Nozzle end broken away. Lightly encrusted.

93 C65.36 Capitolium exterior, E, Level II. Pinkish-buff clay, black slip with a metallic luster. P.L. 0.083 m; Height 0.040 m; Width 0.061 m.

Incomplete, the end of the nozzle, the handle, and part of the side wall of the oil reservoir broken away. Worn and scratched.

94 C65.48 Capitolium exterior, E, Level II. Reddish-buff clay, thin, black slip. P.L. 0.083 m; Height 0.034 m; Width 0.058 m.

Incomplete, the handle and part of the side wall of the oil reservoir broken away. The elongated wick hole is punched off center. Worn.

95 C65.79 Capitolium exterior, E trench, Level II. Pinkish-buff clay, black slip. P.L. 0.095 m; P.H. 0.026 m; P.W. 0.057 m.

Fragment preserving the handle and parts of the top and side wall of the oil reservoir. Worn and scratched. The top of the lamp is concave around the central filling hole; a groove marks the transition. Large, thick, vertical strap handle with raised edges.

96 C65.130 Capitolium exterior, E, S cut, Level II. Buff clay, red slip. P.L. 0.080 m; Height 0.038 m; P.W. 0.035 m.

Incomplete, the handle and part of the side wall of the oil reservoir broken away. Heavily encrusted, surface very worn. The deformed filling hole is smaller than usual.

97 C65.170 Capitolium exterior, E, S cut, Level II. Buff clay, black slip. P.L. 0.077 m; Height 0.035 m; Width 0.063 m.

Incomplete, the end of the nozzle and the handle broken away. Worn and encrusted.

98 C65.185 Capitolium exterior, W trench, Level II. Yellowish-buff clay, black slip mottled to brown in places. P.L. 0.101 m; Height 0.034 m; Width 0.061 m.

Incomplete, the handle and part of the top broken away. Worn and encrusted.

99 C65.193 Capitolium exterior, E, "Pit," Level III. Yellowish-buff clay, black slip. P.L. 0.050 m; Height 0.030 m; Width 0.046 m.

Incomplete, the nozzle, handle, and part of the top broken away. Worn and encrusted.

100 C65.209 Capitolium exterior, W trench, Level III. Yellowish-buff clay, black slip mottled to brown in

places. P.L. 0.082 m; Height 0.036 m; Width 0.062 m.

Incomplete, the end of the nozzle and the handle broken away. High, carelessly turned base. Encrusted and worn.

101 C65.247 Capitolium exterior, NE cut, Level IV. Pinkish-buff clay, black slip mottled to brown in places. P.L. 0.086 m; Height 0.034 m; Width 0.054 m.

Incomplete, the end of the nozzle broken away. Heavy encrustation. Large vertical handle of round section.

102 C65.248 Capitolium exterior, NE cut, Level IV. Pinkish-buff clay, orange-red slip. P.L. 0.086 m; Height 0.036 m; Width 0.054 m.

Incomplete, the end of the nozzle broken away. Worn and encrusted.

103 C65.255 Capitolium exterior, NE cut, Level IV. Pinkish-buff clay, black slip mottled to brown in places. P.L. 0.061 m; Height 0.033 m; Width 0.045 m.

Incomplete, the handle and the end of the nozzle broken away. Worn and encrusted. Graffito on the side of the oil reservoir, incised after firing, letters without serifs: IIVN (see Fig. 135).

104 C65.291 Capitolium exterior, W, Barracks, Level II. Pinkish-buff clay, brownish-red slip. P.L. 0.080 m; Height 0.040 m; Width 0.055 m.

Incomplete, the nozzle, handle, and part of the top of the oil reservoir broken away. Chipped and worn.

105 C65.334 Capitolium exterior, E, Level III. Buff clay, black slip mottled to brown in places. P.L. 0.088 m; Height 0.053 m; Width 0.052 m.

Incomplete, the handle broken away and chips broken from the nozzle. Surface worn and pitted.

106 C66.482 Capitolium exterior, W, Level II. Buff clay, mottled black to brownish-red slip. P.L. 0.080 m; Height 0.034 m; Width 0.054 m.

Incomplete, the end of the nozzle broken away and a hole in the base of the lamp. Chipped and worn. High turned base. Filling hole deformed.

107 C66.483 Capitolium exterior, W, Level II. Cream clay, slip mottled black to brown with a metallic luster. Length 0.091 m; Height 0.035 m; Width 0.060 m.

Incomplete, part of the side of the nozzle broken away.

108 C67.138 Capitolium exterior, E, Level III. Buff clay, black slip. P.L. 0.085 m; Height 0.028 m; Width 0.047 m.

Incomplete, part of the handle broken away and chips missing from the edge of the filling hole. The nozzle is deformed; the carelessly formed wick hole is partially punched through the sloping end of the nozzle. The fabric is unusually thick. The base is not clearly separated from the oil reservoir. Worn; smoke-blackened around wick hole. The handle was a horizontal lug; there is no sign of attachment at the top.

109 C67.145 Capitolium exterior, E, Level II/III. Buff clay, red slip. P.L. 0.091 m; Height 0.037 m; Width 0.057 m.

Incomplete, the end of the nozzle broken away. Surface chipped and worn. Fire-blackened. Large vertical strap handle with slightly raised edges.

110 C67.166 Capitolium exterior, E, Level III. Buff clay, black slip. P.L. 0.065 m; Height 0.043 m; Width 0.055 m.

Incomplete, the handle and end of the nozzle broken away. Worn, chipped, and encrusted.

111 C67.257 Capitolium exterior, W, Level II. Buff clay, mottled black to brown slip. P.L. 0.070 m; Height 0.037 m; Width 0.060 m.

Incomplete, the handle and end of the nozzle broken away. Worn and encrusted.

112 C67.315 Capitolium exterior, E, Level III. Buff clay, mottled dark red slip. P.L. 0.109 m; Height 0.034 m; Width 0.055 m.

Incomplete, the end of the nozzle broken away. Worn, chipped, root-marked, encrusted. Smoke-blackened around wick hole.

113 C69.108 Settling tank of the NW cistern of the fish market. Buff clay, red slip. Length 0.104 m; Height 0.038 m; Width 0.060 m.

Complete lamp. Encrusted, slip peeling.

120–25/20 B.C.

114 CB.1855 Pottery dump, scattered. Orange-buff clay, black slip. P.L. 0.081 m; Height 0.033 m; Width 0.058 m.

Incomplete, the nozzle, part of the adjacent side wall, and top of the oil reservoir broken away. Worn and chipped.

89–70 B.C.

115 C69.50 House of the Skeleton, Main garden trench near portico, Level I. Buff clay, black slip. P.L. 0.093 m; Height 0.033 m; Width 0.053 m.

Two joining fragments preserving most of a

lamp. Part of the handle and right side of the nozzle end are broken away. Worn, encrusted, and chipped.
116 C69.139 House of the Skeleton, Fish pool in the corner of the garden near the portico. Pinkish-buff clay, black slip. P.L. 0.096 m; Height 0.032 m; Width 0.054 m.
Incomplete, the end of the nozzle broken away. Surface very worn and chipped. Lightly encrusted.
117 C70.6 House of the Skeleton, Main garden trench near portico, Level I. Buff clay, black slip. P.L. 0.095 m; Height 0.037 m; Width 0.058 m.
Incomplete, the nozzle broken off. Most of the slip worn away. The disk base was damaged before firing.

25/20 B.C.
118 CEL.199 Atrium Building I, Room 11, Level III. Buff clay, mottled black to reddish-brown slip. P.L. 0.080 m; Height 0.034 m; Width 0.059 m.
Two joining fragments preserving parts of the base and nozzle. Worn.
119 CEL.234 Atrium Building I, Room 16, Level III. Buff clay, mottled black to orange-brown slip. P.L. 0.086 m; Height 0.034 m; Width 0.059 m.
Incomplete, the handle and part of the nozzle broken away. Surface rubbed and chipped.
120 CEL.266 Atrium Building I, Room 11, Level III. Buff clay, black slip. Length 0.105 m; Height 0.036 m; Width 0.056 m.
Two joining fragments preserving parts of all essential features. Slip worn and chipped. Strap handle twisted to one side before firing.

25/20 B.C.–A.D. 50
121 CD.1205 Basilica exterior, NE 4/5, Level II. Orange-buff clay, red slip. P.L. 0.056 m; P.H. 0.033 m; P.W. 0.054 m.
Fragment preserving the nozzle and parts of the top and side wall of the oil reservoir. Worn, chipped, smoke-blackened around the wick hole.
122 CD.1211 Basilica exterior, NE 1, Level III. Orange-buff clay, black slip. P.L. 0.036 m; P.W. 0.038 m.
Fragment preserving the handle and part of the adjoining side wall of the oil reservoir. Worn and chipped.
123 CD.1212 Basilica exterior, NE 1, Level III. Buff clay, mottled black to red slip. P.L. 0.030 m; P.W. 0.036 m.
Fragment preserving the handle and part of the adjoining side wall of the oil reservoir. Worn, chipped, and encrusted.
124 CEL.189 Atrium Building I, Room 24B, cesspit, Level IV. Buff clay, black slip. P.L. 0.040 m; P.W. 0.033 m.
Fragment preserving part of the top and upper side wall of the oil reservoir and nozzle. Very worn, slip worn away in places. A small wedge of clay was cut from the side of the nozzle before firing.
125 CF.847 Atrium Building I, Room 25B, cesspit, Level IV. Buff clay, black slip. P.L. 0.079 m; Height 0.031 m; Width 0.056 m.
Incomplete, the nozzle and part of the side wall of the oil reservoir broken away. Worn, scratched.
126 CF.848 Atrium Building I, Room 25B, cesspit, Level IV. Buff clay, mottled red to black slip. P.L. 0.067 m; Height 0.032 m; Width 0.056 m.
Fragment preserving the handle, parts of the top, side wall of the oil reservoir, and base. Badly rubbed and encrusted.
127 CF.1589 Atrium Building I, Room 25B, cesspit, Level IV. Buff clay, mottled reddish-brown to black slip. P.L. 0.069 m; Height 0.036 m; P.W. 0.048 m.
Fragment preserving the nozzle, base, and part of the side wall of the oil reservoir. Worn and chipped.
128 C69.318 Atrium Building II, Forum NW, Level I. Dark reddish-buff clay, self-slip. Length 0.075 m; Height 0.040 m; Width 0.050 m.
A complete handleless Doughnut Type Lamp. Encrusted, root-marked. Deformed nozzle pushed to the right while the clay was soft.

A.D. 50–225
129 CEL.105 Atrium Building I, Room 15, Level I. Buff clay, black slip. P.L. 0.047 m; P.H. 0.018 m; P.W. 0.035 m.
Fragment preserving parts of the base, lower side wall of the oil reservoir, and nozzle. Worn.
130 CEL.117 Atrium Building I, Room 10, Level I. Pinkish-buff clay, mottled black to brown slip. P.L. 0.067 m; Height 0.033 m; P.W. 0.056 m.
Fragment preserving parts of the base and lower side wall of the oil reservoir and the underside of the nozzle. Worn and chipped.
131 CEL.120 Atrium Building I, Room 10, Level II. Buff clay, black slip. P.L. 0.053 m; Height 0.033 m;

P.W. 0.028 m.

Fragment preserving parts of the base, side, and top of the oil reservoir, and the attachment of the handle. Very worn.

132 CEL.224 Atrium Building I, Room 14, Level I. Buff clay, black slip. P.L. 0.043 m; P.H. 0.020 m; P.W. 0.040 m.

Fragment preserving parts of the base and adjoining side wall of the oil reservoir and nozzle. Slip worn and chipped.

3. CENTRAL-TUBE TYPE LAMPS
(Fig. 9)

(Catalogue Numbers 133–143)

Eleven wheelmade lamps with an open annular reservoir around a central tube have been found at Cosa. The vertical tube through the center of the oil reservoir would have allowed the lamp to be hung on a cord or placed on an upright peg or spike, as well as set on a flat surface. In section the outer wall of the oil reservoir is slightly convex, the tube wall vertical. The top of the central tube is slightly higher than the outer rim. These lamps were a great improvement over their fifth- and fourth-century Greek prototypes, which had a broad, shallow, open well, a short central tube, and a small, spoon-shaped nozzle (see Howland, 52–56, 85–91). The Cosan lamps have deep oil reservoirs, almost twice as deep as they are wide.

Nine of the Cosan lamps have a flat bottom; two have a ring foot; none has a handle. The nozzle is broad and deep with the usual Roman spatulate form. It rises from the bottom of the oil reservoir, and the top of the nozzle is on a plane with the outer rim of the oil reservoir. All the wick holes are large.

The clay is buff, sometimes buff with orange, pink, or gray tints. One has a self-slip; one has a red slip; the other nine all have a black slip. The fabric is thick and hard, which explains why these lamps are unusually well preserved.

One lamp was found in a context dated to before 150 B.C. Eight come from levels dated before 70 B.C., while the remaining two probably belong to the same period, although their contexts have been given extended dating to A.D. 50. Since so few examples of this type have been found, it seems likely that all are of more or less the same date.

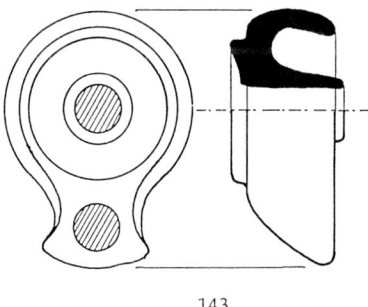

143

Figure 9. Central-Tube Type Lamps, scale 1:2

175–70 B.C.
133 C66.169 Republican houses, V-D west quadrant, Level I. Grayish-buff clay, self-slip. P.L. 0.066 m; Height of side wall 0.026 m, of central tube 0.028 m; Width 0.050 m.

Incomplete, part of the end of the nozzle broken away and minor chips broken from the rim. Worn. High ring foot; the outer face of the foot is vertical; the inner rises to join the central tube.

ca. 150 B.C.

134 CB.829 Temple of Mater Matuta exterior, Level II. Orange-buff clay, black slip. P.L. 0.057 m; P.H. 0.017 m; P.W. 0.063 m.

Fragment preserving the bottom and parts of the lower side wall of the oil reservoir and the central tube. Surface worn and scratched.

150–70 B.C.

135 CB.1726 Capitolium exterior, S, Pronaos, Level II. Orange-buff clay, red slip. P.L. 0.044 m; P.H. 0.022 m; P.W. 0.044 m.

Fragment preserving all but a corner of the nozzle and parts of the upper side wall of the oil reservoir. Worn and scratched. What is preserved of the side wall is vertical.

136 CB.1728 Capitolium exterior, S, Pronaos, Level II. Dark buff clay, black slip. P.L. 0.067 m; Height of side wall 0.029 m, of central tube 0.031 m; P.W. 0.043 m.

Incomplete, part of the outer wall of the oil reservoir broken away. Slip worn. The outer wall of the reservoir is convex.

137 CB.1841 Capitolium exterior, S, Pronaos, Level II. Buff clay, black slip mottled to brown in places. P.L. 0.045 m; P.H. 0.021 m; P.W. 0.050 m.

Fragment preserving the bottom and lower side wall of the oil reservoir and central tube. The lower wall of the tube was beveled with a sharp tool, widening from a diameter of 0.012 m to 0.018 m.

138 CB.1843 Capitolium exterior, S, Pronaos, Level II. Buff clay, black slip. Height 0.028 m; Interior diameter of tube 0.010 m at the top, and 0.016 m at the bottom.

Complete tube of a Central-Tube Type Lamp together with part of the bottom, broken off along the outer edge of the bottom. Worn.

139 C65.109 Capitolium exterior, W trench, Level I. Pinkish-buff clay, blackish-brown slip. Length 0.065 m; Height of side wall 0.030 m, of central tube 0.028 m; Width 0.053 m.

Complete except for minor chipping on the edge of the rim. Slip worn, encrusted. The lamp has been restored and is now in the Museo Archeologico della Maremma at Grosseto.

140 C65.331 Capitolium exterior, S trench, Level III. Orange-red clay, black slip. Length 0.067 m; Height of the side wall 0.032 m; P.H. of tube 0.031 m; Width 0.049 m.

Incomplete, part of the rim and top of the tube broken away. Worn, encrusted, and chipped.

141 C67.247 Capitolium exterior, W, Level III. Buff clay, mottled brown slip. Length 0.067 m; Height of side wall 0.030 m, of central tube 0.031 m; Width 0.048 m.

Complete, except for a minor chip from the rim of the oil reservoir. The bottom is flat, the outer wall slightly convex. The lamp has been restored and is now in the Museo Archeologico della Maremma at Grosseto.

142 C67.349 Capitolium exterior, W, Level III. Buff clay, black slip. Length 0.065 m; Height of side wall 0.029 m, of central tube 0.032 m; Width 0.050 m.

Intact, except for a chip missing at the top of the tube. Slip worn and scratched. The bottom of the lamp is flat. The lower side wall of the oil reservoir is convex but becomes almost vertical toward the top.

89–70 B.C.

143 (Fig. 9) C69.149 House of the Skeleton, Sounding I, Fish pool in corner of garden near the portico, Level II. Buff clay, black slip. Length 0.055 m; Height of the side wall 0.023 m, of the central tube 0.027 m; Width 0.043 m.

Complete, except for minor chipping of the rim. Slip worn and flaking. Heavy encrustation on the bottom; the bottom of the lamp is not covered by the slip. The lamp has a high ring foot; the outer face of the foot is vertical; the inner rises sharply to the inner vertical wall of the central tube.

4. WATCH TYPE LAMPS
(Fig. 10)

(Catalogue Numbers 144–150)

Only seven examples of a type of small wheelmade lamp often called the "Kitchen Lamp" have been found at Cosa. We have termed these Watch Type Lamps because they are different in form and especially in nozzle shape from the usual "Kitchen Lamps" found in large numbers throughout the Greek and Roman worlds.[1] The bun form of the oil reservoir is flattened with a low disk base and a very wide filling hole at the crown, so it resembles a thick, old-fashioned pocket watch. The nozzle is very short, broad, and rounded, rising from the low disk base. The nozzle is integrated with the side wall of the oil reservoir, occupying about one-quarter of its circumference. The large wick hole is very close to the central filling hole. None of these lamps has a handle.

There are variations in the forms of the oil reservoir of the "Kitchen Lamps" found elsewhere: some have high bases; some have oil reservoirs with flattened tops level with the filling holes; some have carinated bodies. The nozzles of most are small, tacked-on appendages, but the nozzles of the Watch Type Lamps from Cosa are an integral part of the lamps.

The clay of five of the seven Watch Type Lamps is

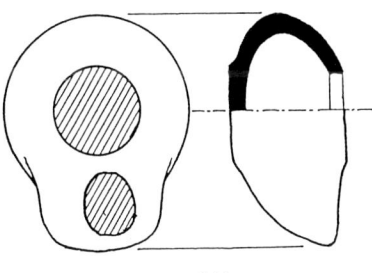

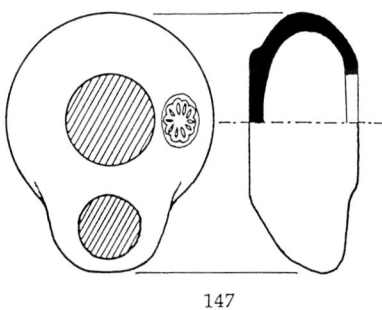

Figure 10. Watch Type Lamps, scale 1:2

1. Bailey 1975, 179–82, pl. 80 nos. Q 405–26. These lamps from Rhodes have carinated bodies; otherwise they are closely related to the Cosan Watch Type Lamps. Similar lamps have been found in Carthage, Athens, and other sites in Italy. See Andrén, 38, pl. 18, no. M, 11b; Bruneau 27, pl. 2, no. 44 (with a small nozzle); Gualandi Genito 1977, 40, p. 13, no. 46; Howland, pp. 98–99, pls. 15, 41 (dated from the second half of the third to mid-second century B.C.; Szentléleky, 37, nos. 18, 19; Taylor, 72, 93, pls. 22, 23; Travagli Visser, 115–34, 165–84; Zaccaria Ruggiu 1980, 20–24, 27–30 (dated from mid-third to beginning of second century B.C.).

buff colored. They all are self-slipped. One of the two remaining lamps was damaged by fire, and the clay is now a grayish red; the clay of the other is orange-red. This lamp is slightly larger than the other six and has a small rosette stamped on the left side of the top near the filling hole.

Two Cosan Watch Type Lamps come from a context dated 225–200 B.C. They were found in the bedding of the street that led to the southeast entrance to the Forum. Two lamps were found in the debris used as terracing fill around the Capitolium after the disaster of 70 B.C. dated 150–70 B.C. The dating of the three remaining lamps is not so secure; one is from material that dates from before 70 B.C. The remaining two come from contexts that might date anywhere from before 70 B.C. to A.D. 225. However, since so few of these little lamps with a non-Roman nozzle have been found at Cosa so far, it is probable that they all should be dated before 70 B.C.

225–200 B.C.

144 C68.719 Forum SE, Street bedding. Dark buff clay. P.L. 0.059 m; Height 0.031 m; P.W. 0.049 m.

Fragment preserving the base, half of the wall of the oil reservoir, an arc of the filling hole, and the start of the nozzle. Worn and encrusted.

145 C68.728 Forum SE, Street bedding. Buff clay. P.L. 0.050 m; Height 0.032 m; Width 0.055 m.

Fragment preserving the base, part of the wall of the oil reservoir, and an arc of the filling hole. The clay of the floor of the oil reservoir is swirled up in a cone, and the bottom is slightly concave. Worn and encrusted.

150–70 B.C.

146 (Fig. 10) C65.88 Capitolium exterior, E, Level II. Buff clay. Length 0.060 m; Height 0.031 m; Width 0.050 m.

Complete, except for small chips from the edge of the filling hole. Worn.

147 (Fig. 10) C67.314 Capitolium exterior, E, Level III. Orange-red clay. Length 0.070 m; Height 0.030 m; Width 0.057 m.

Complete, except for a small chip broken from the edge of the filling hole. There is a small ten-petaled rosette, 0.009 m in diameter, stamped on the left side of the oil reservoir near the filling hole (see Fig. 136). The lamp is slightly larger than the other six examples of the Watch Type (see Taylor, pls. 22, 23, and 31 for examples of small stamped rosettes on black glaze ware).

89–70 B.C.

148 C70.57 House of the Skeleton, Garden rear, Level I. Buff clay. Length 0.058 m; Height 0.031 m; Width 0.044 m.

Complete. Encrusted, smoke-blackened around wick hole. Three small notches were cut in the edge of the base opposite the nozzle after firing.

Before A.D. 225 and probably before 70 B.C.

149 CB.1197 Capitolium exterior, S, Surface. Grayish-red clay, grayed by fire. P.L. 0.035 m; Height 0.030 m; Width 0.043 m.

Four joining fragments forming most of a lamp. Most of the nozzle is broken away.

150 CEL.119 Atrium Building I, Room 10, Impluvium, Level II. Buff clay. P.L. 0.059 m; P.H. 0.026 m; P.W. 0.038 m.

Fragment preserving parts of the top, wall of the oil reservoir, and nozzle, and arcs of the filling and wick holes. Worn and chipped.

5. ESQUILINE TYPE LAMPS
(Fig. 11)

(Catalogue Numbers 151–182)

The fifth type of wheelmade lamp found at Cosa is called the Esquiline Type. It is characterized by a squat cylindrical oil reservoir.[1] Thirty-nine examples have been found, of which thirty-three have been catalogued. Only one of these lamps is from a context dated before 150 B.C. One is from a context dated 150–70 B.C. Nineteen are from contexts dated 120–70 B.C.; and one from the garden in the House of the Skeleton from one dated 89–70 B.C. Four have been dated 100 to 25/20 B.C., and one is from a context of the resettlement period of 25/20 B.C. (see Chronology, page 14). Two lamps are from a context dated 25/20 B.C. to A.D. 50, and four are from disturbed levels that can be dated anywhere from 25/20 B.C. to A.D. 225. Of seven uncatalogued fragments, five are from contexts dated before 70 B.C., and the remaining two from contexts dated 100 to 25/20 B.C.

The clay of all but three of the Cosan Esquiline Type Lamps is the same: hard, coarse, grogged with black and white sand, and brick-red or orange-red in color. The fabric is strong, and these lamps are well preserved, especially their heavy nozzles. These thirty closely related lamps all have a self-slip, except one that has a black slip. They have no handle or base. In the remaining three the clay is fine and rather soft, buff-col-

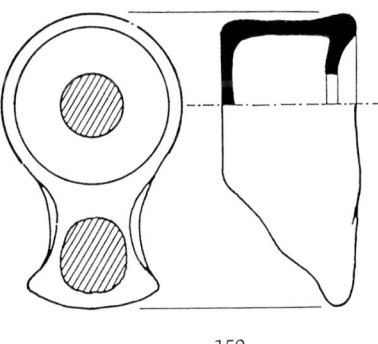

159

Figure 11. Esquiline Type Lamps, scale 1:2

ored with a tint of pink or orange. Two have a black slip; one has self-slip. All have strap handles, and two have disk bases.

All thirty-three of the Cosan Esquiline Type Lamps have cylindrical oil reservoirs. The vertical wall of the oil reservoir rises from a flat bottom, except in three examples that have disk bases. The concave discus with a central filling hole entirely covers the reservoir. The nozzles of some are so long and heavy that there is danger of the lamps tipping over when the reservoirs are empty. The top of the nozzle is horizontal, usually on a plane with the rim, although on some examples the nozzle is slightly higher. It rises steadily from the bottom of the lamp to its tip, occupying about one-quarter of the circumference of the oil reservoir. It is smoothly luted

---

1. Lamps of this type from Isthmia, Delos, and the Athenian Agora were probably produced locally, and lamps of this shape continued to be produced in certain parts of the Roman empire into the first century A.D.

on so that the sides of the nozzle swing out almost imperceptibly from the wall of the oil reservoir, and then curve gently to meet the convex end of the nozzle in blunt flukes. The filling and wick holes are very large.

Four of the Esquiline Type Lamps have inscriptions, of which two were made before and two after firing (Fig. 135). Six lamps have a small stamp centered on the top of the nozzle near the discus. Two stamps are ovals within which is an elongated *S* with a tiny raised dot on either side. Four are circular, one with an *S* with two tiny raised dots on the right side of the *S*, and three with an *SL* with added raised dots (Fig. 136). Two of the six Esquiline Type Lamps with small stamps come from contexts dated 120–70 B.C., four from contexts dated 100–20 B.C. It is likely that they all came from the same pottery. Indeed it is possible that all but three of the Esquiline-Type Lamps found at Cosa were made at the amphora and tile factory owned by the Sestii. Publius Sestius, son of Lucius, had an estate at Cosa. His son, Lucius Sestius Quirinalis, is known to have owned a tile factory. The dating of the Cosan Esquiline Type Lamps would cover three generations of this family. The coarse clay of these lamps is similar to the clay of the Sestius amphoras. Although the location of the factory is unknown, it seems likely that the Sestius amphoras found all over the Roman world were made at or near Cosa.[2]

150–70 B.C.

151 CF.2152 Atrium Building I, Room 15, cesspit, Level III. Orange-red clay. P.L. 0.046 m; P.H. 0.035 m; P.W. 0.044 m.

Fragment preserving the nozzle and part of the side wall of the oil reservoir. Smoke-blackened around wick hole. Worn, encrusted. The right fluke of the nozzle end is deformed.

---

2. For material on the Sestius amphoras, see Will 1956, 224–44; Will 1975, 151; Will 1976, 194; Will 1979, 339–50; and Will, "Ports and Amphoras," *AJA* (1985), 24–25. See also Brown 1980, 71–72; and F. Benoit 1961, 42–70; W. Culican and J. E. Curtis, "The Punic Wreck in Sicily," *International Journal of Nautical Archaeology* 3 (1974), 44–47; D. Manacorda 1978, 122–31. J. Roman, "La place du coloir rhodaniense dans la diffusion des amphores de Sestius," *RAEst* 25 (1974), 125–36. D'Arms, 77–89.

120–70 B.C.

152 CB.1669 Capitolium exterior, S, Level II. Dark brownish-red clay. Length 0.082 m; Height 0.033 m; Width 0.050 m.

Incomplete, most of the bottom broken away. The left fluke of the nozzle and the wick hole are deformed. Worn and chipped.

153 CB.1838 Capitolium exterior, S, Pronaos, Level II. Brick-red clay. P.L. 0.054 m; Height 0.032 m; P.W. 0.041 m.

Fragment preserving the nozzle and parts of the side wall of the oil reservoir, rim, and bottom.

154 CB.1839 Capitolium exterior, S, Pronaos, Level II. Brick-red clay. P.L. 0.043 m; Height 0.031 m; P.W. 0.042 m.

Fragment preserving parts of the discus, including an arc of the filling hole, the rim, the side wall of the oil reservoir, and the bottom. Pitted and worn.

155 CB.1840 Capitolium exterior, S, Pronaos, Level II. Red clay. P.L. 0.044 m; Height 0.038 m; Width 0.052 m.

Fragment preserving half of the discus, including half of the filling hole, parts of the side wall of the oil reservoir and the bottom.

156 CB.1866 Cistern below Arx wall, near Via Sacra. Red clay. P.L. 0.073 m; Height 0.034 m; Width 0.052 m.

Fragment preserving the nozzle, parts of the discus and side wall of the oil reservoir, and base. Worn, chipped, smoke-blackened around wick hole.

157 C65.30 Capitolium exterior, E, Level II. Fine, pale orange-red clay, black slip. Length 0.090 m; Height 0.035 m; Width 0.055 m.

Fragment preserving parts of the discus, the side wall of the oil reservoir, the disk base, and the attachment of a strap handle. Worn, chipped, and encrusted.

158 C65.31 Capitolium exterior, E, Level II. Red clay. Length 0.081 m; P.H. 0.027 m; Width 0.052 m.

Fragment preserving the lower part of a lamp including the base, side wall of the oil reservoir, and most of the nozzle. The bottom and sides of the nozzle were trimmed rectangular, rather than the usual rounded shape. Disk base. Very worn, traces of smoke-blackening around wick hole.

159 (Fig. 11) C65.184 Capitolium exterior, W, Level II. Reddish-buff clay. Length 0.077 m; Height 0.037 m; Width 0.048 m. Now in the Museo Archeologico della Maremma at Grosseto. An almost com-

plete lamp in excellent condition.
160 C65.352 Capitolium exterior, W, Level III. Rather soft, fine, pinkish-buff clay, black slip. P.L. 0.101 m; Height 0.035 m; Width 0.051 m.

Incomplete, the end of the nozzle broken away. Worn and chipped. An unusual Esquiline Type Lamp with a wide fluted strap handle and high disk base. A narrow ridge encircles the discus just within the rim. The lip of the filling hole is slightly raised. Restored, now in the Museo Archeologico della Maremma at Grosseto.

161 C65.432 Capitolium exterior, W trench, Level III. Red clay. P.L. 0.071 m; Height 0.032 m; Width 0.049 m.

Incomplete, the end of the nozzle broken away and minor chipping around the filling hole. Root-marked, smoke-blackened.

162 C65.671 Capitolium exterior, W, Level II. Reddish-buff clay, softer than usual for such lamps. P.L. 0.089 m; Height 0.037 m; Width 0.056 m.

Incomplete, the left fluke of the nozzle broken away. Worn. A *delta* and an *alpha* scratched on the right side of the discus after firing (see Fig. 135). Restored and in the Museo Archeologico della Maremma at Grosseto.

163 C67.7 Capitolium exterior, W, Level II. Red clay. P.L. 0.044 m; P.H. 0.034 m; P.W. 0.041 m.

Fragment preserving the nozzle and part of the side wall of the oil reservoir. The left fluke of the nozzle is deformed. Encrusted, root-marked. A large AL in ligature with a small chevron added at the bottom of the left stroke of the A inscribed on the bottom of the nozzle after firing (see Fig. 135).

164 C67.9 Capitolium exterior, W, Level II. Red clay. Length 0.085 m; Height 0.038 m; Width 0.054 m.

Incomplete, parts of the bottom and side wall of the oil reservoir broken away. Worn, encrusted, root-marked.

165 C67.16 Capitolium exterior, W, Level II/III. Pale buff clay, thin self-slip. P.L. 0.073 m; P.H. 0.019 m; Width 0.042 m.

Fragment preserving the discus, rim, nozzle, parts of the side wall of the oil reservoir, and the attachment of a strap handle. Chipped. This lamp is smaller than usual for the type. The discus is raised around the filling hole.

166 C67.91 Capitolium exterior, W, Level II. Orange-red clay. Length 0.083 m; Height 0.035 m; Width 0.050 m.

A complete lamp. Smoke-blackened around wick hole. Encrusted, root-marked.

167 C67.165 Capitolium exterior, E, Level III. Orange-red clay. P.L. 0.068 m; Height 0.037 m; Width 0.053 m.

Incomplete, the end of the nozzle broken away and minor chipping around the filling hole. An elongated *A* with a very long crossbar scratched on the right side of the oil reservoir after firing (see Fig. 135).

168 C67.332 Capitolium exterior, E, Level III. Red clay. Length 0.089 m; Height 0.041 m; Width 0.054 m.

Three joining fragments forming a complete lamp. Worn and scratched. The nozzle is unusually long, wide, and heavy, and rises slightly higher than the rim of the oil reservoir.

169 C67.595 Capitolium exterior, S, Pronaos, Level III. Orange-red clay. P.L. 0.053 m; P.H. 0.039 m; P.W. 0.044 m.

Fragment preserving the nozzle and parts of the rim and side wall of the oil reservoir. Worn and pitted. Centered on the top of the nozzle near the rim is a small circular stamp, within which are the letters *SL* in relief with two tiny raised dots, one before the *S* and one between the *S* and the *L* at mid-letter (see Fig. 136).

170 C73.1 Capitolium exterior, S, Pronaos, Level II. Red clay. P.L. 0.053 m; Height 0.039 m; P.W. 0.045 m.

Fragment preserving parts of the bottom, side wall of the oil reservoir, nozzle, and rim. Worn and chipped. Centered on the top of the nozzle near the discus is a small circular stamp, within which are the letters *SL* with a tiny raised dot before the *S* and another between the *S* and the *L* (cf. 169 and see Fig. 136).

100–25/20 B.C.

171 CB.1846 Pottery dump, right, Level II/III. Orange-red clay. P.L. 0.060 m; Height 0.040 m; P.W. 0.043 m.

Fragment preserving the nozzle and parts of the rim, side wall of the oil reservoir, and bottom. Worn and encrusted. Centered on the top of the nozzle near the discus is a small circular stamp, within which is an *S* in relief preceded and followed by a tiny raised dot (see Fig. 136).

172 CB.1851 Pottery dump, left center, Level I/II. Orange-red clay. P.L. 0.076 m; Height 0.046 m; P.W. 0.064 m.

Fragment preserving the nozzle, parts of the

rim, side wall of the oil reservoir, and bottom. Worn and encrusted. Smoke-blackened around the wick hole. Centered on the top of the nozzle near the discus is a small elliptical stamp enclosing an elongated *S* in relief with a raised dot on either side (see Fig. 136).

173 CB.1869 Arx surface, from a disturbed area, listed here as dating 100–25/20 B.C. because it is the same type of lamp as those preceding and with an identical stamp on the nozzle. Orange-red clay. P.L. 0.048 m; Height 0.039 m; P.W. 0.044 m.

Fragment preserving the nozzle, parts of the bottom, side wall of the oil reservoir, rim, and discus. Worn and chipped. Centered on the top of the nozzle near the discus is a small elliptical stamp, within which is an elongated *S* in relief with a raised dot on either side. This appears to be the same stamp as the one used on 172 (see Fig. 136).

174 C66.1 Pottery dump outside wall near Tower 9 (cable trench). Orange-red clay. P.L. 0.044 m; Height 0.045 m; P.W. 0.045 m.

Fragment preserving the nozzle, and parts of the rim, side wall of the oil reservoir, and disk base. Chipped and worn. The end of the nozzle and the wick hole are deformed. Centered on the top of the nozzle near the discus is a small circular stamp, within which are the letters *SL* in relief, placed laterally, to be read from the right, with three tiny raised dots placed before, between, and after the letters. The stamp is closely related to that of 169, although that stamp is placed to be read from the left, and lacks the tiny raised dot after the *L*. The letters of the stamp of 169 are not centered as carefully within the circle as the letters on 174. This indicates that there was one stamp for the circle and another for the letters and dots (see Fig. 136).

89–70 B.C.

175 C68.603 House of the Skeleton, Main garden trench near portico. Red clay. Length 0.076 m; Height 0.035 m; Width 0.047 m.

Complete, except for minor chipping. Crevices and pits in the fabric. Root-marked. Smoke-blackened around wick hole.

25/20 B.C.

176 CEL.267 and CE.1473 Atrium Building I, Room 11, Level III. Red clay. P.L. 0.049 m; Height 0.032 m; P.W. 0.042 m.

Two joining fragments preserving the nozzle, and parts of the rim, side wall, and bottom of the oil reservoir. Encrusted, smoke-blackened around the wick hole.

25/20 B.C.–A.D. 50

177 CC.583 Arx, north slope, Medieval ramp, Level I. Orange-red clay. P.L. 0.036 m; P.H. 0.010 m; P.W. 0.021 m.

Fragment preserving parts of the discus and rim. Worn and pitted. There is a graffito on the discus, scratched after firing, the letter *F* inscribed twice; the second is retrograde lacking the top hasta.

178 CEL.253 Atrium Building I, Room 11, cesspit. Orange-red clay. P.L. 0.046 m; P.H. 0.029 m; P.W. 0.045 m.

Fragment preserving the nozzle, parts of the discus, and side wall of the oil reservoir. Pitted, smoke-blackened around wick hole. The center of the end of the nozzle and the flukes have been pinched to make a triangular end.

25/20 B.C.–A.D. 225

179 CD.1249 Basilica exterior, NE 3, Level I. Red clay. P.L. 0.049 m; P.H. 0.029 m; P.W. 0.020 m.

Fragment preserving parts of the discus and upper side wall of the oil reservoir. Encrusted and chipped.

180 CF.1590 Atrium Building I, Room 25B, cesspit, Level IV. Orange-red clay. P.L. 0.069 m; Height 0.034 m; P.W. 0.048 m.

Fragment preserving the nozzle, and parts of the bottom, side wall of the oil reservoir, and rim. Smoke-blackened around the wick hole. Worn.

The two lamps below were found in an area that was farmed in the eighteenth century. This was the site of house ruins left from the destruction of 70 B.C. Therefore the context of these two lamps and two uncatalogued fragments from the same site could be dated anywhere from 175 B.C. to A.D. 225. They could have been turned over by the plow a number of times. It is more than likely, however, that they should be dated before 70 B.C.

181 C66.133 Republican house, V-D west quadrant, Level 0. Red clay. P.L. 0.063 m; Height 0.034 m; P.W. 0.050 m.

Fragment preserving parts of the discus, nozzle, side wall of the oil reservoir, and bottom. Chipped, encrusted. Smoke-blackened around the wick hole.

182 C72.8 Republican house, V-D, Rear of the House of the Treasure, Level 0. Red clay. Length 0.082 m; Height 0.034 m; Width 0.036 m.

Three joining fragments forming a complete lamp. Chipped and worn.

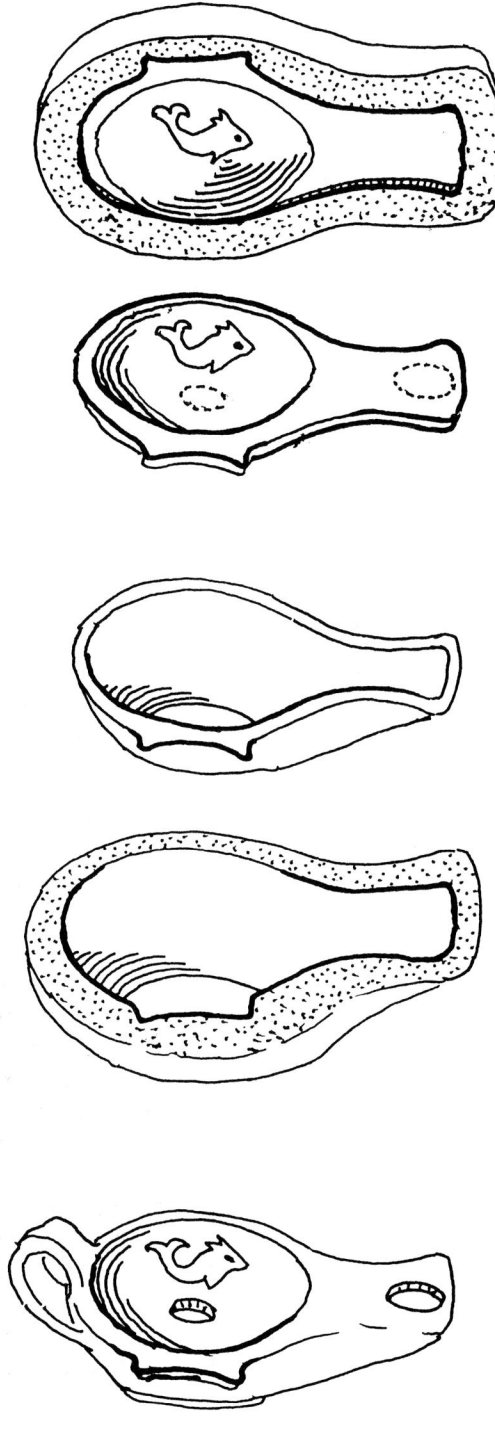

Figure 12. Molded lamp construction

INTRODUCTION TO MOLDMADE LAMPS

(Catalogue Numbers 183–1089)

The first step in the construction of a moldmade lamp was the manufacture of a patrix or prototype, a solid model of the finished lamp and its decoration, if any, carved in wood or stone, or modeled in clay, with the positions of the filling and wick holes indicated. The artisan then cast a two-part matrix (mold) of the upper and lower halves of the lamp with the separation at the widest point. The matrix was usually made of clay or plaster, but limestone molds have been found at some sites, showing that the matrix could also be directly carved in soft stone without a patrix.[1] In both systems the molds carry marks of registration: mortises in the contact surface of one half and matching tenons in the other, so that the two halves of the mold fit together exactly. Another method of registering the two halves was to score the outer edges of the mold to assure a perfect match. Hard-fired clay molds were long-lasting, and the impressions from them remained clear and sharp. Plaster matrices were easier to make but more fragile. Their surfaces were easily scratched and the decorative details became blurred with repeated use.

The original patrix could be used to produce any number of matrices, and since a matrix was out of use until the clay of the lamp being molded inside dried leather hard and could be removed without damage, the lamp maker needed a good supply of molds. He rolled clay into sheets, cut sections roughly into the shape of each half, and pressed the clay into the molds, gently stretching the clay where the mold was deep and filling all the cavities. He then trimmed the clay that overlapped the top of the matrix, scored and painted the edges with slip, which acted as glue, and then pressed the two halves of the registered matrix together with the lamp inside (Fig. 12). For very delicate lamps with very thin walls, the potter may have used a slurry (clay watered to the consistency of heavy cream) to form the hollow lamp. Fingerprints on the inside testify to both kinds of construction and also to the addition of extra smears of clay along the interior seam line or where the discus decoration needed further support. When the clay was firm enough to be handled, the lamp was removed from the matrix and trimmed; then filling and wick holes were punched or carved out. When dry, the lamp could be slipped or glazed and then fired.[2] Some were fired without slip or glaze.

The potter could either make his matrices from his own patrix, or he could obtain his matrices from another potter or shop. He also could pirate a design by mak-

---

1. Robert Bull at the excavations at Caesarea Maritima on the coast of Israel has identified several such soft limestone molds found in a potter's workshop (C Field) during campaigns of excavation in 1978 and 1980.

2. D. M. Bailey, "Pottery Lamps," in D. R. Strong and D. Brown, eds., *Roman Crafts* (London, 1976), 92–103. This chapter contains an excellent summary of casting techniques with illustrations of registered molds.

ing matrices from any lamp that found its way into his hands. Such a lamp could become a patrix by simply closing the filling and wick holes with clay. Such copying was common; patrix, matrix, and the lamps themselves were small and easily transported, which accounts for the widespread dissemination of the same types. At times this even led to reproduction of the original potter's signature or mark, especially in the provinces, where developing local industries met local needs. A parent pottery could also send out a subsidiary pottery to supply local demands.[3]

Although there had been discus reliefs on lamps of the republic, it was in the imperial period that the discus reliefs reached full maturity. Imitating devices on metalwork, pottery, coins, and jewelry, the potters used poinçons (like butter molds) to turn out detailed images of gods and goddesses, scenes from mythology, designs from the natural world and from architecture, genre scenes, and imperial portraits. Once the design was attached to the patrix and copied into the mold, the skilled potter could move on to other work, since unskilled labor could then produce the discus relief from the mold. Eventually both the discus and the shoulder were decorated in the mold.

About A.D. 40–45 the molded handle was introduced, and the outer molding of the rim was widened and turned downward, creating a narrow shoulder to accommodate the new handle. This new rim form was easier to extract from the mold, although the molded handle also created new technical difficulties. The handle was semicircular, and the join line between the upper and lower molds was at the widest projection of the handle (Fig. 12). The seam line along the handle had to be smoothed. Perhaps within a decade after the introduction of the molded handle, a decorative heat shield was added to the face of the handle. This device, borrowed from metal lamps, extended upward at an angle of about 30° to 45° from the horizontal plane of the top of the oil reservoir (see Fig. 70). The upper face of the heat shield was made in the mold of the lamp top,

and the bottom in the lower part, buttressed by plaster built up under it. Since the fabric of these lamps is sometimes quite thin, the mating of the two complex parts had to be executed very carefully. To balance the heat shield, the nozzle was lengthened and broadened, with long, thick volutes extending down the side of the nozzle in cones. The heat shield and the nozzle were easily broken off. To meet the problem, a lamp form was developed with a short, rounded nozzle without volutes. The heat shield was omitted, and the shoulder was widened to accommodate the new nozzle. The discus was somewhat diminished, but there was still a large area left for decoration. Before the end of the first century, the shoulder had also acquired decoration, forming an elaborate frame for the discus relief. This lamp type continued to be produced for another three centuries.

During the fertile period of the first century A.D. other new forms were introduced. Some were failures and did not survive; other innovations enhanced the mainstream of lamp design. The lamp makers experimented with the placing of the volutes, moving them around into new positions on the top of the nozzle and shoulder. Some lamps were given a stemmed handle rising from the center of the discus. One innovation was a wide discus lamp with a short nozzle framed by a continuous volute bent in a right angle (see Fig. 102). There were so-called "plastic lamps" in the shape of a bull's head and a satyr's head (see Figs. 103, 104), and lamps in the form of feet and body parts, although only the first two types have been found so far at Cosa.

Around A.D. 70 a new lamp design was introduced in northern Italy. Plain, angular, strong, cheap, and easily packed for shipping, it could be made by unskilled labor and is called the "Factory Lamp," since it was truly mass-produced. It captured the market in the western Mediterranean and remained a dominant type for more than two hundred years. Three debased examples of the Factory Lamp were found in the Shrine of Liber Pater at Cosa in a context that is dated from A.D 350 to 416, indicating that the lamp form continued in use into the fourth century. However, the majority of the lamps found in the shrine were imported from North Africa or were copies of North African lamps. These lamps were crude, made of thick coarse fabric. The period of fine lamp production in Italy had come to an end.

---

3. W. V. Harris, "Roman Terracotta Lamps: The Organization of an Industry," *JRS* 70 (1980), 126–45. Professor Harris advances many theories of how similar lamp types may have appeared in various regions of the Roman world. E. Haley, "The Lamp Manufacturer Gaius Iunius Draco," *Münsterische Beiträge z. Antiken Handelsgeschichte* 9 (1990), 1–13, has described the production of local copies of Roman lamps at a site in Spain.

6. IMPORTED DELPHINIFORM LAMPS
(Figs. 13–18)

(Catalogue Numbers 183–204)

Among the few examples of "foreign" lamps found at Cosa are twenty-one that probably arrived in a shipment from Sicily before 70 B.C. These handsome lamps are described as delphiniform: the ear on the left side of the oil reservoir resembles the dorsal fin, and the nozzle is roughly in the shape of the tail, while the circular reservoir makes the plump body of the dolphin (Figs. 13–18). The Delphiniform Lamp was imported from Sicily when the lamp industry in Rome was not far advanced. A few molded lamps were being made, but they were crude compared to the Sicilian and Greek lamps of the same period.[1] There are enormous numbers of lamps of this type in the museums of Sicily; some are plain, with sharply carinated bodies; some are like the Cosan lamps with vegetal or geometric decoration; and others have even more intricate designs. One center of production of Delphiniform Lamps was Morgantina;[2] the upper half of a mold (and many lamps) with reliefs of looped vines with flowers in the loops was found there. Several such lamps found at Delos are dated from the last quarter of the second to the first quarter of the first century B.C.[3] Ponsich dates a similar lamp from Tamuda to the first century B.C.[4] The cutoff date for Sicilian lamp manufacture is probably 35 B.C., when Octavian defeated Sextus Pompey and punished the Sicilians for having taken his side.

The clay of the Cosan Delphiniform Lamps is dark gray, finely levigated, and fired very hard. These lamps were fired twice, once in oxydizing conditions, and then again in a reducing atmosphere. They have a black slip, probably applied after the first biscuit firing, and were carefully made from fine molds.

The upper and lower halves of the oil reservoir are shallow truncated cones. The two halves join each other at a sharp angle (carination). The nozzle is long and slender with a horizontal top on a plane with the top of the small recessed discus, although on a few lamps the top slopes slightly upward toward the nozzle. All have a central filling hole. None has the air hole usual on Roman lamps. The majority of these lamps have low disk bases, although a few have a ring base. The side walls of the nozzle flare imperceptibly from the connection with the oil reservoir, and then turn slightly in a reverse curve to meet the straight end of the nozzle in blunt points, similar to, but more refined than, the Roman spatulate nozzle. The underside of the nozzle rises from the bottom of the lamp.

Some of the Cosan Delphiniform Lamps have ribbed strap handles, although the decoration on some was designed for lamps without handles, and the addi-

---

1. In addition to the Sicilian Delphiniform Lamps, see also the Ariston lamp from Athens (1090) found at Cosa.
2. We are grateful to Professor Malcolm Bell of the University of Virginia, Director of the excavations at Morgantina, for permission to see the lamps being catalogued by Professor Shelley Stone and the mold found there.
3. Bruneau, 5.
4. Ponsich, 31–32, 78.

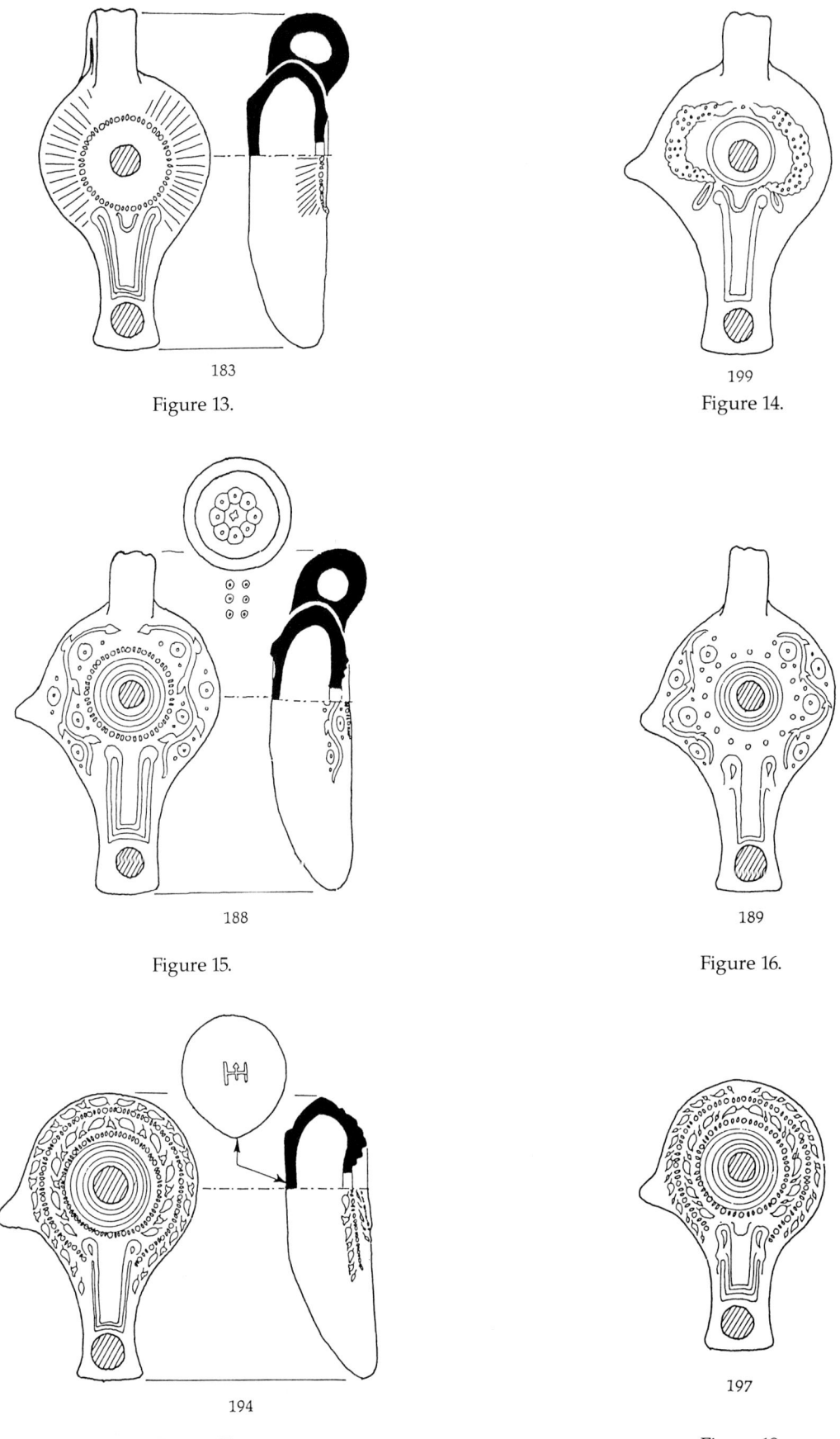

Figures 13–18. Delphiniform Lamps, imported, scale 1:2. Note the difference between figures 17 and 18. Figure 17 has a band of leaves alternating with flowers and Figure 18 has a band of leaves alternating with buds.

tion of the handle interferes with the decoration. All but one have a spurlike ear on the left side of the oil reservoir. The tops of the nozzles are decorated with a pair of narrow fillets with a squared channel between them that stops above the wick hole. At the top near the discus, the moldings loop back on themselves and sometimes form additions that have been interpreted as stylized birds' heads. On most of the lamps in the Sicilian museums these are distinct, but on the Cosan lamps they are blurred.

The wide shoulders of the Delphiniform Lamps are decorated with carefully formed designs of radiating grooves, looped vines with flowers between the loops, or concentric bead-and-reel moldings alternating with bands of stemmed leaves and flowers, interrupted by the nozzle. The relief decoration on some unpublished Delphiniform Lamps in the Museo Nazionale at Syracuse was carried further; instead of using geometric or vegetal designs, four lamps have two gladiators engaged in combat on either side, while toward the nozzle a figure blows a trumpet. On the nozzle top is Hermes, frontal, standing with one leg crossed over the other. Wearing his winged cap and sandals, he holds his caduceus lowered in his right hand, his left hand on his hip. The tiny figures are very fine. Many of the Sicilian lamps have a thunderbolt on the top of the nozzle.

a. DELPHINIFORM LAMPS WITH RADIATING GROOVES

(Catalogue Numbers 183–187)

150–125 B.C.

183 (Fig. 13) CEL.196 Atrium Building I, Room 21, Level IV. Fine, hard, gray clay, black slip. P.L. 0.046 m; P.H. 0.014 m; P.W. 0.028 m.

Fragment preserving part of the discus, the upper part of the oil reservoir, and the attachment of the handle. Worn, chipped, and encrusted. Shoulder decorated with closely spaced grooves that radiate from a bead-and-reel molding separating the small discus from the shoulder.

150–70 B.C.

184 C67.298 Capitolium exterior, E, Level II. Fine, hard, gray clay, black slip. P.L. 0.053 m; P.H. 0.015 m; P.W. 0.050 m.

Fragment broken on all sides, preserving the discus and parts of the shoulder and the attachment of the handle. Shoulder decorated with grooves radiating from a bead molding encircling the discus.

185 C67.350 Capitolium exterior, E trench, Level III. Fine, hard, gray clay, black slip. P.L. 0.069 m; Height 0.026 m; Width 0.056 m.

Incomplete lamp, the nozzle and handle broken away, although the attachment of the handle is preserved slightly off center. Worn. Low disk base, flat underneath. The lamp does not have a side ear. At the top of the shoulder adjoining the narrow bead molding that separates the discus from the shoulder is a narrow bead-and-reel. Radiating from the bead-and-reel are closely spaced grooves that have been smoothed away where the handle was attached. Between the looped fillets on the nozzle near the discus is a horseshoe-shaped molding, the open end toward the discus.

125 B.C.–A.D. 50

186 CEL.384 Atrium Building I, Room 10, Level III. Fine, rather soft, gray clay, black slip. P.L. 0.030 m; P.H. 0.001 m; P.W. 0.015 m.

Fragment preserving parts of the discus and shoulder. Very worn, only traces of slip preserved. Shoulder decorated with grooves radiating from a bead molding encircling the discus.

187 CF.1626 Atrium Building I, Room 25B, cesspit, Level IV. Fine, hard, gray clay, black slip. P.L. 0.032 m; P.H. 0.028 m; P.W. 0.035 m.

Fragment preserving parts of the shoulder and lower side wall of the oil reservoir. Very worn. Shoulder decorated with grooves radiating from the discus.

b. DELPHINIFORM LAMPS DECORATED WITH LOOPED VINES WITH FLOWERS BETWEEN THE LOOPS

(Catalogue Numbers 188–191)

188 (Fig. 15) C65.37 Capitolium exterior, E trench, Level II. Fine, hard, dark clay, black slip. P.L. 0.082 m; P.H. 0.026 m; P.W. 0.058 m.

Incomplete, the end of the nozzle and handle broken away. Worn, encrusted. A bead-and-reel molding encircles the discus at the top of the shoulder. Ring base. Within the foot is a rosette of eight dots, and there are two rows of three bull's eyes under the nozzle, as on 190. Looped vines on either side of the shoulder with a flower in each loop. The buds on the vines are arranged singly and are larger than those on the three lamps listed below. Handmade strap handle carefully attached so as not to interfere with the decoration.

189 (Fig. 16) C67.69 Capitolium exterior, E trench, Level III. Fine, hard, gray clay, black slip. P.L. 0.100 m; P.H. 0.027 m; P.W. 0.057 m.

Incomplete, the end of the nozzle broken away. Slip rubbed. Ring base. Strap handle divided by grooves into three bands. Looped vines with tiny pointed buds, with flowers between the loops.

190 C67.71 Capitolium exterior, W trench, Level III. Fine, hard, gray clay, black slip. P.L. 0.084 m; P.H. 0.065 m; Width with ear 0.057 m.

Incomplete, the handle and end of the nozzle broken away. Worn. Relief on the shoulder the same as on 189. Ring base, within which a rosette of eight small circles with a small circle punched in the center of each. Under the nozzle two rows of three bull's eyes.

191 C67.241 (Fig. 18) Capitolium exterior, W trench, Level II. Hard, gray clay, black slip. P.L. 0.085 m; P.H. 0.027 m; P.W. 0.055 m; Width with ear 0.065 m.

Four joining fragments forming an incomplete lamp. Worn, encrusted. Bead-and-reel molding encircling the small discus. Shoulder decorated with a looped vine with small pointed buds, with flowers between the loops. Ring base with rosette and six bull's eyes under the nozzle, as on 190. The buds on the vine are larger than those on 189 and 190 and are single, not paired.

c. DELPHINIFORM LAMPS WITH CONCENTRIC BEAD-AND-REEL MOLDINGS ALTERNATING WITH BANDS OF STEMMED LEAVES AND BUDS OR BANDS OF STEMMED LEAVES AND FLOWERS

(Catalogue Numbers 192–198)

150–70 B.C.

192 (Fig. 18) CB.1698 Capitolium exterior, Level II. Fine, hard, dark gray clay, black slip. P.L. 0.062 m; P.H. 0.017 m; P.W. 0.035 m.

Fragment preserving half of the lamp top; the lower part is broken away at the mold join. Slip rubbed on raised surfaces. Two narrow bead moldings encircle the central filling hole, sloping upward to a slightly wider molding that separates the discus from the shoulder. On the shoulder are four moldings. The first and third are bead-and-reel; the second and fourth are wider, with alternating stemmed leaves and lotus blossoms. The decoration covers the area where a handle would be attached.

193 C65.404 Capitolium exterior, W trench, Level III. Fine, hard, dark gray clay, black slip. P.L. 0.086 m; Height 0.027 m; Width 0.054 m; Width with ear 0.065 m.

Incomplete, the handle and nozzle broken away. Worn. Decoration the same as 192, with lotus blossoms. Design of parallel string moldings on the top of the nozzle, between which are a horseshoe and anchor in relief.

194 (Fig. 17) C67.146 Capitolium exterior, E trench, Level III. Hard, fine, dark gray clay, black slip. Length 0.091 m; Height 0.028 m; Width 0.058 m; Width with ear 0.065 m.

Complete, except for part of the right side of the nozzle and a small chip from the ear. Low ovoid base, with the point toward the nozzle. On the bottom is impressed a wide capital letter *H* with a vertical arrow, head up, centered on the bar. The shoulder decoration is the same as on 192, with the relief covering the area where a handle would be attached.

195 C67.194 Capitolium exterior, E trench, Level III. Hard, fine, dark gray clay, black slip. P.L. 0.045 m; P.H. 0.015 m; P.W. 0.033 m.

Fragment preserving about one-quarter of the lamp top. Slip rubbed. The decoration is the same as on 192.

196 C67.293 Capitolium exterior, E trench, Level III. Fine, hard, pale gray clay, black slip. P.L. 0.075 m; P.H. 0.025 m; P.W. 0.065 m; Width without ear 0.054 m.

Incomplete, the end of the nozzle and the handle broken away. Worn, encrusted. The decoration is the same as on 192.

197 (Fig. 15) C67.313 Capitolium exterior, Level II/III. Fine, hard, dark gray clay, black slip. P.L. 0.078 m;

P.H. 0.021 m; P.W. 0.053 m; Width with ear 0.062 m.

Incomplete, the end of the nozzle broken away. Worn. Within the small discus are two bead moldings that encircle the central filling hole, sloping upward to the slightly wider bead that separates the discus from the shoulder. The entire lamp slopes slightly up toward the nozzle. Low disk base. The top of the nozzle has complex parallel double string moldings, between which are an anchor and a horseshoe in relief. The shoulder is covered with concentric bead-and-reel moldings alternating with slightly wider bands of stemmed leaves and lotus buds. The decoration covers the area where a handle would be attached.

120–20 B.C.

198 CB.1848 Pottery dump, right, Levels I, II, III. Fine, hard, dark gray clay, black slip. P.L. 0.090 m; P.H. 0.025 m; P.W. 0.060 m; Width with ear 0.069 m.

Incomplete, part of the handle and nozzle broken away. Worn. Remains of a strap handle attachment. Made from a worn mold. Decoration the same as on 192.

d. DELPHINIFORM LAMP DECORATED WITH A GARLAND TIED WITH A RIBBON

(Catalogue Number 199)

199 C67.592 Capitolium exterior, W, Level II. Fine, hard, gray clay, black slip. P.L. 0.062 m; P.H. 0.001 m; P.W. 0.049 m.

Fragment preserving the discus, most of the shoulder, and nozzle top. Worn and chipped. Two looped moldings merge toward the wick hole with a horseshoe-shaped string molding between them. The shoulders are decorated with a garland of flowers tied with a looped ribbon near the nozzle.

e. FRAGMENTS OF DELPHINIFORM LAMPS WITH NO DECORATION PRESERVED

(Catalogue Numbers 200–204)

175–70 B.C.

200 C66.883 Republican house, V-D north quadrant, Sounding 3, cesspool, Level I/III. Fine, hard, dark gray clay, black slip. P.L. 0.071 m; P.H. 0.018 m; P.W. 0.042 m.

Fragment preserving parts of an unprofiled base, the lower side wall of the oil reservoir, the underside of the nozzle, and the underside of the left ear. Slip rubbed; does not completely cover the base.

25/20 B.C.–A.D. 50

201 CEL.236 Atrium Building I, Room 16, Level III. Fine, hard, dark gray clay, black slip. P.L. 0.054 m; P.H. 0.021 m; P.W. 0.038 m.

Fragment preserving part of a nozzle top, from the bead-and-reel molding that encircles the discus to an arc of the wick hole. The lower half of the nozzle is broken away at the mold join. Worn. The moldings that decorate the top of the nozzle of Delphiniform Lamps have been simplified on this example.

202 CEL.205 Atrium Building I, Room 16, Level II. Fine, hard, bluish-gray clay, black slip. P.L. 0.050 m; P.H. 0.027 m; P.W. 0.045 m.

Three joining fragments preserving parts of the base, lower side wall of the oil reservoir, and handle. Very worn. Strap handle, unprofiled base, no decoration preserved.

203 CF.1624 Atrium Building I, Room 25B, cesspit, Level IV. Fine, hard, dark gray clay, black slip. P.L. 0.040 m; P.H. 0.030 m; P.W. 0.038 m.

Fragment preserving a three-ribbed strap handle and parts of the biconical oil reservoir. Worn, chipped, encrusted. The top had decoration, but there is too little preserved, blurred by the attachment of the handle, to be able to identify it. Made from a worn mold.

A.D. 50–ca. 100

204 CEL.387 Atrium Building I, Room 22, Level I. Fine, hard, dark gray clay, black slip. P.L. 0.025 m; P.H. 0.017 m; P.W. 0.034 m.

Fragment preserving parts of the biconical oil reservoir and the attachment of a strap handle. Very worn. Decoration not preserved.

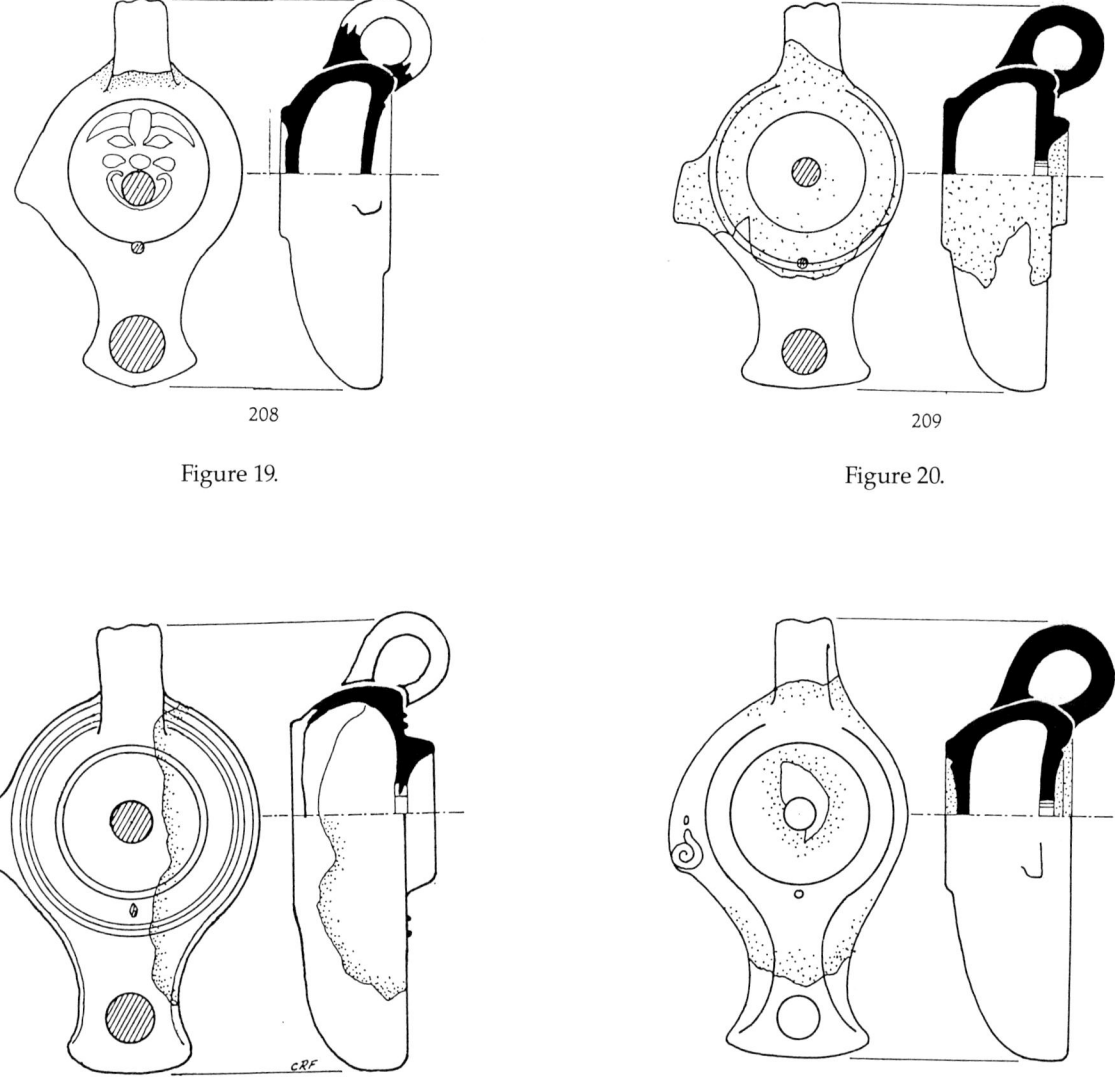

Figures 19–22. Lamps with one ear, cup-shaped oil reservoir, and Roman nozzle, scale 1:2

7. LATE ROMAN REPUBLICAN LAMPS WITH HELLENISTIC FEATURES

(Figs. 19–52)

(Catalogue Numbers 205–323)

   a. LAMPS WITH ONE EAR, CUP-SHAPED OIL RESERVOIR, AND ROMAN NOZZLE
   b. LAMPS WITH ONE EAR AND ROMAN NOZZLE, *WARZENLAMPEN* (RAISED-DOTS LAMPS)
   c. LAMPS WITH CIRCULAR RAISED NOZZLES
   d. LAMPS WITH NOZZLES ENDING IN A TRIANGLE
   e. LAMPS WITH SWALLOWTAIL EARS
   f. LAMPS WITH A BICONICAL BODY AND ROMAN NOZZLE
   g. LAMPS WITH A WIDE, DECORATED DISCUS AND A ROMAN NOZZLE BUT WITHOUT EARS
   h. LAMPS WITH EVOLVING OR PROTO-VOLUTES
   i. MISCELLANEOUS LATE REPUBLICAN LAMPS

The earliest molded lamps found at Cosa come from contexts dated from 150 to 70 B.C. They are the work of potters experimenting with new forms made possible by the use of molds. These new forms were inspired by lamps from the East and from the Greek cities of southern Italy and Sicily, imported or looted. Many of them have such characteristic Hellenistic features as ears, circular raised nozzles (as well as triangular ones), and biconical or other Hellenistic body forms. To several, however, significant elements have been added: a wide concave discus that covers the top of the lamp and a device on either side of the nozzle that is a proto-volute. These two features led directly to the fine Picture Lamps with voluted nozzles of the late first century B.C. and first half of the first century A.D. The largest group of the early molded lamps is the *Warzenlampen* (Raised-Dots Lamp), probably based on a bronze prototype. It continued as a popular type through the early decades of the first century A.D.

a. LAMPS WITH ONE EAR, CUP-SHAPED OIL RESERVOIR, AND ROMAN NOZZLE
(Figs. 19–22)

(Catalogue Numbers 205–219)

There are fifteen lamps in this group with a cup-shaped oil reservoir that has one ear on the left side of the body. Most of these ears are low projections rather like a spur, although two are roughly rectangular. Some represent a cornucopia, the contents indicated by a few short grooves and tiny punched circles.

Nine of the fifteen lamps in this group are from contexts dated 150–70 B.C. which is probably the correct date for the entire group. However, three were found in contexts dating from 25/20 B.C. to A.D. 50, one was found in a context dated A.D. 50 to ca. 100, and two are from levels dated A.D. 50 to 225.

150–70 B.C.
205 CF.2150 Atrium Building I, Room 16, pit, Level III. Buff clay with an orange tint, red slip mottled to black in places. Length 0.108 m; Height 0.029 m; Width 0.066 m.
    Complete lamp; slip scratched and worn. Wide discus encircled by a raised lip along the outer edge that includes the wick hole. Disk base. Three-ribbed strap handle. Very small spur-shaped ear on the left side of the body. Discus plain.

206 C65.49 Capitolium exterior, E trench, Level II. Buff clay, red slip. P.L. 0.085 m; Height 0.029 m; Width 0.067 m.
    Fragment preserving the handle, ear, and most of the discus, base, and side wall of the oil reservoir. Worn. Three-ribbed strap handle. The wide discus is divided by a molding that raises the area around the central filling hole. The outer edge of the discus is lifted into a blunt lip. Cornucopia ear. Discus plain.

207 C65.108 Capitolium exterior, W, Levels I/II. Yellowish-buff clay, brown slip. P.L. 0.100 m; Height 0.029 m; Width 0.059 m.

Complete, except for the end of the nozzle, which is broken away. Worn and scratched. Discus framed by a bead molding that slopes up to the outer raised lip. Strap handle with raised edges. Small spur-shaped ear. Discus plain.

208 (Fig. 19) C65.237 Capitolium exterior, W trench, Level III. Buff clay, red slip. P.L. 0.091 m; Height 0.031 m; Width 0.058 m.

Incomplete, part of the handle broken away. Slip rubbed. Made from a worn mold. Ring base. Small spur-shaped ear. Discus relief: a schematic comic mask, the eyes wide under heavy hornlike brows that curve sharply downward, the end of the nose an oval bead flanked by drop shapes that represent prominent cheekbones, the mouth (the filling hole) embellished by a ridge to give it the grin characteristic of slave masks.

209 (Fig. 20) C65.295 Capitolium exterior, Level III. Dark gray clay (unusual color, perhaps from a fire), dark brown slip. P.L. 0.065 m; Height 0.035 m; Width 0.054 m.

Fragment preserving the discus, disk base, one large, irregularly rectangular ear, most of the side wall of the oil reservoir, and the attachment of the handle. Worn. The discus is divided into two equal parts; the outer half is level, the inner half deeply concave. The two parts are divided by a high ridge. For another example of this divided discus, see Zaccaria Ruggiu 1980, 60 no. 67 a & b.

210 C65.423 Capitolium exterior, W, Level III. Yellow-buff clay, black slip. P.L. 0.086 m; Height 0.029 m; Width 0.053 m.

Incomplete, the handle broken away and chips missing from the large, irregular, rectangular ear. Worn. The small central filling hole was made with a tapered tool, being smaller at the bottom than at the top. The slightly recessed discus is separated from the rim by a groove. There is a groove across the top of the nozzle at the juncture with the body that ends in small circular punch marks. The base is ovoid, the point toward the nozzle.

211 (Fig. 22) C66.359 Republican house, V-D north quadrant, Sounding 3, Levels I/III. Buff clay, red slip mottled to black in places. P.L. 0.079 m; Height 0.026 m; Width 0.062 m.

Incomplete lamp, the handle, end of the nozzle, and chips from the discus broken away. Heavily encrusted. The slightly projecting ear on the left side of the body has a spiral decoration in relief. The connection between the two halves of the mold is not at the top, but lower, creating a narrow sloping shoulder. Discus plain.

212 C67.167 Capitolium exterior, E, Level III. Buff clay, orange-red slip. P.L. 0.060 m; P.H. 0.025 m; P.W. 0.063 m.

Fragment preserving the nozzle and part of the discus, side wall of the oil reservoir, and an ear on the left side of the body. Worn, smoke-blackened around wick hole. The discus is framed by a bead molding, within which is a symmetrical geometric design, only partially preserved. Made from a worn, blurred mold.

213 C67.246 Capitolium exterior, W. Buff clay, orange-red slip. Length 0.111 m; Height 0.031 m; Width 0.067 m.

Incomplete, a corner of the nozzle end broken away. Encrusted; smoke-blackened around wick hole. Low ring foot. Three-ribbed strap handle. Small projecting ear on the left side of the body, decorated with punched circles and string moldings. Two *cyma recta* moldings separate the discus into three almost equal parts. All three slope downward toward the central filling hole. This lamp has been restored and is now in the Museo Archeologico della Maremma at Grosseto.

25/20 B.C.–A.D. 50

214 (Fig. 21) CB.1683 Capitolium exterior, S, Level II. Buff clay, black slip. P.L. 0.081 m; P.H. 0.033 m; P.W. 0.019 m.

Fragment preserving part of the right side of the discus, rim, and upper side wall of the oil reservoir. Worn. The discus is divided into two parts separated by a high ridge; the outer half is flat, the inner deeply concave. This lamp is very closely related to 209. Both have a wide discus divided into two equal parts by a high ridge. Both probably had the same kind of ear and are probably of the same date.

215 CB.1713 Capitolium exterior, S, Level II. Buff clay, red slip. P.L. 0.046 m; P.W. 0.037 m.

Fragment, part of the discus broken on all sides, parts of the rim, and an ear on the left side of the body. Discus relief: A horse galloping to left. The design is crude. Only the head, shoulders, and forelegs are preserved. The filling hole was carelessly punched through the body of the horse.

216 C66.319 Republican house, V-D north quadrant, Level I. Pinkish-buff clay, red slip. P.L. 0.093 m; Height 0.029 m; Width 0.065 m.

Thirteen joining fragments preserving most of a lamp, the end of the nozzle and part of the handle missing. Worn, chipped, and encrusted. Low ring base. A wide undecorated discus separated from a steeply sloping shoulder by a groove. Spur-shaped ear on left side of body decorated with grooves.

A.D. 50–ca. 100

217 CEL.171 Atrium Building I, Room 11, Level I. Buff clay, red slip mottled to black in places. P.L. 0.029 m; P.H. 0.013 m; P.W. 0.009 m.

Fragment preserving an ear and parts of the side wall of the oil reservoir. Worn. Triangular ear with scrolled ends that extend down the body wall.

A.D. 50–225

218 CEL.618 Basilica exterior, W, Level I. Buff clay, brown slip. P.L. 0.042 m; P.H. 0.017 m; P.W. 0.037 m.

Fragment preserving an ear and part of the rim. Very worn. Rim: two rings inside a narrow band, all level. Triangular spur-like ear.

219 C68.646 House of the Skeleton, Garden, Level 0. Buff clay, red slip. P.L. 0.085 m; Height 0.028 m; Width 0.063 m.

Incomplete, the handle and end of the nozzle broken away. Slip flaked in places, encrusted. Made from a worn mold. Small triangular ear on left side of the body. Discus relief: rosette of tongues.

b. LAMPS WITH ONE EAR AND ROMAN NOZZLE, *WARZENLAMPEN* (RAISED-DOTS LAMPS)

(Figs. 23–30)

(Catalogue Numbers 220–270)

(Graviska Type II; Magdalensburg Group II; Dressel/Lamboglia Type 2; Bruneau Delos Group 6 and 7 [in classification "lampes moulés à un seul bec de types divers"])

Seventy-one examples of the late republican and early imperial *Warzenlampen* (Raised-Dots Lamps) have been found at Cosa, and fifty-two have been catalogued. Eighteen are from contexts securely dated before 70 B.C.; four were found in levels that have been dated from 120 to 20 B.C. Twelve are from levels dated from 25 B.C. to A.D. 50; fifteen are from levels dated A.D. 50–100. The remaining three are from contexts loosely dated A.D. 100–225. This lamp type was superseded by the "Picture Lamp," and probably few were made after the turn of the millennium. None was found in the storeroom of the shop that was destroyed in A.D. 40/45. This seems to indicate that they were obsolete before A.D. 45, but since the fabric was thick and strong, they may have survived in use for decades.

The clay is fine and ranges in color from cream to buff, sometimes with a pink or orange cast. The hardness varies from medium soft to hard. The slip is usually red and is often mottled from red to brown due to firing conditions. There are a few dark slips, some with a metallic luster.

The oil reservoir is shaped like a small flattened bun with a sunken discus. All these lamps have a small central filling hole and an air hole at the outer edge of the discus toward the nozzle. The sides of the long nozzle curve out from the oil reservoir and meet the straight or slightly convex end of the nozzle in flukes or points. All but one of these lamps have a small, projecting, spurlike ear on the left side of the body. The exception has none. They all have vertical strap handles, usually divided into three ribs. They usually have a disk base or a ring base, although one rests on three stubby feet, and another has three interlocking disks for a base.

The distinguishing feature of the *Warzenlampen* is the decoration of the bodies with closely spaced, concentric rows of tiny dots in relief. On the finest, and perhaps the earliest, the dots are so small that they are similar to granulation in metalwork and probably based on bronze prototypes.[1] The dots cover the top and side wall of the oil reservoir from the base to the edge of the discus, with some interruption where they were smoothed away at the joining of the two halves. On some of the later lamps the dots become larger, and some have dots only on the top of the lamp.

---

1. The mold for the finest of these lamps, e.g., 235, may have been made directly from a metal lamp.

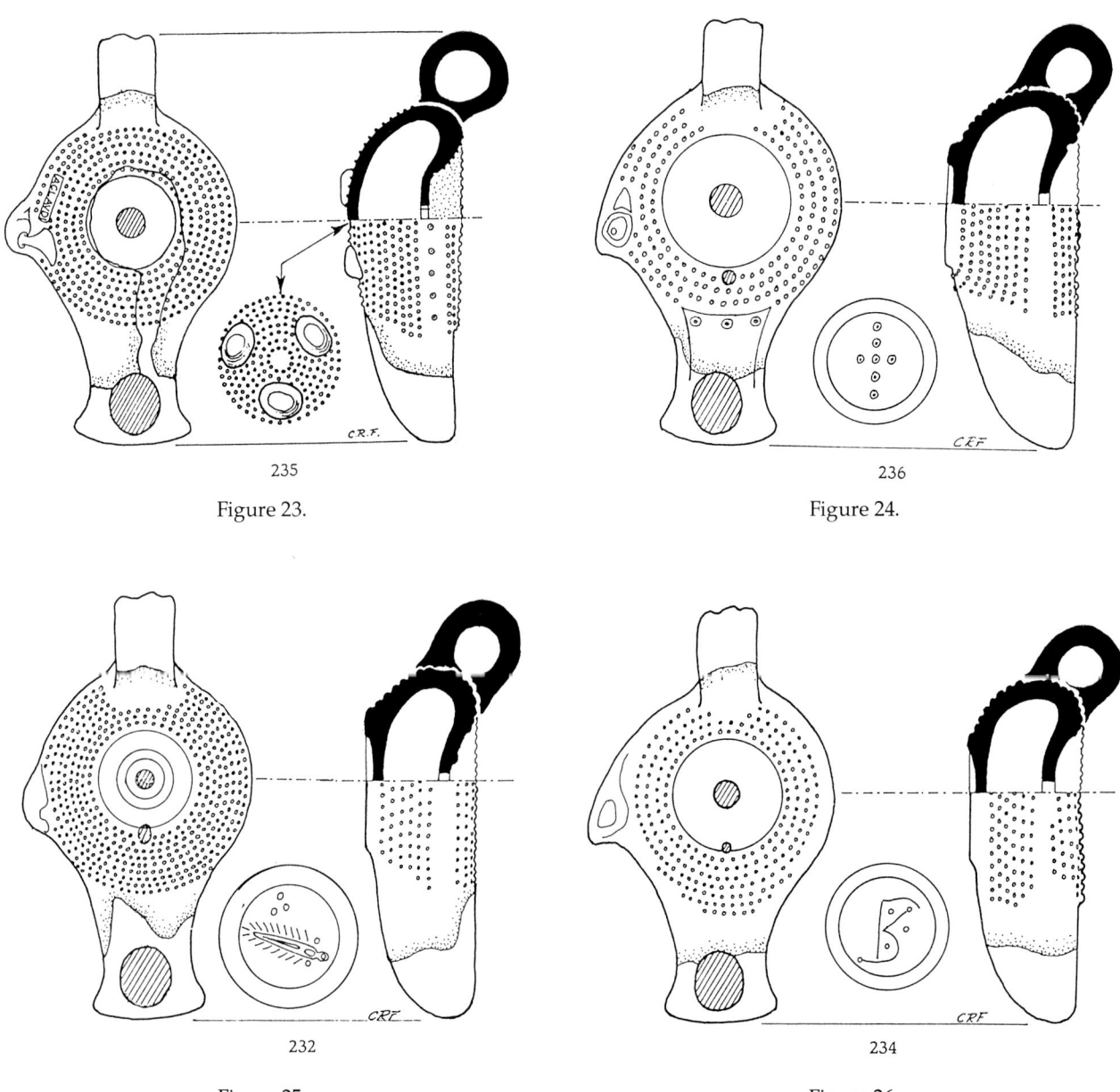

Figures 23–26. Lamps with one ear and Roman nozzle: *Warzenlampen* (Raised-Dots Lamps), scale 1:2

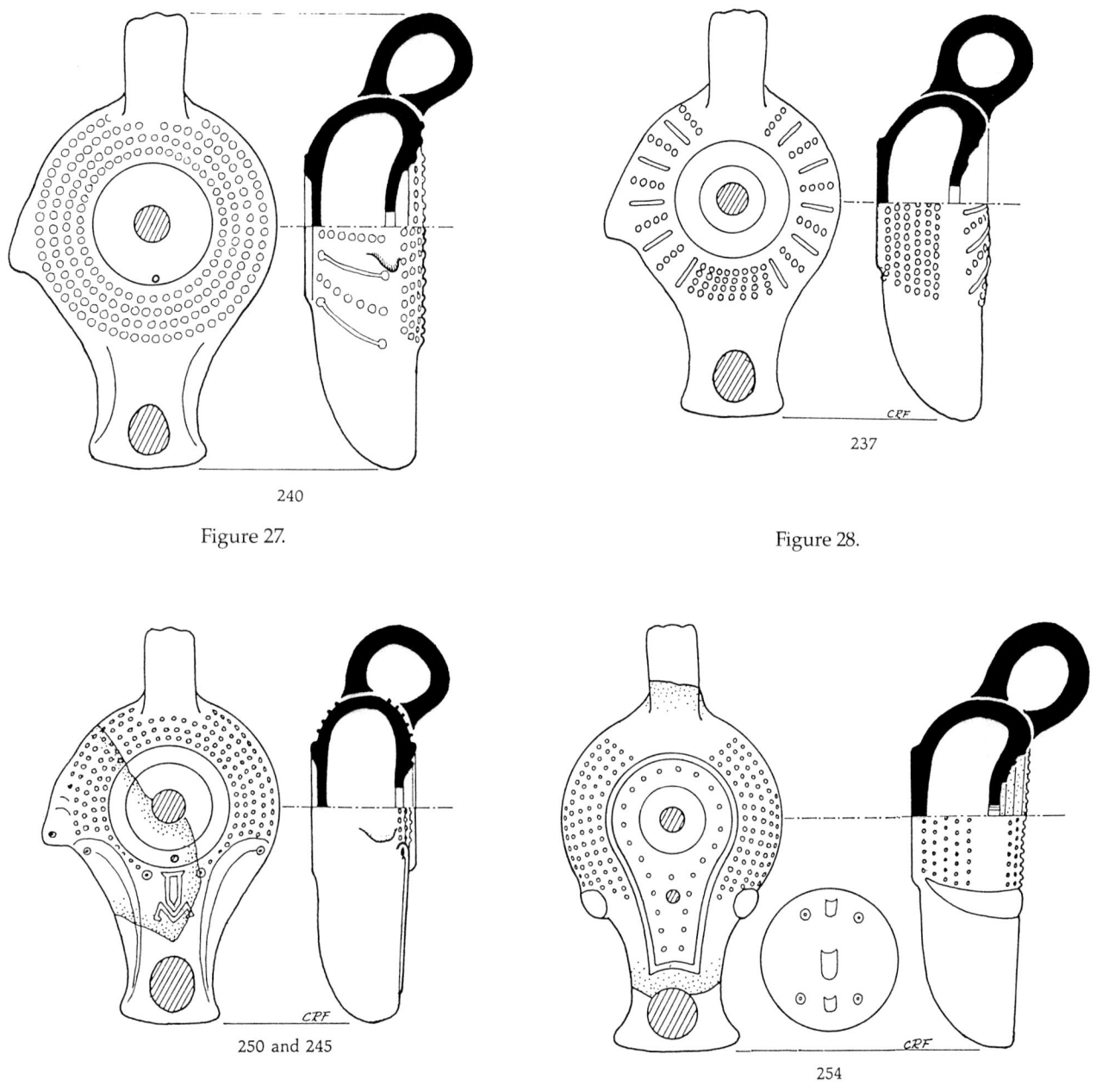

Figures 27–30. Lamps with one ear and Roman nozzle: *Warzenlampen* (Raised-Dots Lamps), different designs, scale 1:2. Lamp 254 is a transitional form without an ear.

There are six lamps on which the potter introduced a new design of radiating rows of dots alternating with a ridge of the same length with a dot at each end.[2] This new design is used either only on the top half or only on the bottom, with the usual concentric rows of dots on the other half. A seventh has long leaves springing from the base instead of ridges and dots. The dots of all seven of these lamps are larger than those on the earlier examples.

Three of the fifty-two *Warzenlampen* are variants. They appear to be experiments with the evolving voluted nozzle.[3] They come from a disturbed stratum laid down probably shortly after the resettlement of the site in 25/20 B.C.

Nineteen of the Cosan *Warzenlampen* have potters' marks of various kinds: small circles or bull's eyes; *TRL* in ligature; *N* with small punched circles at the ends of the strokes; a palm leaf; and an insect. One lamp has the earliest name found on a Cosan lamp—ACLAVDI (235). This beautiful lamp is also unusual in that the name is on the top, not on the base.

175–70 B.C.

220 C66.142 Republican house, V-D W, Level I. Buff clay, red slip. P.L. 0.093 m; Height 0.031 m; Width 0.064 m.

Incomplete, part of the handle broken away. Worn, chipped, and heavily encrusted. There are five rows of the larger-size raised dots on the top of the oil reservoir; the lower side wall is covered to the base with dots. Centered on the top of the nozzle is a small bull's eye.

221 C66.313 Republican house, V-D N, 8–15 NW x 1–15 NE, Level I. Pinkish-buff clay, red slip. P.L. 0.055 m; P.H. 0.008 m; P.W. 0.030 m.

Fragment preserving parts of the base and the lower side wall of the oil reservoir. Worn and chipped. Only parts of the two lowest rows of raised dots are preserved. Ring base. On the base is an incised *N* with small punched circles at the ends of the strokes (cf. 242 for this potter's mark).

222 C66.314 Republican house, V-D N, 8–15 NW x 1–15 NE, Level I. Yellow-buff clay, brown slip. P.L. 0.060 m; P.W. 0.039 m.

Fragment preserving parts of the base and the lower side wall of the oil reservoir. Worn. Unprofiled base, bottom slightly concave. On the bottom of the lamp is an incised *N* with small punched circles at the ends of the strokes and with two additional circles within the triangular interspaces of the *N* (see Fig. 137).

223 C68.510 House of the Birds, Room 3, cesspit, Level I. Buff clay, red slip mottled to brown in places. P.L. 0.094 m; Height 0.033 m; Width 0.068 m.

Incomplete, the handle and parts of the top and side wall of the oil reservoir broken away. Very worn, chipped, and encrusted. Smoke-blackened around wick hole. Ring base.

The top of the lamp has five concentric rows of the larger dots, the two inner rows extending across the top of the nozzle. The lower half of the body is decorated with alternating radiating rows of dots and ridges with a dot marking each end of each ridge. A row of dots encircles the base.

224 C68.714 Republican house, V-D north quadrant, Sounding 7, Room 1, Stratum below floor level. Buff clay, red slip. P.L. 0.030 m; P.W. 0.023 m.

Fragment of a base, flat underneath. Slip rubbed. On the base is part of an incised letter with the ends of the strokes marked by a bull's eye.

225 C68.715 House of the Skeleton, Room 14, Level 0-1. Buff clay, red slip. P.L. 0.054 m; P.H. 0.011 m; P.W. 0.027 m.

Fragment preserving parts of the base and lower side wall of the oil reservoir. Very worn. The interior of the base has high swirls of clay. The bottom of the lamp preserves part of an incised *N* with tiny punched circles marking the ends of the strokes and additional punched circles to either side. It probably had circles in the triangular spaces of the *N* as on 222 and 270, but this part is broken away.

150–70 B.C.

226 CB.1659 Capitolium exterior, S, Level II. Buff clay, reddish-brown slip. P.L. 0.099 m; Height 0.036 m; Width 0.077 m.

Incomplete, the end of the nozzle and handle broken away. Worn. The base is formed of three overlapping disks. Seven concentric rows of tiny raised dots on the top. The rows of dots on the lower half slope up diagonally toward the handle.

---

2. See 223, 237, 240, 251, 252, 258, and 260.
3. See 245, 250, and 254.

227 CB.1867 From the cistern below the retaining wall of the forecourt of the Capitolium. Yellow-buff clay, red slip. P.L. 0.079 m; P.H. 0.023 m; P.W. 0.063 m.

Fragment preserving the handle and parts of the top, side wall of the oil reservoir, and nozzle. Very worn and encrusted. Pits and creases in the fabric. Three-ribbed strap handle. Five concentric rows of tiny dots on the top, the upper two extending across the nozzle. The lower side wall of the oil reservoir is plain.

228 CD.136 Basilica, SW aisle 5, Level I. Pinkish-buff clay, red slip. P.L. 0.046 m; Height 0.034 m; P.W. 0.018 m.

Fragment preserving parts of the top, side wall, and base. Worn; only traces of slip preserved. Five rows of dots on the top; the lower side wall is plain. Ring base.

229 CD.1204 Basilica exterior, NE 5, Level III. Cream clay, brown slip. P.L. 0.071 m; P.H. 0.028 m; P.W. 0.065 m.

Fragment preserving the nozzle and parts of the discus, the top and side wall of the oil reservoir, and the ear. Worn. Five rows of tiny dots on the top; the lower side wall of the oil reservoir is plain.

230 C65.56 Capitolium exterior, E trench, Level II. Buff clay, red slip. P.L. 0.057 m; P.H. 0.031 m; P.W. 0.054 m.

Fragment preserving the nozzle and parts of the top and side wall of the oil reservoir. Encrusted, smoke-stained around the wick hole. Seven concentric rows of tiny raised dots on the upper half of the lamp; the lower is broken away.

231 C65.101 Capitolium exterior, E trench, Level II. Buff clay, red slip. P.L. 0.062 m; P.H. 0.030 m; P.W. 0.049 m.

Fragment preserving the handle and parts of the top and side wall of the oil reservoir. Slip rubbed. The upper half is covered with six rows of tiny raised dots; the lower side wall has only four rows of dots preserved, but others are now broken away.

231A C65.136 Capitolium exterior, E, Level III. Pinkish-buff clay, red slip. P.L. 0.081 m; P.H. 0.032 m; Width 0.058 m.

Incomplete, the base, handle, and part of the nozzle broken away. Worn. The upper half is covered with seven rows of tiny raised dots; the lower side wall of the oil reservoir is plain.

232 (Fig. 25) C65.186 Capitolium exterior, W, Level II. Yellow-buff clay, red slip. P.L. 0.098 m; Height 0.034 m; Width 0.064 m.

Incomplete, the end of the nozzle and part of the handle broken away. Surface rubbed. The upper half of the lamp is covered with eight rows of tiny raised dots, the lower half with six rows. Ring base. Stamped on the bottom is a stylized palm branch or centipedelike insect with small circular punch marks added about the head (see Fig. 137).

233 C65.228 Capitolium exterior, E, Level II. Yellowish-buff clay, red slip. P.L. 0.090 m; Height 0.035 m; Width 0.070 m.

Incomplete, the end of the nozzle and top of the handle broken away. Worn. The upper half is covered with seven rows of tiny raised dots, the lower with six rows. Disk base; the bottom is slightly concave. On the bottom are three grooves of the same length crossing to make a star (see Fig. 135).

234 (Fig. 26) C65.319 Capitolium exterior, E, S cut, Level III. Yellowish-buff clay, red slip. P.L. 0.091 m; Height 0.033 m; Width 0.066 m.

Incomplete, the end of the nozzle and part of the handle broken away. Worn. The upper half is covered with five concentric rows of tiny raised dots, with two short rows added across the top of the nozzle. The lower half of the oil reservoir has five rows of dots. Ring base; within the base *TRL* in ligature, with added punched circles (see Fig. 137). The lamp has been restored and is now in the Museo Archeologico della Maremma at Grosseto.

Cf. Deneauve 1969, 103 and pl. 34 no. 265 for another example of this signature.

235 (Fig. 23) C65.377 Capitolium exterior, E trench, Level II. Yellowish-buff clay, white priming under black slip. P.L. 0.089 m; Height 0.037 m; Width 0.064 m.

Incomplete, the discus, end of the nozzle, and handle broken away. The bottom of the oil reservoir is rounded. The lamp rests on three stubby feet, carefully made and attached. On the ear is decoration in the form of a knotted ribbon, with one end lying flat on the lamp top. The upper half is covered with seven rows of tiny raised dots; the lower half of the oil reservoir is entirely covered with tiny dots, including the rounded bottom, interrupted only by the feet. At the joining of the two halves of the body is a row of evenly spaced bull's eyes added after joining. On the top between the handle and the ear is a small rectangular stamp, within which is the signature *ACLAVDI* in sunken letters (see Fig. 136).

Cf. Bruneau, 98 and pl. 25 no. 4379; and Heres 1969, 39 and pl. 11 no. 103 for other copies of this lamp.

236 (Fig. 24) C67.243 Capitolium exterior, W, Levels II/III. Buff clay, thick, orange-red slip. P.L. 0.091 m; Height at handle end 0.038 m, at nozzle 0.041 m; Width 0.067 m.

Incomplete, the end of the nozzle and handle broken away. Worn. The top of the oil reservoir inclines slightly upward toward the nozzle. The top has four concentric rows of tiny dots, with only three rows extending across the top of the nozzle; at this point three bull's eyes replace the fourth row of dots and mark off the oil reservoir from the nozzle. The lower half of the lamp has eight rows of dots; the lowest two rows completely encircle the base. Ring base. On the base is a cross formed of seven small, punched bull's eyes, five in one line and three in the other (see Fig. 136).

120–20 B.C.

237 (Fig. 28) CB.1854 Pottery dump, Left center, Levels I/II. Cream clay, black slip. P.L. 0.062 m; P.H. 0.032 m; P.W. 0.036 m.

Fragment preserving parts of the discus, the top and lower side wall of the oil reservoir, and the start of the nozzle. Very worn. On the top of the lamp are alternately radiating rows of larger raised dots and ridges of the same length. The lower side wall of the body has the usual concentric rows of dots.

See Gualandi Genito 1977, pls. 21 and 22 nos. 113–16; Lamboglia, fig. 53 no. 25 (Lamboglia dates this lamp to the end of the first century B.C.); Menzel, 23 fig. 21 (with alternating radiating rows of dots and ridges on both the top and the side wall of the oil reservoir); Zaccaria Ruggiu, pl. 67 no. 71. Nos. 252 and 258 from Cosa have the same design.

238 CB.1856 Pottery dump, scattered. Buff clay, red slip mottled to black in places. P.L. 0.007 m; Height 0.029 m near handle, 0.032 m at connection with nozzle; P.W. 0.060 m.

Incomplete, the end of the nozzle and part of the left side of the oil reservoir broken away. Worn. Carelessly made three-ribbed strap handle; the three ribs are of irregular width. The oil reservoir is higher toward the nozzle. The center of the discus and the concentric rows of dots are slightly off-center toward the handle end of the reservoir. The upper half is covered by five concentric rows of slightly larger dots that stop short of the nozzle.

239 CB.1859 Pottery dump, Left center, Level I/II. Cream clay, brown slip. P.L. 0.051 m; P.H. 0.014 m; P.W. 0.032 m.

Fragment preserving parts of the discus, top of the oil reservoir, and nozzle. Very worn. The ridge that separates the discus from the shoulder turns out on either side of the nozzle to form a false channel between the discus and the wick hole. The upper half is covered with six concentric rows of closely set, very small raised dots, interrupted by the false channel above the nozzle.

240 (Fig. 27) CB.1860 Pottery dump, Left center, Levels I/II. Pinkish-buff clay, red slip. P.L 0.066 m; P.H. 0.020 m; P.W. 0.044 m.

Fragment preserving parts of the base and lower side wall of the oil reservoir. Worn. On the lower side wall of the oil reservoir are alternately radiating rows of dots and ridges. A dot marks the end of each ridge. This lamp presumably had concentric rows of dots on the top as on two similar lamps found elsewhere, 223 and 251. Disk base; centered on the bottom is a small punched bull's eye.

25/20 B.C.–A.D. 50

241 CD.1223 Basilica, Exterior NW I, Level II. Buff clay, slip worn away or perhaps a self-slip. P.L. 0.089 m; Height 0.031 m; Width 0.067 m.

Incomplete, the handle and end of the nozzle broken away. Heavily encrusted, as if it had been dropped into coarse sand while still soft. There are five rows of dots on the upper half of the lamp; the lower half of the body is plain. The dots on the top stop short of the nozzle and are replaced by a groove and three small bull's eyes that mark the separation between oil reservoir and nozzle. On the base is a small punched bull's eye, slightly off-center.

242 CD.1237 Basilica exterior, N, Level II. Pale buff clay, red slip. P.L. 0.086 m; P.H. 0.027 m; P.W. 0.048 m.

Fragment preserving parts of the base, lower side wall of the oil reservoir, and the bottom of the nozzle. Encrusted, slip peeling in places. The bottom of the nozzle was trimmed with a sharp instrument. Fire-blackened in places. The lower part of the oil reservoir is plain. Ring base, reworked by hand with a sharp instrument. On the bottom of the lamp is most of an incised *N* with small circles at the ends of the strokes (see Fig. 137).

For other examples of this signature, see 221, 222, 259, 263, 270, and 303; Bailey 1975, pl. 133 nos. Q 714 and Q 715; Gualandi Genito 1977, pl. 21 no. 113; and Carettoni 1957, fig. 34. See *CIL* 15.6535 for an *M* with similar small circles at the ends of the strokes.

243 CEL.201 Atrium Building I, Room 11, Level II. Buff clay with an orange tint, red slip. P.L. 0.023 m; P.H. 0.025 m; P.W. 0.051 m.

Fragment preserving parts of the top and side wall of the oil reservoir and the attachment of the handle. Very worn; only traces of slip preserved. Parts of four rows of tiny raised dots preserved on the upper half.

244 CEL.203 Atrium Building I, Room 11, Level II. Buff clay with an orange tint, red slip. P.L. 0.056 m; P.W. 0.041 m.

Fragment preserving parts of the discus, top, and nozzle. Surface rubbed and scratched. Parts of three rows of tiny raised dots preserved on the top.

245 (Figs. 29, 51) CEL.257 Atrium Building I, Room 11, cesspit, First half meter. Buff clay, black slip with a metallic luster. P.L. 0.057 m; P.H. 0.028 m; P.W. 0.056 m.

Two joining fragments preserving parts of the top, discus, upper side wall of the oil reservoir, nozzle, and ear. Slip in good condition. Made from a worn mold. A bead molding starts near the discus and extends down on either side of the nozzle, like a primitive volute. There is no scroll at the upper end; the lower end is broken away. Five concentric rows of the larger-size raised dots on the top of the lamp are interrupted by this molding. On the top of the nozzle is decoration flanked by bull's eyes.

246 CEL.258 Atrium Building I, Room 11, cesspit. Buff clay, black slip. Length 0.118 m; Height 0.032 m; P.W. 0.052 m.

Three joining fragments preserving the handle and parts of all other essential features. Slip slightly rubbed and chipped. Ring base. On the base are two small punched circles, possibly part of a quincunx, all that remains of a potter's mark.

247 CEL.637 Atrium Building I, Room 11, Level II. Pinkish-buff clay, red slip. P.L. 0.062 m; P.H. 0.023 m; P.W. 0.027 m.

Fragment preserving parts of the base, lower side wall of the oil reservoir, and nozzle. Very worn and chipped; only traces of slip preserved. The fabric is thicker than is usual for this type. High disk base.

248 CG.596 Building L (market building), exterior NW, Level II. Buff clay, blackish-brown slip with a metallic luster. P.L. 0.101 m; Height 0.030 m; Width 0.066 m.

Four joining fragments preserving the discus and nozzle and parts of the top, side wall, base, and attachment of the handle. Worn. The six concentric rows of tiny dots on the top of the oil reservoir stop short of the nozzle. Three bull's eyes mark the separation between the top of the oil reservoir and the nozzle, as on 236 and 270. Disk base. Potter's mark on the base, a quincunx of five small bull's eyes.

249 CG.597 Building L (market building), exterior NW, Level II. Buff clay, red slip. P.L. 0.034 m; P.W. 0.026 m.

Fragment preserving parts of the base and lower side wall of the oil reservoir. Ring base, on the base a central bull's eye (see Fig. 136).

250 (Figs. 29, 51) CG.598 Forum, E corner, NE passage, Surface. Orange-buff clay, red slip. P.L. 0.068 m; P.H. 0.014 m; P.W. 0.051 m.

Fragment preserving the ear and parts of the discus, top of the oil reservoir, and nozzle. Worn. The description is the same as for 245. This lamp may have come from the same mold as 245 but has a different slip.

251 C69.363 Forum, SW, 1.4 SW x 18 NW, Level I. Buff clay, pale reddish-brown slip. P.L. 0.085 m; Height 0.038 m; P.W. 0.072 m.

Three joining fragments making an incomplete lamp, the handle, end of the nozzle, and part of one side of the oil reservoir broken away. Worn. The top of the lamp has four concentric rows of dots. The lower half of the oil reservoir has alternately radiating rows of dots and ridges, as on 223 and 240. Ring base, on the base of the lamp five bull's eyes in a quincunx (see Fig. 136).

See 266 and 288 for examples of the same potter's mark; Zaccaria Ruggiu, pl. on page 63, no. 83; Bailey 1975, pl. 134 nos. Q 721, Q 723, Q 724, Q 726, Q 727, and pl. 135 no. Q 729; Hayes 1980, pl. 21 nos. 208 and 210.

252 C69.310 Forum exterior, NE, VIII-E, Drain channel, Level I. Buff clay with an orange tint, thick reddish-brown slip mottled to dark brown in places. P.L. 0.060 m; P.H. 0.029 m; P.W. 0.037 m.

Fragment preserving most of the discus and parts of the top and the attachment of the handle. Very worn. On the top of the lamp are alternately radiating rows of the larger-size raised dots and ridges of the same length. The lower side wall of the oil reservoir has the usual concentric rows of dots.

See 237 for another example of this lamp.

A.D. 50–ca. 100

253 CB.1136 Capitolium exterior, S, Surface. Buff clay, red slip mottled to black in places. P.L. 0.076 m; P.H. 0.022 m; P.W. 0.054 m; Diameter of base 0.043 m.

Fragment preserving the base and part of the lower side wall of the oil reservoir. Badly worn. Ten rows of tiny raised dots are preserved on the lower side wall. Ring base. On the base of the lamp is an interesting potter's mark, an incised palm branch (see Fig. 137).

Although found in a surface level, this lamp has been catalogued and listed here because it appears to be an early example of a Raised-Dots Lamp. The dots are tiny and closer together than on any other lamp of this type found at Cosa. Two uncatalogued fragments of the same type of lamp with very small raised dots were found in the same context. This lamp and the two fragments are possibly from the debris of the destruction of about 70 B.C.

254 (Figs. 30, 50) CC.458 Arx, N slope, Level I. Greenish-buff clay, black slip. P.L. 0.105 m; Height 0.040 m; Width 0.066 m.

Incomplete, the end of the nozzle and part of the handle broken away. Surface rubbed. The discus is divided into two parts: a small inner area surrounds the central filling hole; the outer part slopes up slightly and extends toward the wick hole in a false channel. The keyhole-shaped outer discus is enclosed by a ridge. There is an unusually large air hole in the false channel. On either side of the top are five concentric rows of the larger-size raised dots that follow the shape of the false channel. On the inner discus and the extension of the false channel is a single row of raised dots that follows the keyhole form. On either side of the lamp at the connection of the oil reservoir and the sides of the nozzle are large cones, as if for scrolls, that extend down to the base, ending in points. But there are no scrolls or volutes. Disk base. On the bottom of the lamp are four small bull's eyes in a rectangle. Between the bull's eyes, lengthwise on axis, are three shields, the shield in the center larger than the others (see Fig. 136). This lamp does not have the usual ear on the left side of the body.

255 CEL.585 Basilica exterior, NW 2 (Atrium Building I, Room 16), Level I. Cream clay, brown slip. P.L. 0.058 m; P.H. 0.018 m; P.W. 0.043 m.

Fragment preserving the ear and parts of the discus, top, and attachment of the nozzle. Worn. A ridge encircles the discus, separating it from the shoulder. The top is covered with five concentric rows of tiny raised dots; the outer three are interrupted on the nozzle and are replaced by three bull's eyes. For the same bull's-eye decoration see 236, 241, and 248.

256 CEL.588 Basilica exterior, NW 2 (Atrium Building I, Room 16), Level I. Grayish-buff clay, brown slip. P.L. 0.057 m; P.W. 0.028 m.

Fragment preserving parts of the discus, top, upper part of the nozzle, and the ear. Worn. The top is covered with five concentric rows of tiny raised dots.

257 CF.2125 Atrium Building I, Room 25 exterior, Level II. Grayish-buff clay, mottled brown slip. P.L. 0.055 m; P.W. 0.029 m.

Fragment preserving parts of the discus and the top of the oil reservoir. Made from a very worn and blurred mold. Discus framed by three ridges. Six concentric rows of tiny raised dots on the top of the oil reservoir.

258 CF.2153 Atrium Building I, Room 25A, Level III. Buff clay, red slip. P.L. 0.060 m; P.W. 0.051 m.

Fragment preserving parts of the discus, top, and nozzle. Worn. On the top of the lamp are alternately radiating rows of the larger-size raised dots and ridges of the same length. The lower half of the lamp is broken away, but it probably had the usual concentric rows of dots, as on 237.

259 CG.590 Building L (market building) exterior, NW, Level I. Orange-buff clay, red slip. P.L. 0.046 m; P.W. 0.025 m.

Fragment preserving parts of the base and the lower side wall of the oil reservoir. Very worn. Ring base. Inscribed on the base is part of a letter *N* with small punch marks at the ends of the strokes.

See 242 and notes for this potter's mark.

260 CG.603 Building L (market building) exterior, NW, Level I. Cream clay, pewter-colored slip with a metallic luster. P.L. 0.040 m; P.H. 0.024 m.

Fragment preserving parts of the oil reservoir and base. Very worn; only traces of slip preserved. The top of the lamp is covered with concentric rows of the larger-size dots; on the lower side wall are elongated leaves that radiate from the base. The leaves are of two kinds: some are long and slender with a central rib; the others are elongated thistle leaves.

261 C68.419 House of the Birds, Olive balk adjoining House of the Skeleton garden, V-D NE 13–17.5. Buff clay, lustrous, dark orange slip. P.L. 0.073 m; P.W. 0.060 m.

Fragment preserving the discus and parts of the top and handle. On the top of the nozzle, scratched after firing, is a rectangle divided in half by a groove. Arcs connect the corners of the rectangle on the long sides (see Fig. 135).

262 C69.34 Forum SW, 21.0 SE by 0.95 SW, Level I. Greenish-buff clay, red slip mottled to brown in places. P.L. 0.102 m; Height 0.030 m.

Two joining fragments preserving the base and parts of the top, side wall of the oil reservoir, the discus, the nozzle, and attachment of the handle. Surface rubbed. The top of the lamp is covered with five concentric rows of tiny raised dots, interrupted at the nozzle by a comic mask in high relief, as on 265.

263 C69.122 House of the Birds, Rooms 2 and 6, Level 0-B. Cream clay, red slip. P.L. 0.056 m; P.H. 0.014 m; P.W. 0.030 m; Diameter of base 0.035 m.

Fragment preserving parts of the base, lower side wall of the oil reservoir, and underside of the nozzle. Worn and encrusted. Only parts of the three lowest rows of tiny raised dots are preserved. The dots stop short of the nozzle, but centered on the bottom of the nozzle is one raised dot. Ring base, within which is an incised *N* with small circles punched at the ends of the strokes and with additional circular punches within the triangular interspaces of the *N* and to either side.

See 242 for this potter's mark.

264 C70.527 Streets VI and D, E, Republican house, Room 20, Level 0. Cream clay, dark reddish-brown slip. P.L. 0.045 m; P.W. 0.042 m.

Fragment preserving part of a ring base. Encrusted. On the base is part of an incised *N*, with small circles at the ends of the strokes.

See 242 for this potter's mark.

265 C71.225 House of the Birds, SW perimeter trench, Level 0-A. Buff clay, red slip. P.L. 0.072 m; P.W. 0.045 m.

Fragment preserving parts of the discus, top of the oil reservoir, and nozzle. Worn; slip preserved only on the top of the nozzle. Smoke-blackened around wick hole, encrusted. Five concentric rows of tiny raised dots on the top of the oil reservoir interrupted at the nozzle. Centered on the nozzle is appliquéd a small comic mask of a slave.

See 262 for another example of a slave mask appliquéd on a nozzle; and Bailey 1980, pl. 133 no. Q 714 for a small boss of a scallop shell. This lamp has the potter's mark *N* with small punched circles at the ends of the hastae (see Fig. 137). Bailey dates this lamp to the second half of the first century B.C.

266 C71.227 House of the Birds, SW perimeter trench. Level 0-A. Gray-buff clay, red slip. P.L. 0.044 m; P.H. 0.016 m; P.W. 0.035 m.

Fragment preserving parts of the base and lower side wall of the oil reservoir. Worn, chipped, root-marked, and encrusted. Low disk base. On the base of the lamp was a quincunx of bull's eyes; only three of the five are preserved. The lower half of the lamp is plain.

267 C71.228 House of the Birds, SW perimeter trench, Level 0-A. Grayish-buff clay, red slip. P.L. 0.078 m; Height 0.030 m; Width 0.068 m.

Five joining fragments preserving most of a lamp; the nozzle, part of the handle, and a chip from the discus are broken away. Slip very worn in places. Most of the surface is fire-blackened. Slightly encrusted and root-marked. The top is covered with five concentric rows of raised dots. Low disk base.

A.D. 100–225

268 CF.1921 Atrium Building I, Room 25, exterior, Level I. Buff clay, red slip. P.L. 0.023 m; P.H. 0.021 m; P.W. 0.008 m.

Fragment preserving part of the top of the oil

reservoir. Worn. The concentric rows of tiny raised dots are spaced farther apart than is usual.

269 CF.2015 Atrium Building I, Room 25, exterior, Level I. Buff clay, red slip mottled to brown in places. P.L. 0.060 m; P.H. 0.014 m; P.W. 0.046 m.

Fragment preserving parts of the discus, top of the oil reservoir, and nozzle. Slip worn and chipped. The concentric rows of tiny raised dots are interrupted at the nozzle.

270 C66.251 Streets V and D, N, Level 0. Cream clay. Length 0.118 m; Height 0.030 m; Width 0.068 m.

Two joining fragments preserving all of a lamp but a few chips broken from the nozzle and the base. Worn and encrusted. There are four concentric rows of the larger-size raised dots on the top of the oil reservoir. The inner three rows continue across the top of the nozzle; the fourth is interrupted by the nozzle and replaced by three bull's eyes. The lower half of the oil reservoir is covered with rows of raised dots to the base. The discus with its encircling rows of dots is off-center, displaced slightly toward the handle. Ring base. On the bottom is an incised N with small punched circles marking the ends of the strokes and additional circles in the triangular interspaces of the N and to either side.

This lamp has been included, although it was found in a surface level, since it has a potter's mark that occurs on a number of lamps that date to the late republic or early empire; see 242.

c. LAMPS WITH CIRCULAR RAISED NOZZLES

(Figs. 31–37)

(Catalogue Numbers 271–278)

The eight lamps in this group all have circular raised nozzles of Hellenistic type. Seven have "biconical" bodies; one has a cup-shaped oil reservoir. Through the distinctive circular raised nozzle the smaller wick hole was punched, leaving a raised rim around the wick hole. Six of the lamps are single-nozzled, one has two nozzles in the front, and one is boat-shaped with a nozzle at either end.

The "biconical" lamps in this group have bodies composed of two flattened truncated cones, base to base, with carination near the midpoint. Six of the eight lamps have an ear on either side of the body, one has a single ear, and one has none. Four of the biconical lamps have small swallowtail ears on either side of the body. All four have a quadrangular discus, usually square or rectangular, but on one the long sides are concave and the short sides convex. All four have strap handles, and all four have shoulder decoration of tiny raised dots.

Two of the eight lamps were found in contexts that have been dated from 150 to 70 B.C.; one is from a context dated 89/85 B.C.; four are from contexts dated from 25/20 B.C. to A.D. 50. One was found on the Arx near the surface, perhaps thrown up from a lower level by a medieval burial.

One of the lamps, 276, is probably from Sicily. The clay and decoration seem closely related to the Sicilian Delphiniform Lamps found at Cosa. The remaining seven were probably made in Rome or nearby.

150–70 B.C.

271 (Fig. 32) CB.1690 Capitolium exterior, S, Level II. Buff clay, red slip. P.L. 0.067 m; P.H. 0.022 m; P.W. 0.056 m.

Fragment broken on all sides, preserving the discus, part of the top of the oil reservoir, and the attachment of the handle. Surface rubbed. Rectangular discus, enclosed on three sides by a double ridge, open on the fourth toward the circular raised nozzle. At the open end, the ridges turn outward but are broken at the break of the fragment. Two semicircular rows of raised dots partially enclose the open end of the discus. The top has six rows of tiny raised dots on either side of the discus. There is a small air hole at the edge of the discus toward the nozzle.

272 C65.405 Capitolium exterior, E, NW cut, Level II. Pinkish-buff clay, red slip. P.L. 0.045 m; P.H. 0.023 m; P.W. 0.051 m.

Fragment, broken on all sides, preserving the discus and part of the top. Slip very worn. Description the same as for 271; these two lamps may be from the same mold.

89/85 B.C.

273 (Fig. 33) C68.627 House of the Skeleton, Main garden trench near the portico. Buff clay, red slip. P.L. 0.095 m; Height 0.034 m; Width across the body 0.070 m; Width including the ears 0.077 m.

Three joining fragments preserving most of a lamp, the handle and part of the nozzle broken

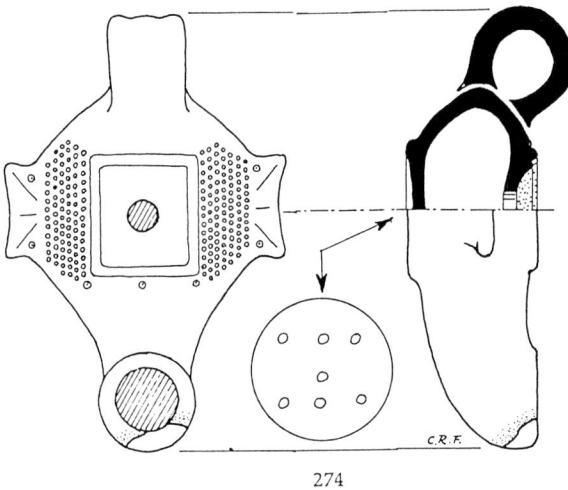

274

Figure 31.

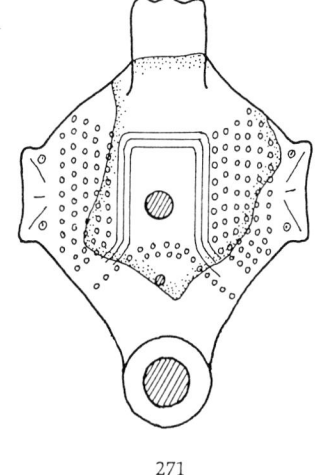

271

Figure 32.

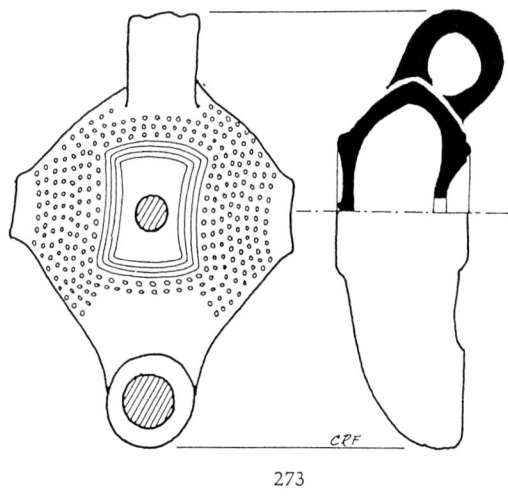

273

Figure 33.

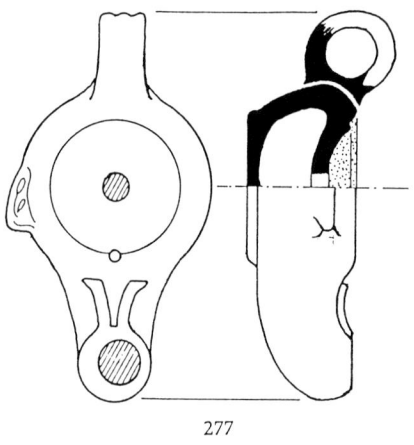

277

Figure 34.

Figures 31–34. Lamps with circular raised nozzles, scale 1:2

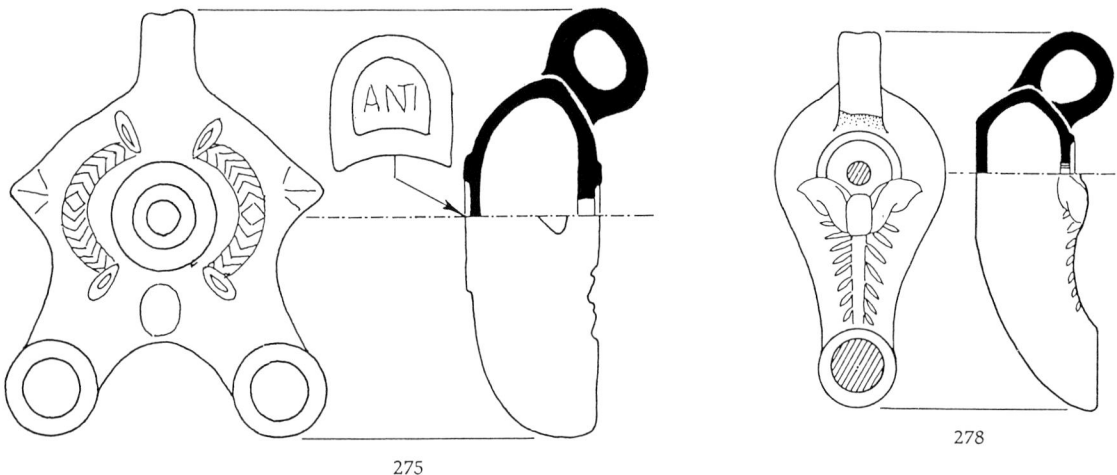

Figure 35.   Figure 36.

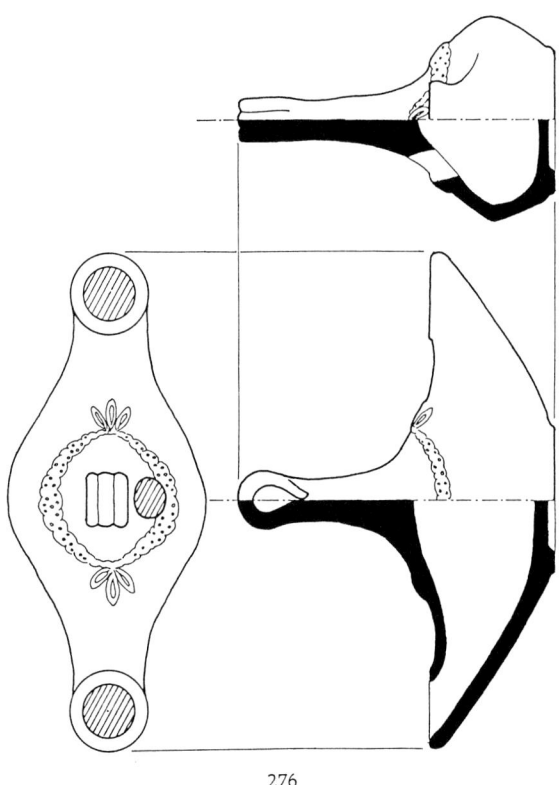

Figure 37.

Figures 35–37. Lamps with circular raised nozzles, scale 1:2

away. Worn, encrusted; slip flaking. No air hole; low disk base. Quadrangular discus enclosed by a ridge, with the long sides concave and the short sides convex. A very small, roughly swallowtail ear on either side. Eight rows of tiny raised dots decorate the top of the oil reservoir following the lines of the discus. The two inner rows completely surround the discus; the remaining six stop short of the circular raised nozzle.

25/20 B.C.–A.D. 50

274 (Fig. 31) CEL.288 Atrium Building I, Room 16 sounding, Level I. Buff clay, red slip mottled to darker red in places. P.L. 0.102 m; Height 0.035 m; Width across body 0.063 m; Width including the ears 0.076 m.

Two joining fragments preserving all of a lamp but the tip of the circular raised nozzle. Slip worn and chipped. Smoke-blackened around the wick hole. The discus is almost square surrounded by a thick ridge. Two swallowtail ears and a three-ribbed vertical strap handle. This lamp does not have an air hole. Disk base, slightly concave. On the base are seven small bull's eyes in three rows, three on each side of one centered between (see Fig. 136). On either side of the discus are six rows of tiny raised dots. Three small bull's eyes are spaced along the outer edge of the discus toward the nozzle, and two bull's eyes are punched at either side of the ears near the juncture with the oil reservoir. Three grooves fan out from the center of each ear.

For comparable lamps with sharply carinated bodies, rectangular disci, and raised dots, see Hanoune, 237–62, pl. 3 no. 5; Lamboglia 1950, 65, fig. 25 no. 3 (Lamboglia dates this lamp "di età cesariana"); Szentléleky, 54–55 no. 48; Pontiroli, pl. 57 no. 71; Bailey 1975, 336, pl. 132 no. Q 710. (This last example has lost its nozzle; however there can be little doubt that it is the same type as 274. Both have carinated bodies, swallowtail ears on either side, and potter's marks of small punched circles or bull's eyes, and neither has an air hole.)

275 (Fig. 35) C71.36 The House of the Birds, Perimeter trench, Level 0-A. Grayish-buff clay, black slip. P.L. 0.085 m; Height 0.037 m; P.W. 0.077 m.

Five joining fragments preserving the handle, discus, base, one ear, parts of the top and side wall of the oil reservoir, the two circular raised nozzles, and the attachment of the other ear. Worn, encrusted. Made from a worn, blurred mold. The relief has been crudely reworked with a sharp instrument. The base is in the shape of the heel of a shoe. On the base is inscribed *ANTI*, the *N* and *T* in ligature (see Fig. 135). Relief: On either side of the discus an unskilled hand has scratched a crude arc of herringbone with a loop of ribbon at each end. The original design of the mold was a floral swag tied with a ribbon at each end. (For an example of this decoration, see Bailey 1975, pl. 135 no. Q 732.) Between the nozzles was a mask in relief, only part of which is preserved.

For examples of a heel-shaped base, see Zaccaria Ruggiu 1980, 32–33 nos. 36, 37, a, b; Bailey 1975, pl. 136 no. Q 733.

276 (Fig. 37) CEL.202 Atrium Building I, Room 11, Level II. Dark gray clay, rather hard, dark orange-red slip mottled to black in places. P.L. 0.133 m; Height 0.086 m; P.W. 0.048 m.

Five joining fragments preserving the handle, and parts of the top and side walls of the oil reservoir, base, and circular raised nozzles. Slip peeling, chipped, and smoke-blackened around the wick holes. A long boat-shaped lamp with a biconical body and a long nozzle at each end. The center of the top rises in a cone and is crowned by the stem of a tall, looped, three-ribbed handle. The filling hole is punched on one side of the handle. Ring base. A double floral swag encircles the top of the lamp and is tied at each end with a ribbon in three loops.

This is the only example of this type that has been found at Cosa. It is probably from Sicily. The clay and profile of the oil reservoir are similar to those of the Delphiniform Lamps imported from Sicily between 120 and 70 B.C. The relief of floral swags closely resembles that on the Sicilian Lamp 199. This unusual lamp was found in a context dated 25/20 B.C.–A.D. 50.

For a similar design see Bailey 1975, pl. 135 no. Q 732; Iconomu, fig. 189 no. 780; and Farka 1977, pl. 24 nos. 1455, 1456.

The lamp below was found near the surface on the Arx, but it has been catalogued and included here as another example of experimentation with new forms by Roman potters during the late republic.

277 (Fig. 34) C67.102 Capitolium exterior, Level I. Fine, buff clay, slip mottled brown to black in places with a metallic luster. P.L. 0.095 m; Height 0.030 m; Width 0.052 m.

Incomplete, part of the strap handle broken away. The top of the lamp is in excellent condition, the lower part worn. Large, plain, concave discus with a central filling hole and an unusually large air hole at the edge of the discus toward the circular raised nozzle. The discus is separated from the narrow, sharply sloping shoulder by a groove. Deep cup-shaped body, splaying slightly toward the top. The raised circular rim surrounding the wick hole divides toward the discus and extends along the top of the nozzle in a V with serifs, stopping short of the rim of the discus. There is a spur-shaped ear on the left side of the body with incised decoration. Disk base.

For other examples of this nozzle form, see Bruneau, pl.12 nos. 2209, 2263; Perlzweig 1963, pl. 6 no. 139, pl. 10 no. 349; Howland, pl. 49 no. 659, pl. 52 no. 759.

278 (Fig. 36) C69.100 Fish Market, SE cistern, settling tank. Soft, fine, orange-buff clay, brownish red slip. P.L. 0.095 m; Height 0.027 m; Width 0.046 m.

Incomplete, part of the handle broken away. Worn, encrusted. Biconical body of about equal elements. The long circular raised nozzle inclines upward toward the wick hole. Small circular discus with a central filling hole. Unprofiled base with flat bottom. Strap handle. This lamp does not have the usual air hole. Relief: A palm branch extends down the top of the nozzle to the rim of the wick hole. It is tied at the discus with a large bow that overlaps the discus.

For comparable lamps, see Bruneau, pl. 13 nos. 2263, 2370, 2423, pl. 14 nos. 2601, 2603, 2620, and 2635; Deneauve, pl. 32 nos. 245–49; Miltner 1930, pl. 11 nos. 7, 9–11; Iconomu, 50 no. 76; Heres 1959, pl. 14 nos. 130, 131, 135; Bernhard, pl. 31.

d. LAMPS WITH NOZZLES ENDING IN A TRIANGLE
(Figs. 38, 39)

(Catalogue Numbers 279, 280)

The two lamps that follow have an ear on the left side of the body and a long nozzle that ends in a triangle. Both have strap handles. The oil reservoirs are different; one is an Ephesus type with a double convex body with carination at about mid-height; the other has a cylindrical body.

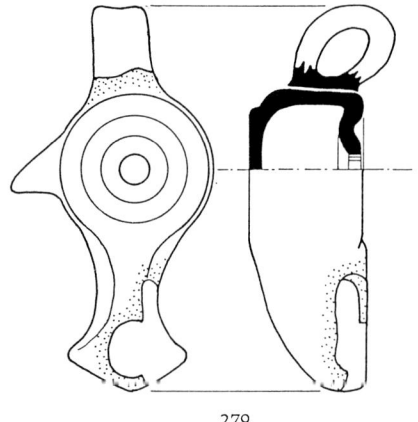

279

Figure 38.

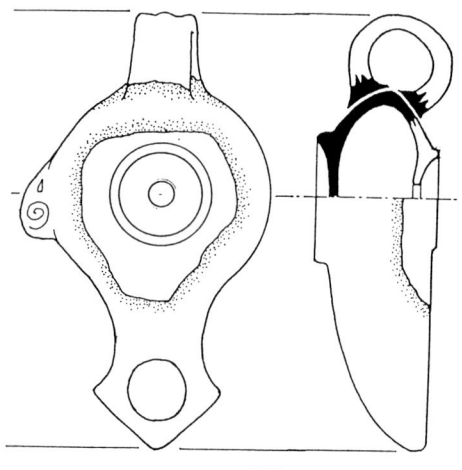

280

Figure 39.

Figures 38, 39. Lamps with nozzles ending in a triangle, scale 1:2

150–70 B.C.

279 (Fig. 38) C67.73 Capitolium exterior, W, Level III. Cream clay with an orange tint, black slip. P.L. 0.085 m; Height 0.032 m; Width without ear 0.041 m.

Incomplete, the right end of the nozzle, a part of the handle, and a chip from the ear broken away. Encrusted. Cylindrical body on a disk base. The discus covers the top of the body. The midsection of the discus is concave, but raised around the filling hole. There is a large, pointed ear on the left side of the body.

25/20 B.C.–A.D. 50

280 (Fig. 39) C65.89 Capitolium exterior, E, Level II. Buff clay, red slip. P.L. 0.101 m; Height 0.031 m; Width 0.067 m.

Incomplete, the center of the top and part of the handle broken away. Ear decorated with a spiral on the left side of the Ephesus-type double convex body. Ring base.

e. LAMPS WITH SWALLOWTAIL EARS

(Figs. 40–44)

(Catalogue Numbers 281–303)

There are twenty-three late Republican molded lamps with swallowtail ears and Roman spatulate nozzles found at Cosa. Each has a wide discus with a simple rim, usually set off from the discus by a groove. The discus and rim cover the top of the cup-shaped oil reservoir. This rests on a low disk base or ring base. All these lamps have vertical strap handles.

The clay is buff to cream colored, and is medium hard. The fabric is thick and strong. The slip is red, brown, or black, and is often mottled. Some of the lamps have decoration in simple geometric designs, usually symmetrical, of small repeated units.

Seven of these lamps were found in contexts dated from 175 to 70 B.C. Three are from contexts dated from 150 to 70 B.C.; two are from the pottery dump dated from 120 to 20 B.C.; one is from a context dated 91–70 B.C. Three are from levels dated 25/20 B.C.–A.D. 50, and four are from contexts that have been dated A.D. 50–ca. 100. The remainder are from contexts loosely dated from A.D. 50 to 225. However, they were probably all made before the end of the first quarter of the first century A.D. Six are from contexts that have been dated A.D. 50–ca. 100, although they too were probably made earlier.

175–70 B.C.

281 C66.227 Republican house, V-D west quadrant. Buff clay, red slip. P.L. 0.104 m; Height 0.030 m; Width 0.070 m.

Incomplete, the end of the nozzle broken away. Very encrusted, worn, and chipped. Low ring base, within which are five tiny punched circles in a quincunx. Discus plain.

For other examples of a quincunx as a potter's mark, see 246, 248, 251, 266, and 288.

282 C66.410 Republican house, V-D north quadrant, Level I. Buff clay with an orange tint, red slip. P.L. 0.081 m; P.H. 0.025 m; P.W. 0.075 m.

Three joining fragments preserving the handle, one ear, and parts of the discus and side wall of the oil reservoir. Very worn; encrusted. Made from a worn mold. Three-ribbed strap handle. Discus relief: Two confronted sea monsters with large open maws (or birds with long open beaks) on either side of the central filling hole, the mouths or beaks toward the handle.

283 (Fig. 42) C66.411 Republican house, V-D north quadrant, Level I. Cream clay, brown slip. P.L. 0.068 m; P.H. 0.013 m; Width 0.075 m.

Two joining and one nonjoining fragments preserving one ear and parts of the other, the discus, nozzle, and attachment of the handle. Worn, encrusted, smoke-blackened around the wick hole. Strap handle. The ears do not match; one ear is the usual swallowtail, the other a small spur. Discus relief: A ship with furled sails facing right. A figure stands on the prow with upraised arms. Only three oars are shown. The details otherwise are carefully drawn: a deck cabin in the rear, the steering oar, oar holes and, toward the prow, a large circular shield, perhaps a fender.

284 C66.469 House of Quintus Fulvius, Room 5, cistern. Buff clay, red slip mottled to black in places. P.L. 0.113 m; Height 0.036 m; Width 0.079 m.

Complete, except for part of the handle. Worn; slightly encrusted. Three small circles are punched at the top of the nozzle near the discus. Ring base, within which five raised dots in a quincunx and a graffito *F* or *E*, perhaps *F* for Fulvius (see Fig. 135). Discus relief: Rosette of bordered

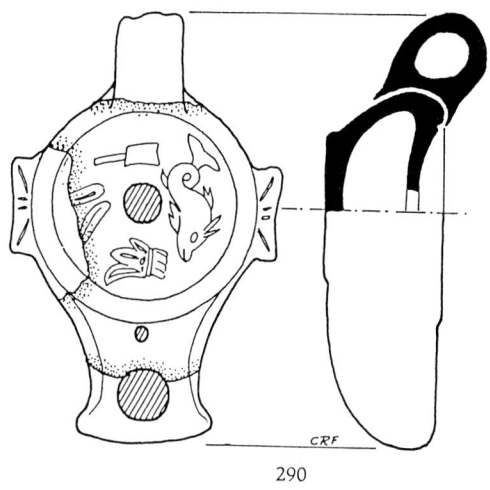

290

Figure 40.

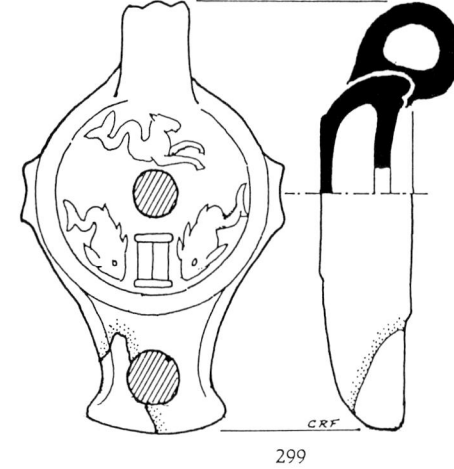

299

Figure 41.

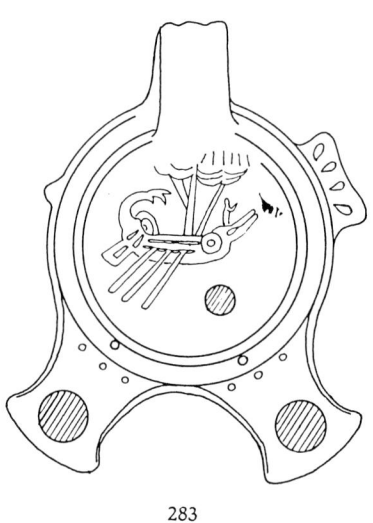

283

Figure 42.

Figures 40–42. Lamps with swallowtail ears, scale 1:2

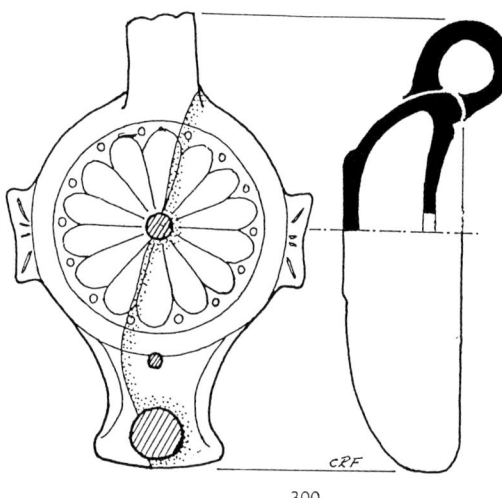

Figure 43.

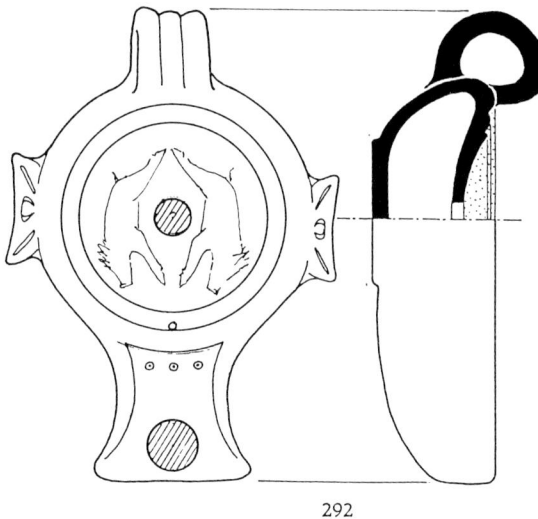

Figure 44.

Figures 43, 44. Lamps with swallowtail ears, scale 1:2

tongues with raised dots at the outer ends and between the tongues.

285 C66.877 House of Quintus Fulvius, Room 5, cistern. Buff clay, black slip. P.L. 0.039 m; P.H. 0.022 m; P.W. 0.024 m.

Fragment preserving part of the side wall of the oil reservoir and the lower part of a swallowtail ear. Broken at the mold join. Very worn; slip rubbed away in places.

286 C68.530 House of Quintus Fulvius, Room 3, cesspit, Level II. Buff clay, mottled brown to black slip. Length 0.122 m; Height 0.033 m; Width 0.072 m.

Three joining fragments making most of a lamp, parts of the base and side wall of the oil reservoir broken away. Surface rubbed and discolored. Three-ribbed strap handle, the outer ribs raised. Discus relief: A dolphin swims to right on the right side of the discus; on the left a sea monster with a lifted head and curling tail ending in a great spiked club swims to left. Under the body is a series of fins.

287 C72.83 Republican house, Streets V/VI-D/E, Room 4, cesspit (later part of the House of the Birds). Cream clay, black slip. P.L. 0.085 m; Height 0.036 m; Width 0.072 m.

Three joining fragments forming most of a lamp, the handle and nozzle broken away. Very worn and encrusted. Discus relief: Around the central filling hole are six objects in relief: toward the handle a scallop shell; flanking this are two amphoras; below the amphoras are two dolphins swimming toward the nozzle. Centered toward the nozzle is another amphora. The mouths of the amphoras point out.

150–70 B.C.

288 CB.1716 Capitolium exterior, S, Level II. Buff clay, reddish-brown slip with a metallic luster. P.L. 0.078 m; Height 0.033 m; P.W. 0.069 m.

Three joining fragments forming most of a lamp, the nozzle, handle, parts of the side wall of the oil reservoir, and part of the discus and rim broken away. Worn and chipped. The attachment of the handle and one rectangular ear are preserved. Low disk base, flat underneath; on the base are small bull's eyes in a quincunx. Discus relief: Around the central filling hole are a dolphin, a ship's beak, an octopus, and a steering oar. Cf. 290 and Fig. 40.

289 CB.1773 Arx, Cistern near the Via Sacra below the retaining wall. Pink-buff clay, red slip. P.L. 0.097 m; Height 0.036 m; Width 0.066 m.

Incomplete lamp, the right side of the nozzle and handle broken away. Worn, chipped, and scratched. Made from a worn mold. An example of proto-volutes. These are long and narrow with a scroll only at the edge of the discus. Ring base, within the ring is inscribed an *N* with punched circles added at the ends of the strokes, to either side, and within the triangular spaces of the *N* (see Fig. 137). Discus relief: A rosette of seven deeply bordered petals with central ribs and one complex veined leaf toward the handle.

For similar lamps, see Gualandi Genito 1977, pl. 20 no. 108; Lamboglia 1950, 65 fig. 25; Marsa, pl. 1 nos. 79–80.

290 (Fig. 40) CD.1006 Basilica exterior, NE 5, Level III. Cream clay, black slip. P.L. 0.080 m; P.W. 0.045 m.

Two joining fragments preserving most of the discus, and parts of the rim and nozzle. Worn and chipped. This lamp is identical with 288, made from the same or same generation of molds.

120–20 B.C.

291 CB.1853 Pottery dump, left center, Levels I/II. Cream clay, light brown slip. P.L. 0.036 m; Height 0.031 m; P.W. 0.069 m.

Fragment preserving parts of the handle, discus, side wall of the oil reservoir, base, and attachment of the two ears. Worn and encrusted. Low disk base. Discus relief: Twenty-two grooves radiating from the central filling hole.

292 (Fig. 44) CB.1861 Pottery dump, scattered. Pinkish-buff clay, red slip. P.L. 0.085 m; Height 0.031 m; P.W. 0.085 m.

Two joining fragments preserving the discus, rim, side wall of the oil reservoir, base, one intact ear, and parts of the other. Worn. Low disk base. Discus relief: Two boars running toward the nozzle above and below the central filling hole, belly to belly.

119/91–70 B.C.

293 C66.875 Republican house, V-D east quadrant, Room 21, sounding 4-E in a buried dolium. Buff clay, red slip mottled to black in places. P.L. 0.072 m; Height 0.035 m; P.W. 0.038 m.

Fragment preserving the right ear and parts of the discus, side wall of the oil reservoir, and base. Worn; slip worn away in places. Encrusted. The ear has three grooves fanning from the juncture with the oil reservoir. Discus plain. This lamp was found with two uncial asses minted 119–91 B.C.

25/20 B.C.–A.D. 50

294 CD.1207 Basilica exterior, NE 3, Level III. Buff clay, red slip. P.L. 0.052 m; P.H. 0.028 m; P.W. 0.043 m.

Two joining fragments preserving one ear and parts of the discus, rim, side wall of the oil reservoir, and base. Worn; slightly chipped. Rim: A wide rope twist, then a bead molding, then a wide outer rim, all sloping up to the outer edge. Two grooves radiate to the corners of the ears, and two raised dots mark the connection of the center of the ear with the body. Discus plain.

295 CD.1224 Basilica exterior, NW I, Level II. Grayish-buff clay, thick black slip. P.L. 0.069 m; P.H. 0.028 m; P.W. 0.025 m.

Fragment preserving one ear and parts of the discus and side wall of the oil reservoir. Slip chipped and peeling in places. Ear decorated with three grooves fanning from the center at the juncture with the body of the lamp. Rim: A twisted rope molding sloping up to a narrow bead molding. Discus relief too fragmentary to identify.

296 CD.1623 Atrium Building I, Room 25B, pit, Level IV. Cream clay, brown slip. P.L. 0.052 m; P.H. 0.028 m; P.W. 0.056 m.

Fragment preserving the handle and parts of the discus, side wall of the oil reservoir, and one ear. Very worn; only traces of slip preserved. The handle was carelessly attached and cracked across the top before firing. Smoke-blackened in places. Three-ribbed strap handle. Discus relief: Only the tip of a wing or palm branch is preserved.

A.D. 50–ca. 100

297 CD.1253 Basilica exterior, NE 3, Level I. Buff clay, red slip. P.L. 0.056 m; P.H. 0.017 m; P.W. 0.033 m.

Fragment preserving one ear, part of the discus, and attachment of the nozzle. Worn; a chip missing from the ear. Discus plain.

298 CEL.313 Atrium Building I, Room 16, Level I. Buff clay, red slip mottled to reddish-brown in places. P.L. 0.059 m; P.H. 0.020 m; P.W. 0.021 m.

Fragment preserving parts of the discus, side wall of the oil reservoir, nozzle, and one ear. Slip worn, peeling, and chipped. Smoke-blackened around the wick hole. This lamp has protovolutes; a raised ridge on either side of the nozzle ends in an elementary scroll at the discus. Discus relief: The outer edge of the discus has a border of raised dots framing a geometric design, but too little is left for identification.

299 (Fig. 41) CG.601 Building L (market building) exterior, NW, Level I. Buff clay with an orange tint, red slip. P.L. 0.097 m; Height 0.029 m; Width 0.067 m.

   Incomplete, the handle and end of the nozzle broken away. Condition good except for minor scratches. Low disk base, concave underneath. Discus relief: At the center toward the handle is a hippocamp facing right. In the lower part of the discus are two dolphins confronted around a central altar.

   Cf. Deneauve, pl. 34 no. 272; Bailey 1975, pl. 134 no. Q 724.

300 (Fig. 43) CG.602 Building L (market building) exterior, NW, Level I. Cream clay, pewter-colored slip with a metallic luster. P.L. 0.099 m; P.H. 0.021 m; P.W. 0.043 m.

   Fragment preserving one ear, parts of the discus, nozzle, upper side wall of the oil reservoir, and attachment of the handle. Very worn; only traces of slip preserved. Discus relief: Rosette of fourteen concave petals, with raised dots between the outer ends of the petals (parts of seven petals preserved).

A.D. 50–225

301 CEL.190 Atrium Building I, Room 24, Level IV. Cream clay, black slip. P.L. 0.054 m; P.H. 0.023 m; P.W. 0.029 m.

   Fragment preserving an ear, parts of the discus, and side wall of the oil reservoir. Surface rubbed and chipped. Encrusted. Discus plain.

302 CEL.589 Basilica exterior, NW 2, Level I. Buff clay, red slip mottled to brown in places. P.L. 0.054 m; P.H. 0.021 m; P.W. 0.023 m.

   Fragment preserving a swallowtail ear and part of the upper side wall of the oil reservoir. Worn and chipped.

303 C69.440 House of the Skeleton, Rear of garden, Surface. Cream clay, red slip. P.L. 0.074 m; Height 0.031; P.W. 0.035 m.

   Fragment preserving one ear, parts of the discus, side wall of the oil reservoir, base, nozzle, and handle. Worn and encrusted. Edge of rim damaged in one place before firing. Four raised dots set off the ear from the rim. Ring base, within which is part of an incised letter, a stroke, perhaps of an N, with a tiny bull's eye at its end. Discus plain. For other examples of this mark, see 221, 222, 224, 242, and 270.

f. LAMPS WITH A BICONICAL BODY AND ROMAN NOZZLE
(Figs. 45–47)

(Catalogue Numbers 304–307)

Four lamps have been found at Cosa made of a pale gray, brittle, lightweight, soft, micaceous clay. All have a black slip; one has two slips, black over green. All have biconical bodies, with carination occurring at midheight, a small depressed discus with a central filling hole, a broad spatulate Roman nozzle with flukes, and a strap handle. Three have disk bases; the fourth has a ring base. The shoulders are decorated with unevenly spaced radiating grooves. Marking the separation between the oil reservoir and nozzle on three of these lamps are a pair of transverse grooves, the space between them divided into five squares by short vertical grooves. The fourth lamp has only a single transverse groove at this point.

Three of these biconical lamps come from contexts dated 150–70 B.C. One was found near the surface, but in an area near the Capitolium where medieval burials have disturbed the strata.

Donald Bailey (Bailey 1975, 335) gives a number of examples of this lamp from various sites and observes that "three unnumbered examples in the Museo Nazionale at Taranto point to a south Italian manufacturing source."

150–70 B.C.

304 (Fig. 45) C65.168 Capitolium exterior, W trench, S cut, Level II. Soft, brittle gray clay, black slip. P.L. 0.063 m; Height 0.031 m; Width 0.051 m.

   Incomplete, the end of the nozzle and part of the handle broken away. Worn. The filling hole is punched slightly off center. A band of five squares in relief extends across the top of the nozzle, marking the juncture of the nozzle and oil reser-

74   Cosa: The Lamps

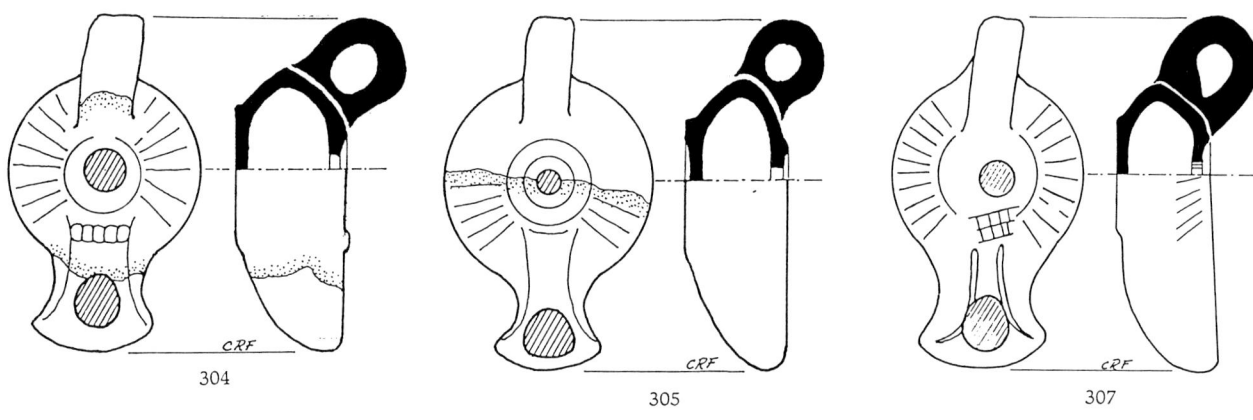

Figure 45.   Figure 46.   Figure 47.

Figures 45–47. Lamps with a biconical body and Roman nozzle, scale 1:2

voir. There are eight grooves on the left shoulder and seven on the right radiating from the center.
   Cf. Bruneau, pl. 26 no. 3367 for a similar lamp.

305 (Fig. 46) C67.596 Capitolium exterior, W, Levels II/III. Soft, brittle, gray clay, black slip. P.L. 0.067 m; Height 0.028 m; P.W. 0.055 m.
   Fragment preserving the nozzle, most of the base, and half of the oil reservoir and discus, including half of a very small central filling hole. Very worn. Ring base. A short straight transverse groove marks the juncture of the oil reservoir and nozzle. Only five radiating grooves of the left shoulder and three of the right are preserved.
   Cf. Deneauve 1959, pl. 20 nos. 3407 and 3410, closely related to this lamp, although both have double nozzles.

306 C70.396 Forum SE, Level II, Square IX-E. Pale gray brittle clay, black slip over a pale green slip. Length 0.092 m; Height 0.024 m; Width 0.052 m.
   Complete, except for a chip at one end of the nozzle. Worn. Made from a crudely reworked mold. A band of five squares in relief extends across the top of the nozzle marking the joint of the nozzle and oil reservoir. There are eleven grooves on the left side of the shoulder and nine on the right.

307 (Fig. 47) CB.1384 Capitolium exterior, S, Surface. Pale gray, soft, brittle clay, black slip. Length 0.064 m; Height 0.026 m; Width 0.052 m.
   Complete. Slip rubbed; smoke-stained around the wick hole. Filling hole punched off center and the handle twisted to the right before firing. A ridge partially encircles the discus and extends out to the corners of the nozzle. There are two bands of squares in relief across the top of the nozzle. They have been crudely reworked and are not evenly spaced or aligned.

g. LAMPS WITH A WIDE DECORATED DISCUS AND A ROMAN NOZZLE BUT WITHOUT EARS
(Figs. 48, 49)
(Catalogue Numbers 308–316)

Nine lamps have been found at Cosa that are only a short step from the Picture Lamp that was developed during the Augustan period. They have a large discus that covers the top of the cup-shaped oil reservoir, providing an ideal surface for decoration. They have lost the ear or ears that occurred on earlier Roman molded lamps, but they have kept the Roman spatulate nozzle.
   One of the lamps in this group is from a context dated 150–70 B.C. Seven are from the pottery dump, dated 100–25/20 B.C. Another was found in a context that has been dated A.D. 50–100.

150–70 B.C.
308 CB.1774 Cistern below the Arx Wall, near the

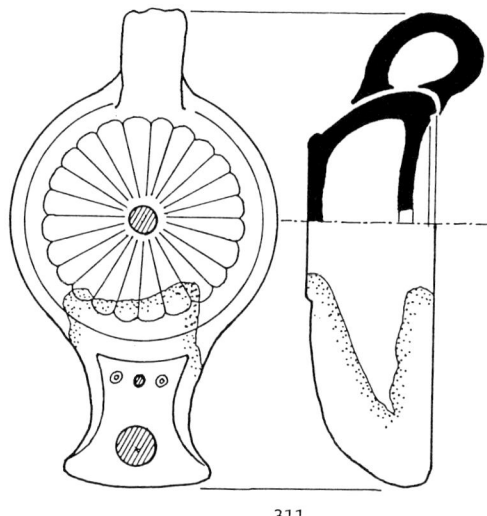

311

Figure 48.

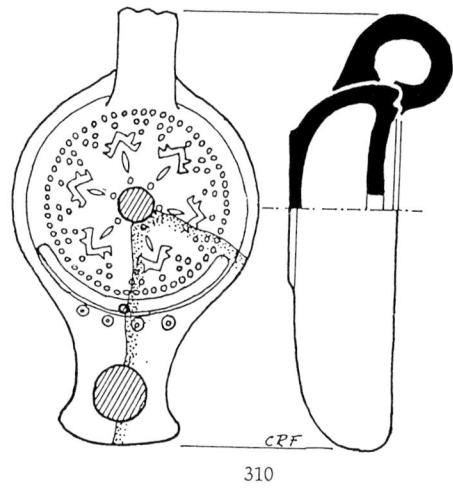

310

Figure 49.

Figures 48, 49. Lamps with a wide, decorated discus and a Roman nozzle but without ears, scale 1:2

Sacra Via. Buff clay, brown slip mottled to black in places. P.L. 0.104 m; Height 0.028 m; Width 0.060 m.

Incomplete, part of the handle broken away. Worn, scratched, and chipped. Made from a worn, blurred mold. A lamp with a wide, decorated discus edged with a lip and a Roman spatulate nozzle. Low ring base. Strap handle. Discus relief: A wreath of laurel leaves tied in groups of three, with the design starting on each side of the handle.

100–25/20 B.C.

309 CB.1847 Pottery dump, right, Levels I/III. Buff clay, brown slip mottled to black in places. P.L. 0.057 m; P.W. 0.028 m.

Fragment preserving parts of the discus, rim, and nozzle. Very worn; made from a worn, blurred mold. Rim: A narrow bead molding sloping up to a wider one. Discus relief: A rosette of twenty-four petals, parts of seven preserved.

310 (Fig. 49) CB.1849 Pottery dump, right, Levels I/II/III. Buff clay, black slip. P.L. 0.063 m; P.W. 0.032 m.

Fragment preserving the right side of a nozzle and a wedge of the discus and rim, including an arc of the central filling hole. Surface rubbed. Rim: An inner bead molding sloping up to a slightly wider one. Four bull's eyes mark the juncture between discus and nozzle. There is a proto-volute on either side of the nozzle. Discus relief: At the outer edge of the discus is a ring of raised dots; within this is a hexagonal design of raised dots and small chevrons making a six-pointed star around the filling hole. The dots are arranged in triangles pointing toward the filling hole.

311 (Fig. 48) CB.1850 Pottery dump, right, Levels I/II/III. Buff clay, red slip. P.L. 0.056 m; Height 0.034 m; P.W. 0.036 m.

Two joining fragments preserving the nozzle and parts of the discus, side wall of the oil reservoir, and base. Worn and chipped. Across the nozzle at the juncture with the body are three bull's eyes, the central one punched through the fabric to make the air hole. Low ring base. Discus relief: A rosette of twenty-four petals, parts of five preserved.

312 CB.1858 Pottery dump, left center, Levels I/II. Cream clay, brown slip. P.L. 0.042 m; Height 0.025 m; P.W. 0.063 m.

Fragment preserving parts of the discus, side wall of the oil reservoir, handle, and base. Slip worn away in places. Low base ring. Rim: Two narrow bead moldings. Discus plain.

313 (Fig. 52) CB.1862 Pottery dump, scattered. Buff clay, black slip. P.L. 0.082 m; Height 0.030 m; Width 0.066 m.

Three joining fragments preserving parts of the discus, rim, side wall of the oil reservoir, base, start of handle, and nozzle, including the scroll of a proto-volute. Discus plain.

The two lamps below are more refined than the others in this group from the pottery dump and are probably Augustan.

314 CB.1852 Pottery dump, left center, Levels I/II. Grayish-buff clay, black slip. P.L. 0.039 m; P.W. 0.022 m.

Fragment preserving parts of a discus and rim. Surface rubbed. Rim: A high bead molding encircling a flat discus. Discus relief: A linen-fold pattern with the folds radiating from the center. Made from a fine mold, carefully executed.

315 CB.1857 Pottery dump, scattered. Buff clay, brown slip. P.L. 0.023 m; P.W. 0.026 m.

Fragment preserving parts of a discus and rim. Surface rubbed. Made from a fine mold. Rim: A narrow bead molding between slightly wider flattened ones. Discus relief: A wreath of olive leaves, four leaves and parts of two more preserved.

A.D. 50–100

316 CF.2145 Atrium Building I, Room 15, Level II. Buff clay with an orange tint, red slip. P.L. 0.079 m; P.H. 0.011 m; P.W. 0.058 m.

Fragment preserving parts of the discus, rim, attachment of the nozzle, and handle. Very worn and encrusted. Shallow concave discus separated from a convex rim by a groove. Discus plain.

h. LAMPS WITH EVOLVING OR PROTO-VOLUTES

The five lamps listed below are fully described in the sections to which they belong, but are listed here because they all have proto-volutes that may be an attempt to create a design that would unite the nozzle with the discus visually as well as physically (Figs. 50–52). From these attempts came the fully developed volute that appeared on Roman Picture Lamps from 25/20 B.C. through the first quarter of the first century A.D. These five lamps all have the Roman spatulate nozzle.

100–20 B.C.

310 (Fig. 49) CB.1849 Pottery dump. A wide, decorated discus lamp without ears and with proto-volutes.

313 (Fig. 52) CB.1862 Pottery dump. A wide, plain discus without ears and with proto-volutes.

25/20 B.C.–A.D. 50

245 (Fig. 51) CEL.257 Atrium Building I, Room 11, cesspit. A *Warzenlampe* with rounded body, one ear, and proto-volutes.

250 (Fig. 51) CG.598 Forum E. Corner, NE passage, Surface. A *Warzenlampe* from the same mold or the same generation of molds as 245.

25/20 B.C.–A.D. 225

254 (Fig. 50) CC.458 Arx, W slope, Level I. An anomalous lamp with a keyhole-shaped discus, a form of *Warzenlampe* with a large horn, as if for a scroll, on either side of the nozzle, but without the scroll or volute.

i. MISCELLANEOUS LATE REPUBLICAN LAMPS

(Catalogue Numbers 317–323)

The three lamps listed below have potters' marks on their bases. The upper parts of the lamps are not preserved. They were all found in contexts that antedate the destruction of Cosa in about 70 B.C.

150–70 B.C.

317 CB.1693 Capitolium exterior, S, Level II. Buff clay with a grayish tint, red slip. P.L. 0.077 m; P.W. 0.047 m.

Fragment preserving the base, lower part of the nozzle, and part of the lower wall of the oil reservoir. Surface rubbed. Roman spatulate nozzle. Ovoid ring base, within which are eight small circular punches, six punches in a circle with one in the center and one toward the point of the ovoid ring (see Fig. 136).

318 CB.1699 Capitolium exterior, S, Level II. Buff clay with a pink tint, red slip. P.L. 0.062 m; P.H. 0.027 m; Width 0.066 m.

Fragment preserving a ring base and most of the side wall of the oil reservoir up to the join with the discus, where the break occurs. Worn.

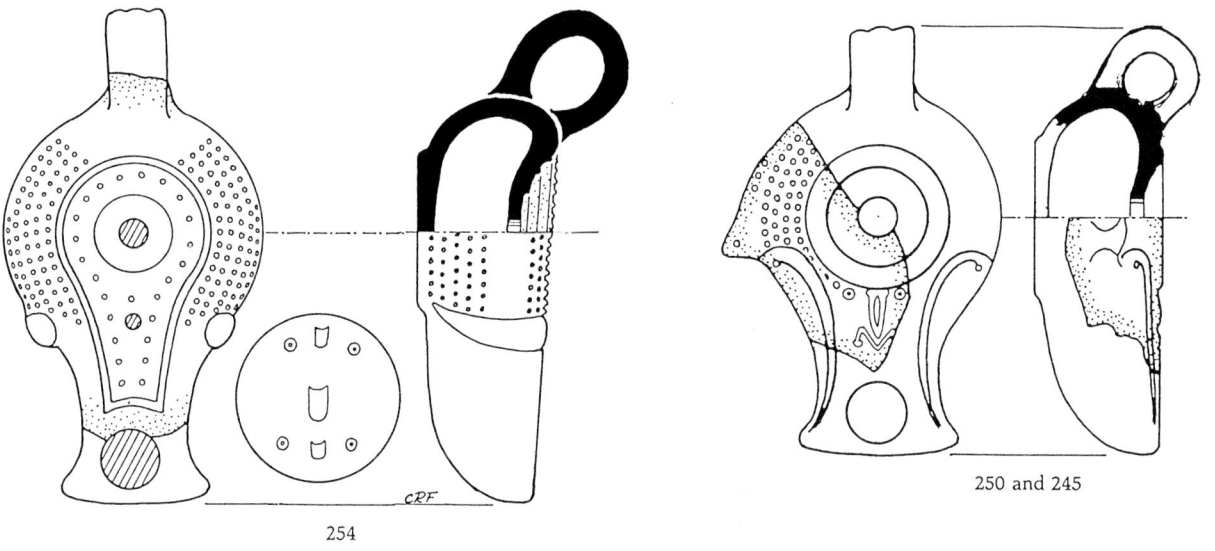

Figure 50.   254

Figure 51.   250 and 245

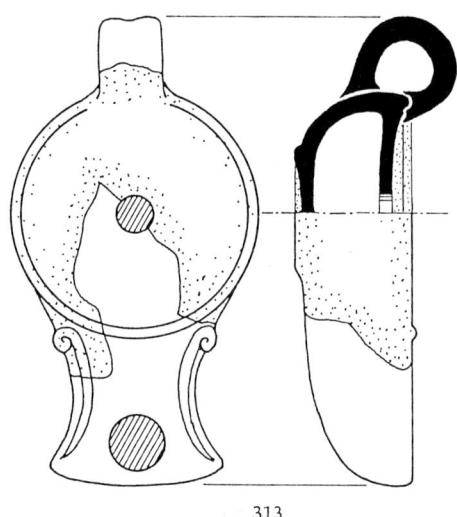

313

Figure 52.

Figures 50–52. Lamps with evolving or proto-volutes, scale 1:2

78 Cosa: The Lamps

Slip worn away in places. The side wall of the oil reservoir is almost vertical. Ring base, within which are the letters *TRL* in ligature with added tiny punch marks (see Fig. 137). The same signature is found on a *Warzenlampe*, 234.

319 CD.1044 Basilica exterior, NE 6, Level IV. Buff clay, red slip mottled to brown in places. P.L. 0.080 m; P.H. 0.042 m; P.W. 0.066 m.
   Two joining fragments preserving the base, parts of the lower and upper side wall of a deep Ephesus type body, and part of a handle. Very worn. Wide ring base, within which is *MR* in ligature (see Fig. 135).

The next four catalogue entries are fragments of late Republican lamps. One is a lamp of a new form that was not successful, and of which this is the only example found at Cosa thus far. One fragment is of a handle with some adjoining parts, and the other two are pre-volute, spatulate, Roman nozzles.

120–70 B.C.

320 CB.1845 Capitolium exterior, S, Pronaos, Level II. Buff clay, red slip. P.L. 0.057 m; P.H. 0.037 m; P.W. 0.048 m.
   Fragment preserving a three-ribbed strap handle, part of the side wall of the oil reservoir, and the top. Very worn. The wall of the oil reservoir of this angular lamp is in three straight stages, the lowest is inclined sharply outward, the broad middle stage inclined only slightly outward, the third inclined inward.

91–70 B.C.

321 C66.876bis V-D east quadrant, Sounding 4 E, Room 21, Dolium. Buff clay, red slip. P.L. 0.053 m; Height 0.041 m; P.W. 0.044 m.
   Fragment preserving part of a handle, the side wall of the oil reservoir, the base, and the outer edge of the rim. Worn and chipped. The handle is divided into three ribs; the center one is flat, decorated with raised dots, the two outer ribs rounded.

25 B.C.–A.D. 50

322 CF.2151 Atrium Building I, Room 15, pit, Level III. Cream clay, dark reddish-brown slip. P.L. 0.032 m; P.H. 0.027 m; P.W. 0.037 m.
   Fragment preserving a spatulate Roman nozzle. Surface chipped. Fire-blackened. The nozzle is straight across the end, wider and shorter than usual.

A.D. 50–ca. 100

323 CD.1238 Basilica exterior, N, Level II. Buff clay with a pinkish tint, red slip. P.L. 0.039 m; P.W. 0.024 m.
   Fragment preserving the left half of a nozzle broken down the center. Chipped; otherwise the surface is in good condition. A spatulate pre-volute Roman nozzle.

8. BIRDS'-HEADS LAMPS (*VOGELKOPFLAMPEN*)

(Fig. 53)

(Catalogue Numbers 324–344)
(Dressel Types 2, 4, and 22; Deneauve Types I and II; Leibundgut Type I;
Haken Types 1 and 10; Sartorio Type 1; Menzel Types 70 and 71; Gravisca
Type 2; Magdalensburg Group II)

Twenty-one Birds'-heads Lamps and fragments have been found at Cosa and catalogued, together with a number of uncatalogued fragments. None of these lamps is complete, but all the essential features are preserved in various fragments. The drawing at the head of this chapter is a composite, with eleven different rim profiles. The parts of these lamps that survive best are the nozzles, as their fabric is thick and is reinforced by the reliefs of the birds' heads, although most of these are broken down the center of the channel separating the two heads.

Two Birds'-heads Lamps have been found at Cosa in contexts that predate the destruction of the town in 70 B.C. This date is earlier than has been generally advanced for the introduction of this type of lamp. The evidence, however, seems incontrovertible, since one was found in a cistern sealed over by debris from the destruction of 70 B.C., and the other in Level IV at the rear of the Basilica. Twelve of these lamps were found in contexts dated from 25 B.C. to A.D. 50. Five come from contexts dated from A.D. 50 to ca. 100, while the remaining two are from contexts loosely dated from A.D. 50 to 225.

The clay of the Cosan Birds'-heads Lamps ranges from cream to buff in color, occasionally with a pink, orange, or gray tint. The clay is finely levigated and rather soft. Fourteen lamps of the twenty-one have a red slip; five have a dark brown or black slip, three of these with a metallic luster. One lamp of this group has a pale green slip and one a self-slip.

The body of the Birds'-heads Lamps is deep and cup-shaped. The large concave discus that covers the top of the oil reservoir is either ovoid or circular, with a central filling hole. The bases seem to match the shape of the discus, either ovoid or circular, although few bases have been preserved. The rims are a series of rings of different widths, rounded or flat, with one band almost always decorated with a rope twist. The rims slope up toward the exterior and vary in width from 0.012 m to 0.019 m. The range of their profiles is shown in Fig. 53. The earlier rim profiles are the more complex; a wider, simpler rim molding with fewer rings indicates a later development, and would make extraction from the mold easier. Only unusual rims are described in the catalogue.

The distinguishing feature of this type of lamp is the nozzle decoration. There are addorsed birds' heads in relief flanking a channel on top of the nozzle. The necks are bent sharply down near the discus. The heads extend toward the wick hole; the long bills are pressed against the necks. Four kinds of bird are identifiable: swans, geese, storks, and pelicans. This design may have first appeared on Delphiniform Lamps, although on the Cosan Delphiniform Lamps the birds' heads are not distinct or are so abstracted that they are unrecognizable, whereas on some Delphiniform Lamps from Sicily birds' heads are very distinct. The ends of the nozzles are the usual spatulate Roman form that preceded the voluted nozzle, with straight or slightly curved ends flanked by short flukes.

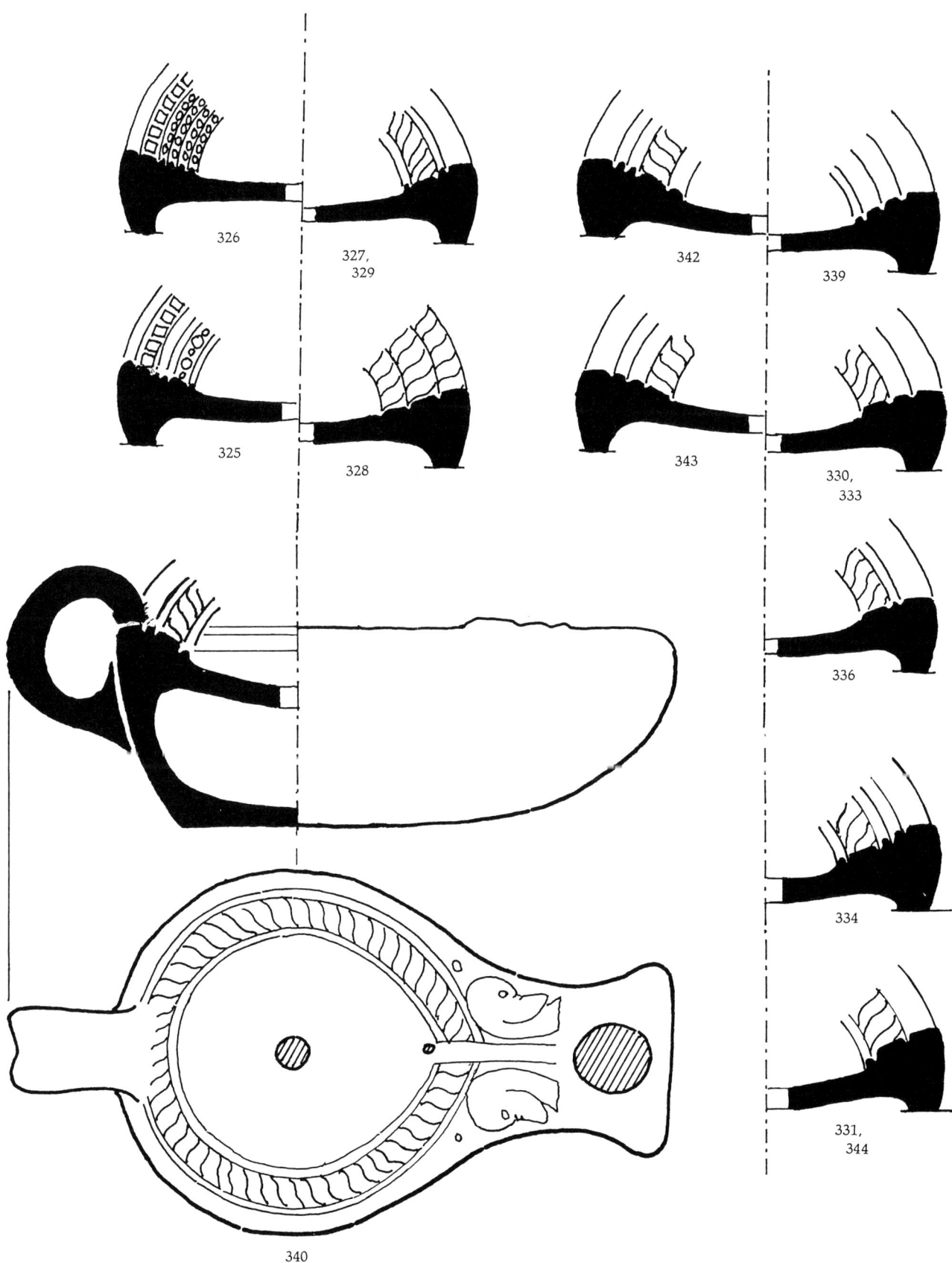

Figure 53. Birds'-heads Lamps (*Vogelkopflampe*), full scale

Only parts of four handles that can be assigned to Birds'-heads Lamps have survived. Three of the four are strap handles; the fourth was made in the mold. All lamps of this type have a small air hole either in the discus toward the nozzle or in the bottom of the nozzle channel. Seven bases are preserved, either entire or partial. Four of these have a signature on the bottom inscribed with a sharp instrument in elongated letters: *SIC* or *SICI*.

Birds'-heads Lamps have been found at many sites in Italy, Sicily, and the western Roman empire, very few in the East. They probably originated in or near Rome.

175–70 B.C.

324 C66.878 House of Quintus Fulvius, cistern under Room 5, Level I/II. Buff clay with an orange tint, red slip mottled to darker red in places. P.L. 0.054 m; P.H. 0.031 m; P.W. 0.043 m.

Fragment preserving parts of the rim, side wall of the oil reservoir, base, and handle. Worn, chipped, and encrusted. Low circular disk base, separated from the side wall of the oil reservoir by a groove. The handle is very carefully made by hand. The outer edges are raised; the broader central section is flat and decorated with small raised dots in a quincunx.

150–70 B.C.

325 CD.871 Basilica exterior, NE 1, Level IV. Buff clay with a pinkish tint, red slip. P.L. 0.053 m; P.H. 0.034 m; P.W. 0.060 m.

Three joining fragments preserving most of the base and side wall of the oil reservoir, and parts of the discus and handle. Chipped and worn. Rim: An inner ring, then a border alternating smaller and larger dots, then two rings, then a narrow band with a checkered design, and finally a narrow outer ring (Fig. 53). All slope upward. Ovoid unprofiled base with the point under the nozzle end. (The discus, which is not preserved, was probably also ovoid.) On the bottom is a signature incised in elongated letters, not clearly legible, perhaps *RILISCI*. This signature may be that usually abbreviated to *SIC* or *SICI* (see Fig. 135).

For the signature, see *CIL* 15.6691. Lamps with this signature have been found at various sites in Rome, on the bank of the Tiber, on the Mausoleum of Augustus, on the Palatine, in the Forum, and in graves at Porta Praenestina. There are examples in the Museo Nazionale Romano (delle Terme). Two lamps of this type with *SIC* and *SICI* are in the Römisch-Germanisches Zentral Museum in Mainz, published by Menzel.

25/20 B.C.–A.D. 50

326 CD.1210 Basilica exterior, NE 1, Level IV. Cream clay, red slip. P.L. 0.061 m; Height 0.031 m; Width 0.066 m.

Incomplete, the end of the nozzle and handle broken away. A hole is worn through the base, and the entire lamp is very worn, and made from a worn, blurred mold. Round discus. Rim: Four concentric rows of tiny raised dots, a slightly wider band of small squares, and a narrow outer ring (Fig. 53). Low circular disk base, separated from the body by a groove. The birds' heads are of pelicans. Just below the heads are cones that extend down the side wall of the nozzle, like the scrolls of a volute.

See Fremersdorf, pl. 41, for a similar rim.

327 CD.1221 a and b Basilica exterior, NW 1, Level II. Cream clay, red slip. P.L. a 0.065 m, b 0.045 m; P.H. 0.013 m; P.W. a 0.044 m, b 0.019 m.

Two nonjoining fragments preserving parts of the discus, rim, and nozzle. Worn, slip worn away on raised surfaces. Ovoid discus. Rim: Fig. 53. The heads are of storks.

328 CD.1222 Basilica exterior, NW 1, Level II. Cream clay, brownish-black slip with a metallic luster. P.L. 0.071 m; P.H. 0.024 m; P.W. 0.030 m.

Fragment preserving parts of the discus and upper side wall of the oil reservoir, and the left side of the nozzle. Very worn; only traces of slip preserved. Smoke-blackened around the wick hole. Rim: Fig. 53. Discus design on the preserved part is too little to identify. The heads are of storks.

329 CD.1225 Basilica exterior, NW 1, Level II. Buff clay, red slip. P.L. 0.079 m; P.H. 0.022 m; P.W. 0.028 m.

Fragment preserving parts of the discus, rim, body, and nozzle. Worn and chipped. Made from a worn, blurred mold. Rim: Fig. 53. The birds' heads are unidentifiable, because the mold is worn.

330 CEL.242 Atrium Building I, Room 6, Level II. Buff clay, red slip. P.L. 0.054 m; P.W. 0.030 m.

Fragment preserving parts of the left side of the nozzle, rim, and discus. Very worn. Made from a worn, blurred mold. Ovoid discus. Rim: Fig. 53. Above the bird's head at the outer edge of the lamp was something in relief, but the mold was too worn for this to be identifiable. The head is of a pelican.

See Menzel 1969, fig. 22 nos. 1–3, for a similar relief.

331 CEL.254 Atrium Building I, Room 16, Level II. Buff clay, red slip.

Fragment preserving part of the base and lower side wall of the oil reservoir. Worn. Low disk base, separated from the side wall of the body by a groove. Rim: Fig. 53. On the base are incised the elongated letters *SIC*, part of the *C* broken away. There is space for another letter after *C* (see Fig. 135).

See Menzel 1969, fig. 22 no. 1, for *SICI* in the same elongated letters, and 325, 335, and 338 for other examples of this signature from Cosa.

332 CEL.256 Atrium Building I, Room 11, cesspit, Level first half meter. Buff clay with a pinkish tint, self-slip. P.L. 0.060 m; P.H. 0.035 m; P.W. 0.058 m.

Two joining fragments preserving parts of the discus, rim, oil reservoir, base, handle, and nozzle, in fairly good condition. The discus and base are ovoid. Three-ribbed strap handle.

333 CEL.282 Atrium Building I, Room 21, Level II. Buff clay, red slip. P.L. 0.044 m; P.W. 0.029 m.

Three fragments, two joining and one nonjoining, preserving parts of the discus, rim, and nozzle. Very worn. Rim: Fig. 53. The discus is circular. The heads are crane or stork heads, placed high, cutting into the rim.

334 CEL.594 Basilica exterior, NW 2, Level II. Buff clay, brown slip with a metallic luster. P.L. 0.096 m; P.H. 0.023 m; P.W. 0.058 m.

Two joining fragments preserving parts of all essential features. Worn, chipped, and encrusted. Rim: Fig. 53. Unprofiled base, slightly ovoid. The head is of a swan. Handle included in the mold.

This lamp is probably Claudian, as the molded handle does not appear earlier at Cosa (see Introduction, p. 7).

335 C71.140 Street M, drain sediment. Cream clay, red slip. P.L. 0.045 m; P.W. 0.022 m.

Fragment preserving half of a disk base. Inscribed on the bottom in elongated letters is part of a vertical stroke and a *C*, probably to be restored as *SIC* (see Fig. 135).

Cf. 325, 331, and 338 for the same mark.

336 C71.229 a and b House of the Birds, Perimeter trenches A 11 and B 10. Cream clay, pale green slip. P.L. a 0.043 m, b 0.034 m; P.H. a 0.008 m, b 0.031 m; P.W. a 0.031 m, b 0.037 m.

Two nonjoining fragments preserving the right half of the nozzle, and parts of the discus and rim. Slip slightly rubbed. Encrusted, smoke-blackened around wick hole. Rim: Fig. 53. The head is of a stork.

337 C71.230 House of the Birds, V/VI-D/E, Perimeter trench 12. Cream clay, brown slip. P.L. 0.054 m; P.H. 0.023 m; P.W. 0.028 m.

Fragment preserving the left half of the nozzle and part of the rim. Worn; only traces of slip preserved. The stork head is in unusually high relief.

A.D. 50–ca. 100

338 CD.1216 Basilica exterior, NE 1, Level II. Pinkish-buff clay, red slip. P.L. 0.057 m; P.H. 0.028 m; P.W. 0.033 m.

Fragment preserving parts of the base and lower side wall of the oil reservoir. Chipped and encrusted. Low disk base. On the bottom of the lamp in attenuated letters is *SIC*, part of the *C* broken away, and room for another letter on the missing part (see Fig. 135).

339 CE.2211 Atrium Building I, Rooms 15 and 16, Level I. Cream clay, red slip mottled to brown in places. P.L. 0.039 m; P.W. 0.048 m.

Two joining fragments preserving part of the nozzle, including both birds' heads, and parts of the discus and rim. Very worn. Rim: Fig. 53. This is the only lamp of this type without a decorative molding as part of the rim. The interior of the discus is flat. The heads are of storks.

340 (Fig. 53) CEL.142 Atrium Building I, Room 11, Level I. Cream clay, dark brown slip. P.L. 0.054 m; P.H. 0.023.m; P.W. 0.028 m.

Fragment preserving the left side of the nozzle and parts of the rim and discus. Very worn; smoke-blackened around wick hole. The discus is ovoid. The heads are of geese.

341 CEL.143 Atrium Building I, Room 11, Level I. Cream clay, dark brown slip. P.L. 0.040 m; P.H. 0.029 m; P.W. 0.019 m.

Fragment preserving the right side of a nozzle. Very worn. The head is of a stork.

342 CEL.162 Atrium Building I, Room 11, Level I.

Cream clay, dark brownish-black slip with a metallic luster. P.L. 0.051 m; P.H. 0.010 m; P.W. 0.034 m.

Two joining fragments preserving parts of the discus, rim, and nozzle. Slip worn away on raised surfaces. Circular discus. Rim: Fig. 53. The heads are of storks. The interior of the discus is flat.

A.D. 50–225

343 CF.844 Atrium Building I, Room 25B, Level III. Grayish-buff clay, red slip mottled to brown in places. P.L. 0.062 m; P.H. 0.024 m; P.W. 0.033 m.

Two joining fragments preserving parts of the discus, rim, and nozzle. Worn and chipped. Rim: Fig. 53. The heads are of storks.

344 CG.599 IX-E, Forum, E corner cistern, Level I. Buff clay, red slip mottled to brown in places. P.L. 0.043 m; P.W. 0.046 m.

Fragment preserving parts of the discus and nozzle, including parts of both birds' heads. Slip slightly rubbed and chipped. Rim: Fig. 53. The heads are of storks.

9. TRIANGULAR NOZZLE LAMPS

(Figs. 54–61)

(Catalogue Numbers 345–511)
(Loeschcke Type I; Bailey Type A; Broneer Type XXII; Deneauve Type IV; Dressel/Lamboglia Type 9; Goldman/Jones Type XII; Heres Type B; Ivanyi Type I; Leibundgut Types V–VIII; Lerat 2d Series A; Provoost Type IV; Walters Forms 78–80)

In 70 B.C. Cosa lay in ruins; it seems to have been almost deserted from the time disaster struck until it was resettled during the Augustan period ca. 25/20 B.C. It is at this time that the Triangular Nozzle Lamp appears at Cosa, already fully developed, and of very fine quality. The most refined and elegant lamps were produced from the time of the resettlement through about A.D. 75. The reliefs in miniature on the disci of these lamps were often executed with great skill and attention to detail.

The oil reservoir of the lamp is now completely covered by the discus and the rim. The lamps all have shallow, wide oil reservoirs (*infundibula*), although the earlier ones tend to be deeper. They have rather short nozzles, with volutes that have a scroll only at the end adjoining the rim (one-scroll volutes). At their outer end, the volutes taper to two points of a triangle whose third point is the tip of the nozzle, hence the name given the type. The nozzle and its volutes do not encroach on the rim. These lamps are handleless. All have a small air hole centered on the top of the nozzle near the rim, or sometimes punched through the rim near the nozzle. Because the rims on the earlier Triangular Nozzle Lamps are complex, extracting the lamps from the mold without damage must have been difficult. The rims become standardized and simplified with time. Ideally it should be possible to date these lamps by the rims; however, if a potter had a good supply of molds of a given type, he would use them until they became worn and had to be discarded, rather than invest in new fashions as soon as they came on the market. Thus a lamp type could continue in manufacture long beyond its invention. Only four of these lamps have survived with bases more or less intact. Three have ring bases; one has a disk base.

Triangular Nozzle Lamps were carefully made from finely levigated clay, the color ranging from cream to buff, sometimes with a pinkish, yellowish, or grayish tint. The fabric is very thin except at the rims, in the reliefs on the disci, and at the nozzles, where the volutes provided reinforcement. The side walls and bottoms of the oil reservoirs as a rule are shattered. The lamps are slipped in red, brown, grayish-brown, or black. The slip is often mottled as a result of poor firing. The dark-colored slips sometimes have a metallic luster, as if the potters were trying to imitate bronze.

Cosan Triangular Nozzle Lamps fall into three groups, designated A, B, and C. Group A (not catalogued by Loeschcke, since it did not appear at Vindonissa) is the earliest, with a relatively narrow nozzle and long, slender volutes extending out along the rim. Group B represents the next step in the development; the nozzle is wider, and the volutes are thicker and shorter. Examples of both Groups A and B were found at Cosa with Augustan material, although only two Group B lamps were of this early date. Groups A and B have been subdivided into: (1) those that have a channel from the discus toward the wick hole, and (2) those without a channel. Group C lamps have a prominent, short, thick nozzle that is as wide as the reservoir. At

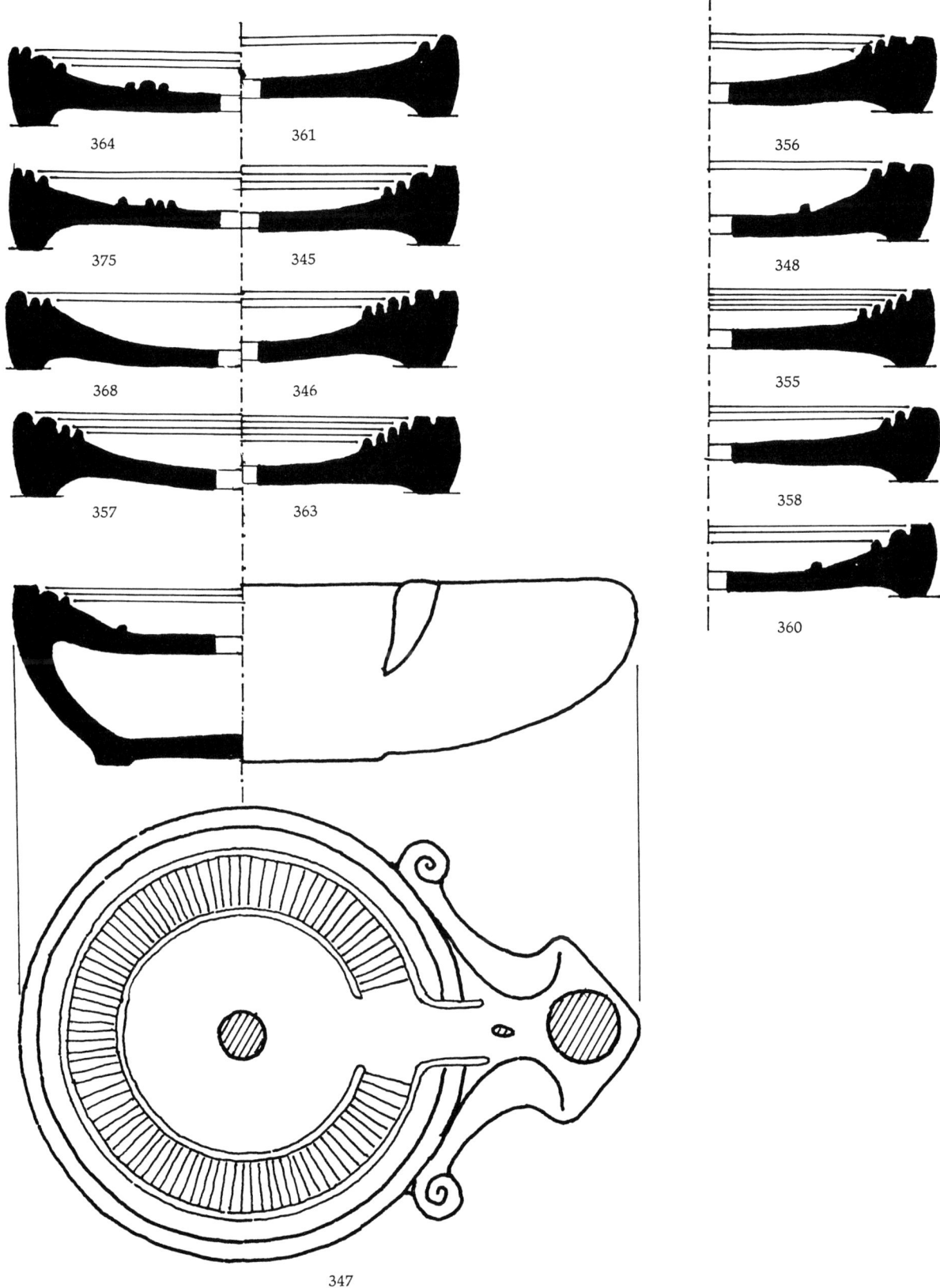

Figure 54. Triangular Nozzle Lamps A1 and rim profiles, full scale

Cosa, Group C lamps probably date from the middle of the first century A.D. Each group is treated separately, with drawings showing the variations of rim profiles.

Molded lamps with decorated disci appeared at Cosa before 70 B.C. They had rather crude, simple reliefs.[1] The fabric was thick; the nozzles were the usual Roman spatulate nozzle; and the lamps often had ears. They usually had strap handles. At some time during the hiatus at Cosa between 70 and 25/20 B.C., the fine Roman "Picture Lamp" with voluted nozzle came into production. The lamps found at Cosa that date from the resettlement of 25/20 B.C. are already fully developed, although there is still experimentation with the rims (there are forty-eight rim varieties in Group A2 alone). Such sophistication of design could hardly have been developed all at once.

The reliefs on some of the Triangular Nozzle Lamps probably illustrate well-known sculptures. They could copy reliefs on various small objects: bowls, armor, jewelry, etc., but these were adapted to fit the circular form of the discus of the lamp. (For example, see 385 and 386 with Europa and the bull; 472 and 491 with a hunter and his dog; and 483 with a kneeling horse.) They include scenes from mythology, the Greco-Roman divinities, geometric designs, vegetal patterns, animals, marine life, gladiators, and genre scenes, including erotica. The fineness of the clay, the crisp execution, and the sophistication of design testify to its being the golden era of Roman lamp production.

Triangular Nozzle Lamps have been studied, published, and classified by a number of scholars. One of the earliest studies and still of great importance is Siegfried Loeschcke's publication of the lamps of Vindonissa, a Tiberian fortress in Switzerland; the Cosan Groups A1 and A2 from the Augustan period, however, represent types not found at Vindonissa.[2]

a. GROUP A1: TRIANGULAR NOZZLE LAMPS WITH NARROW NOZZLE, WIDESPREAD NARROW VOLUTES, AND A CHANNEL

(Fig. 54)

(Catalogue Numbers 345–376)

Thirty-two examples of Group A1 of the Triangular Nozzle Lamps have been found at Cosa. They have short, narrow nozzles with long, slender volutes that stretch out along the rim and end in scrolls. They have channels opening out along the nozzles from the discus toward the wick hole. The nozzles are often broken down the center of the channel. The disci of only nine lamps in this group have been more or less preserved. One of these has a geometric design on the outer part of a concave discus; eight have angular disci divided into two zones: a flat inner zone around the central filling hole, and an outer zone that slopes up regularly to the rim. These two zones are separated by one or more rings. The outer zone on five of the Group A1 lamps is decorated with radiating grooves. The rims of these lamps are decorated with a series of rings in close succession, sometimes as few as three, but often more. These tend to step up, or slope up, from one another toward the exterior, but the outermost are often in a single plane. The inner rings tend to be rounded, but the outermost ring or pair of rings is commonly flat, and when a pair in a single plane. The rims vary in width from 0.005 m to 0.016 m, and their range is shown in Fig. 54. Only unusual rims are described in the catalogue.

Seven of the Triangular Nozzle Lamps in Group A1 were found in contexts dated to the resettlement period of 25/20 B.C.; twelve come from contexts dated 25 B.C.–A.D. 50. Twelve come from contexts dated A.D. 50–ca. 100; one is from material dated A.D. 50–225. None was found in the storeroom of the hardware and pottery shop that was sealed over in A.D. 40/45.

25/20 B.C.

345 CEL.9 Atrium Building I, Room 21, Level IV. Cream clay, reddish-brown, metallic slip. P.L. 0.080 m; Height 0.029 m; Width 0.067 m.

Eight joining fragments preserving most of the oil reservoir and rim, and parts of the discus, channel, and nozzle. Slip rubbed and chipped.

---

1. The exceptions were the fine Sicilian Delphiniform Lamps and the Athenian Ariston lamp.
2. See Loeschcke 1919, 213 (25).

Rim: Fig. 54. Discus relief: None preserved.
346 CEL.228 Atrium Building I, Room 21, Level III. Buff clay, orange-red slip. P.L. 0.037 m; P.H. 0.016 m; P.W. 0.032 m.

Fragment preserving parts of the discus, rim, and nozzle, including the upper part of the left volute and the left half of the channel. Slip worn. Rim: Fig. 54. In the channel at the edge of the discus is a small scallop shell in relief. Discus relief: None preserved.

For reliefs in the channel, see Bailey 1980, pl. 1 nos. Q 754, Q 755.

347 CEL.229 Atrium Building I, Room 21, Level III. Cream clay, red slip. P.L. 0.023 m; P.W. 0.019 m.

Fragment preserving parts of the discus, rim, nozzle, and channel. Very worn. Discus relief: None preserved.

348 (Fig. 54) CEL.238 Atrium Building I, Room 16, Level III. Grayish-cream clay, brown slip. P.L. 0.046 m; P.H. 0.012 m; P.W. 0.040 m.

Fragment preserving parts of the discus, rim, nozzle, and left half of the channel. Very worn. Discus relief: Angular discus, the inner zone level and plain, the outer decorated with radiating grooves.

For this design see Broneer 1930, 77, fig. 37 no. 422; Deneauve, pl. 42 no. 369, pl. 55 no. 540; Perlzweig 1961, pl. 2 no. 22; Oziol 1977, pl. 10 no. 166.

349 CEL.268 Atrium Building I, Room 11, Level III. Cream clay, purplish-brown slip. P.L. 0.043 m; P.W. 0.019 m.

Fragment of a shallow discus preserving an arc of the central filling hole. Very worn. Only traces of slip preserved. Discus relief: A rosette of six bordered lentoid tongues with central ribs. There was decoration in raised dots between the tongues.

350 CEL.504 Atrium Building I, Room 16, Level III. Pinkish-buff clay, red slip. P.L. 0.038 m; P.W. 0.017 m.

Fragment preserving parts of the discus and rim. Only faint traces of slip preserved. Discus relief: An angular discus with radiating grooves in the outer zone, as on 348.

351 CEL.521 Atrium Building I, Room 21, Level III. Buff clay, red slip. P.L. 0.020 m; P.W. 0.018 m.

Fragment preserving part of a discus, including an arc of the central filling hole. Discus relief: Three rings separate the inner level zone and the outer beveled zone of the angular discus, but the discus relief is too fragmentary to identify.

25/20 B.C.–A.D. 50

352 CD.1219 Basilica exterior, NW, Level II. Pinkish-buff clay, mottled dark to light red slip. P.L. 0.043 m; P.H. 0.012 m; P.W. 0.033 m.

Fragment preserving the nozzle and part of the rim. Slip rubbed. Discus relief: None preserved.

353 CEL.71 Atrium Building I, Room 21, Level I/III. Buff clay, mottled light to dark-brown slip. P.L. 0.074 m; P.W. 0.038 m.

Three joining fragments preserving parts of the discus and rim. Slip rubbed. Discus relief: An angular discus with radiating grooves, like 348.

354 CEL.342 Atrium Building I, Room 21, Level II. Cream clay, brown slip. P.L. 0.027 m; P.W. 0.023 m.

Fragment preserving parts of the discus, rim, nozzle, and channel. Very worn. Discus relief: None preserved.

355 CEL.351 Atrium Building I, Room 21, Level II. Grayish-cream clay, red slip. P.L. 0.021 m; P.W. 0.029 m.

Fragment preserving parts of the rim and nozzle, and half of the channel. Very worn. Rim: Fig. 54. Discus relief: None preserved.

356 CEL.346 Atrium Building I, Room 21, Level II. Buff clay, brown slip. P.L. 0.032 m; P.W. 0.026 m.

Fragment preserving parts of the rim and nozzle, and half of the channel. Very worn. Rim: Fig. 54. Discus relief: None preserved.

357 CEL.399 Atrium Building I, Room 21, Level II. Grayish-buff clay, dark brown slip. P.L. 0.030 m; P.W. 0.032 m.

Fragment preserving parts of the discus, rim, and nozzle. Very worn. Rim: Fig. 54. Discus relief: None preserved.

358 CEL.416 Atrium Building I, Room 21, Level II. Cream clay, dark-brown, metallic slip. P.L. 0.046 m; P.H. 0.024 m; P.W. 0.034 m.

Two joining fragments preserving parts of the discus, rim, and nozzle, and half of the channel. Very worn; only traces of slip preserved. Rim: Fig. 54. Discus relief: None preserved.

359 CEL.428 Atrium Building I, Room 21, Level II. Grayish-cream clay, brown slip. P.L. 0.029 m; P.W. 0.026 m.

Fragment preserving parts of the rim and nozzle, and half of the channel. Very worn; smoke-blackened. Discus relief: None preserved.

360 CEL.429 Atrium Building I, Room 21, Level II. Grayish-buff clay, brown slip. P.L. 0.035 m; P.W. 0.042 m.
  Fragment preserving parts of the discus, rim, and nozzle, and half of the channel. Very worn; only traces of slip preserved. Rim: Fig. 54. Discus relief: An angular discus. The only decoration is a narrow bead molding between two rings separating the two zones.
361 CEL.462 Atrium Building I, Room 21, Level II. Pinkish-buff clay, dark brown slip. P.L. 0.036 m; P.W. 0.030 m.
  Fragment preserving parts of the discus and rim. Very worn; only traces of slip preserved. Rim: Fig. 54. Discus relief: A wreath of two branches of oak leaves and flowers, tied at the top.
362 CEL.550 Atrium Building I, Room 11, Level II. Buff clay, red slip. P.L. 0.025 m; P.W. 0.021 m.
  Fragment preserving parts of the discus, rim, and nozzle, and half of the channel. Very worn. Discus relief: None preserved.
363 CF.1628 Atrium Building I, Room 25A, Level IV. Pinkish-buff clay, red slip. P.L. 0.030 m; P.H. 0.014 m; P.W. 0.029 m.
  Fragment preserving parts of the rim and nozzle, including half of the channel. Very worn. Rim: Fig. 54. Discus relief: None preserved.

A.D. 50–ca. 100

364 CD.1234 Basilica exterior, N, Level II. Cream clay, red slip. P.L. 0.051 m; P.H. 0.013 m; P.W. 0.044 m.
  Fragment preserving parts of the discus, rim, nozzle, and the upper side wall of the oil reservoir. Slip worn on raised surfaces. Smoke-blackened on the nozzle. Rim: Fig. 54. Discus relief: The discus is angular, the two zones separated by a narrow bead molding between rings. The outer zone is decorated with radiating grooves, like 348.
365 CD.1235 Basilica exterior, N, Level II. Pinkish-cream clay, red slip. P.L. 0.048 m; P.H. 0.017 m; P.W. 0.022 m.
  Fragment preserving parts of the discus, rim, nozzle, and upper side wall of the oil reservoir. Worn, smoke-blackened around the wick hole. Discus relief: An angular discus, no decoration preserved.
366 CEL.67 Atrium Building I, Room 22, Level I. Buff clay, dark-brown, metallic slip. P.L. 0.037 m; P.W. 0.027 m.
  Fragment preserving parts of the discus, rim, and nozzle, and half of the channel. Very worn. Discus relief: Too fragmentary to identify.
367 CEL.149 Atrium Building I, Room 11, Level I. Buff clay, brown, metallic slip. P.L. 0.044 m; P.H. 0.017 m; P.W. 0.029 m.
  Fragment preserving parts of the discus, rim, and nozzle, and half of the channel. Slip worn on upper surfaces. Discus relief: None preserved.
368 (Pl. I) CEL.243 Atrium Building I, Room 6, Level I. Cream clay, brown slip. P.L. 0.056 m; P.H. 0.013 m; P.W. 0.025 m.
  Fragment preserving parts of the discus, rim, nozzle, and half of the channel. Very worn, only traces of slip preserved. Rim: Fig. 54. Discus relief: A geometric design of zigzags separated by tiny palmettes, perhaps remains of a rosette, encircling the concave discus.
369 CEL.296 Atrium Building I, Room 21, Level I. Pinkish-buff clay, red slip. P.L. 0.049 m; P.H. 0.020 m; P.W. 0.038 m.
  Fragment preserving parts of the discus, rim, and nozzle. Very worn. Discus relief: An angular discus, the two zones separated by a narrow bead molding between rings. The outer zone was decorated with a band of radiating grooves.
370 CEL.314 Atrium Building I, Room 16, Level I. Cream clay, red slip. P.L. 0.028 m; P.W. 0.019 m.
  Fragment preserving parts of the discus, rim, and nozzle, and half of the channel. Worn. Discus relief: None preserved.
371 CEL.488 Atrium Building I, Room 21, Level I. Cream clay, brown slip. P.L. 0.035 m; P.W. 0.024 m.
  Fragment preserving part of a discus. Very worn. Discus relief: An angular discus, the center broken away. There is a band of radiating grooves on the beveled outer zone. Probably like 348.
372 CEL.515 Atrium Building I, Room 21, Level I. Buff clay, reddish-brown slip. P.L. 0.021 m; P.W. 0.030 m.
  Fragment preserving part of the discus. Slip rubbed. Discus relief: An angular discus; three rings separate the inner and the outer zones. The beveled outer zone had relief, but too little is left for identification.
373 CEL.520 Atrium Building I, Room 21, Level I. Cream clay, brown slip. P.L. 0.036 m; P.W. 0.021 m.
  Fragment preserving part of the discus. Worn. Discus relief: An angular discus, the two zones separated by three rings. The outer zone had

relief, but it is too fragmentary to identify.
374 CEL.523 Atrium Building I, Room 21, Level I. Cream clay, brown slip. P.L. 0.019 m; P.W. 0.011 m.
Fragment preserving part of the discus. Very worn. Discus relief: Three rings around the central filling hole, the rest of the discus broken away. An angular discus lamp.
375 C70.674 Intersection of Streets 5 and M, Sewer. Cream clay, pale brown slip. P.L. 0.041 m; P.W. 0.033 m.
Fragment preserving parts of the discus, rim, and nozzle, including half of the channel. Very worn. Rim: Fig. 54. Discus relief: An angular discus; three rings separate the two zones of the discus. The outer zone is decorated with radiating grooves like 348.

A.D. 50–225
376 CEL.510 Atrium Building I, Room 10, Level I. Pinkish-buff clay, red slip. P.L. 0.024 m; P.W. 0.023 m.
Fragment preserving parts of the discus, rim, and nozzle, including half of the channel. Very worn. Discus relief: Too fragmentary to identify.

b. GROUP A2: TRIANGULAR NOZZLE LAMPS WITH NARROW NOZZLE AND WIDESPREAD, NARROW VOLUTES, WITHOUT A CHANNEL
(Figs. 55, 56, 57)

(Catalogue Numbers 377–451)

Triangular nozzle lamps of Group A2 are like those in A1, except that they do not have a channel from the discus toward the wick hole, and the discus is usually decorated with relief. They have a relatively narrow nozzle with long slender volutes extending out along the rim of the oil reservoir. The rims tend to be flatter than those of Group A1 but are still composed of a series of rings, those in the interior of rounded profile, the outermost sometimes flat and sometimes rounded. They vary in width from 0.006 m to 0.020 m, and their range is shown in Figs. 55 and 56. There are seventy-five lamps in Group A2. Five of these are from contexts dated 25/20 B.C.; seven are from contexts dated 25/20 B.C.–A.D. 40/45. Twenty-five are from contexts that are dated 25/20 B.C.–A.D. 50; twenty-four are from contexts dated A.D. 50–ca. 100, and fourteen are from contexts dated A.D. 50–225.

25/20 B.C.
377 CEL.198 Atrium Building I, Room 21, Level IV. Cream clay, reddish-brown slip. P.L. 0.035 m; P.W. 0.032 m.
Fragment preserving parts of the discus, rim, and nozzle. The large wick hole was punched through the inner edges of the volutes. Worn. Discus relief: Too fragmentary to identify.
378 (Fig. 55; Pl. VIII) CEL.230 Atrium Building I, Room 21, Level III. Cream clay, dark brown slip. P.L. 0.099 m; Height 0.032 m; Width 0.086 m.
Nineteen joining fragments preserving all but the tip of the nozzle. Very worn; only traces of slip preserved. Ring base. Rim: Inner ring and a narrow bead molding sloping upward to two rings, a bead molding, and an outer ring. Discus relief: A griffin bounding to the right.
For other examples of this relief, see Bachofen, pl. 45 no. 1; Leibundgut 1977, pl. 32 no. 112; Loeschcke 1919, pl. 12 nos. 470–71; Deneauve, pl. 37, figs. 306–9; Oziol 1977, pl. 12 nos. 208–10.
379 CEL.397 Atrium Building I, Room 21, Level III. Buff clay, brown slip. P.L. 0.070 m; P.W. 0.040 m.
Two joining fragments preserving parts of the discus, rim, and nozzle. Worn. Rim: Fig. 56. Discus relief: None preserved.
380 CEL.479 Atrium Building I, Room 16, Level III. Cream clay, red slip. P.L. 0.026 m; P.W. 0.012 m.
Fragment preserving parts of the discus and rim. Very worn. Discus relief: A scallop shell.
For other examples of this relief, see Gualandi Genito 1977, pl. 37 no. 255, pl. 38 no. 267. Cf. 420; Loeschcke 1919, pl. 14 nos. 551, 554, 556, 559, 568.
381 CEL.516 Atrium Building I, Room 21, Level III. Buff clay, red slip. P.L. 0.039 m; P.W. 0.021 m.
Fragment preserving parts of the discus, rim, and the upper side wall of the oil reservoir. Worn; only traces of slip preserved. Rim: Fig. 55. Discus relief: A wreath of two olive branches tied at the top. The leaves are pointed with a central rib. There are either fruits or flowers on the branches.
For other examples of this relief, see 361, 406, 467, 509, 640, etc.; Loeschcke 1919, pl. 11 no. 189.

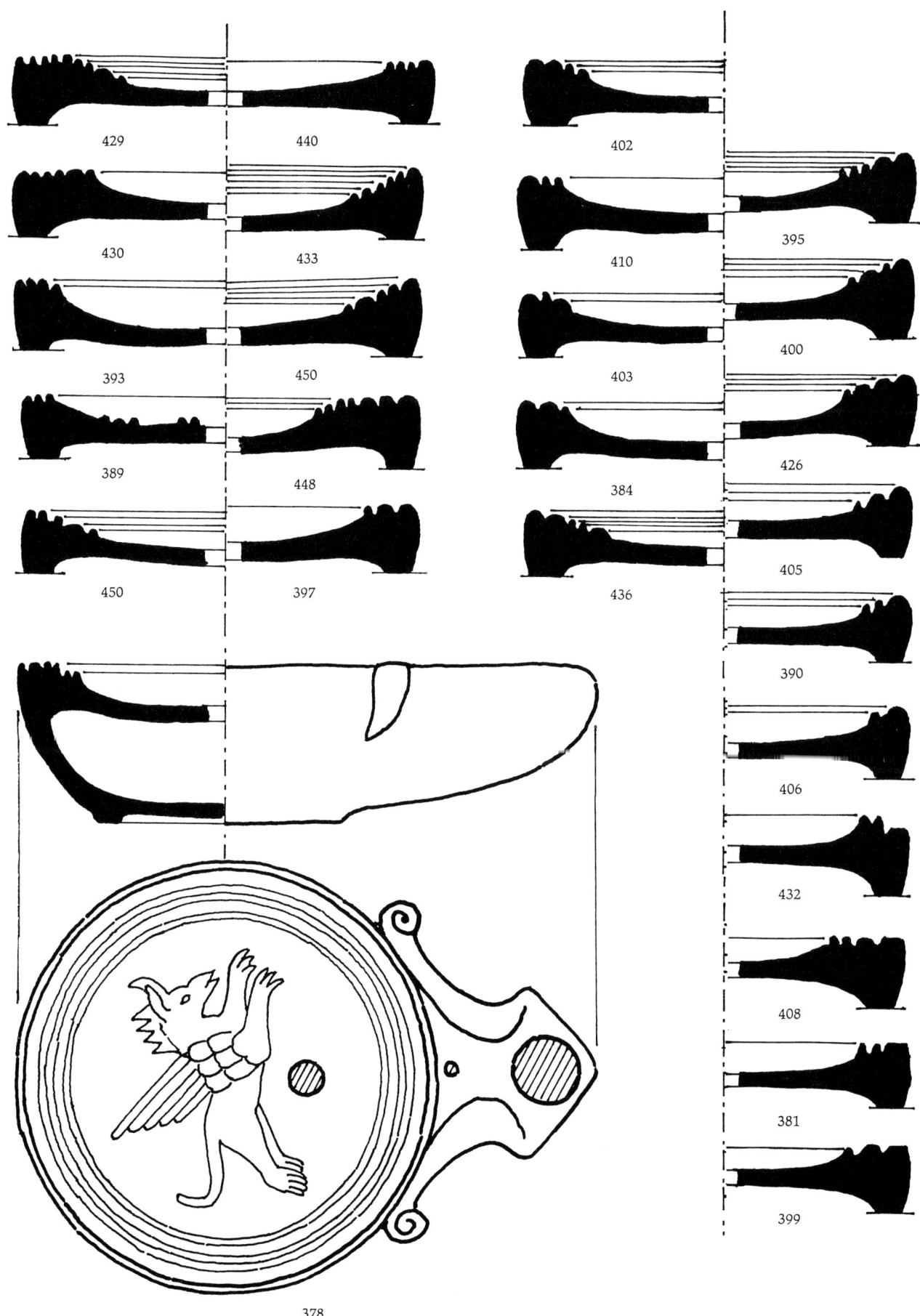

Figure 55. Triangular Nozzle Lamps A2 and rim profiles, full scale

Triangular Nozzle Lamps 91

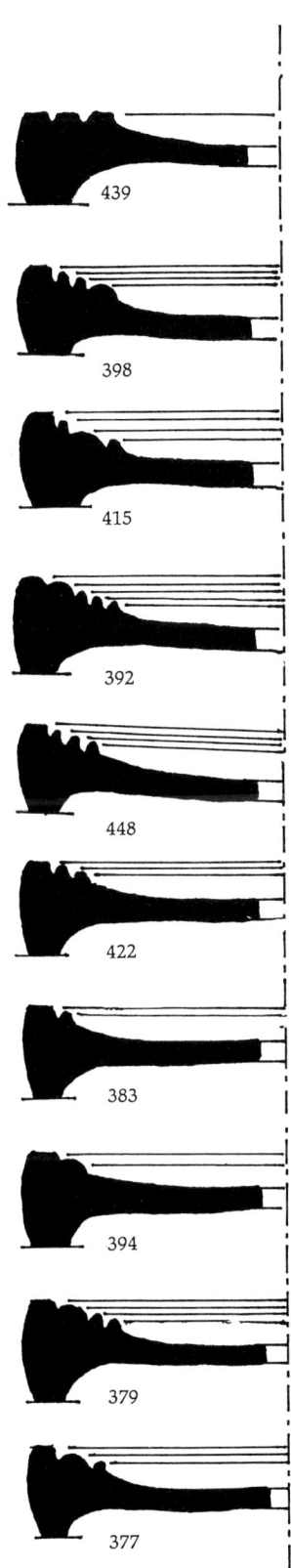

Figure 56. Additional rim profiles of Triangular Nozzle Lamps A2, full scale

25/20 B.C.–A.D 40/45

382 (Pl. VI) CEL.41 Atrium Building I, Room 22, Level II. Buff clay, brown slip with a metallic luster. P.L. 0.079 m; P.W. 0.054 m.
   Three joining fragments preserving parts of the discus, rim, and nozzle. Slip rubbed. Discus relief: A scallop shell.
   See 380 for another example of this decoration.

383 (Pl. VIII) CEL.46 Atrium Building I, Room 22, Level II. Buff clay, dark brown slip with a metallic luster. P.L. 0.035 m; P.W. 0.042 m.
   Fragment preserving part of the discus and rim. Slip worn. Rim: Fig. 56. Discus relief: Centaur or horse crouching with feet tucked under the body. The head and upper part of the relief are broken away, but above the back of the animal is a trace of drapery that might be a cloak.
   Cf. Heres l972a, pl. 2 no. 71.

384 (Pl. III) CEL.55 Atrium Building I, Room 22, Level II. Pinkish-buff clay, red slip. P.L. 0.101 m; Height 0.037 m; Width 0.077 m.
   Six joining fragments preserving the rim, base, and parts of the discus, nozzle, and oil reservoir. Very worn and chipped. Rim: Fig. 55. Ring base. Discus relief: Two Lares, facing each other on either side of an altar, perhaps dancing. The left hand of the right figure and the right hand of the left figure are raised high holding *rhyta*; the opposite hands are extended toward each other holding *paterae*. The figures are dressed in short tunics with scarves draped over the lifted arms, falling in folds behind to the thighs. Both figures are broken away below the thighs, but the feet are preserved. An arc of the filling hole is preserved between the figures at thigh level.
   For other examples of this group, see 506, 527, 546; Loeschcke 1919, pl. 6 no. 390; Ponsich, pl. 22 no. 308; Bailey 1977, pl. 7 no. Q 834; Leibundgut 1977, pl. 27 no. 45.

385 (Pl. II) CEL.57 Atrium Building I, Room 22, Level II. Buff clay, red slip mottled to brown in places. P.L. 0.082 m; P.W. 0.073 m.
   Two joining fragments preserving parts of the discus, rim, and nozzle. Slip worn and discolored. Discus relief: Europa seated sidesaddle on the bull, facing front; the bull moves to the left, tail lifted. Ground line indicated. Europa's right arm is extended, grasping the bull's horn; her left arm is raised holding a veil that floats above her head.

She wears a chiton fastened on her left shoulder, leaving the right breast bare; the chiton is belted at the waist with an overfold.

For examples of the same group, see 386; Perlzweig 1961, pl. 3 no. 63; Bachofen, pl. 18 no. 3; Deneauve, pl. 88 no. 971; Oziol 1977, pl. 15 nos. 260–62; Leibundgut 1977, pl. 25 no. 22; Walters, 124, fig. 150 no. 826; Brants, pl. 4 no. 431; Gualandi Genito 1977, pl. 25 no. 148, pl. 32 no. 217.

386 (Pl. III) CEL.58 Atrium Building I, Room 22, Level II. Grayish-cream clay, metallic dark brown slip. P.L. 0.033 m; P.W. 0.028 m.

Two joining fragments preserving part of the discus. Discus relief: Europa, the same relief as 385, the hindquarters of the bull broken away.

387 CEL.334 Atrium Building I, Room 22, Level II. Cream clay, red slip mottled to brown in places. P.L. 0.067 m; P.H. 0.028 m; P.W. 0.036 m.

Fragment preserving parts of the discus and rim. Slip worn. Discus relief: Rosette of sixteen concave tongues with raised edges, four of the sixteen preserved.

Cf. Menzel, fig. 28 no. 13.

388 CEL.454 Atrium Building I, Room 22, Level II. Cream clay, metallic brown slip. P.L. 0.027 m; P.W. 0.027 m.

Fragment preserving parts of the discus and rim. Slip slightly worn. Discus relief: Part of the head of a goat is preserved, including one eye, the horns, and an ear.

25/20 B.C.–A.D. 50

389 CD.1208 Basilica exterior, NE 1, Level III. Buff clay, self-slip. P.L. 0.105 m; P.H. 0.012 m; P.W. 0.061 m.

Fragment preserving parts of the discus, rim, and nozzle. Encrusted and root-marked. Rim: Fig. 55. Discus relief: An angular discus. The central filling hole is encircled by two rings, and three rings separate the discus into two zones.

390 CEL.279 Atrium Building I, Room 21, Levels II/III. Cream clay, purple-brown slip. P.L. 0.036 m; P.W. 0.035 m.

Two joining fragments preserving parts of the discus, rim, and nozzle. Worn and scratched. Rim: Fig. 55. Discus relief: Only a hand and part of a ground line are preserved.

391 CEL.347 Atrium Building I, Room 21, Level II. Cream clay, brown slip. P.L. 0.046 m; P.W. 0.049 m.

Fragment preserving most of the nozzle and part of the rim. Slip worn away in places.

392 CEL.352 Atrium Building I, Room 21, Level II. Cream clay, brown slip. P.L. 0.026 m; P.H. 0.018 m; P.W. 0.055 m.

Fragment preserving parts of the discus, rim, and nozzle. Slip worn on raised surfaces. Rim: Fig. 56. Discus relief: None preserved.

393 CEL.353 Atrium Building I, Room 21, Level II. Buff clay, brown slip. P.L. 0.035 m; P.W. 0.034 m.

Two joining fragments preserving parts of the discus and rim. Slip worn away on raised surfaces. Rim: Fig. 55. Discus relief: A lifted wing is preserved.

394 (Pl. V) CEL.354 Atrium Building I, Room 21, Level II. Cream clay, brown slip. P.L. 0.050 m; P.W. 0.040 m.

Two joining fragments preserving parts of the discus, rim, and nozzle. Worn. Rim: Fig. 56. Discus relief: Boxer, body three-quarters frontal, head to right, in fighting stance. Left arm bent at elbow, fist at chest, right arm out thrust. Legs spread wide, short belted skirt. The head, part of the left arm, and the left leg are broken away.

For other examples of this relief, see Brants, 233; Menzel, 119; Perlzweig 1961, pl. 3 no. 64; Broneer 1930, 172 fig. 97.

395 CEL.358 Atrium Building I, Room 21, Level II. Buff clay, dull red slip. P.L. 0.055 m; P.H. 0.020 m; P.W. 0.083 m.

Two joining fragments preserving parts of the discus, rim, and nozzle. In fairly good condition. Rim: Fig. 55. Discus relief: None preserved.

396 CEL.362 Atrium Building I, Room 21, Level II. Cream clay, mottled brown slip. P.L. 0.050 m; P.H. 0.025 m; P.W. 0.050 m.

Fragment preserving parts of the rim and nozzle. Worn. Discus relief: None preserved.

397 (Pl. II) CEL.366 Atrium Building I, Room 21, Level II. Cream clay, brownish-black metallic slip. P.L. 0.078 m; P.W. 0.049 m; Diameter 0.068 m.

Two joining fragments preserving parts of the discus, rim, and nozzle. Chipped and slightly worn. Rim: Fig. 55. Discus relief: Near the center of the discus is a plump, dancing, male nude in three-quarters back view. Left arm extended with fingers spread. Right hand appears in front at the waist. An arc of the filling hole is preserved just below and to the left of the figure.

398 CEL.367 Atrium Building I, Room 21, Level II. Cream clay, metallic dark brown slip. P.L. 0.085 m;

P.W. 0.086 m; Diameter 0.089 m.

Four joining fragments preserving parts of the discus, rim, and nozzle. Worn and scratched. Rim: Fig. 56. Discus relief: Only a bit of the ground line is preserved.

399 (Pl. I) CEL.370 Atrium Building I, Room 21, Level II. Cream clay, purple-brown slip. P.L. 0.100 m; P.W. 0.074 m; Diameter 0.084 m.

Ten joining fragments preserving parts of the discus, rim, and nozzle. Slip very worn. Shallow discus, flattened in the center. Rim: Fig. 55. Discus relief: The central filling hole is framed by a lozenge with double addorsed volutes at its points, extensions of the sides bound together where they meet. This figure is enclosed by three rings that separate the discus into two zones.

400 CEL.373 Atrium Building I, Room 21, Level II. Buff clay, purple-brown slip. P.L. 0.086 m; P.H. 0.016 m; Width 0.081 m.

Three joining fragments preserving the discus and rim, except for minor chipping. Slip rubbed. Rim: Fig. 55. Discus relief: Four lanceolate leaves with stems curving outward arranged in a square around the central filling hole.

401 (Pl. VI) CEL.375 a and b Atrium Building I, Room 21, Level II. Buff clay, red slip. P.L. 0.065 m; P.W. 0.074 m; Diameter 0.080 m.

Four fragments, three joining, one nonjoining, preserving parts of the discus and rim. Worn. Discus relief: A charioteer, frontal, right hand to head crowning himself. Figure is broken away just below the waist, and the left hand is missing. He wears a long-sleeved garment with the charioteer's corset around the chest. His left arm is extended downward and to right.

See Heres 1972a, pl. 57 no. 526 for a rather crude version of this relief.

402 CEL.396 Atrium Building I, Room 21, Level II. Cream clay, metallic reddish-brown slip. P.L. 0.037 m; P.W. 0.034 m.

Fragment preserving parts of the discus, rim, and nozzle. Worn. Rim: Fig. 55. Discus relief: Only a pair of greaves crossed at the ankles is preserved, presumably part of a design of gladiatorial armor encircling the discus.

See Broneer 1930, pl. 25 no. 427; Heres 1972a, pl. 7 no. 33, for more complete examples of this relief.

403 CEL.421 Atrium Building I, Room 21, Level II. Pale grayish-buff clay, metallic gray to black mottled slip. P.L. 0.042 m; P.H. 0.022 m; P.W. 0.029 m; Diameter 0.075 m.

Fragment preserving parts of the discus, rim, upper side wall of the oil reservoir, and nozzle. Worn. Made from a worn, blurred mold. Rim: Fig. 55. Discus relief: Radiating grooves around the central filling hole.

404 CEL.424 Atrium Building I, Room 21, Level II. Cream clay, metallic brown slip. P.L. 0.082 m; P.W. 0.048 m; Diameter 0.080 m.

Three joining fragments preserving parts of the discus, rim, and nozzle. Slip worn on raised surfaces. Discus relief: Remains too little to identify.

405 CEL.426 Atrium Building I, Room 21, Level II. Pinkish-buff clay, red slip mottled to brown in places. P.L. 0.030 m; P.W. 0.041 m.

Fragment preserving parts of the discus, rim, and nozzle. Slip rubbed. Rim: Fig. 55. Discus relief: What remains may be the feet of an animal.

406 (Pl. VII) CEL.456 Atrium Building I, Room 21, Level II. Cream clay, dark brown slip. P.L. 0.026 m; P.W. 0.049 m.

Fragment preserving parts of the discus and rim. Very badly worn. Slip survives only in grooves. Rim: Fig. 55. Discus relief: A wreath of laurel, only partially preserved.

407 CEL.460 Atrium Building I, Room 21, Level II. Cream clay, brown slip. P.L. 0.027 m; P.W. 0.023 m.

Fragment preserving parts of the discus and rim. Very worn; only traces of slip preserved. Rim: Fig. 55. Discus relief: A flower with raised center surrounded by five ribbed petals; part of the stem preserved. This is near the outer edge of the discus; the flower was perhaps held by a figure now broken away.

408 CEL.485 Atrium Building I, Room 11, cesspool, Level I. Cream clay, dark brown slip. P.L. 0.028 m; P.W. 0.019 m.

Fragment preserving parts of the discus and rim. Only traces of slip preserved. Rim: Fig. 55. Discus relief: A rosette of narrow concave tongues with raised edges.

409 CEL.487 Atrium Building I, Room 21, Level II. Buff clay, red slip. P.L. 0.037 m; P.W. 0.024 m.

Two joining fragments preserving parts of the discus and rim. Very worn, only traces of slip preserved. Discus relief: Rosette of thirty bordered tongues, five preserved, the center broken away.

410 CEL.489 Atrium Building I, Room 21, Level II.

Cream clay, dark brown slip. P.L. 0.025 m; P.W. 0.030 m.

Fragment preserving parts of the discus and rim. Very worn. Rim: Fig. 55. Discus relief: Rosette of concave tongues.

411 CEL.500 Atrium Building I, Room 21, Level II. Cream clay, only traces of a dark metallic slip. P.L. 0.039 m; P.W. 0.023 m.

Fragment preserving parts of the discus and rim. Very worn. Made from a new, crisp mold. Discus relief: Rosette of concave tongues with borders, only partially preserved.

412 CEL.524 Atrium Building I, Room 21, Level II. Cream clay, dark brown slip. P.L. 0.037 m; P.H. 0.011 m; P.W. 0.016 m.

Fragment preserving parts of the discus, rim, and upper side wall of the oil reservoir. Discus relief: Rosette of thirty concave tongues, only partially preserved.

413 C69.355 House of the Skeleton, Room 19, Level IIA. Buff clay, thin black-brown slip. P.L. 0.075 m; P.W. 0.061 m.

Incomplete, chips missing from the rim and nozzle. Worn, encrusted, and discolored. A lamp with wide discus and voluted nozzle. Rim like that of 514. Discus relief: A sacrifice. A frontal male figure wearing the exomis straddles a kneeling victim, the animal facing right. The man's left hand is on the animal's head, right arm down holding knife. The ground line is an irregular ridge.

This lamp is an intrusion into an earlier context.

A.D. 50–ca. 100

414 (Pl. VI) CEL.40 Atrium Building I, Room 22, Level I. Cream clay, orange-red slip mottled to dark brown in places. P.L. 0.074 m; P.H. 0.022 m; P.W. 0.048 m; Diameter 0.072 m.

Three joining fragments preserving parts of the discus, rim, oil reservoir, base, and nozzle. Chipped and worn. Discus relief: Stylized scallop shell with hinge toward the nozzle. Small filling hole punched off center just inside the hinge of the shell.

Cf. Loeschcke 1919, pl. 14 nos. 551, 554, 556, 559, 568.

415 CEL.141 a and b Atrium Building I, Room 11, Level I. Cream clay, red slip mottled to purple in places. P.L. 0.080 m; P.H. 0.010 m; Width 0.082 m.

Four fragments, three joining, preserving parts of the discus and rim. Slip worn away in places. Rim: Fig. 56. Discus relief: An angular discus, the two zones separated by a narrow bead molding between rings. The outer zone is decorated with an assortment of gladiatorial armor.

Cf. Bruneau, pl. 28 no. 4573; Deneauve, pl. 56 no. 456, pl. 36 no. 325; Heres 1972a, pl. 18 no. 142; Leibundgut 1977, pl. 43 no. 236; Oziol 1977, pl. 17 nos. 303, 311.

416 CEL.167 Atrium Building I, Room 11, Level I. Pinkish-buff clay, red slip mottled to brown in places. P.L. 0.035 m; P.W. 0.029 m.

Fragment preserving parts of the discus and rim. Slip slightly rubbed. Discus relief: Grooves radiating from a ring around the central filling hole.

417 CEL.289 Atrium Building I, Room 21, Level I. Buff clay, red slip mottled to brown in places. P.L. 0.065 m; P.W. 0.025 m.

Two joining fragments preserving parts of the discus and rim. Slip rubbed. Discus relief: A rosette of thirty-six concave tongues, ten preserved.

418 CEL.304 Atrium Building I, Room 21, Level I. Buff clay, dark brown slip. P.L. 0.040 m; P.W. 0.056 m; Diameter 0.072 m.

Fragment preserving parts of the discus, rim, and nozzle. Slip worn on raised surfaces. Chipped. Discus relief: Only part of an altar and a foot are preserved.

419 CEL.394 Atrium Building I, Room 21, Level I. Cream clay, red slip mottled to brown in places. P.L. 0.038 m; P.W. 0.021 m.

Fragment preserving parts of the discus, rim, and nozzle. Very worn; only traces of slip preserved. Discus relief: A wreath of laurel, tied at the top, only two leaves preserved.

420 CEL.473 Atrium Building I, Room 11, Level I. Cream clay, red slip. P.L. 0.042 m; P.W. 0.022 m; Diameter 0.072 m.

Fragment preserving parts of the discus, rim, and nozzle. Very worn. Discus relief: A scallop shell with the hinge toward the nozzle.

See 414 for a similar relief.

421 CEL.484 Atrium Building I, Room 21, Level I. Buff clay, dark brown slip. P.L. 0.062 m; P.W. 0.025 m; Diameter 0.080 m.

Three joining fragments preserving parts of the

discus and rim. Very worn; only traces of slip preserved. Discus relief: Rosette of thirty concave tongues radiating from three rings around the central filling hole, eleven of the thirty tongues preserved.

422 CEL.491 Atrium Building I, Room 21, Level I. Buff clay, metallic brown slip. P.L. 0.052 m; P.W. 0.025 m.
Two joining fragments preserving parts of the discus and rim. Slip rubbed. Rim: Fig. 56. Discus relief: Rosette of thirty concave tongues radiating from three rings around the central filling hole, nine tongues preserved.

423 CEL.501 Atrium Building I, Room 11, Level I. Buff clay, red slip mottled to brown in places. P.L. 0.026 m; P.W. 0.020 m.
Fragment preserving parts of the discus, rim, and nozzle. Very worn. Discus relief: Rosette of twenty-four concave tongues, parts of only three preserved.

424 CEL.503 Atrium Building I, Room 11, Level I. Grayish-cream clay, dark slip. P.L. 0.025 m; P.W. 0.020 m.
Fragment preserving parts of the discus, rim, and nozzle. Worn; only traces of slip preserved. Discus relief: Rosette of narrow concave tongues, parts of three preserved.

425 CEL.514 Atrium Building I, Room 16, Level I. Buff clay, red slip. P.L. 0.030 m; P.H. 0.011 m; P.W. 0.013 m; Diameter 0.080 m.
Fragment preserving parts of the discus, rim, and upper side wall of the oil reservoir. Slip slightly rubbed. Discus relief: Rosette of narrow concave tongues.

426 CEL.599 A. Atrium Building I, Room 11, Level I. Grayish-cream clay, dark metallic slip. P.L. 0.038 m; P.W. 0.022 m; Diameter 0.076 m.
Fragment preserving parts of the discus and rim. Very worn; only traces of slip preserved. Rim: Fig. 55. Discus relief: Rosette of concave tongues, the tips of only two preserved.

427 C70.324 House of the Skeleton, drain from Room 21 to Street 5 (41 NE x 15.5 SE). Cream clay, red slip. P.L. 0.069 m; P.W. 0.073 m.
Five joining fragments preserving most of the discus and parts of the rim. Worn; slip worn away on raised surfaces. Discus relief: Athene Promachos, frontal in long drapery, head turned to left, Corinthian helmet pushed back from forehead. Left hand holds vertical spear; right arm bent at elbow, forearm and hand outstretched, originally to steady a shield now broken away. Left knee slightly bent. Very fine mold with delicate modeling of drapery.

428 C70.336 V-E, Intersection of Streets 5 and M, Sewer. Cream clay, red slip. P.L. 0.032 m; P.W. 0.045 m.
Fragment preserving part of the discus. Worn and encrusted. Discus relief: Europa seated facing front on bull moving to the left. Europa holds on to one of the bull's horns. Her veil, now partially broken away, billows in an arc over her head.
For the same motif, see 385 and 386.

429 C70.666 V-E, Street M, Sewer. Grayish-buff clay, red slip. P.L. 0.064 m; P.W. 0.065 m.
Three joining fragments preserving parts of the discus, rim, and nozzle. Slip rubbed, encrusted, smoke-blackened around wick hole. Rim: Fig. 55. Discus relief: None preserved.

430 C70.667 V-E, Intersection of Streets 5 and M, Sewer. Pinkish-buff clay, red slip. P.L. 0.049 m; P.W. 0.045 m.
Fragment preserving parts of the discus, rim, and nozzle. Very worn; only traces of slip preserved. Encrusted. Rim: Fig. 55. Discus relief: None preserved.

431 C70.668 V-E, Street M, Sewer. Cream clay, red slip. P.L. 0.040 m; P.W. 0.029 m.
Fragment preserving parts of the discus. Slip rubbed. Angular discus, the two zones separated by a narrow bead molding between rings. Discus relief: The outer zone of the discus is decorated with a ring of gladiatorial armor, parts of three objects preserved.
Cf. Loeschcke 1919, pl. 11 no. 164; Walters, pl. 20 no. 562; Oziol 1977, pl. 17 nos. 303–11.

432 C70.672 a and b V-D Intersection of Streets 5 and M, Sewer. Cream clay, red slip. P.L. a 0.031 m, b 0.025 m; P.W. a 0.036 m, b 0.033 m.
One nonjoining and two joining fragments preserving parts of the discus and rim. Worn. Rim: Fig. 55. Discus relief: An angular discus with three rings encircling the central filling hole. The outer zone of the discus is decorated with a wreath of ivy tied in clusters of six leaves with berries between clusters.
Cf. Heres 1972a, pl. 57 no. 533.

433 C70.677 V-D Intersection of Streets 5 and M,

Sewer. Buff clay, red slip. P.L. 0.071 m; P.W. 0.037 m.

Two joining fragments preserving parts of the discus and rim. Worn. Rim: Fig. 55. Discus relief: Ten elongated hearts arranged in a rosette around the central filling hole.

Cf. Oziol 1977, pl. 31 no. 542.

434 C70.679 a and b Intersection of Streets 5 and M, Sewer. Cream clay, black slip. P.L. a 0.033 m, b 0.037 m; P.W. a 0.043 m, b 0.034 m.

Two nonjoining fragments preserving parts of the discus, rim, and nozzle. Slip worn and scratched. The air hole at the inner edge of the rim is not punched completely through. Discus relief: Gladiatorial armor: two pairs of greaves, crossed at the ankles, on opposite sides of the discus; between the greaves are swords; only a part of the hilt of a curved sword is preserved.

For a complete example of this relief, see Bailey 1980, fig. 57 no. Q 764; Heres 1972a, pl. 7 no. 33. These lamps have two swords, one straight and one curved, on either side of the paired greaves.

435 C71.141 V-D Street M, drain sediment of sewer. Cream clay, brown slip. P.L. 0.072 m; P.H. 0.032 m; P.W. 0.045 m.

Fragment preserving parts of the discus, rim, upper side wall of the oil reservoir, and attachment of the handle. This is the only Triangular Nozzle Lamp with a handle that has been found at Cosa. Very worn. A delicate vertical strap handle with two grooves down the center, only partially preserved. Discus relief: Superimposed on a rosette of narrow concave tongues is a wreath of two branches of laurel tied at the top.

436 C71.142 V-D Street M, drain sediment of sewer. Cream clay, red slip. P.L. 0.082 m; P.W. 0.057 m.

Three joining fragments preserving parts of the discus, rim, and nozzle. Slightly worn. This was made from a very fine mold. Rim: Fig. 55. Discus relief: Apollo enthroned, profile to right. Only the front leg of throne with a lion's-paw foot is shown, at the top of which is a large volute that supports the seat. Drapery over the thighs of the figure; legs bare. The upper part of the figure is broken away, but in other examples of this relief Apollo is shown playing the lyre.

Cf. Oziol 1977, pl. 25 no. 464; Walters, fig. 307 no. 1360; Bailey 1980, pl. 37 no. Q 1057.

437 C71.231 a and b House of the Birds, Perimeter trench 15. Cream clay, brown slip. P.L. a 0.036 m, b 0.031 m; P.W. a 0.027 m, b 0.023 m.

Two nonjoining fragments preserving parts of the discus, rim, and nozzle. Worn and encrusted. Only traces of slip preserved. Rim: An inner ring and a narrow bead molding sloping up to a narrow outer fillet. (Loeschcke has only a wide version of this rim profile; 377 has the same rim.) Discus relief: Rosette of thirty narrow concave petals with borders, parts of seven preserved.

A.D. 50–225

438 CD.1230 Basilica exterior, NW 1, Level II. Cream clay, brown slip with a yellowish-white slip or underglaze. P.L. 0.066 m; P.W. 0.051 m.

Fragment preserving parts of the discus, rim, and nozzle. Worn. Discus relief: A wreath of laurel, only the lower part preserved, but the remains indicate that there were two branches tied at the top.

For parallels, see 406; Bailey 1980, pl. 29 no. Q 1010. For the same relief on a heat shield lamp, see Goldman/Jones, pl. 98 no. 142.

439 (Fig. 57) CD.1236 Basilica exterior, N, Level II. Cream clay, red slip. P.L. 0.050 m; P.H. 0.021 m; P.W. 0.060 m.

Fragment preserving the nozzle, parts of the rim, and upper side wall of the oil reservoir. Worn, chipped, smoke-blackened around wick hole. Crevice in fabric. Rim: Fig. 56. The volutes are unusual; the two raised inner edges merge at a point midway along the nozzle, forming a V.

For a similar nozzle, see Bruneau, pl. 26 no. 4573; Bailey 1980, pl. 7(c).

440 CD.1239 Basilica exterior, N, Level II. Cream clay, metallic, dark brownish-gray slip. P.L. 0.080 m; P.H. 0.026 m; Width 0.082 m.

Two joining fragments preserving parts of the discus, rim, and upper side wall of the oil reservoir. Chipped; most of the slip is worn away. Rim: Fig. 55; cf. 441. Discus relief: An angular discus; the outer zone is decorated with griffins running away from the nozzle; one griffin and parts of two others of perhaps six are preserved.

For bands of animals on an angular discus, see Deneauve, pl. 37 no. 311; Leibundgut 1977, pl. 32 no. 113.

441 CD.1242 Basilica exterior, N, Level II. Cream clay, metallic brownish-gray slip. P.L. 0.069 m; Height

Triangular Nozzle Lamps 97

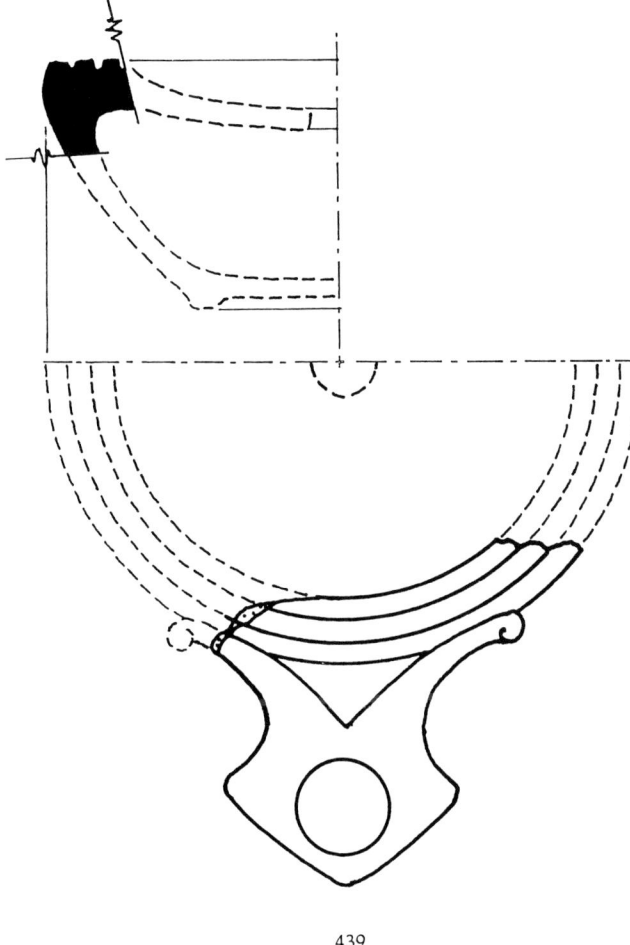

Figure 57. Variant form of Triangular Nozzle Lamp A2, full scale

0.030 m; P.W. 0.026 m.
Fragment preserving parts of the discus, rim, oil reservoir, base, and nozzle. Very worn and chipped. Rim: Like that of 440; Fig. 55. Discus relief: Too fragmentary to identify.

442 CD.1244 Basilica exterior, N, Level II. Buff clay, red slip.
Fragment preserving parts of the discus, rim, and nozzle. Slip slightly rubbed; fire-blackened in places. Discus relief: An angular discus, but the decoration is too fragmentary to identify.

443 CEL.601 Basilica exterior, NW 1, Level II. Buff clay, brown slip. P.L. 0.025 m; P.W. 0.027 m.
Fragment preserving parts of the discus and rim. Very worn. Discus relief: A wreath of oak or laurel branches tied at the top, only the tie and stems at the top preserved.
See Deneauve, pl. 41 no. 364.

444 CEL.608 Basilica exterior, NW 2, Level III. Buff clay, brown slip. P.L. 0.059 m; P.H. 0.023 m; P.W. 0.042 m.
Fragment preserving part of a nozzle. Very worn.

445 CEL.617 a and b Basilica exterior, W 1, Level I. Buff clay, red slip. P.L. a 0.050 m, b 0.035 m; P.H. a 0.010 m, b 0.010 m; P.W. a 0.025 m, b 0.020 m.
Two nonjoining fragments preserving parts of the discus, rim, and nozzle. Slip very worn. Discus relief: Rosette of narrow concave tongues.

446 (Pl. I) CEL.630 Basilica exterior, W, Level I. Buff clay, red slip. P.L. 0.089 m; P.H. 0.028 m; Width 0.079 m.
Five joining fragments preserving the rim, all of the discus, except for a small chip, and part of the nozzle. Slip worn on raised surfaces. The central filling hole carelessly punched off center. Discus relief: Three rings encircle the filling hole, radiating from which is a rosette of twenty-one concave tongues.

447 CEL.843 Atrium Building I, Room 25B, Level III. Grayish-cream clay, mottled brown slip. P.L. 0.041 m; P.W. 0.036 m.
Fragment preserving part of a nozzle. Very worn.

448 CF.1973 Basilica exterior, NW 2, Level II. Buff clay, red slip mottled to black and yellow in places. P.L. 0.031 m; P.H. 0.019 m; P.W. 0.045 m.
Fragment preserving parts of the discus, rim, and nozzle. Rim: Fig. 55. Discus relief: Angular discus. The outer zone is decorated with a band of ovules, the open ends outward. The inner zone of the discus is broken away.

449 C69.456 House of the Skeleton, Rear of the garden, Surface. Buff clay, red slip. P.L. 0.071 m; P.H. 0.013 m; Width 0.078 m.
Three joining fragments preserving parts of the discus, rim, and upper side wall of the oil reservoir. Discus relief: Rosette of twelve long pointed and bordered leaves. Only three leaves are preserved, and each is different: one has a central rib, one has two ribs, and one has a herringbone pattern.

450 C69.457 House of the Skeleton, Rear of the garden,

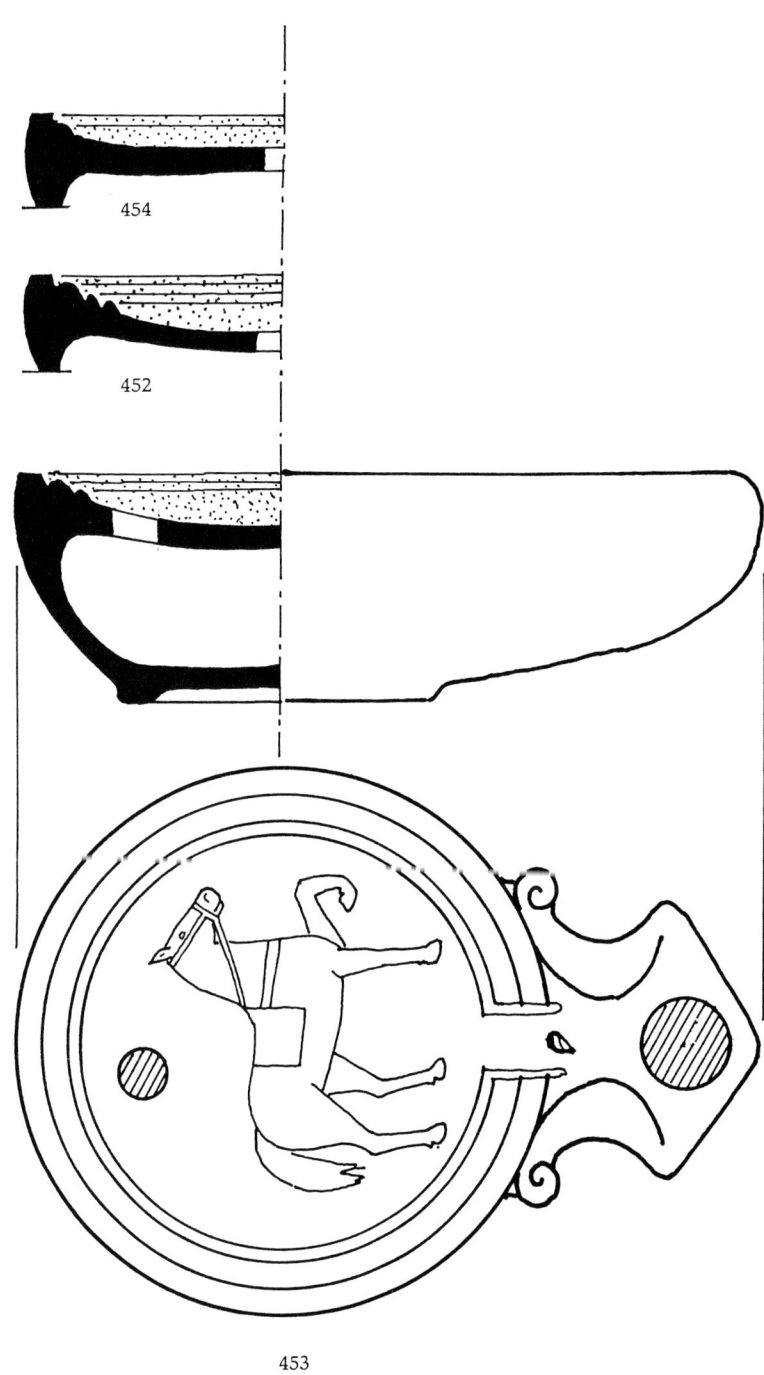

Figure 58. Triangular Nozzle Lamps B1 and rim profiles, full scale

Surface. Cream clay, self-slip. P.L. 0.034 m; P.H. 0.008 m; P.W. 0.015 m.

Fragment preserving parts of the discus, rim, and upper side wall of the oil reservoir. Very worn. Rim: Fig. 55. Discus relief: None preserved.

451 C71.123 V-D Street M, Level 0. Cream clay, brown slip. P.L. 0.041 m; P.W. 0.038 m.

Fragment preserving parts of the discus and rim. Slip rubbed. Discus relief: Two cornucopias filled with grapes flanking the central filling hole. Most of one cornucopia is preserved; part of the other is broken away.

For a similar relief see Loeschcke 1919, pl. 4 no. 342, but with caduceus between the cornucopias.

c. GROUP B1: TRIANGULAR NOZZLE LAMPS WITH WIDE NOZZLE, THICK, SHORT VOLUTES, AND A CHANNEL
(Fig. 58)
(Catalogue Numbers 452–454)

(Loeschcke Type Ia; Broneer Type XXII; Deneauve Type IV A; Dressel/Lamboglia Form 9; Bailey Type A; Heres Type B; Provoost Type IV 1 and 2)

Triangular Nozzle Lamps of Group B1 have a wider nozzle than those of Group A, the volutes being thicker and shorter. There is a channel extending from the discus to the wick hole. The rims are rather plain, composed of a few rings of varying width, the outermost on the Cosan examples always flat. They vary in width from 0.006 m to 0.013 m, and their range is shown in Fig. 58. Only three lamps of Group BI have been found at Cosa. The form with a channel, popular in the earlier Group A1, has almost disappeared in this later version.

25/20 B.C.–A.D. 40/45

452 CEL.64 Atrium Building I, Room 22, Levels I/II. Greenish-cream clay, brown slip, mottled to black in places. P.L. 0.049 m; P.H. 0.026 m; P.W. 0.048 m.

Two joining fragments preserving parts of the rim and nozzle. Very worn, only traces of slip preserved. Rim: Fig. 58. The inner ring turns outward, cutting through the others and forming the walls of the channel. Discus relief: None preserved.

25/20 B.C.–A.D. 50

453 (Fig. 58) C68.520 House of the Birds, Foot of stairs, Level I. Buff clay, red slip, slightly mottled. P.L. 0.095 m; Height 0.030 m; P.W. 0.070 m.

Nine joining fragments preserving all essential features. Worn, chipped, and fire-blackened. The inner ring of the rim turns outward, cutting through the others, to form the walls of the channel. Ring base. Discus relief: A horse, bridled and saddle-blanketed, prancing to the right. The left front hoof is lifted very high. The filling hole is punched off center to accommodate the relief.

For other examples of this relief, see Bailey 1980, pl. 1 no. Q 759 and fig. 87 on p. 79; Oziol 1977, pl. 20 no. 375 (where the horse prances to the left).

A.D. 50–100

454 CE.2215 Atrium Building I, Rooms 15, 16, Level I. Cream clay, red slip mottled to brown in places. P.L. 0.067 m; P.W. 0.049 m.

Two joining fragments preserving parts of the discus, rim, and nozzle. Slip rubbed on raised surfaces. Rim: Fig. 58. Discus relief: Rosette of four elements: two small palmettes above and below the small filling hole, and two rounded bordered petals to the left and right.

For a parallel to this relief, see Ponsich 1963, pl. 9 no. 89.

d. GROUP B2: TRIANGULAR NOZZLE LAMPS WITH WIDE NOZZLE AND THICK, SHORT VOLUTES, WITHOUT A CHANNEL
(Figs. 59, 60)
(Catalogue Numbers 455–493)

Triangular Nozzle Lamps of Group B2 have a wider nozzle than those of Group A, and the volutes are thicker and shorter. There is no channel from discus to nozzle in Group B2 lamps. The rims are decorated with a series of close-set rings of varying width, as few as two or as many as six, the inner ones rounded in profile, the outermost either rounded or flat. The rims vary in width from 0.007 m to 0.015 m, and their range is shown

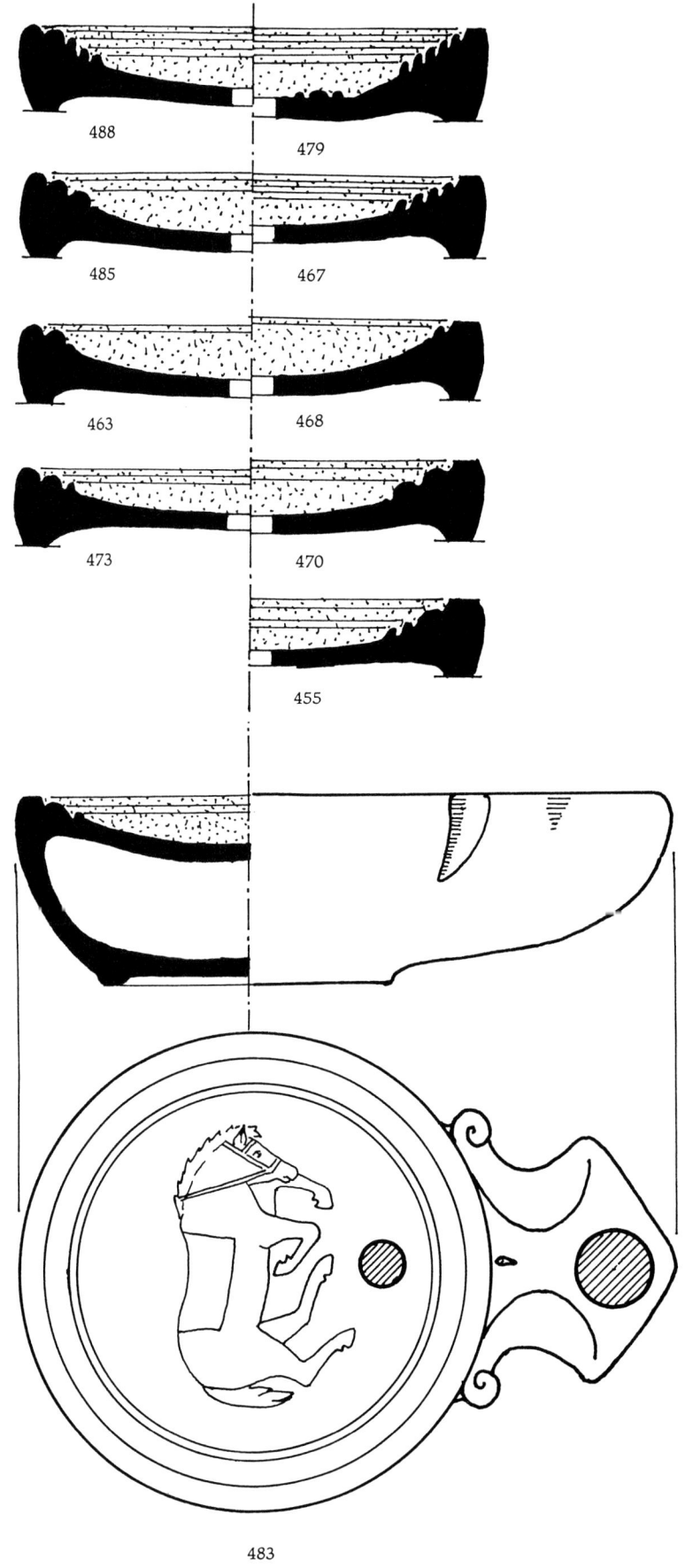

Figure 59. Triangular Nozzle Lamps B2 and rim profiles, full scale

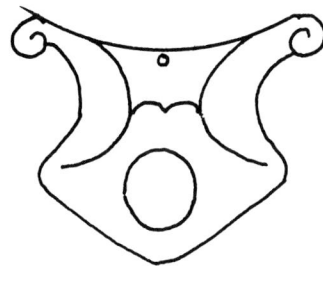

462

Figure 60. Variant form of Triangular Nozzle Lamp B2, full scale

in Fig. 59. Only unusual rims are described in the catalogue. Thirty-nine lamps of this group have been found at Cosa: two were found in contexts dated 25/20 B.C., five in contexts dated from 25/20 B.C. to A.D. 40/45, ten in contexts dated from 25/20 B.C. to A.D. 50, the greatest number, twenty, in contexts dated from A.D. 50 to 100, and only two in contexts dated from A.D. 50 to 225.

25/20 B.C.

455 CEL.237 Atrium Building I, Room 16, Level III. Cream clay, red slip mottled to brown in places. P.L. 0.044 m; P.H. 0.017 m; P.W. 0.042 m.
  Fragment preserving parts of the discus, rim, and nozzle. Very worn. Rim: Fig. 59. Discus relief: Only the lower legs and hoofs of a running horse are preserved.

456 (Pl. V) CEL.239 Atrium Building I, Room 21, Levels III/IV. Buff clay, brown slip with a metallic luster. P.L. 0.074 m; P.H. 0.028 m; P.W. 0.049 m.
  Six joining fragments preserving parts of the discus, rim, nozzle, and upper side wall of the oil reservoir. Discus relief: Warrior stringing his bow. Figure frontal, seated to the right, right leg out to the left and left leg tucked under the body. The left hand is held to the chest; the right arm is down supporting the body, the right hand holding a bow. Figure wears a long, sleeved caftan and a soft Phrygian cap. The face is worn away. The filling hole is punched to the left of the figure.
  For other examples of this relief, see Leibundgut 1977, pl. 36 no. 159; Ivanyi, pl. 2 no. 3; and Vessberg, pl. 2 no. 2.

25/20 B.C.–A.D. 40/45

457 CEL.36 a and b Atrium Building I, Room 22, Level II. Cream clay, metallic dark brown slip. P.L. a 0.047 m, b 0.046 m; P.H. a 0.022 m, b 0.022 m; P.W. a 0.025 m, b 0.020 m.
  Three fragments, two joining, preserving parts of the discus, rim, and nozzle. Very worn. Discus relief: Rosette of concave petals.

458 CEL.69 Atrium Building I, Room 22, Level II. Buff clay, orange-red slip mottled to brown and yellow in places. P.L. 0.059 m; Height 0.030 m; P.W. 0.023 m.
  Fragment preserving parts of the discus, rim, nozzle, oil reservoir, and base. Surface slightly rubbed and chipped. Disk base, flat underneath. Discus relief: An erotic symplegma, only part of the couch with a bell-shaped couch leg is preserved.

459 CEL.356 Atrium Building I, Room 22, Level II. Cream clay, brown slip. P.L. 0.092 m; P.H. 0.015 m; P.W. 0.067 m.
  Six joining fragments preserving parts of the discus, rim, and nozzle. Very worn. Discus relief: Rosette of sixteen concave tongues, the center broken away.

460 CEL.401 Atrium Building I, Room 22, Level II. Cream clay, brown slip. P.L. 0.034 m; P.W. 0.033 m.
  Fragment preserving parts of the discus, rim, and nozzle; worn. Discus relief: None preserved.

461 CEL.505 Atrium Building I, Room 22, Level II. Buff clay, dull red slip. P.L. 0.041 m; P.W. 0.029 m.
  Fragment preserving parts of the discus, rim, and nozzle. Slip rubbed on raised surfaces. Discus relief: Rosette of sixteen concave tongues, parts of four preserved.

25/20 B.C.–A.D. 50

462 (Fig. 60) CD.1220 Basilica exterior, NW 1, Level II. Buff clay, red slip. P.L. 0.038 m; P.H. 0.025 m; P.W. 0.034 m.
  Fragment preserving most of a nozzle. Very worn. The right side was damaged by a sharp tool before firing. An unusual Triangular Nozzle Lamp nozzle of intermediate width, the two inner edges of the volutes connected by a pair of arcs at the point of their greatest width.
  In the Museum of the City of London, case 3, is an unpublished lamp of this type with a similar nozzle and an angular discus, the outer zone decorated with arms and armor.

463 CD.1227 Basilica exterior, NW I, Level II. Grayish-buff clay, red slip. P.L. 0.053 m; P.H. 0.019 m; P.W. 0.025 m.

Fragment preserving parts of the discus, rim, nozzle, and upper side wall of the oil reservoir. Worn; only traces of slip preserved. Rim: Fig. 59. Discus relief: Rosette of narrow concave tongues.

464 CEL.344 Atrium Building I, Room 21, Level II. Cream clay, reddish-brown slip.

Fragment preserving the nozzle of a group B2 lamp.

465 CEL.348 Atrium Building I, Room 21, Level II. Grayish-buff clay, brown slip. P.L. 0.043 m; P.W. 0.050 m.

Fragment preserving parts of the discus, rim, and nozzle. Worn. Discus relief: None preserved.

466 CEL.349 Atrium Building I, Room 21, Level II. Cream clay, brown slip. P.L. 0.038 m; P.W. 0.032 m.

Fragment preserving parts of the discus and rim. Very worn. Discus relief: Four rings surround the central filling hole; radiating from these is a rosette of eight hearts with the points outward, only one and part of a second preserved.

467 (Pl. VII) CEL.350 Atrium Building I, Room 21, Level II. Cream clay, red slip mottled to brown in places. P.L. 0.033 m; P.W. 0.026 m.

Fragment preserving parts of the discus and rim. Slip rubbed. Rim: Fig. 59. Discus relief: Wreath of two branches of oak tied at the top, with ribbed lanceolate leaves and flowers. Two leaves and one flower are preserved.

See Deneauve, pl. 54 no. 533, for another example of the relief.

468 (Pl. IV) CEL.379 Atrium Building I, Room 21, Level II. Buff clay, red slip. P.L. 0.100 m; P.W. 0.089 m; Diameter 0.098 m.

Thirteen joining fragments preserving parts of the discus and rim. Slip worn on raised surfaces. Rim: Fig. 59. Discus relief: A horse galloping to left; astride it is a bald man looking backward. He wears pointed shoes and ankle-length drapery that leaves the left forearm bare; one end of the drapery blows out behind his waist. Left arm, elbow bent, holds a winnowing fan over the left shoulder; from the end of the fan hangs a basket of vegetables. Upraised right hand (arm missing) holds a short object. Under horse is a broken wine jug, and a small child in a short tunic runs left toward jug. Filling hole carefully punched between child's head, horse's belly, and the leg of the rider. On the right edge of the discus in a curving band in raised letters: *CVPD . . . NIV*, to be restored *CVPDICENIV* (see Fig. 138).

For other examples of this lamp, see Loeschcke 1919, pl. 7 no. 401; Heres 1972a, pl. 17 no. 132, pl. 57 no. 529; Leibundgut 1977, pl. 35 no. 152. Hellmann 1985, pp. 12–13 no. 9, interprets the signature on a similar lamp as Quintus Cup[i]di Geniu[s]; this lamp has a circular base with *planta pedis* inside.

469 CEL.400 Atrium Building I, Room 21, Level II. Cream clay, dull red slip. P.L. 0.053 m; P.H. 0.021 m; P.W. 0.045 m.

Two joining fragments preserving parts of the discus, rim, and nozzle. Very worn. Discus relief: None preserved.

470 CF.846 Atrium Building I, Room 25A, Level IV. Buff clay, red slip mottled to brown in places. P.L. 0.039 m; P.W. 0.026 m.

Fragment preserving parts of the nozzle and rim. Rim: Fig. 59.

471 C68.589 House of the Birds, cesspit, Level I. Grayish-cream clay, mottled brown to black slip. P.L. 0.087 m; Height 0.028 m; Width 0.084 m.

Seven joining fragments preserving parts of the discus, rim, side wall of the oil reservoir, nozzle, and base. Very worn; only traces of slip preserved. Low ring base. Discus relief: Two gladiators facing each other in combat. Both wear *subligacula* and elaborate crested helmets, and both carry short rectangular shields. The one to the left wears a sleeveless upper garment and greaves. The one to the right holds a short sword in his left hand ready to strike; his arm has a protective padding; he has advanced his right leg with his foot behind the leg of his opponent and seems about to trip him. The right arm and right leg of the gladiator to left are broken away.

A.D. 50–ca. 100

472 CD.675 Basilica exterior, NW 1, Level II. Cream clay, grayish-black metallic slip. P.L. 0.047 m; P.W. 0.044 m.

Fragment preserving the central part of a discus. Worn. Discus relief: A hunter and his dog running to left. The hunter, bending forward, holds the dog's collar with his right hand; his left arm is drawn back and up holding a spear. He is nude, except for a cloak fastened around his neck that flies out behind. The dog is large, short-haired, with pointed ears. He leaps forward, his forefeet lifted. Ground line indicated.

For other examples of this relief, see 491; Menzel, 31 fig. 27 no. 18; Bachofen, pl. 22 fig. 4; Leibundgut 1977, pl. 35 no. 150; Loeschcke 1919, pl. 9 no. 102.

473 CEL.24 Atrium Building I, Room 22, Level I. Buff clay, red slip. P.L. 0.025 m; P.W. 0.026 m.

Fragment preserving parts of the discus and rim. Very worn. Rim: Fig. 59. Discus relief: Along the outer edge of the discus is a band of ovules, the blunt ends outward, bordered by two rings.

474 (Pl. I) CEL.28 Atrium Building I, Room 22, Level I. Buff clay, red slip mottled to black in places. P.L. 0.058 m; P.H. 0.016 m; P.W. 0.032 m.

Fragment preserving parts of the discus, rim, and the upper side wall of the oil reservoir. Worn. Discus relief: A deep angular discus with a band of radiating grooves in the outer zone.

475 CEL.155 Atrium Building I, Room 11, Level I. Buff clay, brownish-red metallic slip. P.L. 0.031 m; P.W. 0.047 m.

Fragment preserving part of the discus and rim. Slip rubbed. Discus relief: Urn rising above acanthus leaves, only partially preserved. See 481 for a more complete example of this relief and the rim. These two lamps are from the same mold or closely related molds.

476 CEL.176 Atrium Building I, Room 11, Level I. Cream clay, metallic brown slip. P.L. 0.065 m; Height 0.023 m; P.W. 0.050 m.

Two joining fragments preserving the nozzle and parts of the rim, base, and oil reservoir. Slip worn and scratched. Smoke-blackened around wick hole. Low ring base. Discus relief: Too fragmentary to identify.

477 CEL.194 Atrium Building I, Room 21, Level I. Cream clay, red slip mottled to brown in places.

Fragment preserving part of a nozzle. Slip rubbed.

478 CEL.221 Atrium Building I, Room 22, Level I. Cream clay, brown slip.

Fragment preserving part of a nozzle. Worn and smoke-blackened.

479 CEL.252 a and b Atrium Building I, Room 6, Level I. Buff clay, metallic brown slip. P.L. a 0.032 m, b 0.055 m; P.H. a 0.013 m, b 0.013 m; P.W. a 0.048 m, b 0.032 m.

Two nonjoining fragments preserving parts of the discus, rim, and nozzle. Slip rubbed. Rim: Fig. 59. Discus relief: Angular discus; three rings separate the two zones.

480 CEL.270 Atrium Building I, Room 5, Level II. Buff clay, red slip mottled to brown in places. P.L. 0.050 m; P.H. 0.011 m; P.W. 0.042 m.

Two joining fragments preserving parts of the discus, rim, and nozzle. Slip worn and chipped. Discus relief: None preseved.

481 (Pl. VII) CEL.291 Atrium Building I, Room 21, Level I. Cream clay, brown slip. P.L. 0.079 m; P.W. 0.088 m; Diameter 0.096 m.

Four joining fragments preserving parts of the discus and rim. Very worn. Discus relief: Large, elaborate covered urn rising above a clump of acanthus leaves and flanked by horizontal and vertical pairs of curling palm branches.

Cf. Goldman/Jones, pl. 100 no. 175; Brants, pl. no. 238; Heres 1972a, pl. 44 no. 404; Bruneau, pl. 26 nos. 4625, 4596.

482 (Pl. VII) CEL.295 Atrium Building I, Room 21, Level I. Cream clay, brown slip. P.L. 0.083 m; P.H. 0.013 m; P.W. 0.055 m.

Two joining fragments preserving parts of the discus, rim, and nozzle. Very worn. Discus relief: A squat *scyphos* flanked by what appear to be a pair of Hercules's clubs.

For this discus relief, see Loeschcke 1919, pl. 3 no. 72, pl. 7 no. 72.

483 (Pl. VIII; Fig. 59) CEL.302 Atrium Building I, Room 21, Level I. Buff clay, dull red slip. P.L. 0.084 m; P.H. 0.027 m; P.W. 0.062 m.

Three joining fragments preserving parts of the discus, rim, and nozzle. Discus relief: A horse, forelegs buckling under body, head down, bridled and with a saddle blanket. The original relief, of which this is an adaptation, showed a wounded Amazon about to fall from her horse, her right hand held to her head, left hand dropping the reins. The horse without rider on the Cosan lamp nicely fits the circular space.

For an exact parallel, see Broneer 1930, pl. 25 no. 446; Heres l972a, pl. 7 no. 32. For scene including the Amazon, see Bailey 1980, pl. 37 no. Q 1068, and pl. 3 no. Q 779 for horse alone.

484 CEL.303 Atrium Building I, Room 21, Level I. Cream clay, brown slip. P.L. 0.073 m; P.W. 0.068 m; Diameter 0.074 m.

Three joining fragments preserving parts of the discus, rim, and nozzle. Slip worn on raised surfaces. Discus relief: Curtius on horse plunging into chasm. The center of the discus is broken away, but one of the horse's forefeet, a hand brandishing a spear, and flying drapery are preserved.

For complete examples of this relief, see Loeschcke 1919, pl. 7 nos. 81–83; Bailey 1980, pl. 4 no. Q 795 (and drawing and discussion of subject on p. 41).

485 CEL.402 Atrium Building I, Room 11, Level I. Buff clay, red slip. P.L. 0.035 m; P.H. 0.012 m; P.W. 0.042 m.

Fragment preserving parts of the discus, rim, and nozzle. Very worn. Rim: Fig. 59. Discus relief: None preserved.

486 CEL.403 Atrium Building I, Room 6, Level I. Cream clay, brown slip. P.L. 0.036 m; P.W. 0.025 m.

Fragment preserving parts of the discus, rim, and nozzle. Slip rubbed. Discus relief: To the right is a booted human foot, the rest of the figure broken away.

487 CEL.404 Atrium Building I, Room 21, Level I. Buff clay, brown slip. P.L. 0.026 m; P.W. 0.032 m.

Fragment preserving parts of the discus, rim, and nozzle. Very worn. Discus relief: None preserved.

488 CEL.496 Atrium Building I, Room 11, Level I. Pinkish-buff clay, red slip. P.L. 0.052 m; P.W. 0.036 m.

Fragment preserving parts of the discus and rim. Slip rubbed. Rim: Fig. 59. Discus relief: An angular discus, the inner level zone broken away, the outer zone undecorated.

489 CEL.519 Atrium Building I, Room 11, Level I. Cream clay, brown slip. P.L. 0.025 m; P.W. 0.019 m.

Fragment preserving parts of the discus and rim. Very worn. Discus relief: None preserved.

490 CEL.522 Atrium Building I, Room 11, Level I. Grayish-cream clay, black slip. P.L. 0.034 m; P.W. 0.030 m; Diameter 0.096 m.

Fragment preserving parts of the discus and rim. Very worn. Discus relief: Rosette of thirty-six concave petals radiating from at least one ring around the central filling hole, the center broken away.

491 C69.265 House of the Skeleton, Room 20, Level B. Buff clay, red slip. P.L. 0.116 m; Height 0.025 m; Width 0.086 m.

Incomplete, the end of the nozzle and part of the right side of the oil reservoir broken away. Slip rubbed on raised surfaces. Encrusted. Low ring base. Discus relief: The same as 472, hunter and dog. Although the slip is different on these two lamps, they may have been made from the same mold.

A.D. 50–225

492 CD.868 Basilica exterior, N, Level I. Cream clay, brownish-red slip. P.L. 0.062 m; P.W. 0.069 m.

Three joining fragments preserving parts of the discus, rim, and nozzle. Slip rubbed on high surfaces. Discus relief: Fighting cock facing right. Small filling hole punched above the body of the cock.

493 C70.314 V-D Street M, Levels 0-I. Cream clay, brownish-black slip. P.L. 0.051 m; P.W. 0.039 m.

Fragment preserving parts of the discus and rim. Worn; only traces of slip preserved. The mold was new and crisp, but rather crude in execution. Discus relief: On the left side of the discus is an Eros moving left. The face and upper torso are frontal. The right hand holds a torch [?], the left lifts a bunch of grapes upside down by the stem. There is space for another figure, now broken away, to the right.

e. GROUP C: TRIANGULAR NOZZLE LAMPS WITH VERY WIDE NOZZLE AND THICK, SHORT VOLUTES
(Fig. 61)

(Catalogue Numbers 494–511)

There are seventeen lamps in Group C of the Triangular Nozzle Lamps found at Cosa. They are made of the same clay as the lamps in Groups A and B, and the slips are similar. The fabric is very thin, with the exception of the rims, nozzles, and reliefs. The bowls of the lamps in this group tend to be wider and shallower than those in Groups A and B. In this later development of Triangular Nozzle Lamps, the nozzle is very wide and the volutes are very broad. The width across the nozzle at the reservoir end of the volutes is the same as the width across the scrolls at the wick end of the volutes. The rim has become standardized, made up of one or two inner rings and a wide bead molding sloping up to a wide outer fillet. None of these lamps has a handle.

Nine of the seventeen lamps in this group come

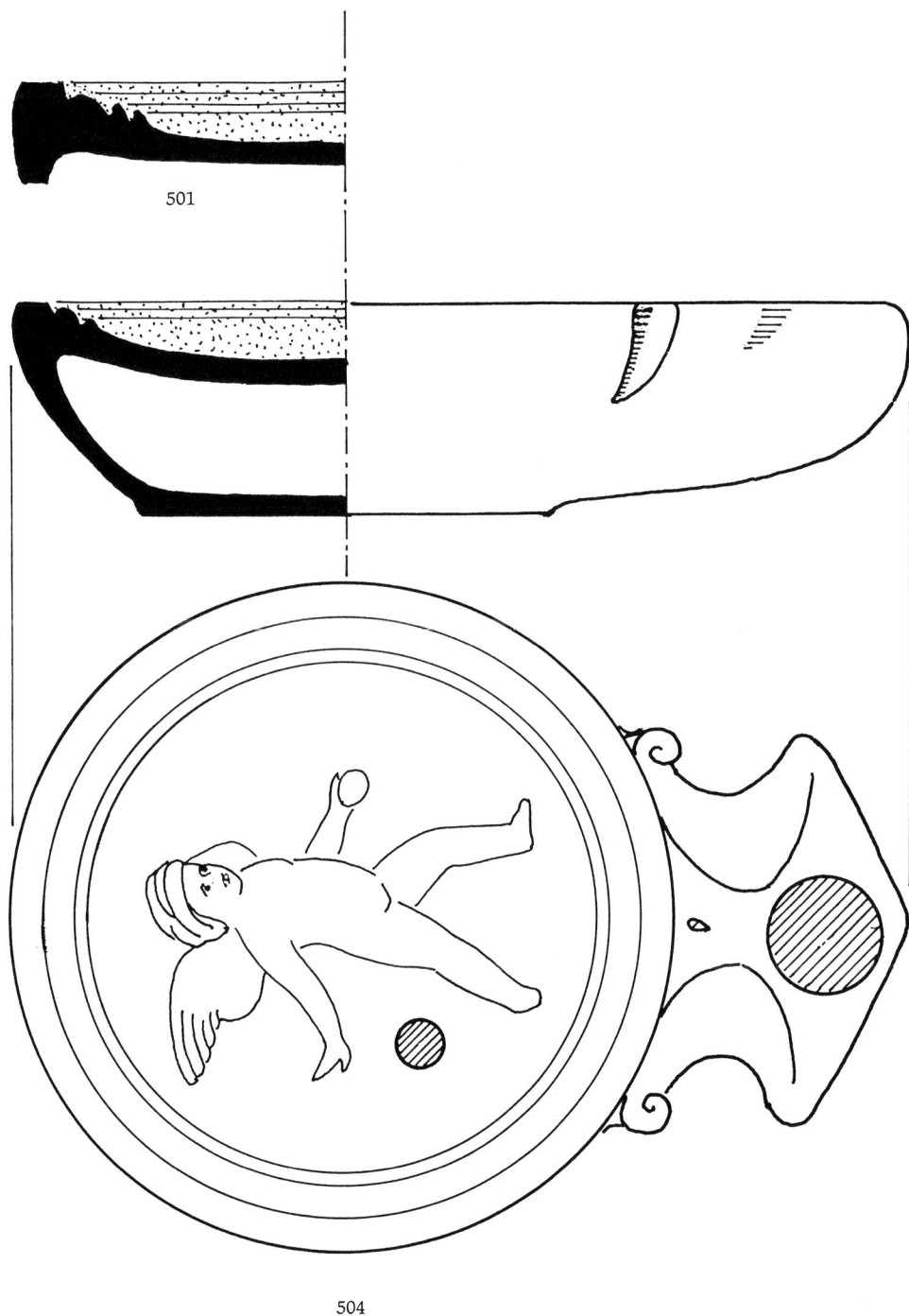

Figure 61. Triangular Nozzle Lamps C and rim profiles, full scale

from contexts securely dated 25/20 B.C.–A.D. 40/45. Seven are from contexts dated A.D. 50–100, while one is from a level that can be only loosely dated A.D. 50–225.

25/20 B.C.–A.D. 40/45

494 CEL.7 Atrium Building I, Room 22, Level II. Yellow-buff clay, brown metallic slip. P.L. 0.060 m; Height 0.026 m; P.W. 0.063 m.

Three joining fragments preserving parts of the discus, rim, oil reservoir, base, and nozzle. Very worn; only traces of slip preserved. Fire-blackened in places, but not at wick hole. Ring base. Discus relief: None preserved, although an arc of the filling hole appears at the lower edge of the discus to accommodate a relief.

495 CEL.43 a, b, and c Atrium Building I, Room 22, Level II. Cream clay, dark brown metallic slip. P.L. a 0.041 m, b 0.022 m, c 0.023 m; P.W. a 0.052 m, b 0.027 m, c 0.033 m.

Three nonjoining fragments preserving parts of the discus and rim. Very worn. Discus relief: A wreath of two oak branches with their leaves and acorns tied at the top.

See 743 for a similar relief.

496 (Pl. VI) CEL.44 Atrium Building I, Room 22, Level II. Cream clay, dark brown metallic slip. P.L. 0.085 m; Height 0.024 m; Width 0.074 m.

Seven joining fragments preserving most of the discus, oil reservoir, and parts of the nozzle. Slip very worn. Low disk base. Discus relief: A crab in high relief, with claws pointing upward, legs and swimmers outspread.

For other examples of this relief, see Loeschcke 1919, 405, pl. 14 nos. 539–49; Ivanyi, pl. 15 no. 6; Oziol 1977, pl. 18 no. 320; Goldman/Jones, pl. 100 no. 165; Ponsich 1963, pl. 8 no. 96; Deneauve, pl. 54 no. 531; Leibundgut 1977, pl. 50 no. 322.

497 CEL.47 Atrium Building I, Room 22, Level II. Greenish-cream clay, dark brown slip. P.L. 0.048 m; P.W. 0.035 m; Diameter 0.088 m.

Fragment preserving parts of the discus and rim. Slip rubbed. Discus relief: Bust of Jupiter and eagle, only the left side of the head preserved. Frontal, bearded, with carefully arranged curly hair.

For other examples of this relief, see Deneauve, pl. 14 no. 403, pl. 56 nos. 544, 545, pl. 60 nos. 578, 579; Leibundgut 1977, pl. 22 no. 1045; Menzel, fig. 33 nos. 1, 20; Oziol 1977, pl. 25 no. 472, pl. 28 no. 523; Loeschcke 1919, pl. 4 nos. 329, 651.

498 (Pl. VII) CEL.214 Atrium Building I, Room 22, Level II. Cream clay, red slip mottled to brown in places. P.L. 0.085 m; P.W. 0.068 m.

Six joining fragments preserving parts of the discus, rim, and nozzle. Worn; slip rubbed away on raised surfaces. Discus relief: An erotic symplegma.

For other examples of this relief, see Deneauve, pl. 81 no. 889; Joly 1974, pl. 28 no. 727; Leibundgut 1977, pl. 37, no. 174.

499 CEL.329 Atrium Building I, Room 22, Level II. Cream clay, metallic black slip. P.L. 0.064 m; P.H. 0.019 m; P.W. 0.048 m.

Fragment preserving parts of the discus, rim, and nozzle. Worn; only traces of slip preserved. Discus relief: None preserved.

500 CEL.407 Atrium Building I, Room 22, Level II. Buff clay, red slip mottled to black in places. P.L. 0.046 m; P.W. 0.052 m.

Two joining fragments preserving parts of the discus and rim. Slip worn and chipped. Discus relief: None preserved.

501 CEL.442 Atrium Building I, Room 22, Level II. Cream clay, metallic brown slip. P.L. 0.081 m; P.H. 0.028 m; P.W. 0.051 m; Diameter 0.096 m.

Fragment preserving parts of the discus, rim (Fig. 61), side wall of the oil reservoir, and nozzle. Worn and scratched. Discus relief: Preserved at the left edge of the discus is the turned leg of a bed, indicative of an erotic symplegma.

502 CEL.509 Atrium Building I, Room 22, Level II. Cream clay, mottled dark to light brown slip. P.L. 0.050 m; P.H. 0.025 m; P.W. 0.018 m.

Fragment preserving parts of the discus, rim, and side wall of the oil reservoir. Surface very worn. Discus relief: Rosette of bordered tongues, only partially preserved.

503 Withdrawn.

A.D. 50–ca. 100

504 (Pl. III; Fig. 61) CEL.48 Atrium Building I, Room 22, Levels I/II. Cream clay, red slip mottled to brown in places. Length 0.111 m; Height 0.029 m; Width 0.078 m.

Nineteen joining fragments preserving most of a lamp. Chips are broken from the rim, the side wall of the oil reservoir, and the nozzle. Smoke-blackened around the wick hole. Made from a worn and blurred mold. Low disk base, flat underneath. Slip partially worn away. Discus relief: An Eros, three-quarters frontal, running to right, nude, except for a turban. Right arm stretched backward with fingers outstretched; left forearm extended forward holding a scallop shell. (This figure is shown on some lamps holding a jug.)

For other examples of this relief, see Loeschcke 1919, pl. 5, no. 22; Deneauve, pl. 60 nos. 587–88; Oziol 1977, pl. 32 no. 572; Leibundgut 1977, pl. 8 no. 692 (on a lamp of different type).

505 (Pl. V) CEL.150 Atrium Building I, Room 11, Level I. Cream clay, orange-red slip mottled to brown in places. P.L. 0.035 m; P.W. 0.059 m.

Fragment preserving parts of the rim, discus, and nozzle. Worn. Discus relief: Boxer in fighting stance, only the lower legs and feet preserved. Left foot in profile to right with bent knee, right leg extended with foot frontal.

For a more complete example of the relief, see 394.

506 (Pl. III) CEL.152 Atrium Building I, Room 11, Level I. Buff clay, red slip. P.L. 0.064 m; P.H. 0.028 m; P.W. 0.065 m; Diameter 0.076 m.

Five joining fragments preserving parts of the discus, rim, upper side wall of the oil reservoir, and base. In fairly good condition. Discus relief: Dancing Lares facing each other across an altar. Only the one on the right is preserved, dressed in a short tunic and scarf blowing back. Right arm raised above head holding a rhyton, left hand missing, destroyed by filling hole punched at that place. Made from a poor reworked mold.

For other examples of this relief, see 384, 527; Loeschcke 1919, pl. 6 nos. 390–91.

507 CEL.159 Atrium Building I, Room 11, Level I. Pinkish-cream clay, red slip mottled to black in places. P.L. 0.072 m; P.H. 0.019 m; P.W. 0.073 m.

Two joining fragments preserving parts of the nozzle, rim, and upper side wall of the oil reservoir. Slip slightly rubbed. Discus relief: None preserved.

508 CEL.240 Atrium Building I, Room 21, Levels I/II. Buff clay, red slip mottled to brown in places. P.L. 0.065 m; P.H. 0.013 m; P.W. 0.056 m.

Four joining fragments preserving parts of the discus and rim. Very worn. Discus relief: Horse galloping to left, head down. Filling hole below belly.

For similar reliefs, see De Brun and Gagnière, pl. 7 no. 99; Deneauve, pl. 40 no. 347, pl. 53 no. 512; Leibundgut 1977, pl. 47 no. 282; Loeschcke 1919, pl. 12 nos. 242–55.

509 (Pl. VII) CEL.293 Atrium Building I, Room 21, Levels I/III. Cream clay, brown slip. P.L. 0.085 m; P.W. 0.039 m; Diameter 0.090 m.

Fragment preserving parts of the discus and rim. Slip very worn. Discus relief: Wreath of two branches of oak tied at the top; the leaves are ribbed and pointed, and the branches bear fruit. Only part of one branch is preserved.

For other examples of this relief, see 361, 381, 406, 467, 640; Deneauve, pl. 54 no. 533.

510 (Pl. VIII) CEL.305 & CE.1018 Atrium Building I, Room 21, Levels I/III. Buff clay, brown slip. P.L. 0.079 m; Width 0.080 m.

Three joining fragments preserving the discus, parts of the rim, and nozzle. Very worn. Discus relief: Small horse galloping to left, head down and tail up. Filling hole punched off center under belly of horse.

The relief of 508 is similar, except that the horse's tail is more horizontal.

A.D. 50–225

511 CEL.624 Basilica exterior, W I, Level I. Buff clay, red slip. P.L. 0.056 m; P.W. 0.040 m.

Fragment preserving parts of the nozzle and rim. Worn. Discus relief: None preserved.

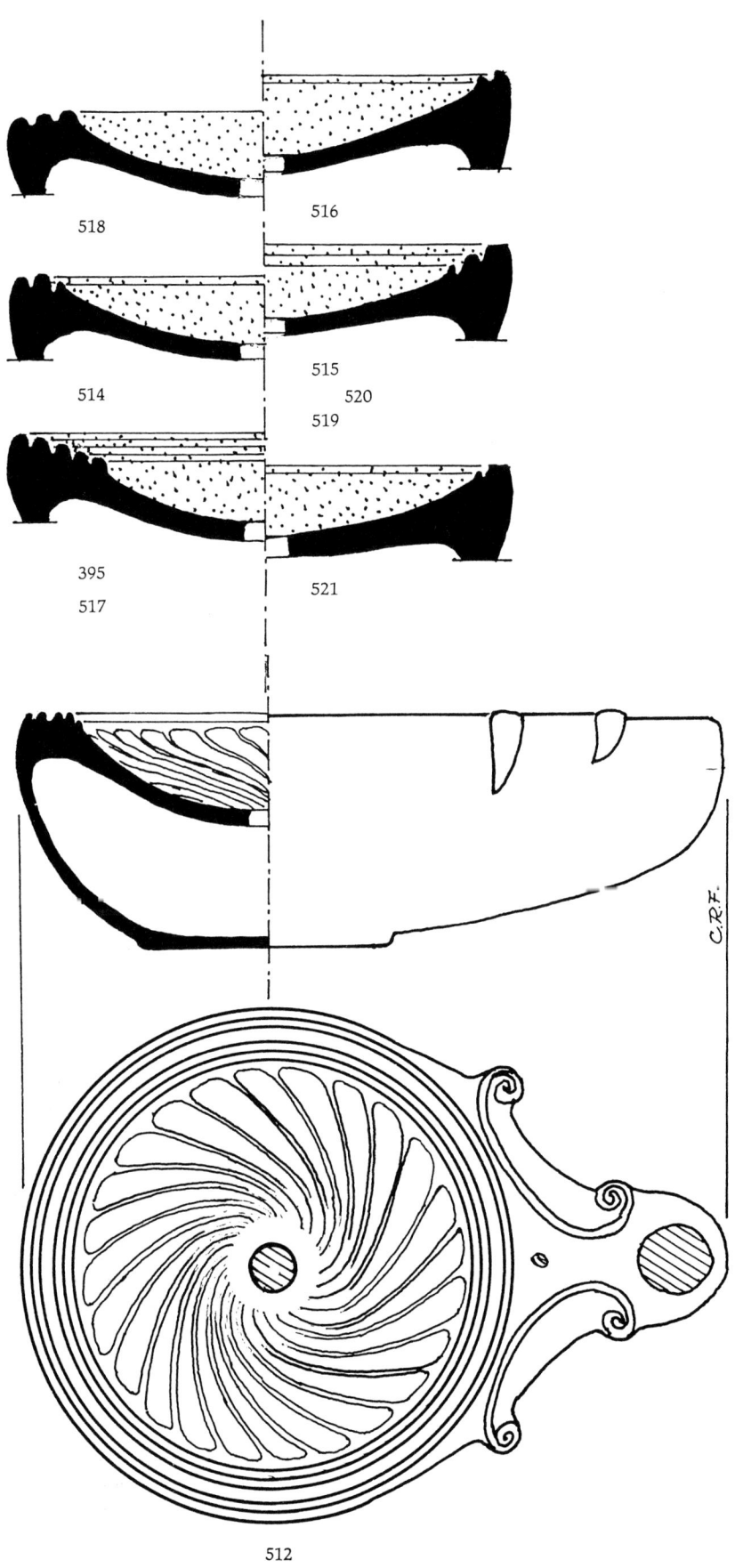

Figure 62. Lamps with a long, slender, voluted nozzle with a rounded end, and decorated discus, full scale

10. LAMPS WITH A LONG, SLENDER, VOLUTED NOZZLE WITH A ROUNDED END, AND DECORATED DISCUS

(Fig. 62)

(Catalogue Numbers 512–521)
(Bailey Type 4B, Group I; Goethert-Polaschek Type X b; Leibundgut Forms XII and XIII; Dressel Types 11 and 14; Heres Type G; Provoost Type IV; Loeschcke Type IV)

Ten lamps have been found at Cosa that have long, narrow nozzles with a rounded end. The nozzles have long, slender, widespread volutes with a scroll at each end. These lamps are closely related to early Triangular Nozzle Lamps, the only difference being in the nozzle end. Some writers place these lamps with the Pouter Pigeon Lamps. We prefer, however, to keep them as a separate early experiment that did not survive for long, but that led directly to the more practical and popular Pouter Pigeon Lamps with their shorter, broader, and stronger nozzles.

All these lamps have complex rims composed of rings and bead moldings with the outermost often a crisply squared fillet. They have concave disci that, with the rim, cover the top of the oil reservoir. Only one lamp (512) is preserved almost complete. It does not have a handle, and one can assume that the others, like the early Triangular Nozzle Lamps, did not have handles. This particular lamp has been almost miraculously preserved; the fabric is incredibly thin for terra-cotta.

Two of these beautiful, delicate lamps were found in contexts dated 25/20 B.C.–A.D. 40/45. Six are from contexts that are dated 25/20 B.C.–A.D. 50. The remaining two are from contexts dated A.D. 50–ca. 100. Bailey assigns these lamps to Augustan and Tiberian times: "The earliest lamps of Type B are Augustan, although this round nozzled lamp Type was not as popular in this period as the contemporary angle-nozzled lamps of Type A. Indeed the earliest examples are anomalies, the Type only becoming standardized in Tiberian times."[1]

1. Bailey 1980, 154.

25/20 B.C.–A.D. 40/45

`512 (Pl. I; Fig. 62) CEL.255 Atrium Building I, Room 22, Level II. Buff clay, brown slip mottled to black in places. Length 0.106 m; P.H. 0.023 m; Width 0.080 m.
 Fifteen joining fragments preserving most of a lamp, the base and chips from the nozzle and discus broken away. Slip rubbed on raised surfaces. Smoke-blackened around wick hole. Rim: An inner ring sloping up to four rings in the same plane divided into pairs by a wide groove. The fabric is extremely thin; the fact that so much of the lamp remains must be due to the texture of the clay and careful firing. This is a very fine lamp, very carefully executed from an elegant mold, produced by a master potter. Discus relief: A rosette of twenty petals swirling counterclockwise.

513 CEL.338 Atrium Building I, Room 22, Level II. Buff clay, brown slip.
 Fragment preserving most of a long, slender nozzle with long, thin, spreading volutes with a scroll at each end. The end is rounded. Surface worn.

25/20 B.C.–A.D. 50

514 CD.734 Basilica exterior, NW 1, Level II. Cream clay, brown slip. P.L. 0.085 m; P.H. 0.029 m; P.W. 0.059 m.
 Two joining fragments preserving the nozzle, and parts of the discus, rim, and side wall of the oil reservoir. Surface very worn; only traces of slip

preserved. Smoke-blackened around the wick hole. Rim: An inner ring sloping up to two narrow beads in the same plane (Fig. 62). The usual air hole on the top of the nozzle near the discus. Long, slender, voluted nozzle, with scrolls at each end of the long, thin, spreading volutes. Discus relief: None preserved.

515 CD.1226 Basilica exterior, NW 1, Level II. Cream clay, red slip.

Fragment preserving parts of a discus, side wall of the oil reservoir, and nozzle, including one volute. Slip worn on high surfaces; encrusted and scratched. Smoke-blackened around wick hole. A very fine, large lamp with a long, narrow nozzle and long, slender, spreading volutes. The cone of the scroll of the upper volute extends down the side wall of the oil reservoir and crosses under the nozzle to connect with the opposite cone. A delicate narrow ring base, with an added interior ring. Rim: Fig. 62. Discus relief: A rosette of thirty-two bordered petals in very low relief.

This is the only example found at Cosa of a lamp with a ridge crossing under the nozzle connecting the cones under the scrolls.

516 CD.1245 Basilica exterior, N, Level II. Pinkish-buff clay, mottled light to dark red slip. P.L. 0.067 m; P.H. 0.029 m; P.W. 0.021 m.

Fragment preserving parts of the discus, rim, side wall of the oil reservoir, base, and upper part of one volute. Surface worn away in places. Rim: Fig. 62. Discus relief: Radiating grooves swirled counterclockwise.

517 CD.1246 Basilica exterior, N, Level II. Buff clay, red slip. P.L. 0.054 m; P.H. 0.028 m; P.W. 0.021 m.

Fragment preserving parts of discus and rim. Very worn and encrusted. Rim: Fig. 62. Discus relief: Rosette of narrow concave petals swirled counterclockwise, the design closely related to that of 512. The two parts of the mold used for this lamp did not match. The lower half was smaller than the upper, making the join of the two irregular.

518 CEL.134 Atrium Building I, Room 4, Level II. Cream clay, dark brown slip. P.L. 0.041 m; P.H. 0.018 m; P.W. 0.040 m.

Fragment preserving parts of the discus, rim, and nozzle. Very worn. Rim: Fig. 62 (Loeschcke I). Small circular air hole at edge of rim. Long, slender volutes, the scrolls broken away. Discus relief: Only a short semicircular ridge remains.

519 CEL.135 Atrium Building I, Room 4, Level II. Cream clay, dark brown slip. P.L. 0.042 m; P.H. 0.014 m; P.W. 0.047 m.

Fragment preserving parts of a rim and nozzle. Surface very worn. One long, slender, spreading volute partially preserved, with a small scroll at the reservoir end, the lower scroll broken away. Small circular air hole at edge of rim. Rim: Fig. 62.

A.D. 50–ca. 100

520 CEL.218 Atrium Building I, Room 21, Level I. Buff clay, red slip. P.L. 0.057 m; P.H. 0.015 m; P.W. 0.084 m.

Three joining fragments preserving parts of the rim, discus, and nozzle. Very worn. Rim: Fig. 62. Discus relief: None preserved.

521 CEL.482 Atrium Building I, Room 11, Level I. Buff clay, red slip. P.L. 0.068 m; P.H. 0.012 m; P.W. 0.028 m.

Two joining fragments preserving parts of the discus, rim, and upper side wall of the oil reservoir. Surface worn. Rim: Fig. 62. Discus relief: A rosette of twenty concave petals swirled counterclockwise.

Made from the same mold or the same generation of molds as 512. The two parts of the mold used for this lamp did not match. The lower half was smaller than the upper, making the join irregular.

11. LAMPS WITH POUTER PIGEON VOLUTED NOZZLES

(Figs. 63–66)

(Catalogue Numbers 522–598)
(Bailey Type B; Broneer Type XXIII; Deneauve Type II b; Dressel/Lamboglia Type 14; Leibundgut Type XII; Lerat 2d series B; Loeschcke Type IV; Ponsich Type II B)

Seventy-seven handsome lamps have been found at Cosa that have wide decorated disci and short, wide, voluted nozzles with a rounded end and small scrolls at both ends of the broad volutes. These volutes were described as "Pouter Pigeon" by Eric Baade in his work on the lamps of Cosa in 1952. They strongly resemble two pouter pigeons confronted breast to breast.

The finely levigated, micaceous clay from which these lamps were made is the usual cream-to-buff color of central Italy, sometimes with a pink or orange tint. The fabric is extremely thin, and the preservation is poor. All the Pouter Pigeon Voluted Lamps have either a red or a brown slip; some of the dark slips have a metallic luster.

The wide discus and the rim cover the top of the oil reservoir on lamps of this type. The joining of the two parts of the lamp is just below the rim.

Lamps with rims with a narrow bead for outer molding have been placed first in this catalogue. Although the date of the earliest context in which they have been found is after A.D. 50, lamps with these rims are an earlier development than those with a plain outer band. As should be clear from the drawing at the head of this chapter, the rim profiles have become much simpler than those of Groups A and B of the Triangular Nozzle Lamps. There is a further change: the outer rim has become a narrow shoulder sloping downward and outward (Fig. 64). This design would enable the potter to extract the lamp from the top of the mold with greater ease than was possible when the rims consisted of a complex series of delicate rings and grooves that extended up to the outer edge. Three Pouter Pigeon Lamps have an earlier rim profile, with the outer rim a narrow bead molding. Seventeen have rim profiles with an outer fillet. Fifty-seven have the new rim with sloping shoulder and a variety of inner rings and grooves, the large number being an indication of the popularity of the new type. The rims vary in width from 0.007 m to 0.024 m, and the range of their profiles is shown in Fig. 63. Only unusual rims are described in the catalogue.

Very few of these lamps have a handle, and for those that do, the handle was made in the mold. There are very few bases left attached to a body, and most of the side walls of the oil reservoirs are lost. The disci and rims are better preserved, because the clay of these parts is thicker than that of the rest of the lamp. The reliefs are very fine.

Eleven lamps of this type were found in the storeroom of the hardware and pottery shop in Atrium Building I sealed over by debris from the collapse of the Basilica in A.D. 40/45. Another five are from levels dated 25/20 B.C.–A.D. 50, while twelve are from levels dated A.D. 50–ca. 100. The remainder are from contexts that can be dated only loosely A.D. 50–225, although probably very few Pouter Pigeon Lamps were made after the first century A.D.

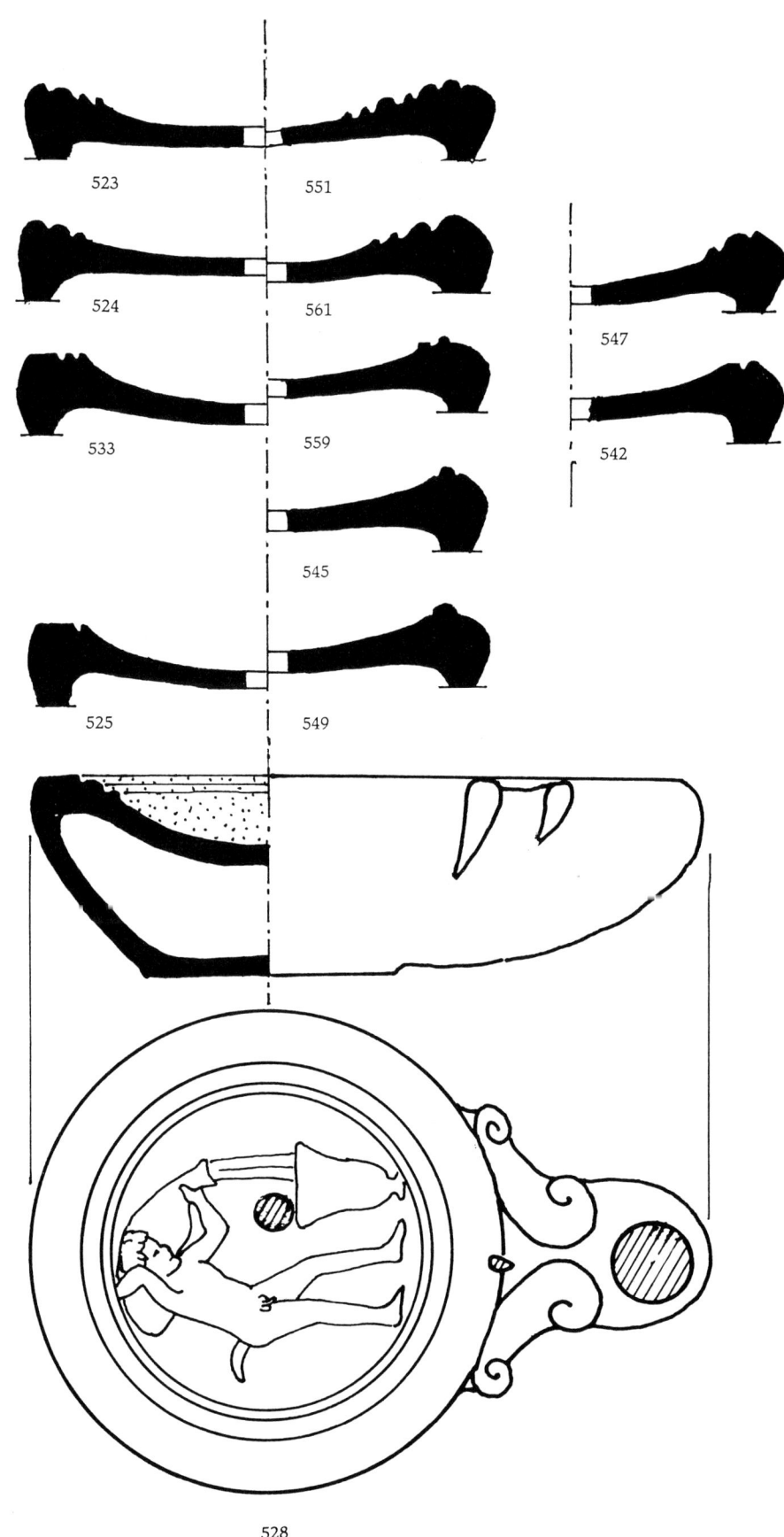

Figure 63. Lamps with Pouter Pigeon voluted nozzles and rim profiles, full scale

Figure 64 Additional Pouter Pigeon Lamp, full scale

a. POUTER PIGEON LAMPS WITH A BEAD MOLDING FOR RIM OUTER BORDER

A.D. 50–ca. 100

522 CD.804 Basilica exterior, NE 3, Level I. Buff clay, brown slip. P.L. 0.104 m; P.H. 0.027 m; Width 0.078 m.

Five joining fragments preserving parts of the discus, rim, side wall of the oil reservoir, and nozzle. Worn, lime-encrusted; smoke-blackened around the wick hole. Rim identical with 524. Discus relief: Mercury, three-quarters frontal, running to left. Both arms are bent at the elbow, the caduceus in the right held close to the chest, the purse in the left. The filling hole is punched between the legs.

523 (Pl. IV) CEL.169 Atrium Building I, Room 11, Level I. Buff clay, red slip. P.L. 0.053 m; P.W. 0.048 m.

Two joining fragments preserving parts of the discus, rim, and left volute. Worn and chipped. Rim: Fig. 63. Discus relief: A Victory, preserved from the hips down, turned three-quarters left with drapery blowing out to right. This is remains of a Victory holding a shield.

For other examples of this relief, see 525; Loeschcke 1919, pl. 6 nos. 384–88; Menzel, pl. 66 no. 207; Evelein, pl. 3 no. 21; Bailey 1980, pl. 7 no. Q 829, pl. 10 no. Q 855, pl. 11 no. Q 870, pl. 21 no. Q 957 (a version with different attributes); Goethert-Polaschek, pl. 26 nos. 96, 176, 278.

524 (Pl. VI) CEL.231 Atrium Building I, Rooms 16/21, Level I. Buff clay, dark brown slip with a metallic luster. P.L. 0.090 m; P.W. 0.048 m.

525

Figure 65. Additional Pouter Pigeon Lamp, scale 1:2

Two joining fragments preserving parts of the discus, rim, and nozzle, including part of the right volute. Slip rubbed on raised surfaces. Rim: Fig. 63. Low ring base. Mold very worn and details blurred. Discus relief: Driver and chariot, racing to left. Only the right side of the discus is preserved with the driver and part of the chariot. The charioteer's extended right hand, now broken away, held the reins; the left hand is raised above the head holding the whip. He wears a tunic and the charioteer's corselet.

For other examples of this relief, see Bailey 1980, pl. 4 no. Q 796; Brants, pl. 2 no. 218; Deneauve, pl. 39 no. 329; Menzel, fig. 27 no. 6, 114; Oziol 1977, pl. 13 no. 224.

b. POUTER PIGEON LAMPS WITH A FLAT BAND OR FILLET FOR RIM OUTER BORDER

The first lamp listed in this group of lamps with a fillet as outer rim border is the earliest as far as the type is concerned, as it has two ears, a survival from the Hellenistic types. The volutes do not encroach on the rim, as they do on the later examples of the Pouter Pigeon Voluted Lamps.

25/20 B.C.–A.D. 45

525 (Pl. IV; see Fig. 66) CEL.52 Atrium Building I, Room 22, Level II. Cream clay with a greenish tint, dark to light brown slip with a metallic luster. P.L. 0.107 m; Height 0.027 m; P.W. 0.105 m.

Twelve fragments, some joining, some nonjoining, preserving parts of the discus, rim, oil reservoir, base, nozzle, and one ear (there may have been two). Slip worn on raised surfaces. Low ring base. Rim: Fig. 63 (Loeschcke Type IVb). Discus relief: A New Year's greeting lamp. The only part of the Victory preserved is her hand holding the shield to the left. The amphora of honey and two coins are also preserved on the left side of the discus. The upper, smaller coin has a figure, perhaps Mercury, while the lower has clasped hands holding a caduceus.

For a complete example of the relief, see 657 with the Victory, Janus coin, and a fig on the right of the discus (Fig. 67). On the shield is inscribed *ANNV(M) NOVVM FAVSTV(M) FELICE(M) TIBI*. Cf. Bailey 1980, pl. 21 nos. Q 957–59; Bachofen, pl. 12 no. 12; Brants, pl. 4 no. 429; Ivanyi, pl. 43 no. 14; Roux-Barré, no. 1 (with ears of a different design).

526 CEL.39 Atrium Building I, Room 22, Level II. Buff clay, red slip. P.L. 0.095 m; Height 0.032 m; P.W. 0.065 m.

Six joining fragments preserving parts of the discus, rim, nozzle, side wall of the oil reservoir, and base. Worn. Rim: Identical with that of 525 (Fig. 63), a narrow version of Loeschcke IVb. Discus relief: The central filling hole is encircled by a narrow bead between rings, from which radiates a rosette of twenty-four petals swirled clockwise.

For another example of this relief, see Oziol 1977, pl. 17 no. 293.

527 (Pl. III) CEL.54 Atrium Building I, Room 22, Level II. Cream clay, purplish-red slip with a metallic luster. P.L. 0.062 m; P.W. 0.087 m.

Three joining fragments preserving parts of the discus, rim, and nozzle. In good condition. Rim: A narrower version of Loeschcke IIIb. Discus relief: Two Lares, frontal, wearing knee-length tunics, blown back, and boots with toes pointing upward. The figures are broken away above the thigh. The complete relief shows two dancing Lares pouring a libation on either side of an altar.

Cf. Loeschcke 1919, pl. 6 nos. 390–91; Mercando, pl. 7 (the same relief on a different type of lamp); Deneauve, pl. 61 no. 594; Walters, pl. 18 no. 543; Joly 1974, fig. 216 no. 1064.

528 (Pl. II; Fig. 63) CEL.56 Atrium Building I, Room 22, Level II. Buff clay, red slip mottled to black in places. Length 0.103 m; Height 0.027 m; Width 0.073 m.

The top of the lamp is intact, except for the right end of the nozzle; there are chips missing from the side wall of the oil reservoir, the bottom of the nozzle, and parts of the base. Rubbed. Rim: Loeschcke IIIb. Disk base. Discus relief: A nude satyr facing right, pouring wine from a wineskin into a bell-shaped crater. Small filling hole punched between the satyr and the crater.

Cf. Loeschcke 1919, pl. 5 no. 361, pl. 15 no. 360.

529 CEL.66 Atrium Building I, Room 22, Level II. Cream clay, red slip, discolored to brown in places, with a metallic luster. P.L. 0.045 m; P.W. 0.055 m.

Fragment preserving parts of the discus, rim,

and nozzle. Worn. Rim: A narrow version of Loeschcke IIIb. Discus relief: Too fragmentary to identify.

530 (Pl. I) CEL.211 Atrium Building I, Room 22, Level II. Cream clay, brown slip. P.L. 0.071 m; P.W. 0.088 m.

Four joining fragments preserving parts of the discus, rim, and nozzle. Both volutes are preserved. Slip very worn. Rim: Loeschcke IIIb. Discus relief: Three rings around the central filling hole, from which radiates a rosette of sixteen bordered tongues.

531 CEL.411 Atrium Building I, Room 22, Level II. Buff clay, dull red slip. P.L. 0.067 m; P.W. 0.047 m.

Fragment preserving parts of the rim and nozzle. Surface rubbed. Rim: Loeschcke IIIb.

25/20 B.C.–A.D. 50

532 (Fig. 64) CD.925 Basilica exterior, NE 2, Level III. Buff clay, brown slip. P.L. 0.076 m; Width 0.072 m.

Two joining fragments preserving most of the top of a lamp, the end of the nozzle and part of the rim broken away. Worn and encrusted. Rim: Loeschcke IIIb. Discus relief: Mercury moving to right, head turned right, but body almost frontal. Caduceus held out in left hand, purse in right down at side. He wears a cloak thrown back over his shoulders, winged sandals, and *petasus*. The upper part of the head is missing.

533 CD.1229 Basilica exterior, NW I, Level II. Buff clay with a pink tint, red slip. P.L. 0.061 m; P.H. 0.013 m; P.W. 0.046 m.

Fragment preserving parts of the discus, rim, and upper side wall of the oil reservoir. Slip worn and peeling away in places. Rim: Fig. 63 (Loeschcke I). Discus relief: Fallen gladiator, body preserved below the hips. He leans on right hand that holds a short sword. Legs protected by wrappings.

The relief is the same as that of 536 and 543. Cf. Deneauve, pl. 49 nos. 459–60; Loeschcke 1919, pl. 10 no. 444.

534 CEL.602 Basilica exterior, NW 2, Level II. Buff clay, red slip. P.L. 0.038 m; P.W. 0.041 m.

Fragment preserving parts of the rim and nozzle. Worn and scratched.

A.D. 50–ca. 100

535 CD.1247 Basilica exterior, N, Level II. Buff clay, red slip. P.L. 0.079 m; P.W. 0.056 m.

Two joining fragments preserving parts of the rim, upper side wall of the oil reservoir, and nozzle. Slightly worn, chipped, and encrusted. Rim: Loeschcke IIIb. Discus relief: None preserved.

536 CEL.395 Atrium Building I, Room 21, Level I. Buff clay, dull red slip.

Fragment of discus, broken on all sides. Discus relief: Legs of fallen gladiator as in 533 and 543.

Cf. Deneauve, pl. 49 nos. 459–60; Loeschcke 1919, pl. 10 no. 444.

537 CEL.410 Atrium Building I, Room 21, Level I. Cream clay, dark brown slip. P.L. 0.045 m; P.W. 0.036 m.

Fragment preserving parts of the discus, rim, and nozzle. Very worn; only traces of slip preserved. Rim: Loeschcke IIIb. Discus relief: Too little to identify. A hand holding a rod, perhaps a spear, is all that remains.

538 CEL.435 Atrium Building I, Room 22, Level I. Buff clay, dark brown slip. P.L. 0.043 m; P.W. 0.039 m.

Fragment preserving parts of the rim and nozzle. Worn. Rim: A narrow version of Loeschcke IIIb.

A.D. 50–225

539 CD.771 Basilica exterior, NE 3, Level I. Buff clay, red slip. Length 0.116 m; Height 0.028 m; Width 0.083 m.

Five joining fragments preserving most of a lamp. The discus, the left side of the nozzle end, and chips from the side wall of the oil reservoir are broken away. Slip slightly worn on raised surfaces. Smoke-blackened around the wick hole. Rim: The same profile as 524 (Fig. 63). Low disk base, bottom flat. On the bottom in *planta pedis* the letters *VV*. The discus is broken away.

540 CD.1250 Basilica exterior, NE 3, Level I. Buff clay with a pinkish tint, red slip. P.L. 0.085 m; P.H. 0.024 m; Width 0.073 m.

Two joining fragments preserving parts of the discus, rim, side wall of the oil reservoir, and nozzle. Very worn in places. Rim: Loeschcke IIIb.

541 C68.525 Arx, west slope, Structure, Level I. Buff clay, red slip. Length 0.118 m; Height 0.028 m; Width 0.081 m.

Incomplete, chips broken from the left side of the oil reservoir and nozzle. Rim: A narrow version of Loeschcke IIIb. Discus relief: Bust of a

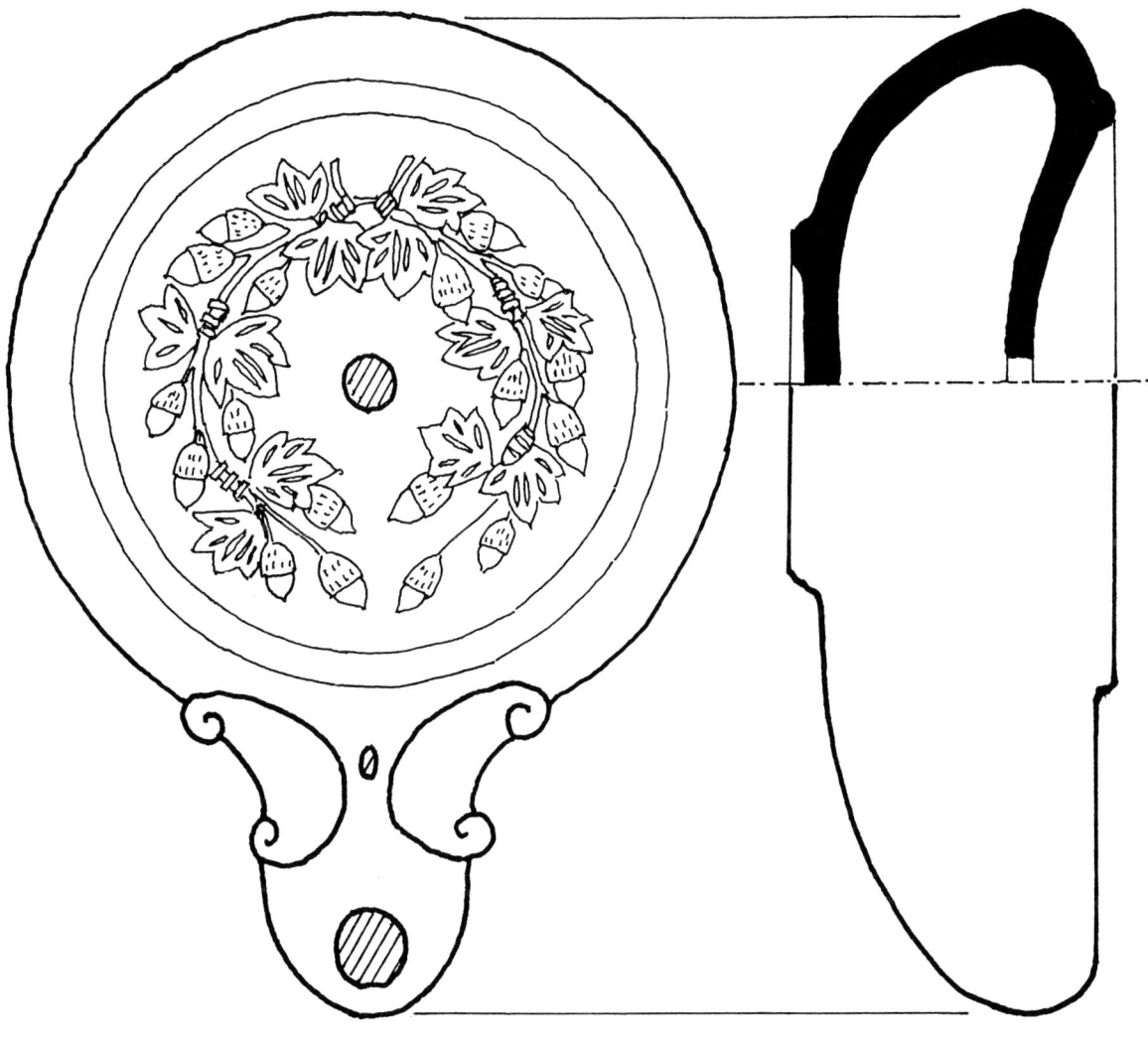

Figure 66. Additional Pouter Pigeon Lamp, full scale

female divinity with carefully detailed drapery and hair facing left, holding a cornucopia in her right hand. Made from a good, new matrix.

c. POUTER PIGEON LAMPS WITH NARROW BEVELED SHOULDERS
(Fig. 65)

The seventeen lamps below have narrow beveled shoulders, Loeschcke Rims V–VII, Broneer Rim 6.

25/20 B.C.–A.D. 40/45

542 CEL.33 Atrium Building I, Room 22, Level II. Cream clay, red slip, discolored to reddish-brown in places. P.L. 0.088 m; P.H. 0.018 m; Width 0.073 m.

Six joining fragments preserving parts of the discus, rim, and nozzle. Surface worn. Rim: Fig. 63 (Loeschcke VIIb). Discus relief: Rosette of nineteen petals in relief radiating from the central filling hole.

Cf. Menzel, 39 no. 182; fig. 31 no. 16.

543 (Pl. V) CEL.59 Atrium Building I, Room 22, Level II. Cream clay, bronze metallic slip partly discolored to dark brown. P.L. 0.084 m; P.H. 0.016 m; Width 0.080 m.

Two joining fragments preserving the nozzle and two-thirds of the discus. Surface worn in places. Rim: Loeschcke VIa. Discus relief: Fallen gladiator seated frontal, wearing the *subligaculum,* a crested helmet, and gauntlets; legs padded. His right arm is down by his side holding a short sword; his left hand holds his rectangular shield out to the right. The filling hole is punched below the figure.

For other examples of this relief, see 533, 536; Loeschcke 1919, nos. 444–47; Menzel, no. 190; Fremersdorf, figs. 86, 87; Goethert-Polaschek, pl. 54 no. 488.

544 CEL.65 Atrium Building I, Room 22, Level II. Cream clay with a greenish tint, bronze metallic slip. P.L. 0.033 m; P.W. 0.028 m.

Fragment preserving parts of discus and rim, and one volute. Slip rubbed. Rim: Loeschcke VIIb. Discus relief: None preserved.

545 CEL.554 Atrium Building I, Room 22, Level II. Cream clay, dark brown slip with a metallic luster. P.L. 0.030 m; P.W. 0.034 m.

Fragment preserving parts of the discus, rim, and nozzle. Slip very worn. Rim: Fig. 63 (Loeschcke VIIa). Discus relief: None preserved.

25 B.C.–A.D. 50

546 CEL.136 Atrium Building I, Room 4, Level II. Cream clay, mottled brown slip. P.L. 0.040 m; P.W. 0.023 m.

Fragment preserving parts of the discus and rim. Worn and chipped. Rim: Loeschcke VIIa, Broneer 7. Discus relief: Two Lares dancing, flanking an altar. Part of one leg, an elbow, and the scarf of the left Lar are preserved.

For another example of this relief, see 527.

547 (Pl. VI) CEL.374 Atrium Building I, Room 21, Level II. Cream clay, brown slip. P.L. 0.053 m; P.W. 0.063 m.

Three joining fragments preserving parts of the discus and rim. Very worn; surface poorly preserved. Rim: Fig. 63 (Loeschcke VIa). Discus relief: Victory driving chariot to left, her drapery blowing behind her. The horses are not preserved. The matrix was very worn.

For other examples of this relief, see Goldman/Jones, no. 428; Bartoli, no. 29; Brants, no. 256.

548 CEL.378 Atrium Building I, Room 21, Level II. Buff clay with a pinkish tint, red slip. P.L. 0.063 m; P.W. 0.088 m.

Eight joining fragments preserving parts of the discus, rim, and nozzle. Slip worn. Rim: Loeschcke VIa. Discus relief: On the left is part of a smoking altar with pulvinate end. The center of the relief is missing, but near the edge of the discus at the bottom are two feet, frontal, and on the right are remains of a shield and spear [?].

A.D. 50–ca. 100

549 (Fig. 65) CD.606 Basilica exterior, NE 2, Level II. Buff clay, red slip. P.L. 0.076 m; P.H. 0.025 m; P.W. 0.084 m.

Six joining fragments preserving most of the discus, part of the rim, and part of the upper wall of the oil reservoir. Worn; slightly chipped. Rim: Loeschcke VIa. Discus relief: A wreath of two oak branches with acorns, tied at the top.

Cf. Bruneau, pl. 29 no. 4595.

550 CD.1243 Basilica exterior, N, Level II. Cream clay,

brown slip mottled to black in places. P.L. 0.061 m; P.H. 0.028 m; P.W. 0.018 m.

Fragment preserving parts of the discus, rim, upper side wall of the oil reservoir, and nozzle. Worn. Rim: Loeschcke VIa. Discus relief: Too fragmentary to identify.

551 CD.1248 Basilica exterior, N, Level II. Buff clay, red slip. P.L. 0.065 m; P.W. 0.082 m.

Fragment preserving parts of the discus, rim, and nozzle. Slip slightly rubbed. Rim: Fig. 63. Discus relief: None preserved.

552 CEL.247 Atrium Building I, Room 6, Level I. Grayish-cream clay, brown slip mottled light to dark brown with a metallic luster. P.L. 0.024 m; P.W. 0.021 m.

Fragment preserving part of the rim and one volute. Very worn.

553 CEL.556 Atrium Building I, Room 11, Level I. Buff clay, dull red slip. P.L. 0.036 m; P.W. 0.048 m.

Fragment preserving parts of the discus, rim, and nozzle. Worn. Rim: Loeschcke VIIb. Discus relief: None preserved.

A.D. 50–225

554 CD.408 Basilica exterior, NE 3, Level I. Cream clay, red slip. P.L. 0.097 m; Height 0.030 m; Width 0.084 m.

Complete, except for the end of the nozzle. Slip rubbed and discolored in places. Rim: Loeschcke VIa. Low disk base. Discus relief: Two gladiators in rear view, heads turned to the left, gesturing with their left hands. The left figure salutes with elbow bent and hand to forehead; the right figure salutes with arm outstretched and held upward. Both wear the *subligaculum*. The left figure wears greaves; the right does not. The left figure holds a pelta at chest height and wears a pointed Phrygian cap. The right figure wears a helmet with a wide brim and carries a short sword in his right hand. His rectangular shield rests on the ground. The small filling hole is punched between the legs of the left figure.

Cf. Menzel, fig. 32 no. 5; Deneauve, pl. 38 no. 323 (the right figure), no. 317 (the left figure); Leibundgut 1977, pl. 41 no. 213 (the right figure); Heres 1972, pl. 13 no. 82 (both figures).

555 CEL.276 Atrium Building I, Room 5, Level I. Buff clay, brown slip. P.L. 0.067 m; P.H. 0.023 m; P.W. 0.036 m.

Two joining fragments preserving parts of a discus, rim, and upper side wall of the oil reservoir. Slip very worn. Rim: Loeschcke VIIb. Discus relief: None preserved.

556 CG.605 Building L (market building) exterior, NE, Level I. Buff clay, pewter-colored metallic slip. P.L. 0.056 m; P.H. 0.028 m; P.W. 0.049 m.

Fragment preserving part of a nozzle. Worn and chipped.

557 C66.862 V-D, Houses, east quadrant, Level 0/I. Buff clay, red slip. P.L. 0.080 m; Height 0.027 m; Width 0.072 m.

Fifteen joining fragments forming most of a lamp, the end of the nozzle, a part of the discus, and chips from the side wall of the oil reservoir missing. Worn. Rim: Loeschcke VIa. Discus relief: An erotic scene (about one-third missing). A crouching woman looks back over her right shoulder at her partner; the rest of the figure from the waist down is missing, as is the male figure, except for his hand and forearm, on which he rests his weight. Only a small part of the bed is preserved. The scene is not shown from the nozzle end, the usual point of view, but from the left side of the lamp.

A.D. 50–383

558 CEL.133 Atrium Building I, Room 4, Level I (found with four coins dating from A.D. 14–37 to 364–383). Cream clay, brown slip.

Fragment preserving parts of a rim and one volute. Very worn. Rim: Only the narrow beveled shoulder is preserved.

d. PROBABLE POUTER PIGEON LAMPS

The thirty-eight lamps below are all probably Pouter Pigeon Lamps, although none has retained any part of the nozzle with its distinctive volutes. The evidence for their being Pouter Pigeon Lamps is that all have Loeschcke shoulders V, VI, and VII, including the first one listed, 559, from a context dated 25/20 B.C., which has a Loeschcke V shoulder. But rims with beveled shoulders do not appear this early, and 559 should probably be dated 25/20 B.C.–A.D. 50.

25/20 B.C.

559 CEL.470 Atrium Building I, Room 21, Level III.

Buff clay, red slip mottled to brown in places. P.L. 0.038 m; P.W. 0.028 m.

Fragment preserving parts of the discus and rim. Slip discolored and slightly worn. Rim: Fig. 63 (Loeschcke V). Discus relief: A rosette of twelve raised petals, the center missing.

25/20 B.C.–A.D. 40/45

560 Withdrawn.
561 (Pl. III) CEL.53 Atrium Building I, Room 22, Level II. Cream clay with a pink tint, red slip mottled to black in places. P.L. 0.055 m; P.W. 0.068 m.

Two joining fragments preserving parts of the discus and rim. Slip very worn. The face and arms of the figure on the discus were damaged before firing, or the mold had been damaged. Rim: Fig. 63; a variation on Loeschcke VIa. Discus relief: An Eros, dancing or running, three-quarters left, with right arm raised aloft and left holding a torch. The filling hole is punched between the feet.

Cf. Brants, pl. 3 no. 241.

562 (Pl. V) CEL.60 Atrium Building I, Room 22, Level II. Buff clay, red slip mottled to black in places. P.L. 0.062 m; Width 0.080 m.

Two joining fragments preserving parts of the discus and rim. Rim: Loeschcke VIb. Discus relief: Gladiator, frontal, head turned right, wearing a crested helmet. On the left arm a rectangular shield; the right arm is raised across the body, holding short sword to deliver a back-handed slash. The right arm is padded.

563 CEL.322 Atrium Building I, Room 22, Level II. Buff clay with a pinkish tint, red slip mottled to brown in places. P.L. 0.033 m; P.W. 0.035 m.

Fragments preserving part of a discus and rim. Worn. Rim: Loeschcke VIa. Discus relief: The left side of the discus preserves a palm branch and underneath it a small bull's eye, which may be the eye of an animal or bird.

564 CEL.339 Atrium Building I, Room 22, Level II. Cream clay, dark brown slip. P.L. 0.028 m; P.H. 0.025 m; P.W. 0.026 m.

Fragment preserving parts of the discus, rim, upper side wall of the oil reservoir, and handle. Rim: Loeschcke VIIb. Molded handle with a V-shaped groove in front that divides the handle into three ribs as it extends along the handle. This is one of very few handles that occur on these early fine lamps. Discus relief: None preserved.

565 CEL.412 Atrium Building I, Room 22, Level II. Cream clay, red slip mottled to purple-brown in places. P.L. 0.032 m; P.H. 0.014 m; P.W. 0.025 m.

Fragment preserving parts of the discus, rim, and a tiny part of a volute. Slip very worn. Rim: Loeschcke VIa. Discus relief: Only a bell-shaped leg of a bed is preserved, presumably remains of an erotic symplegma.

566 CEL.494 Atrium Building I, Room 22, Level II. Buff clay, dark brown slip. P.L. 0.030 m; P.W. 0.027 m.

Fragment preserving parts of the discus and rim. Slip worn on high surfaces. Rim: Loeschcke VIIa. Discus relief: A rosette of thirty-six deeply concave petals, four preserved, center broken away.

567 CEL.508 Atrium Building I, Room 22, Level II. Buff clay, red slip. P.L. 0.032 m; P.W. 0.024 m.

Fragment preserving parts of the discus and rim. Very worn and encrusted. Rim: Loeschcke VIb. Discus relief: Only the outer edge of a rosette of lily-and-tongue pattern is preserved.

568 CEL.517 Atrium Building I, Room 22, Level II. Cream clay with a greenish tint, dark brown slip with a metallic luster. P.L. 0.053 m; P.W. 0.022 m.

Fragment preserving parts of the discus and rim. Worn. Rim: Loeschcke VIIb. Discus relief: Too little left to identify.

569 CEL.553 Atrium Building I, Room 22, Level II. Buff clay, brown slip with a metallic luster. P.L. 0.046 m; P.W. 0.034 m.

Fragment preserving parts of the discus and rim. Slip rubbed on the shoulder. Rim: Loeschcke VIIb. Discus relief: None preserved.

25/20 B.C.–A.D. 50

570 CEL.6 Atrium Building I, Room 21, Level II. Cream clay, dark brown slip. P.L. 0.022 m; P.W. 0.015 m.

Fragment preserving parts of the discus and rim. Very worn. Rim: Loeschcke V. Discus relief: Rosette of raised petals, tips of two preserved.

571 Withdrawn.
572 CEL.433 Atrium Building I, Room 21, Level II. Grayish-buff clay, red slip. P.L. 0.030 m; P.W. 0.040 m.

Fragment preserving parts of the discus and rim. Very worn. Rim: Loeschcke VIIb. Discus relief: An erotic symplegma with only the bell-shaped leg of a bed preserved, the rest of the relief broken away.

573 CEL.492 Atrium Building I, Room 11, Level II. Cream clay with a grayish tint, brown slip. P.L. 0.028 m; P.W. 0.018 m.

Fragment preserving parts of the discus and rim. Only traces of slip preserved. Smoke- and fire-blackened. Rim: Loeschcke VIIb. Discus relief: Rosette of concave petals, parts of two preserved.

A.D. 50–ca. 100

574 CEL.145 Atrium Building I, Room 11, Level I. Buff clay, red slip mottled to black in places. P.L. 0.068 m; P.H. 0.027 m; P.W. 0.045 m.

Two joining fragments preserving parts of the discus and rim. Slip rubbed. Rim: Loeschcke VIIb. Discus relief: An erotic symplegma. The bell-shaped leg of a bed is preserved at the lower left, the rest of the relief broken away.

575 CEL.307 Atrium Building I, Room 16, Level I. Buff clay with a pinkish tint, red slip. P.L. 0.085 m; P.W. 0.048 m.

Fragment preserving parts of the discus and rim. Worn. Rim: Loeschcke VIa. Discus relief: A rosette of eighteen petals, each with a central rib, only partially preserved.

576 CEL.468 Atrium Building I, Room 21, Level I. Buff clay with a pinkish tint, red slip mottled to brown in places. P.L. 0.042 m; P.W. 0.021 m.

Fragment preserving parts of the discus and rim. Slip rubbed. Rim: Loeschcke VIa. Discus relief: Rosette of large petals, probably twelve in all, with part of only one preserved.

577 CEL.476 Atrium Building I, Room 21, Level I. Buff clay, brown slip with a metallic luster. P.L. 0.047 m; P.W. 0.019 m.

Fragment preserving parts of the discus and rim. Very worn. Rim: Loeschcke VIIa. Discus relief: Rosette of large raised petals.

578 (Pl. VI) CEL.481 Atrium Building I, Room 11, Level I. Buff clay with a pink tint, red slip. P.L. 0.047 m; P.W. 0.039 m.

Fragment preserving parts of the discus and rim. Slip slightly worn. Rim: Loeschcke VIIb. Discus relief: A stylized scallop shell.

Cf. Gualandi Genito 1977, pl. 37 no. 255, pl. 38 no. 267.

579 CEL.490 Atrium Building I, Room 21, Level I. Buff clay with a pink tint, brown slip. P.L. 0.019 m; P.W. 0.017 m.

Fragment preserving parts of the discus and rim. Slip very worn. Rim: Loeschcke VIa. Discus relief: A rosette of narrow petals.

580 CEL.499 Atrium Building I, Room 21, Level II. Buff clay, red slip. P.L. 0.033 m; P.W. 0.028 m.

Fragment preserving parts of the discus and rim. Very worn. Rim: Loeschcke V. Discus relief: Rosette of twenty-four concave petals, three preserved, with the center broken away.

581 CEL.512 Atrium Building I, Room 22, Level I. Buff clay, red slip mottled to brown in places. P.L. 0.028 m; P.W. 0.021 m.

Fragment preserving parts of the discus and rim. Worn. Rim: Loeschcke VIIa. Discus relief: An outer band of radiating grooves. The central part of the discus is not preserved.

582 CEL.570 a and b Atrium Building I, Room 21, Level I. Cream clay, dark brown slip. P.L. a 0.055 m, b 0.022 m; P.W. a 0.024 m, b 0.023 m.

One nonjoining and two joining fragments preserving parts of the discus and rim. Very worn; only traces of slip preserved. Rim: Loeschcke V. Discus relief: Remains are too little to identify, but the filling hole is off-center to accommodate the relief.

583 CEL.597 Basilica exterior, NW 2, Level II. Buff clay, red slip. P.L. 0.076 m; P.W. 0.050 m.

Fragment preserving the discus, parts of the rim, and the handle. Slip rubbed. Rim: Loeschcke VIIa; the shoulder is almost horizontal, sloping only slightly. Molded pierced handle. Discus relief: A duck or goose facing right. The filling hole is punched off center below the body of the bird.

584 C70.671 VI-D, Sewer at the corner of Streets 5 and M. Cream clay, red slip. P.L. 0.061 m; P.W. 0.031 m.

Fragment preserving parts of the discus and rim. In good condition, made from a crisp, new matrix. Rim: Loeschcke VIIa. Discus relief: An erotic scene. On the left is a male figure kneeling on a bed facing right, body erect, his right hand on the back of his hip. The rest of the relief is broken away. The bed has the usual bell-shaped legs and bolster at one end.

Cf. Leibundgut 1977, pl. 38 no. 179; Oziol 1977, pl. 14 nos. 233–35, pl. 21 no. 399.

A.D. 50–225

585 CB.1682 Capitolium exterior, S, Level II. Buff clay,

brown slip mottled to black in places. P.L. 0.052 m; P.W. 0.036 m.

Fragment preserving a molded handle, parts of the discus, and the rim. Worn. Rim: Loeschcke VIIa. Discus relief: A comic mask in high relief, almost complete.

586 CB.1714 Capitolium exterior, S, Level I. Buff clay, red slip. P.L. 0.052 m; P.W. 0.021 m.

Fragment preserving parts of the discus and rim. Worn and chipped. Rim: Loeschcke VIIa. Discus relief: Too little remains to identify.

587 (Pl. VIII) CD.867 Basilica exterior, N, Level I. Cream clay, red slip. P.L. 0.049 m; P.W. 0.065 m.

Three joining fragments preserving parts of the discus and rim. Worn. Rim: Loeschcke VIb. Discus relief: A bear running to right. Filling hole punched below the belly of the bear.

Cf. Loeschcke 1919, pl. 12 no. 233; Ponsich 1963, pl. 14 no. 147; Deneauve, pl. 52 nos. 507–8; Gualandi Genito 1977, pl. 29 no. 185, pl. 31 no. 203.

588 CD.880 Basilica exterior, N, Level I. Cream clay, purple-brown slip. P.L. 0.067 m; P.W. 0.046 m.

Two joining fragments preserving most of the discus and parts of the rim. Chipped and worn. Rim: Loeschcke VIIa. Discus relief: Bust of Polyphemus, frontal, wearing crown or turban.

Cf. Deneauve, pl. 71 no. 746.

589 (Pl. I) CEL.631 a, b, and c Basilica exterior, W, Level I. Grayish-buff clay, red slip mottled to dark brown in places. P.L. 0.088 m; Height 0.028 m; P.W. 0.062 m.

Four joining and two nonjoining fragments preserving parts of the discus, rim, side wall of the oil reservoir, and base. Rim: Loeschcke VIIb. Ring base. Discus relief: Central filling hole framed by a bead molding between rings, radiating from which is a rosette of thirty concave tongues.

590 CG.539 Forum, NE passage, Level I. Buff clay, red slip. P.L. 0.047 m; P.W. 0.041 m.

Fragment preserving most of the discus and part of the rim. Slip only slightly rubbed in a few places. Rim: Loeschcke V. Made from a crude matrix. Discus relief: An erotic symplegma of two pygmies, one male, the other male or female. Snake to left.

Cf. Deneauve, pl. 50 nos. 484–85, pl. 51 nos. 486–90. The bedding is arranged differently on these lamps.

591 C70.245 VI-D, Street M, Trench 35–7 SE, Level 0. Fine, rather soft cream clay, light brown slip.

Fragment of discus. Slip worn on high relief. Discus relief: Two-horse cart with seated driver moving left.

See 592, made from the same matrix or a matrix of the same generation, for a full description of this relief.

592 C70.318 VI-D, Street M. Cream clay, red slip. P.L. 0.073 m; P.H. 0.027 m; Width 0.075 m.

Three joining fragments preserving the handle, parts of the rim, and side wall of the oil reservoir. Slip rubbed on raised surfaces. Smoke- or fire-blackened in places. Rim: Loeschcke VIIa. Molded handle with two grooves along the back converging at the top, scratched before firing. Discus relief: A cart with seated driver, reins in one hand, whip in the other, pulled by two galloping horses moving left. The wheels of the cart have four spokes, and there is a hood over the rear of the cart. The matrix is rather crude, but all the parts of the scene are carefully indicated, possibly representing the government mail service.

Cf. 591 for the same relief.

593 C72.140 VI-D, Street N, E/W trench, in front of House E. Buff clay, red slip. P.L. 0.054 m; P.W. 0.046 m.

Fragment preserving parts of the discus and rim. Worn and chipped. Rim: Loeschcke VIIa. Discus relief: A peacock, frontal, with spread tail; the tail fills the upper arc of the discus. Filling hole punched to the left of the body.

594 C72.141 VI-D, Street N, E/W trench, in front of House E. Buff clay with a pink tint, red slip. P.L. 0.040 m; P.W. 0.022 m.

Fragment preserving parts of the discus and rim. Worn; slip peeling and discolored. Rim: Loeschcke VIIa. Discus relief: Only a forearm and hand holding out a large bunch of grapes is preserved.

595 C72.142 VI-D, Street N, E/W trench, in front of NE House. Cream clay, red slip. P.L. 0.060 m; P.W. 0.036 m.

Fragment preserving parts of the discus and rim. Slip worn. Rim: Loeschcke VIIb. Discus relief: A little foliage survives, probably part of a laurel wreath.

596 C72.143 VI-D, N, E/W trench, in front of NE

House. Cream clay, brown slip. P.L. 0.040 m; P.W. 0.048 m.

Fragment preserving parts of the discus and rim. Slip worn and discolored. Rim: Loeschcke VIIa. Discus relief: An urn with close-set handles that do not rise above the mouth. The neck is decorated with bands of triangular design, and there is further decoration on the shoulder.

597 C72.144 VI-D, Street N, E/W trench, in front of NE House. Cream clay, red slip. P.L. 0.037 m; P.W. 0.021 m.

Fragment preserving parts of the discus and rim. Slip worn and chipped. Rim: Loeschcke VIIb. Discus relief: A rosette of bordered tongues, parts of two preserved of a probable eight.

598 C72.145 VI-D, Street N, E/W trench, in front of NE House. Cream clay, red slip mottled to black in places. P.L. 0.032 m; P.W. 0.033 m.

Fragment preserving parts of the discus and rim. Worn, encrusted, and discolored. Rim: Loeschcke VIIb. Discus relief: Rosette of nine concave petals, parts of two preserved.

12. DECORATED DISCUS FRAGMENTS FROM LAMPS WITH TRIANGULAR, ROUNDED, OR POUTER PIGEON NOZZLES

(Catalogue Numbers 599–652)

25/20 B.C.–A.D. 40/45

599 CEL.316 Atrium Building I, Room 22, Level II. Buff clay, red slip. P.L. 0.032 m; P.W. 0.029 m.
  Fragment preserving part of a discus. Worn and chipped. Shallow flattish discus with a central filling hole. Discus relief: A helmet, parts of a sword, and a javelin are preserved, part of a design of gladiatorial armor that encircled the discus.
  Cf. Loeschcke 1919, 374, pl. 11 no. 164; Heres 1972, 38, pl. 18 no. 142; Bailey 1980, 137, pl. 3 Q 776, pl. 28 Q 1005 (military equipment), 209, pl. 29 Q 1011, Q 1012; Walters, 561; Leibundgut 1977, pl. 43 nos. 231, 236; Deneauve, pl. 38 nos. 324–25; Bachofen, pl. 34 no. 1.

600 (Pl. III) CEL.317 Atrium Building I, Room 22, Level II. Buff clay, red slip mottled to brown in places, with a metallic luster. P.L. 0.036 m; P.W. 0.041 m.
  Fragment of discus. Worn and chipped. Discus relief: Eros, frontal, upper torso bent to left, right arm crossed over body and holding Hercules's [?] club on the left shoulder. Head and left foot broken away, right foot missing before slipping (made from a damaged matrix).

601 CEL.321 Atrium Building I, Room 22, Level II. Buff clay, red slip mottled to brown in places. P.L. 0.041 m; P.W. 0.029 m.
  One nonjoining and two joining fragments preserving parts of the discus and rim. Discus relief: A ring and a narrow bead molding frame the central filling hole; radiating from these is a rosette of fifteen bordered tongues, parts of six preserved.

602 CEL.393 Atrium Building I, Room 22, Level II. Cream clay, brown slip. P.L. 0.026 m; P.W. 0.016 m.
  Fragment of a discus with an arc of the filling hole preserved off center. Slip worn on high surfaces. Discus relief: Victory, frontal, alighting on a globe. Only her skirt swirling about her legs is preserved.
  Cf. Loeschcke 1919, pl. 6 no. 389; Goldman/Jones, pl. 100 nos. 163–64; Waagé 1941, pl. 87 no. 6; Roux-Barré, pl. 41; Evelein, pl. 4 no. 12; Deneauve, pl. 36 no. 299; Heres 1977, pl. 16 nos. 120–21; Broneer 1930, pl. 25 no. 437; Bailey 1980, pl. 30 no. Q 1015; Bachofen, pl. 17 no. 2.

603 CEL.469 Atrium Building I, Room 22, Level II. Buff clay, reddish-brown slip with a metallic luster. P.L. 0.024 m; P.W. 0.028 m.
  Fragment preserving part of a discus. Worn. Discus relief: Radiating from the central filling hole is a rosette of concave tongues, parts of three preserved.

604 CEL.475 Atrium Building I, Room 22, Level II. Buff clay, dark brown slip. P.L. 0.023 m; P.W. 0.019 m.
  Fragment preserving parts of a discus and rim. Very worn; only traces of slip preserved. Discus relief: Rosette of thirty-six concave petals, parts of only three preserved.

605 (Pl. I) CEL.480 Atrium Building I, Room 22, Level II. Buff clay, red slip. P.L. 0.045 m; P.W. 0.024 m.

Two joining fragments preserving part of a discus. Slip rubbed on high surfaces. Discus relief: A rosette of six almond-shaped bordered petals with central ribs. Raised dots appear between the petals.

Identical with 349.

606 CEL.551 Atrium Building I, Room 22, Level II. Cream clay, brown slip. P.L. 0.032 m; P.W. 0.023 m.

Fragment preserving part of a discus. Worn. Made from a worn, blurred mold. Discus relief: A ring and a narrow bead frame the central filling hole, from which radiates a rosette of sixteen bordered tongues, parts of three preserved.

Cf. Loeschcke 1919, pl. 15 no. 302; Heres 1977, pl. 44 no. 405 (a Fat Lamp).

25/20 B.C.–A.D. 50

607 CB.1680 Capitolium exterior, S, Level II. Buff clay, brown slip. P.L. 0.036 m; P.W. 0.053 m.

Fragment preserving part of a discus. Worn. Discus relief: An Eros, body frontal, head turned three-quarters right. His right wing and arm are outstretched; he holds an inverted torch or quiver in his right hand.

Cf. Leibundgut 1977, pl. 8 no. 92 (a Fat Lamp with short, unvoluted nozzle); Loeschcke 1919, pl. 5 nos. 22–24, 353–54; Deneauve, pl. 60 nos. 587–88; Bachofen, pl. 15 no. 4 (unnumbered).

608 CB.1681 Capitolium exterior, S, Level II. Buff clay, red slip. P.L. 0.046 m; P.W. 0.059 m.

Fragment preserving part of a discus. Worn. Discus relief: A head of Sol, frontal, with carefully rendered hair. Rays radiate from the head, the lowest turned down at an angle, ending at the break. The filling hole is punched to the right of the neck. Classicizing style.

For motif of Sol, but smaller and less refined, see Bailey 1980, 208, pl. 29 no. Q 1009; Deneauve, pl. 35 no. 282 (lowest rays horizontal).

609 (Pl. II) CEL.355 Atrium Building I, Room 21, Level II. Grayish-buff clay, reddish-brown slip. P.L. 0.039 m; P.W. 0.031 m.

Fragment preserving part of a discus. Slip worn. Discus relief: Ulysses offering a scyphos to Polyphemus, who does not appear. Figure complete, except for the left foot. Ulysses holds out the cup and faces right, while his body is frontal and his legs turn left; the right knee is bent ready to run. Ulysses bearded, wearing *pilleus* and short tunic. An arc of the filling hole to right of the figure.

Cf. Loeschcke 1919, pl. 7 no. 399 (with Polyphemus); Lavage 1970, 703–4 figs. 15–17 (*MEFRA* 83).

610 (Pl. VIII) CEL.360 Atrium Building I, Room 21, Level II. Cream clay, brown slip. P.L. 0.041 m; P.W. 0.042 m.

Fragment preserving part of a discus. High surfaces rubbed. Discus relief: A lion attacking the back of a horse or ass, which has been forced to its knees, left hind leg extended to the rear. The heads of both animals are missing. Filling hole under the belly of the horse.

Cf. Menzel, 31, fig. 27 no. 21; Fremersdorf, 29, fig. 30, 136, fig. 93; Loeschcke 1919, pl. 12 nos. 484–88; Brants, pl. 2 no. 165; Heres 1977, pl. 18 no. 136; De Brun/Gagnière, pl. 7 no. 118; Deneauve, pl. 51 no. 497; Bailey 1980, 161–62, pl. 11 no. Q 866; Walters, 693.

611 CEL.365 Atrium Building I, Room 22, Level II. Grayish-buff clay, black slip. P.L. 0.023 m; P.W. 0.016 m.

Fragment preserving part of a discus. Very worn. Discus relief: A tiny Pegasus near the outer edge of the discus, flying right, head turned to the left. Under him may be a cloud. This was probably one of four or six in a narrow band around the discus. Or there may have been other mythological animals.

Cf. Fremersdorf, 29, fig. 28.

612 CEL.443 Atrium Building I, Room 22, Level II. Buff clay, brown slip. P.L. 0.025 m; P.W. 0.026 m.

Fragment preserving part of the discus and rim. Very worn. Discus relief: Too little remains to identify.

613 (Pl. VIII) CEL.444 a and b Atrium Building I, Room 22, Level II. Buff clay, red slip. P.L. 0.025 m; P.W. 0.029 m.

Two nonjoining fragments preserving part of a discus. Very worn; only traces of slip preserved. Discus relief: Hippocamp to left, fragment *a* preserving the coiled tail, fragment *b* the legs and shoulders.

Cf. Deneauve, pl. 48 nos. 449–51 (with Eros on the back of the hippocamp), pl. 61 nos. 608–9 (hippocamp without a rider); Bachofen, pl. 9 no. 3.

614 (Pl. V) CEL.455 Atrium Building I, Room 21, Level

II. Cream clay, dark brown slip with a metallic luster. P.L. 0.026 m; P.W. 0.022 m.

Fragment preserving part of a discus. Very worn. Discus relief: Nude male torso, frontal, lower part of body, top of head, and parts of arms broken away.

615 CEL.458 Atrium Building I, Room 21, Level II. Buff clay with a pinkish tint, reddish-brown slip with a metallic luster. P.L. 0.028 m; P.W. 0.018 m.

Fragment preserving part of a discus. Slip worn away on raised surfaces. Discus relief: Eros facing left, with outstretched arms. The legs, most of the wings, and whatever he held are missing.

616 CEL.472 Atrium Building I, Room 21, Level II. Buff clay with a pinkish tint, red slip mottled to brown in places. P.L. 0.024 m; P.W. 0.028 m.

Fragment preserving part of a discus. Slip slightly rubbed. Discus relief: Scallop shell, the hinge toward the handle.

Cf. 578; Gualandi Genito, pl. 37 no. 255, pl. 38 no. 267.

617 CEL.477 Atrium Building I, Room 21, Level II. Buff clay, red slip. P.L. 0.022 m; P.W. 0.020 m.

Fragment preserving part of a discus. Very worn. Discus relief: A rosette of twenty-four concave petals, two preserved, the center missing

618 CEL.506 Atrium Building I, Room 21, Level II. Buff clay, red slip. P.L. 0.022 m; P.W. 0.018 m.

Fragment preserving part of a discus. Slip slightly worn. Discus relief: Rosette of concave petals radiating from central filling hole.

619 CEL.555 Atrium Building I, Room 21, Level II. Cream clay, dark brown slip. P.L. 0.042 m; P.W. 0.029 m.

Fragment preserving part of a discus. Only traces of slip preserved. Discus relief: Possibly a statue mounted on a base, only the lower part preserved. There is drapery in high relief that falls over a horizontal edge, perhaps a throne. Enthroned goddess?

25/20 B.C.–A.D. 50

620 C71.153 VI-D, Streets 5 and M in front of the House of the Skeleton, Sewer, sediment. Cream clay, pale green under brown slip. P.L. 0.041 m; P.W. 0.042 m.

Fragment preserving part of a discus. Worn; only traces of slip preserved. The mold was old and blurred. Discus relief: Erotic symplegma, the woman seated facing left, with torso bent forward, left arm behind left knee pulling leg back at an acute angle, man broken away, except for a leg. The bed is only partially preserved.

A.D. 50–ca. 100

621 CD.558 Basilica exterior, N, Level II. Buff clay, red slip. P.L. 0.066 m; P.W. 0.063 m.

Two joining fragments preserving the major part of a discus and one framing ring. Slightly rubbed on high surfaces. Made from a very fine new mold. Discus relief: Hercules moving right, head in profile, body three-quarters frontal, wearing fillet with long ends. Left arm extended out to right, draped with lion's skin. The hand held something now broken away. Right arm down by side, hand holding spear [?] nearly vertical. To the right is an amphora. The filling hole is punched between the amphora and Hercules's legs.

622 CD.674 Basilica exterior, NW 1, Level II. Buff clay, reddish-brown slip. P.L. 0.042 m; P.W. 0.041 m.

Fragment preserving the central part of a discus. Slip slightly rubbed. Discus relief: Gladiator, frontal, head three-quarters left, wearing the *subligaculum*. Rectangular shield in left hand, short sword in right pointing across body at chest height toward the shield. Arm guard on right arm. Left leg raised, as if stepping up. Lower legs and feet broken away. An arc of the filling hole is preserved between the legs.

Cf. 791.

623 CD.733 Basilica exterior, NW 1, Level II. Buff clay, red slip. P.L. 0.051 m; P.W. 0.033 m.

Fragment preserving the right side of a discus and one framing ring. Worn. Discus relief: A wild boar to left, ears laid back, standing in the mouth of a cave on a rocky ledge; a tree bends over the boar following the curve of the edge of the discus, cutting off the hindquarters of the boar with its trunk. Meleager and the Calydonian boar?

Cf. Deneauve, pl. 94 no. 1037 (Meleager to the right and the boar running toward a rocky outcrop, similar to the rocky ledge of 623).

624 CD.1231 Basilica exterior, NW 1, Level II. Buff clay, grayish-black slip with a metallic luster. P.L. 0.032 m; P.W. 0.052 m.

Fragment preserving parts of the discus and rim. Worn; only traces of slip preserved. An angular discus, the inner zone separated from the outer beveled zone by a bead molding framed by rings. Discus relief: The outer zone is decorated with a series of motifs: a fruit with two leaves, possibly a pomegranate, a bird to left, and a plant. A ground line for each is included.

625 CD.1241 Basilica exterior, N, Level II. Cream clay, red slip. P.L. 0.036 m; P.W. 0.034 m.

Fragment preserving the center of a discus. Very worn. Discus relief: A fighting cock, moving to the right, with a vertical palm branch behind. The head and feet of the cock and top of the palm branch are broken away.

Cf. Ponsich 1962, pl. 13 no. 135; Oziol 1977, pl. 2 no. 189; Deneauve, pl. 41 no. 360; Leibundgut 1977, pl. 51 no. 336.

626 CE.2212 Atrium Building I, Rooms 15, 16, Level I. Buff clay, orange-red slip. P.L. 0.028 m; P.W. 0.027 m.

Fragment preserving the center of a discus. In good condition, only slightly rubbed on high surfaces. Discus relief: Head and upper torso of Fortuna, body turned three-quarters left, head in profile to left. She holds a large cornucopia cradled in the crook of her left elbow. Right arm broken away at elbow. She wears a belted peplos with an overfold reaching almost to the belt.

For a complete example of this relief that shows Mercury facing her and Hercules standing to the right behind her, see Bailey 1980, 174, pl. 16 no. Q 921 (a Pouter Pigeon Lamp).

627 CE.2213 Atrium Building I, Rooms 15, 16, Level I. Buff clay, purplish-red slip. P.L. 0.034 m; P.W. 0.026 m.

Fragment preserving part of a discus. Slightly worn and chipped; fire-blackened on the interior. Discus relief: A *murmillo* moving left, head bowed. He carries a large rectangular shield in front of him; his body is broken away below the thighs, and the top of the head is missing. He wears only the *subligaculum*. There may have been another gladiator balancing him on this discus.

Cf. Oziol 1977, pl. 13 no. 216 (a Triangular Nozzle Lamp); Deneauve, pl. 38 no. 321 (a single gladiator on a Triangular Nozzle Lamp of Group B); Bachofen, pl. 33, lower left (with two gladiators, the one to the left wearing greaves and helmet with a short square shield in his right hand and a short curved sword in his left).

628 (Pl. II) CEL.153 Atrium Building I, Room 11, Level I. Cream clay with a pink tint, red slip. P.L. 0.040 m; P.W. 0.039 m.

Fragment preserving part of a discus. Slip rubbed on raised surfaces. Discus relief: On the right side of the discus is a young, nude Bacchus, three-quarters left. His right knee is bent, his left arm extended back, the hand missing; the right arm is bent at the elbow holding a cantharus. Over both arms is a cloak that falls to the ground behind the figure. On the ground before the figure crouches a female panther, looking back and up at Bacchus. The filling hole is punched over the body of the panther.

Cf. Walters, fig. 100 no. 528.

629 (Pl. II) CEL.156 Atrium Building I, Room 11, Level I. Cream clay, thin red slip. P.L. 0.045 m; P.W. 0.037 m.

Fragment preserving part of a discus. Very worn; only traces of slip preserved. Discus relief: Venus wearing the girdle of beauty in right profile. Left leg lifted, arms down, fastening her sandal on her lifted foot. Hair loose below shoulders. Face and both feet broken away.

630 CEL.161 a and b Atrium Building I, Room 11, Level I. Buff clay, red slip. P.L. a 0.042 m, b 0.028 m; P.W. a 0.021 m, b 0.025 m.

Two nonjoining fragments preserving part of a discus. Slip very worn. Discus relief: A series of moldings; starting at the center is a thick bead or torus framed by narrow rings, a scotia, and remains of a second torus with framing rings. The rest is broken away. Such a decoration is more than likely on a Triangular Nozzle Lamp.

631 CEL.165 Atrium Building I, Room 11, Level I. Buff clay with an orange tint, red slip. P.L. 0.032 m; P.W. 0.030 m.

Fragment preserving part of a discus. Only slightly worn. Made from a worn and blurred mold. Surface pitted and pocked with air bubbles. Discus relief: Right profile of a bearded head, probably Jupiter.

632 CEL.166 Atrium Building I, Room 11, Level I. Cream clay, brown slip. P.L. 0.022 m; P.W. 0.042 m.

Fragment preserving part of a discus and rim. Very worn; only traces of slip preserved. Discus relief: Wreath of two branches of myrtle tied at the top; the pointed leaves are ribbed, and the branches bear fruit. Part of only one branch is preserved.

Cf. 361, 406, 467, 509, 640; Deneauve, pl. 54 no. 533; Bailey 1980, pl. 20 no. Q 950.

633 (Pl. I) CEL.175 Atrium Building I, Room 11, Level I. Cream clay, purple-brown slip. P.L. 0.038 m; P.W. 0.027 m.

Two joining fragments preserving parts of the discus and rim. Very badly rubbed. Discus relief: A rosette of double-bordered tongues alternating with three-leaved palmettes (or schematic lilies).

634 (Pl. VII) CEL.215 Atrium Building I, Room 21, Level I. Buff clay, red slip mottled to brown in places. P.L. 0.040 m; P.W. 0.041 m.

Fragment of a discus. Slip rubbed. Discus relief: An erotic symplegma; a bed with bell-shaped legs; only a knee and hand of the woman and a knee of the man are preserved.

Cf. Perlzweig 1961, pl. 2 no. 41; Leibundgut 1977, pl. 38 no. 176; Heres 1977, pl. 24 no. 193; Menzel, no. 216; Miltner 1930, no. 2; Loeschcke 1919, nos. 94, 406, 410; Oziol 1977, pl. 21 no. 400.

635 (Pl. II) CEL.222 Atrium Building I, Room 22, Level I. Buff clay, red slip. P.L. 0.043 m; P.W. 0.018 m.

Fragment preserving part of a discus. Worn. Discus relief: A nude male figure facing front, head looking down to right. Left arm extends down and out, forearm and hand broken away. Right arm broken off at shoulder, as also right leg and lower left leg and foot. The complete relief showed Hercules and the Hydra. He grasps the serpent with his left hand and lifts his right arm holding his club, preparing to strike off the head of the serpent.

For the complete relief, see Loeschcke 1919, pl. 7 no. 71; Deneauve, pl. 45 nos. 411–12; Walters, 207, fig. 319; Gualandi Genito 1977, pl. 33 no. 220.

636 CEL.300 Atrium Building I, Room 21, Level I. Cream clay, brown slip. P.L. 0.030 m; P.W. 0.021 m.

Fragment preserving parts of a discus. Worn. Discus relief: Two horses with a rider on the near horse galloping to the right. The rider's right arm is held back and bent at the elbow, holding a whip and whipping the horse; his left hand holds the reins. The man's head and knee and the horse's forequarters are broken away.

Cf. Fremersdorf, 91, typ. 153; Leibundgut 1977, 172, pl. 44 no. 248 (reversed).

637 (Pl. II) CEL.301 Atrium Building I, Room 21, Level I. Buff clay, brown slip with a metallic luster. P.L. 0.026 m; P.W. 0.036 m.

Two nonjoining fragments preserving parts of the discus and rim. High surfaces worn. Rim: Only the inner framing ring is preserved. Discus relief: On the larger fragment Omphale in three-quarters back view sleeping on Hercules's lion skin surrounded by three sleeping Erotes. Her arms encircle her head, which rests on her left hand. The upper torso and head are missing. Legs bent and covered with drapery. On the smaller fragment are one bare foot and the arrows of Hercules, whose club lies nearby.

For the complete relief, see Loeschcke 1919, pl. 7 no. 396; Perlzweig 1961, pl. 3 no. 56; Waage 1941, fig. 87 on p. 80; Bachofen, pl. 54 no. 1; Leibundgut 1977, pl. 25 no. 21.

638 (Pl. V) CEL.312 Atrium Building I, Room 16, Level I. Cream clay, dark brown slip. P.L. 0.048 m; P.W. 0.039 m.

Fragment preserving part of a discus. Worn and encrusted. Made from a poor, worn mold. Discus relief: A gladiator moving left, right knee bent and leg lifted as if stepping up, perhaps onto the body of his opponent. His right hand holds a rectangular shield, his left a curved sword pointing left at waist height. He wears greaves and thigh padding [?], and a cloak fastened at the right shoulder, leaving the left shoulder bare. Most of the head and the left foot are broken away.

Cf. 917; Fremersdorf, 91, typ. 16; Bachofen, pl. 33 no. 3; Brants, pl. 2 no. 227; Deneauve, pl. 38 fig. 318.

639 CEL.453 a and b Atrium Building I, Room 11, Level I. Cream clay, brown slip. P.L. a 0.029 m, b 0.019 m; P.W. a 0.014 m, b 0.011 m.

Two nonjoining fragments preserving part of a discus. Slip rubbed. Discus relief: A wreath of pointed leaves and berries, myrtle or olive [?], only one leaf and one berry preserved.

640 (Pl. VII) CEL.459 Atrium Building I, Room 21, Level I. Buff clay, brown slip. P.L. 0.025 m; P.W. 0.035 m.

Two joining fragments preserving parts of the discus and rim. Slip rubbed. Rim: Only the inner framing ring is preserved. Discus relief: One almond-shaped ribbed leaf and one thistlelike flower or pomegranate are preserved, probably of a wreath of two branches, tied at the top.

641 CEL.461 Atrium Building I, Room 21, Level I. Cream clay, brown slip. P.L. 0.022 m; P.W. 0.011 m.

Fragment preserving part of a discus. Very

worn. Discus relief: A laurel wreath, only four leaves and part of the stem preserved.

642 (Pl. V) CEL.463 Atrium Building I, Room 11, Level I. Buff clay, red slip. P.L. 0.027 m; P.W. 0.027 m.

Fragment preserving part of a discus and rim. Worn. Rim: Only the inner framing ring is preserved. Discus relief: Male head facing right, the rest of the figure broken away, probably the boxer of 915.

643 CEL.467 Atrium Building I, Room 11, Level I. Buff clay, dark brown slip. P.L. 0.052 m; P.W. 0.039 m.

Fragment preserving parts of a discus and rim. Very badly worn. Rim: Only a ring is preserved. Discus relief: A rosette of fourteen concave petals radiating from a ring around the central filling hole.

644 CEL.471 Atrium Building I, Room 21, Level I. Cream clay, brown slip. P.L. 0.030 m; P.W. 0.019 m.

Fragment preserving part of a discus. Very worn. Discus relief: Three rings framing the central filling hole, from which radiates a rosette of petals.

645 CEL.474 Atrium Building I, Room 11, Level I. Cream clay, brown slip. P.L. 0.049 m; P.W. 0.024 m.

Fragment preserving part of a discus. Slip rubbed and chipped. Discus relief: A rosette of fourteen concave petals as on 643, parts of four preserved.

646 CEL.493 Atrium Building I, Room 11, Level I. Buff clay, dark brown slip. P.L. 0.013 m; P.W. 0.019 m.

Fragment preserving part of a discus and rim. Very worn. Rim: Only the inner ring is preserved. Discus relief: Rosette of small concave tongues, parts of three preserved.

647 (Pl. IV) CEL.599 Basilica exterior, NW 2, Level II. Cream clay, brown slip. P.L. 0.034 m; P.W. 0.032 m.

Fragment preserving the center of a discus. Slip worn on high surfaces. Discus relief: Seated fisherman facing left, his legs pulled back under his body. He wears a cloak over his left shoulder, his right shoulder bare. His extended right hand holds a fishing rod; the left arm is bent at the elbow with a basket hanging from the forearm. The head and feet are broken away.

Cf. Loeschcke 1919, pl. 3 no. 103; Leibundgut 1977, pl. 35 no. 148.

648 CF.1951 Atrium Building I, Room 21, Level I. Buff clay with a pinkish tint, red slip. P.L. 0.040 m; P.W. 0.027 m.

Fragment preserving part of a discus. Very worn. Discus relief: Radiating from a plain sunken area around the central filling hole is a rosette of concave petals.

649 C69.264 House of the Skeleton, Room 15, Level I. Buff clay, red slip. P.L. 0.057 m; P.W. 0.042 m.

Fragment preserving parts of a discus and rim. Encrusted. Rim: Only two rings preserved. Discus relief: The front half of a bridled and saddled horse bounding left, both forefeet lifted. One back lower leg is preserved under the body, the rest broken away. Filling hole punched under body.

Cf. Brants, pl. 2 no. 217.

A.D. 50–225

650 C68.554 VD East House "corridor", Sounding 5, Level 0. Buff clay, orange-red slip. P.L. 0.031 m; P.W. 0.032 m.

Fragment preserving part of a discus. Worn, encrusted. Discus relief: A fox in high relief, curled up sleeping, nose and tail touching the filling hole.

651 C70.484 VI-D. 12.50 NE x 20 SE, Level 0. Buff clay, slipped. P.L. 0.050 m; P.W. 0.045 m.

Two joining fragments preserving parts of a discus. Worn. Discus relief: A frenzied maenad, her upper torso frontal, the legs and head in profile. The left arm is broken away at the shoulder, the right arm at the elbow. Swirling drapery exposing the right leg to mid-thigh and left breast. Her robe trails behind her, and her hair flies out behind. The filling hole is punched to the right of the figure.

652 C70.496 VI-D east quadrant, Corridor 2 exterior, Level 0. Buff clay, grayish slip. P.L. 0.042 m; P.W. 0.031 m.

Three joining fragments preserving parts of a discus. Worn, slightly encrusted. Discus relief: Actaeon attacked by his dogs leaping up from the left. Actaeon, antlers sprouting from his forehead, lifts his club above his head in his right hand; his left holds a spear. His cloak is draped over his left arm and falls to cover his left foot.

13. LAMPS WITH SIMPLE VOLUTES WITH ONLY ONE SCROLL

(Figs. 67–68)

(Catalogue Numbers 653–662)
(Bailey Type C; Broneer Type XXIV; Deneauve Type V D; Dressel/Lamboglia Form 16; Goethert-Polaschek Type XI; Heres Type D; Leibundgut Form XV; Loeschcke Type V; Pavolini Type D; Provoost Type IV; Walters Form 85)

Ten lamps have been found at Cosa that have simple volutes with a scroll only where the nozzle meets the oil reservoir. The volutes curve in and up toward the discus, covering the lower part of the shoulder. The upper ends of the volutes run into the outer groove of the framing molding of the discus or stop short of the framing molding and are connected by an arc that parallels the line of the discus.

The oil reservoirs are wide and shallow. The lower walls are convex, curving in sharply to a low disk base. The bases are flat. These lamps all have wide, concave disci and narrow sloping or beveled shoulders left plain. The disci are separated from the shoulders by a bead molding, by two rings, or by a groove (Loeschcke rim profiles V–VII). These are not described in the catalogue unless they are unusual. The broad nozzles are long and flat on top with rounded ends.

One of these lamps does not have a handle; three have molded pierced handles set on the shoulder, extending down the body as a spine. The handles have two longitudinal grooves giving them a ribbed look. Whether the other five lamps had handles is unknown.

The clay of these simple voluted lamps is very fine, rather soft, and cream to buff in color. They are slipped red or brown. They probably all date to mid-first century A.D. Only one was found in the sealed deposit in Atrium Building I, Room 22, Level II.

25/20 B.C.–A.D. 40/45
653 CEL.331 Atrium Building I, Room 22, Level II. Cream clay, dark brown slip with a metallic luster. P.L. 0.045 m; P.H. 0.018 m; P.W. 0.048 m.
Fragment preserving parts of the discus, rim, and top of the nozzle. Very worn. Discus relief: None preserved.

25/20 B.C.–A.D. 50
654 CEL.502 a and b Atrium Building I, Room 21, Level II. Cream clay, brown slip with a metallic luster. P.L. a 0.034 m, b 0.056 m; P.H. a 0.011 m, b 0.018 m; P.W. a 0.026 m, b 0.032 m.
Two nonjoining fragments preserving parts of the rim and nozzle. Very worn. Discus relief: None preserved.

A.D. 50–ca. 100
655 (Fig. 67) CD.602 Basilica exterior, NE 1, Level II. Buff clay, red slip mottled to brown in places. P.L. 0.084 m; P.H. 0.025 m; P.W. 0.062 m.
Fragment preserving the handle, most of the discus, parts of the shoulder, and one semi-volute. Worn. Discus relief: Bust of Mercury, frontal, wearing a small winged cap and *bulla*. His caduceus is to the left, purse to the right. The filling hole is punched between the head and the caduceus.
Cf. Deneauve, pl. 60 no. 580 (an exact parallel); Bachofen, pl. 30, fig. 2; Ponsich 1963, pl. 8 no. 77, pl. 12 no. 121.

656 CD.1240 Basilica exterior, N, Level II. Buff clay,

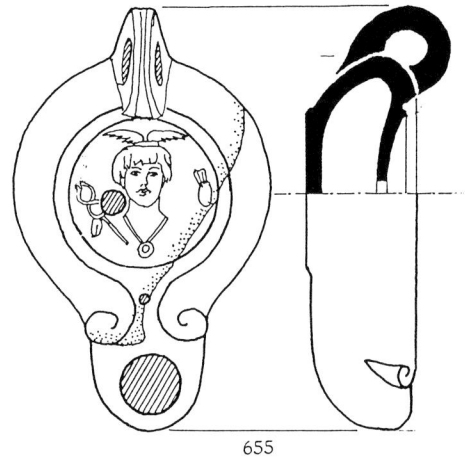

Figure 67.

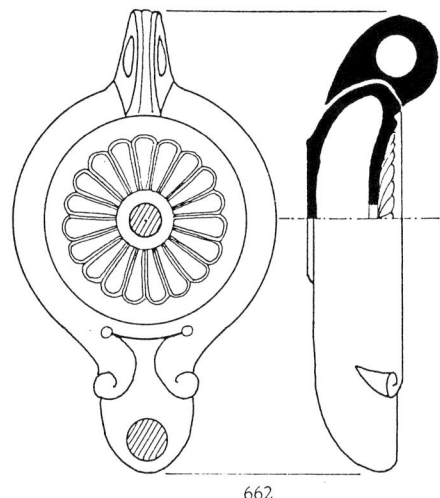

Figure 68.

Figures 67, 68. Lamps with simple volutes with only one scroll, scale 1:2

red slip. P.L. 0.063 m; P.W. 0.059 m.

Fragment preserving the discus, parts of the shoulder, and nozzle. Slip rubbed in places. Discus relief: Undecorated.

657 (Fig. 66) CE.2083 Atrium Building I, Room 16, Level I. Buff clay, red slip mottled to brown in places. P.L. 0.102 m; Height 0.025 m; Width 0.094 m.

Seven joining fragments preserving the oil reservoir, rim, parts of the discus, and nozzle. Slip worn. Discus relief: A New Year's greeting lamp; a winged Victory, three-quarters left, head in profile, wearing a peplos that has slipped from her left shoulder with skirt blown back. Left hand holds palm branch, right is broken away, but on similar lamps the right holds a round shield with greetings inscribed on it. The usual gifts of coins, an amphora of honey, and a cake on the left side of the discus are also broken away. On the right is a Janus coin, and suspended below it is a fig.

See 525 for the left side of this relief; Leibundgut 1977, pl. 23 no. 2; Deneauve, pl. 46 no. 418 (examples of this relief on a different lamp type); Bailey 1980, pl. 22 no. Q 963; Menzel, fig. 33 no. 3; Heres 1977, pl. 26 no. 209.

658 CEL.292 Atrium Building I, Room 21, Level I. Pinkish-buff clay, red slip. P.L. 0.055 m; P.W. 0.035 m.

Fragment preserving parts of the discus, rim, and nozzle. Rim: Discus separated from the beveled shoulder by a ring. Discus relief: None preserved.

659 C70.355 Sewer in front of House of the Skeleton on Street 5. Buff clay, red slip. P.L. 0.105 m; Height 0.030 m; Width 0.075 m.

Incomplete, the end of the nozzle broken away and chips broken from the shoulder and base. Encrusted, root-marked. Low disk base. Molded handle with two parallel grooves along the spine, the hole of the handle unusually large. Discus relief: Dolphin swimming to right, with lifted tail. The filling hole is punched off center to avoid the relief.

Cf. Heres 1977, pl. 14 no. 101; Bailey 1980, pl. 23 no. Q 972.

A.D. 50–225

660 CEL.613 Basilica exterior, W, Level I. Cream clay, brown slip. P.L. 0.043 m; P.W. 0.055 m.

Fragment preserving parts of the discus, rim, and nozzle. Very worn. Discus relief: Too little left to identify.

661 CEL.621 Basilica exterior, W, Level I. Buff clay, brown slip. P.L. 0.032 m; P.H. 0.022 m; P.W. 0.032 m.

Fragment preserving parts of the rim and nozzle. Very worn. Discus relief: None preserved.

662 (Fig. 68) CF.2143 Atrium Building I, Room 15, Level I. Buff clay, red slip mottled to dark brown in places. Length 0.124 m; Height 0.026 m; Width 0.075 m.

Three joining fragments preserving all but a small part of the base. Very worn. Molded pierced handle with two grooves along the spine. Discus relief: Rosette of nineteen concave tongues around the small central filling hole.

14. LAMPS WITH VOLUTES IN NEW POSITIONS

(Fig. 69)

(Catalogue Numbers 663–670)
(Loeschcke Type V; Broneer Type XXIV D; Bailey Type C, Group V)

The eight lamps in this group are almost identical, with small variation in the sizes of three. The clay is very fine and ranges in color from cream to buff. The fabric is very thin, and the lamps are carefully made from new molds that show little wear. All are slipped red or brown.

The small concave disci are plain with a central filling hole and set off by a bead molding framed by grooves. The shoulders are wide and convex, rising from the discus, then dropping to meet the lower half of the lamp at a sharp angle, their outer and inner limits on the same plane. The oil reservoirs are shallow; the lower walls curve in sharply to meet the low disk base; all have flat bases. The nozzles are wide and flat on top, with rounded ends. All have molded pierced handles with two grooves running down the spine. There are small air holes on the axes of the nozzles near the discus.

The volutes of these lamps are flattened with the upper scrolled ends tangent to the discus and the lower ends at the outer edges of the juncture between body and nozzle. The scrolls at the lower ends extend down the body as cones. The volutes mark the limits of the shoulders. A band of elongated, bordered tongues radiates around the discus. These decorative bands are interrupted by the upper scrolls of the volutes.

Five of the eight lamps in this group were found in the storeroom of the hardware and pottery shop that was sealed in A.D. 40/45. One comes from a context dated 25/20 B.C.–A.D. 50, while the remaining two are from contexts that have been dated A.D. 50–ca. 100.

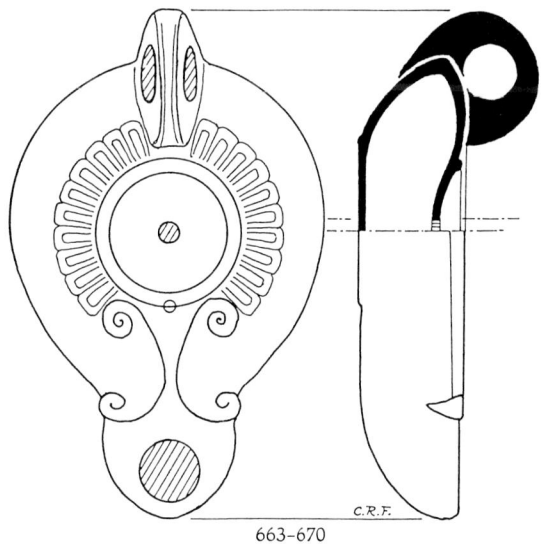

Figure 69. Lamps with volutes in new positions, scale 1:2

However, since this type was so short-lived, and since all these lamps are of the same generation, it seems likely that they were from a single shipment and five still in stock in the storeroom when the roof collapsed.

25/20 B.C.–A.D. 50
663 CEL.297 Atrium Building I, Room 21, Level II. Pinkish-cream clay, brown slip. P.L. 0.072 m; P.W. 0.052 m.

Three joining fragments preserving parts of the shoulder and nozzle. Slip rubbed.

25/20 B.C.–A.D. 40/45

664 CEL.18 Atrium Building I, Room 22, Level II. Cream clay, red slip mottled to purplish-brown in places. P.L. 0.073 m; P.W. 0.052 m; Diameter 0.090 m.
Six joining fragments preserving the handle and parts of the right side of the discus, shoulder, and nozzle. Slip worn and discolored.

665 CEL.19 Atrium Building I, Room 22, Level II. Buff clay, brown slip. P.L. 0.034 m; P.W. 0.032 m; Diameter 0.090 m.
Fragment preserving a handle and part of a shoulder. Slip very worn.

666 CEL.20 Atrium Building I, Room 22, Level II. Light pinkish-buff clay, red slip. P.L. 0.073 m; P.W. 0.059 m; Diameter 0.090 m.
Two joining fragments preserving the discus and parts of the shoulder and lower side wall of the oil reservoir.

667 CEL.209 Atrium Building I, Room 22, Level II. Cream clay, brown slip. P.L. 0.076 m; Height 0.029 m; P.W. 0.078 m; Diameter 0.084 m.
Two joining fragments preserving parts of all features, except the nozzle. Slip worn.

668 CEL.332 Atrium Building I, Room 22, Level II. Cream clay, brown slip. P.L. 0.111 m; Height 0.031 m; P.W. 0.078 m; Diameter 0.088 m.
Six joining fragments preserving the discus, handle, parts of the shoulder, lower side wall of the oil reservoir, base, and nozzle. Worn and chipped.

A.D. 50–ca. 100

669 CEL.158 Atrium Building I, Room 11, Level I. Buff clay, red slip. P.L. 0.128 m; Height 0.030 m; Width 0.083 m.
Ten joining fragments preserving the nozzle, and parts of the shoulder, discus, lower side wall of the oil reservoir, handle, and base. Slip rubbed.

670 CEL.299 Atrium Building I, Room 21, Level I. Pinkish-buff clay, brown slip. P.L. 0.063 m; P.W. 0.056 m.
Two joining fragments preserving parts of the shoulder and framing bead molding of the discus. Worn.

15. LAMPS WITH LONG, VOLUTED NOZZLES AND HEAT SHIELDS

(Figs. 70–77)

(Catalogue Numbers 671–735)
(Bailey Type D; Broneer Type XXI; Deneauve Type V B; Dressel/Lamboglia Types 12 and 13; Goethert-Polaschek Type X A; Ivanyi Type III; Loeschcke Type III)

Ninety-one lamps and parts of lamps have been found at Cosa that have wide disci, one or more long, voluted nozzles, and a heat shield above the handle.[1] Eight have been reconstructed from fragments and are complete enough to project the whole lamp, including the shape of the heat shield. Twenty-seven others preserve all essential elements except the heat shield. The remaining fifty-six are simply heat shields.

These lamps were carefully made from fine molds. The fabric of the bodies and the underside of the nozzles is very thin. The clay was finely levigated and rather soft, the color ranging from cream to buff, occasionally with a pinkish tint. All are slipped in red, brown, or black, the slip often mottled, due to imperfect firing. The darker slip colors often have a metallic luster, as if the potters were trying to duplicate the color of a bronze prototype. Despite the complexity of these lamp forms, only two-part molds were used. The bottom mold formed the oil reservoir, the underside of the nozzle or nozzles, and the lower part of the cone-shaped scrolls at each end of the volutes. The bottom mold also included the handle, which extends as a support up the stem and underside of the heat shield. The top mold included the discus and its relief, if any, the rim, the crowns of the nozzles and volutes, and the face of the heat shield and its stem (Fig. 70).

The oil reservoir of these lamps is wide and shallow. The sides curve up and out from the low disk or ring base to the mold join near the crown of the lamp. The nozzles are wide and long, with long wide volutes decorated with scrolls that extend down the sides of the body and nozzle as cones. The nozzles and volutes are flat on top. The disci are concave, very often without any decoration. The decoration is occasionally only a molding around the filling hole, but often a rosette radiating from a molding around the filling hole; the rosettes are of various, more or less conventional designs. Only once, on 700, is there a different sort of discus relief. The rims are a series of rings of varying width; usually these are more or less rounded, but the outermost is often flat. The rims vary in width from 0.006 m to 0.017 m; the range of their profiles is shown on Figs. 71–73, and they are not described individually in the catalogue unless they are unusual. There is sometimes a narrow beveled shoulder beyond the rim, and on one example, 702, this is decorated with a band of ovules. Most heat shields are either triangular or lunate in form with occasional other shapes, such as a siren or a female head. The relief decoration on the triangular heat shields includes palmettes and acanthus leaves, often executed in fine detail. The shields are attached above the molded pierced handles, extending up and back at a thirty- to forty-five degree angle. All these lamps have small air holes punched either through the rim or at the edge of the discus toward the nozzle and in the lower part of the hollow heat shield. Some fragments preserve part of the continuous volute that con-

---

1. In the bronze prototype of these lamps, this shield would have served as a light reflector; on clay lamps it served mainly as decoration, although it provided a handle to protect the hand when the lamp was carried.

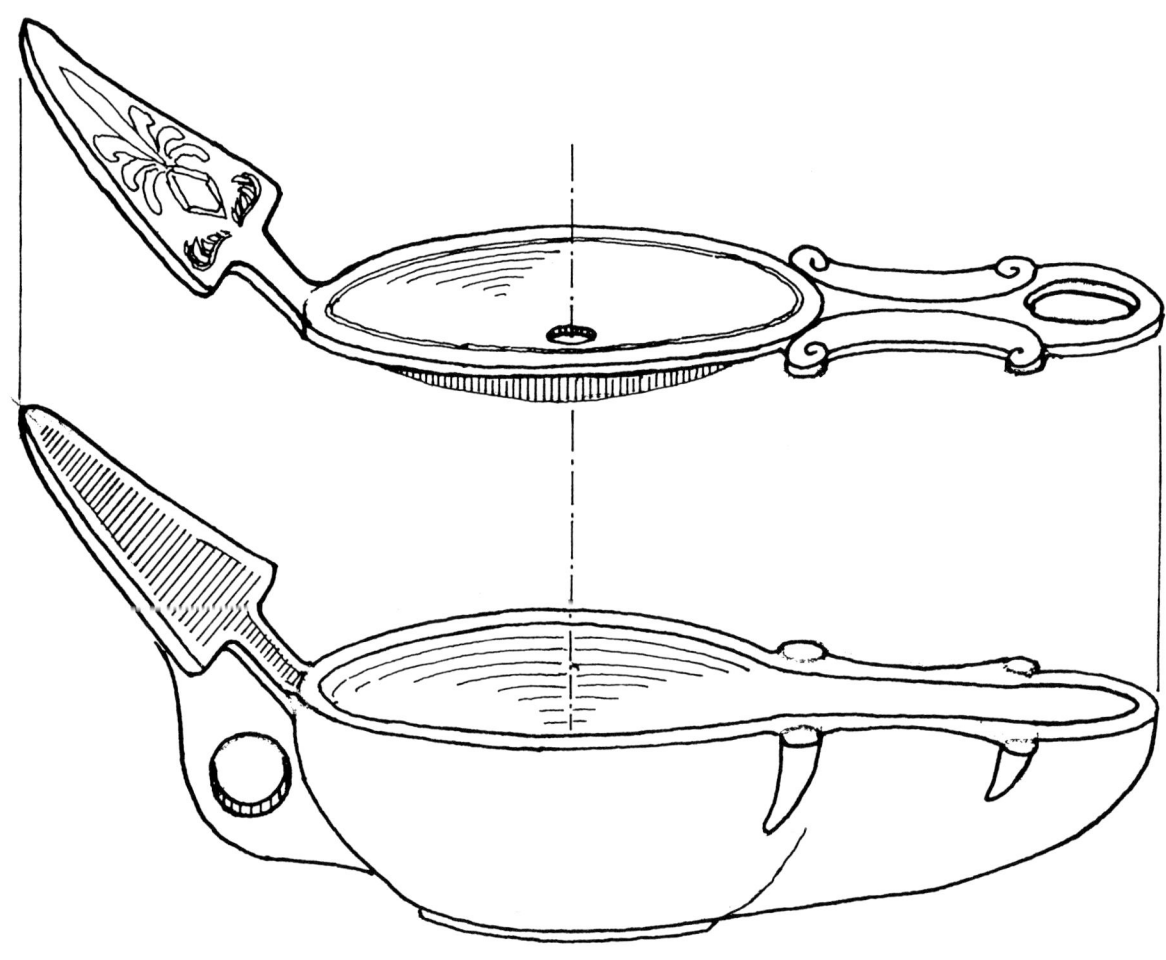

Figure 70. Lamps with a long, voluted nozzle and a heat shield showing the two parts before joining in the mold

nected the two nozzles of a double-nozzle version (*dilynchnos*) of this type. On lamps with two or more nozzles there is usually a decorative relief between the volutes.

Thirty-one lamps of this class were found in Room 22 of Atrium Building I in a level sealed off by the debris from the collapse of the northwest wall of the Basilica in ca. A.D. 40/45. Eight are from contexts that are dated 25/20 B.C.–A.D. 50. Twenty-two are from contexts dated A.D. 50–ca. 100. The remaining thirty lamps of this type can be only loosely dated A.D. 50–225. From this evidence it is clear that these lamps were available and popular in Cosa during the Claudian and Neronian eras, but ceased to be as popular during the last quarter of the first century A.D. It also seems evident that this was a period of prosperity at Cosa, as these lamps must have been expensive to make and use. A two-nozzle lamp would burn fuel twice as quickly as one with only one nozzle. A seven-nozzle lamp—such as the Cosan example (Fig. 71)—would amount to conspicuous luxury. The quick acceptance and popularity of the plain, strong, inexpensive Factory Lamps when they were introduced at Cosa toward the end of the first century A.D. meant the end of this "baroque" type, although crude copies were made in the provinces as late as the end of the second or beginning of the third century A.D.

The Cosan lamps with long, voluted nozzles and heat shields have been divided into two groups, followed by the unattached heat shields: a. lamps with two or more nozzles (Fig. 72); b. lamps with one nozzle (Fig. 73). Heat shields and handles broken away from the bodies of their lamps are grouped into: 1. Triangular Heat Shields; 2. Lunate Heat Shields; 3. Unusual Heat Shields. Sixteen other handles with part of a heat shield attached were catalogued.

a. LAMPS WITH TWO OR MORE NOZZLES AND A HEAT SHIELD
(Figs. 71, 72)

(Catalogue Numbers 671–693)

25/20 B.C.–A.D. 40/45

671 (Pl. IX; Fig. 71) CEL.22 Atrium Building I, Room 22, Level II. Greenish cream clay, self-slip mottled dark to light brown, slightly metallic luster. Length 0.204 m; Height 0.038 m; Width 0.201 m.

Twenty-seven fragments preserving most of a large seven-nozzled lamp. The handle with its heat shield, the base, the discus, and two of the nozzles are preserved, with parts of the other five nozzles, the rim, and sides of the oil reservoir. Surface rubbed and discolored. Concave discus; central filling hole framed by a flattened bead between rings. Rim: Three inner rings sloping up to a pair of bead moldings between two rings. The nozzles partially encircle the discus, set at about a forty-three degree angle from one another. The heat shield occupies approximately the space of one nozzle; the others are spaced at equal intervals. The volutes are continuous between nozzles, with scrolls only at either side of the wick holes. A lunate heat shield with a broad fillet marks off a wide border.

Cf. Bisi Ingrassia, 83 type 7c.

672 CEL.10 Atrium Building I, Room 22, Level II. Cream clay, red slip mottled to brown in places. P.L. 0.145 m; Height 0.031 m.

Thirteen joining fragments preserving the handle and heat shield, parts of the discus, rim, two nozzles, side wall of the oil reservoir, and base. Worn. Shallow concave discus without relief. Low disk base. Rim: Fig. 72. Two nozzles with the volutes continuous between the nozzles. Lunate heat shield with a sunken crescent marked off by a groove.

673 CEL.11 Atrium Building I, Room 22, Level II. Cream clay, light reddish brown slip mottled to dark brown in places with a metallic luster. P.L. 0.143 m; Height 0.028 m; P.W. 0.069 m; Diameter 0.086 m.

Eleven joining fragments preserving the base and parts of the discus, rim, two nozzles, and handle with a fragment of a triangular heat shield. Very worn; only traces of slip preserved. Rim: Fig. 72. Shallow concave discus without relief, with small filling hole punched slightly off center. Low disk base. Two nozzles, with the volutes continuous between them.

674 CEL.35 Atrium Building I, Room 22, Level II. Pinkish-buff clay, red slip. P.L. 0.165 m; Height 0.054 m; P.W. 0.075 m.

Nine joining fragments preserving parts of the discus, rim, oil reservoir, base, handle, and heat shield of an unusually large lamp. Slip slightly worn and chipped. Deep concave discus; central

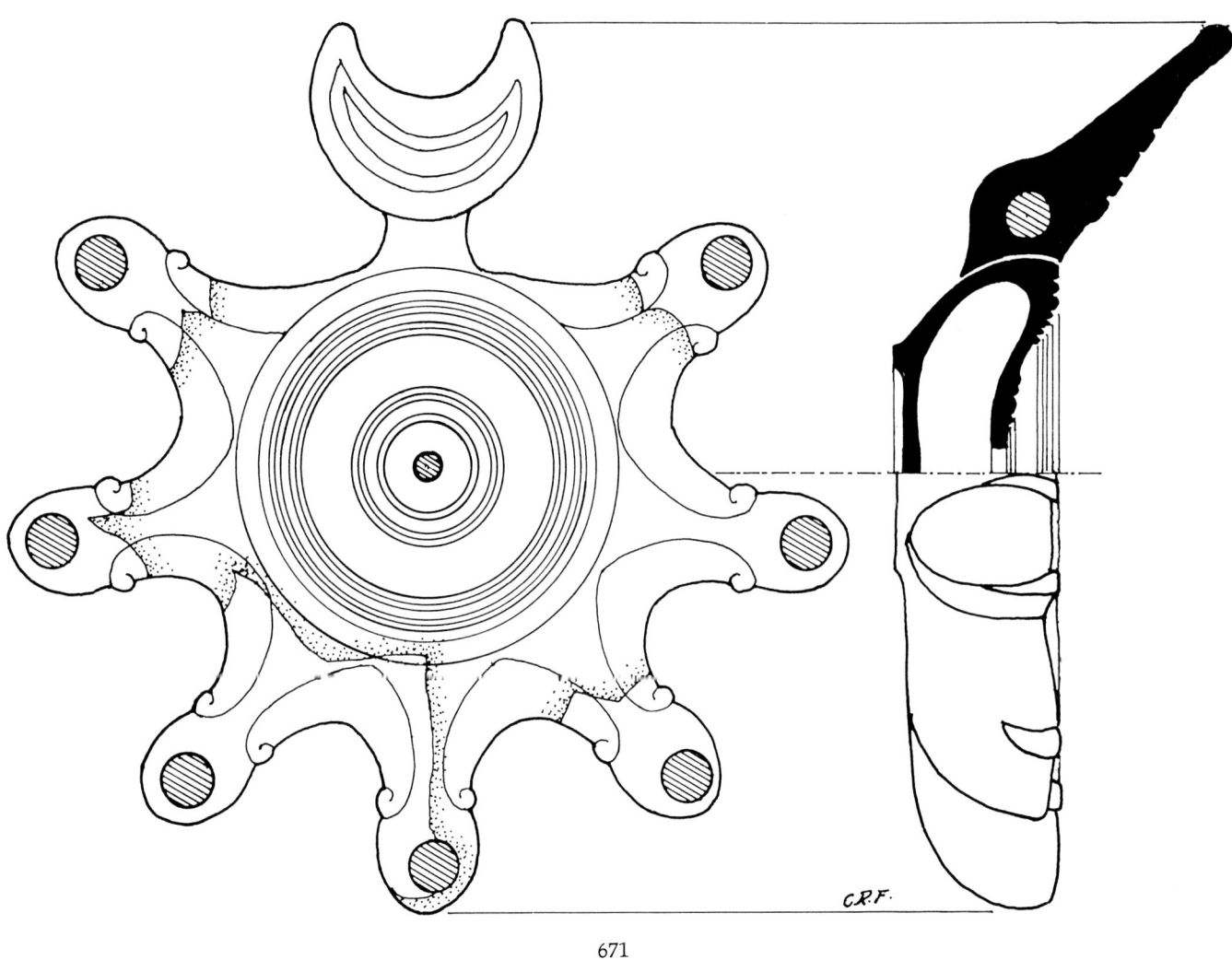

Figure 71. Lamp with seven long, voluted nozzles and a heat shield, scale 1:2

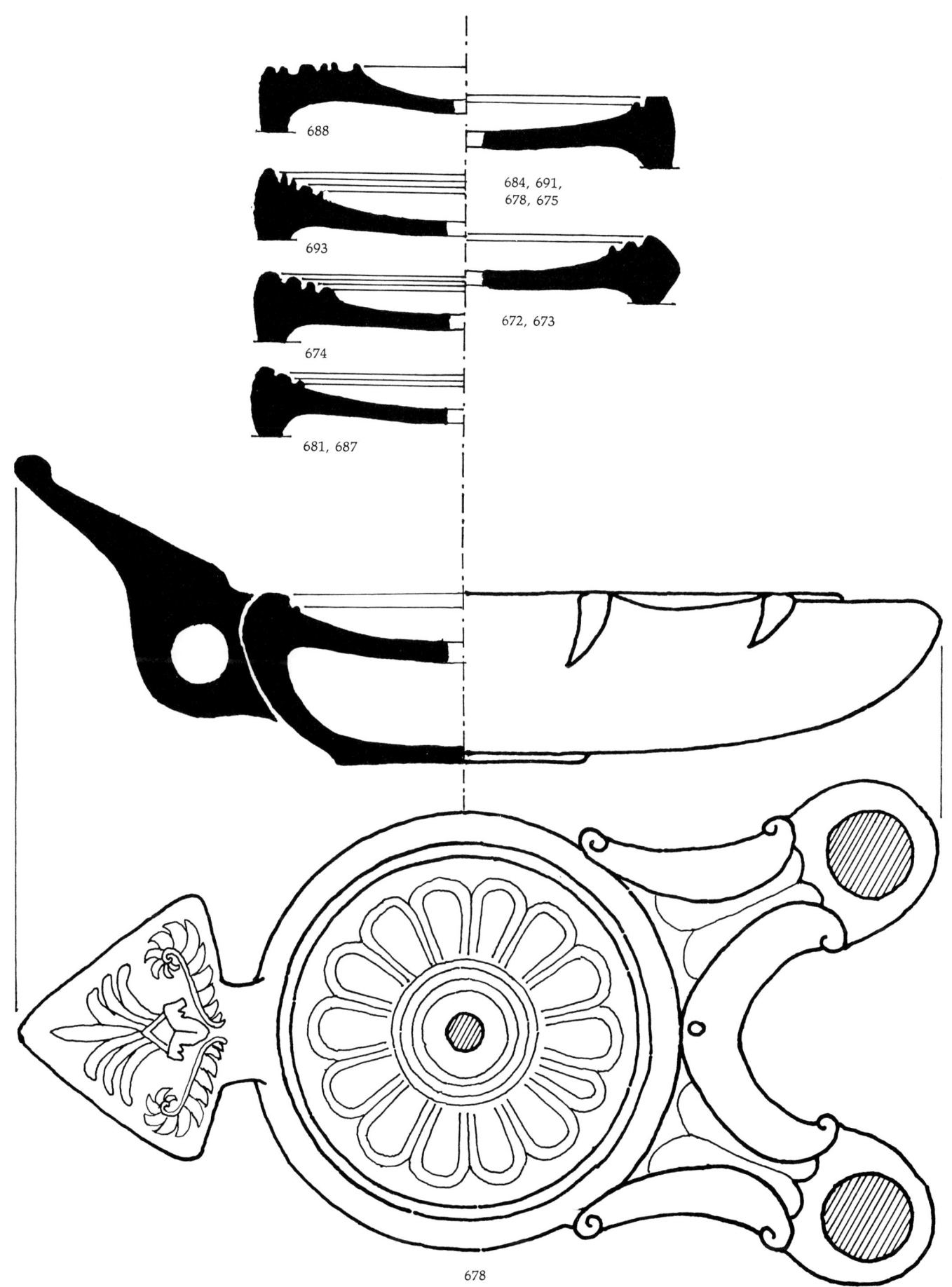

Figure 72. Lamp with two long, voluted nozzles and a heat shield, with rim profiles, full scale

filling hole framed by a narrow bead molding bordered by rings from which radiates a rosette of twenty-five tongues, seven preserved. Low ring base. Rim: Fig. 72. The lower part of a triangular heat shield preserving parts of a palm branch. The design would have been a palmette rising above a pair of horizontal palm branches.

675 CEL.61 & CEL.62 Atrium Building I, Room 22, Level II. Pinkish-buff clay, red slip. CEL.61: P.L. 0.125 m; CEL.62: P.L. 0.133 m.

Rim: Fig. 72. Parts of two long, voluted nozzles. CEL.61 is composed of five joining fragments, CEL.62 a single one. These fragments must be parts of the same lamp. The clay and slip are similar, and these are the only fragments found of so large a lamp. Cf. Brants, pl. 3 no. 260; Deneauve, pl. 57 no. 550.

676 CEL.208 Atrium Building I, Room 22, Level II. Cream clay, light reddish-tan slip mottled to brownish-black in places, with a metallic luster. P.L. 0.078 m; P.H. 0.026 m; P.W. 0.075 m.

Three joining fragments preserving parts of the discus, rim, and two nozzles. Very worn; only traces of slip preserved. Shallow concave discus without relief.

Cf. Rosenthal/Sivan, 20 no. 43; Heres 1972a, pl. 6 no. 22.

677 CEL.210 Atrium Building I, Room 22, Level II. Buff clay, red slip mottled to brown in places. P.L. 0.047 m; P.W. 0.072 m.

Two joining fragments preserving parts of the discus, rim, and two nozzles. Slip worn on raised surfaces. Shallow concave discus without relief. Base broken away.

678 (Fig. 72) CEL.212 Atrium Building I, Room 22, Level II. Buff clay, red slip. P.L. 0.141 m; Height 0.032 m; Width 0.080 m.

Twelve joining fragments preserving most of the lamp, except for the ends of the nozzles and some chips from the discus and rim. Slip worn on raised surfaces. Rim: Fig. 72. Shallow concave discus with central filling hole framed by three rings from which radiates a rosette of fourteen bordered tongues of unequal width, one very narrow. Low disk base. Triangular heat shield decorated with a palmette rising between two palm branches curling up at their ends.

679 CEL.213 Atrium Building I, Room 22, Level II. Pinkish-buff clay, red slip mottled to brown in places. P.L. 0.152 m; Height 0.031 m; Width 0.083 m.

Three joining fragments preserving most of a lamp, the end of one nozzle and parts of the handle and heat shield broken away. Worn, scratched, and encrusted. Shallow concave discus without relief. Low disk base. Rim: The same as 672 (Fig. 72).

680 CEL.315 Atrium Building I, Room 22, Level II. Cream clay, light brown slip. P.L. 0.123 m; Height 0.038 m; Width 0.086 m.

Eighteen joining fragments preserving parts of all essential features, except the heat shield, which is broken away. Very worn, chipped, and scratched. Deep concave discus with central filling hole framed by two rings from which radiates a rosette of sixteen concave tongues. A lanceolate leaf with a central rib in relief between the volutes on each nozzle. Low disk base.

681 CEL.318 Atrium Building I, Room 22, Level II. Pinkish-buff clay, red slip. P.L. 0.069 m; P.W. 0.045 m.

Three joining fragments preserving parts of the discus, rim, and one nozzle, with part of the continuous volute that joined the two nozzles. Slip slightly rubbed. Deep concave discus without relief. Rim: Fig. 72.

682 CEL.323 Atrium Building I, Room 22, Level II. Pinkish-buff clay, red slip. P.L. 0.123 m; P.H. 0.028 m; P.W. 0.029 m.

Three joining fragments preserving parts of the discus, rim, oil reservoir, two nozzles, handle, and heat shield. The ends of the nozzles are broken away, and only the stem of the heat shield is preserved. Worn and chipped. Shallow concave discus without relief.

683 CEL.333 Atrium Building I, Room 22, Level II. Buff clay, red slip. P.L. 0.087 m; Height 0.028 m.

Six fragments, five joining, one nonjoining, preserving parts of the discus, rim, two nozzles, and base. Deep concave discus without relief. Low disk base, slightly concave.

684 CEL.406 Atrium Building I, Room 22, Level II. Buff clay, red slip mottled to brown in places. P.L. 0.038 m; P.W. 0.058 m.

A fragment preserving parts of the discus, rim, and one nozzle with a part of the continuous volute that connected two nozzles. Slip rubbed. No discus relief preserved. Rim: Fig. 72.

685 CEL.427 Atrium Building I, Room 22, Level II. Cream clay, brown slip with a metallic luster. P.L. 0.035 m; P.W. 0.023 m.
  Fragment preserving parts of the rim, nozzle, and continuous volute connecting the two nozzles. Slip worn.

25/20 B.C.–A.D. 50

686 CEL.357 Atrium Building I, Room 21, Level II. Cream clay, reddish-brown slip. P.L. 0.066 m; P.H. 0.028 m; P.W. 0.035 m.
  Fragment preserving one nozzle and part of a second.

687 C68.560 V, VI-D/E House of the Birds, Room 4, at bottom of steps, Level IB. Buff clay, red slip mottled to brown in places. P.L. 0.130 m; Height 0.035 m; Width 0.110 m.
  Many joining fragments preserving parts of the discus, two nozzles, and the rim. The surface is very worn. Encrusted. Rim: Fig. 72. Discus relief: Rosette of four hearts, the points toward the central filling hole.
  Cf. Bailey 1980, pl. 29 no. Q 1008; Heres 1972a, pl. 6 no. 26 (five hearts); Menzel 1969, fig. 25 no. 5.

A.D. 50–ca. 100

688 CEL.174 Atrium Building I, Room 11, Level I. Buff clay, brownish-red slip. P.L. 0.093 m; P.H. 0.025 m; P.W. 0.060 m.
  Five joining fragments preserving one nozzle and parts of a second, the discus, and the rim. Worn and encrusted. Smoke-blackened around wick hole. The central part of the plain discus is level. Rim: Fig. 72. This elaborate combination of rings, grooves, and bead moldings is similar to the earlier Augustan rims.
  Cf. Bailey 1980, pl. 28 no. Q 998.

689 CEL.177 Atrium Building I, Room 11, Level I. Buff clay, brownish-red slip. P.L. 0.062 m; P.W. 0.086 m.
  Fragment preserving a nozzle and part of the continuous volute that connected it with another. Badly worn; smoke-blackened around wick hole.

690 CEL.219 Atrium Building I, Room 21, Level I. Pinkish-buff clay, red slip. P.L. 0.084 m; P.H. 0.021 m; P.W. 0.064 m.
  Fragment preserving parts of the base, the lower side wall of the oil reservoir, and the undersides of two nozzles. Very worn. Low ring base.

691 CEL.414 Atrium Building I, Room 11, Level I. Buff clay, red slip. P.L. 0.056 m; P.H. 0.018 m; P.W. 0.018 m.
  Fragment preserving parts of the discus, rim, nozzles, and side wall of the oil reservoir. Slip slightly worn. Shallow concave discus. Rim: Fig. 72.

A.D. 50–225

692 CEL.113 Atrium Building I, Room 15 drain, Level I. Cream clay, brown slip. P.L. 0.068 m.
  Four joining fragments preserving parts of a nozzle and the continuous volute that connected two nozzles. Worn and encrusted.

693 C69.246 Atrium Building V, Level 0. Buff clay, dull black slip. P.L. 0.125 m; Height 0.035 m; Width 0.070 m.
  Many joining fragments preserving most of a lamp, the ends of the two nozzles and the heat shield broken away. Worn, encrusted, and root-marked. Low base of three rings. Rim: Fig. 72. Discus relief: A series of concentric rings around the central filling hole.
  Cf. Bailey 1980, pl. 28 no. Q 998.

b. LAMPS WITH ONE NOZZLE AND A HEAT SHIELD
(Fig. 73)
(Catalogue Numbers 694–705)

25/20 B.C.–A.D. 40/45

694 CEL.13 Atrium Building I, Room 22, Level II. Cream clay, red slip mottled to brown in places. P.L. 0.105 m; Height 0.033 m; P.W. 0.069 m.
  Eleven joining fragments preserving parts of the discus, rim, oil reservoir, base, nozzle, and handle with a part of the stem of the heat shield. Very worn. Concave discus without relief, the filling hole punched slightly off center. Low disk base. Rim: Fig. 73. Relief ridge on nozzle top between volutes echoing the curve of the inner edge of the volutes. This is the only example of this decoration on a single-nozzle lamp of this type found at Cosa.

695 CEL.29 Atrium Building I, Room 22, Level II. Cream clay, brown slip discolored to pale yellow-

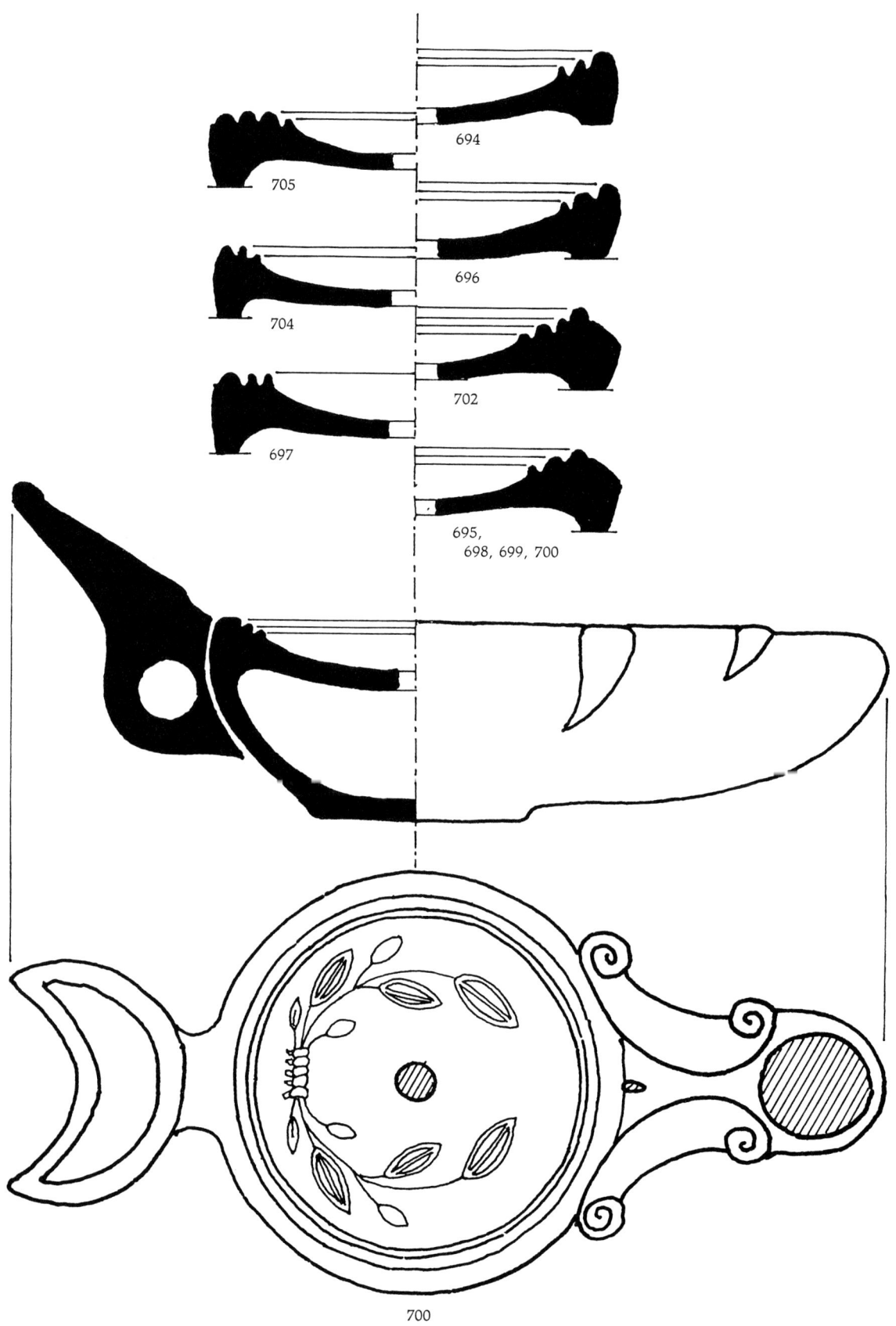

Figure 73. Lamps with one long, voluted nozzle and a heat shield, with rim profiles, full scale

brown in places, with a metallic luster. Length 0.155 m; Height 0.028 m; Width 0.074 m.

Twelve joining fragments preserving all essential parts of the lamp, the left half of the nozzle and chips from the discus and rim broken away. Shallow concave discus with central filling hole. Low disk base. Rim: Fig. 73. Discus relief: Closely spaced grooves radiating from a ring around the central filling hole. Molded pierced handle with triangular heat shield decorated with a palmette. Flanking the base of the palmette are two dolphins, confronted, with tails curling up.

For similar heat shield decorations, see 723; Menzel, no. 87; Miltner 1930, pl. 11 no. 56.

696 CEL.34 Atrium Building I, Room 22, Level II. Cream clay, dark brown slip. P.L. 0.045 m; P.W. 0.071 m.

Two joining fragments preserving parts of the discus, rim, upper side wall of the oil reservoir, handle, and stem of a heat shield. Very worn. Deep concave discus without relief. Rim: Fig. 73.

697 CEL.74 Atrium Building I, Room 22, Level II. Buff clay, dark brown slip with a metallic luster. P.L. 0.062 m; P.H. 0.020 m; P.W. 0.044 m.

Fragment preserving handle, heat shield, parts of the discus, rim, and upper side wall of the oil reservoir. Slip rubbed. Deep concave discus. Rim: Fig. 73. Lunate heat shield with a wide plain border. No indication of the number of nozzles.

698 CEL.408 Atrium Building I, Room 22, Level II. Cream clay, red slip mottled to brown in places. P.L. 0.052 m; P.W. 0.039 m.

Three joining fragments preserving parts of the discus, rim, and stem of the heat shield. Slip rubbed on raised surfaces. Shallow concave discus without relief. Rim: Fig. 73. No indication of the number of nozzles.

25/20 B.C.–A.D. 50

699 CEL.376 Atrium Building I, Room 21, Level II. Pinkish-buff clay, red slip. P.L. 0.128 m; Height 0.028 m; Width 0.077 m.

Twelve fragments, eleven joining and one nonjoining, preserving the discus, base, parts of the oil reservoir, rim, handle, nozzle, and one volute. Slip rubbed and chipped. Deep concave discus without relief, the filling hole not quite centered. Rim: Fig. 73. The volutes encroach on the rim. Low disk base, the bottom slightly recessed. On the bottom is a cross in relief, the arms of equal length.

A.D. 50–ca. 100

700 (Fig. 73) CEL.306 & CE.1019 Atrium Building I, Room 16, Level I. Pinkish-buff clay, mottled purple-red slip. P.L. 0.138 m; Height 0.031 m; Width 0.074 m.

Eight joining fragments preserving all essential features, except the heat shield. Chipping on discus, rim, and upper side wall of oil reservoir. Condition good, except for minor rubbing of the surface on ridges. Deep concave discus with central filling hole. Low disk base. Rim: The same as 695, 698, and 699 (Fig. 73). The volutes encroach slightly on the rim. Discus relief: A wreath of two olive branches with olives and centrally ribbed leaves, tied at the top.

Cf. Menzel, 26, fig. 24; Oziol 1977, pl. 28 no. 517; Bailey 1980, pl. 29 no. Q 1010.

A.D. 50–225

701 CD.869 Basilica exterior N, Level I. Cream clay, brown slip. P.L. 0.112 m; P.H. 0.005 m; P.W. 0.054 m.

Three joining fragments preserving the heat shield, most of the discus, parts of the side wall of the oil reservoir, and the nozzle. Very worn; only traces of slip preserved. Concave discus without relief, with central filling hole. Triangular heat shield decorated with relief of an acanthus leaf that fills the triangle.

702 CEL.115 Atrium Building I, Room 15, Level I of drain B. Buff clay, dark brown slip with a metallic luster. P.L. 0.027 m; P.H. 0.028 m; P.W. 0.065 m.

Two joining fragments preserving the handle, heat shield, parts of the discus, rim, and upper side wall of the oil reservoir. Very worn; only traces of slip preserved. Deep concave discus without relief. Rim: Fig. 73. The beveled shoulder is decorated with a band of ovules. Triangular heat shield with a short stem decorated with an elaborate design of a palmette, leaves and fronds extending to the edge of the shield (see Fig. 74).

Cf. Hayes 1980, 47, pl. 21 no. 214.

703 CEL.616 Basilica exterior W, Level I. Pinkish-buff clay, red slip mottled to brown in places. P.L. 0.056 m; P.W. 0.065 m.

Two joining fragments preserving parts of the rim and nozzle. Slip worn away in places. A

144   Cosa: The Lamps

groove extends across the nozzle connecting the inner edges of the long volutes. Centered above the groove is a small punched circle.

704 C67.535 a and b Arx, west slope, Level 0-I. Buff clay, grayish-brown slip. P.L. a 0.065 m, b 0.065 m; P.W. a 0.040 m, b 0.050 m.

Two nonjoining fragments preserving the heat shield and parts of the base, side wall of the oil reservoir, discus, rim, and upper part of one long volute. Very worn. Base of three rings. Rim: Fig. 73. Triangular heat shield decorated with a thistle leaf with a central stem.

705 C68.376bis Arx, west slope. Level 0-I. Buff clay, grayish-black slip. P.L. 0.105 m; Height 0.035 m; Width 0.071 m.

Fourteen joining fragments preserving the discus, the rim, the base, parts of the long, voluted nozzle, the molded pierced handle, and the stem of a heat shield. Rim: Fig. 73. Discus relief: An angular discus with plain inner field separated from the outer zone by a ring and a narrow bead molding. The outer zone has a band of radiating grooves.

c. TRIANGULAR HEAT SHIELDS
(Figs. 74, 75)

(Catalogue Numbers 706–732)

Below are twenty-seven triangular heat shields broken away from their lamps.

25/20 B.C.–A.D. 40/45

706 (Fig. 74) CEL.81 Atrium Building I, Room 22, Level II. Cream-colored clay, brown slip with a metallic luster.

Fragment preserving a molded pierced handle and heat shield. Very worn and chipped. Decoration: A palmette springing from a pair of horizontal palm branches that curl up at their ends. On the reverse is a small vent hole.

For a similar design, see 711, 714, 715.

707 (Fig. 74) CEL.82 Atrium Building I, Room 22, Level II. Buff clay, purple-red slip with a metallic luster.

Two joining fragments preserving parts of the handle and heat shield, the left side of the shield broken away. Worn and discolored. Decoration: A palmette with leaves that curl up and in, springing from a pair of thick reversing S-spirals at its base.

Cf. 708; Deneauve, pl. 58 no. 557.

708 CEL.83 Atrium Building I, Room 22, Level II. Buff clay, red slip mottled to dark brown in places.

Two joining fragments preserving heat shield. Very worn. Decoration: the same as 707.

709 (Fig. 74) CEL.84 Atrium Building I, Room 22, Level II. Cream clay, red slip mottled to brown in places.

Fragment preserving the handle and heat shield of gentle S-curve profile. Slip very worn. Decoration: Stylized acanthus leaf filling the triangular space, with a stem extending down the stem of the shield.

Cf. Menzel, pl. 25 no. 8; Brants, pl. 9; Perlzweig 1961, pl. 2 no. 31.

710 (Fig. 74) CEL.206 Atrium Building I, Room 22, Level II. Cream clay, red slip mottled to brown in places.

Fragment preserving the center and right side of a triangular heat shield. Worn. Decoration: Small palmette, above a horizontal ridge curling up at the ends.

For the same design, see 732.

711 CEL.529 Atrium Building I, Room 22, Level II. Buff clay, red slip.

Fragment preserving part of the right side of a triangular heat shield. Worn. Decoration: Palmette springing from a pair of horizontal palm branches that curl up at their outer ends.

For a similar design, see 706, 714, 715.

712 (Fig. 75) CEL.535 Atrium Building I, Room 22, Level II. Buff clay, red slip.

Fragment preserving most of a triangular heat shield. Worn. Decoration: Palmette of seven leaves, sword-and-sickle, with lozenge base springing from a pair of horizontal palm branches that curl up at their outer ends. The fronds rise above the stalk.

For the same design, see 713, 726, 729, 731.

713 CEL.543 Atrium Building I, Room 22, Level II. Buff clay, red slip.

Two joining fragments preserving part of a triangular heat shield. Decoration: Palmette springing upward from a pair of horizontal palm branches that curl up at their ends with fronds above the stalk.

For the same design, see 712, 726, 729, 731.

Lamps with Long, Voluted Nozzles 145

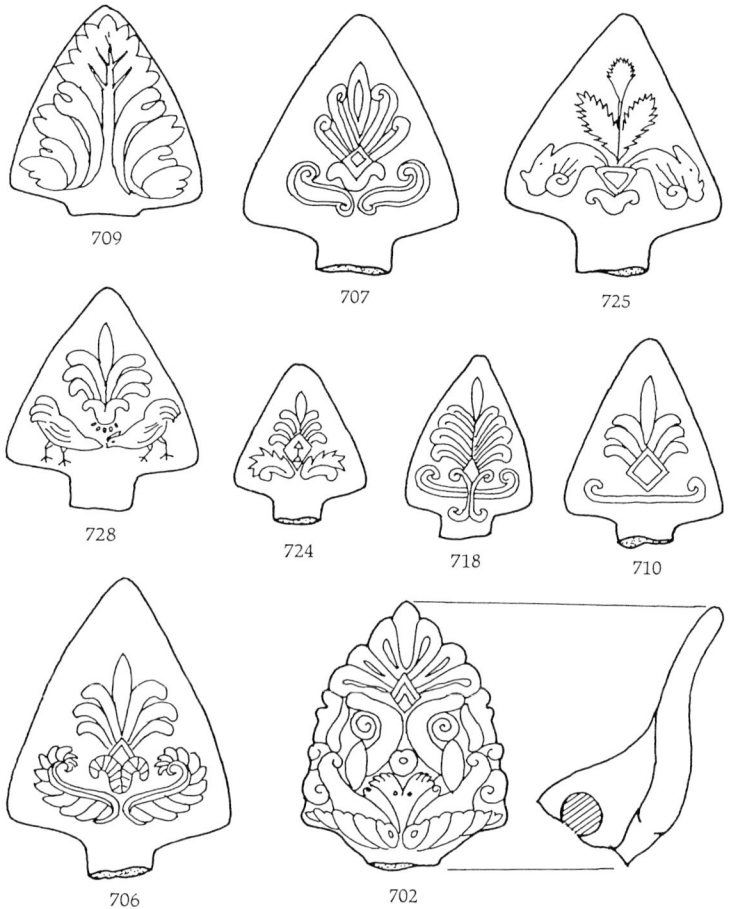

Figure 74. Triangular heat shields, scale 1:2

714 CEL.544 Atrium Building I, Room 22, Level II. Pinkish-buff clay, red slip.

Fragment preserving part of a triangular heat shield. Worn and chipped. Decoration: Palmette springing from a pair of horizontal palm branches that curl up at their outer ends with fronds below the stem.

The same design as 706, 711, and 715.

715 CEL.557 Atrium Building I, Room 22, Level II. Pinkish-buff clay, red slip.

Fragment preserving the left side of a triangular heat shield. Worn and chipped. Decoration: Palmette springing from a pair of horizontal palm branches that curl up at their outer ends with fronds below the stem.

The same design as 706, 711, and 714.

25/20 B.C.–A.D. 50

716 (Fig. 75) CD.1209 Basilica exterior, NE I, Level III. Cream clay, brown slip.

Fragment preserving part of a molded pierced handle and a triangular heat shield. Slip worn away on raised surfaces. Decoration: Palmette springing from a horizontal double-bordered ridge curled up at its ends.

717 CD.1228 Basilica exterior, NW I, Level II. Buff clay, red slip.

Fragment preserving a triangular heat shield and part of the handle. Slip rubbed on raised surfaces. Decoration: Palmette springing from a pair of horizontal palm branches that curl down at their outer ends with fronds above the stem.

718 (Fig. 74) CEL.369 Atrium Building I, Room 21, Level II. Buff clay, brown slip.

146 Cosa: The Lamps

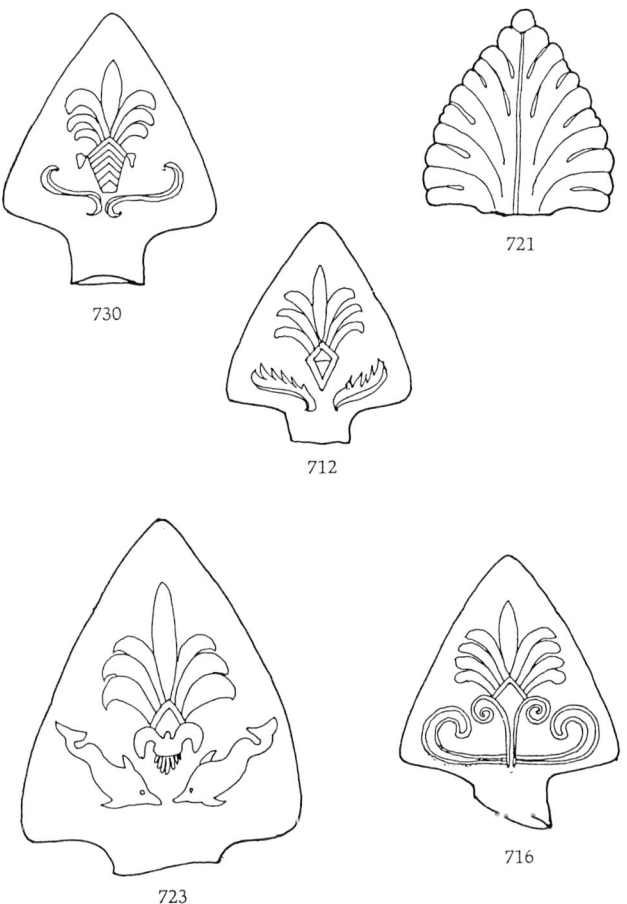

Figure 75. Triangular heat shields, scale 1:2

Fragment preserving handle and heat shield. Worn and scratched. Decoration: Palmette, rising from a stem that divides into scrolls at both ends. This is superimposed on a double horizontal ridge that curls up at its ends.

Cf. 722; Szentléleky 1969, no. 56; Deneauve 1969, pl. 58 no. 563.

719 CEL.372 Atrium Building I, Room 21, Level II. Cream clay, slip mottled dark to light brown.

Fragment preserving a triangular heat shield of gentle S-profile. Very worn and chipped. Decoration: Acanthus leaf with the stem extending down the stem of the shield. The stylized leaf fills the triangle.

For the same design, see 720; for a similar design, see 709.

720 CEL.531 Atrium Building I, Room 21, Level II. Buff clay, dark brown slip.

Fragment preserving part of a triangular heat shield. Very worn; no trace of slip preserved. Decoration: The same as 719.

A.D. 50–ca. 100

721 (Fig. 75) C70.669 V-D House of the Skeleton, Room 17, Sounding I, Level 0. Cream clay, brown slip.

Fragment preserving a triangular heat shield of gentle S-curve profile, broken from the lamp at the top of the stem. Shield in the shape of a thistle leaf, the edge of the shield cut to follow the shape of the leaf.

This shield is in the antiquarium at Cosa.

722 CD.1233 Basilica exterior, N, Level II. Cream clay, grayish-brown slip with a metallic luster.

Fragment preserving most of a large triangular

heat shield, the tip and part of the molded handle broken away. Worn; only traces of slip preserved. Decoration: Palmette, cradled at the base, rising between a pair of large scrolls terminating vertical ridges that curl in scrolls in the opposite direction below.

See 718 for a smaller version of the same design.

723 (Fig. 75) CE.2214 Atrium Building I, Rooms 15/16, Level I. Pinkish-buff clay, thin, red slip.

Two nonjoining fragments preserving parts of a triangular heat shield. Decoration: Palmette flanked at the base by a pair of confronted dolphins.

For heat shields with dolphins, see Bailey 1980, pl. 36 no. Q 1048; Oziol, pl. 28, figs. 518, 519.

724 (Fig. 74) CEL.160 Atrium Building I, Room 11, Level I. Pinkish-buff clay, orange-red slip.

Fragment preserving the handle and heat shield. Very worn and encrusted. Decoration: Palmette rising from a pair of thick, short palm branches that curl down at their ends with fronds above the stalk.

For the same design, see Menzel, pl. 25 no. 1; Bruneau, pl. 35 no. 4749.

725 (Fig. 74) CEL.217 Atrium Building I, Room 21, Level I. Pinkish-buff clay, red slip.

Fragment preserving handle and triangular heat shield. Very worn and encrusted. Decoration: Thistlelike plant with a flower at the top above a pair of saw-toothed leaves, with curious half-animal, half-vegetable forms flanking the triangular base.

See Broneer 1930, 170, fig. 96 for a similar design.

726 CEL.533 Atrium Building I, Room 21, Level I. Cream clay, brown slip.

Fragment preserving part of a triangular heat shield. Worn; only traces of slip preserved. Decoration: Palmette springing from a pair of horizontal palm branches that curl up at their outer ends, with fronds above the stems.

For the same design, see 712.

727 C68.471 V,VI-D/E House of the Birds, Room 3, cesspit, Level I. Buff clay, red slip mottled to orange-red in places.

Fragment preserving a triangular heat shield of slightly concave profile and part of the handle. Worn, encrusted. Decoration: Acanthus leaf that fills the triangle with the outer edge of the shield cut following the jagged form of the leaf.

Cf. 709.

A.D. 50–225

728 (Fig. 74) CB.793 Capitolium exterior, S, Surface. Buff clay, reddish-brown slip.

Decoration: Palmette flanked at the base by a pair of chickens, the heads down and beaks touching.

729 CEL.263 Atrium Building I, Room 14, Level I. Buff clay, red slip.

Fragment preserving parts of a handle and the right side of a triangular heat shield. Slightly worn. Decoration: Palmette rising from a pair of horizontal palm branches that curl up at their outer ends, with fronds above the stem, as on 712.

730 (Fig. 75) CEL.626 Basilica exterior, W I, Level I. Pinkish-buff clay, red slip.

Fragment preserving the upper right side of a triangular heat shield. Worn and chipped. Decoration: Palmette above a pair of reversing S-spirals.

731 C67.483 Arx, W slope, Level 0. Cream clay, slip mottled brown to black.

Fragment preserving part of a triangular heat shield. Worn. Decoration: Palmette springing from a pair of horizontal palm branches curled up at their ends with fronds above the stem.

732 C68.401 V-D, East House, Room 2, "the corridor," Level 0-B. Pinkish-buff clay, red slip.

Fragment preserving parts of a handle and a triangular heat shield. Worn and chipped. Decoration: Palmette rising from a wide horizontal ridge that curls up at the outer ends, as on 710.

d. LUNATE HEAT SHIELDS
(Fig. 76)

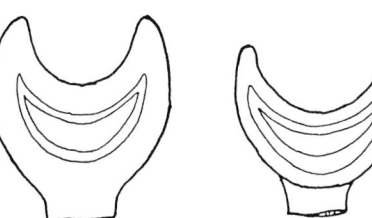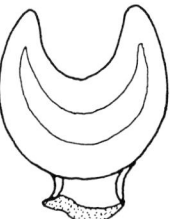

Figure 76. Lunate heat shields, scale 1:2

Twenty-six lunate heat shields have been found at Cosa broken from their lamps. Eight are from levels dated 25/20 B.C.–A.D. 40/45. Seven come from contexts dated 25/20 B.C.–A.D. 50. Nine are from levels dated A.D. 50–ca. 100. The remaining two can be only loosely dated A.D. 50–225. Only three of these shields were drawn, showing the three variations represented. Nineteen were found in Atrium Building I, Rooms 4, 11, 21, and 22. Seven were recovered from the exterior south of the Capitolium (see Fig. 76).

e. HEAT SHIELDS WITHOUT KNOWN PARALLELS AT COSA
(Fig. 77)

(Catalogue Numbers 733–735)

A.D. 50–ca. 100

733 (Fig. 77) CD.1232 Basilica exterior, N, Level II. Cream clay, light brown slip. Length of shield 0.070 m; Width 0.056 m; Maximum Thickness 0.024 m.

Fragment preserving a heat shield and part of the handle. Slip very worn; crevices in the fabric. A thick bulbous shield, the flat top face divided in half by a vertical groove, around which a broad lentoid shape frames a lanceolate inset.

For parallels, see Bachofen, pl. 18 no. 4; Bailey 1980, pl. 32 no. Q 1025, pl. 36 no. Q 1050; Farka 1977, pl. 55 no. 620, pl. 18 no. 620 (drawing); Leibundgut 1977, pl. 7 no. 368; Menzel, fig. 25 no. 11.

734 (Fig. 77) CEL.311 Atrium Building I, Room 16, Level I. Pinkish-buff clay, red slip. Length of shield 0.061 m; Width 0.060 m.

Fragment preserving the heat shield and part of the molded pierced handle. Slip worn and chipped on raised edges. Shield in the form of a siren, frontal, with human head and breast and bird body. The wings are lifted in a lunate form; the head projects above the crescent. The figure appears to stand on the stem of the heat shield. The feathers of the wings are indicated by five curved ridges.

For a similar siren shield, see Deneauve 1969, pl. 59 no. 574. The ridges that indicate feathers completely cover the crescent in the Carthage example, instead of only partially, as on the Cosan shield.

735 (Fig. 77) C68.270 V-D House of the Skeleton, 3.70 NE x 13.75 SE, Level 0. Buff clay, reddish-brown slip. Length of shield 0.061 m; Width 0.034 m.

Fragment preserving a heat shield and part of its stem. Shield in the form of a female head with an elaborate hairdress rising to great height and width, with a row of curls over the forehead and two rows of combs centered one over the other.

Cf. Bailey 1980, 221, pl. 36 no. Q 1051.

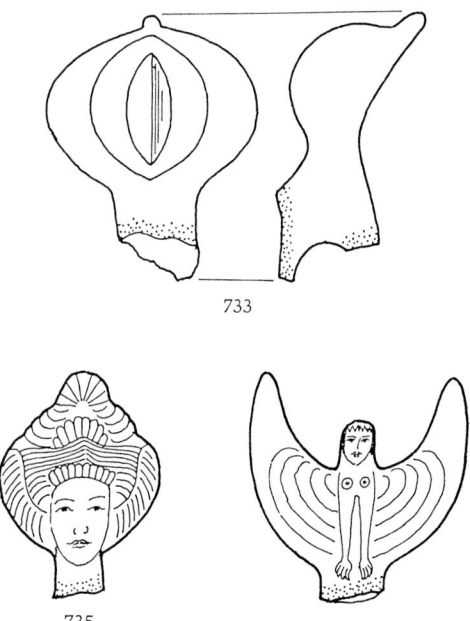

Figure 77. Heat shields without known parallels at Cosa, scale 1:2

16. FAT LAMPS, OR LAMPS WITH SHORT, ROUNDED, UNVOLUTED NOZZLES

(Figs. 78–101)

(Catalogue Numbers 736–983)
(Bailey Types O, P, and Q; Brants Type XVII; Broneer Type XXV; Dressel Forms 17, 18, 19, 24, and 27; Deneauve Types VII and VIII, A to D; Evelein Type V; Gualandi Genito Groups A, B, and C; Goethert-Polaschek Type XIX; Heres Type E with subgroups A to F; Ivanyi Type VII; Leibundgut Form XX; Loeschcke Type VIII; Niessen Type X; Ponsich Type III; Walters Forms 96 and 100; Vessberg Types 13, 14, and 15)

The last of the series of fine Julio-Claudian Picture Lamps to be developed was Loeschcke Type VIII, or Fat Lamps. Two hundred forty-seven examples of this type found at Cosa have been catalogued. They appear at Cosa earliest in the sealed storeroom of Atrium Building I in a context dated 25/20 B.C.–A.D. 40/45 and continued in use until the final days of the town. This lamp type has a shallow circular body with a concave discus and a simple rim with beveled shoulder. The shoulder takes up part of the lamp top, but leaves ample room for relief decoration on the discus. The distinctive feature of the type is a very short, rounded nozzle without volutes that occupies part of the shoulder and projects only slightly beyond the body of the lamp. This new nozzle was not so prone to breakage as the long, voluted nozzles of the preceding types, and the new form quickly became dominant. These lamps continued to be popular for several centuries throughout the Roman empire.

All early examples of the Fat Lamp were carefully made of finely levigated clay, cream to buff in color. The fabric is thin, and all have a slip, usually red or brown. Some of the darker slips have a metallic luster. The shoulders of early Fat Lamps are narrow. They gradually became wider, and by the late second century they assumed almost as much importance as the discus, with elaborate relief decoration. All have a small air hole, usually on the discus near the nozzle. The earliest examples of this lamp do not have handles. Only two examples with molded handles date before A.D. 50. By the early Neronian period, however, most lamps of this type had a pierced molded handle.[1] The handle is set on the shoulder opposite the nozzle. It projects beyond the body and extends down the lower side wall of the oil reservoir as a spine, ending in a point near the base. The handle has two grooves on the front that converge near the crest and continue down the spine as a single groove.

Only three fragments of bases have been found in a context that is dated before A.D. 50. One is unprofiled; two are low disk bases. The later lamps of this type, where the bases have been preserved, all have ring bases. Many have impressed signatures.

Seven forms of these short nozzles have been classified (Fig. 78). Heres's classification seems to fit the Cosan examples best, with the exception of his no. 7, but it is impossible to classify the Cosan Fat Lamps by their nozzles, since so few are preserved, and the only organization possible is by shoulder decoration. The classifications of Heres, Loeschcke, Bailey, and the oth-

---

1. From the evidence of the sealed storeroom in Atrium Building I at Cosa, the molded handle seems to have been introduced shortly before A.D. 40/45. Ten lamps from Trier and two in the Berlin Museum have a bust of Agrippina on the discus; they all have molded handles. These were proba- bly made after the death of Claudius in A.D. 54, but while Agrippina was still alive. Within the decade following the collapse of the Basilica wall in A.D. 40/45, molded handles became common.

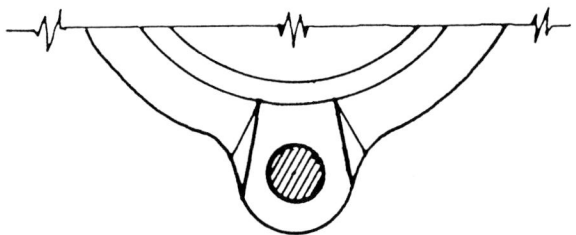

Heres type Ea, Loeschcke R,
Bailey type O, group ii,

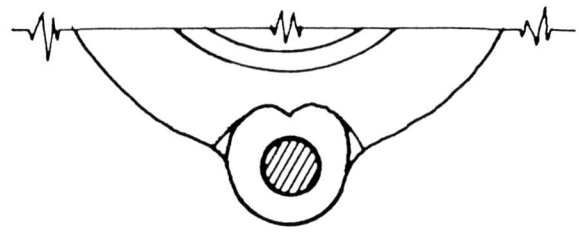

Heres type Ee, Loeschcke H,
Bailey type Q.

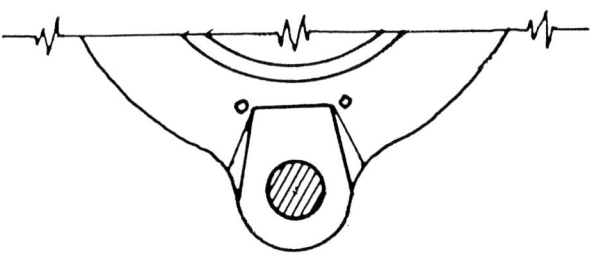

Heres type Eb, Loeschcke L 1,
Bailey type P.

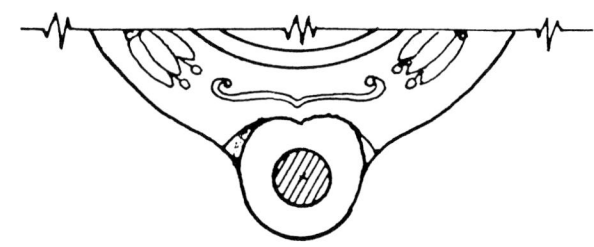

Heres type Ef
Bailey type Q, group viii.

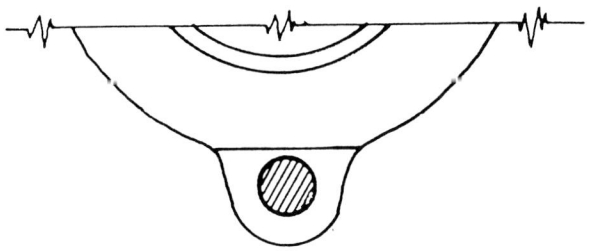

Heres type Ec, Loeschcke L 2,
Bailey type O, group iii.

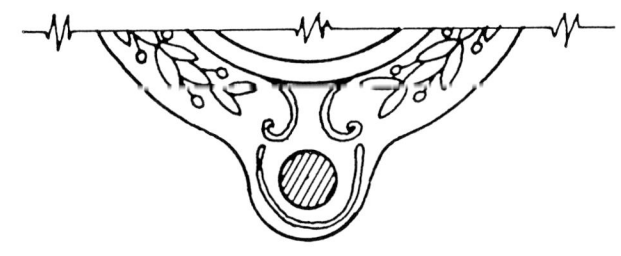

Bailey type Q, group viii.

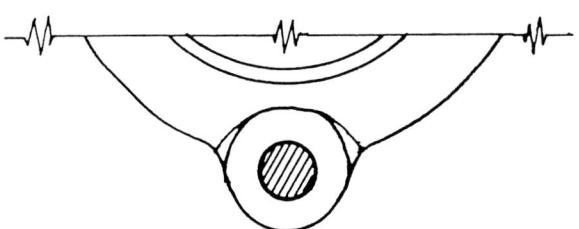

Heres type Ed, Loeschcke K,
Bailey type O, group i.

Figure 78. Fat Lamps: Nozzle classification, reduced

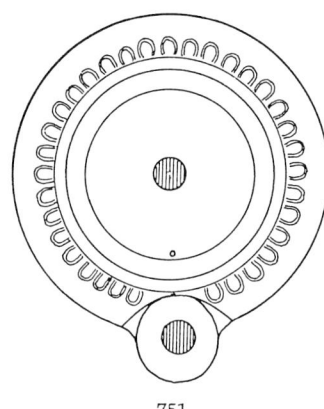

751

Figure 79. Fat Lamps: a. Shoulders decorated with a band of ovules, scale 1:2

ers accompany the drawings illustrating the different nozzle forms in Fig. 78.

Of the two hundred forty-nine Fat Lamps found at Cosa, twenty are from levels dated 25/20 B.C.–A.D. 40/45. Eleven are from contexts dated 25/20 B.C.–A.D. 50. Fifty-four are from levels dated A.D. 50–100, ninety-one from levels dated A.D. 100–225, and ten from contexts dated from the late second century A.D. to 225. Sixty-three are from contexts of A.D. 225–416, the end of Cosa as a town. Thus the archaeological evidence shows that the Fat Lamps were a favored type at Cosa during the first four centuries of the Roman empire.

a. FAT LAMPS: SHOULDERS DECORATED WITH A BAND OF OVULES
(Fig. 79)

(Catalogue Numbers 736–772)

The thirty-seven lamps in this group all have a band of ovules decorating the top of the narrow shoulder. Seventeen are earlier and of better quality with narrower shoulders. The other twenty are coarser and have wider shoulders. Some have handles; some do not. Only four examples preserve their nozzles. One is Heres Type E a; two are E b; and one is E e; they are Bailey Type O, Groups i, ii, iii.

25/20 B.C.–A.D. 40/45

736 CEL.14 Atrium Building I, Room 22, Level II. Buff clay, dark brown slip with a metallic luster.
   Fragment preserving parts of a rim and a plain discus. Very worn.

737 CEL.15 Atrium Building I, Room 22, Level II. Cream clay, black slip, discolored.
   Fragment preserving parts of a plain discus. Worn.

738 CEL.16 Atrium Building I, Room 22, Level II. Buff clay, red slip mottled to dark brown in places.
   Fragment preserving parts of a rim and a plain discus. Surface rubbed.

739 CEL.25 Atrium Building I, Room 22, Level II. Cream clay, black slip. P.L. 0.035 m; P.W. 0.038 m.
   Fragment preserving parts of a rim and a decorated discus. Surface worn on high relief. Angular discus; three rings separate the inner level zone from the outer zone that slopes up to two framing rings, beyond which a bead molding separates the discus from the shoulder.

740 CEL.26 Atrium Building I, Room 22, Level II. Buff clay, red slip mottled to black in places. P.L. 0.040 m; P.W. 0.012 m.
   Fragment preserving parts of a rim and a plain discus. Slip rubbed and chipped. Nozzle, partially preserved: Heres Type E b, or Loeschcke L 1.

741 CEL.27 Atrium Building I, Room 22, Level II. Cream clay, red slip mottled to brown and black in places. P.L. 0.053 m; Height 0.035 m; P.W. 0.041 m.
   Fragment preserving parts of a rim, a handle, and a plain discus. Worn. Molded pierced handle with two grooves that converge at the crest.

742 CEL.38 Atrium Building I, Room 22, Level II. Buff clay, orange-red slip.
   Fragment preserving parts of the discus and rim. Discus relief: Rosette of four hearts. For discus relief, see Maccario 1980, pl. 18 no. 229 (with five hearts); Brugnoli/De Carolis 1977, pl. 15 no. 1; Goethert-Polaschek 1985, pl. 72 no. 696.

743 (Pl. VII) CEL.42 Atrium Building I, Room 22, Level II. Buff clay, dark slip, only traces preserved. P.L. 0.052 m; Width 0.080 m.
   Four joining fragments preserving parts of the discus and rim. Chipped and worn. Narrow beveled shoulder; no handle. Discus separated from the shoulder by a narrow bead molding. Discus relief: A wreath of two oak branches bound

together at the top, only partially preserved.
See Bailey 1980, pl. 57 no. Q 1212 for a similar lamp, but with a handle; Goethert-Polaschek 1985, pl. 72 no. 692.

744 CEL.327 Atrium Building I, Room 22, Level II. Cream clay, purplish-brown slip. P.L. 0.036 m; P.W. 0.018 m.
Fragment preserving parts of a rim and a plain discus.

745 CEL.566 Atrium Building I, Room 22, Level II. Buff clay, brown slip.
Fragment preserving parts of a rim and a plain discus. Very worn.

746 CEL.568 Atrium Building I, Room 22, Level II. Cream clay, dark slip, only traces preserved.
Fragment preserving parts of a rim and a plain discus. Surface rubbed.

25/20 B.C.–A.D. 50

747 CEL.368 Atrium Building I, Room 21, Level II. Cream clay, red slip mottled to brown in places. P.L. 0.046 m; P.H. 0.011 m; P.W. 0.039 m.
Three joining fragments preserving parts of a rim and a plain discus. Slip rubbed.

A.D. 50–ca. 100

748 CEL.157 Atrium Building I, Room 11, Level I. Cream clay, brown slip. P.L. 0.076 m; P.W. 0.045 m.
Three joining fragments preserving parts of a rim and a plain discus. Very worn.

749 CEL.246 Atrium Building I, Room 6, Level I. Cream clay, brownish-red slip. P.L. 0.037 m; P.W. 0.022 m.
Fragment preserving parts of a rim and a plain discus. Surface rubbed.

750 CEL.567 Atrium Building I, Room 6, Level I. Cream clay, dark brown slip. P.L. 0.046 m; P.W. 0.023 m.
Fragment preserving parts of a rim and a plain discus. Worn.

751 (Fig. 79) CEL.593 a and b Basilica exterior, NW 2, Level II. Cream clay, dark brown slip. P.L. 0.091 m; P.H. 0.025 m; P.W. 0.088 m.
Seven fragments, six joining, preserving parts of a plain discus, rim, and nozzle. Surface worn. Nozzle: Heres Type E a; Loeschcke R.

All the Fat Lamps of Loeschcke type VIII listed above have narrow rounded shoulders with carefully spaced ovules around the top of the shoulder. Most probably did not have a handle. The lamps listed below are not so well made, and probably most of them had a molded pierced handle. Sometimes the ovules are not so carefully spaced, and the shoulder is wider.

A.D. 100–225

752 CD.1252 Basilica exterior, NE 3, Level I. Cream clay, light brown slip. P.L. 0.041 m; P.W. 0.038 m.
Fragment preserving parts of a rim and a plain discus, shoulder, and handle. Slip worn away in places. Crevices in fabric. Handle delicately molded, with two grooves on the face converging at the crest.

753 CEL.561 Atrium Building I, Room 25 C, Level II. Buff clay, orange slip. P.L. 0.046 m; P.W. 0.016 m.
Fragment preserving part of a rim. Very worn, made from an old worn mold.

754 CEL.609 Basilica exterior, NW 2, Level III. Orange-red clay, red slip. P.L. 0.024 m; P.W. 0.032 m.
Fragment preserving part of a rim and a decorated discus. Very worn; made from an old worn mold. Discus relief: Bust of Athena with a Corinthian helmet pushed back from face, identical with 765.
Cf. Bailey 1988, 7 nos. Q 3258–61; Menzel, nos. 536, 545; Goldman/Jones, pl. 102 no. 209; Broneer 1930, pl. 12 no. 582.

755 CEL.1934 Atrium Building I, Room 25 B, Level III. Buff clay, red slip. P.L. 0.025 m; P.W. 0.027 m.
Fragment preserving parts of the rim and upper side wall of the oil reservoir. Surface rubbed.

756 CF.1660 Atrium Building I, Room 25 D, Level II. Orange-buff clay, red slip. P.L. 0.048 m; Height 0.023 m; P.W. 0.046 m.
Fragment preserving parts of the rim, side wall of the oil reservoir, base, and handle. Slip very worn. Excess clay trimmed away very carelessly at the mold join. Molded pierced handle with two grooves on the face converging at the crest and extending down the spine as a single groove. There is a raised dot on either side of the handle just before the band of ovules.

757 CF.1644 Atrium Building I, Room 25 D, Level II. Buff clay, orange slip. P.L. 0.083 m; Height 0.026 m; Width 0.084 m.
Four joining fragments preserving all but part of the nozzle. Slip rubbed. Nozzle: Heres Type E

b, Loeschcke L 1. Molded pierced handle with two grooves converging at the crest and extending down the spine of the handle at the rear as a single groove. Disk base, slightly concave, with a small stamped pelta (see Fig. 136). Discus relief: Four pointed leaves, bordered, forming a rosette around the central filling hole. Filling hole carelessly punched slightly off center.

For this relief, see Gualandi Genito 1986, pl. 45 no. 331.

758 CF.1647 Atrium Building I, Room 25 D, Level II. Buff clay, orange slip. P.L. 0.083 m; Height 0.028 m; P.W. 0.079 m.

Four joining fragments preserving the handle, parts of the discus, rim, side wall of the oil reservoir, and unprofiled base. Surface rubbed; made from an old worn mold. Discus relief: A rosette of sixteen petals around the central filling hole; very faint.

759 CF.1937 Atrium Building I, Room 25, Level II. Grayish-buff clay, slip worn away. P.L. 0.046 m; P.W. 0.053 m.

Fragment preserving parts of discus and rim. Very worn. Discus relief: An animal, perhaps a lion, moving left; too little survives for certain identification.

Late Second Century–A.D. 225

760 CF.69 Atrium Building I, Room 16, exterior, Level I. Buff clay, orange-red slip. Length 0.087 m; Height 0.023 m; Width 0.063 m.

Complete lamp, made from an old worn mold. The surface is pitted and scratched. Heart-shaped nozzle, Heres Type E e, Loeschcke Type H. Shoulder decorated with elongated ovules. Ring base, within which is impressed an illegible signature with a bull's eye centered above and below it. Discus relief: Rosette, the design too faint to determine the number of petals.

Cf. Joly 1974, pl. 25 no. 655; Deneauve, pl. 84 no. 929, pl. 85 no. 932. The ovules on the shoulders of the Deneauve lamps are as long as those on 760.

761 CF.831 Atrium Building I, Room 25, Level I. Pinkish-buff clay, red slip. P.L. 0.033 m; P.W. 0.024 m.

Fragment preserving parts of a rim and a plain discus. Surface worn. Rim: The edge of the discus rises above the shoulder in an unprofiled margin.

762 CF.1924 Atrium Building I, Room 25, Level I. Cream clay, slip worn away. P.L. 0.029 m; P.W. 0.028 m.

Fragment preserving parts of a rim and a plain discus. Very worn. Rim: The edge of the discus rises above the shoulder forming an unprofiled margin.

763 CF.1928 Atrium Building I, Room 25, Level II. Cream clay, brown slip. P.L. 0.067 m; P.H. 0.016 m; P.W. 0.027 m.

Two joining fragments preserving parts of a rim, and the upper side wall of the oil reservoir and a plain discus. Worn; only traces of slip preserved.

764 CF.1979 Atrium Building I, Room 25 exterior NW, Level II. Buff clay, orange slip mottled to brown in places.

Fragment preserving parts of the shoulder and handle. Slip rubbed. Molded pierced handle with two grooves converging at the crest, but on this lamp a groove does not continue down the spine. Discus relief: None preserved.

765 CF.2119 Atrium Building I, Room 25 exterior, Level II. Buff clay, orange slip mottled to dark brown in places. P.L. 0.063 m; P.W. 0.054 m.

Fragment preserving parts of the discus, rim, and handle. Very worn; made from a worn mold. Discus relief: Bust of Athena in left profile, with Corinthian helmet pushed back from face, as on 754.

Late Second Century–A.D. 416

766 CEL.562 Atrium Building I, Room 25 exterior, Wall cleaning. Pinkish-buff clay, slip worn away. P.L. 0.022 m; P.W. 0.028 m.

Fragment preserving parts of the rim and a plain discus. Very worn.

767 (Pl. II) CF.2016 Atrium Building I, Room 25 exterior, Level I. Buff clay, orange slip. P.L. 0.056 m; P.W. 0.035 m.

Fragment preserving parts of the discus and rim. Slip worn. The ovules are more widely spaced than is usual. Discus relief: On the left side of the discus a nude warrior, with a cloak over his left shoulder and a band around his upper right arm, wears a crested helmet with long cheek pieces. Both arms down at sides; the right hand holds an undecipherable object, the left a spear. The feet and lower legs are broken away. *Comparanda* show a Fortuna on the right side of the discus.

See 771 for a part of the Fortuna figure on a

lamp made from the same (or same generation) mold. Cf. Heres 1972a, pl. 35 no. 312; Brants, pl. 5 no. 953.

768 (Pl. II) CF.2019 Atrium Buiding I, Room 25 exterior, Level I. Buff clay, red slip. P.L. 0.053 m; P.W. 0.066 m.

Two joining fragments preserving most of the discus and parts of the rim. Very worn; only traces of slip preserved. Made from an old worn mold. The ovules are widely and unevenly spaced. Discus relief: Female bust in right profile, wearing a laurel wreath and a mantle fastened on breast. The filling hole is punched below and to the left of the head and neck. A tiny circular air hole is at the bottom edge of the discus. The head projects beyond the edge of the discus. This seems to be copied from a coin of the classical period, but the archetype is unknown, and the lamp is, so far as is known, unique.

769 CF.2022 Atrium Building I, Room 25 exterior, Level I. Buff clay, orange-red slip. P.L. 0.058 m; P.W. 0.061 m.

Fragment preserving parts of the discus, rim, and handle. Slip rubbed. Handle has the usual two grooves that converge on the crest and extend down the spine as a single groove. Discus relief: Too little survives to identify.

770 CF.2114 Atrium Building I, Room 25 exterior, Level I. Grayish-buff clay, red slip. P.L. 0.052 m; P.W. 0.054 m.

Fragment preserving parts of the discus, rim, and handle. Very worn, only traces of slip preserved. Molded pierced handle with two grooves converging on the crest. Discus relief: Too fragmentary to identify.

771 (Pl. II) CF.2120 a and b Atrium Building I, Room 25 exterior, Level II. Buff clay, slip mottled from yellow to brown. P.L. a 0.057 m, b 0.061 m; P.H. 0.025 m; P.W. a 0.045 m, b 0.024 m.

Two nonjoining fragments preserving parts of the discus, rim, and nozzle. Slip rubbed on raised surfaces. Bubbles in grooves of the rim. Nozzle: Heres Type E b, Loeschcke Type L 1. There are bull's eyes at the ends of the groove at the top of the nozzle. The ovules on the shoulder are more widely spaced than is usual. Discus relief: On fragment a are two feet with long drapery blowing to the right. The ground line is indicated. On fragment b is part of the nude torso of a warrior, as on 767. The lower legs and feet, the left shoulder, and part of the head are broken away. This lamp was made from the same (or same generation) mold as 767.

772 CF.2129 Atrium Building I, Room 25 exterior, Level II. Buff clay, orange slip. P.L. 0.049 m; Height 0.028 m; P.W. 0.057 m.

Fragment preserving the handle and parts of the rim, side wall of the oil reservoir, and base. Surface worn. Ring base. Handle has the usual two grooves that converge on the crest and extend down the spine as a single groove.

b. FAT LAMPS: DECORATED DISCI AND PLAIN SHOULDERS
(Figs. 80–82)
(Catalogue Numbers 773–814)

25/20 B.C.–A.D. 40/45

773 CEL.21 Atrium Building I, Room 22, Level II. Cream clay, light reddish-brown slip. P.L. 0.037 m; Width 0.068 m.

Three joining fragments preserving parts of the discus and rim. Surface worn and chipped. Discus set off from the narrow shoulder by a groove. Discus relief: A crescent moon partially encircles the central filling hole.

Cf. Bailey 1980, pl. 70 no. Q 1307; Deneauve 1969, pl. 70 nos. 739–41 (but these also have a star); Gualandi Genito 1986, pl. 42 no. 312 (also with a star); Szentléleky 1969, no. 148; Goldman/Jones 1950, pl. 102 no. 203.

774 CEL.37 Atrium Building I, Room 22, Level II. Buff clay, red slip. P.L. 0.057 m; P.H. 0.014 m; P.W. 0.024 m.

Fragment preserving parts of the discus and rim. Worn. Nozzle: Heart-shaped, Heres Type E e; Loeschcke, Type H. Discus relief: Rosette of fourteen concave petals, parts of seven preserved.

775 (Pl. VIII; Fig. 82) CEL.45 Atrium Building I, Room 22, Level II. Cream clay, purplish-brown slip with a metallic luster. P.L. 0.063 m; P.H. 0.023 m; Width 0.075 m.

Three joining fragments preserving parts of the discus, rim, upper side wall of the oil reservoir, and nozzle. Slip very worn. Rim: An inner ring

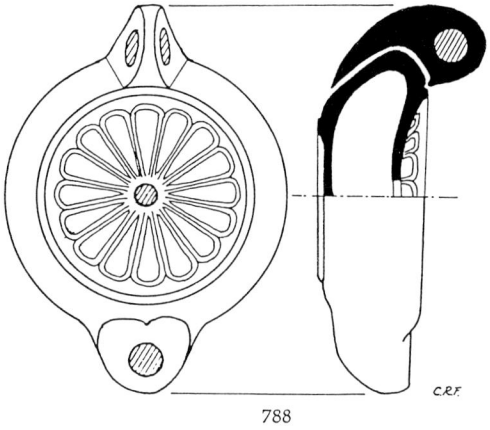

788

Figure 80.

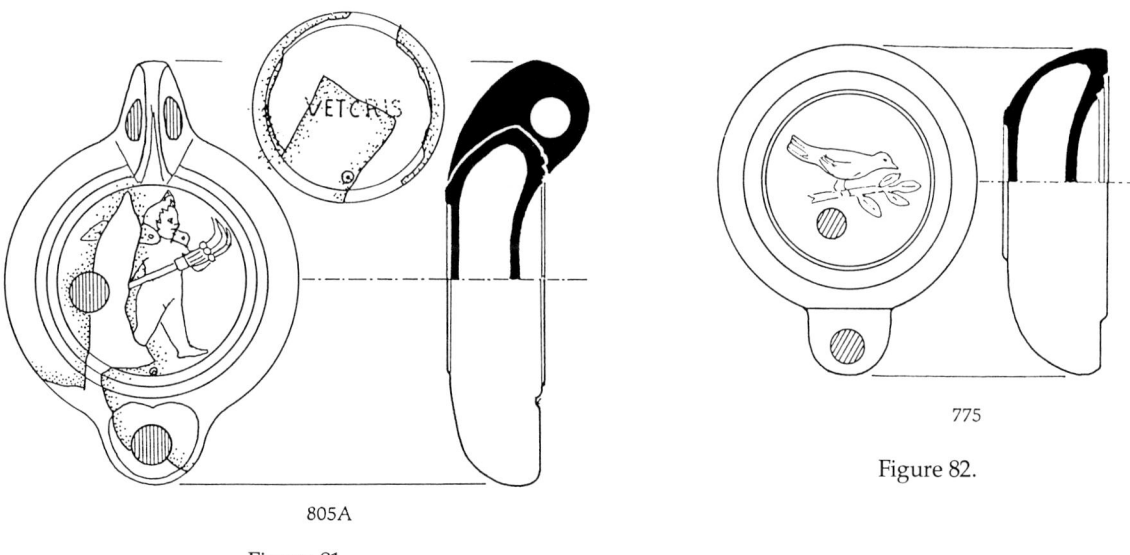

805A

Figure 81.

775

Figure 82.

Figures 80–82. Fat Lamps: b. Decorated discus and plain shoulder, scale 1:2

and a bead molding sloping up to a plain outer fillet. The nozzle is separated from the edge of the shoulder by a straight groove, Heres Type E c, Loeschcke Type L 2. Discus relief: A bird facing right on a spray of leaves. The small filling hole is punched below the relief.

For another example of this relief, see Bailey 1965, pl. 4 no. 11, pl. 5 nos. 47, 48, 68; Bailey 1980, pl. 70 no. Q 1310; Ponsich 1963, pl. 8 no. 83; Deneauve 1969, pl. 53 nos. 522–23.

776 CEL.207 Atrium Building I, Room 22, Level II. Cream clay, dark brown slip with a metallic luster. P.L. 0.091 m; P.H. 0.019 m; P.W. 0.063 m.

Four joining fragments preserving the nozzle, parts of the discus, and rim. Slip rubbed and discolored. Nozzle heart-shaped, Heres Type E e; Loeschcke Type H. Discus relief: Rosette of fourteen concave petals, parts of seven preserved; made from the same (or same generation) mold as 774.

Cf. Zaccaria Ruggiu 1977, pl. 115 no. 12; Heres 1972a, pl. 37 no. 330; Maccario, pl. 18 no. 225.

777 CEL.319 Atrium Building I, Room 22, Level II. Cream clay, purplish-brown slip with a metallic luster. P.L. 0.047 m; P.W. 0.035 m.

Two joining fragments preserving parts of the discus and rim. Slip worn. Discus relief: Rosette of eight large bordered tongues or petals, parts of two preserved.

778 CEL.328 Atrium Building I, Room 22, Level II. Cream clay, purplish-brown slip. P.L. 0.039 m; P.W. 0.026 m.

Fragment preserving parts of the discus and rim. Slip rubbed. Discus relief: the same as 774, 776.

779 CEL.335 Atrium Building I, Room 22, Level II. Cream clay, dark slip, only traces preserved. P.L. 0.058 m; P.H. 0.019 m; P.W. 0.024 m.

Fragment preserving parts of the discus and rim. Slip very rubbed. Discus relief: Laurel wreath, four leaves preserved.

Cf. Bailey 1980, pl. 64 nos. Q 1253, Q 1254.

25/20 B.C.–A.D. 50

780 CEL.607 Basilica exterior, NW 2, Level III. Buff clay, red slip. P.L. 0.058 m; P.H. 0.024 m; P.W. 0.072 m.

Fragment preserving the nozzle and parts of the discus and rim. Slip rubbed. Nozzle: Heres Type E b, Loeschcke Type L 1. Discus relief: Bust of Jupiter, frontal, with eagle on a thunderbolt below, only the thunderbolt and eagle's feet preserved.

For complete examples of this relief, see Brants 1913, pl. 5 no. 865; Bailey 1980, pl. 64 nos. Q 1250, Q 1251; Heres 1972a, pl. 28 no. 230, pl. 61 nos. 580–81; Zaccaria Ruggiu 1977, pl. 289 no. 10.

781 CEL.611 Basilica exterior, NW 2, Level III. Orange-buff clay, mottled orange slip. P.L. 0.037 m; P.H. 0.012 m; P.W. 0.036 m.

Fragment preserving parts of the plain [?] discus, rim, and nozzle. Worn. Smoke-blackened around the wick hole. Nozzle: Heres Type E d, Loeschcke Type K.

A.D. 50–ca. 100

782 C70.678 Sewer at the intersection of Streets 5 and M. Buff clay, purplish-red slip.

Two joining fragments preserving parts of the discus, rim, and nozzle. Worn. Nozzle: Short, rounded with groove across the top, Heres Type E b, Loeschcke Type L 1. Discus relief: Gladiator to right, the head, lower right leg, and right hand preserved. He holds a dagger or short sword vertically behind his body in his right hand and wears a crested helmet. His legs are bandaged, and a cloak falls behind the body.

783 CEL.191 Atrium Building I, Room 4, Level I. Cream clay, red slip mottled to black in places.

Four joining fragments preserving the handle, parts of the shoulder, side wall of the oil reservoir, and base. Slip rubbed. Disk base inscribed *LMVN*. . . This could be completed *LMVNPHILI*, *EMVNSVC*, or *LMVNTHRE* (see Fig. 140).

For this signature, see 963; Bailey 1980, pl. 61 no. Q 1237, pl. 76 no. Q 1321; also *CIL* 2.6526.38, *CIL* 8.22644.223, *CIL* 11.6699.123, *CIL* 13.10001.217, *CIL* 15.6562.

784 CEL.294 Atrium Building I, Room 21, Level I. Cream clay, brown slip. P.L. 0.085 m; Width 0.088 m.

Five fragments, two joining and three nonjoining, preserving most of the rim and parts of the discus and nozzle. Slip very worn. Nozzle: Heres Type E d, Loeschcke Type K. Discus relief: A rosette of fourteen concave petals around the central filling hole.

785 CEL.389 Atrium Building I, Room 11, Level I. Buff clay, red slip. P.L. 0.025 m; P.W. 0.031 m.

Discus relief: None preserved.

786 CEL.464 Atrium Building I, Room 11, Level I. Buff clay, dark brown slip. P.L. 0.042 m; P.H. 0.026 m; P.W. 0.045 m.

Fragment preserving parts of the discus, rim, and handle. Very worn. The handle has two grooves that converge at the crest, but the usual single groove does not extend down the spine. Discus relief: At the top of the discus is a small head with a crescent moon at the top of the forehead. The complete relief might show Selene and Endymion.

787 CEL.465 Atrium Building I, Room 11, Level I. Cream clay, red slip. P.L. 0.045 m; P.W. 0.020 m.

Fragment preserving parts of the right side of the discus and rim. Surface rubbed. Discus relief: The bridled head and one forefoot of a galloping horse, moving right, the rest broken away.

788 (Fig. 80) CEL.483 Atrium Building I, Room 11, Level I. Buff clay, red slip mottled to brown and black in places. P.L. 0.069 m; P.W. 0.038 m.

Two joining fragments preserving parts of the discus, rim, and nozzle. Very worn. Nozzle: heart-shaped, Heres Type E e, Loeschcke Type H. Discus relief: Rosette of sixteen concave petals, parts of eight preserved, radiating from a ring around the central filling hole.

789 CF.1642 Atrium Building I, Room 25 C, Level III. Cream clay, reddish-brown slip mottled darker in places. P.L. 0.034 m; P.W. 0.019 m.

Fragment preserving parts of the discus and rim. Slip worn. Discus relief: Rosette of fourteen concave petals in high relief.

790 CF.1940 Atrium Building I, Room 25 C, Level III. Grayish-buff clay, black slip. P.L. 0.038 m; P.W. 0.026 m.

Fragment preserving parts of the discus and rim. Worn and chipped. Discus relief: The feet and legs of a cock, the rest broken away.

A phallic dwarf appears on the discus relief of the four lamps below. Three are very similar, but the fourth is different. They are probably all of the same date.

791 (Pl. IV) CEL.635 Basilica exterior, NW 2, Level II. Buff clay, red slip. P.L. 0.045 m; P.W. 0.068 m.

Fragment preserving parts of the discus and rim. In good condition. Discus relief: A nude hunchbacked dwarf with grotesque features and a large phallus who wears an odd hat and kneels in a crescent-shaped boat. The left hand holds a pair of short rods before his face; the right hand and arm extend back also holding a pair of rods. According to Doro Levi, the figure is protecting himself from the evil eye. See Doro Levi, *Antioch-on-the-Orontes* 3.220-32, "The Evil Eye and the Lucky Hunchback."

Cf. Bachofen, fig. 10 no. 1; Goldman/Jones, no. 273; Menzel, pl. 61 no. 12; Brants, pl. 5 no. 761; Bailey 1980, pl. 79 no. Q 1368; Heres 1972a, pl. 65 no. 654 (the same subject but not the same relief); Ponsich 1963, pl. 5 no. 36.

792 (Pl. IV) CF.1961 Atrium Building I, Room 25, Level III. Buff clay, orange slip mottled to brown in places. P.L. 0.058 m; P.H. 0.040 m; P.W. 0.066 m.

Fragment preserving the handle and parts of the discus and rim. Slip rubbed. Discus relief: A phallic dwarf kneeling in a boat. Identical with 791, but only the head and the right hand holding rods are preserved.

793 CD.607 Basilica exterior, NW 2, Level II. Buff clay with a pink tint, orange-red slip. P.L. 0.068 m; P.W. 0.044 m.

Fragment preserving most of a discus and parts of the rim. Surface rubbed. Discus relief: A phallic hunchbacked dwarf, as on 791 and 792. A series of oar holes is indicated along the gunwales of the boat. The filling hole is punched through the bottom of the boat.

A.D. 100–225

794 CF.1923 Atrium Building I, Room 25, Level I. Cream clay, orange slip. P.L. 0.048 m; P.W. 0.029 m.

Fragment preserving parts of the discus and rim. Slightly worn. Discus relief: Only one hand holding a pair of rods is preserved, but this relief is doubtless the hunchbacked phallic dwarf running or dancing to the right with the rods held in front of and behind the body. The hand with the rods is the same as that on a lamp in the British Museum.

Cf. Bailey 1980, pl. 79 no. Q 1368; Brants, pl. 5 no. 761; Bachofen, pl. 10 no. 1; Goldman/Jones, no. 273; Menzel, pl. 61 no. 12; Loeschcke 1919, no. 432.

795 CD.772a Basilica exterior, NE 3, Level I. Buff clay, red slip. P.L. 0.056 m; P.W. 0.029 m.

Fragment preserving parts of the discus and

shoulder. Slip worn. Mold worn and blurred. Discus relief: An Eros wearing a turban moving right, both hands carrying a large bundle in front of him, held by a loop at the top. The lower torso and legs are broken away.

796 CEL.118 Atrium Building I, Room 10, Level I. Grayish-buff clay, red slip. P.L. 0.047 m; P.W. 0.058 m.

Two joining fragments preserving parts of the discus and rim. Very worn; made from an old, blurred mold. Discus relief: A bull running right, attacked by a bear.

Cf. Goethert-Polaschek, pl. 18 nos. 11–12, pl. 19 (all photographs), pl. 20 nos. 50, 64–66, 71–74, and drawing and description on p. 251. These lamps all have the same relief as 796, but they are all Triangular Nozzle Lamps.

797 CEL.264 Atrium Building I, Room 14, Level I. Buff clay, brown slip. P.L. 0.048 m; P.H. 0.025 m; P.W. 0.049 m.

Fragment preserving parts of the handle, discus, and rim. Slip worn away in places. Discus relief: At the top of the discus is a crudely modeled warrior or gladiator holding a sword vertically. The body is broken away below the waist.

798 CEL.628 Atrium Building I, Room 5, Level I. Buff clay, red slip. P.L. 0.031 m; P.W. 0.022 m.

Fragment preserving parts of the discus and rim. Very worn. Discus relief: A wreath of two branches of laurel, only partially preserved.

799 (Pl. III) CF.1645 Atrium Building I, Room 25 D, Level II. Buff clay, orange slip mottled to brown in places. P.L. 0.095 m; Height 0.027 m; Width 0.098 m.

Three joining fragments preserving the handle and parts of the discus, rim, side wall of the oil reservoir, and disk base. Slip worn; made from an old, blurred mold. Molded pierced handle, with two grooves that converge on the crest and extend down the spine as a single groove. Discus relief: A winged Eros, nude, to the right, supporting the infant Bacchus to the left, both moving left. Bacchus, three-quarters frontal, wears a short tunic and a wreath. His right arm is extended holding up a bunch of grapes.

Cf. Bachofen, pl. 3 no. 1; Deneauve 1969, pl. 82 no. 906 (but the figures move to the right, instead of to the left).

800 CF.1938 Atrium Building I, Room 25 A, Level II. Orange clay, orange-red slip. P.L. 0.029 m; P.W. 0.026 m.

Fragment preserving parts of the discus and rim. Slip slightly rubbed. Discus relief: A geometric design, semicircular, divided into two parts. The lower part is a pelta, divided into three wedges. The upper part is oval; the lower curve of the oval fits into the upper curve of the pelta.

801 CF.2288 Atrium Building I, Room 22 exterior, Level II. Buff clay, orange slip. P.L. 0.051 m; Height 0.029 m; P.W. 0.047 m.

Three joining fragments preserving the handle and parts of the rim, side wall of the oil reservoir, and base. Made from a new crisp mold. Ring base with a smaller interior ring inscribed: BASAV..., to be completed as BASAVGV, with bull's eyes centered above and below the inscription (see Fig. 141).

Cf. Bailey 1980, 99 and fig. 108; Mercando 1962, 434; Sotgiu 1968, 122–23. See also CIL 3.12012.71; CIL 5.8114.105; and CIL 9.6081.

802 CF.2298 Atrium Building I, Room 22 exterior, Level III. Cream clay, red slip. P.L. 0.068 m; Height 0.028 m; P.W. 0.037 m.

Two joining fragments preserving parts of the discus, rim, handle, side wall of the oil reservoir, base, and nozzle. Worn, chipped, and flaked. Made from a crude mold; the grooves flanking the bead defining the shoulder have been reworked unevenly. Nozzle: heart-shaped, Heres Type E e, Loeschcke Type H. Low ring base, within which is part of a signature: ...CLID to be completed ERACLID (see Fig. 141). Discus relief: Bust of Julia Domna as Luna, with a crescent moon on her forehead. She faces right, her hair elaborately waved and caught up in a large knot at the back. She wears long earrings and a necklace and is dressed in a tunic or stola, with a mantle or palla off the shoulders held together below the breasts, making a circular frame for the upper body. The relief of the features is chipped and blurred. The filling hole is carelessly punched to the right cutting slightly into the chin. Two tiny circular air holes are punched at the edge of the discus near the rim.

A number of lamps with busts of Julia Domna as Luna and Septimius Severus as Sol, and with Julia Domna alone, are preserved in various collections. These must all have been made during the reign of Septimius Severus, A.D. 193–211. For other examples, see Hanoune 1970, pl. 4 no. 18 (also with the signature ERACLID); Heres 1972a, pl. 47 no. 442 (with both figures as Luna and Sol, also signed *ERACLID*); Heres 1972a, pl. 43 no. 385 (a portrait of the empress with ovules on the shoulder of the lamp), and pl. 48 nos. 451–54 for other portraits of the empress with various decorations on the shoulders of Loeschcke Type VIII Lamps. Cf. Bailey 1980, 97 and fig. 104 for *ERACLID*.

803 CF.2146 Atrium Building I, Room 15, Level II. Buff clay, red slip. P.L. 0.031 m; P.W. 0.042 m.

Fragment preserving parts of the discus and rim. Slip worn away on raised surfaces. Discus relief: The head and neck of a goat facing left, the rest broken away.

See Farka 1977, pl. 44, for the same goat turned to the right.

804 (Pl. VIII) CF.2299 Atrium Building I, Room 22 exterior, Level IV. Hard, orange-buff clay, red slip. P.L. 0.102 m; Height 0.027 m; P.W. 0.067 m.

Fragment preserving the handle, and most of the right side of the lamp, except the nozzle, of which only the upper part of the right volute survives. Top of handle damaged before firing. Molded pierced handle; two grooves on face converging at the crest, then dividing, and then converging again near the base. Lower part of handle set off from body wall by narrow molding. Voluted nozzle, the end broken away and underside decorated with grooves and looped string molding. Ring base with a smaller interior ring inscribed: *LCAES*..., to be completed *LCAESAE*, for Lucius Caecilius Saecularis (see Fig. 139). Discus relief: A peacock, frontal, displaying his tail, which fills the upper arc of the discus (cf. 593, a Pouter Pigeon Lamp).

Cf. *CIL* 2.4969.13; *CIL* 5.8114.17; *CIL* 8.22644.52; *CIL* 9.6081.13; Bailey 1980, 91 and fig. 103.

805 CG.315 Curia, SE room of basement, Mithraeum, Level III. Buff clay, red slip mottled to brown in places. P.L. 0.031 m; P.W. 0.029 m.

Fragment preserving parts of the discus and rim. Worn. Discus relief: Sol facing left on the right side of the discus, the left side broken away. This relief may have shown portraits of Julia Domna and Septimius Severus as Luna and Sol (see 802).

805A (Fig. 81) CC.159 Arx, N Slope, medieval ramp, Level I. Buff clay with a pinkish tint, brown slip. P.L. 0.112 m; Height 0.026 m; Width 0.080 m.

Incomplete, end of nozzle and parts of discus, side wall, and base broken away. Plain shoulder, molded handle. Nozzle: heart-shaped, Heres Type E e. Ring base with inscription *VETCRIS*, parts of the last three letters broken away (see Fig. 141). Discus relief: Eros walking right holding a flaming torch held almost horizontally in his right hand. Filling hole punched to the left of the figure.

806 CG.527 Forum, NE passage, Level I. Buff clay with an orange tint, red slip. Length 0.104 m; Height 0.025 m; Width 0.069 m.

Complete, except for a chip broken from the left end of the nozzle. Very worn; smoke-blackened around the wick hole. The top of the handle was damaged before firing. A narrow bead molding marks off the shoulder from the discus. The nozzle has a horizontal groove across the top with two bull's eyes at each end, Heres Type E b, Loeschcke Type L 1. Low disk base inscribed *CLOSVC* with a phallus beneath (see Fig. 139). Discus relief: Female bust, frontal, with elaborate hairdress, above a crescent moon, perhaps Julia Domna. Bailey identifies the head as Luna.

For the relief, see Bailey 1980, pl. 68 no. Q 1289. For the signature, see Bailey 1980, pl. 24 no. Q 985, pl. 40 no. Q 1106, fig. 104, and notes on pp. 93–94; Brants 1913, nos. 763 and 925; Deneauve, pl. 1, pp. 83–93; p. 88 nos. 420, 579. See also Heres 1972a, pl. 27 no. 215, pl. 32 no. 272, pl. 58 no. 543.

807 CG.593 Forum, NE passage, Level I. Buff clay, red slip. Length 0.105 m; Height 0.024 m; P.W. 0.070 m.

Incomplete, part of the side wall of the oil reservoir and a small part of the base broken away. Slip worn. Low disk base with an illegible signature of probably eight letters.

808 C68.416 Arx, W. slope, Level 0-I. Buff clay, red slip.

Four joining fragments preserving most of a lamp, the top of the handle broken away. Worn and chipped. Made from an old, worn mold. Nozzle: heart-shaped, Heres Type E e, Loeschcke Type H. Four rings separate the discus from the beveled shoulder. Ring base. Discus relief: A large bitch, recumbent, nursing pups, the design too blurred to count the pups. The filling hole is punched below the group.

For a clearer example of this relief, see Leibundgut 1977, pl. 47 no. 290, with the relief reversed.

809 C68.470 Arx, W. slope, Level 0-I. Buff clay with a pink tint, reddish-orange slip.
Fragment preserving parts of the discus, rim, handle, body, and base. Slip rubbed. Made from an old, blurred mold. Ring base. Discus relief: Bust of a goddess, frontal, too indistinct to identify any attribute.

A.D. 350–416

810 (Pl. II) CF.462 Atrium Building I, Room 25, Level I. Buff clay with an orange tint, red slip. P.L. 0.036 m; P.W. 0.027 m.
Fragment preserving parts of a discus and rim. Worn. Discus relief: Bust of Athena, wearing a Corinthian helmet pushed back from her face, head turned left. Very fine mold.
Cf. 754, 765; Goldman/Jones 1950, pl. 102 no. 209; Heres 1972a, pl. 52 nos. 485–86; Broneer 1930, pl. 12 no. 582 (a Corinthian lamp); Menzel 1969, nos. 536, 545.

811 CF.836 Atrium Building I, Room 25, Level I. Buff clay with an orange tint, orange slip mottled to brown in places. P.L. 0.068 m; Height 0.026 m; P.W. 0.068 m.
Fragment preserving the handle and parts of the rim, side wall of the oil reservoir, base, and discus. Worn. Disk base. Discus relief: Only a small part of the relief is preserved, possibly the end of the tail of a dolphin.

812 CF.1926 Atrium Building I, Room 25, Level I. Cream clay, slip worn away. P.L. 0.069 m; Height 0.036 m; P.W. 0.064 m.
Fragment preserving parts of the discus, rim, handle, side wall of the oil reservoir, and base. Very worn. Made from a worn, blurred mold. Discus relief: A female bust, frontal, left shoulder draped, too badly worn for identification.

813 CF.2004 Atrium Building I, Room 25 exterior NW, Level I. Buff clay, red slip. P.L. 0.035 m; P.W. 0.030 m.
Fragment preserving parts of the discus and rim. Slip worn. Discus relief: A frenzied maenad to right, the legs from the hips down preserved. The carefully modeled drapery swirls about the legs.
Cf. Goethert-Polaschek, pl. 52 no. 509; Bailey 1980, pl. 3 no. Q 787 (the figure on this Triangular Nozzle Lamp facing left); Heres 1972a, pl. 8 nos. 37, 40 (also a Triangular Nozzle Lamp).

814 CF.2020 Atrium Building I, Room 25 exterior NW, Level I. Buff clay, orange-red slip. P.L. 0.080 m; Height 0.021 m; P.W. 0.067 m.
Four joining fragments preserving parts of the discus, rim, side wall of the oil reservoir, and base. Very worn; made from an old, blurred mold. Discus relief: A dolphin with lifted tail.
Cf. Joly 1974, pl. 13 no. 339.

c. FAT LAMPS: UNDECORATED DISCI AND SHOULDERS

(Fig. 83)

(Catalogue Numbers 815–823)

25/20 B.C.–A.D. 50

815 CEL.610 Basilica exterior, NW 2, Level III. Buff clay, brown slip. Length 0.100 m; Width 0.081 m.
Two joining fragments preserving the nozzle, and parts of the discus, rim, and handle. Worn and chipped. Molded pierced handle. Nozzle: Heres Type E b, Loeschcke Type L 1.

A.D. 50–ca. 100

816 CEL.249 Atrium Building I, Room 6, Level I. Buff clay, red slip. P.L. 0.047 m; P.H. 0.020 m; P.W. 0.034 m.
Fragment preserving parts of the discus, rim, and nozzle. Surface very worn. Probably this lamp had no handle. Nozzle: Heres Type E c, Loeschcke Type L 2.

817 CF.476 Atrium Building I, Room 25 A, Level III. Buff clay, orange slip. Length 0.108 m; Height 0.023 m; P.W. 0.077 m.
Four joining fragments preserving the handle, base, and parts of the discus, rim, side wall of the oil reservoir, and nozzle. Surface worn. Made from an old, worn mold; the molding that would have separated the discus from the shoulder and grooves on the top of the handle erased by wear. Unprofiled base.

818 CF.1630 Atrium Building I, Room 25 A, Level IV. Buff clay, orange-red slip. P.L. 0.081 m; Height 0.023 m; Width 0.080 m.
Twelve joining fragments preserving everything but chips from the nozzle, discus, and rim. Surface rubbed. Made from a worn mold. Molded pierced handle. Nozzle: Heres Type E b, Loeschcke Type L 1. Unprofiled base stamped with an illegible signature.

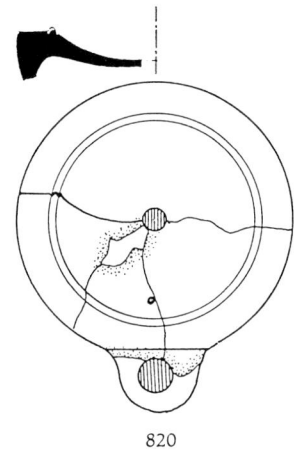

Figure 83. Fat Lamps: c. Undecorated discus and shoulder, scale 1:2

819 CF.1632 Atrium Building I, Room 25 C, Level II. Cream clay, slip worn away. P.L. 0.042 m; P.H. 0.022 m; P.W. 0.049 m.

Fragment preserving the nozzle and part of the rim. Very worn. Nozzle: heart-shaped, Heres Type E e, Loeschcke Type H.

820 (Fig. 83) CF.1639 Atrium Building I, Room 25 C, Level III. Cream clay, red slip mottled to brown in places. P.L. 0.078 m; P.H. 0.020 m; Width 0.074 m.

Eight joining fragments preserving the plain discus, rim, and part of the nozzle. Surface rubbed. Nozzle: Heres Type E c, Loeschcke Type L 2. This lamp did not have a handle.

821 CF.2273 Atrium Building I, Room 16 exterior, Level V. Buff clay, brown slip. P.L. 0.082 m; Height 0.027 m; P.W. 0.054 m.

Three joining fragments preserving parts of the discus, rim, nozzle, side wall of the oil reservoir, and base. Made from a worn mold; all detail of the nozzle is worn away. Unprofiled base.

822 CF.2276 Atrium Building I, Room 16 exterior, Level V. Grayish-buff clay, orange slip mottled to black in places. P.L. 0.069 m; Height 0.025 m; P.W. 0.071 m.

Fragment preserving the nozzle and parts of the rim and base. Surface worn. Nozzle: heart-shaped, Heres Type E e, Loeschcke Type H.

A.D. 100–225

823 CEL.185 Atrium Building I, Room 1, Level I. Buff clay, self-slip. P.L. 0.095 m; Height 0.032 m; P.W. 0.082 m.

Fragment preserving the base, handle, and parts of the discus and rim. Made from a very old, worn mold.

d. FAT LAMPS: SHOULDERS DECORATED WITH TOOTHED LEAVES OBLIQUELY SET
(Fig. 84)
(Catalogue Number 824)

25/20 B.C.–A.D. 40/45

824 (Fig. 84) CEL.50 a, b, and c Atrium Building I, Room 22, Level II. Cream clay, dark brown slip.

One nonjoining and two joining fragments preserving parts of the discus and rim. Worn. Shoulder decorated with toothed leaves set obliquely to the bead molding that separates the discus from the shoulder. Discus relief: Victory, frontal, wearing long *peplos*. Right hand holds a wreath, left hand down at side holding palm branch. Only partially preserved.

For complete relief, see Bailey 1980, pl. 71 no. Q 1321. The relief on this lamp is the same, but the lamp has a panel on the sides (Bailey Type P, Group iii). The shoulder decoration occurs on Bailey Type O, Group v. His example, Q 1228 on pl. 60, has oak leaves alternating with acorns.

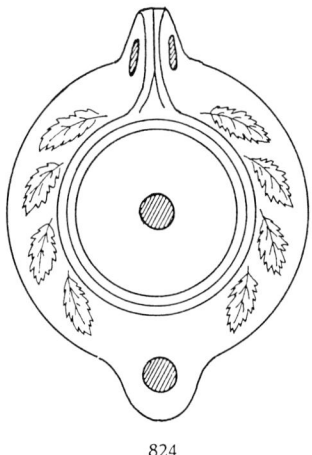

Figure 84. Fat Lamps: d. Shoulders decorated with toothed leaves obliquely set, scale 1:2

e. FAT LAMPS: SHOULDERS DECORATED WITH LANCEOLATE LEAVES WITH DOUBLE OUTLINES OBLIQUELY SET

(Fig. 85)

(Catalogue Numbers 825, 826)

25/20 B.C.–A.D. 40/45

825 (Fig. 85) CEL.72 Atrium Building I, Room 22, Level II. Cream clay, self-slip.

Fragment preserving parts of discus and shoulder. Worn and scratched. Discus separated from the shoulder by two narrow bead moldings, the inner one slightly narrower. The shoulder is decorated with obliquely set lanceolate leaves with a double outline and a central rib. Discus relief: None preserved.

For examples of this shoulder decoration, see Menzel 1969, fig. 38; Heres 1972a, pl. 28 no. 227; Oziol 1977, pl. 26 nos. 489–90; Bailey 1980, pl. 60 no. Q 1232.

A.D. 50–ca. 100

826 CEL.298 Atrium Building I, Room 21, Level I. Cream clay, brown slip.

Fragment preserving part of a shoulder decorated with obliquely set lanceolate leaves with a central rib, like 825.

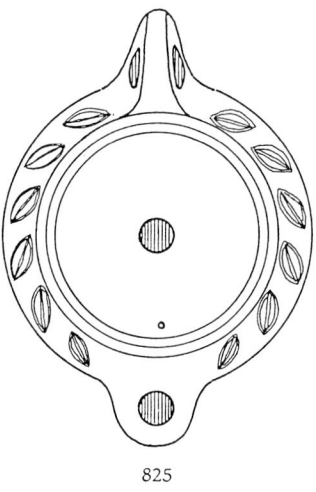

Figure 85. Fat Lamps: e. Shoulders decorated with lanceolate leaves with double outlines obliquely set, scale 1:2

f. FAT LAMPS: SHOULDERS DECORATED WITH LANCEOLATE LEAVES OBLIQUELY SET

(Fig. 86)

(Catalogue Number 827)

A.D. 350–416

827 (Fig. 86) CF.2116 Atrium Building I, Room 25, Level I. Buff clay, slip worn away. P.L. 0.032 m; P.H. 0.042 m; P.W. 0.055 m.

Fragment preserving the handle and parts of the discus, rim, and upper side wall of the oil

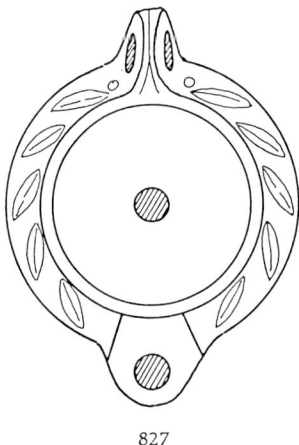

Figure 86. Fat Lamps: f. Shoulders decorated with lanceolate leaves obliquely set, scale 1:2

reservoir. Very worn, scratched. Handle has two grooves converging at the crest and extending down the spine as a single groove. Shoulder decorated with obliquely set laurel leaves with a single outline and a central rib; a small circle, perhaps a berry, flanks the handle on either side.

Although this fragment comes from a context dated A.D. 350–416, it is clearly of the first half of the first century A.D. and must be regarded as intrusive.

g. FAT LAMPS: SHOULDERS DECORATED WITH A BAND OF HEARTS, POINTS OUTWARD

(Fig. 87)

(Catalogue Numbers 828, 829)

25/20 B.C.–A.D. 50

828 CEL.17 a, b, and c Atrium Building I, Room 16, Level II. Buff clay, red slip. P.L. 0.064 m; P.W. 0.060 m.

Three fragments, two joining, preserving parts of the discus and rim. Slightly worn; scratched. Shoulder decorated with a band of small hearts with the points outward and a tiny circle at each point.

Cf. Heres 1972a, pl. 29 no. 242; Goethert-Polaschek 1985, pl. 73 no. 648; Gualandi Genito 1986, pl. 50 no. 372; Ivanyi 1935, pl. 27 no. 10; Farka 1977, pl. 21, no. 674; Iconomu 1967, fig. 124 on p. 120; Cahn-Klaiber 1977, pl. 29 nos. 281, 283; Bailey 1980, pl. 61, nos. Q 1234, Q 1235; Ponsich 1961, pl. 30 no. 455; Deneauve, pl. 64 no. 634; Leibundgut 1977, pl. 8 no. 663.

A.D. 50–ca. 100

829 (Fig. 87) CEL.486 Atrium Building I, Room 22, Level I. Buff clay, red slip. P.L. 0.033 m; P.W. 0.021 m.

Fragment preserving parts of the rim. Surface rubbed. Shoulder decorated with a band of small hearts with the points outward and a tiny circle at each point.

h. FAT LAMPS: SHOULDERS DECORATED WITH A BAND OF HEARTS, POINTS INWARD

(Fig. 88)

(Catalogue Number 830)

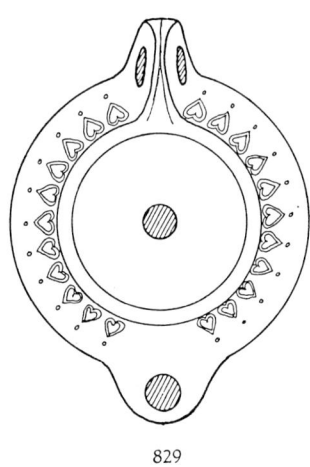

829

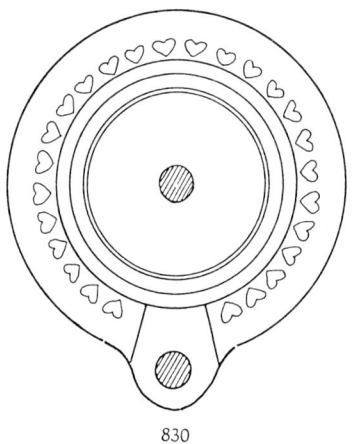

830

Figure 87. Fat Lamps: g. Shoulders decorated with a band of hearts, points outward, scale 1:2

Figure 88. Fat Lamps: h. Shoulders decorated with a band of hearts, points inward, scale 1:2

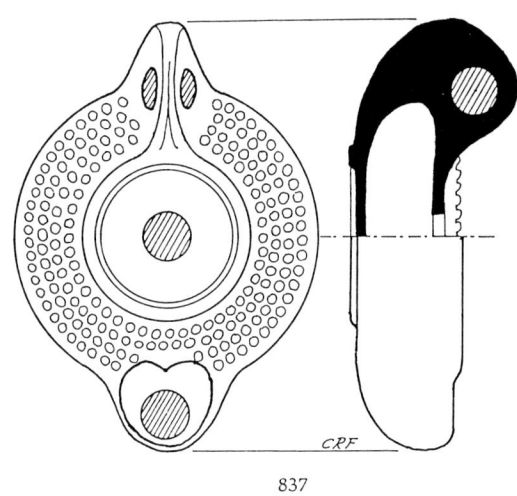

Figure 89. Fat Lamps: i. Shoulders decorated with raised dots, scale 1:2

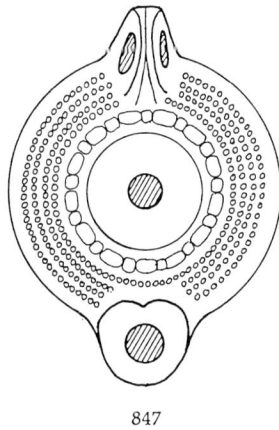

Figure 90. Fat Lamps: i. Shoulders decorated with raised dots separated from the discus by a bead-and-reel molding, scale 1:2

A.D. 50–ca. 100

830 (Fig. 88) CEL.569 Atrium Building I, Room 21, Level I. Cream clay, red slip. P.L. 0.035 m; P.W. 0.023 m.

Fragment preserving parts of the discus and rim. Very worn. The upper part of the shoulder is decorated with a band of small hearts with the points inward.

Cf. Bailey 1980, pl. 73 no. Q 1328 (closely related, but the hearts are more widely spaced).

i. FAT LAMPS: SHOULDERS DECORATED WITH RAISED DOTS

(Figs. 89, 90)

(Catalogue Numbers 830A–847)

(Bailey Type O, Group x; Dressel/Lamboglia Type 30 A)

Parts of eighteen Fat Lamps with wide shoulders covered by concentric rows of raised dots have been found at Cosa. They have small plain disci with a central filling hole. The bodies are all of Loeschcke Type VIII, and all probably had molded pierced handles. Only four bases have been preserved, all ring bases. Four of the five nozzles that survive are heart-shaped, Heres Type E e; the fifth is Heres Type E b with a horizontal groove across the top.

The clay is coarse and ranges in color from buff to cream. The lamps are carelessly made, with pits and crevices in the thick fabric. They have red, orange-red, or brown slip. Two of the eighteen, 846 and 847, are more carefully made than the others. These two have a bead-and-reel molding framed by a ring on either side that separates the shoulder from the discus. All eighteen lamps probably date from the late second century to A.D. 225, although several come from contexts that could be as late as the Constantinian village (A.D. 330–416). Bailey dates these lamps Severan or later.

For other examples of these lamps, see Bailey 1980, pl. 86 nos. Q 1421, Q 1422; Hayes, pl. 28 no. 249; Gualandi Genito 1986, pl. 55 nos. 406–7; Zaccaria Ruggiu 1977, pl. 289 no. 915; Joly 1974, pl. 16 nos. 430, 432, pl. 24 nos. 637–39, 642–43; Heres 1972a, pl. 35 no. 309; Deneauve, pl. 90 nos. 992, 997, pl. 91 no. 999; Ponsich 1961, pl. 24 no. 327, pl. 25 no. 341; Szentléleky, no. 146.

A.D. 100–225

830A CEL.122 Atrium Building I, Room 10, Level III. Buff clay with a pinkish tint, red slip. P.L. 0.034 m; P.W. 0.037 m.

Fragment preserving parts of the rim and nozzle. Slip very worn; smoke-blackened around wick hole. Nozzle: heart-shaped, Heres Type E e, Loeschcke Type H. Shoulder decorated with concentric rows of small raised dots.

Late Second Century–A.D. 225

831 CEL.124 Atrium Building I, Room 13 exterior, Level I. Buff clay, slip worn away. P.L. 0.032 m; P.W. 0.026 m.

Fragment preserving parts of the rim. Very worn. Shoulder decorated with four rows of larger-size raised dots on shoulder.

832 CEL.195 Atrium Building I, Room 13 exterior, Level I. Buff clay, dull brown slip. P.L. 0.049 m; P.W. 0.044 m.

Fragment preserving parts of the discus and rim. Slip rubbed. Shoulder decorated with six rows of irregularly spaced small raised dots.

833 CEL.286 Atrium Building I, Room 12, Level I. Cream clay, slip worn away. P.L. 0.035 m; P.W. 0.035 m.

Fragment preserving part of shoulder. Very worn. Shoulder decorated with four rows of larger-size raised dots on shoulder.

834 CF.465 Atrium Building I, Room 25, Level I. Buff clay, orange slip. P.L. 0.039 m; P.W. 0.040 m.

Fragment preserving parts of the discus and rim. Worn. Shoulder decorated with three rows of larger-size raised dots.

835 CF.469 Atrium Building I, Room 25 A, Level II. Grayish-buff clay, slip worn away. P.L. 0.091 m; Height 0.025 m; Width 0.062 m.

Seven joining fragments preserving the handle and parts of all essential features. Very worn. Nozzle: heart-shaped, Heres Type E e and Loeschcke Type H. Molded pierced ring handle does not have the usual grooves. Shoulder decorated with three rows of large raised dots. Ring base, within which is impressed *LMARMI* (see Fig. 140).

CF. Bailey 1980, 97–98, fig. 107; Mercando 1962, 432.

836 CF.1838 Atrium Building I, Room 25 D, Level II. Buff clay, slip worn away. P.L. 0.028 m; P.W. 0.016 m.

Fragment preserving part of rim. Very worn. Shoulder decorated with widely spaced, small raised dots.

837 (Fig. 89) CF.2010 Atrium Building I, Room 22 exterior, Level III A. Buff clay, orange-red slip. P.L. 0.069 m; Height 0.028 m; Width 0.078 m.

Two joining fragments preserving parts of the discus, rim, side wall of the oil reservoir, base, and nozzle. Surface very worn. Nozzle: heart-shaped, Heres Type E e, Loeschcke Type H. Shoulder decorated with four rows of larger-size raised dots. Ring base, within which is impressed an illegible signature with a bull's eye centered above and below it.

838 CF.2124 Atrium Building I, Room 25 exterior, Level II. Grayish-buff clay, yellow-brown slip. P.L. 0.039 m; P.H. 0.017 m; P.W. 0.032 m.

Fragment preserving parts of the discus and rim. Very worn. Shoulder decorated with three rows of larger-size raised dots.

839 CF.2289 Atrium Building I, Room 22 exterior, Level V. Buff clay, orange slip. P.L. 0.046 m; P.W. 0.050 m.

Fragment preserving parts of the rim, nozzle, side wall of the oil reservoir, and base ring. Slip worn. Nozzle: heart-shaped, Heres Type E e, Loeschcke Type H. Shoulder decorated with four rows of larger-size raised dots.

Late Second Century–A.D. 416

840 CEL.571 Atrium Building I, Room 25 exterior, Level I. Buff clay, red slip. P.L. 0.081 m; P.W. 0.071 m.

Two joining fragments preserving parts of the discus, rim, and handle. Worn. Shoulder decorated with four rows of larger-size raised dots.

841 CEL.572 Atrium Building I, Room 25 exterior, Level I. Cream clay, dark slip. P.L. 0.048 m; P.W. 0.038 m.

Fragment preserving parts of the discus and rim. Very worn; only traces of slip preserved. Shoulder decorated with four rows of larger-size raised dots.

842 CF.2012 Atrium Building I, Room 25 exterior, Level I. Buff clay, brown slip. P.L. 0.062 m; Width 0.081 m.

Two joining fragments preserving the upper half of the handle and parts of the discus and rim.

Slip worn. Two grooves converging at the crest of the handle. Shoulder decorated with four rows of larger-size raised dots.

843 C.F.2013 Atrium Building I, Room 25 exterior, Level I. Buff clay, dark brown slip. P.L. 0.081 m; Height 0.030 m; Width 0.082 m.

Six joining fragments preserving parts of the discus, rim, nozzle, and base. Slip worn. Shoulder decorated with four rows of larger-size raised dots, the tops of some dots broken away.

844 C.F.2024 Atrium Building I, Room 25 exterior, Level I. Buff clay, red slip. P.L. 0.031 m; P.W. 0.029 m.

Fragment preserving parts of the rim. Chipped and worn. Shoulder decorated with four rows of larger-size raised dots.

845 C.F.2112 Atrium Building I, Room 25 exterior, Level I. Buff clay, red slip. P.L. 0.074 m; Height 0.030 m; P.W. 0.076 m.

Two joining fragments preserving parts of the discus, rim, and handle. Slip worn. Two grooves converge on the crest of the molded pierced handle. Shoulder decorated with four rows of larger-size raised dots.

The two lamps that follow, 846 and 847, are of finer quality. The dots are more carefully shaped and spaced, and the shoulder is separated from the discus by a bead-and-reel molding framed by rings.

A.D. 100–225

846 C.F.475 Atrium Building I, Room 25 A, Level III. Buff clay, red slip. P.L. 0.051 m; P.W. 0.034 m.

Fragment preserving parts of the discus and rim. In good condition. Shoulder marked off from discus by a bead-and-reel molding between rings and decorated with at least four rows of small raised dots, but there may have been more.

Late Second Century–A.D. 225

847 (Fig. 90) C.F.2121 Atrium Building I, Room 25 exterior, Level II. Grayish-buff clay, brown slip. P.L. 0.050 m; P.W. 0.029 m.

Fragment preserving parts of the discus and rim. Very worn. The bead-and-reel molding marking off the discus is not so carefully executed as that on 846, composed in effect of bead molding of two sizes, and there is a wide groove between the ring bordering the bead-and-reel and the shoulder with the first row of small raised dots. Only two rows of small raised dots are preserved.

For another example of this lamp, see Zaccaria Ruggiu 1980, 105 no. 66.

j. FAT LAMPS: SHOULDERS DECORATED WITH LOOPED VINES, WITH GRAPES AND LEAVES WITHIN LOOPS

(Fig. 91)

(Catalogue Numbers 848–861)

Fourteen Fat lamps from Cosa all have designs of looped ivy on the shoulder. Within each loop is a leaf or a cluster of berries. The rather crudely executed design starts at the handle and ends short of the nozzle. Above the nozzle is a tightly wound coil, as of fine cord, ending on either side in a bull's eye. The clay is coarse and ranges from hard to soft; it is buff in color, sometimes with a reddish or grayish tint. The lamps are carelessly made, with pits and crevices in the fabric.

One of the lamps in this group was found in a context dated ca. A.D. 100–225. Four are from levels dated from the late second century to A.D. 225. Nine are from contexts dated late second century to A.D. 416.

There is one example of this lamp in the British Museum; Bailey (Bailey 1980, 337) has classified it as Group i of his Type Q and dates it early Antonine to Severan.

A.D. 100–225

848 C.F.842 Atrium Building I, Room 25 B, Level III. Buff clay, with a reddish tint, red slip. P.L. 0.048 m; P.W. 0.076 m.

Three joining fragments preserving parts of the plain discus, rim, and handle. Worn and chipped. The mold has been reworked rather clumsily.

Late second century–A.D. 225

849 C.F.1635 Atrium Building I, Room 25 C, Level II. Buff clay, with a reddish tint, red slip. P.L. 0.038 m; P.W. 0.032 m.

Fragment preserving part of the rim. Slip worn.

850 C.F.1648 Atrium Building I, Room 25 D, Level II. Cream clay, self-slip. P.L. 0.076 m; P.W. 0.063 m.

Fragment preserving parts of the plain (?) discus and rim. Very worn.

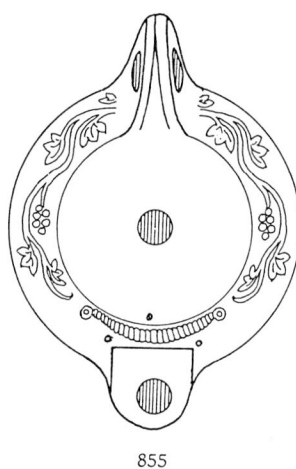

855

Figure 91. Fat Lamps: j. Shoulders decorated with looped vines, with grapes and leaves within loops, scale 1:2

851 CF.1831 Atrium Building I, Room 25 D, Level II. Buff clay, slip worn away. P.L. 0.049 m; P.W. 0.028 m.
   Fragment preserving parts of the handle, plain [?] discus, and rim. Very worn.
852 CF.1839 Atrium Building I, Room 25 D, Level II. Buff clay, orange-red slip. P.L. 0.031 m; P.W. 0.027 m.
   Fragment preserving part of the rim and nozzle. Surface rubbed. Nozzle: Heres Type E b, Loeschcke Type L 1.

Late Second Century–A.D. 416
853 CEL.590 Basilica exterior, NW 2, Level I. Buff clay, orange slip. P.L. 0.033 m; P.W. 0.040 m.
   Fragment preserving parts of the discus, rim, and handle. Very worn. Made from an old, blurred mold. Discus relief: Too little remains to identify.
854 CEL.596 Basilica exterior, NW 2, Level II. Buff clay, black slip with a metallic luster. P.L. 0.060 m; P.W. 0.042 m.
   Fragment preserving parts of the discus and rim. Surface rubbed. Discus relief: Rosette of eighteen concave petals radiating from central filling hole.
   Cf. 865; Heres 1972a, pl. 36 no. 317, pl. 46 nos. 431–32; Bailey 1980, pl. 72 no. Q 1327. For other examples of lamps with the same shoulder decoration, see Deneauve, pl. 89 no. 985; Joly 1974, pl. 26 no. 709; Hanoune, pl. 6 no. 33.
855 (Fig. 91) CF.468 Atrium Building I, Room 25, Level I. Grayish-buff clay, reddish-brown slip mottled to dark brown in places. P.L. 0.101 m; Height 0.033 m; P.W. 0.083 m.
   Five joining fragments preserving a plain discus and handle, and parts of the rim, nozzle, and disk base. Surface rubbed. Nozzle: Heres Type E b, Loeschcke Type L 1.
856 CF.2001 Atrium Building I, Room 25 exterior NW, Level I. Buff clay, red slip. P.L. 0.037 m; P.W. 0.038 m.
   Fragment preserving parts of the rim and a plain discus. Very worn.
857 CF.2113 Atrium Building I, Room 25 exterior, Level I. Buff clay, orange-red slip. P.L. 0.039 m; P.W. 0.024 m.
   Fragment preserving part of a rim.
858 CF.2272 Atrium Building I, Room 16 exterior, Level V. Buff clay, orange slip. P.L. 0.050 m; P.W. 0.040 m.
   Fragment preserving parts of the discus and rim. Very worn. Made from an old, worn mold.
859 CF.2277 Atrium Building I, Room 16 exterior, Level V. Grayish-buff clay, brown slip. P.L. 0.037 m; P.W. 0.041 m.
   Fragment preserving part of the rim. Very badly rubbed.
860 CF.2290 Atrium Building I, Room 16 exterior, Level III. Buff clay, orange slip. P.L. 0.080 m; P.W. 0.054 m.
   Fragment preserving parts of the plain discus, rim, and nozzle. Surface rubbed. Nozzle: Heres Type E b, Loeschcke Type L 1.
861 CF.2297 Atrium Building I, Room 22 exterior, Level III A. Grayish-buff clay, dull gray slip, overfired. P.L. 0.042 m; P.W. 0.054 m.
   Fragment preserving parts of the discus, rim, and handle. Surface worn. Discus relief: Victory facing left, the head, upper part of the body, and wings preserved. This is probably part of a New Year's greeting lamp.

k. FAT LAMPS: SHOULDER DECORATED WITH A WREATH OF OLIVE LEAVES AND OLIVES, WITH A CIRCULAR BOSS AROUND THE CENTRAL FILLING HOLE (FIG. 92)

(Catalogue Numbers 862–865)

(Bailey Type Q)

Four Fat Lamps found at Cosa have a small circular boss in the center of the discus through which the filling hole was punched. This was not a functional design, since oil would be trapped in the discus unless great care was used in filling the lamp. There is a ring molding dividing the discus into two equal parts. The shoulder is decorated with bands of ribbed olive leaves arranged in clusters of three, the central one flanked by stemmed olives. The shoulder is separated from the discus by a narrow bead molding.

Figure 92. Fat Lamps: k. Shoulder decorated with a wreath of olive leaves and olives; with a circular boss around the central filling hole, scale 1:2

Late second century–A.D. 416

862 CEL.565 Atrium Building I, Room 25 exterior, Level I. Grayish-buff clay, dark slip, only traces preserved. P.L. 0.041 m; P.W. 0.059 m.
Fragment preserving parts of the discus and rim. Very worn.
Lamp identical with 865.

863 C.F. 834 Atrium Building I, Room 25 exterior, Level I. Buff clay, brown slip. P.L. 0.026 m; P.W. 0.014 m.
Fragment preserving part of the rim. Very worn.
Lamp identical with 865.

864 C.F.2115 Atrium Building I, Room 25 exterior, Level I. Buff clay, red slip. P.L. 0.044 m; P.W. 0.049 m.
Fragment preserving the handle and parts of the discus and rim. Slip rubbed. Pierced molded handle, with two grooves converging toward the crest.
Lamp identical with 865.

865 (Fig. 92) C.F.2117 Atrium Building I, Room 25 exterior, Level I. Cream clay, black slip. P.L. 0.056 m; P.H. 0.018 m; P.W. 0.060 m.
Fragment preserving parts of the discus, rim, and nozzle. Slip very worn, only traces preserved. Made from a handsome new mold. The shoulder is almost horizontal, decorated with ribbed olive leaves arranged in groups of three, with an olive on either side of the longer central leaf. Design starts at the handle and ends over the nozzle, almost touching the opposite half. Nozzle: heart-shaped, Heres Type E e, Loeschcke Type H. Discus: A ring divides the discus into two equal parts. There is a small circular boss in the center of the discus through which the filling hole was punched.

For other examples of this type of lamp, see Brants 1913, pl. 6 no. 991; Heres 1972a, pl. 46 no. 428; Deneauve 1969, pl. 91 nos. 1005, 1009–11; Ponsich 1963, pl. 17 no. 198 (with Heres Type E b nozzle), no. 324 (with an E f nozzle), pl. 25 nos. 337 and 344 (both with E f nozzles). Bailey 1980, pl. 73 no. Q 1333 has the characteristic central boss but a different shoulder decoration.

l. FAT LAMPS: SHOULDER DECORATED WITH A WREATH OF OLIVE LEAVES IN CLUSTERS OF THREE

(Fig. 93)

(Catalogue Number 866)

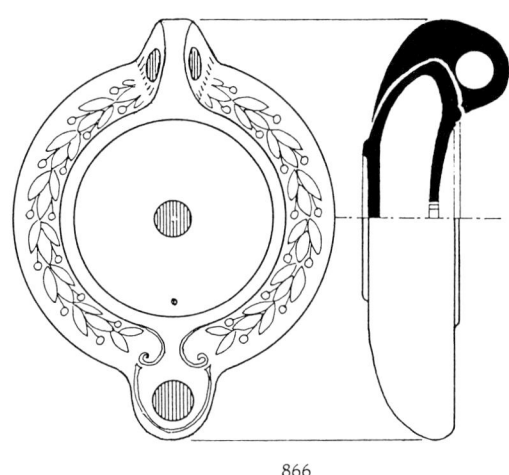

866

Figure 93. Fat Lamps: l. Shoulder decorated with a wreath of olive leaves in clusters of three, scale 1:2

Only one example of a Fat Lamp with shoulder decoration of a band of olive leaves and a decorated discus has been found at Cosa. A string molding is curled in volutes at the base of the nozzle, and a ridge arches from these around the wick hole. The upper part of the nozzle is without definition.

A.D. 118–225

866 (Fig. 93) CF.470 Atrium Building I, Room 25 A, Level II. Coin dated 118 found here. Grayish-buff clay, reddish-brown slip. P.L. 0.046 m; P.H. 0.015 m; P.W. 0.031 m.

Fragment preserving parts of the discus, rim, and nozzle. Slip worn. Shoulder separated from the discus by a bead molding and decorated with a band of olive leaves arranged in clusters of three, with an olive on either side of the longer central leaf. The leaves are unribbed. The decoration starts at the handle and ends short of volutes in string molding that flank the band over the nozzle. The outer edge of the shoulder is framed by a ridge, and another arches around the wick hole of the short, rounded, unprofiled nozzle (Cosan nozzle Type 7). Discus relief: Only part of the lower right side of the discus is preserved. On that part is a ground line and the lower part of a draped figure. The three Fates appear on the two examples of this lamp in the British Museum; per-

haps this relief was the same.

For parallels, see Bailey 1980, pl. 83 nos. Q 1392, Q 1393; Deneauve 1969, pl. 92 no. 1021 (with Apollo Citharoedus); Ivanyi 1935, pl. 35 no. 8; Heres 1972a, pl. 48 no. 452 (with a bust of Julia Domna).

m. FAT LAMPS: SHOULDER DECORATED WITH A BAND OF RADIATING GROOVES TERMINATING IN SMALL CIRCULAR PUNCHES
(Fig. 94)

(Catalogue Numbers 867, 868)

Late Second Century–A.D. 416

867 (Fig. 94) CF.839 Atrium Building I, Room 25 exterior, Level I. Cream clay, dark brown slip. P.L. 0.044 m; P.W. 0.043 m.

Two joining fragments preserving the handle and parts of the discus and rim. Surface worn and chipped. Molded pierced handle with two grooves converging at the crest. Shoulder decorated with a band of radiating grooves with a small

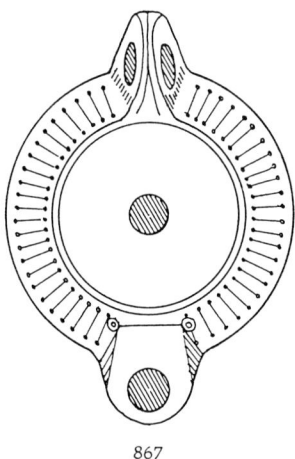

867

Figure 94. Fat Lamps: m. Shoulder decorated with a band of radiating grooves, scale 1:2

circular punch mark at each end.
868 CF.1972 Atrium Building I, Room 25 exterior NW Sidewalk, Level II. Cream clay, self-slip, or the slip is completely worn away. P.L. 0.045 m; P.W. 0.043 m.

Fragment preserving parts of the discus, rim, and nozzle. Very worn. Shoulder decorated with a band of radiating grooves with small circular punch marks at each end. Nozzle: Heres Type E b, Loeschcke Type L 1, with a bull's eye at each end of the groove at the top of the nozzle.

For lamps with the same shoulder decoration, see Deneauve, pl. 77 nos. 835–40, pl. 34 (misprint for 84) nos. 920, 925; Joly 1974, pl. 15 nos. 402, 406, 417; Ponsich 1963, pl. 17 nos. 192–93, pl. 28 nos. 315, 319.

n. FAT LAMPS: SHOULDER DECORATED WITH A BAND OF RECTANGLES AND RAISED DOTS
(Fig. 95)

(Catalogue Number 869)

Late Second Century–A.D. 416

869 (Fig. 95) CF.1978 Atrium Building I, Room 25 exterior NW Sidewalk, Level II. Orange-buff clay, orange slip. P.L. 0.060 m; P.W. 0.048 m.

Fragment preserving parts of the discus, shoulder, and nozzle. Slip rubbed on high relief. Unprofiled, short, semicircular nozzle (Cosan Type 8). The shoulder is divided into two bands, the outer plain, the inner decorated with a broad continuous ring of small radiating panels framed by raised ridges, each containing one or two raised dots or a pair of oblique ridges. The ring narrows toward the nozzle and turns at an angle to extend across the top of the nozzle as a straight band containing a series of raised dots. Discus relief: None preserved, but the filling hole is at the extreme left of the discus to avoid the relief.

o. FAT LAMPS: SHOULDER DECORATED WITH OLIVES AND OLIVE LEAVES BOUND IN THREES, WITH DISCUS RELIEF
(Fig. 96)

(Catalogue Numbers 870–899)

Thirty Fat Lamps or fragments of lamps of Loeschcke Type VIII have been found at Cosa with relief decora-

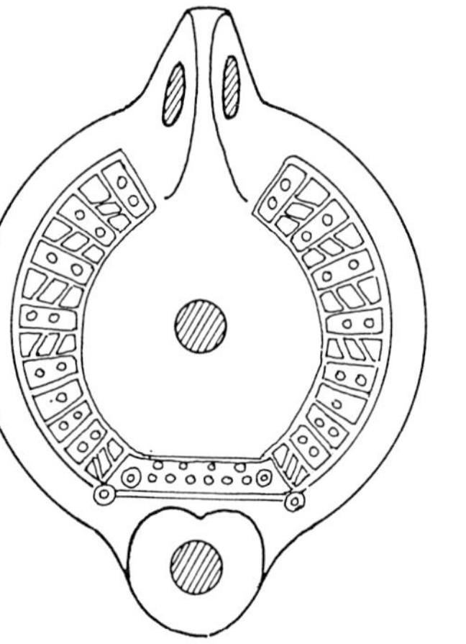

Figure 95. Fat Lamps: n. Shoulder decorated with a band of rectangles and raised dots, scale 1:2

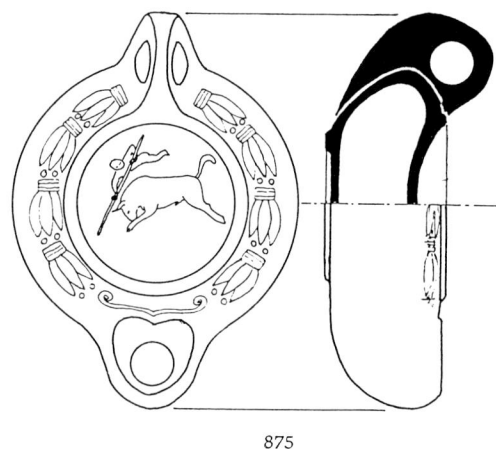

Figure 96. Fat Lamps: o. Shoulder decorated with olives and olive leaves bound in threes, with discus relief, scale 1:2

tion on the shoulder of a series of olive leaves in clusters of three bound together at the stem end by a band, forming a very stylized wreath. Between the ends of each three leaves are two olives. The design starts on either side of the molded pierced handle and ends short of the nozzle. On some of these lamps at the nozzle a thread molding with volute ends is added above the heart framing the nozzle to fill the space between the ends of the wreath. All the nozzles that are preserved are Heres Type E e or E f, or Loeschcke Type H. The fabric is thick and coarse. The color of the clay is buff or cream; the lamps are slipped in red, orange, or brown, often mottled. The clay was carelessly packed in the mold, and there are frequent pits and crevices in the fabric. The molds are crude compared with Julio-Claudian examples.

Eleven of these lamps were found in contexts dated A.D. 100–225. One lamp has a portrait bust of Julia Domna, which can be securely dated to the reign of Septimius Severus (A.D. 193–211). The remainder of this group can be only loosely dated from the late second century to A.D. 416.

This group of lamps corresponds to Bailey Type Q, Groups viii and ix. The only difference between these two groups seems to be that Group ix are smaller (see Bailey 1980, 364–66, 371–72, for a discussion of these two groups). Bailey dates these lamps late Antonine to mid-third century. However, the evidence of the Cosan examples indicates that this date must be extended into the fourth century.

A.D. 100–225

870 CEL.131 Atrium Building I, Room 1, Level I. Buff clay, dark brown slip. P.L. 0.047 m; P.W. 0.073 m.
   Fragment preserving parts of the handle and rim. Very worn; only traces of slip preserved. Handle has two grooves converging at the crest.

871 CEL.181 Atrium Building I, Room 24, Level I. Buff clay, dark brown slip. P.L. 0.039 m; P.W. 0.015 m.
   Fragment of a rim. Very worn.

872 (Pl. VI) CEL.269 Atrium Building I, Room 5, Level I. Buff clay, orange slip. P.L. 0.026 m; P.W. 0.030 m.
   Fragment preserving parts of the discus and rim. Slip rubbed. Discus relief: Racing biga, only the two horses' heads preserved.
   For the complete relief, see Loeschcke 1919, pl. 6 nos. 55, 57.

873 CEL.558 Atrium Building I, Room 22 exterior, Level IV. Buff clay with an orange tint, orange slip. P.L. 0.040 m; P.W. 0.047 m.
   Fragment preserving the handle and parts of the discus and rim. Very worn; made from a worn mold. Discus relief: Too little left for identification.

874 CF.473 Atrium Building I, Room 25 A, Level III. Buff clay, orange-red slip. P.L. 0.054 m; P.H. 0.024 m; P.W. 0.060 m.
   Fragment preserving the nozzle and parts of the discus, rim, and upper side wall of the oil reservoir. Surface worn. Nozzle: heart-shaped, Heres Type E f. Discus relief: The hind legs of a horse galloping right, the rest broken away. The filling hole is at the bottom center of the discus.

875 (Fig. 96) CF.1638 Atrium Building I, Room 25 B, Level IV. Buff clay, brown slip. P.L. 0.071 m; P.W. 0.047 m.
   Fragment preserving parts of the discus, rim, and nozzle. Very worn. Made from an old, blurred mold. Nozzle: Heres Type E f. Discus relief: Man pole-vaulting over a bull that charges left with its head lowered. The pole is placed just in front of the bull. The man is almost horizontal over the bull's back.
   For exact parallels, see Bailey 1980, pl. 83 no. Q 1390 and Heres 1972a, pl. 47 no. 447.

876 CF.1941 Atrium Building I, Room 25 A, Level III. Buff clay, red slip. P.L. 0.034 m; Height 0.024 m; P.W. 0.032 m.
   Fragment preserving the handle and parts of the rim and base. Worn. Ring base, only partially preserved. Handle with two grooves converging at the crest.

877 CF.2148 Atrium Building I, Room 15, Level II. Buff clay, self-slip. P.L. 0.031 m; P.H. 0.014 m; P.W. 0.022 m.
   Fragment preserving parts of the rim and nozzle. Very worn. Nozzle: heart-shaped, Heres Type E f.

878 CF.2283 Atrium Building I, Room 22 exterior, Level IV. Buff clay, orange-red slip. P.L. 0.048 m; P.W. 0.031 m.
   Fragment preserving parts of the plain discus, rim, and nozzle. Nozzle: heart-shaped, Heres Type E f.

879 CF.2296 Atrium Building I, Room 22 exterior, Level III A (found with three coins dated A.D. 134–38, 177–78, and 187–93). Buff clay, orange slip. P.L. 0.029 m; P.W. 0.026 m.
   Fragment preserving part of the rim. Slip worn.

Made from an old, blurred mold.
880 CF.2118 Atrium Building I, Room 25 exterior, Level II. Grayish-buff clay, red slip mottled to black in places. P.L. 0.027 m; P.W. 0.035 m.

Fragment preserving part of the left side of a discus and the rim. Worn. Discus relief: On the left a bust of Julia Domna facing right, with an elaborate hairdress, earrings, and drapery fastened on the left shoulder. The top of her head is broken away, but she probably had a crescent there, identifying her as Luna. On the right side of the discus Septimius Severus should appear as Sol.

Cf. Heres 1972a, pl. 47 no. 442 (this relief on a lamp signed *LCAECSAE*). Nos. 451 and 454 have profiles of Julia Domna alone facing right, no. 451 signed *LCAECSAE*, no. 454 signed *ERACLID*.

Late Second Century–A.D. 416

881 CEL.546 Atrium Building I, Room 25 exterior, Level I. Buff clay, red slip mottled to black in places. P.L. 0.034 m; P.W. 0.035 m.

Fragment preserving parts of the discus and rim. Very worn. Discus relief: A wing, perhaps of an Eros, the rest broken away.

882 CEL.547 Atrium Building I, Room 25 exterior, Level I. Buff clay, orange slip mottled to brown in places. P.L. 0.049 m; P.W. 0.044 m.

Fragment preserving parts of the rim and nozzle. Very worn; made from a worn mold. Nozzle: heart-shaped, Heres Type E f.

883 CEL.560 Atrium Building I, Room 25, Level I. Buff clay, dark brown slip. P.L. 0.045 m; P.W. 0.039 m.

Fragment preserving the handle and parts of the discus and rim. Very worn. Discus relief: The remains are too fragmentary and the mold too worn for identification.

884 (Pl. VII) CF.463 Atrium Building I, Room 25, Level I. Buff clay, orange-red slip. P.L. 0.048 m; P.W. 0.035 m.

Fragment preserving parts of the discus, rim, and nozzle. Surface worn. Nozzle: heart-shaped, Heres Type E f. Discus relief: Two large bunches of grapes hanging from a pole around which grape tendrils twine. Only the bunch of grapes to the left is preserved. Large filling hole punched lower center.

For the complete relief, see Bailey 1980, pl. 82 no. Q 1387. See also 895.

885 CF.830 Atrium Building I, Room 25, Level I. Buff clay, red slip. P.L. 0.025 m; P.W. 0.031 m.

Fragment preserving parts of the rim and discus. Surface rubbed. Discus relief: Too little remains to identify.

886 CF.838 Atrium Building I, Room 25, Level I. Buff clay, red slip. P.L. 0.050 m; P.W. 0.052 m.

Fragment preserving parts of the discus and shoulder. Very worn; surface pitted. Made from an old, worn mold. Discus relief: A large bird, perhaps a crane, running left, attacked by a bear that has leaped on the back of the bird from the right. Filling hole near the edge of the discus toward the nozzle.

887 CF.1633 Atrium Building I, Room 25, Level I. Buff clay, red slip. P.L. 0.030 m; P.W. 0.028 m.

Fragment preserving parts of the discus and rim. Very worn; only traces of slip preserved. Discus relief: Eros to the right supporting the infant Bacchus, who holds a bunch of grapes.

Cf. 799.

888 CF.1649 Atrium Building I, Room 25 D, Level II. Buff clay, orange slip. P.L. 0.045 m; P.W. 0.042 m.

Fragment preserving parts of the discus, rim, and nozzle. Slip rubbed on raised surfaces. Nozzle: Heres Type E f. Discus relief: Bust of Jupiter above an eagle mounted on a thunderbolt. Only the thunderbolt and part of the eagle's right wing are preserved.

For the complete relief on lamps with a different nozzle, see Bailey 1980, pl. 64 nos. Q 1250, Q 1251.

889 CF.1661 Atrium Building I, Room 25 D, Level II. Buff clay, orange slip. P.L. 0.081 m; P.W. 0.050 m.

Two joining fragments preserving parts of the discus, rim, handle, and nozzle. Surface rubbed. Nozzle: heart-shaped, Heres Type E f. Discus relief: Too fragmentary to identify.

890 CF.1974 Atrium Building I, Room 25 exterior, NW sidewalk, Level II. Buff clay, orange slip. P.L. 0.018 m; P.W. 0.014 m.

Fragment preserving part of the rim.

891 CF.1977 Atrium Building I, Room 25 exterior, NW Sidewalk, Level II. Buff clay, self-slip. P.L. 0.042 m; P.W. 0.030 m.

Fragment preserving parts of the discus, rim, and handle. Very worn. Discus relief: A feline attacking an antelope from the rear.

For a complete example of this relief, see 897.

892 CF.1981 Atrium Building I, Room 25 exterior NW, Level I. Cream clay, brown slip. P.L. 0.040 m; P.W. 0.034 m.

Fragment preserving parts of a plain discus, rim, and nozzle. Very worn.

893 (Pl. IV) CF.2003 Atrium Building I, Room 25 exterior NW, Level I. Buff clay, brown slip. P.L. 0.034 m; P.W. 0.046 m.

Fragment preserving a handle of the usual form with grooves converging on the crest and part of the rim.

894 CF.2005 Atrium Building I, Room 25 exterior NW, Level I. Buff clay, with a reddish tint, orange slip. P.L. 0.041 m; P.W. 0.041 m.

Fragment preserving parts of the discus, rim, and nozzle. Worn; made from an old, blurred mold. Discus relief: Perhaps a bunch of grapes. Too worn to identify positively.

895 CF.2011 Atrium Building I, Room 25 exterior, Level I/II. Buff clay, orange slip. P.L. 0.062 m; P.H. 0.030 m; P.W. 0.059 m.

Fragment preserving the nozzle and parts of the discus, rim, and upper side wall of the oil reservoir. The mold is very worn, except for the discus relief, which has been reworked. Slip worn. Nozzle: heart-shaped, Heres Type E f. Discus relief: Two bunches of grapes hanging from a pole around which grape tendrils twine. The design has been reworked, and the grape forms are clear, but they are smaller than those on 884, made from the same (or same-generation) mold.

896 CF.2018 Atrium Building I, Room 25 exterior, Level I. Buff clay, red slip mottled to brown in places. P.L. 0.089 m; P.W. 0.069 m.

Two joining fragments preserving the handle, and parts of the discus and rim. Discus relief: Two large bunches of grapes hanging from a pole, the same relief as on 884 and 895.

897 (Pl. VIII) CF.2122 Atrium Building I, Room 25 exterior, Level II. Buff clay, orange slip. Length 0.107 m; Height 0.024 m; Width 0.076 m.

A complete lamp, in good condition, probably preserved because it was unusable. The signature was pressed too hard on the base of the lamp and broke through the fabric. Nozzle: heart-shaped, Heres Type E f, with vine tendrils over the nozzle forming a volute. Molded pierced handle with two grooves converging on the crest. Discus relief: Feline attacking an antelope, both moving left. The antelope looks back at the attacking animal, which has leaped on the antelope's back and sunk its teeth into its back. Ring base, with carelessly scratched circles within the outer ring. The signature *CRISPINI* is impressed on the base, with a bull's eye above and below the signature (see Fig. 141).

Cf. Joly 1974, pl. 13 no. 365, pl. 30 no. 794; Bonnet, fig. 17 no. 10; Bailey 1980, pl. 11 no. Q 866 (on a lamp of another type).

898 CF.2127 Atrium Building I, Room 25 exterior, Level II. Buff clay, red slip mottled to black in places. P.L. 0.038 m; P.W. 0.027 m.

Fragment preserving parts of the discus and rim. Very worn; discolored. Plain discus with central filling hole.

899 CF.2284 Atrium Building I, Room 25 exterior, Level I. Buff clay, red slip. P.L. 0.026 m; P.W. 0.025 m.

Fragment preserving parts of the discus and shoulder. Fire-blackened; worn. Made from a worn, blurred mold. Discus relief: Too fragmentary to identify.

p. FAT LAMPS: SHOULDER DECORATED WITH ALTERNATING BUNCHES OF GRAPES AND LEAVES, CUT FROM VINE
(Fig. 97)
(Catalogue Numbers 900–906)

Seven Fat Lamps have shoulders decorated with alternating bunches of grapes and grape leaves. Each has been cut from the parent vine with a bit of the vine still attached, and the stem end is toward the handle. Several lamps have a discus relief. None preserves its nozzle, but the four examples of lamps with this shoulder decoration in the British Museum collection all have heart-shaped nozzles; see Bailey 1980, Q 1397–98, Q 1416–17.

A.D. 100–225

900 (Pl. VIII; Fig. 97) CEL.182 Atrium Building I, Room 19, Level II. Buff clay, red slip. P.L. 0.070 m; P.H. 0.022 m; P.W. 0.053 m.

Two joining fragments preserving parts of the

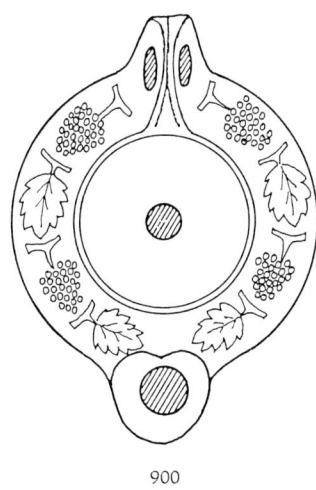

Figure 97. Fat Lamps: p. Shoulder decorated with alternating cut bunches of grapes and leaves, scale 1:2

discus and rim. Very worn. Discus relief: A long-legged fighting cock in high relief, walking right. Rather crudely executed; the feathers are indicated with coarse striation.

901 CEL.564 Atrium Building I, Room 16 exterior, Level V. Buff clay, red slip mottled to black in places. P.L. 0.049 m; P.W. 0.053 m.
  Fragment preserving the handle and part of the rim.

902 CF.1662 Atrium Building I, Room 25 D, Level II. Buff clay, orange slip. P.L. 0.046 m; P.W. 0.061 m.
  Fragment preserving the handle and parts of the rim. Slip rubbed.

903 (Pl. II) CF.1835 Atrium Building I, Room 25 D, Level II. Buff clay, red slip. P.L. 0.052 m; P.W. 0.034 m.
  Fragment preserving parts of the discus, rim, and handle. Very worn; only traces of slip preserved. Discus relief: Aeneas in three-quarters view moves right, carrying Anchises on his left shoulder and leading Ascanius with his right hand; Aeneas looks down at Ascanius. Some of the relief is broken away; Ascanius is missing, and Aeneas is preserved only from the waist up.
  For a complete example of this relief, see Bailey 1980, pl. 83 no. Q 1394. Bailey writes that Aeneas wears a short tunic, probably a cuirass, a cloak, and boots, and that Ascanius wears a short tunic, a cloak, and cap, and carries a *pedum*. He dates this lamp late Antonine to mid-third century.

904 CF.1936 Atrium Building I, Room 25 A, Level II. Buff clay with a reddish tint, self-slip. P.L. 0.039 m; P.W. 0.034 m.
  Fragment preserving part of the rim. Very worn.

Late Second Century–A.D. 416

905 CF.832 Atrium Building I, Room 25, Level I. Buff clay, red slip. P.L. 0.023 m; P.W. 0.017 m.
  Fragment preserving part of the rim. Slip rubbed.

906 CF.1927 Atrium Building I, Room 25, Level I. Buff clay, red slip. P.L. 0.031 m; P.W. 0.020 m.
  Fragment preserving parts of the discus and rim. Very worn; made from an old, blurred mold.

q. FAT LAMPS: SHOULDER DECORATED WITH A BAND OF LOTUS BUDS AND PALMETTES
(Fig. 98)
(Catalogue Number 907)

A.D. 50–ca. 100

907 (Fig. 98) CEL.612 Basilica exterior, NW 2, Level III. Buff clay, brown slip. Length 0.112 m; Height 0.045 m; Width 0.076 m.
  Two joining fragments preserving all essential features. Very worn. Made from an old, blurred mold. Molded pierced handle, the grooves usually on the crest worn away. Nozzle: heart-shaped, Heres Type E e, Loeschcke Type H. The shoulder is decorated with a band of tiny palmettes alternating with lotus buds, and the discus marked off from the shoulder by a narrow bead molding. Discus relief: Rosette of twenty-two concave petals radiating from the central filling hole.
  Cf. Gualandi Genito 1977, pl. 55 no. 409 (who described the decoration of the shoulder as ovules).

r. FAT LAMPS: SHOULDER DECORATED WITH LOOPED VINES WITH GRAPES OR A LEAF IN ALTERNATE LOOPS ENCLOSED BY THREAD MOLDINGS

(Fig. 99)

(Catalogue Number 908)

The Fat Lamp below has a shoulder decorated with a continuous design of looped grapevines with a bunch of grapes and a leaf in alternating loops, with unprofiled nozzle.

A.D. 50–ca. 100

908 (Fig. 99) CEL.173 Atrium Building I, Room 11, Level I. Buff clay, orange slip. P.L. 0.043 m; P.W. 0.047 m.

Fragment preserving parts of the discus, rim, and nozzle. Surface worn, pitted, and chipped. Discus marked off from the shoulder by a narrow bead molding. The shoulder is decorated with a carefully rendered grapevine wound in loops, ending in a spiral tendril at the nozzle. Within the loops of the vine a bunch of grapes alternates with a leaf. A narrow ridge frames the outer edge of the shoulder decoration and ends at the unprofiled nozzle in scrolls that make a false channel from discus to nozzle. Discus relief: Two large bunches of grapes hanging from a twining vine. Only part of the relief is preserved.

For a complete example of the discus, see Bailey 1980, pl. 82 no. Q 1386 (but with different shoulder decoration).

s. FAT LAMPS: SHOULDER DECORATED WITH A CRUDE ZIGZAG DESIGN

(Fig. 100)

(Catalogue Number 909)

A.D. 330–416

909 (Fig. 100) C68.106 Forum, SE, Shrine of Liber Pater, Level 0. Buff clay, orange slip mottled to brown in places. Length 0.093 m; Height 0.027 m; Width 0.069 m.

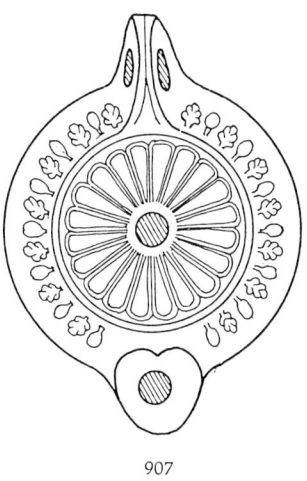

Figure 98. Fat Lamps: q. Shoulder decorated with a band of lotus buds and palmettes, scale 1:2

Figure 99. Fat Lamps: r. Shoulder decorated with looped vines with grapes or a leaf in alternate loops enclosed by thread moldings, scale 1:2

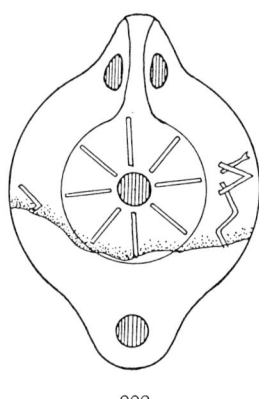

909

Figure 100. Fat Lamp: s. Shoulder decorated with a crude zigzag design, scale 1:2

Two joining fragments preserving most of a lamp, the top of the nozzle and part of the rim broken away. Encrusted; made from a crude mold. Unprofiled base. Molded pierced handle without grooves. Shoulder decorated with uneven crude irregular ridges in a zigzag. Discus relief: A ring of eight ridges, evenly spaced, radiating from the central filling hole.

t. FAT LAMPS: DISCI UNASSOCIATED WITH OTHER ELEMENTS

(Catalogue Numbers 910–932)

25/20 B.C.–A.D. 40/45

910 CEL.388 Atrium Building I, Room 22, Level II. Cream clay, brown slip. P.L. 0.051 m; P.W. 0.027 m.
  Two joining fragments preserving parts of a discus. Very worn. Discus relief: Three bead moldings encircle the central filling hole.

25/20 B.C.–A.D. 50

911 CEL.68 Atrium Building I, Room 21, Level II. Buff clay, brown slip. P.L. 0.037 m; P.W. 0.030 m.
  Fragment preserving part of the discus, including an arc of the filling hole. Worn. Discus relief: A hippocamp, only partially preserved, rather crudely executed.
  Cf. Bailey 1980, pl. 3 no. Q 784 (on a Triangular Nozzle Lamp).

912 CEL.497 Atrium Building I, Room 21, Level II. Cream clay, red slip. P.L. 0.039 m; P.W. 0.021 m.
  Fragment preserving part of a discus. Slip very worn. Discus relief: Central filling hole encircled by a bead molding framed by two rings. The outer part of the discus is broken away.

A.D. 50–ca. 100

913 CEL.108 Atrium Building I, Room 15, Level I, drain. Buff clay with a pink tint, red slip. P.L. 0.032 m; P.W. 0.035 m.
  Fragment preserving part of a discus. Worn; made from a crude mold. Discus relief: A fighting cock, only the feet, legs, and part of the lower body preserved.

914 (Pl. VIII) CEL.130 Atrium Building I, Room 8, Level II. Cream clay, red slip. P.L. 0.029 m; P.W. 0.045 m.
  Fragment preserving part of a discus. Worn; made from a worn, crude mold. Discus relief: A lion to left, right front paw raised, the top of the head and tail broken away.
  Cf. Deneauve, pl. 63 no. 622.

915 (Pl. V) CEL.154 Atrium Building I, Room 11, Level I. Cream clay, brown slip. P.L. 0.038 m; P.W. 0.021 m.
  Fragment preserving part of a discus. Surface very worn. Discus relief: Boxer, frontal, legs apart, arms down at sides, forearms and hands heavily bandaged. He wears a belted kilt, but the upper body is nude. Head, right hand, both feet, and lower right leg are broken away. Filling hole punched between legs.

916 CEL.223 Atrium Building I, Room 22, Level I. Buff clay, red slip. P.L. 0.024 m; P.W. 0.032 m.
  Fragment preserving part of a discus. Slip rubbed. Discus relief: Vegetation and part of a crocodile, perhaps part of a fight between a crocodile and another animal.

A.D. 50–225

917 (Pl. V) CEL.164 Atrium Building I, Room 11, Level I. Buff clay, red slip. P.L. 0.043 m; P.W. 0.032 m.
  Fragment preserving discus center. Slip worn away on raised surfaces. Discus relief: Gladiator, frontal, with left leg forward, knee bent, and foot on fallen opponent. The fallen gladiator is broken away, except for a foot. The head, arms, and right foot of the victorious gladiator are broken away. He wears greaves, a *subligaculum*, thigh padding, and a twisted belt [?].

Cf. Loeschcke 1919, pl. 9 no. 127; Goethert-Polaschek, pl. 30 nos. 122, 235, 282, pl. 64 no. 570; Deneauve, pl. 38 nos. 317, 320; Menzel, fig. 31 no. 6; Heres 1972a, pl. 59 no. 552; Loeschcke 1919, pl. 10 nos. 435, and 129 (with the victor alone).

918 CG.529 Forum, NE passage. Buff clay, red slip. P.L. 0.047 m; P.W. 0.041 m.

Fragment preserving most of the discus and part of two framing rings separating the discus from the plain beveled shoulder. Fair condition. Made from a crude mold. Discus relief: An erotic symplegma.

Cf. Deneauve, pl. 1 nos. 484–85, pl. 11 nos. 486–87. Except for the arrangement of the bedding, the design is the same.

919 CG.534 Forum, NE passage. Buff clay, red slip. P.L. 0.042 m.

Fragment preserving parts of a discus and rim. Worn. Discus relief: Bust of Sol, frontal, with radiate crown. Probably Septimius Severus as Sol.

Cf. Leibundgut 1977, pl. 26 no. 33.

920 CG.535 Forum, NE passage. Buff clay, red slip. P.L. 0.039 m; P.W. 0.038 m.

Fragment preserving part of a discus. Slip worn. Discus relief: Mounted warrior galloping left. Warrior looks back, holding round shield in left hand and a vertical sword in right. Figure wears trousers, presumably a barbarian.

Cf. Deneauve, pl. 38 nos. 326–27; Leibundgut 1977, pl. 44 no. 246 (a cruder example of this relief with the warrior carrying an oblong or rectangular shield).

921 CG.606 Building L (market building), Exterior NE, Level I. Cream clay, red slip mottled to brown in places. P.L. 0.026 m; P.W. 0.035 m.

Fragment preserving part of a discus. Slip worn. Discus relief: A fighting cock facing right, with a vertical palm branch behind the bird. Made from a crude mold.

921A CG.607 Building L (market building), Exterior NW, Level I. Buff clay, purplish-red slip. P.L. 0.033 m; P.W. 0.030 m.

Fragment preserving part of a discus. Slip rubbed. Discus relief: A double-curved rope [?] ending in a circular form at one end and a three-pronged object at the other, possibly part of a relief of a retiarius or his equipment.

922 C68.413 Arx, W slope, Level 0-I. Cream clay, red slip. P.L. 0.036 m; P.W. 0.032 m.

Fragment preserving part of the discus and rim. Very worn. Discus relief: Eros walking left, wearing drapery looped around hips and tied in a swag behind. The left hand behind the body holds the knot of the garment. The head, left foot, and right arm are broken away.

923 C68.432 Arx, W slope, Level 0-I. Buff clay, grayish-black slip. P.L. 0.041 m; P.W. 0.043 m.

Fragment preserving part of a discus. Slip rubbed. Discus relief: Bear attacking a bull. Bull moving right, bear attacking from left.

For an example of the same relief from the same (or same-generation) mold, see 796.

924 C68.433 Arx, W slope, Level 0-I. Buff clay, black slip. P.L. 0.035 m; P.W. 0.038 m.

Fragment preserving right part of discus. Slip worn. Discus relief: Pegasus flying left. On the bit remaining of the left side of the discus appears to be part of another winged horse, so perhaps a confronted pair.

925 C68.531 Arx, W slope, Level 0-I. Buff clay, red slip. P.L. 0.046 m; P.W. 0.037 m.

Fragment preserving part of a discus. Slip worn. Discus relief: Sacrifice of a sheep on an altar with a nude male bending over from the left, knife held aloft, left knee holding the animal down.

926 C68.539 Arx, W slope, Structure, Level I. Buff clay, red slip. P.L. 0.040 m; P.W. 0.036 m.

Fragment preserving parts of the discus and shoulder. Very worn. Discus separated from the beveled shoulder by a ring. Discus relief: Panther running left, spots indicated by punch marks. Crude, but fresh mold.

A.D. 100–225

927 CD.772b Basilica exterior, NE 3, Level I. Buff clay, red slip. P.L. 0.037 m; P.W. 0.034 m.

Fragment preserving part of the discus and rim. Very worn. Discus relief: On the deck of a ship a nude Eros, preserved from the hips down, strides to the right. He carries a large lantern, or perhaps a bundle, behind him, over his shoulder on a stick. The ship is indicated by six oblique oar holes.

928 CEL.451 Atrium Building I, Room 19, Level I. Buff clay, red slip. P.L. 0.016 m; P.W. 0.018 m.

Fragment preserving part of a discus. Worn and chipped. Discus relief: Heavily maned lion's head, frontal.

929 CEL.632 Basilica exterior, W, Level I. Buff clay, red slip. P.L. 0.033 m; P.W. 0.028 m.

Fragment preserving part of a discus. In good condition. Discus relief: Rosette of narrow concave tongues, radiating from three rings around the central filling hole.

930 CF.1646 Atrium Building I, Room 25 D, Level II. Buff clay, red slip. P.L. 0.057 m; P.W. 0.036 m.

Fragment preserving the central part of a discus. Slip worn. Discus relief: The infant Bacchus walking left, holding out a bunch of grapes in his right hand. (Some lamp reliefs show the infant Bacchus supported by an Eros on the right.)

931 CEL.1836 Atrium Building I, Room 25 D, Level II. Grayish-buff clay, dark slip, only traces remaining. P.L. 0.031 m; P.W. 0.032 m.

Fragment preserving part of the discus. Very worn, made from a worn, crude mold. Discus relief: A dolphin swimming right with lifted tail. He has a very large eye, with eyelashes indicated by short strokes.

Cf. Joly 1974, pl. 13 no. 339.

932 CF.1930 Atrium Building I, Room 25 C, Level II. Buff clay, red slip. P.L. 0.026 m; P.W. 0.032 m.

Fragment preserving part of a discus, including an arc of the filling hole. Very worn. Discus relief: A horned animal, perhaps an ibex, running left. Part of the head and the feet are broken away.

Cf. Joly 1974, pl. 13 no. 365, pl. 30 no. 794 (the same animal, but running right).

u. FAT LAMPS: PLAIN SHOULDER AND DISCUS WITH A VITREOUS GREEN GLAZE

(Fig. 101)

(Catalogue Number 933)

A.D. 100–225

933 (Fig. 101) CD.600 a–e Basilica exterior, NE 1, Level I. Cream clay, vitreous green glaze. P.L. 0.110 m; Height 0.041 m; Width 0.090 m.

Six joining and nonjoining fragments preserving parts of all essential features. Two lumps of puddled glaze on the top of the rim and nozzle show that the lamp was fired upside down. In good condition. Rim: A ring framed by grooves

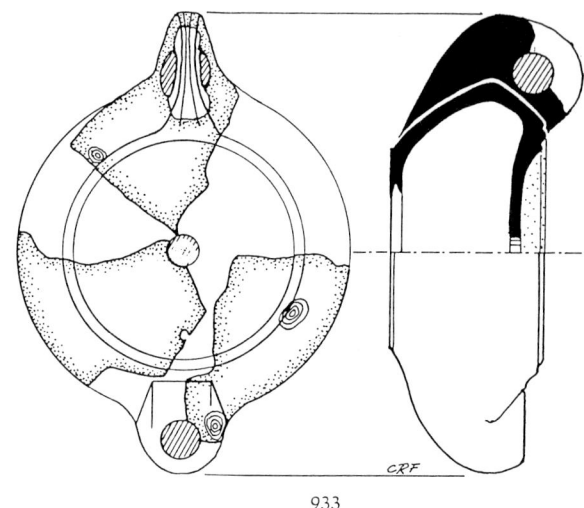

Figure 101. Fat Lamp: t. Plain shoulder and discus with a vitreous green glaze, scale 1:2

separates the discus from the wide, beveled shoulder. Short unprofiled nozzle and unprofiled base. Molded pierced handle without the usual grooves. Discus plain.

This is the only lamp found at Cosa that has a vitreous glaze. It is included in the publication of the glass from Cosa by David F. Grose.

v. FAT LAMPS: FRAGMENTS OF BASES WITH SIGNATURES

(Catalogue Numbers 934–983)

25/20 B.C.–A.D. 50

934 CB.1577 Capitolium exterior S, Level II. Buff clay with a pink tint, red slip. P.L. 0.044 m; P.W. 0.040 m.

Fragment preserving part of a base. Worn. Low disk base with part of an impressed signature: *COPRES* to be completed *COPRESTI* for Gaius Oppius Restitutus. See Fig. 139. See Bailey 1980, 99 and fig. 108, for this signature.

935 CEL.377 Atrium Building I, Room 21, Level II. Fine, buff-colored clay, dark-brown slip with a metallic luster.

Four joining fragments preserving parts of ring base and lower side wall of oil reservoir. Ring base formed of three rings. Across the center is impressed either the upper or lower half of an illegible signature, of perhaps six letters.

936 CEL.605 Basilica exterior, NW 2, Level III. Buff clay, brown slip. P.L. 0.081 m; Height 0.022 m; P.W. 0.069 m.

Fragment preserving the handle and parts of the discus, base, and side wall of the oil reservoir. Worn. Molded, pierced handle with two grooves converging on crest. Disk base with an illegible impressed signature, with a bull's eye centered above and below the signature.

A.D. 50–100

937 CEL.91 Atrium Building I, Room 22, Level I. Cream-colored clay, brown slip. P.L. 0.037 m; P.H. 0.009 m; P.W. 0.027 m; Base diameter 0.045 m.

Fragment preserving parts of ring base and lower side wall of oil reservoir. Very worn, only traces of slip preserved. The first two letters of an impressed signature are preserved: *LM*, with the upper part of the *M* broken away, to be completed *LMADIEC* for Lucius Munatius Adiectus, or *LMVNPHILE* for Lucius Munatius Philemon. Below the signature, centered, a vertical palm branch. See Fig. 140.

Cf. 974 (from the Basilica); Menzel, 56; Bailey 1980, 98 and fig. 107.

938 CEL.92 Atrium Building I, Room 22, Level I. Buff-colored clay, very faint traces of a dark slip. P.L. 0.044 m; P.H. 0.020 m; P.W. 0.026 m; Base diameter 0.044 m.

Fragment preserving parts of disk base and lower side wall of oil reservoir. Very worn. On the base is impressed the upper half of an *M*, the top angle cut by horizontal lines (see Fig. 140).

939 CEL.106 Atrium Building I, Room 15, Level I. Buff clay with an orange tint, self-slip. P.L. 0.059 m; P.H. 0.024 m; P.W. 0.043 m.

Fragment preserving parts of the base, lower side wall of the oil reservoir, and lower part of the nozzle and handle. Worn. Low disk base. On the bottom of the lamp is a part of an impressed signature: *LSV* . . . perhaps for Lucius Successus. See Fig. 140.

Cf. Bailey 1980, 101 and fig. 109.

940 CEL.232 Atrium Building I, Room 22, Level I. Fine, cream-colored clay, dark brown slip with a metallic luster. P.L. 0.048 m; P.H. 0.024 m; P.W. 0.035 m; Base diameter 0.038 m.

Fragment preserving parts of sloping convex shoulder, oil reservoir, and base. Disk base with part of an impressed signature: . . . *MASC*, probably for Lucius Fabricius Masculus. See Fig. 139.

Cf. Bailey 1980, 95 and fig. 105.

941 CEL.248 Atrium Building I, Room 6, Level I. Fine, cream-colored clay, black or dark brown slip with a metallic luster P.L. 0.032 m; P.W. 0.020 m; Base diameter 0.038 m.

Fragment preserving parts of base and lower side wall of oil reservoir. Disk base; impressed on base is part of a signature, the vertical stroke of an *I* or *L*, a dot, and the top of an *A* or *M*. See Fig. 140.

942 CEL.277 Atrium Building I, Room 5, Level I. Cream clay, brown slip.

Fragment preserving part of a base. Worn. Ring base, within which are impressed three illegible letters.

943 CEL.278 Atrium Building I, Room 5, Level I. Cream clay, brown slip.

Two joining fragments preserving part of a base. Very worn, made from an old, blurred mold. Ring base, within which is impressed an illegible signature.

944 CEL.280 Atrium Building I, Rooms 12 A, cistern, Level I. Hard, coarse, red clay, red slip. P.L. 0.058 m; Height 0.030 m; P.W. 0.062 m.

Fragment preserving nozzle and parts of base, side wall of oil reservoir, and shoulder. Slip rubbed; smoke-blackened around wick hole. Short rounded nozzle with groove across top. Beveled shoulder decorated with a band of bordered ovules. Ring base, set off by grooves, enclosing an impressed bull's eye that would have been centered above or below a signature.

945 CEL.381 Atrium Building I, Room 25 A, Level III. Buff clay, orange slip. P.L. 0.051 m; P.W. 0.049 m.

Fragment preserving part of a disk base, slightly concave, on which is impressed an illegible signature, with a bull's eye centered above and below the signature.

946 CEL.584 Basilica exterior, NW 2, Level I. Fine, hard, orange-buff clay, red slip. P.L. 0.027 m; P.W. 0.030 m.

Fragment preserving part of a base with two complete impressed letters and parts of two others. First is the horizontal stroke of an *L*, followed by *ER* and the first part of an *N* or *M* (*LERN*). See Fig. 139.

947 CG.589 Forum, NE passage, E corner, Level II. Buff clay, red slip mottled to brown in places. P.L. 0.029 m; P.W. 0.025 m.

Fragment preserving parts of the base and lower side wall of the oil reservoir. Slightly worn and chipped. Low disk base with part of an impressed signature: . . . *IEC*, to be completed *LMADIEC* for Lucius Munatius Adiectus. See Fig. 140.

For this signature, see Bailey, pl. 62 no. Q 1239, pl. 64 no. Q 1251, fig. 107, and notes on p. 98. See also *CIL* 5.8114.87; *CIL* 8.22644.219; *CIL* 10.8053; *CIL* 11.6699.130; *CIL* 12.5682.71; *CIL* 13.10001.216; *CIL* 15.6560.

948 C70.83 V-D Street M, between House of the Skeleton and House of Quintus Fulvius. Cream clay, dark brown slip. P.L. 0.040 m; P.H. 0.015 m; P.W. 0.034 m.

Fragment preserving parts of the base and lower side wall of the oil reservoir. Worn and chipped. Low disk base with a single impressed letter, *A*, surviving from a possible five, possibly to be restored *LMVNA*. See Fig. 140.

Cf. the Arretine pottery stamp Oxé-Comfort, no. 1031.

A.D. 100–225

949 CD.1206 Basilica exterior, NW I, Level II. Cream clay, reddish-brown slip. P.L. 0.032 m; P.W. 0.035 m.

Fragment preserving part of a base and the lower side wall of the oil reservoir. Worn. Ring base enclosing an illegible impressed signature.

950 CD.1217 Basilica exterior, W, Level I. Cream clay, brown slip. P.L. 0.035 m; P.W. 0.022 m.

Fragment preserving parts of a base and the lower side wall of the oil reservoir. Worn, only traces of slip preserved. Low disk base with an impressed signature, the last two letters of a possible three, . . . *HR*, the rest broken away. See Fig. 139.

951 CD.1218 Basilica exterior, NE I, Level I. Cream clay, blackish-brown slip. P.L. 0.029 m; P.W. 0.031 m.

Fragment preserving parts of the base and lower side wall of the oil reservoir. Worn, only traces of slip preserved. Low disk base; on the flat bottom is impressed a signature: . . . *MADIEC*, to be completed *LMADIEC* for Lucius Munatius Adiectus. See Fig. 140.

Cf. Bailey 1980, 98, 198, and fig. 107 on p. 116.

952 CF.471 Atrium Building I, Room 25 A, Level II. Fine, orange-buff clay, red slip. P.L. 0.046 m; P.H. 0.016 m; P.W. 0.025 m.

Fragment preserving parts of base and lower wall of the oil reservoir. Ring base with the last letter of an impressed signature, *E*. See Fig. 139.

953 CF.472 Atrium Building I, Room 25 A, Level II. Fine, orange-buff clay, orange-red slip. P.L. 0.050 m; P.H. 0.012 m; P.W. 0.019 m.

Fragment preserving parts of base and lower wall of oil reservoir. Ring base within which is an impressed *C* followed by a vertical stroke.

954 CF.840 Atrium Building I, Room 25 B, Level III. Buff clay, orange-red slip. P.L. 0.030 m; P.W. 0.027 m.

Fragment preserving part of a base. Worn and chipped. Very narrow ring base, within which is part of an impressed signature: *LCAEC*. . . , probably to be completed *LCAECSAE* for Lucius Caecilius Saecularis. The usual form of his signature is *LCAESAE*. See Fig. 139.

Cf. Bailey 1980, 91 and fig. 103.

955 CF.1631 Atrium Building I, Room 25 C, Level II. Hard, coarse, orange-red clay, orange-red slip. P.L. 0.057 m; P.H. 0.023 m; P.W. 0.046 m.

Fragment preserving parts of base and lower side wall of oil reservoir. Worn; clay has pits and crevices. Ring base, impressed within which are the last two letters of a signature: . . . *NI*, with a bull's eye centered below (and probably above also, now broken away). Perhaps to be completed: *CRISPINI*. See Fig. 141.

Cf. Bailey 1980, 94 and fig. 104.

956 CF.1672 Atrium Building I, Room 25 D, Level II. Orange-red clay, orange slip. P.L. 0.057 m; P.H. 0.019 m; P.W. 0.036 m.

Fragment preserving parts of base and side wall of oil reservoir. Clay pitted and creviced. Ring base, within which are parts of one or two letters, either the beginning or end of a signature, with a stamped bull's eye above or below. Two short vertical strokes are all that remain.

957 CF.1840 Atrium Building I, Room 25 D, Level II. Buff clay, orange-red slip. P.L. 0.034 m; P.H. 0.013

m; P.W. 0.038 m.

Fragment preserving parts of base and lower side wall of oil reservoir. Ring base, within which are impressed the last two letters of a signature: . . . *FL*. See Fig. 141.

958 CF.2130 Atrium Building I, Room 25 exterior, Level II. Buff clay, orange-red slip mottled to brown in places. P.L. 0.038 m; P.W. 0.031 m.

Two joining fragments preserving part of a base. Worn. Ring base, within which is part of an impressed signature . . . *INI*, probably to be completed *CRISPINI*. See Fig. 141.

Cf. Bailey 1980, 94 and fig. 104.

959 CF.2131 Atrium Building I, Room 25 exterior, Level II. Buff clay, with perhaps a self-slip. P.L. 0.030 m; P.W. 0.028 m.

Fragment preserving part of a base. Very worn. Ring base, within which are the first three letters of an impressed signature with a bull's eye above and below: *CRI*. . . , probably to be completed *CRISPINI*. See Fig. 141.

Cf. Bailey 1980, 94 and fig. 104.

960 CF.2287 Atrium Building I, Room 22 exterior, Level II. Cream clay, red slip. P.L. 0.033 m; P.W. 0.029 m.

Fragment preserving part of a base. Worn. Ring base, within which are the first two letters of an impressed signature: *CL*. . . This signature could be *CLOHELI*, for Clodius Heliodorus, or *CLOSVC*, for Gaius Clodius Successus. See Fig. 139.

Cf. Bailey 1980, 92 and fig. 104.

961 CG.524 Forum, NE passage, E corner, Level I. Grayish-cream clay, red slip. P.L. 0.089 m; Height 0.026 m; Width 0.097 m.

Incomplete, nozzle broken away. Fire-blackened in places. Worn. Made from a crude mold. Very low disk base with an impressed signature: *LFABRICMAS*, with a phallus above the signature. The completed name would be Lucius Fabricius Masculus. See Fig. 139. Discus relief: Eros striding left, carrying a huge club aloft in his left hand, a spear in his right. Ground line indicating rocky terrain.

For another example of this relief, see Bailey 1980, pl. 68 no. Q 1293. For examples of this signature, see Bailey 1980, pl. 67, nos. Q 1282–83, pl. 68 no. Q 1295, and pl. 70 no. Q 1312. Q 1312 reads *LFABRMASCL*, the others all *LFABRICMAS*. See also Deneauve, 89 (index of marks); *CIL* 2.6256.19; *CIL* 5.8114.46; *CIL* 8.22644.101; *CIL* 10.8053.74; *CIL* 11.6999.78; *CIL* 12.5682.40; *CIL* 13.10001.127; *CIL* 15.6433.

962 CG.526 Forum, NE Passage, Level I. Grayish-buff clay, brown slip with a metallic luster. P.L. 0.047 m; P.H. 0.011 m; P.W. 0.038 m.

Fragment preserving parts of a low disk base and lower side wall of the oil reservoir. Worn. Low disk base with the impressed signature: . . . *NPHILE*, to be completed *LMVNPHILE*, for Lucius Munatius Philemon. A phallus is centered above the signature. See Fig. 140.

For examples of Fat Lamps with this signature, see Bailey 1980, pl. 61 no. Q 1237 and pl. 71 no. Q 1321, also fig. 107 and p. 98; *CIL* 2.6526.38; *CIL* 8.22644.223; *CIL* 11.6699.123; *CIL* 13.10001.217; *CIL* 15.6562.

963 CG.591 Forum NW, Building L (market building) exterior, Level I. Buff clay with an orange tint, red slip. P.L. 0.039 m; P.W. 0.024 m.

Fragment preserving parts of the base and lower side wall of the oil reservoir. Very worn, only traces of slip preserved. Low disk base with the impressed signature: *MVN*. . ., the rest broken away. The complete signature would be Lucius Munatius Philemon. See Fig. 140.

Cf. Bailey 1980, 98 and fig. 107.

964 CG.592 Forum NE passage, Level I. Buff clay with an orange tint, red slip. Length 0.105 m; Height 0.026 m; Width 0.064 m.

Incomplete, part of the discus and side wall of the oil reservoir broken away. Worn and chipped. Made from a worn, blurred mold. Low disk base with the impressed signature: *CLOSVC*, an abbreviation of Gaius Clodius Successus. See Fig. 139. Discus relief: Bust of Luna, frontal, in crescent moon.

For a similar relief, see 806; Bailey 1980, pl. 68 no. Q 2189; Brants, pl. 5 no. 589. For this signature, see Bailey 1980, 92 and fig. 104.

965 CG.594 Forum, NE passage, E corner, Level I. Buff clay, brown slip. P.L. 0.049 m; P.H. 0.016 m; P.W. 0.027 m.

Fragment preserving parts of the base, lower side wall of the oil reservoir, and underside of the nozzle. Very worn; only traces of slip preserved. Two concentric ring bases, the outer wider, with part of an impressed signature: . . . *NIA*, perhaps to be completed as *GABINIA*. See Fig. 139.

Cf. Bailey 1980, 96 and fig. 106.

966 CG.595 Forum, NE passage, E corner, Level I. Buff clay, red slip. P.L. 0.031 m; P.W. 0.022 m.

Fragment preserving parts of the base, lower side wall of the oil reservoir, and underside of the nozzle. Surface worn. Low disk base with an impressed signature, parts of four illegible letters preserved.

967 CG.600 IX-E, Building L (market building), Exterior NW, Level I. Fine, soft, cream-colored clay, red slip. P.L. 0.014 m; P.W. 0.025 m.

Fragment preserving part of a low disk base with a part of a worn signature, the tops of three letters, perhaps *LCE*. See Fig. 140.

968 C67.10 Capitolium W, Level I. Buff clay, red slip. P.L. 0.061 m; P.W. 0.053 m.

Fragment preserving parts of the discus, rim, side wall of the oil reservoir, base, and handle. Worn and encrusted. Molded pierced handle without the usual grooves. Disk base; on the bottom are the upper halves of the last four letters of an impressed signature: ...*DIEC*, probably to be completed as *LMADIEC* for Lucius Munatius Adiectus. See Fig. 140. Discus relief: Too fragmentary to identify.

Cf. Bailey 1980, 98 and fig. 107.

969 C70.133 V-D House of the Skeleton, Level 0. Fine buff clay, brown slip. P.L. 0.043 m; P.W. 0.031 m.

Fragment preserving parts of the base and lower side wall of the oil reservoir. Worn; only traces of slip preserved. Ring base; on the bottom is part of a signature in impressed slanted strokes not easily identifiable as letters; perhaps *VAISI*, although this signature is unknown (see Fig. 135).

970 C70.244 V-D Street M, between the House of the Skeleton and the House of Quintus Fulvius. Buff clay, brownish-black slip. P.L. 0.054 m; P.W. 0.043 m.

Fragment preserving most of the base and part of the lower side wall of the oil reservoir. Very worn. Very low disk base, slightly convex, causing unusual wear of the signature, which is illegible, perhaps five letters.

971 C70.319 Street M, between the House of the Skeleton and the House of Quintus Fulvius. Cream clay, red slip. P.L. 0.058 m; P.W. 0.037 m.

Fragment preserving parts of the base and lower side wall of the oil reservoir. Worn, encrusted, and scratched. Low disk base; impressed on the bottom are the first three letters of a signature: *CAE*..., probably to be completed *CAESAE* for L. Caecilius Saecularis. See Fig. 139.

Cf. Bailey 1980, 112 fig. 103; pp. 91, 350, 366–67, 372–73 (all Loeschcke VIII Fat Lamps).

972 C70.358 V-D Street 5 in front of the House of the Skeleton, Level I. Buff clay, red slip. P.L. 0.064 m; P.H. 0.019 m; P.W. 0.034 m.

Two joining fragments preserving parts of the base and lower side wall of the oil reservoir. Encrusted, root-marked. Low disk base; impressed on the flat bottom is part of a signature: part of *N* and *IA*, probably to be completed *GABINIA*. See Fig. 139.

Cf. Bailey 1980, 96 and fig. 106.

973 C70.498 Forum exterior, SW, Fish Market, Level I. Buff clay, dark, reddish-brown slip. P.L. 0.080 m; P.W. 0.052 m.

Three joining fragments preserving parts of the base, side wall of the oil reservoir, and handle. Worn. Ring base, within which is part of an impressed signature: *VX*; the rest is broken away. See Fig. 140.

974 CD.598 Basilica exterior, NE I, Level I. Cream clay, red slip mottled to black in places. P.L. 0.054 m; P.W. 0.045 m.

Fragment preserving parts of the base and lower side wall of the oil reservoir. Worn. Low disk base with an impressed signature: *MADIEC* to be completed *LMADIEC* for L. Munatius Adiectus. See Fig. 140.

Cf. Bailey 1980, 98 and fig. 107.

975 CD.881 Basilica exterior, N, Level I. Cream clay, purplish-red slip. P.L. 0.059 m; P.H. 0.032 m; P.W. 0.073 m.

Three joining fragments preserving parts of the base, side wall of the oil reservoir, shoulder, and handle. Worn. Molded pierced handle with two grooves converging at the crest and extending down the spine as a single groove. Low disk base with an impressed signature: *LMADIEC*, for L. Munatius Adiectus. The signature is not carefully centered on the base. See Fig. 140.

Cf. Bailey 1980, 98 and fig. 107.

976 C69.303 Basilica exterior, NE, Level I. Buff clay, red slip. P.L. 0.037 m; P.W. 0.030 m.

Fragment preserving part of a base and lower side wall of the oil reservoir. Worn. Low disk base; on the bottom are the first four letters of an impressed signature: *COPR*....The complete signature would be *COPRESTI* for Gaius Oppius Restitutus. See Fig. 139.

For this signature, see Bailey 1980, 99 and fig. 108.

977 C69.358 Basilica exterior, NE, Level I/II. Buff clay, thin, nut-brown slip. P.L. 0.024 m; P.W. 0.052 m.

Two joining fragments preserving parts of the rim, side wall of the oil reservoir, and base. Worn and encrusted. Ring base divided into three parts, within which is part of an impressed signature: ...*NA*. See Fig. 140.

A.D. 350–416

978 CEL.634 Basilica exterior, NW 2, Level I. Buff clay, orange slip.

Fragment preserving parts of the discus, rim, side wall of the oil reservoir, base, and nozzle. Made from an old, blurred mold. Nozzle: heart-shaped, Heres Type E e, Loeschcke Type H. Ring base, within which is an impressed signature, very worn, perhaps *BASAVGV*. See Fig. 141.

979 CF.464 Atrium Building I, Room 25, Level I. Buff clay with an orange tint, orange-red slip. P.L. 0.032 m; P.W. 0.029 m.

Fragment preserving part of a base and the lower side wall of the oil reservoir. Very worn. Ring base, within which is part of an impressed signature: ...*NI*. See Fig. 141. There were several potters this might be (Crispini, Fortuni, Sabini, Sereni), but the evidence weighs in favor of *CRISPINI*.

Cf. Bailey 1980, 94 and fig. 104.

980 CF.1918 Atrium Building I, Room 25, Level I. Pinkish-buff clay, brown slip. P.L. 0.036 m; P.W. 0.014 m.

Fragment preserving parts of a ring base and the lower side wall of the oil reservoir. At the outer edge of the base are remains of a horizontal stroke, perhaps part of an *L*.

981 CF.1919 Atrium Building I, Room 25, Level I. Buff clay, dark brown slip. P.L. 0.026 m; P.H. 0.008 m; P.W. 0.027 m.

Fragment preserving parts of the base and lower side wall of the oil reservoir. Ring base; impressed on remaining fragment of the base are traces of one or two letters, two short vertical strokes, either above or below which is part of a stamped bull's eye.

982 CF.2017 Atrium Building I, Room 25, exterior, Level I. P.L. 0.032 m; P.W. 0.031 m.

Fragment preserving part of ring base. Impressed on the bottom are the last four letters of a signature: ...*PINI*, the first part broken away, probably to be completed as *CRISPINI*. See Fig. 141.

Cf. Bailey 1980, 94 and fig. 104.

983 CF.2028 Atrium Building I, Room 25 exterior, Level I. P.L. 0.036 m; P.W. 0.031 m.

Fragment preserving parts of disk base and lower wall of oil reservoir, the part toward the nozzle. Disk base: off center toward the nozzle is a bull's eye. Several potters used this device above and below their signatures; however, this does not seem to have been one of them, since the fragment is large enough that some of the letters would have appeared.

17. DEEP-BODIED LAMP WITH A RIGHT-ANGLED NOZZLE

(Fig. 102)

(Catalogue Number 984)

Only one example of a Bailey Type F Lamp has been found at Cosa, and that in fragments. However, enough remains to make the identification certain. The body is deep, with a discus divided into two zones meeting at an angle. The nozzle is a right-angle triangle, with the hypotenuse of the triangle replaced by the curve of the rim of the lamp. The wick hole is centered in the angle. A continuous, narrow ribbon extends along the outer edge of the nozzle ending in large scrolls at the edge of the oil reservoir.

25/20 B.C.–A.D. 50

984 (Fig. 102) CEL.71 and CEL 418 a and b Atrium Building I, Room 21, CEL.71 found in Level I/III; CEL.418 found in Level II. Fine cream clay, mottled light to dark brown slip. CEL.71: P.L. 0.069 m; P.W. 0.034 m; CEL.418 a: P.L. 0.044 m; P.W. 0.028 m; CEL.418 b: P.L. 0.025 m; P.W. 0.008 m.

Three joining and two nonjoining fragments preserving parts of the discus, rim, and nozzle. Slip worn away on high relief, and minor chipping. Angular discus, the inner level zone marked off from the outer beveled zone by a bead molding framed by rings. Rim: Two inner rings, a narrow bead and a narrow outer fillet, all moldings in a single plane. A narrow ribbon of bead molding borders the outer edge of the nozzle and ends in large scrolls where the nozzle meets the oil reservoir. Discus relief: The outer zone of the discus is decorated with radiating grooves.

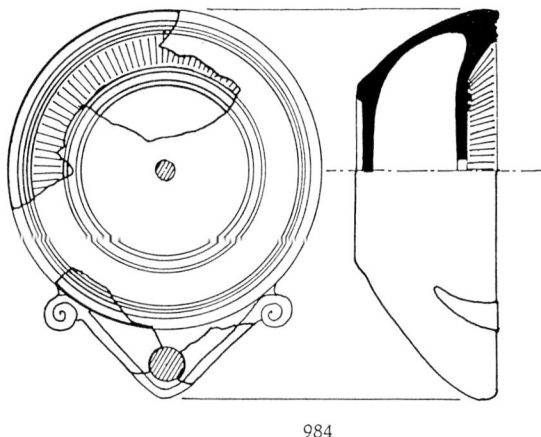

Figure 102. Deep-bodied lamp with a right-angled nozzle, scale 1:2

For close parallels to this lamp, see Bailey 1980, 231–32 and pl. 38 nos. Q 1090–91; Farka 1977, 325–26, pl. 24 and pl. 57 no. 1458.

18. PLASTIC LAMPS

(Figs. 103, 104)

(Catalogue Numbers 985, 986)

Only two plastic lamps have been found at Cosa, one in the shape of a bull's head, the other in the shape of a barbarian's head. The bull's head was found in the Basilica, Level I, in a context dated A.D. 50–100; the barbarian's head is from a context dated 25/20 B.C.–A.D. 50.

A.D. 50–100

985 (Fig. 103) CD.409 a and b Basilica, ENE 3, Level I. Light buff clay, brown slip. a: P.L. 0.065 m; P.H. 0.030 m; b: P.L. 0.006 m; P.H. 0.042 m.

Two nonjoining fragments, each preserving one of the eyes of a three-dimensional bull's head that was the body of a lamp. Worn. Each eye is fringed top and bottom with schematic lashes. There are carefully drawn tufts of hair carved into the clay above the ridge bones over and between the eyes. Parts of a filling hole are preserved on each fragment atop the crown of hair, framed by a beveled fillet sloping inward. Smear marks on the interior show the potter's fingermarks. Two lines of five wrinkles above the nostrils are preserved on fragment b.

The *comparanda* show a wick hole centered on the tongue or stubby forehooves as double wick holes at the end of a nozzle. They also show short triangular horns, a lunate or triangular heat shield attached above the horns by a stem, and a flat base.

Cf. Bailey 1980, 254–56, 258–59, pl. 47 nos. Q

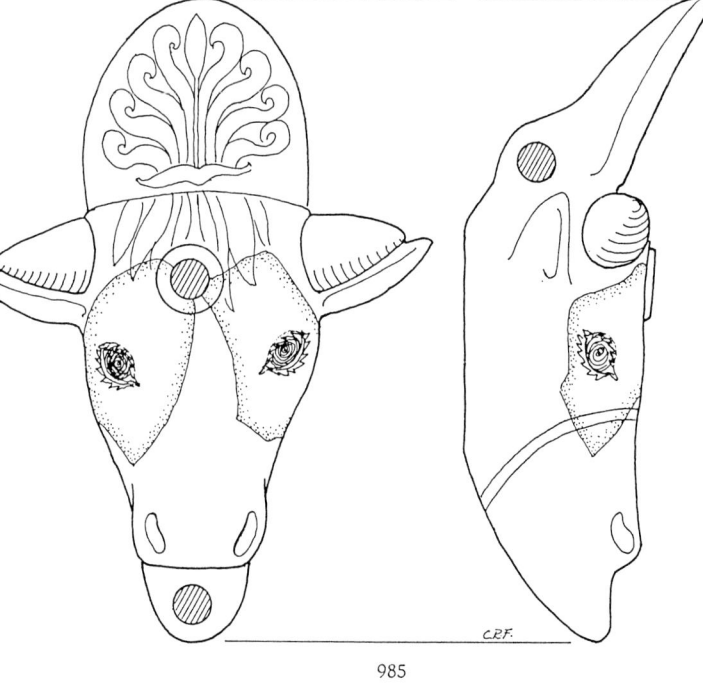

Figure 103. Plastic lamp in the form of a bull's head, scale 1:2

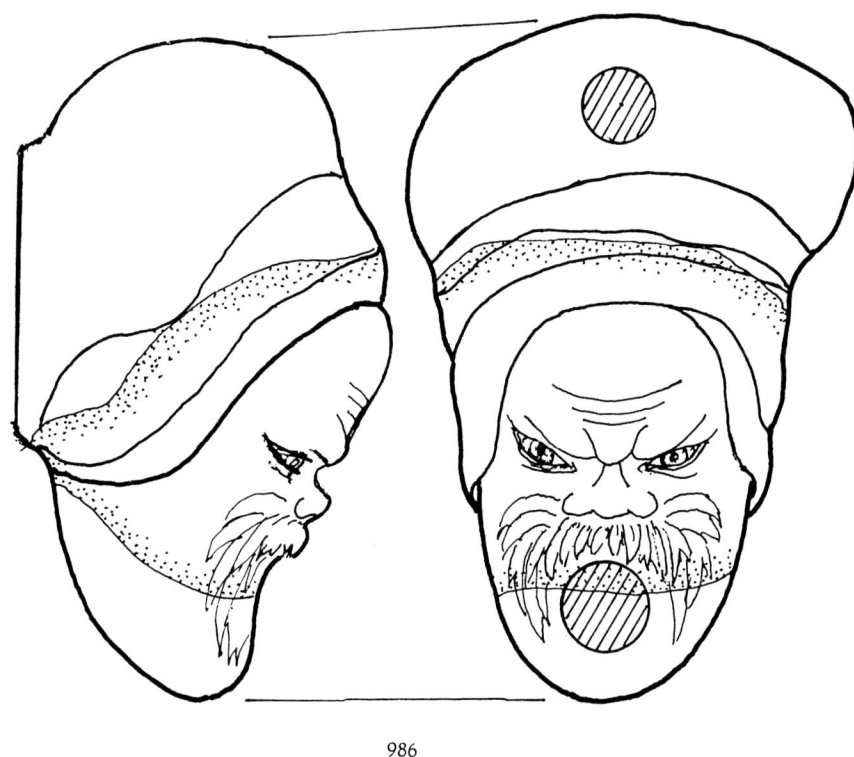

Figure 104. Plastic lamp in the form of a barbarian's head, full scale

1141–43; pl. 96 no. Q 1143 with Q 1048 (Townley drawing with triangular heat shield).

25/20 B.C.–A.D. 50

986 (Fig. 104) CC.122 Capitolium exterior, S, Forecourt, Level I. Grayish-cream clay, reddish-brown slip. P.L. 0.059 m; P.H. 0.051 m; P.W. 0.046 m.

Incomplete, the top of the head and the jaw broken away. Encrusted. A beautifully modeled head of a scowling and screaming barbarian. Exaggerated mustache but no beard, snub nose, slanted oriental eyes, and high wrinkled forehead under a turbanlike cap. The top of the turban and lower part of the face with the wick hole are conjectural, based on *comparanda*.

Cf. Bailey 1980, pl. 45 no. Q 1133, and pl. 104 no. Q 743.

19. LAMPS WITH "INCHWORM EARS" AND A CHANNEL

(Fig. 105)

(Catalogue Numbers 987–998)
(Bailey Type G; Broneer Isthmia Type XXIV B; Loeschcke Type V; Deneauve Type V G; Goldman/Jones Group XIV; Leibundgut Type XVII; Goethert-Polaschek Type XII)

Twelve lamps with double-curved "inchworm ears" and channels opening from the discus to the nozzle have been found at Cosa. One is almost complete; the others are fragmentary but are easily identifiable, since the side projections and the form of the channel make them unlike any other lamp type.

Four of these lamps come from contexts dated 25/20 B.C.–A.D. 40/45. Two are from a context that has been dated 25/20 B.C.–A.D. 50. Six are from contexts that have been dated A.D. 50–ca. 100. However, it is probable that all twelve are to be dated mid-first century A.D. since the A.D. 40/45 dating of the destruction of the storeroom in Atrium Building I is secure.

These lamps are copies of a Cnidian lamp.[1] They are made of finely levigated clay ranging in color from cream to buff. The slip is usually mottled, ranging from red or reddish-brown to brown or black. The concave disci are wide with either narrow beveled shoulders or level rims. The moldings that separate the discus from the shoulder open out on top of the nozzle to form the walls of a short channel. The channel walls flare sharply at an angle and end before they reach the wick hole. There is a small air hole in the channel.

On either side of the oil reservoir are ears or handles that suggest double-curved inchworms; the central part curves outward in an arc, and the ends turn out in reverse curves. Only a part of one base is preserved; it is low with a small raised pelta, one of three or four that served as feet.[2]

25/20 B.C.–A.D. 40/45

987 (Fig. 105) CEL.3 Atrium Building I, Room 22, Level II. Cream clay, red slip mottled to dark brown in places with a metallic luster. P.L. 0.097 m; Height 0.032 m; P.W. 0.098 m; Diameter without ears 0.083 m.

Six joining fragments preserving most of a lamp. The end of the nozzle, parts of the lower wall of the oil reservoir, the base, and parts of one ear are broken away. Slip worn away on high

---

1. Photographs and a description of Cosan lamp 987 were sent to Judith Perlzweig by Eric Baade in 1954. In reply to Baade's inquiry about this lamp type she wrote, "these are copies of a Knidian original," identifying the Cosan lamp on the basis of the photograph. She graciously sent photographs of two lamps found in the Agora at Athens as examples of this type "probably made in Knidos." Henry S. Robinson has dated these two Cnidian lamps (L 2104 and L 2768) to the early first century A.D. The ears of the Cnidian lamps have a pierced central arc; the ears of the Cosan example are solid. Perlzweig wrote that the solid form of the ear is later than the pierced one and also indicated that since the clay and slip of the Cosan lamp are typical of Roman lamps of the period, it was probably Roman-made, not Cnidian.

2. Agora lamp L 2768 has three peltate feet like that of Cosan lamp 987.

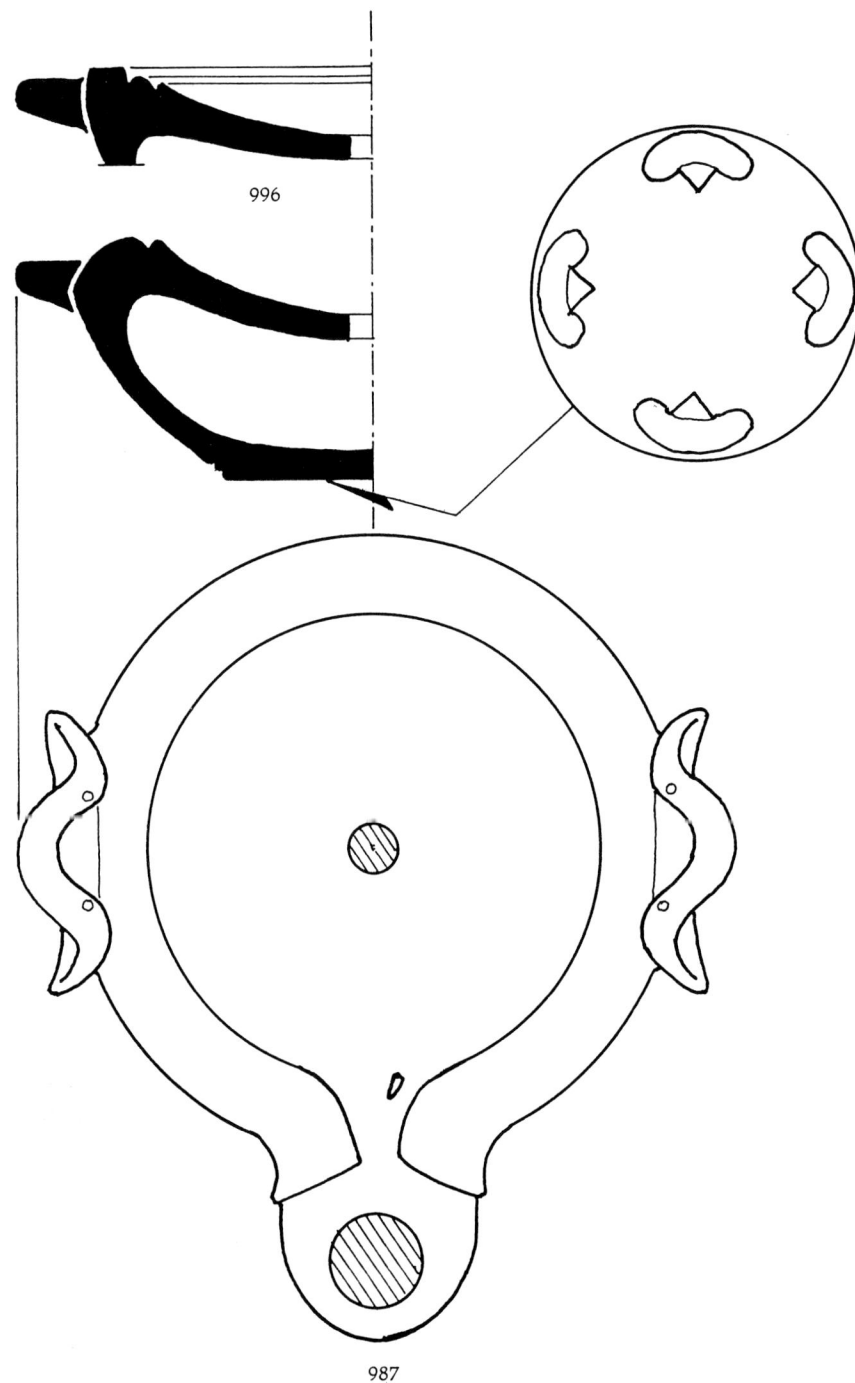

Figure 105. Lamps with "inchworm ears" and a channel from the discus toward the wick hole, full scale

relief. Beveled shoulder marked off from the discus by a groove. Low disk base with peltate feet. Only one pelta is preserved of three or four. For Athenian Agora lamp with peltate feet, see Perlzweig 1961, pl. 4, no. 82.

988 CEL.5 Atrium Building I, Room 22, Level II. Cream clay, red slip mottled to purple in places with a metallic luster. P.L. 0.057 m; P.W. 0.029 m.

Fragment preserving one ear, parts of the discus, and the shoulder. Slip rubbed. Discus, rim, and ear as in 987.

989 CEL.326 Atrium Building I, Room 22, Level II. Cream clay, dark brown slip. P.L. 0.029 m; P.W. 0.038 m.

Fragment preserving parts of the discus, rim, and channel. Badly worn. Discus, rim, and channel as in 987.

990 CEL.337 Atrium Building I, Room 22, Level II. Cream clay, brown slip with a metallic luster. P.L. 0.072 m; Height 0.031 m; P.W. 0.052 m.

Three joining fragments preserving one ear, and parts of the discus, shoulder, side wall of the oil reservoir, and the base. Slip rubbed on high spots. Plain disk base. The discus, shoulder, and ear as in 987. There are small bull's eyes added to either side of the arc of the ear.

25/20 B.C.–A.D. 50

991 CEL.172 Atrium Building I, Room 11, Level I. Buff clay, dull mottled brown slip. P.L. 0.041 m; P.H. 0.012 m; P.W. 0.035 m.

Fragment preserving parts of the discus, shoulder, and one ear. Slip rubbed. Discus, shoulder, and ear as in 987.

992 C70.675 V-D, Sewer at intersection of Streets 5 and M. Buff clay with a pinkish tint, red slip. P.L. 0.064 m; P.W. 0.036 m.

Fragment preserving one ear, and parts of the discus and shoulder, as in 987. Worn and encrusted. Discus relief: Lares dancing on either side of an altar, only the left Lar preserved. He is frontal with head turned toward the altar. The right hand holds a rhyton high, pouring a libation. He wears a belted tunic and a long scarf in a loop behind the body. The right figure would have been the mirror image of this one.

Cf. Bailey 1980, pl. 38 no. Q 1095; Leibundgut 1963, pl. 27 no. 45. The Lares on the British Museum lamp stand on a plinth without an altar.

A.D. 50–ca. 100

993 CEL.73 Atrium Building I, Room 22, Level I. Buff clay, dark brown slip with a metallic luster. P.L. 0.060 m; P.H. 0.025 m; P.W. 0.025 m.

Fragment preserving one ear and part of the rim. Very worn. Rim: Inner ring and bead sloping up to a wide, plain outer fillet.

For an example with a similar rim, see Bailey 1980, pl. 38 no. Q 1093.

994 CEL.140 Atrium Building I, Room 15, Level I. Cream clay, brown slip. P.L. 0.044 m; P.H. 0.020 m; P.W. 0.029 m.

Two joining fragments preserving one ear, and parts of the discus and shoulder, as in 987. Very worn; only traces of slip preserved. The ear is decorated with bull's eyes as in 990.

995 CEL.220 Atrium Building I, Room 21, Level I. Buff clay, brown slip. P.L. 0.055 m; P.W. 0.028 m.

Fragment preserving parts of one ear and the shoulder. Badly rubbed. The shoulder and ear are as in 987.

996 CEL.290 Atrium Building I, Room 21, Level I. Pinkish-buff clay, orange slip. P.L. 0.079 m; P.H. 0.010 m; P.W. 0.088 m.

Six joining fragments preserving one ear and parts of the discus and rim. Slip very worn. Rim: Fig. 105. The ear has decorative bull's eyes as in 990.

997 CEL.127 Atrium Building I, Room 13, Level I. Buff clay, dull red slip. P.L. 0.038 m; P.H. 0.029 m; P.W. 0.018 m.

Fragment preserving part of one ear. Slip rubbed.

998 CEL.620 Atrium Building I, Room 5, Level I. Cream clay, dark brown slip with a metallic luster. P.L. 0.048 m; P.H. 0.011 m; P.W. 0.019 m.

Two joining fragments preserving one ear.

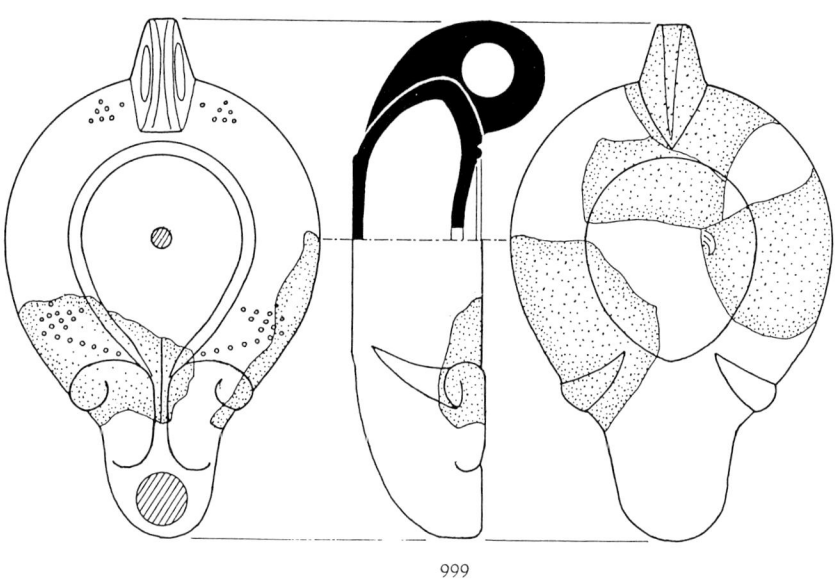

Figure 106. Lamp with ovoid discus and base, scale 1:2

20. LAMP WITH OVOID DISCUS AND BASE
(Fig. 106)

(Catalogue Number 999)
(Bailey Type K; Brants Type XIV; Fabricotti, E, Group 1B, 16)

The following lamp is the only one of its type that has been found at Cosa. It is a stray from south Italy, possibly brought by a traveler. The type has been dated variously from the middle of the first century A.D. to the beginning of the third.

A special study of this lamp type was made by E. Fabbricotti (Fabbricotti 1974a). She examined drawings of the Cosan example and observed that it was very similar to her Potenza 16, but the dots were arranged in a pattern, while her examples had random dots.

A.D. 118–225

999 (Fig. 106) C.F.644 a–d Atrium Building I, Room 25, Level III. Buff clay, orange slip. P.L. a 0.060 m, b 0.038 m, c 0.056 m, d 0.044 m; P.H. a 0.028 m, c 0.026 m, d 0.019 m; P.W. a 0.045 m, b 0.044 m, c 0.025 m, d 0.036 m.

Five fragments, three nonjoining, two joining, preserving parts of the base, side wall of the oil reservoir, shoulder, discus, channel, and one volute. Very worn; the surface is flaked and chipped. A large oval lamp with wide decorated shoulder, ovoid discus, and base. The discus ends in a point toward the nozzle and leads into a narrow, nonfunctioning channel. The volutes, which form the walls of the channel, have a scroll only at the body end; this extends down the side of the body as a pointed cone. Low ovoid base, flat below, narrow end toward nozzle. Molded pierced handle with grooves extending down the lower part of the handle, the upper part broken away. Wide convex shoulder decorated with a design in raised dots.

This lamp was found with a coin of A.D. 118.

21. WALL LAMPS

(Fig. 107)

(Catalogue Numbers 1000–1002)
(Bailey Type M, Group ii; Leibundgut Form XXVIII; Provoost Type 3, Variant I)

Only three examples of Wall Lamps have been found at Cosa, and these are fragmentary. These lamps get their descriptive name from the way in which they could be used: they could be hung from a bracket or nail driven into a wall as well as placed on a flat surface. The transverse handle was set at right angles to the lamp's axis and pierced horizontally front to back, so that the lamp, if hung, would project out at a right angle to the wall. The Wall Lamp and the late *Vogelkopflampe*, possibly its predecessor, are the only lamps in the Roman potter's repertory that could be used in this way. The Wall Lamp is usually included together with the late *Vogelkopflampe* (also called Flat Fish) as a single type. The relationship between the two lamp types, however, is very tenuous, the handle being the only feature that they have in common.[1]

The clay of the three Wall Lamps from Cosa is a soft, fine pinkish-buff. All three have an orange-red slip. The discus is less than a full circle, the transverse handle covering part of the discus circle. The discus is framed by a bead that also marks it off from the sloping, rounded shoulder. The shoulder meets the side wall of the oil reservoir at an angle. The nozzle is wide and rounded, with simple volutes without scrolls. The

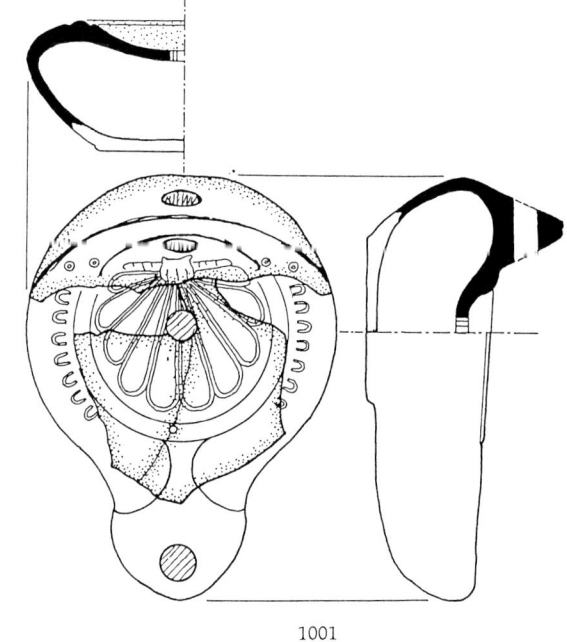

Figure 107. Wall Lamps, scale 1:2

---

1. The bodies and nozzles of late *Vogelkopflampen* or "Flat Fish Lamps" and Wall Lamps are different; the *Vogelkopflampe* has an unprofiled base, while the Wall Lamp has a ring base, and there is nothing left of the schematic channel and bird's heads of the late *Vogelkopflampe* on the Wall Lamp. The *Vogelkopflampe* is unslipped; the Wall Lamp is slipped.

shoulder is decorated along the sides with a series of ovules. A scallop shell in relief fills the discus, with the flattened hinge of the shell toward the handle.

The three Cosan Wall Lamps were found in contexts dated from mid-first century A.D. to A.D. 225. Bailey dates the example in the British Museum collection Antonine to Severan.[2] This lamp is a very close parallel to the Cosan examples, the only difference being that the British Museum lamp has bull's eyes at either end of the band of ovules on the shoulder. A similar lamp found at Ostia in the Terme del Nuotatore has been dated A.D. 225–250 by Provoost.

A.D. 100–225

1000 CEL.281 Atrium Building I, Room 25 exterior, Level II. Soft, pinkish-buff clay, orange-red slip. P.L. 0.044 m; P.H. 0.029 m; P.W. 0.061 m.

Fragment preserving the handle and parts of the discus, rim, and shoulder. Slip rubbed away on high surfaces. Concave discus separated from the sloping shoulder by a bead set off by a groove on either side. The filling hole is near the handle end, slightly off-center. Discus relief: A scallop shell with the hinge of the shell toward the transverse handle. Only the upper part of the shell is preserved. Pairs of bull's eyes mark the transition between shoulder and handle. On either side of the shoulder along the bead is a row of ovules, two preserved.

Cf. Bailey 1980, pl. 50 no. Q 1158.

1001 (Fig. 107) CEL.583 Basilica, Exterior NW 2, Level I. Soft pinkish-buff clay with occasional impurities, orange-red slip. P.L. 0.065 m; P.H. 0.041 m; P.W. 0.072 m.

Three joining fragments preserving the handle, and parts of the discus, shoulder, and top of the nozzle including the upper part of the volutes. Worn; only traces of slip preserved. Encrusted. Description the same as for 1000.

1002 CF.1976 Atrium Building I, Exterior of Room 25, sidewalk, Level II. Soft pinkish-buff clay with occasional impurities, orange-red slip. P.L. 0.029 m; P.H. 0.024 m; P.W. 0.032 m.

Fragment preserving part of a transverse pierced handle. Very worn and chipped.

---

2. Bailey dates the British Museum example to the last quarter of the second century A.D. on the basis of the signature *CVNBIT*, a potter who was active at that time, and other examples from dated contexts.

22. FACTORY LAMPS (*FIRMALAMPEN*)

(Figs. 108–110)

(Catalogue Numbers 1003–1041)
(Loeschcke Type X (*Normalformen* or Standard form), (Loeschcke Type IX has not been found at Cosa); Buchi Type X a & b; Iconomu Type XII; Brants Type XIII; Leibundgut Types XXVI, XXX, and XXXII; Bailey Type N; Broneer Type XXVI; Dressel/Lamboglia Type 5; Walters Forms 90–94; Ponsich Type V; Deneauve Type IX)

Around A.D. 70 a new type of moldmade lamp appeared in northern Italy, the so-called Factory Lamp or *Firmalampe*. Plain and angular, these lamps were efficient, strong, easy to make, and presumably cheap. Mass production of lamps had started with the introduction of the mold. However, it was only with the invention of the simple Factory Lamp that unskilled labor could carry out the complete manufacture from mixing the clay to the finished product.

This lamp quickly became popular, indication of a change in taste. The most popular lamps of the Julio-Claudian period had been the fragile, elegant ones with decorated disci and voluted nozzles, culminating in the most difficult of all to make, the lamp with a long voluted nozzle and heat shield. These intricate lamps were time-consuming to produce and probably costly. The Factory Lamp filled the need for a cheaper and more durable product. They were produced originally in northern Italy; one of the centers of production was Mutina, modern Modena. The clay of the original north Italian lamps is coarse, hard, and brick-red in color. The fabric is thick and often has pits and crevices due to careless or unskilled workmen. The lamps are unslipped or have a thin self-slip. Within a very short time the potters of central Italy were producing copies of Factory Lamps.[1] The clay of the central Italian product ranges from coarse to fine, and from fairly hard to soft. The color varies from cream to buff, sometimes with tints of orange, red, or gray. The fabric is thick with pits and crevices, as in the north Italian originals. The copies are all slipped. Eleven of the Factory Lamps found at Cosa are from northern Italy; the remaining twenty-five were made in central Italy.

With two exceptions, the Cosan Factory Lamps are

---

1. According to Bailey, "Loeschcke Type IX lamps of north Italian manufacture appear to be largely of the Flavian period, extending into Trajanic times, *circa* AD 75 to 100. . . *Firmalampen* were exported from north Italy to many parts of the Roman Empire, and were copied and made by many local lampmakers in those areas, both during the period of Italian manufacture and after this ceased. . . . It is difficult to believe that the lampmaker Fortis, for example, or the north Italian workshop to which he gave his name, had much to do with the immense number of provincial lamps signed *FORTIS* made in many parts of the Empire, from Britain to Bulgaria, over a period of at least one hundred and fifty years." (Bailey 1980, 274–75). Bailey goes on to say that both the north Italian Factory Lamps and their copies in the provinces spread to areas north, east, and west of Italy, present-day Britain, France, Belgium, Germany, Hungary, Yugoslavia, and Bulgaria, but that in the western provinces Factory Lamps with handles seem to have been preferred (*ibid.* 276). Broneer notes that they "were the most common kind in the West toward the end of the first century A.D. [but] were never imported to Greece in great numbers, chiefly because the local industries filled the need for cheap lamps" (Broneer 1930, 87).

the fully developed type, Loeschcke's Type X *Normalform* or standard form.² The exceptions are the later shorter nozzle or *Kurzform* lamps. The oil reservoirs are deep with side walls that are straight, flaring slightly toward the top. A sharp angle is formed at the join where the side wall of the oil reservoir meets the outer edge of the shoulder. The shoulder slopes up and in to a ridge at the top. This continuous ridge or fillet circles the discus with its central filling hole and runs along the channel that connects the discus and the wick hole and around the wick hole, making a continuous enclosure around both openings. Any oil that was spilled here would be contained and drain back into the reservoir.

The nozzle is long, deep, and wide; it merges smoothly into the body of the lamp. The end of the nozzle is rounded. Some of the bases of these lamps are unprofiled; some have base rings. The bronze prototype of the Factory Lamp had three equidistant pierced lugs on the shoulder, which allowed it to be suspended from a wall bracket or lamp stand by cords or chains. These suspension lugs were carefully copied on the clay lamps, but they were seldom pierced and functional. None of the Cosan lamp lugs is pierced.

Only two of the Factory Lamps from Cosa are complete. The others are fragmentary. The two complete lamps are from north Italy, neither with a handle. One of the two has three lugs, the other only two, the axial one having been omitted. This omission would enable the potter to attach a handle at the proper place. The Factory Lamps found at the frontier fortress of Vindonissa have strap handles, but recent chemical analysis of the composition of these lamps by X-ray fluorescence has shown that most of the Vindonissan lamps were not produced at Vindonissa, but at factories in Modena, Lyon, or Trier.³

Perhaps most of the Factory Lamps exported from the north were without handles, since their omission would make for less breakage and greater ease in packing and shipping. Four of the Cosan central Italian Factory Lamps have strap handles, while one of the lamps from north Italy and two of the central Italian ones have molded pierced handles.

Nine of the Factory Lamps found at Cosa have signatures or parts of signatures in relief, centered on the base of the lamp to be read with the nozzle pointing up, like most Factory Lamp signatures. One, a later *Kurz-*

---

2. For the development of the Factory Lamp, see Buchi, Types IX to X a, b, and c (Buchi, xxv–xxvii); see also Leibundgut, Types 23–27 and 30–32. The Cosan Factory Lamps are Buchi's Type X a and b, and Leibundgut's Type 26.

3. The Factory Lamps found at the frontier fortress of Vindonissa have strap handles. Vindonissa was established by Tiberius and abandoned ca. A.D. 101. The Factory Lamps found at Vindonissa were Type IX with very narrow closed channels. They are earlier than Type X, the type found at Cosa. Gerwulf Schneider of the Freie Universität in Berlin has been experimenting with the use of X-ray fluorescence in attempting to determine the provenance of Factory Lamps from Vindonissa and other sites. He summarizes his results as follows: "The chemical composition of a ceramic artifact is specific according to its place of manufacture. It can be determined by wavelength-dispersive X-ray analysis or by any other analytical method allowing the precise and accurate analysis of at least fifteen chemical elements." From the analysis of *Firmalampen* from Vindonissa (G. Schneider, B. Hoffmann, E. Wirz, "Significance and Dependability of Reference Groups for Chemical Determinations of Provenance of Ceramic Artefacts" in *Proceedings of the Eighteenth International Symposium on Archaeometry and Archaeological Prospection* [*Archaeophysika* 10], Bonn 1978, 269–83) it was clear that most of these lamps were produced at only three places, lamps of Loeschcke's technique A and B very probably in Modena, lamps of his technique C in the Lyon area, and lamps of technique D in only one Rhenish center, probably Trier. Loeschcke's hypothesis of local manufacture of lamps of technique B could no longer be maintained. Only few of the *Firmalampen* in Vindonissa may have been made by *surmoulage* in Switzerland but not in Vindonissa, because none of the *Firmalampen* matches one of the compositions of the local Roman pottery.

"An increased number of analyses of *Firmalampen* from various sites in the Germanias and in Raetia yielded more general results (G. Schneider, E. Wirz, *Chemical Answers to Archaeological Questions—Roman Terracotta Lamps as Documents of Economic History* [Doc. et Trav.IGAL no. 15] Paris 1992, 1–44): The lampmaking center Modena exported lamps to Regensburg certainly after A.D. 179, and the firm of *FORTIS* thus must have existed in Modena for more than one hundred years. *Firmalampen* identified as locally made, bearing local names or in fewer cases north Italian lampmakers' names, are almost generally of a bad quality, made for local use and clearly distinguishable from imported lamps of the three lampmaking centers mentioned. In our opinion these centers represent organised production in branches of the large firms. The larger firms, like *FORTIS, STROBILVS, ATIMETVS* and *COMMVNIS* made lamps at these three centers, others at only one or two of them. No other places of any importance were yet detected for the supply of the region under investigation. The study will be continued to get information on the number of branches of such large lampmaking firms as *FORTIS*."

form lamp, has an impressed signature. Four of these ten are from north Italy; six are from central Italy. The central Italian lamps could have been made by branches of the north Italian potteries established in or near Rome, or they could have been pirated by Roman potters making molds from northern lamps, including the signatures.

One of the central Italian Factory Lamps comes from material that was sealed by the debris from the Basilica that collapsed ca. A.D. 40–45. This is obviously intrusive or a mistake in the location, since this date is too early even for any Factory Lamp. The earliest, Type IX with a closed channel, was introduced ca. A.D. 60, according to Buchi and Fremersdorf, while Loeschcke and Evelein date its introduction ca. A.D. 75. The Factory Lamps found at Cosa are the fully developed type with a true channel, Type X. If one allows a few years for Type X to evolve from Type IX, A.D. 80 seems a conservative date for the first appearance of Factory Lamps at Cosa.

Two of the north Italian Factory Lamps and four central Italian ones were found in contexts dated A.D. 50–ca. 100. Three north Italian Factory Lamps and fourteen central Italian ones were found in contexts dated A.D. 50–225. Two north Italian lamps were found in Level II of the Mithraeum, dated A.D. 80–395/400. Two central Italian Factory Lamps were found in the Shrine of Liber Pater, dated A.D. 330–395/400. The remainder of these lamps can be dated as late as A.D. 416, when Cosa was abandoned.

The evidence of the Cosan finds indicates that north Italian Factory Lamps were in use in Cosa before A.D. 100 and continued in use to the city's end. The evidence also indicates that by the time the north Italian Factory Lamp was introduced to Cosa, central Italian potters had entered the market with their version, and that the competition between northern and central Italy for the market extended perhaps through the second century.

a. FACTORY LAMPS FROM NORTH ITALY

(Fig. 108)

(Catalogue Numbers 1003–1014)

A.D. 50–100

1003 C.F.1588 Atrium Building I, Room 25 B, pit, Level

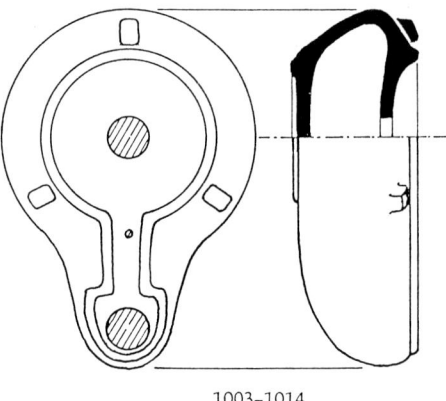

Figure 108. Factory Lamps from north Italy, scale 1:2

IV. Brick-red clay. P.L. 0.044 m; P.H. 0.012 m; P.W. 0.057 m.

Fragment preserving parts of the discus and shoulder, including one suspension lug. Surface worn, pitted, chipped, and scratched. Handleless.

1004 C67.3 Capitolium West, Surface to Level II. Brick-red clay. P.L. 0.068 m; Height 0.031 m; Width 0.060 m.

Two joining fragments preserving the side wall of the oil reservoir, the shoulder, most of the base, the attachment of the nozzle, and the handle. Made from a new crisp mold. The two suspension lugs are threaded with a short ribbon of clay. Molded pierced handle. Multiple ring base with part of a signature in relief: . . . *BIANI*, to be completed as *VIBIANI* (see Fig. 138).

This is the best made of all the Cosan Factory Lamps. There is a similar lamp from Rusellae with this signature in the Museo Archeologico della Maremma at Grosseto dated A.D. 125–150. For other examples, see Bailey 1980, 286, pl. 54 no. Q 1178; Larese, 60–70, 88 no. 103, 90 no. 118, 92–93 nos. 126–31, 100 nos. 172–74. Buchi believes that Vibianus was one of the later north Italian makers of Factory Lamps, whose workshop flourished from the middle of the second century to its end. Szentléleky asserts that the signature of Vibianus was among the early ones of the beginning of the second century. Cf. Marsa, pl. 13 nos. 178–80, pl. 14 no. 181, pl. 17 (for signatures only).

A.D. 100–225

1005 CF.1670 Atrium Building I, Room 25 D, Level II. Brick-red clay, red slip mottled to brown in places. P.L. 0.045 m; P.H. 0.032 m; P.W. 0.042 m.

Fragment preserving the nozzle of a Factory Lamp. Slip rubbed and scratched.

1006 CF.2123 Atrium Building I, Room 25 exterior, Level II. Brick-red clay. P.L. 0.060 m; P.H. 0.019 m; P.W. 0.028 m.

Fragment preserving parts of the discus, shoulder, channel, upper side wall of the oil reservoir, and one suspension lug. Good condition. The ridge surrounding the discus, channel, and wick hole is a well-defined fillet. The lamp was made from a good, crisp, new mold.

1007 CG.281 Curia cellar, SE Room, Mithraeum, Level II. Brick-red clay. Length 0.089 m; Height 0.035 m; Width 0.064 m.

Seven joining fragments preserving a complete lamp. Smoke-blackened around the wick hole. The end of the nozzle is deformed and the filling hole punched off center. Only two suspension lugs; no handle. Ring base, within which are three letters in relief: *QGC*. See Fig. 138.

For examples of this signature, see Buchi, 96–101 (he lists sixty-one examples of Factory Lamps with this signature, which he interprets as Q. Gavius Cerialis or Q. Gavius Communis as possible interpretations; see his bibliography, p. 97); Larese, 63 and 91 no. 122.

1008 CG.282 Curia cellar, SE Room, Mithraeum, Level II. Brick-red clay. Length 0.081 m; Height 0.032 m; Width 0.057 m.

Complete lamp in good condition, except for minor chipping. No evidence of use. Made from a damaged mold; the rim is partially broken away around the wick hole. Three suspension lugs. Ring base, unsigned.

1009 C68.740 Arx, west slope, structure, Level 0. Brick-red clay. P.L. 0.026 m; P.W. 0.040 m.

Fragment preserving parts of the ring base and lower side wall of the oil reservoir. Worn. On the bottom are parts of the first two letters of a signature in relief, a vertical hasta and the lower part of an *R*, perhaps to be completed as *FRONTO*. See Fig. 138.
Cf. Larese, 57, 69 nos. 89, 166, 177.

A.D. 225–416

1010 Withdrawn.

1011 CEL.125 Atrium Building I, Room 13 exterior, Level I. Brick-red clay. P.L. 0.040 m; P.H. 0.025 m; P.W. 0.026 m.

Fragment preserving parts of the shoulder, the side wall of the oil reservoir, and the attachment of the nozzle. Condition good. The angle between the shoulder and the lower side wall is very sharp.

1012 CEL.126 Atrium Building I, Room 13 exterior, Level I. Brick-red clay. P.L. 0.047 m; P.H. 0.027 m; P.W. 0.022 m.

Fragment preserving parts of the side wall of the oil reservoir and the base. Scratched and worn. Double ring base, the center broken away.

1013 CEL.132 Atrium Building I, Room 4, Level I. Brick-red clay. P.L. 0.059 m; P.H. 0.016 m; P.W. 0.024 m.

Fragment preserving parts of the discus, shoulder, side wall of the oil reservoir, and one suspension lug.

1014 CF. 461 Atrium Building I, Room 25, Level I. Brick-red clay. Length 0.081 m; P.H. 0.025 m; P.W. 0.041 m.

Fragment preserving the base, the lower side wall of the oil reservoir, and the underside and side wall of the nozzle of a small Factory Lamp. Encrusted. Handleless. Unprofiled base, concave bottom. On the bottom in relief is the signature *FORTVNI* in two lines, *NI* centered below *FORTV*, with a palm branch, also in relief, above. See Fig. 138.

b. ROMAN COPIES OF FACTORY LAMPS FROM CENTRAL ITALY

(Fig. 109)

(Catalogue Numbers 1015–1039)

Twenty-five Roman copies of the Factory Lamp have been found at Cosa. Both the original north Italian type and the Roman copy seem to have reached the market at Cosa in the last half of the first century A.D., and they continued in competition down to the end of Cosa in 416.

A.D. 50–100

1015 (Fig. 109) CEL.179 Atrium Building I, Room 16, Level I. Buff clay, brown slip with a metallic luster. P.L. 0.053 m; P.H. 0.031 m; P.W. 0.064 m.

198 Cosa: The Lamps

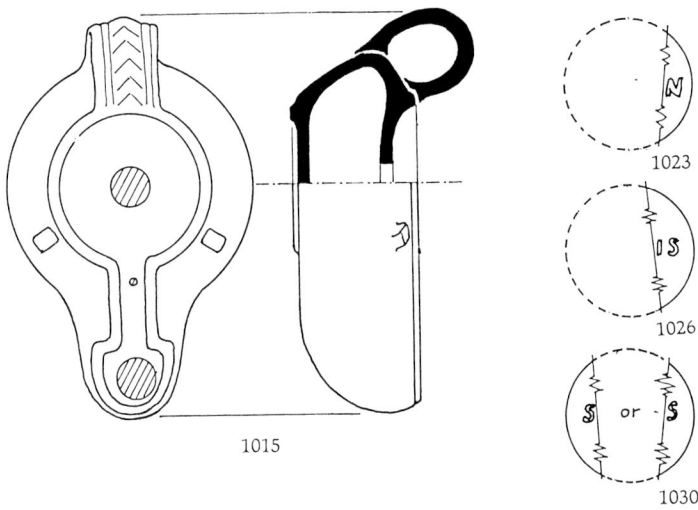

Figure 109. Roman copies of Factory Lamps from central Italy, scale 1:2

Two joining fragments preserving the handle and parts of the discus, shoulder including one suspension lug, and side wall of the oil reservoir. Surface rough due to impurities and coarseness of the clay. The ridge outlining the discus, channel, and wick hole is less pronounced than usual. Wide strap handle with broad central band decorated with impressed herringbone framed by two narrow ridges.

1016 CEL.233 Atrium Building I, Room 22, Level I. Cream clay, brown slip. P.L. 0.035 m; P.H. 0.010 m; P.W. 0.019 m.

Fragment preserving parts of the discus and shoulder, including one suspension lug. Very worn. The shoulder is slightly convex. The suspension lug is semicircular and divided into equal parts by a groove.

1017 CEL.261 Atrium Building I, Room 14, Level I. Grayish-buff clay, reddish-orange slip mottled to brown in places. P.L. 0.027 m; P.H. 0.007 m; P.W. 0.017 m.

Fragment preserving parts of the shoulder, including one suspension lug and the ridge that marks the shoulder off from the discus. The ridge is angular, wide, and level on top. Very worn.

1018 CEL.340 Atrium Building I, Room 22, Level II (an obvious intrusion, as Level II in Room 22 was sealed in A.D. 40/45, a date too early for this lamp type). Buff clay with an orange tint, red slip. P.L. 0.042 m; P.H. 0.008 m; P.W. 0.029 m.

Fragment preserving parts of the ring base and the underside of the nozzle. Very worn. The center of the base is broken away.

A.D. 100–225

1019 CEL.123 Atrium Building I, near the impluvium in the atrium, Level III. Grayish-cream clay, dark brown slip. P.L. 0.040 m; P.H. 0.010 m; P.W. 0.019 m.

Fragment preserving parts of the discus, shoulder, and one suspension lug. Worn; only traces of slip preserved. The ridge outlining the discus, channel, and wick hole is less pronounced than usual and rounded. The shoulder is slightly convex.

1020 CEL.603 Basilica exterior, NW 2, Level II. Buff clay with a reddish tint, self-slip. P.L. 0.056 m; P.H. 0.008 m; P.W. 0.017 m.

Fragment preserving parts of the discus, shoulder, including one suspension lug, and the attachment of the nozzle. The fabric has crevices due to careless packing of the clay in the mold. Very worn.

1021 C.F.2282 Atrium Building I, Room 22 exterior, Level IV. Buff clay with an orange tint, orange slip. P.L. 0.053 m; P.H. 0.014 m; P.W. 0.026 m.

Fragment preserving parts of the discus, shoulder, including one suspension lug, and the upper side wall of the oil reservoir. Slip rubbed, encrusted, and chipped. The shoulder is slightly convex. The discus had some decoration, but too little is left for identification.

1022 C.F.2285 Atrium Building I, Room 22 exterior, Level II. Buff clay with an orange tint, red slip. P.L. 0.032 m; P.H. 0.014 m; P.W. 0.015 m.

Fragment preserving part of the shoulder, including one suspension lug. Very worn; only traces of slip preserved. Surface pitted and crevices in fabric.

1023 C.F.2293 Atrium Building I, Room 16 exterior, Level II. Buff clay with an orange tint, red slip. P.L. 0.051 m; P.H. 0.024 m; P.W. 0.029 m.

Fragment preserving parts of a ring base and the lower side wall of the oil reservoir. Very worn. On the fragment of the base preserved is an *N* in relief. There is space for five or six more letters before the *N*. See Fig. 138.

1024 C.F.2295 Atrium Building I, Room 22 exterior, Level III. Buff clay, brown slip. P.L. 0.054 m; P.H. 0.018 m; P.W. 0.049 m.

Fragment preserving parts of the discus, shoulder, and upper part of the nozzle, including an arc of the wick hole. Worn; only traces of slip preserved. Encrusted.

1025 C67.452 Arx, west slope, Trial trench I, Level I. Buff clay with an orange tint, self-slip. P.L. 0.075 m; P.H. 0.006 m; Width 0.055 m.

Upper half of a Factory Lamp broken at the mold join, the tip of the nozzle broken away. Encrusted and root-marked. Smoke-blackened around wick hole. Three suspension lugs.

1026 C72.146 Street N, House of the Birds, front trench, Level 0. Buff clay, red slip. P.L. 0.054 m; P.H. 0.021 m; P.W. 0.029 m.

Fragment preserving parts of the base and lower side wall of the oil reservoir. Slip rubbed. Ring base. On the base are two letters in relief, *IS*, the rest broken away. These are probably the last two letters of a signature of six or seven letters, perhaps *FORTIS*. See Fig. 138.

For the signature *FORTIS*, see Bailey 1980, 96 and fig. 106, nos. 256, 260, and 262.

A.D. 330–410

1027 C68.678 Forum SE, Shrine of Liber Pater. Dark grayish-brown clay with a soft flaky surface, slip not preserved or self-slip. P.L. 0.058 m; P.H. 0.013 m; P.W. 0.052 m.

Fragment preserving more than half of the top of a lamp, including parts of the discus, shoulder, and two suspension lugs. Worn, encrusted, root-marked. The ridge marking the discus off from the shoulder is high, but not well defined. The narrow, sharply sloping shoulder is slightly concave.

See also 1028 and note.

1028 C68.680 Forum SE, Shrine of Liber Pater. Dark grayish-brown clay with a soft flaky surface like 1027, slip not preserved. P.L. 0.068 m; P.H. 0.011 m; P.W. 0.057 m.

Three joining fragments preserving the discus, most of the shoulder, and part of the channel leading to the nozzle. The lower part of the lamp is broken away at the mold join. Chipped; the surface is worn away; encrusted and root-marked. This is a debased copy of a Factory Lamp without suspension lugs or handle. The ridge marking off the discus from the shoulder and outlining the channel is very high, but poorly defined. The narrow shoulder slopes sharply and is slightly concave.

Nos. 1027 and 1028 are very closely related, and the clay of both is unlike that of any other lamp from Cosa. The shoulders of both these lamps have a slight concavity, and the ridges surrounding the disci, channels, and wick holes are higher than is usual but poorly defined.

A.D. 350–416

1029 CEL.186 Atrium Building I, Room 11, Level I. Buff clay with a reddish tint, red slip. P.L. 0.075 m; Height 0.034 m; Width 0.056 m.

Four joining fragments preserving parts of the discus, shoulder, side wall of the oil reservoir, base, nozzle, attachment of the strap handle, and one suspension lug. Made from a worn, crude mold; the surface is pitted and scratched; only traces of slip preserved. Smoke-blackened around wick hole. Ring base, the center broken away. The ridge outlining the discus, channel, and wick hole is low and poorly defined. The shoulder is decorated with a carelessly inscribed zigzag.

1030 CEL.287 Atrium Building I, Room 12, Level I. Buff clay with an orange tint, dark brown slip. P.L. 0.062 m; P.H. 0.025 m; P.W. 0.029 m.

Fragment preserving parts of the base and lower side wall of the oil reservoir. Worn; only traces of slip preserved. Pitted. Ring base. Only a small part of the interior is preserved, including an S in relief, the beginning or end of a signature of five or six letters (see Fig. 138).

1031 CEL.582 Atrium Building I, Room 25 exterior, Level I. Grayish-buff clay, red slip. P.L. 0.015 m; P.H. 0.013 m; P.W. 0.015 m.

Fragment preserving parts of the discus and shoulder. Slip very worn. The shoulder is slightly convex.

1032 CEL.615 Basilica exterior, W, Level I. Grayish-buff clay, red slip mottled to brown in places. P.L. 0.030 m; P.H. 0.008 m; P.W. 0.023 m.

Fragment preserving parts of the discus and shoulder. Worn; the surface is uneven, probably the result of a damaged mold. The discus is shallow and flat, then rises vertically to the top of the low ridge that separates the discus from a slightly convex shoulder.

1033 CEL.591 Basilica exterior, NW 2, Level I. Buff clay with an orange tint, red slip. P.L. 0.066 m; P.H. 0.017 m; P.W. 0.061 m.

Fragment preserving the molded pierced handle and parts of the discus, shoulder, side wall of the oil reservoir, and one low, crudely formed suspension lug. Fire-blackened, chipped, and worn.

1034 CEL.641 & CD.784 Basilica exterior, NW 2, Level I. Buff clay with reddish tint, red slip. P.L. 0.099 m; Height 0.034 m; P.W. 0.063 m.

Four joining fragments preserving most of a lamp. A part of the left side and the handle are broken away. Slip rubbed; smoke-blackened around the wick hole. Made from a worn mold; the suspension lug is only a low protrusion, and the ridge outlining the discus, channel, and wick hole is very low and blurred. Ring base; within the ring was a signature of probably five raised letters, but it is illegible.

1035 CF.2025 Atrium Building I, Room 25 exterior, Level I. Brownish-buff clay with a reddish tint, gray-black slip. P.L. 0.048 m; P.H. 0.019 m; P.W. 0.014 m.

Fragment preserving parts of the discus, shoulder, upper side wall of the oil reservoir, and one suspension lug. Made from a new mold. The rectangular suspension lug is unusually long and thin, divided by a groove.

1036 CF.2026 Atrium Building I, Room 25 exterior, Level I. Buff clay, red slip. P.L. 0.043 m; P.H. 0.014 m; P.W. 0.042 m.

Fragment preserving parts of the discus, shoulder with one suspension lug, and upper part of the channel. Very worn. The shoulder is slightly concave.

1037 CF.2027 Atrium Building I, Room 25 exterior, Level I. Buff clay, red slip. P.L. 0.075 m; P.H. 0.017 m; P.W. 0.060 m.

Fragment preserving part of the discus, shoulder, one suspension lug, and complete nozzle. The surface is rough and worn, with crevices and pits. The filling and wick holes were punched with a tapered tool. The small air hole is punched off center in the bottom of the channel.

1038 CF.2292 Atrium Building I, Room 16 exterior, Level I. Buff clay with an orange tint, red slip. P.L. 0.079 m; P.H. 0.033 m; P.W. 0.066 m

Fragment preserving the discus, shoulder, parts of the handle, and top of the nozzle. The bottom part of the lamp is broken away at the mold join. Worn and chipped; the surface is pitted with air bubbles. Made from a worn mold. Strap handle, with broad central area decorated with herringbone bordered on either side by a narrow bead. The shoulder is slightly convex. Suspension lug is poorly defined.

1039 CF.2300 Atrium Building I, Room 16 exterior, Level I. Buff clay with an orange tint, red slip. P.L. 0.089 m; P.H. 0.035 m; P.W. 0.067 m.

Nine joining fragments preserving the discus, the base, most of the side wall of the oil reservoir, the shoulder, part of the nozzle, and the attachment of the handle. Worn and chipped. Made from a worn mold. The two suspension lugs are low protrusions, and the ridge outlining the discus, channel, and wick hole is very low and poorly defined. Unprofiled flat base.

c. FACTORY LAMPS WITH A SHORT NOZZLE (*KURZFORM*)
(Fig. 110)
(Catalogue Numbers 1040, 1041)

(Loeschcke *Kurzform* Type X; Dressel Form 6; Provoost Typologie IV, 5, 23; Buchi Type X, *forma corta*, variant of Type XaI; Bailey Type N; Leibundgut Form XXXII)

A later development of Type X of the Factory Lamp or *Firmalampe* was the shorter nozzle lamp or *Kurzform*. Only two examples of the *Kurzform* have been found at Cosa. In addition to the shorter nozzle, the oil reservoir is wider and not so deep as in the *Normalform*. The *Kurzform* lamps keep the characteristic continuous ridge that outlines the discus and wick hole, forming the walls of a connecting channel. They also keep a suspension lug on each side of the shoulder, but a molded pierced handle has replaced the central axial lug. Both of these lamps were probably made in central Italy. The clay is buff-colored, coarse and hard, grogged with black and white sand with some mica.

One of the two examples of the short nozzle form of the Factory Lamp was found with a coin of A.D. 118. This lamp can then be dated A.D. 118–225, after which time very few inhabitants remained on the site of Cosa. The other lamp was found in Level I of a shop that was repaired and reopened during the partial revival of life at Cosa around A.D. 350. This lamp can be dated 350–416.

A.D. 118–225
1040   C.F.1659 Atrium Building I, Room 25 D, Level II. Buff clay with a reddish tint, red slip mottled to darker red in places. P.L. 0.062 m; P.H. 0.021 m; P.W. 0.048 m.

Fragment preserving the handle and parts of the discus, shoulder with one suspension lug, and upper side wall of the oil reservoir. Made from a worn mold. Pits and crevices in the clay. Worn. The molded pierced handle has two grooves that converge at the crest and extend down to the base as a single groove. The suspension lugs are placed on the shoulder near the center of the side.

A.D. 350–416
1041   (Fig. 110) C.F.460 Atrium Building I, Room 25 D,

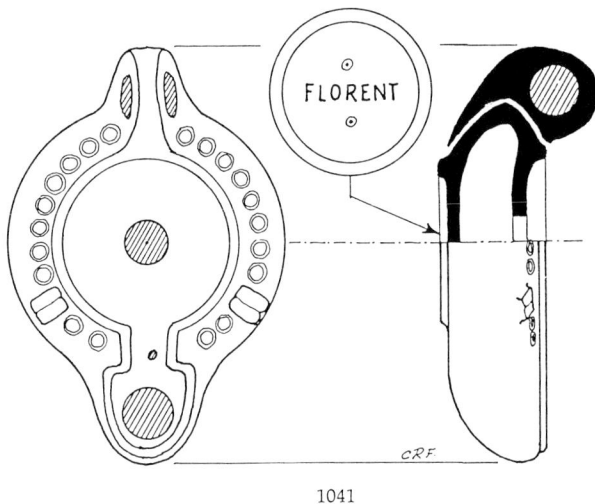

Figure 110. Factory Lamps with a short nozzle (*Kurzform*), scale 1:2

Level I. Buff clay, brown slip with a metallic luster. P.L. 0.098 m; Height 0.027 m; Width 0.078 m.

Incomplete, the end of the nozzle broken away. Slip very worn. Crevices and pits in the clay. Made from a worn and damaged mold. The groove marking off the ridge from the shoulder was reworked with a sharp tool. The suspension lugs are located forward toward the nozzle. The two lugs and the molded pierced handle form an equilateral triangle. The upper part of the shoulder is decorated with a band of impressed circles, unevenly spaced. There are ten on one side and eleven on the other. Ring base. On the bottom within the ring is the signature *FLORENT* in sunken letters with a bull's eye centered above and below the signature. See Fig. 141.

For the signature *FLORENT*, which also appears on late Fat Lamps from the end of the first century A.D. to ca. 250, see *CIL* 3.6008.23; *CIL* 5.8114.52; *CIL* 7.1330.14; *CIL* 10.8053.81; *CIL* 11.6699.85; *CIL* 12.5682.48; *CIL* 13.10001.135; *CIL* 15.6445; Bailey 1980, 95 and fig. 105.

23. PINECONE LAMPS

(Fig. 111)

(Catalogue Numbers 1042–1053)
(Loeschcke Type X; Bailey Type T; Provoost Type 12, variant 3; Buchi Type X)

Parts of twelve lamps molded in the shape of a pinecone have been found at Cosa. The clay is rather hard and coarse, and the fabric thick. The color of the clay is buff, or buff with an orange tint. Eleven of the Cosan Pinecone Lamps are slipped red or brown; the surface of the twelfth is worn away, but it was probably also slipped. Seven of these fragmentary lamps have preserved some part of their base: four rest on a ring base; one has a disk base; two stand on feet made by elongating three of the scales at appropriate places. On two of the bases are parts of a signature in relief; one is *FORTIS* retrograde, the other too fragmentary to be legible. On another base is part of a signature in incised letters, and on a fourth are two stamped peltae. Fortis was one of the early Factory Lamp manufacturers in northern Italy. The lamp with this signature was probably pirated or made in a branch of the Fortis workshop in central Italy, since the clay of all twelve Pinecone Lamps appears to be typical of the clay of central Italy.

There is a continuous ridge that partially encloses the areas around the filling and wick holes and forms the walls of a channel that connects them, similar to the channel of the Factory Lamp. However, the discus of the Pinecone Lamp is reduced to a very small area around the filling hole. There was probably the usual tiny air hole in the bottom of the channel, although this feature has not been preserved on any Cosan lamp. One side of the ridge near the filling hole swells and humps in a semicircle and is pierced, forming a handle. Both tapering ends of the cones are smooth, one being elongated into the nozzle. The lozenge-shaped scales are in realistic relief. At the crest of each scale is a small circle or bull's eye.

One of the twelve lamps was found in a context dated A.D. 50–ca. 100. Three are from contexts dated A.D. 50–225. Five are from contexts dated A.D. 118–225, and the remaining three are from contexts associated with the Constantinian revival of life on the site. Buchi dates the Pinecone Lamps from Aquileia from the end of the second century A.D. to the end of the third century. The dating of Factory and Pinecone Lamps from Aquileia is the best available at this time. From the evidence at hand and that from Aquileia, it seems safe to date the Pinecone Lamps of Cosa A.D. 118–ca. 350.

Terra-cotta Pinecone Lamps are copies of bronze lamps in the same shape. Several of these have been found: two are in the British Museum, one is in the Eisenstadt collection, and one is in the Antiquarium Comunale in Rome, published by Mercando. Loeschcke and Buchi put the Pinecone Lamp together with the Factory Lamp. Bailey separates the two and assigns the letter T to his classification of the Pinecone Lamps and the letter N to the Factory Lamps.

The drawing at the head of this chapter is a composite made from parts of various Cosan Pinecone Lamps with addition of missing parts from examples in other publications.

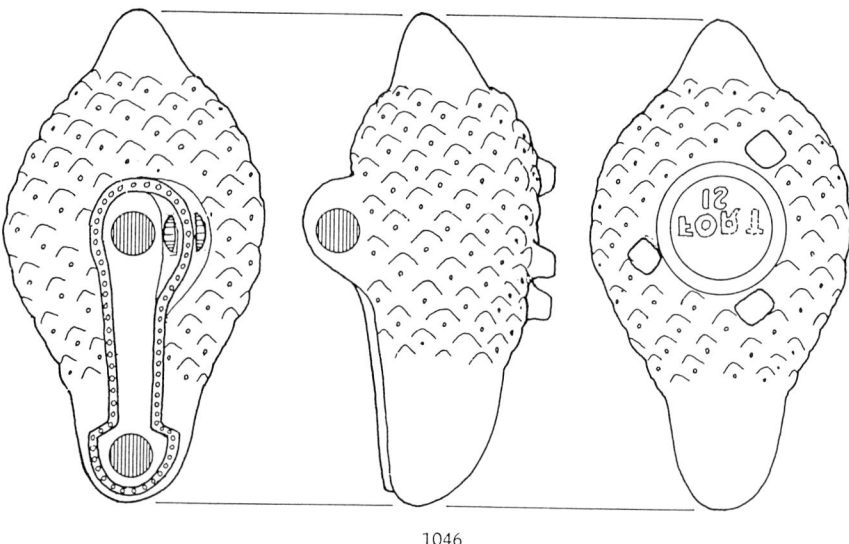

1046

Figure 111. Pinecone Lamps, scale 1:2

A.D. 50–ca. 100

1042 CEL.309 Atrium Building I, Room 16, Level I. Buff clay with an orange tint, red slip. P.L. 0.035 m; P.W. 0.041 m.

Fragment preserving parts of a disk base and the lower side wall of the oil reservoir. Worn. A tiny punched circle crowns each scale.

A.D. 50–225

1043 CEL.629 Basilica exterior, NW 3, Level I. Buff clay with a pinkish tint, red slip. P.L. 0.043 m; P.H. 0.016 m; P.W. 0.058 m.

Fragment preserving half of the base and parts of the lower side wall of the oil reservoir. Only traces of slip preserved. There is a small bull's eye on the apex of each scale. Low ring base, within which are impressed two peltae (see Fig. 136).

A potter's mark of a single pelta occurs on another lamp from Cosa, 757.

1044 CF.74 Atrium Building I, Room 22 exterior, Level II. Buff clay with an orange tint, brown slip. P.L. 0.055 m; P.H. 0.039 m; P.W. 0.060 m.

Fragment preserving parts of the bottom and lower side wall of the oil reservoir. Very worn; only traces of slip preserved. This lamp stood on three or four feet, only one of which, made by elongating a scale, is preserved. There is a tiny punched circle in the center of each scale.

For examples of Pinecone Lamps with three feet, see 1048; Buchi 1975, 205–7 nos. 1587, 1593, 1598; Menzel, 76 and fig. 61; Evelein, pl. 16 nos. 11, 13, 14.

1045 CF.2279 a and b Atrium Building I, Room 16 exterior, Level IV (from an area disturbed by the digging of foundations for a late buttress for the Basilica wall). Pinkish-buff clay, red slip. P.L. a 0.051 m, b 0.071 m; P.H. a 0.061 m, b 0.017 m; P.W. a 0.033 m, b 0.026 m.

Two nonjoining fragments preserving parts of the underside of the nozzle, the oil reservoir, the base, and the stem end of the cone. Very worn; only traces of slip preserved. The scales are in low relief and flattened on top, with a small circle at the apex of each scale. The ends of the cone are smooth. The ring base is divided into two unequal parts by an uneven groove that was retouched with a sharp tool. On the bottom is a small part of an illegible incised signature or mark.

A.D. 118–225

1046 (Fig. 111) CF.1935 Atrium Building I, Room 25 A, Levels II/III (found with a coin of A.D. 118). Buff clay with an orange tint, orange-red slip. P.L. 0.118 m; P.H. 0.060 m; P.W. 0.059 m.

Five joining fragments preserving parts of the base, the lower side wall of the oil reservoir, and the bottom of the smooth tapering stem end of the cone. Very worn. There is a tiny circle at the apex of each scale. Ring base, within which is the signature *FORTIS* in retrograde relief, *ROF* in one line, with *SI* below, the T broken away. See Fig. 138.

For examples of *FORTIS* retrograde, see Szentléleky, nos. 121, 124, 132, and 134 (from Budapest).

1047 CF.1952 Atrium Building I, Room 25 A, Levels II/III. Buff clay with an orange tint, red slip. P.L. 0.059 m; P.H. 0.043 m; P.W. 0.068 m.

Three joining fragments preserving parts of the discus, including an arc of the filling hole, parts of the channel, the molded pierced handle, and the upper part of the side wall of the oil reservoir. Slip worn away on raised surfaces. A continuous ridge encloses the discus and wick hole and forms the side wall of the channel; it swells and humps up in a semicircle on one side of the channel to make a molded pierced handle. The top of the rim is decorated with a series of tiny punched circles. There is a small bull's eye at the apex of each scale.

1048 CF.1953 Atrium Building I, Room 25 A, Levels II/III. Pinkish-buff clay, red slip mottled to brown in places. P.L. 0.087 m; P.H. 0.047 m; P.W. 0.068 m.

Two joining fragments preserving parts of the bottom and lower side wall of the oil reservoir and three feet. Very badly worn and encrusted. The feet are made by extending three scales. There is a small bull's eye at the apex of each scale.

1049 CF.1954 Atrium Building I, Room 25 A, Levels II/III. Pinkish-buff clay, dark slip with a metallic luster. P.L. 0.025 m; P.H. 0.039 m.

Fragment preserving part of the side wall of the oil reservoir. Very worn and discolored.

1050 CF.1958 Atrium Building I, Room 25 A, Levels II/III. Buff clay, brown slip. P.L. 0.038 m; P.H. 0.025 m.

Fragment preserving part of the smooth stem end of a pinecone, and one scale. Very badly worn. There is a small circle at the apex of the scale.

A.D. 225–416

1051 CF.2128 Atrium Building I, Exterior of Room 25, Level II (found with three coins of A.D. 134–38, 177–78, and 187–93). Buff clay, red slip. P.L. 0.044 m; P.W. 0.030 m.

Two joining fragments preserving part of the side wall of the oil reservoir. Very worn; only traces of slip preserved. A tiny circle is punched at the apex of each scale.

A.D. 350–416

1052 CF.2023 Atrium Building I, Exterior of Room 25, Level I (found with five coins of A.D. 64–66, 163–64, 228, 231–35, and 244–49). Buff clay, red slip. P.L. 0.047 m; P.H. 0.042 m; P.W. 0.037 m.

Fragment preserving parts of the base, smooth stem end of the cone, and bottom and side walls of the oil reservoir. Slip rubbed. There is a tiny circle punched at the apex of each scale. Part of the letter *S* in relief is preserved within the ring base. See Fig. 138 and cf. 1046.

1053 CF.2029 Atrium Building I, Exterior of Room 25, Level I. Buff clay with an orange tint, dull red slip. P.L. 0.040 m; P.H. 0.028 m.

Fragment preserving parts of the bottom wall of the oil reservoir and the smooth bottom of the nozzle. Slip worn. The scales are in low relief and are flattened on the top, with a tiny bull's eye at the apex of each scale.

24. FAT GLOBULAR (*KUGELFORM*) LAMPS

(Figs. 112, 113)

(Catalogue Numbers 1054–1063)
(Bailey Type R; Dressel Form 30; Leibundgut Form XXXV; Provoost Type 4; Zaccaria Ruggiu Type 4)

Ten crude, sturdy lamps that are almost circular in plan and section have been found at Cosa. They are descriptively called Fat Globular Lamps (or *Kugelform*). The very short nozzle and the handle project only slightly beyond the circle of the body. These lamps have a small, plain, sunken discus framed by a bead. The wide, rounded shoulders slope to meet the lower half of the body at mid-height. They have ring bases; one is ovoid in shape with the narrow end toward the nozzle, but the others are round. The semicircular molded handles are set on the shoulder and extend down the body of the lamp to end in points at the base. Seven handles of ten are pierced; one is unpierced; two are only partially pierced. The filling and wick holes are large. The shoulders of these lamps are decorated with three or four concentric rows of large raised dots, sometimes carelessly spaced and aligned.

All the Fat Globular Lamps from Cosa are made of a coarse, sandy, micaceous clay that is buff in color, sometimes yellowish or pinkish buff. The fabric is very thick. Four lamps have a brown slip, two a dark orange slip, and four a self-slip.

This lamp type appears in large numbers all over the Roman empire from the late third century to the early fifth century A.D. The Fat Globular Lamps from Cosa were found in contexts dated from the second century A.D. to A.D. 416. The second century, however, is too early for this lamp to make its appearance, and a mid-third century date is more probable.

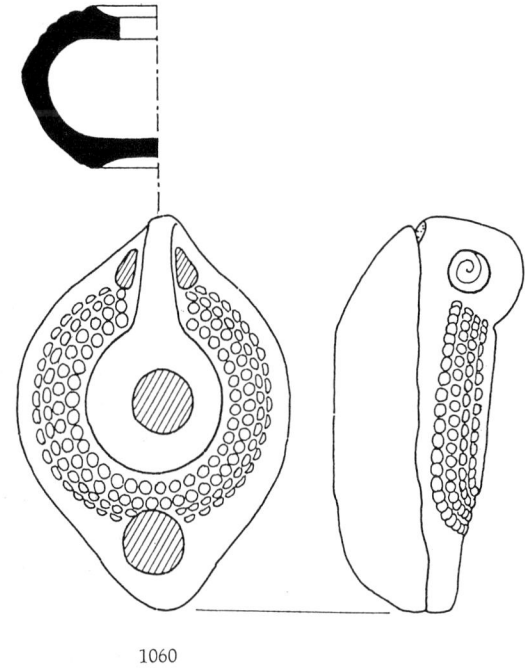

1060

Figure 112. Fat Globular Lamps, scale 1:2

Late Third Century–A.D. 416

1054 CE.1015 Atrium Building I, Room 18, Level I. Pinkish-buff clay, self-slip. Length 0.095 m; Height 0.055 m; Width 0.075 m.
   Complete, worn, encrusted. Four rows of large

raised dots on the shoulder.

1055 (Fig. 113) CEL.259 Atrium Building I, Room 18, Level I. Pinkish-buff clay, self-slip. Length 0.088 m; Height 0.036 m; Width 0.068 m.

Twelve joining fragments preserving an almost complete lamp. Chips are missing from the top, nozzle, and discus. Worn; made from a worn, blurred mold. The pierced handle was bent slightly out of alignment before firing. Four rows of raised dots on the shoulder.

1056 CF.2294 Atrium Building I, Exterior Room 22, Level IIIA (Buttress foundation area). Grayish-buff clay, brown slip. P.L. 0.078 m; P.H. 0.030 m; P.W. 0.079 m.

Fragment preserving the pierced handle and parts of the discus and shoulder. Slip rubbed. Four rows of large raised dots on the shoulder.

1057 CF.2301 Atrium Building I, Exterior of Rooms 16 and 22, Levels IV/V (Buttress foundation). Buff clay, brown slip. P.L. 0.082 m; Height 0.034 m; Width 0.080 m.

Three joining fragments preserving the pierced handle and parts of the discus, shoulder, side wall of the oil reservoir, and base. Slip rubbed. Clay pitted. Worn. Ovoid ring base, the pointed end toward the nozzle. Three rows of large raised dots on the shoulder, unevenly spaced.

1058 CG.291 Curia, SE basement room, Mithraeum, Level II. Pinkish-buff clay, orange slip. P.L. 0.093 m; P.H. 0.023 m; Width 0.083 m.

Two joining fragments preserving the handle and parts of the discus, shoulder, and lower side wall of the oil reservoir. Worn. Handle pierced with a tapering tool. Four rows of large raised dots on the shoulder, unevenly spaced.

1059 CG.304 Curia, SE basement room, Mithraeum, Level II. Buff clay, self-slip. P.L. 0.075 m; Height 0.038 m; Width 0.080 m.

Fragment preserving the pierced handle, discus, side wall of the oil reservoir, base, and start of the nozzle. Worn.

A.D. 330–410

1060 (Fig. 112) C68.107 Forum SE, Shrine of Liber Pater. Buff clay, brown slip. Length 0.103 m; Height 0.040 m; Width 0.077 m.

Four joining fragments preserving a lamp complete except for minor chipping. Worn, encrusted, root-marked, smoke-blackened around the wick

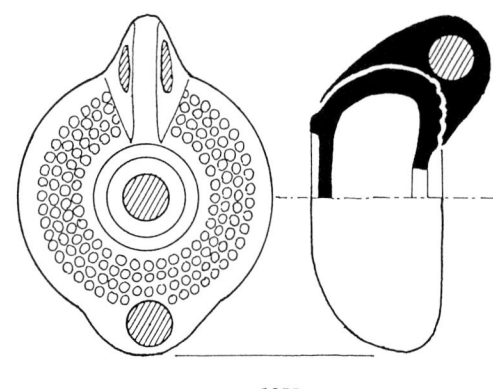

1055

Figure 113. Fat Globular Lamps, scale 1:2

hole. Central filling hole carelessly punched off center. The handle is partially punched from both sides, not pierced through. Four rows of large raised dots on the shoulder.

1061 C68.675 Forum SE, Shrine of Liber Pater. Yellow-buff clay, dark orange slip. Length 0.105 m; P.H. 0.030 m; Width 0.074 m.

Four joining fragments preserving the upper half of a lamp. Worn, encrusted, root-marked. Handle unpierced. Three rows of large raised dots on the shoulder.

1062 C68.676 Forum SE, Shrine of Liber Pater. Yellow-buff clay, self-slip. Length 0.092 m; P.H. 0.031 m; Width 0.070 m.

Fragment preserving the upper half of a lamp. Worn, encrusted. Handle only partially pierced from both sides. Three rows of large raised dots on the shoulder.

1063 C68.677 Forum SE, Shrine of Liber Pater. Yellow-buff clay, brown slip. P.L. 0.079 m; P.H. 0.024 m; P.W. 0.039 m.

Fragment preserving the handle and parts of the discus and shoulder. Worn, encrusted, root-marked. The handle is only partially pierced from both sides. Three rows of large raised dots on the shoulder.

25. NORTH AFRICAN LAMPS

(Figs. 114–124)

(Catalogue Numbers 1064–1077)
(Bailey 1980, Type S; Broneer 1930, Type XXXI; Deneauve Type VII; Dressel Type 30; Hayes Type 1; Pohl Type 1; Salomonson Type K)

A building at the center of the southeast side of the Forum was excavated in 1967–68 by Jacquelyn Collins-Clinton.[1] The building had been inserted into one of the original entrances of the Forum, occupying the space between and incorporating the side walls of buildings flanking it. This building appears to have been abandoned and destroyed very suddenly; all of its contents were discovered *in situ* under the debris of fallen building material. From its contents it was identified as a shrine of Liber Pater.[2] The abrupt destruction of this pagan shrine might have been the deliberate work of Christian zealots.[3]

One hundred nine bronze coins were found in the shrine. Most of these are from a single location, perhaps from a collection box. The earliest was minted in A.D. 317. Two, not from the collection box, were minted between A.D. 425 and 455. Coins of Constantius II appear in quantity and coins of Valentinian I and his immediate successors in even greater quantity.[4] The number of coins struck during the last third of the fourth century is greater than that of those from the first two-thirds. No coin has been found at Cosa that dates between the two of the fifth century just mentioned and those found in graves of the tenth century.

Eleven lamps found in the Shrine of Liber Pater, two found in the Mithraeum, and one from the exterior of Room 25 of Atrium Building I were imported from North Africa.[5] The fabric is thick and strong, and the lamps are in good condition. Several are complete. The clay ranges from fine to coarse and is orange-red in color. They have a self-slip. The bodies are ovoid in plan and rounded in section with one exception (the body of 1074 is shallower than the others and has a sharper angle where the upper and lower halves are joined). They all have concave disci and sloping shoulders. The disci are frequently ornamented with relief, and on the shoulders of twelve lamps are sunken panels of single or herringbone hatching (Hayes Type 1; Pohl Type 2 and variants; Graziani Abbiani Type 2, Variant a or d of North African lamps). The nozzles are broad with rounded ends and are flat on top; those that have been preserved are all smoke-blackened around

---

1. Collins-Clinton 1977. See pages 5–13 for description of the shrine and finds, and 57–71 for a discussion of the lamps.
2. According to Collins-Clinton, the coins and pottery (including the lamps) are contemporaneous, but the other furnishings of the shrine are much earlier. There are seven marble sculptures of the first century A.D. and a small Doric capital, a terra-cotta lion's head spout, and an antefix of the third or second century B.C. One of the marble sculptures is a young Bacchus; there were ritual snake vessels and an inscription with the name of Liber Pater.
3. Paganism was outlawed by Theodosius in two edicts of A.D. 391 and 392.
4. Buttrey 1980, 34, 53–55.
5. Two North African lamps were found in the Mithraeum in the southeast basement of the Curia.

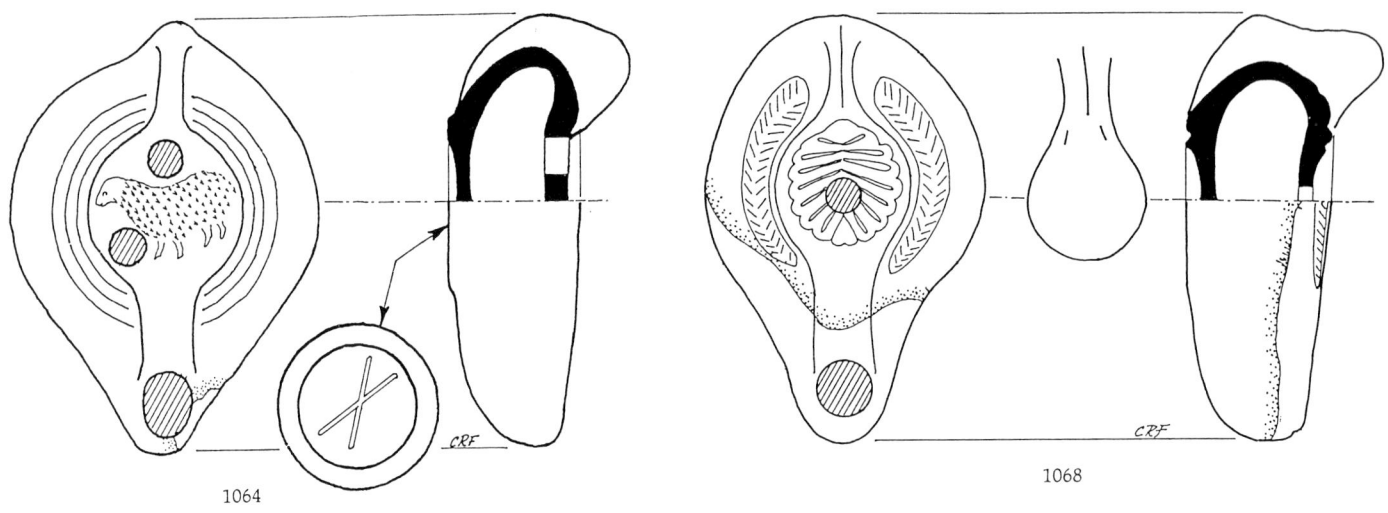

Figure 114.

Figure 115.

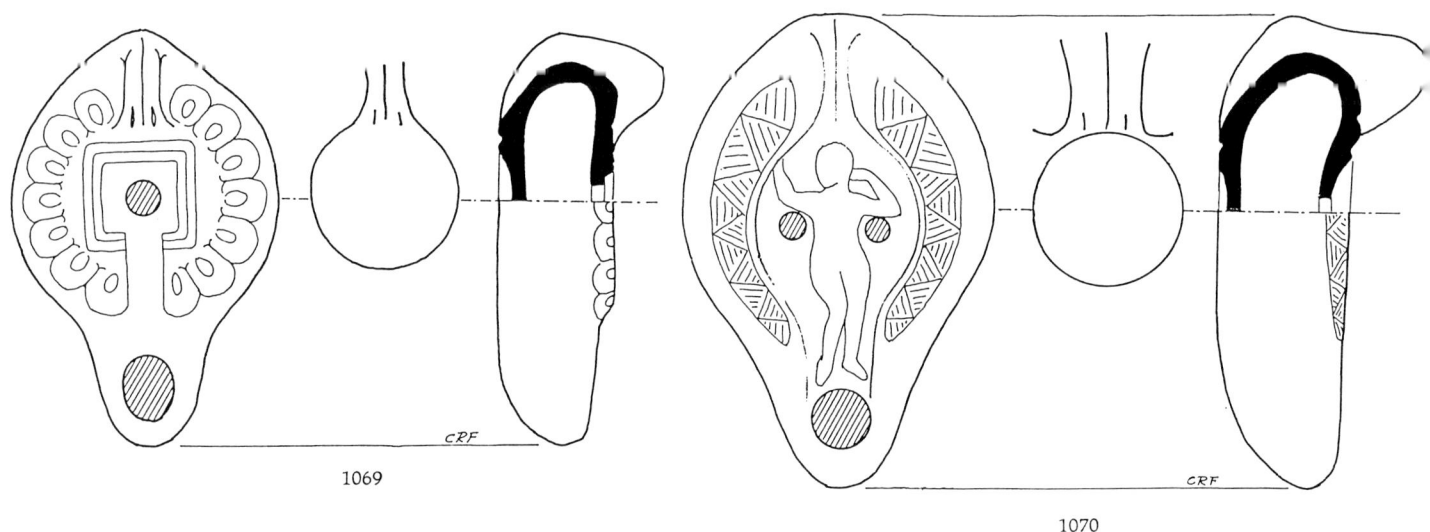

Figure 116.

Figure 117.

Figures 114–117. North African Lamps, scale 1:2

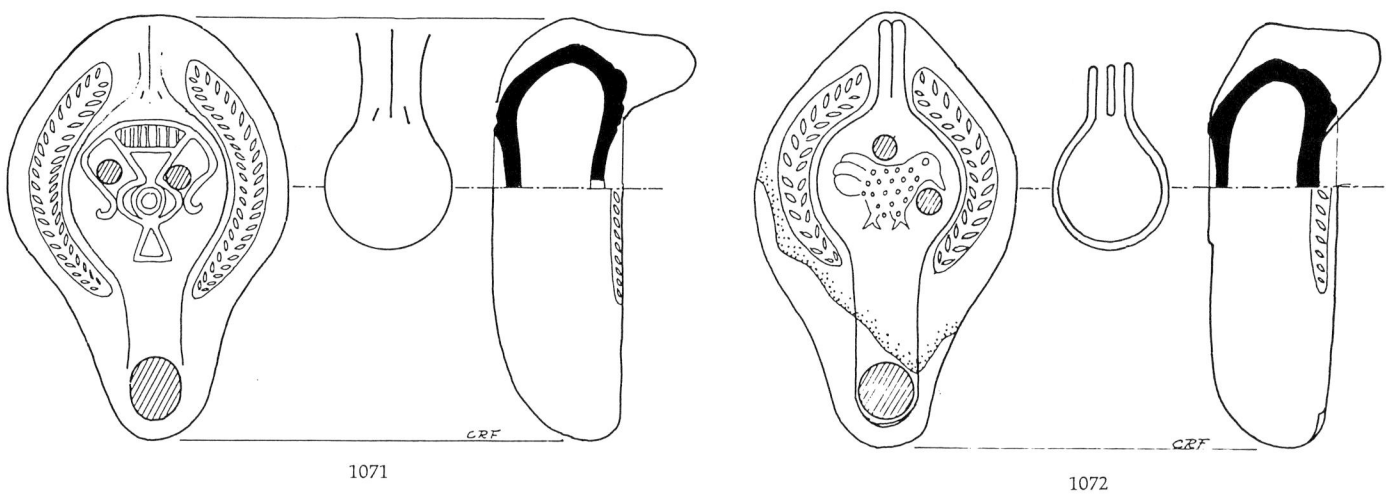

Figure 118.   1071

Figure 119.   1072

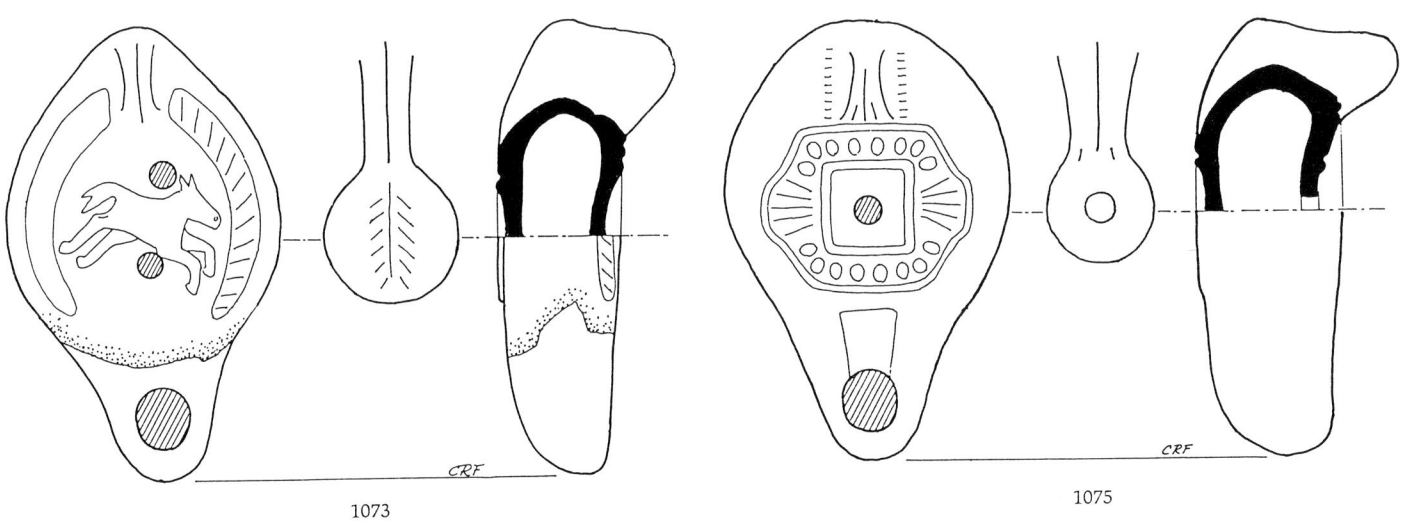

1073

Figure 120.

1075

Figure 121.

Figures 118–121. North African Lamps, scale 1:2

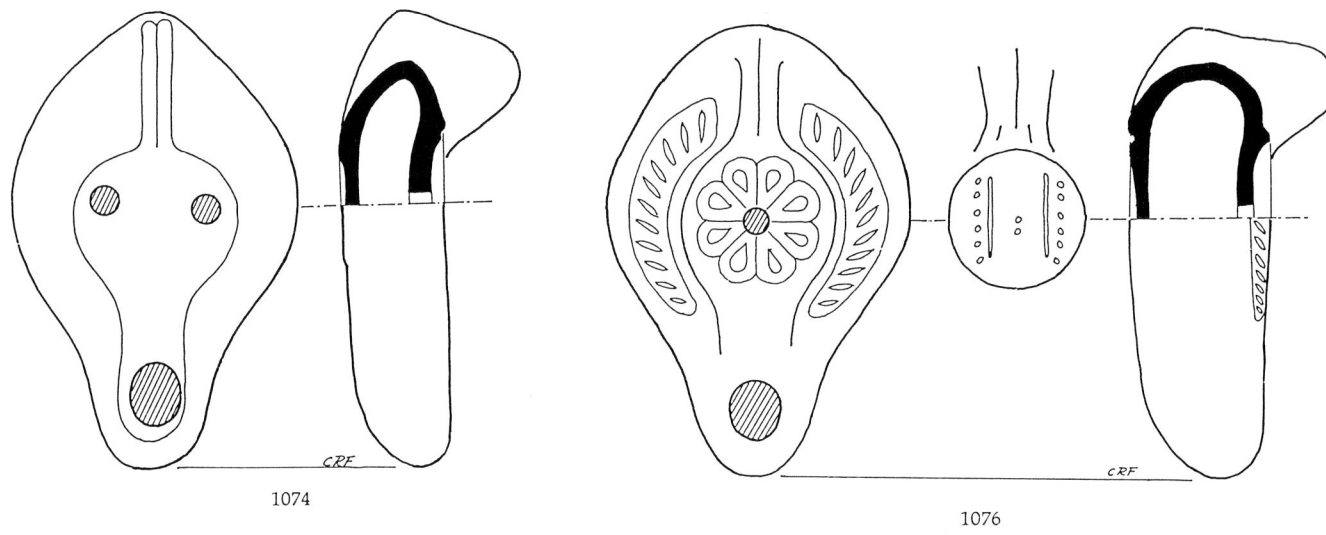

Figure 122.

Figure 123.

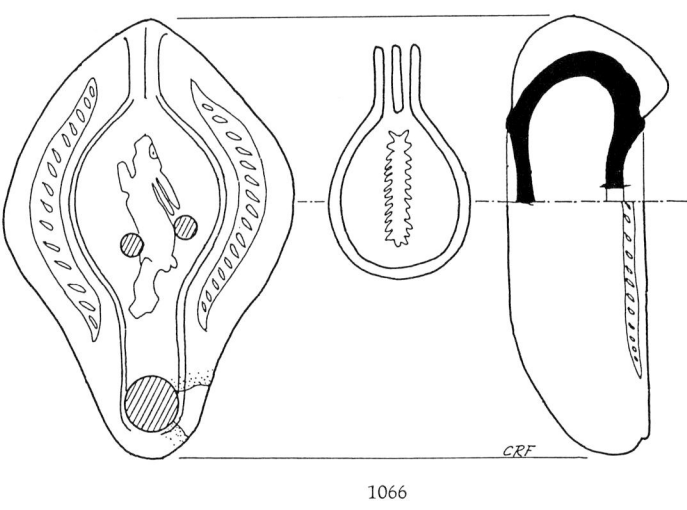

Figure 124.

Figures 122–124. North African Lamps, scale 1:2

the wick hole from use. These lamps have the sensible design of a continuous ridge enclosing the discus and wick hole and a channel between these, a feature borrowed from the north Italian Factory Lamp. They all have moldmade handles set on the shoulder with a groove on top. These do not project beyond the body and are unpierced with one exception, and that one is only partially pierced from one side. The lamps have unprofiled bases that are outlined by a groove that encircles the bottom of the oil reservoir, then opens out and extends up the wall under the handle; another groove is sometimes added to the base inside this.

One of the African Lamps, 1064, is different: the body is almost circular in plan, and the handle extends beyond the body, extending down to a ring base as a ridge. This is an example of Salomonson's North African Lamp Type K, which Salomonson dates second half of the third century A.D. to first half of the fourth.

A.D. 330–410

1064 (Fig. 114) C68.126 Forum, SE, Shrine of Liber Pater. Hard, brick-red clay, self-slip. Length 0.115 m; Height 0.035 m; Width 0.083 m.

Complete, except for a chip from the left side of the nozzle. Worn; smoke-blackened around wick hole. Within the low ring base on the concave bottom are two grooves that cross at their centers making a 15-degree angle. The discus is framed by a triple bead; the inner one cuts through the two outer beads and becomes the ridge that encloses the discus and wick hole. Discus relief: A sheep with curly wool walking left. The relief is rather crude and worn.

For a close parallel, see Salomonson 1966, fig. 2 no. 3, fig. 6 no. 3 (the sheep faces right); Ennabli 1976, 73–85, pl. on 72 no. 100, pl. on 73 nos. 101–2 (in the Musée Bardo); Provoost 1970, 2–55, pls. 1–9.

1065 CF.2014 Atrium Building I, Room 25 exterior, Level I. Hard, orange-red clay, red slip. P.L. 0.048 m; Height 0.045 m; P.W. 0.053 m.

Four joining fragments preserving the handle, and parts of the discus, shoulder, oil reservoir, base, and nozzle. Crude mold; imperfections due to careless packing of the mold and damage to the handle before firing. Molded pierced handle extending beyond the body and continuing down to the base as a spine, ending in a point. Two grooves on the upper part of the handle converge at the crest, separate again into two down the spine, and converge again at the base. Long, heavy nozzle, the top broken away. On the shoulder is a band of elongated ovules. Low disk base, within which are impressed three letters of a signature: . . . *BIT* with a bull's eye centered above (one below would be broken away). This is probably the signature *C.IVN.BIT* (see Fig. 141).

Cf. Bonnet 1988, 107–9, 108 fig. 34.

1066 (Fig. 124) CG.284 Curia, SE basement room, Mithraeum, Level II. Dark orange-red clay, self-slip. Length 0.117 m; Height 0.036 m; Width 0.080 m.

Fourteen joining fragments preserving most of a lamp. A chip is broken away from the side of the nozzle. Worn and encrusted. Low ring base with extension up the wall of the oil reservoir under the handle, joined at the base by a third central ridge creating a triple bead. On the axis of the bottom is a band of herringbone so dense it resembles a caterpillar (cf. 1067). On the shoulder are arched bands of oblique hatching. Discus relief: A rabbit with ears laid back running left toward the handle, very crudely drawn. Two filling holes, one above and one below the relief.

For the same relief, but running right, see Joly 1974, pl. 46 no. 1044.

1067 CG.287 Curia, SE basement room, Mithraeum, Level I. Orange-red clay, self-slip. Length 0.118 m; Height 0.040 m; Width 0.070 m.

Thirteen joining fragments making most of a lamp. Chips broken away from discus and base. Worn. Low undefined ring base with extension up body wall under handle in parallel ridges. On the axis of the bottom is a band of dense herringbone like that on 1066. One side of the handle is partially pierced. Discus relief: Possibly a horse to right, but very worn and blurred.

1068 (Fig. 115) C68.111 Forum, SE, Shrine of Liber Pater. Rather fine, orange-red clay, self-slip. Length 0.114 m; Height 0.038 m; Width 0.076 m.

Three joining fragments making most of a lamp, parts of the lower wall of the oil reservoir and top of the nozzle broken away. Worn and encrusted. Discus relief: Stylized scallop shell with a central filling hole punched through the shell. Arched bands of herringbone hatching on the shoulder.

1069 (Fig. 116) C68.112 Forum, SE, Shrine of Liber Pater.

Coarse orange-red clay, self-slip. Length 0.109 m; Height 0.032 m; Width 0.073 m.

Complete lamp in good condition. Smoke-blackened around wick hole. Central filling hole. On either side on the shoulder is an arched band of seven large, deeply bordered ovules. Discus relief: Small depressed square discus framed by a double bead with an opening toward the nozzle.

For an exact parallel, see Ivanyi, pl. 46 no. 14.

1070 (Fig. 117) C68.113 Forum, SE, Shrine of Liber Pater. Coarse, hard, orange-red clay, self-slip. Length 0.125 m; Height 0.035 m; Width 0.084 m.

Complete lamp. Worn and encrusted. Smoke-blackened around wick hole. On the shoulder are arched bands of hatched triangles. Discus relief: Venus, nude, standing with raised arms. Very worn and crudely executed. A small filling hole on either side of the figure at breast height.

For similar shoulder decorations, see Ponsich 1963, pl. 32 no. 380; Ivanyi, pl. 40 no. 2.

1071 (Fig. 118) C68.116 Forum, SE, Shrine of Liber Pater. Fine, hard, orange-red clay, self-slip. Length 0.112 m; Height 0.035 m; Width 0.076 m.

Complete lamp. Surface slightly worn and encrusted. Smoke-blackened around wick hole. Arched bands of herringbone hatching on the shoulder. Discus relief: Stylized cantharus in profile, the belly decorated with a circle. Two small filling holes punched inside the handles of the cantharus.

1072 (Fig. 119) C68.122 Forum, SE, Shrine of Liber Pater. Fine, hard, orange-red clay, self-slip. P.L. 0.096 m; Height 0.034 m; Width 0.069 m.

Four joining fragments preserving the handle, discus, parts of the shoulder, body, nozzle, and base. Encrusted. Chipped. Arched bands of herringbone hatching on the shoulder. Discus relief: A crudely drawn bird to right. Two filling holes, one above the back of the bird and the other under the breast.

Cf. Ivanyi, pl. 39 no. 4 (a rooster, similar in theme, not in style).

1073 (Fig. 120) C68.125 Forum, SE, Shrine of Liber Pater. Clay misfired from brownish-buff to brownish-black, slip of same color. P.L. 0.089 m; Height 0.034 m; P.W. 0.075 m.

Incomplete lamp, nozzle broken away. Worn and encrusted. Made from a worn mold. On the base is incised a schematic palm branch (see Fig. 120). Arched bands of hatching on the shoulder. Discus relief: A horse cantering to right, poorly drawn and blurred. Two filling holes, one just behind the head, the other under the chest and forelegs.

For the same horse, see Joly 1974, pl. 46 no. 1033; Graziani Abbiani, pl. 3 fig. 11, pl. 20 fig. 78; Ivanyi, pl. 39 no. 5 (with the horse facing left). For the potter's mark, see Ivanyi, pl. 39; Graziani Abbiani, pl. 3 fig. 12.

1074 (Fig. 122) C68.127 Forum, SE, Shrine of Liber Pater. Fine, orange-red clay, self-slip. Length 0.121 m; Height 0.029 m; Width 0.077 m.

Complete lamp. Worn, pitted, encrusted. Smoke-blackened around wick hole. This lamp is different from the others in this group: the body is shallower, with a sharp angle where the two halves join. The shoulder is wider at the handle end, distending the circular form of the discus. The handle is unusually long, extending from the edge of the discus to the outer edge of the body. The lamp has a low ring base, not clearly defined, that extends up toward the handle in parallel ridges. An illegible decoration on the shoulder. Discus relief: Worn and blurred, not identifiable. Two filling holes, symmetrically placed.

1075 (Fig. 121) C68.130 Forum, SE, Shrine of Liber Pater. Orange-red clay, self-slip. Length 0.117 m; Height 0.039 m; Width 0.078 m.

Complete lamp. Encrusted; smoke-blackened around wick hole. In the center of the base is a small impressed circle. There is a truncated channel leading from the wick hole toward the discus and lines of short hatching on either side of the handle. Discus relief: The discus is divided into two zones. There is a small, square, inner area, plain, with a central filling hole. This is framed by a bead molding. Around it is a symmetrical collar of irregular shape approaching an octagon also framed by a bead molding. This collar is decorated on the narrow sides toward handle and nozzle with rows of eight small oval depressions, and on the deeper sides between these with fans of radiating grooves.

For a similar lamp, see Joly 1974, pl. 46 no. 1032. The lines of hatching on either side of the handle are missing on the Joly example, but the mold in which this lamp was made was very worn, and they may have been erased by use. For the mark on the base, see Menzel, 95, fig. 79 no. 3, and cf. 92, fig. 77 nos. 1–5, 7, 10 (circles in relief).

1076 (Fig. 123) C68.131 Forum, SE, Shrine of Liber Pater. Coarse, orange-red clay, self-slip. Length 0.119 m; Height 0.035 m; Width 0.083 m.

Complete lamp. Worn and encrusted. Smoke-blackened around wick hole. On the base, parallel to the axis, are two widely spaced grooves that almost cut off quarter segments of the circle, each with six small circular punch marks along it within the segment. There are also two punch marks centered between these on the axis. There are arched bands of hatching on the shoulder. Discus relief: Rosette of eight bordered petals, radiating from the central filling hole.

For the same discus relief, see Graziani Abbiani, pl. 6 fig. 22; Hayes 1980, pls. 34–35 no. 281 (top and bottom views); Ivanyi, pl. 40 no. 1; Alvarez Ossorio, pl. 285 no. 13, fig. 5 no. 12; Broneer 1930, pl. 21 no. 1457.

1077 C68.682 Forum, SE, Shrine of Liber Pater. Fine, orange-red clay, self-slip. P.L. 0.080 m; Height 0.035 m; Width 0.077 m.

Two joining fragments preserving parts of the discus, shoulder, side wall of the oil reservoir, base, and handle. Encrusted and worn. Shoulder decorated with arched bands of hatching. Discus relief: A crudely drawn dolphin with a large round eye facing left. The outline of the dolphin is scalloped. Single filling hole off center above dolphin.

Cf. Hayes 1980, pls. 34–35 no. 283 (top and bottom views).

26. ROMAN COPIES OF NORTH AFRICAN LAMPS

(Figs. 125–130)

(Catalogue Numbers 1078–1089)
(Hayes Type 1 and 2)

The following twelve lamps found at Cosa are Roman imitations of North African Lamps. The clay is fine, rather soft, and ranges in color from cream to buff, sometimes with an orange tint. The slip is orange, brownish-orange, or brown. The bodies of these lamps are ovoid, as are their prototypes, but three are smaller and slenderer than the prototypes. One copies the form of Salomonson Type K. The others closely follow the North African Hayes Type I lamps. They are from contexts dated ca. A.D. 330–410.

Other differences, aside from clay and slip, between North African Lamps and their Roman imitations are the following: Roman copies usually have ring bases, while North African Lamps have unprofiled bases; Roman copies have pierced handles, while North African Lamp handles are unpierced; and North African handles have a groove on the top, while the imitations have none.

ca. A.D. 330–410

1078 (Fig. 127) CEL.180 and C68.124, from the same or same-generation molds. Atrium Building I, Room 23, Level I. Buff clay, self-slip. P.L. 0.078 m; Height 0.030 m; Width 0.054 m.

Three joining fragments preserving the handle, base, parts of the discus, shoulder, and side wall of the oil reservoir. Worn and chipped. Shoulder decorated with a series of slender lanceolate leaves, set obliquely. Discus relief: Eight petaled rosettes radiating around central filling hole. A second filling hole is on axis toward the nozzle just beyond the rosette.

This lamp was made from the same (or same-generation) mold as 1084.

1079 (Fig. 129) CG.286 and C68.110, from the same or same-generation molds. Curia, SE basement room, Mithraeum, Level II. Buff clay with a pinkish tint, dull orange slip. P.L. 0.103 m; Height 0.035 m; Width 0.079 m.

Four joining fragments preserving the handle, parts of the discus, shoulder, side wall of the oil reservoir, and base. Surface worn and scratched. Unprofiled base. The shoulder and discus are plain.

1080 (Fig. 126) C68.108 and C68.129, from the same or same-generation molds. Forum, SE, Shrine of Liber Pater. Buff clay with an orange tint, orange slip. Length 0.104 m; Height 0.032 m; Width 0.062 m.

Complete, except for a chip from the top of the handle. Worn. The ring base opens out under the handle and extends up the wall of the body as a double bead. Two symmetrically placed filling holes on the cross axis of the plain discus. Shoulder decorated with arcs of lanceolate leaves set obliquely with pairs of leaves at the handle end.

1081 (Fig. 130) C68.109 and C68.681, from the same or same-generation molds. Forum, SE, Shrine of Liber Pater. Buff clay with an orange tint, deep orange slip. P.L. 0.082 m; Height 0.044 m; P.W. 0.066 m.

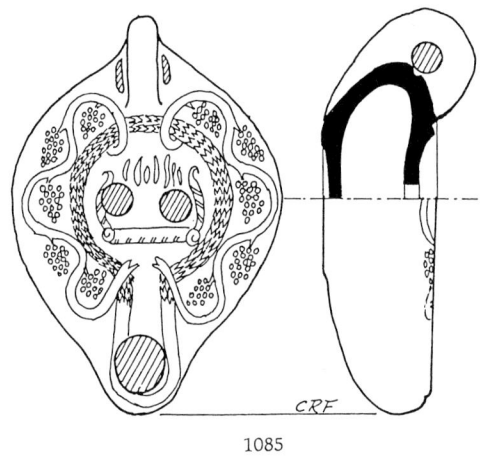

1085

Figure 125.

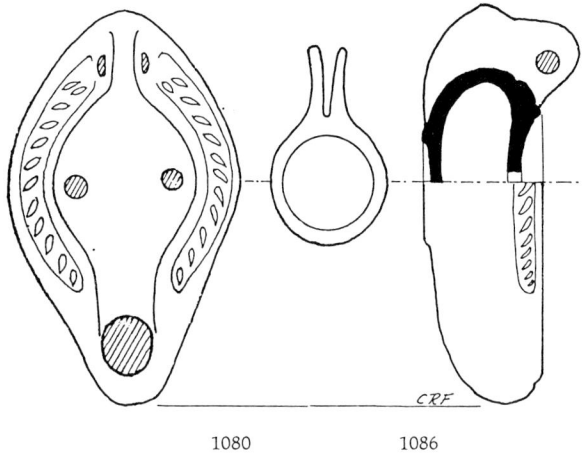

1080   1086

Figure 126.

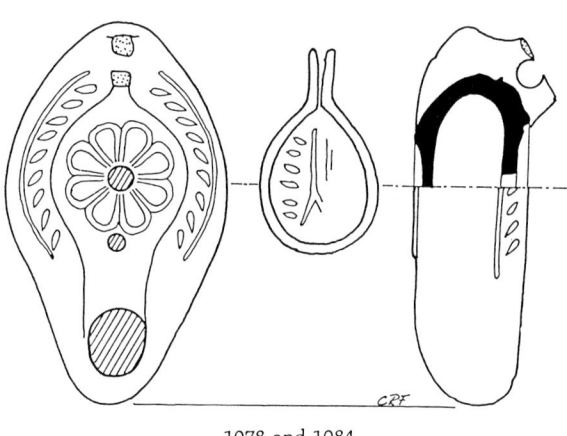

1078 and 1084

Figure 127.

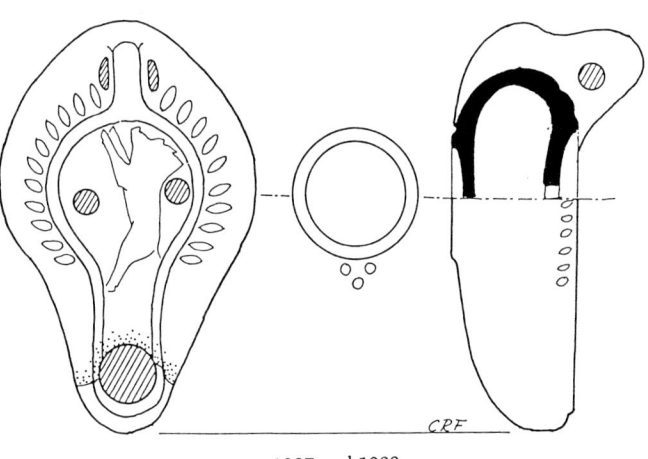

1087 and 1088

Figure 128.

Figures 125–127. Roman copies of North African Lamps, scale 1:2

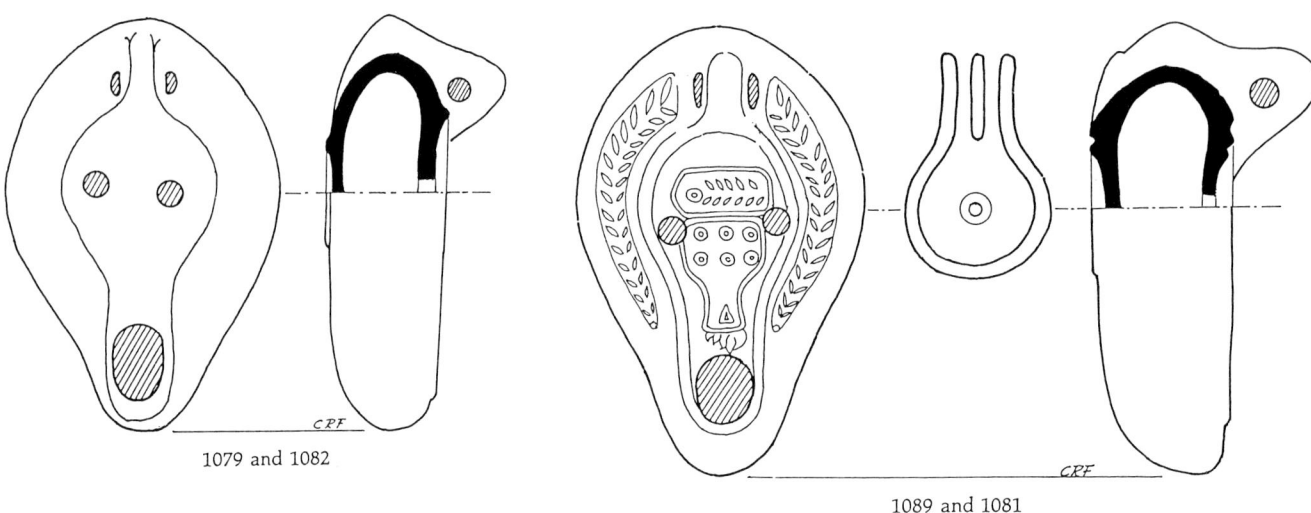

Figure 129. Figure 130.

Figures 129, 130. Roman copies of North African Lamps, scale 1:2

Incomplete, the nozzle, parts of the discus, shoulder, and base broken away. Worn; encrusted. Body rounded in profile, ovoid in plan. Base ring opens, extending up body under handle with an added ridge in the center, making a triple bead. Within the base is a small circle in relief. The shoulder is decorated with a double file of slender oval leaves set like chevrons. Discus relief: See 1089 for a complete description of the discus of a lamp from the same (or same-generation) mold.

1082 (Fig. 129) C68.110 and CG.286, from the same or same-generation molds. Forum, SE, Shrine of Liber Pater. Buff clay, deep orange slip. Length 0.108 m; Height 0.031 m; Width 0.074 m.

Complete, except for minor chipping on one side of the oil reservoir. Worn and encrusted. Crudely formed ring base opens under the handle, extending up the lower body of the lamp as parallel ridges. Discus framed by a molding that opens out toward the nozzle and encloses the wick hole, forming a channel between the two. Two filling holes punched on the cross axis of the discus. The shoulder and discus are plain.

This lamp is closely related to 1079.

1083 C68.123 Curia, SE basement room, Mithraeum, Level II. Buff clay, dull orange slip. Length 0.102 m; Height 0.030 m; Width 0.060 m.

Complete, except for minor chipping. Worn and encrusted. Ring base opens out under handle, extending up the wall of the oil reservoir as a pair of ridges. Arcs on either side of the shoulder decorated with hatching. Discus relief: A flaming altar. Two filling holes punched above the altar encroach on the relief. For the more complete discus relief, cf. 1085.

1084 (Fig. 127) C68.124 and CEL.180, from the same or same-generation molds. Curia, SE basement room, Mithraeum, Level II. Buff clay, mottled dark to light brown slip. Length 0.101 m; Height 0.030 m; Width 0.060 m.

Complete, except for a chip from the top of the handle. Encrusted. This lamp is smaller than usual for this lamp type. Low ovoid ring base opens under handle, extending up the wall of the oil reservoir as a pair of beads. Within the base are two palm sprays, that to the left very blurred. The shoulder is decorated with arcs of palm sprays with fronds only on the discus side of the stem. Discus relief: A rosette of eight bordered petals radiating from a central filling hole; a second filling hole is punched on axis toward the nozzle just beyond the rosette.

Cf. 1078; Joly 1974, 179, pl. 45 no. 1026; Graziani Abbiani, 56, pl. 16, fig. 22, and 114, pl. 16 fig. 62, and 131, pl. 20 fig. 80; Breccia, 31, pl. 28 figs. 1–3; Leibundgut 1963, 294, pl. 15 no. 950; Gualandi Genito 1986, 222–23, pl. 79 nos. 612–13; Ivanyi, pl. 39 no. 8 and pl. 40 no. 1; Hayes 1980, pl. 34 no. 281.

1085 (Fig. 125) C68.128 Forum, SE, Shrine of Liber Pater. Buff clay with an orange tint, slip mottled from brown to reddish-brown. Length 0.105 m; Height 0.030 m; Width 0.073 m.

Complete, except for minor chipping. Slightly worn. Oil reservoir rounded in plan, with a short rounded nozzle. Low ring base that extends up the body in a ridge that merges with the handle, which extends beyond the edge of the body. A wreath shown as a band of imbrication at small scale, probably to suggest laurel, frames the discus and opens out along the channel to the wick hole, continuing then as a plain bead around the wick hole. A serpentine ribbon or grapevine decorates each shoulder, with a bunch of grapes in each loop. Discus relief: A flaming altar or a schematic lyre. Two filling holes punched in the middle interfere with the design.

This lamp is a copy of Salomonson Type K; see North African Lamps Introduction and 1064.

For a lamp with a similar shoulder decoration but different discus, see Bruneau, pl. 34 no. 4717 (Bruneau dates this lamp fifth to seventh century); Hayes 1972, Type 1; Pohl Type 2; Graziani Abbiani Type 2. For the discus relief, cf. 1083.

1086 (Fig. 126) C68.129 and C68.108, from the same or same-generation molds. Forum, SE, Shrine of Liber Pater.

Identical with 1080; these two lamps may have been made from the same (or same-generation) mold.

1087 (Fig. 128) C68.154 Forum, SE, Shrine of Liber Pater. Buff clay with an orange tint, self-slip. P.L. 0.098 m; Height 0.034 m; Width 0.070 m.

Incomplete, the nozzle with part of the body broken away. Heavily encrusted and surface flaking. Low ring base. Near the base under the nozzle are three large raised dots in a triangle. Shoulder decorated with single rows of lanceolate leaves set obliquely. Discus relief: A boar bounding toward the handle. The mold is old and worn.

For the same discus relief, see Graziani Abbiani, pl. 22 no. 88.

1088 (Fig. 128) C68.674 Forum, SE, Shrine of Liber Pater. Buff clay, misfired to grayish-buff in places, dull orange slip. Length 0.109 m; Height 0.034 m; Width 0.069 m.

Four joining fragments preserving a complete lamp, except for chips broken from side wall of the oil reservoir and part of the nozzle. Surface flaking.

Discus relief and shoulder decorations identical with 1087, made from the same (or same-generation) mold.

1089 (Fig. 130) C68.681 and C68.109, from the same or same-generation molds. Forum, SE, Shrine of Liber Pater. Buff clay with an orange tint, deep orange slip. P.L. 0.112 m; Width 0.078 m.

Four joining fragments preserving most of the top of a lamp. Worn and encrusted. Shoulder decoration identical with 1081. Discus relief: Enigmatic. Pointing toward the nozzle is a shape like a jug-shaped torchere or an irregular arula from which liquid or flames issue; the body is decorated with two rows of three bull's eyes each, evenly spaced, while the neck has a triangle enclosing a smaller triangle. Above this and tangent to it is an oblong with rounded corners to the right and a rounded end to the left on which is a double row of small leaves set in chevrons with a bull's eye at the end toward the rounded end. There is a filling hole to either side of the relief.

27. THREE FOREIGN LAMPS

(Figs. 131–133)

(Catalogue Numbers 1090–1092)

a. ATHENIAN LAMP BY ARISTON

(Fig. 131)

(Catalogue Number 1090)

This very fine lamp was found in a dump outside the city walls below the Arx, between Towers 9 and 10. The material in the dump had probably been thrown over the wall in the cleanup during the resettlement of Cosa between 25 and 20 B.C. This debris was from the destruction of the city ca. 70 B.C. The lamp was made in Athens in the workshop of the potter Ariston. Howland, who published the Greek lamps from the Agora at Athens, dates Ariston between the late second century B.C. and 86 B.C. Ariston's workshop, and perhaps Ariston himself, did not survive the capture and sack of Athens by Sulla in 86 B.C.

(Bailey 1975, 63, pl. 20 no. 104; Bruneau, 44–46, pl. 10 nos. 2051, 2056 [see Chapter 6, in which Bruneau deals with the different arrangements of the letters in Ariston's signatures; on some lamps all the letters are on one line, on others on two, and on some the letters are arranged in a circle]; Howland, 175–77, pl. 50 no. 691; Hayes 1980, 15–16, pl. 7 no. 57 [a simpler lamp without an ear]; Scheibler, 161 and 164, figs. 9–10 [see 164 for Ariston's signature with the letters in a circle].)

120–25/20 B.C.
1090 (Fig. 131) CB.1772 Pottery dump. Fine, hard, buff

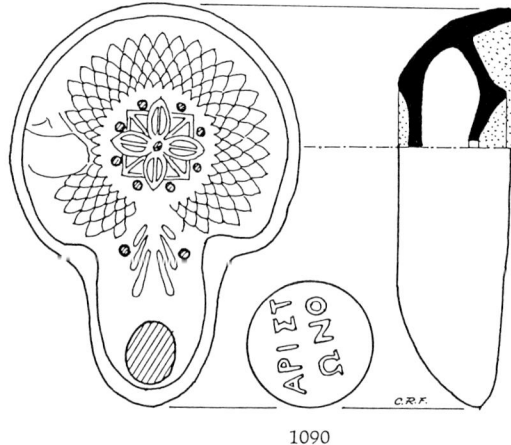

Figure 131. Athenian Lamp by Ariston, scale 1:2

clay, thin self-slip. P.L. 0.084 m; Height 0.031 m; Width 0.073 m.

Four joining fragments preserving the nozzle and parts of the discus, shoulder, lower side wall of the oil reservoir, base, and an added collar of a Triangular Nozzle Lamp. Worn. Biconical body, forming an angle where the two halves join. Small concave discus. Horn-shaped ear on the left side of the body, the ear and outline of the body obscured by the attachment of a handmade collar that surrounds the top, including the nozzle. The collar also blunts the points of the triangular nozzle. This was a crude device to prevent oil spillage.

The discus is decorated with a small, four-petaled rosette superimposed on a square. In the center is a very small filling hole, with eight small holes all the same size in a circle flanking the ends of the petals. Three additional holes have been punched, one for the wick and one on either side of the nozzle to drain the sunken area formed by the collar. The shoulder around the rosette is decorated with a deep band of flowerlike imbrication in five rows of pointed scales, interrupted toward the nozzle where there is an elongated palmette of six club-shaped leaves, lacking a center leaf.

Unprofiled base, slightly concave, with the signature *ARISTONO* in Greek characters in relief. The letters are arranged in two lines, *ARIST* above and *ONO* below.

b. CORINTHIAN LAMP BY LOUKIOS
(Fig. 132)

(Catalogue Number 1091)

(Broneer Type XXVII, Group I; Loeschcke Type VIII; Deneauve Type VII; Dressel/Lamboglia Type 25)

This fine Corinthian Lamp is the only one of its kind that has been found in Cosa so far and may have been brought there by a traveler. It comes from a deposit around the foundation of the buttress of the northwest wall of the Basilica. When the soil was filled in around the buttress foundation, it included later material on the bottom, while Augustan and Tiberian material was found above. Therefore the dating of this lamp must depend upon evidence from other sites. Broneer has published two hundred forty lamps made in Corinth of this type. Eight of these are signed, as is the Cosan example with the name *LOUKIOU* in Greek characters, indicating the workshop. Broneer writes that these lamps, produced originally about the end of the first century A.D., were fully developed under Hadrian and were the commonest type in Greece during the Antonine period. Lamps of this type have been found not only in Corinth, but also at Isthmia, the Agora in Athens, and other sites. Broneer writes that Corinthian Lamps appear as "a fully developed product of superior craftsmanship in the early years of the second century . . . [and] continued to be made throughout the second century and well into the third."[1]

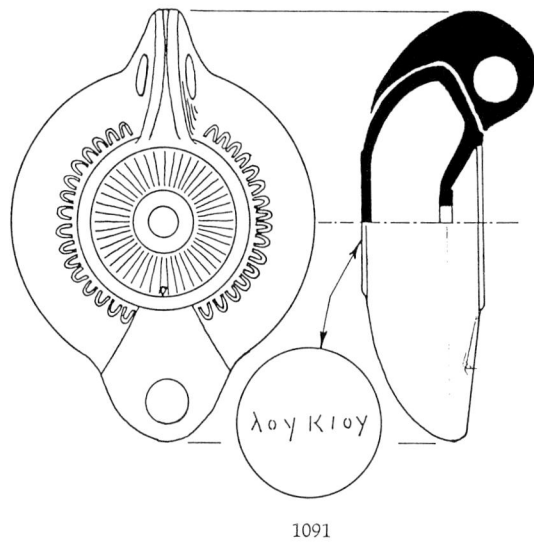

1091

Figure 132. Corinthian Lamp by Loukios, scale 1:2

The Corinthian Lamp was developed from the Loeschcke Type VIII Roman Lamp, presumably by Roman potters who had settled in Corinth. The body shape of Type VIII was retained, with its wide shoulder, decorated concave discus, and molded pierced handle with two grooves converging at the crest of the handle.

The nozzle is set into the shoulder as far as the edge of the discus, with straight sides flaring from the discus to the outer edge of the lamp as in Loeschcke's form R of his Type VIII, and Heres's Type E a.

The discus and shoulder were decorated, and the shoulder on later lamps of this type often has the suspension lugs of the Factory Lamp. The Cosan lamp is an early form of Broneer Type XXVII and does not have suspension lugs.

This lamp is of very high quality, made from carefully prepared clay in a fine mold. Although lamps of this type were never able to compete with the local Roman product in Italy, they were very popular in the eastern Mediterranean.[2]

---

1. Broneer 1930, 90–97 nos. 582, 603, 745–49; Broneer 1977, 64–65.
2. When Corinth was resettled by Julius Caesar around 46 B.C., the colonists were Roman veterans and freedmen. It is likely that the potter Loukios was a descendant of one of these.

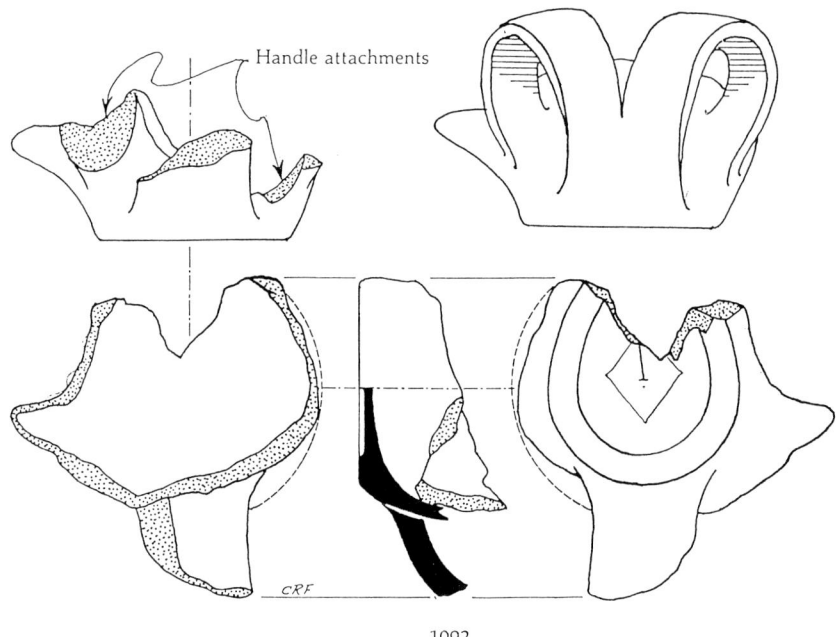

Figure 133. Split-handled lamp probably from Cnidus, scale 1:2

End of the First Century A.D.– Early Second Century

1091 (Fig. 132) CF.2274 Atrium Building I, Room 16 exterior, Buttress foundation, Level V. Fine, cream clay, slightly yellow in tint, self-slip. P.L. 0.101 m; Height 0.033 m; P.W. 0.082 m (when intact 0.086 m).

Six joining fragments preserving the discus and parts of all other essential features of a Fat Lamp. New crisp mold. Smoke-blackened around the wick hole. Angular, funneled discus, the sides flaring from a narrow level ring around the central filling hole. A bead molding separates the discus from the sloping shoulder. The shoulder meets the lower side wall of the oil reservoir at an acute angle. Low disk base. Molded pierced handle, the upper part of the handle ungrooved, the lower part with two grooves (the reverse of what is usual on these lamps). Short nozzle, slightly raised and with rounded end, set over the shoulder starting at the edge of the discus, separated from the shoulder by straight sides that flare from the edge of the discus to the outer edge of the shoulder. There is the usual Roman air hole at the edge of the discus toward the nozzle. Discus relief: A ring of grooves radiating from central filling hole. Around the shoulder just beyond the bead marking it off from the discus is a band of tiny bordered ovules.

Inscribed on the base in Greek characters: *LOUKIOU*.

c. SPLIT-HANDLED LAMP, PROBABLY FROM CNIDUS

(Fig. 133)

(Catalogue Number 1092)

A fragment of a large lamp has an unusual handle for which there seems to be no known parallel. The lower part is a normal, but broad strap handle; this then divides into two parts and separates, each half returning to attach low on the side of the oil reservoir about one-quarter of the circumference apart. All three attachments for the handle have been preserved and can be seen in the accompanying drawing (Fig. 133).

The clay is similar to that of the Delphiniform Lamps from Sicily (see Chapter 6), and evidently similar to that of a group of lamps from Cnidus, excavated by Newton and Smith in 1858 in the "Temenos of

Demeter." These Cnidian lamps, the Delphiniform Lamps, and the Cosan fragment were fired twice (oxidation/reduction technique), resulting in a dark gray color.

The handles of the Cnidian lamps were made of two circular ropes of clay, attached side by side, and bound together at the highest point of the handle by two small rings of clay. The Cnidian lamps are in the British Museum and were published by Bailey (see Bailey 1975, 151–58; pls. 62–67).

120–70 B.C.
1092 (Fig. 133) C65.159 Arx, T.J.E. trench, Level III. Hard, dark, gray clay, black slip. P.L. 0.087 m; P.H. 0.040 m; P.W. 0.086 m; Width of base 0.052 m.

Fragment of a large molded lamp, broken on all sides. Preserved are two-thirds of a wide ovoid ring base, a part of the thick lower wall of the oil reservoir, including part of an ear, three handle attachments, and about three centimeters of the lower part of a wide vertical strap handle. The handle obviously divided into two parts, and each part returned to the side of the oil reservoir at about 45° from its axis.

The interior of the base is recessed, and within this is a potter's mark, an incised *I* in the center of a lozenge.

28. IRON LAMP

(Catalogue Number 1093)

Only one metal lamp has been found at Cosa, a large iron lamp found in Atrium Building I, Room 22, Level II, a storeroom, its contents sealed by the collapse of the Basilica wall in A.D. 40/45. The lamp had a heat shield and a long single nozzle with volutes. The seven joining fragments have been well enough preserved to indicate the general shape, despite their being badly corroded.

1093 CEL.1 Atrium Building I, Room 22, Level II. Badly corroded and encrusted iron. P.L. 0.199 m; Height 0.038 m; Width 0.106 m.
   Seven joining fragments preserving the discus, base, nozzle, parts of the handle with its heat shield, the rim, and most of the side walls of the oil reservoir. All forms are distorted by corrosion. Shallow concave discus with small central filling hole. Decoration, if any, now rusted away. Unprofiled base.

29. THE COSAN LANTERN
(Fig. 134)

(Catalogue Number 1094)

A part of a lantern has been found at Cosa that appears to be the only lantern surviving from antiquity with a built-in lamp. The other known examples of lanterns, also called lamp holders or lamp houses, have only a floor or shelf on which a lamp was placed.

(Bailey 1965, no. 200; Bailey 1975, 225–27, pl. 98 nos. Q 495–96; Baur, 73, figs. 35–36, pl. 13 no. 421 (from Dura Europus); Hayes 1980, 144, pl. 68 nos. 565–68; Loeschcke 1909b, pl. 35; Flinders Petrie, pl. 52A nos. 155–57; Rosenthal/Sivan 1978, nos. 623–25.

120–70 B.C.
1094 (Fig. 134) CA.958 Capitolium exterior, Pronaos, Level II. Coarse gray clay. P.L. 0085 m; P.H. 0.061 m; P.W. 0.096 m.

Part of a lantern, with the lamp built in. Fragment preserving the nozzle, the oil reservoir, the filling hole, and part of the side wall of the lantern. The nozzle is centered in the base of the lantern; the oil reservoir is also in the interior, while a protuberance containing the filling hole and a pipe to the reservoir appears on the exterior. The lamp was shaped by hand, but the lantern was thrown on the wheel. The lantern was circular; almost a quarter of the circumference of the flaring base is preserved. The bottom is open. The cylindrical wall narrows as it rises to the break in the fabric. The wall of the lantern was pierced, as was usual for lanterns, with small circular holes; two are complete, and parts of four more are preserved. The same small circular tool that made the holes in the wall of the lantern seems to have been used repeatedly to punch a filling hole with an opening just large enough to admit the oil.

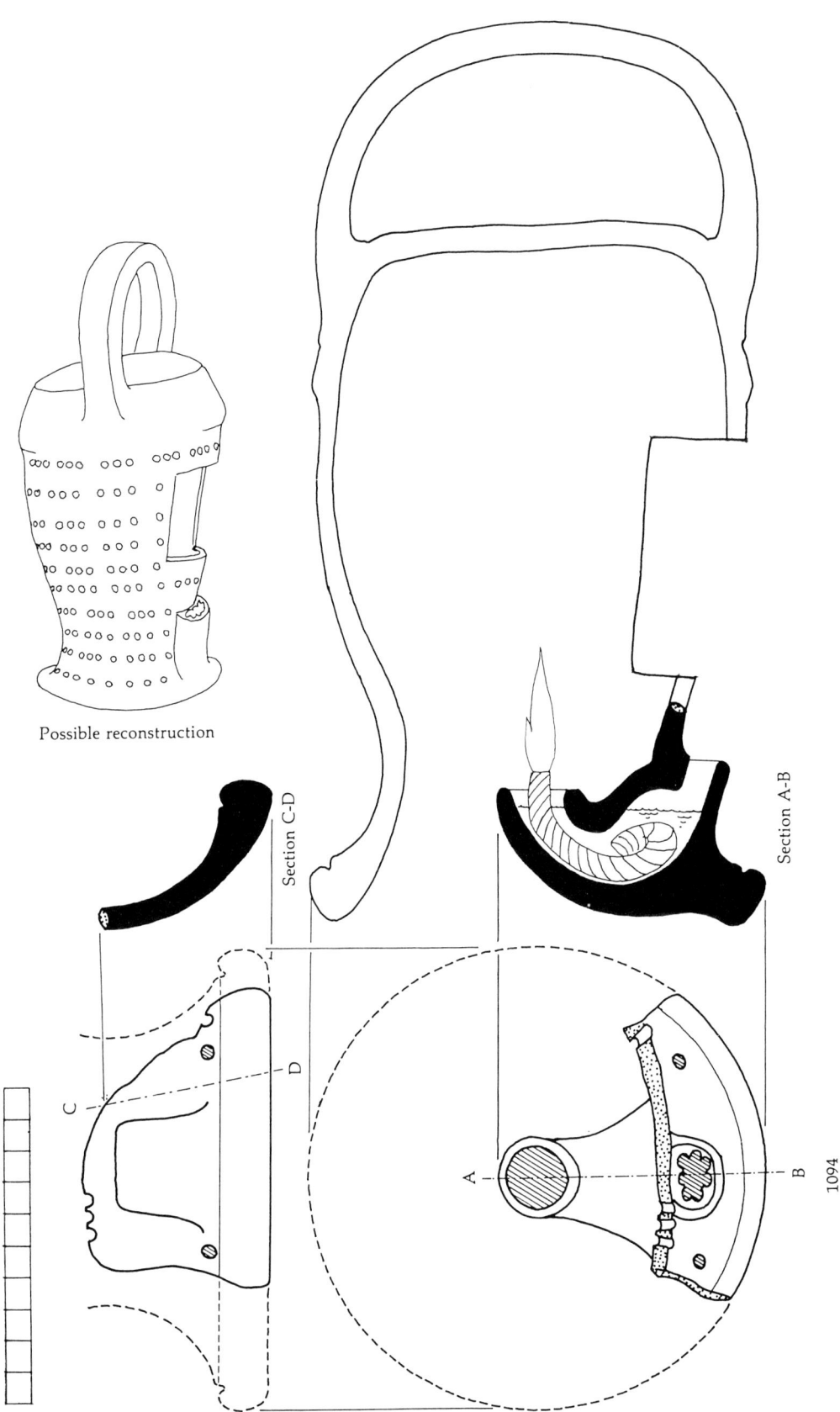

Figure 134. The Cosan Lantern, scale 1:2

NOTE ON THE COSAN LAMP MARKS AND SIGNATURES

Marks and signatures on the Cosan lamps identify the potteries and potters who produced some of the late republican and imperial lamps. Most Cosan lamps are unsigned, and we have only one complete lamp with a complete signature. Many of the marks and signatures appear on bases without other parts preserved, making the identification of the lamp type to which the base belonged impossible. Donald Bailey, in *The Catalogue of Lamps in the British Museum,* has identified several of the Cosan signatures. Jacqueline Bonnet in her recent work, *Lampes céramiques signées,* tracing the signed picture lamps from various sites in the Roman world, is not of great assistance in throwing light on the Cosan lamp signatures, since we cannot with certainty correlate our discus reliefs with signatures.

A few of the signatures give complete names, usually in the genitive case, as in the case of the two Greek lamps, one by Ariston (*ARISTONO*) and the other by Loukios (*LOUKIOU*). Complete, or nearly complete, names appear in some signatures, such as *FORTVNI, FLORENT, ERACLID,* and some in which the praenomen has been abbreviated to a single letter: *ACLAVDI, LCAEC..., LCAES...* Several lamps are signed in the abbreviated style of partial tria nomina, with praenomen, nomen, and cognomen run together: *COPRESTI* (Gaius Oppius Restitutus), *LFABRICMAS* (Lucius Fabricius Masculus). Some reconstructions of names are extremely speculative, because the bases were recovered in fragments.

Some signatures appear as initials only, such as *QGC,* or bound in ligature, such as *ANTI* and *TRL;* some marks are single letters or letters decorated with bull's eyes. Some appear only as symbols: feathers, herringbone patterns, leaves, a footprint, circles, lines, or dots.

Donald Bailey writes, "It is very unfortunate... that so few kiln sites with inscribed products have been found in Italy; many must be buried beneath the suburbs of Rome."[1] We can only echo that regret in regard to the pottery workshop of Sestius at Cosa, which must have produced the Sestius amphoras and probably also domestic pottery, including lamps, but so far it has not been located.

1. Bailey 1980, 89.

Inscriptions and marks made before firing.

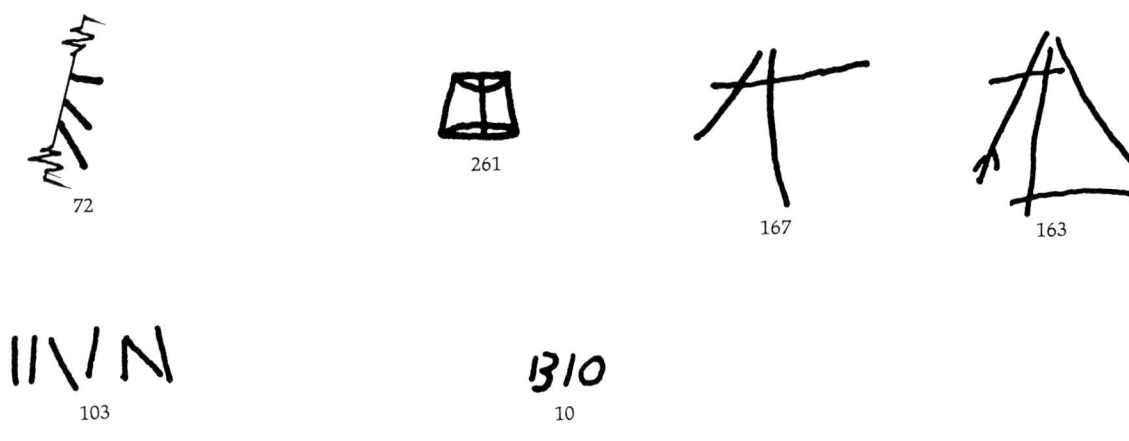

Inscriptions and marks made after firing.

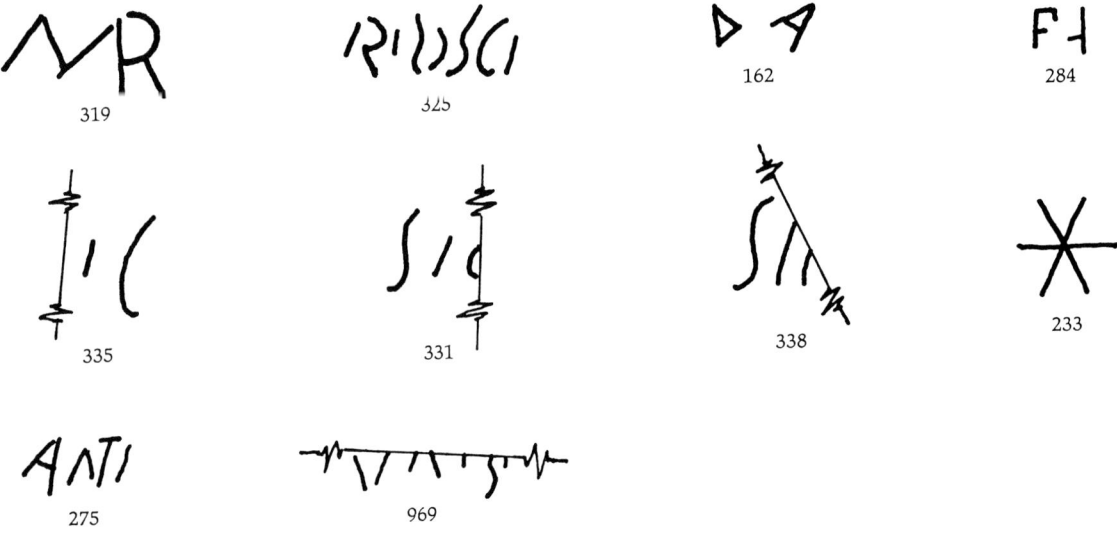

Figure 135. Inscriptions and marks made before and after firing, full scale

The four marks shown above are from Roman Republican wheel made lamps.

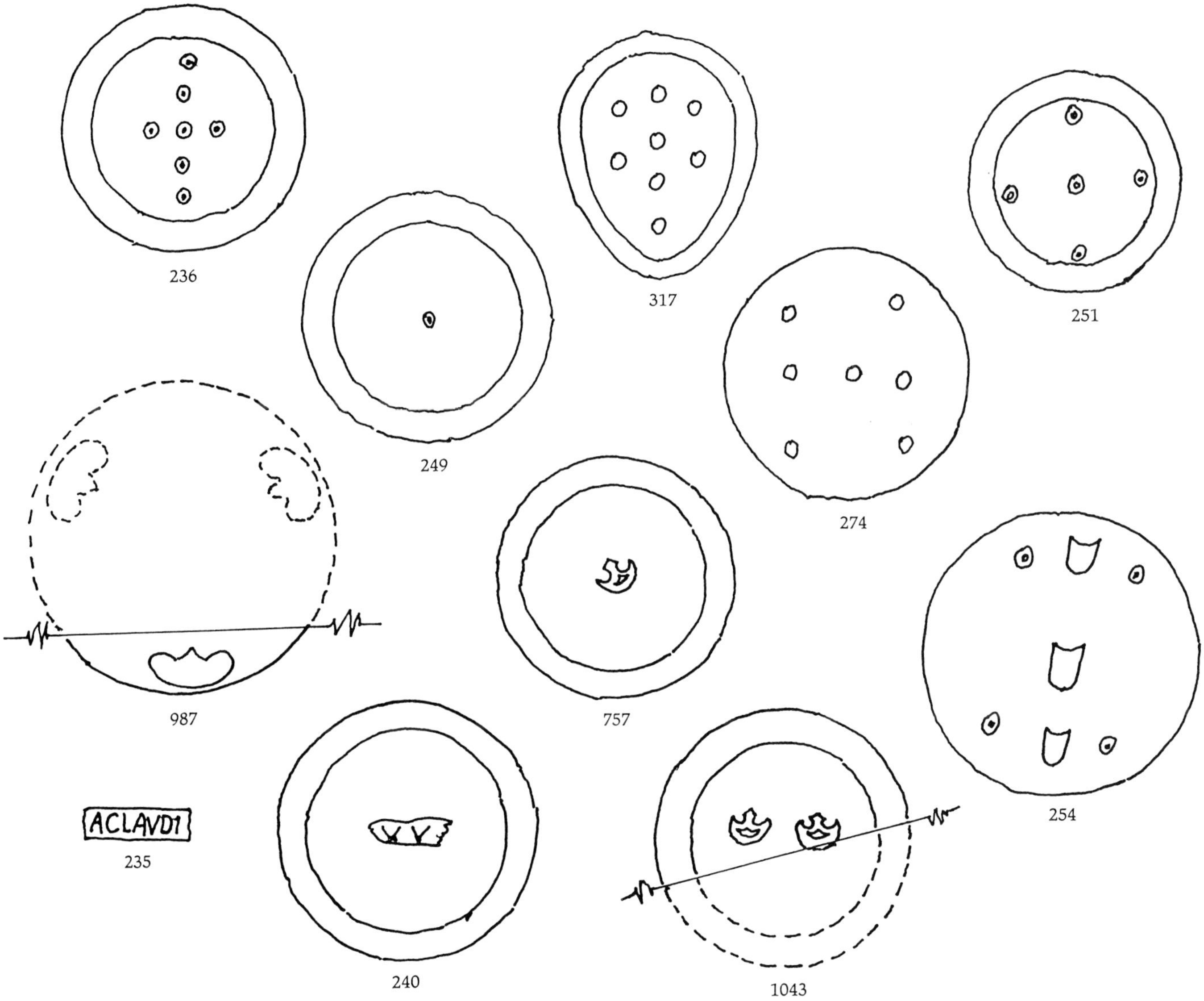

The marks shown above are from Roman Republican or early Empire moldmade lamps.

Figure 136. Marks from Roman Republican wheelmade and moldmade lamps, full scale

Figure 137. Incised and stamped marks, late Republican, full scale

The Fortis lamp is a pirated copy of a Pine Cone Lamp in retrograde. No. 468 is from the discus of a Triangular Nozzle Lamp

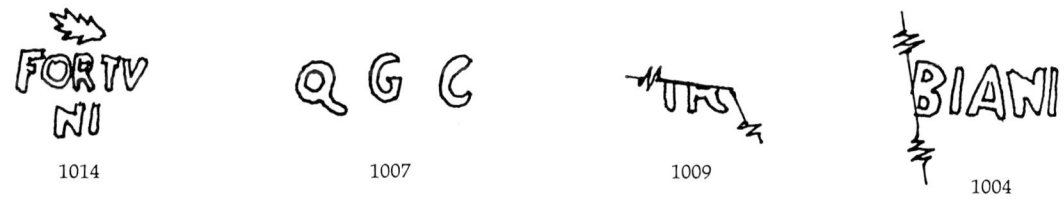

The four signatures above are from North Italian Factory Lamps.

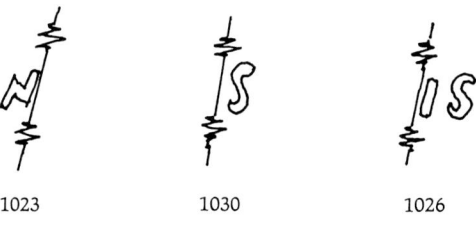

The three fragmentary signatures above are from Roman copies of North Italian Lamps.

Figure 138. Marks and makers' signatures in relief, full scale

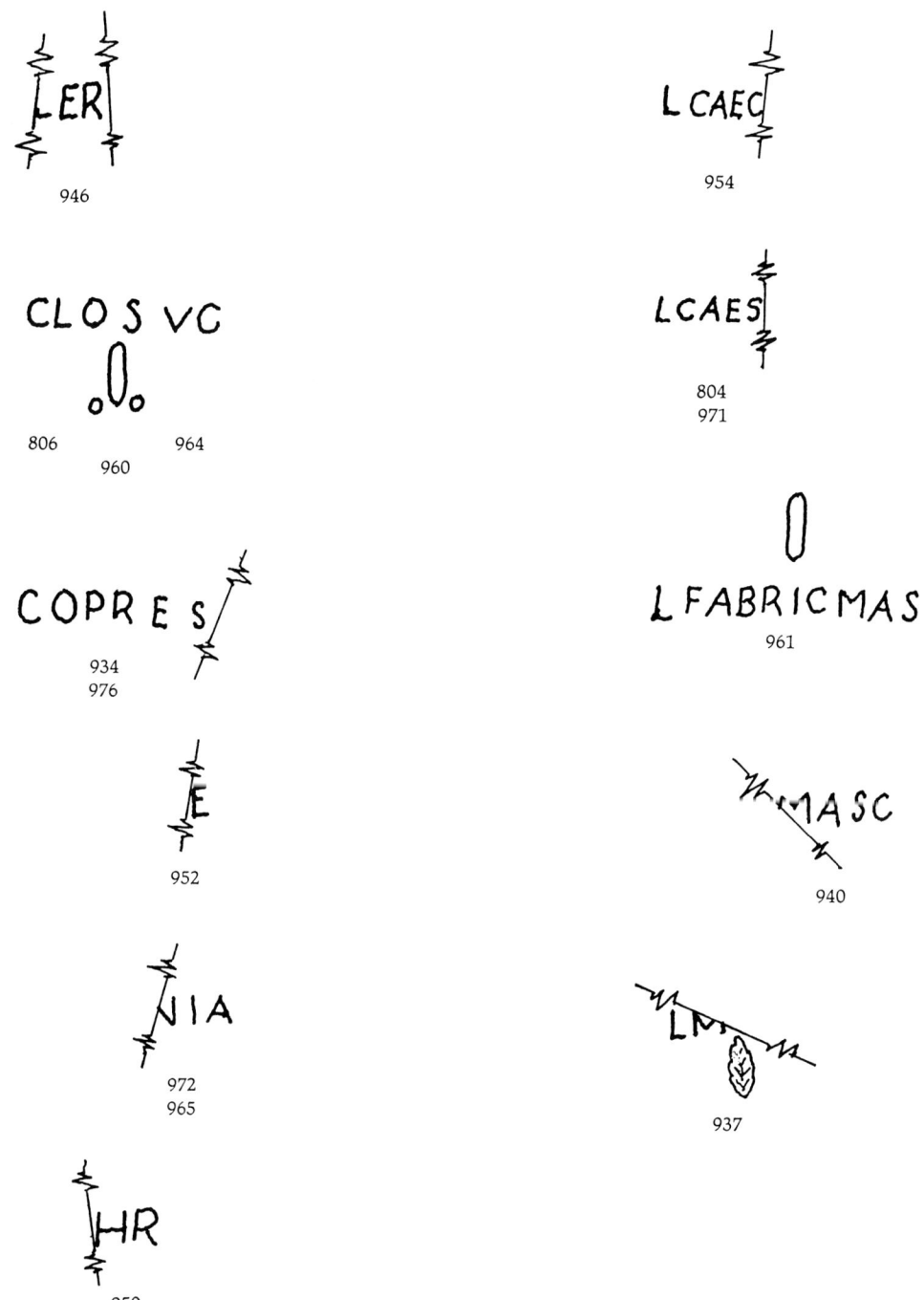

Figure 139. Makers' names and initials, full scale

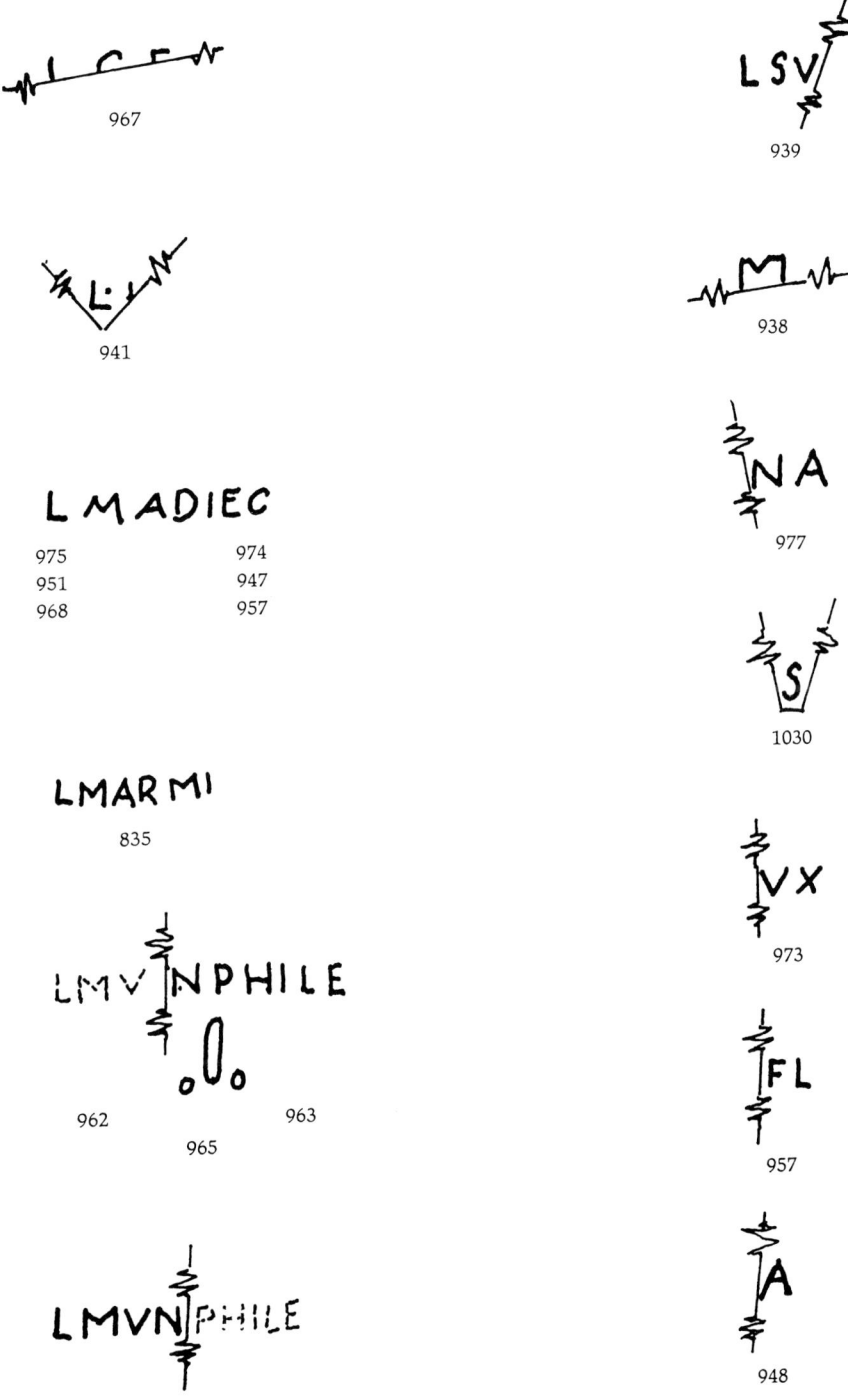

Figure 140. Makers' names and initials, full scale

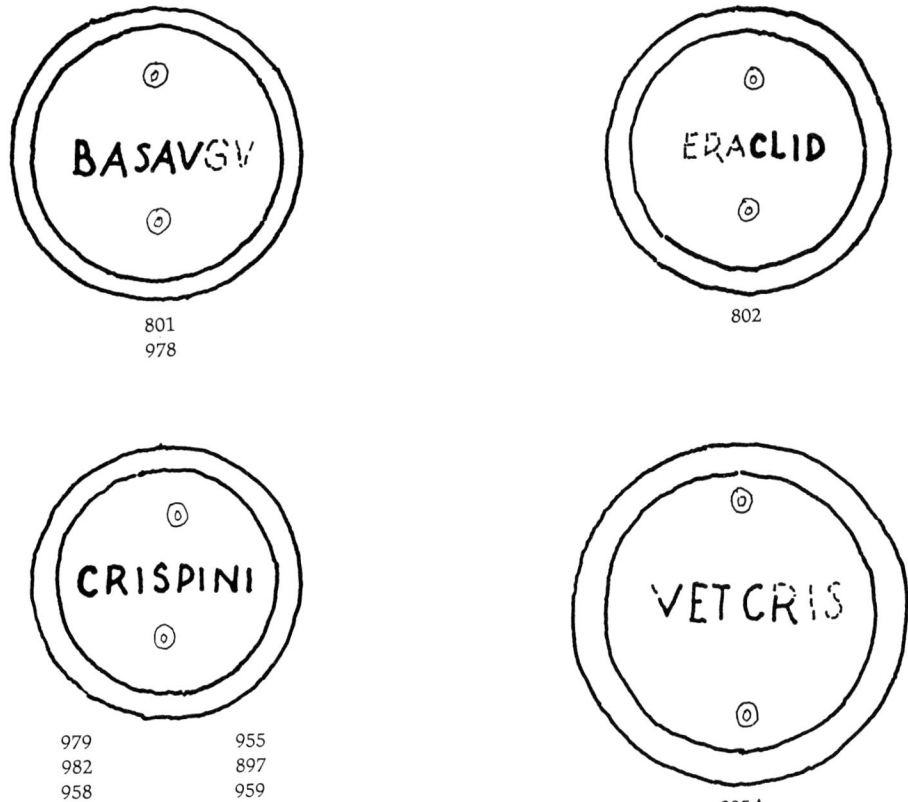

The four signatures above are from "Fat Lamps"

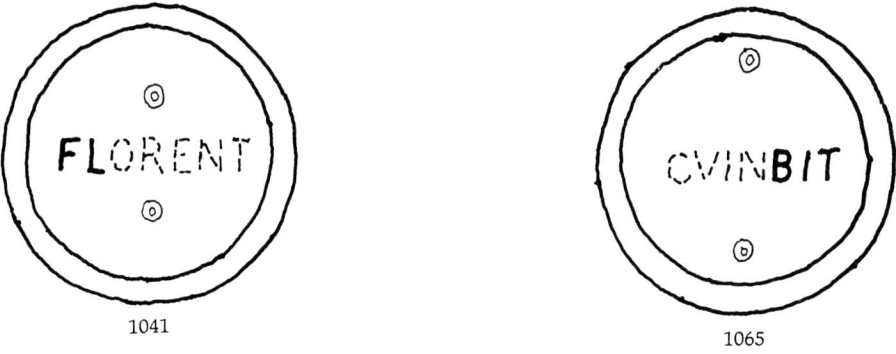

The signature FLORENT is from a "Factory Lamp,"
CUINBIT is from a North African Lamp.

Figure 141. Makers' signatures with a bull's eye centered above and below, full scale

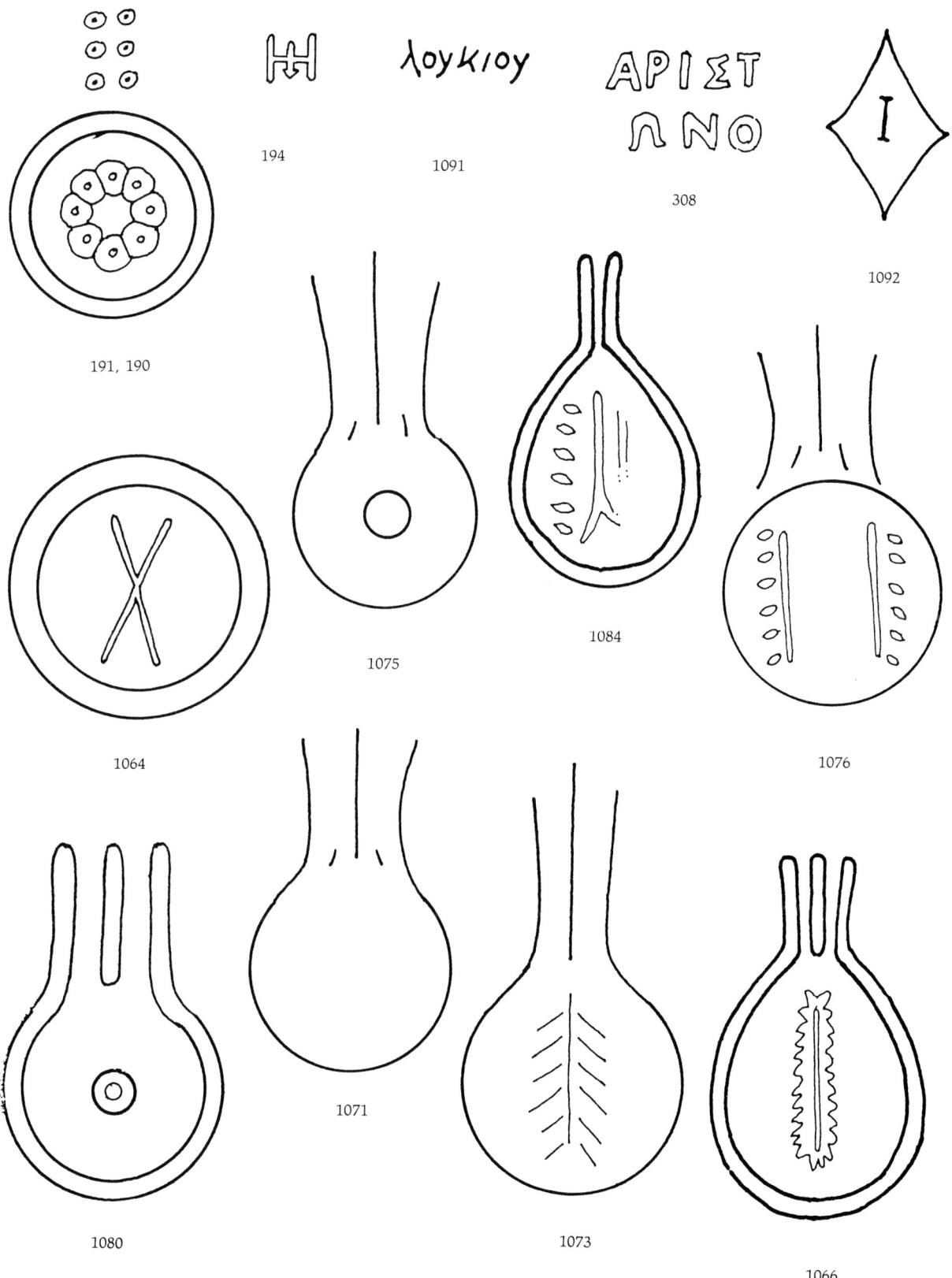

Figure 142. Marks and makers' signatures on imported or foreign lamps, full scale

THE PLATES

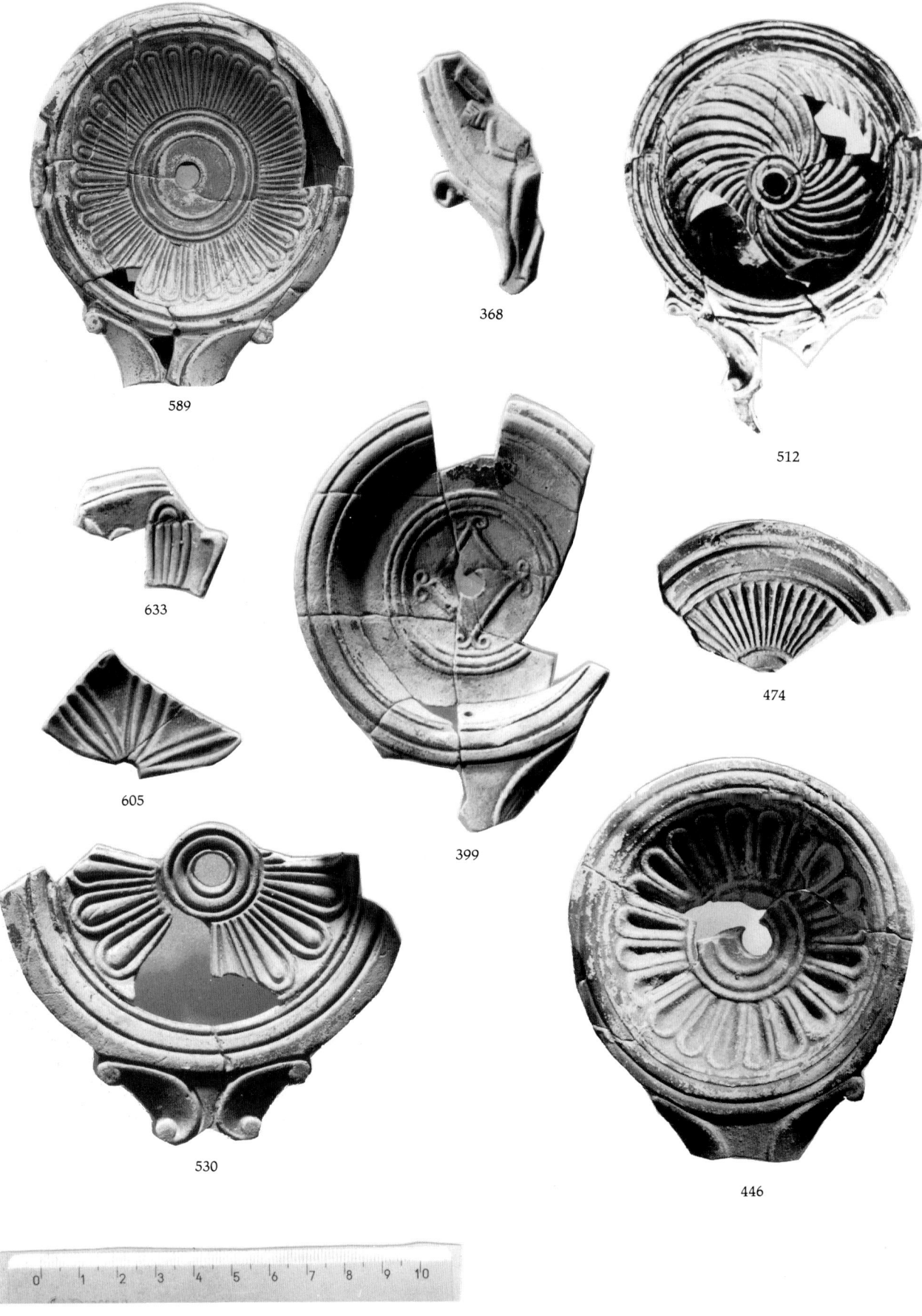

Plate I. Geometric designs

Plate II. Myths, gods, goddesses, and heroes

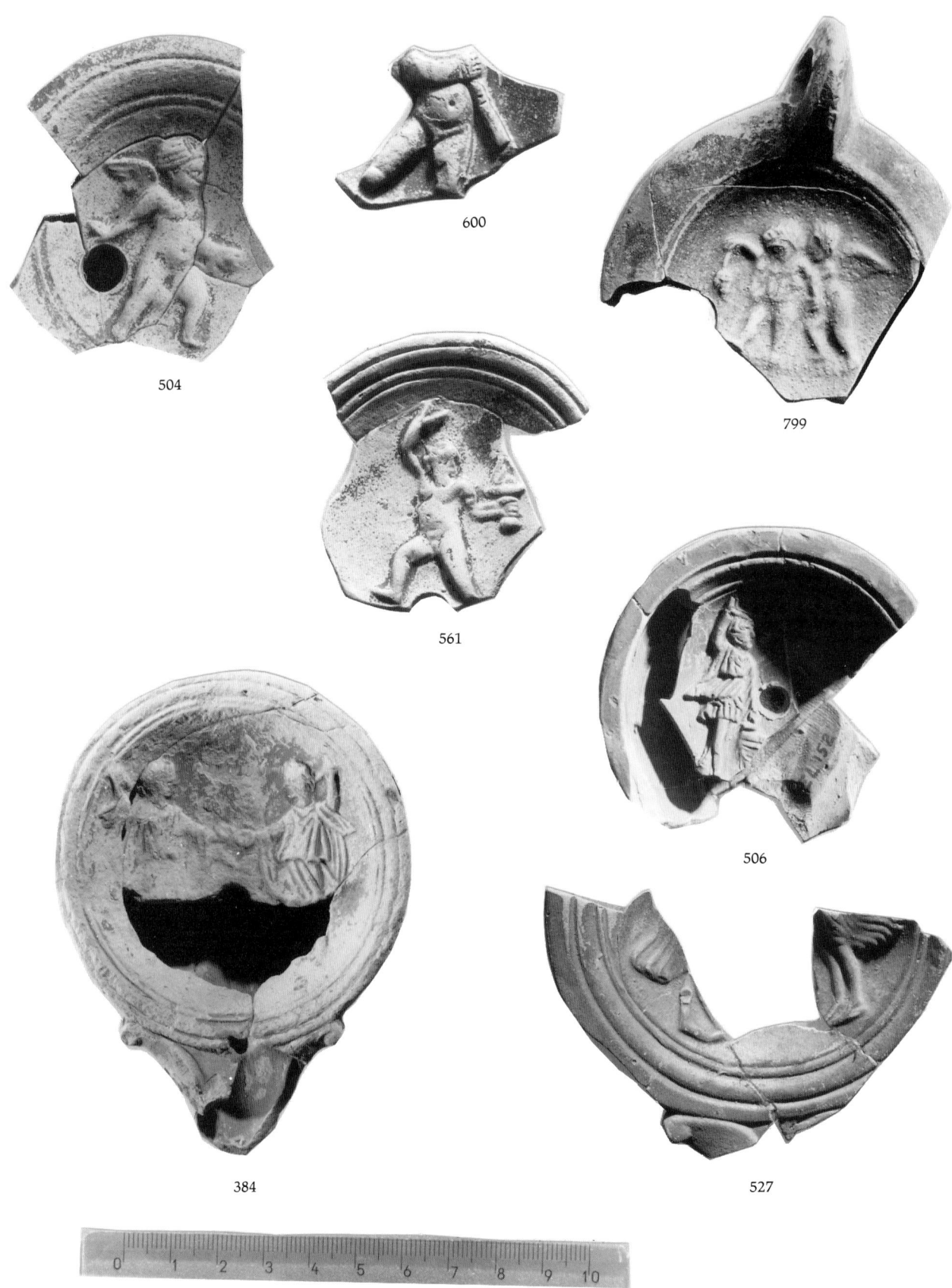

Plate III. Minor divinities

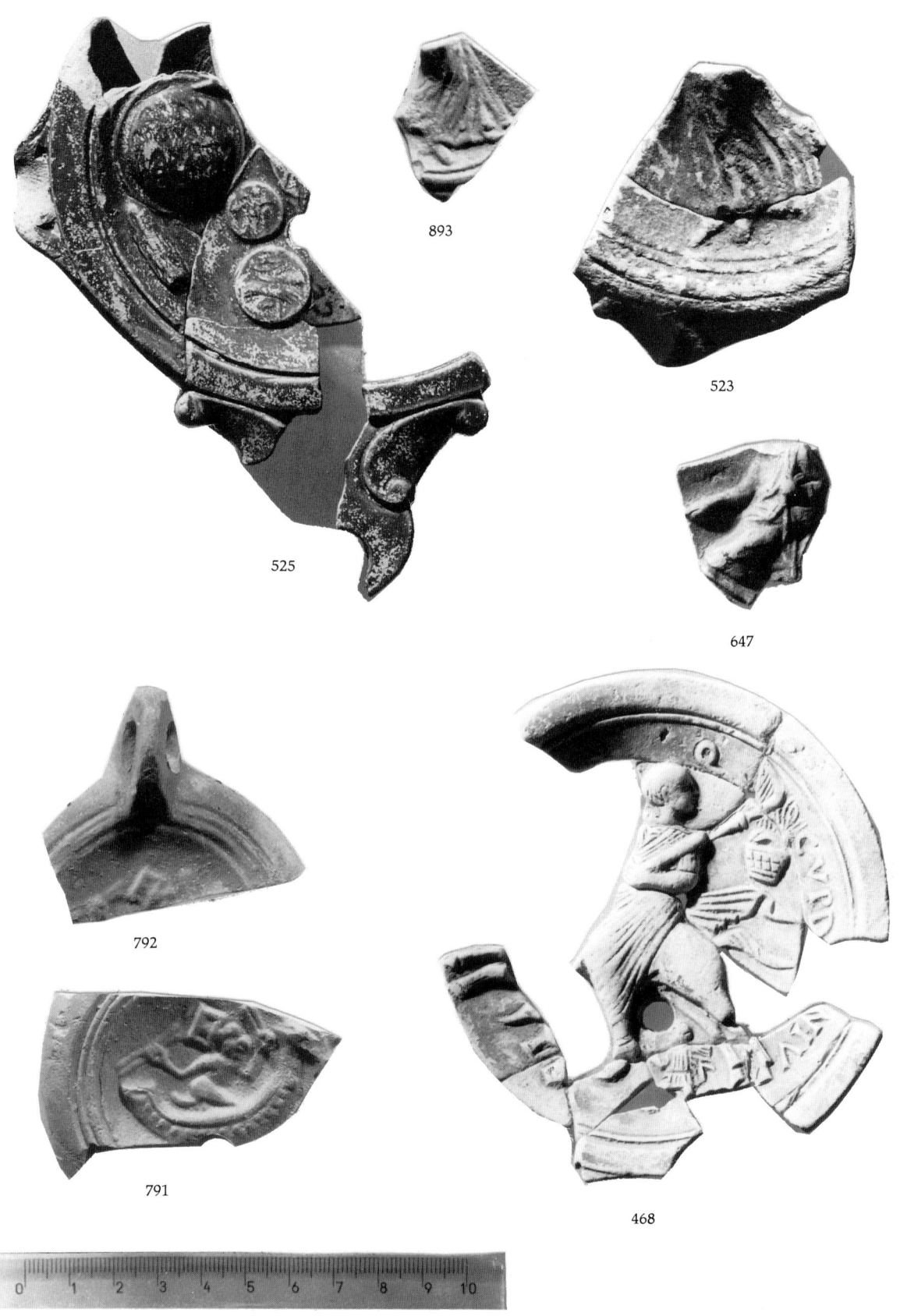

Plate IV. New Year's greetings; hunchback dwarf; maenad; horse and rider; fisherman

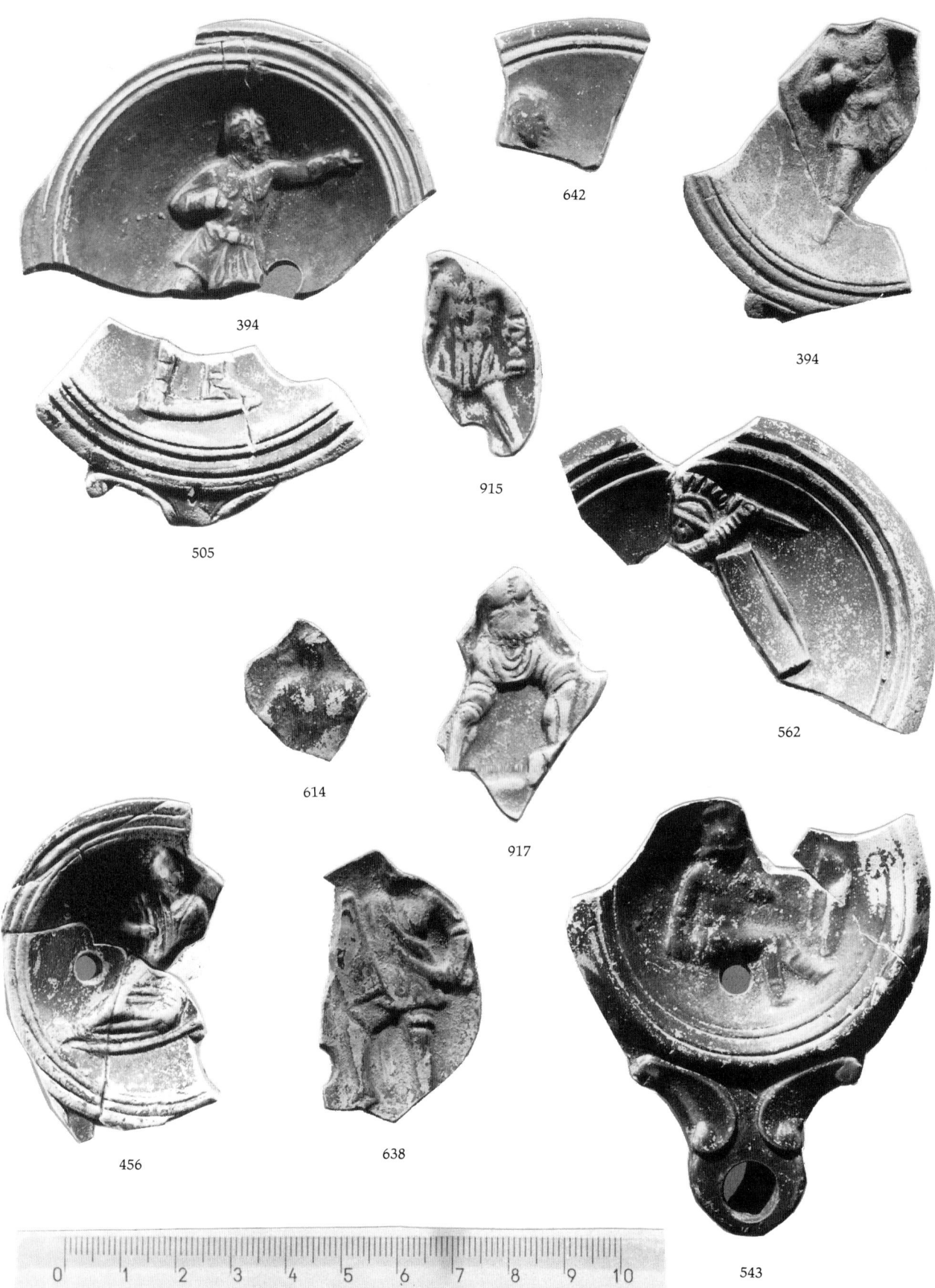

Plate V. Gladiators; Parthian stringing his bow

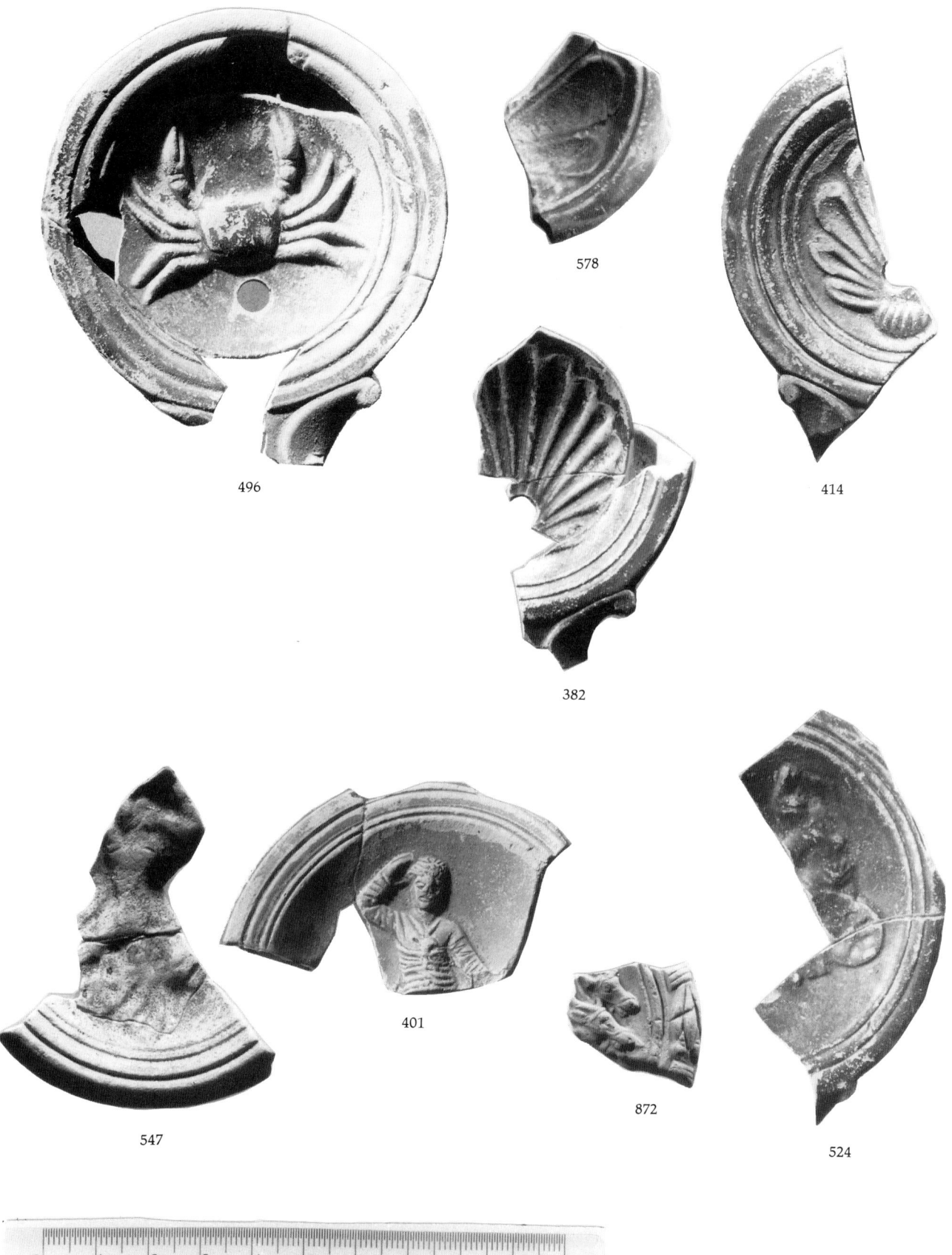

Plate VI. Marine life; charioteers

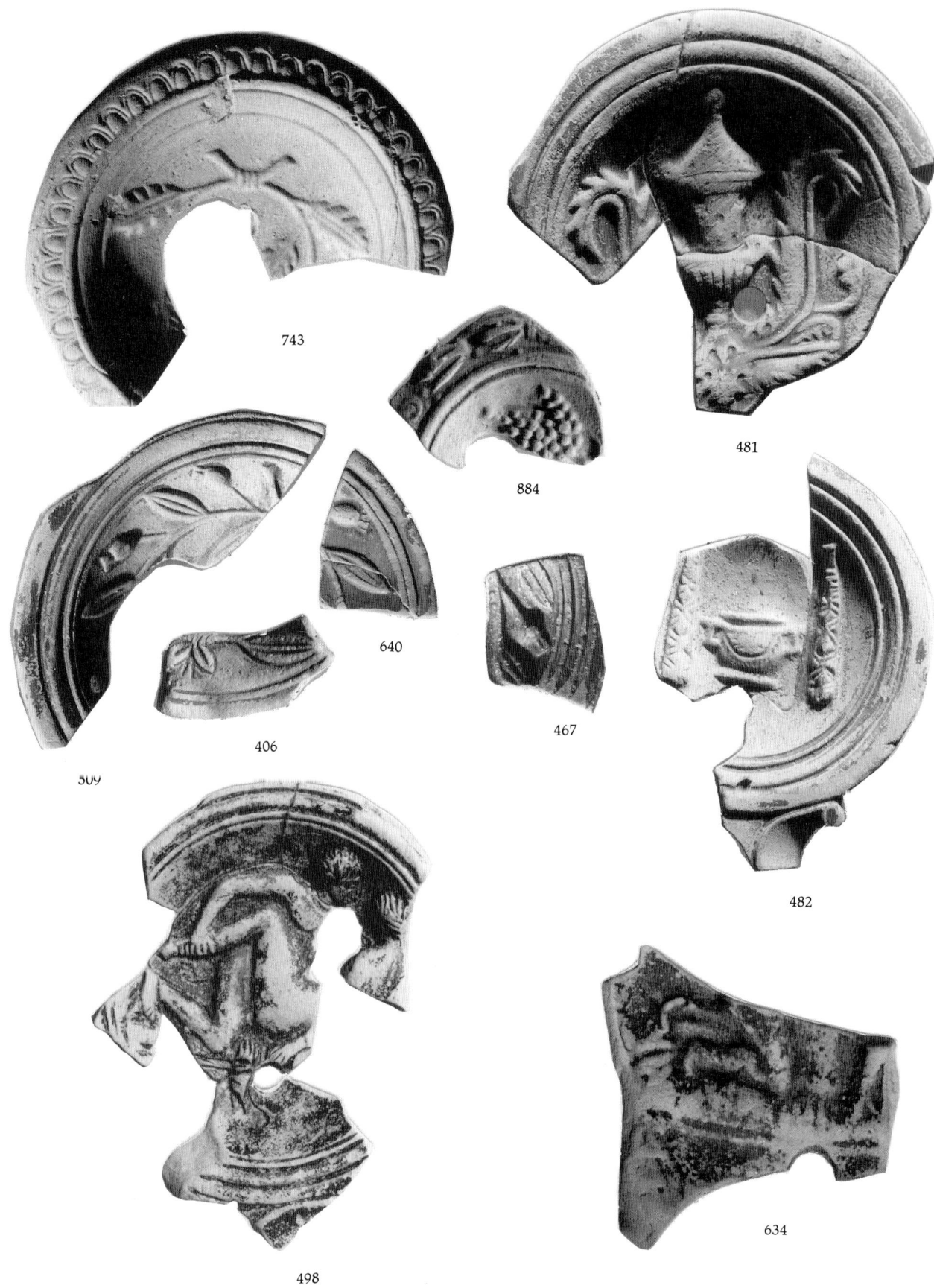

Plate VII. Wreaths and plants; erotic symplegmata

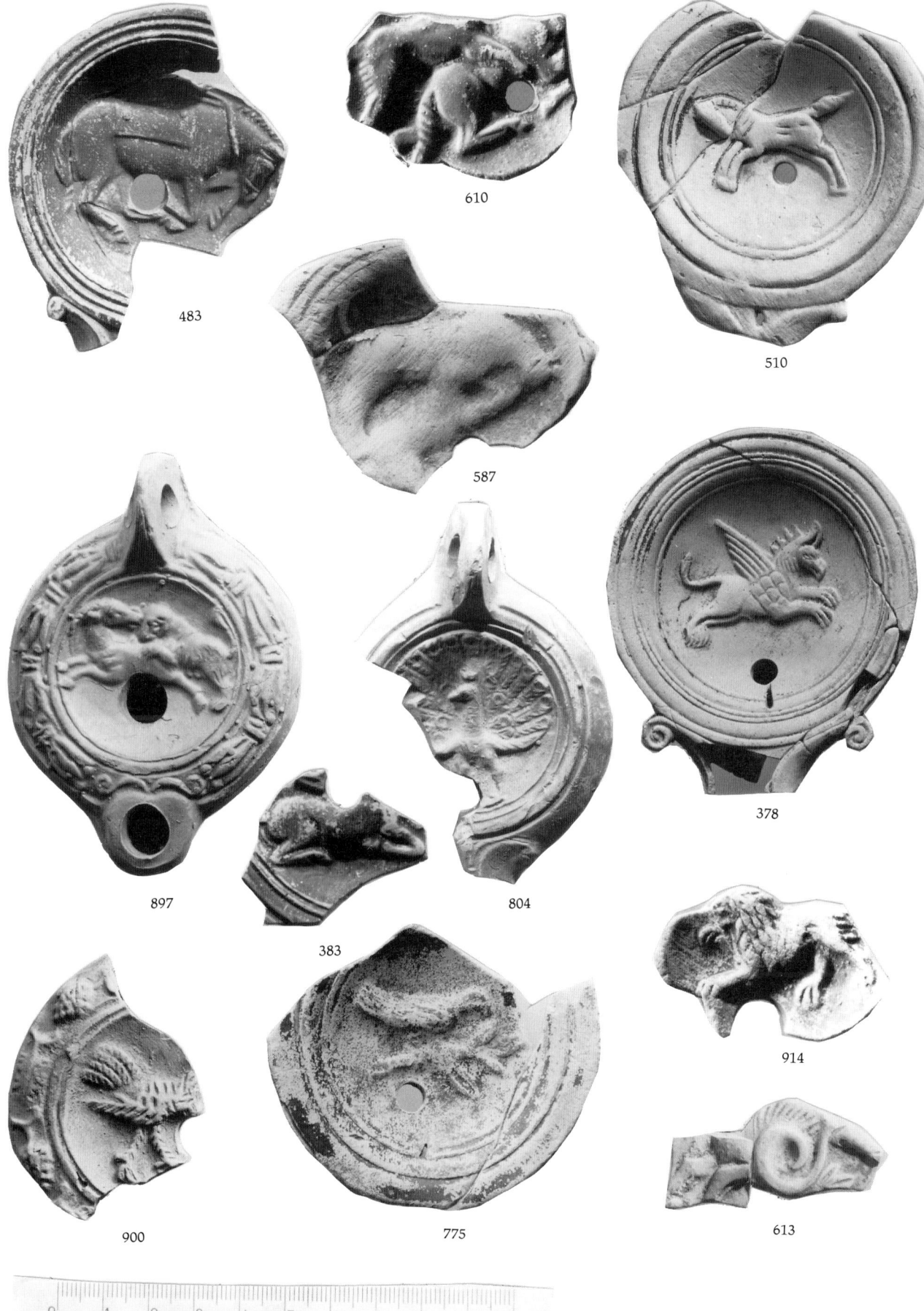

Plate VIII. Animals and birds

Plate IX. Lamp with seven nozzles

CONCORDANCE

Artifact Inventory Number	This Book Number	Artifact Inventory Number	This Book Number	Artifact Inventory Number	This Book Number	Artifact Inventory Number	This Book Number
CA.722	12	CB.1716	288	CB.1856	238	CD.734	514
CA.958	1094	CB.1725	15	CB.1857	315	CD.771	539
CB.476	72	CB.1726	135	CB.1858	312	CD.772a	795
CB.540	73	CB.1728	136	CB.1859	239	CD.772b	927
CB.556	74	CB.1729	16	CB.1860	240	CD.784	1034
CB.606	75	CB.1772	1090	CB.1861	292	CD.804	522
CB.610	76	CB.1773	289	CB.1862	313	CD.867	587
CB.793	728	CB.1774	308	CB.1865	92	CD.868	492
CB.829	134	CB.1835	17	CB.1866	156	CD.869	701
CB.1136	253	CB.1836	91	CB.1867	227	CD.871	325
CB.1197	149	CB.1837	18	CB.1869	173	CD.880	588
CB.1384	307	CB.1838	153	CC.122	986	CD.881	975
CB.1577	934	CB.1839	154	CC.159	805A	CD.925	532
CB.1659	226	CB.1840	155	CC.458	254	CD.1006	290
CB.1669	152	CB.1841	137	CC.583	177	CD.1044	319
CB.1679	90	CB.1843	138	CD.136	228	CD.1185	65
CB.1680	607	CB.1845	320	CD.408	554	CD.1186	66
CB.1681	608	CB.1846	171	CD.409a&b	985	CD.1187	67
CB.1682	585	CB.1847	309	CD.558	621	CD.1196	77
CB.1683	214	CB.1848	198	CD.598	974	CD.1198	78
CB.1690	271	CB.1849	310	CD.600a-e	933	CD.1199	79
CB.1692	14	CB.1850	311	CD.602	655	CD.1200	80
CB.1693	317	CB.1851	172	CD.606	549	CD.1201	13
CB.1698	192	CB.1852	314	CD.607	793	CD.1202	81
CB.1699	318	CB.1853	291	CD.674	622	CD.1204	229
CB.1713	215	CB.1854	237	CD.675	472	CD.1205	121
CB.1714	586	CB.1855	114	CD.733	623	CD.1206	949

Artifact Inventory Number	This Book Number	Artifact Inventory Number	This Book Number	Artifact Inventory Number	This Book Number	Artifact Inventory Number	This Book Number
CD.1207	294	CE.1018	510	CEL.44	496	CEL.113	692
CD.1208	389	CE.1019	700	CEL.45	775	CEL.115	702
CD.1209	716	CE.1404	51	CEL.46	383	CEL.117	130
CD.1210	326	CE.1409	52	CEL.47	497	CEL.118	796
CD.1211	122	CE.1473	176	CEL.48	504	CEL.119	150
CD.1215		CE.2083	657	CEL.50a-c	824	CEL.120	131
CD.1212	123	CE.2211	339	CEL.52	525	CEL.122	830A
CD.1216	338	CE.2212	626	CEL.53	561	CEL.123	1019
CD.1217	950	CE.2213	627	CEL.54	527	CEL.124	831
CD.1218	951	CE.2214	723	CEL.55	384	CEL.125	1011
CD.1219	352	CE.2215	454	CEL.56	528	CEL.126	1012
CD.1220	462	CEL.1	1093	CEL.57	385	CEL.127	997
CD.1221a&b	327	CEL.3	987	CEL.58	386	CEL.130	914
CD.1222	328	CEL.5	988	CEL.59	543	CEL.131	870
CD.1223	241	CEL.6	570	CEL.60	562	CEL.132	1013
CD.1224	295	CEL.7	494	CEL.61	675	CEL.133	558
CD.1225	329	CEL.9	345	CEL.62	675	CEL.134	518
CD.1226	515	CEL.10	672	CEL.64	452	CEL.135	519
CD.1227	463	CEL.11	673	CEL.65	544	CEL.136	546
CD.1228	717	CEL.13	694	CEL.66	529	CEL.140	994
CD.1229	533	CEL.14	736	CEL.67	366	CEL.141a&b	415
CD.1230	438	CEL.15	737	CEL.68	911	CEL.142	340
CD.1231	624	CEL.16	738	CEL.69	458	CEL.143	341
CD.1232	733	CEL.17a-c	828	CEL.71	984	CEL.145	574
CD.1233	722	CEL.18	664	CEL.72	825	CEL.149	367
CD.1234	364	CEL.19	665	CEL.73	993	CEL.150	505
CD.1235	365	CEL.20	666	CEL.74	697	CEL.152	506
CD.1236	439	CEL.21	773	CEL.81	706	CEL.153	628
CD.1237	242	CEL.22	671	CEL.82	707	CEL.154	915
CD.1238	323	CEL.24	473	CEL.83	708	CEL.155	475
CD.1239	440	CEL.25	739	CEL.84	709	CEL.156	629
CD.1240	656	CEL.26	740	CEL.91	937	CEL.157	748
CD.1241	625	CEL.27	741	CEL.92	938	CEL.158	669
CD.1242	441	CEL.28	474	CEL.93	53	CEL.159	507
CD.1243	550	CEL.29	695	CEL.94	54	CEL.160	724
CD.1244	442	CEL.33	542	CEL.95	55	CEL.161a&b	630
CD.1245	516	CEL.34	696	CEL.96	56	CEL.162	342
CD.1246	517	CEL.35	674	CEL.98	57	CEL.164	917
CD.1247	535	CEL.36a&b	457	CEL.99	58	CEL.165	631
CD.1248	551	CEL.37	774	CEL.100	59	CEL.166	632
CD.1249	179	CEL.38	742	CEL.101	60	CEL.167	416
CD.1250	540	CEL.39	526	CEL.103	61	CEL.169	523
CD.1252	752	CEL.40	414	CEL.104	62	CEL.171	217
CD.1253	297	CEL.41	382	CEL.105	129	CEL.172	991
CD.1623	296	CEL.42	743	CEL.106	939	CEL.173	908
CE.1015	1054	CEL.43a-c	495	CEL.108	913	CEL.174	688

Artifact Inventory Number	This Book Number	Artifact Inventory Number	This Book Number	Artifact Inventory Number	This Book Number	Artifact Inventory Number	This Book Number
CEL.175	633	CEL.232	940	CEL.294	784	CEL.350	467
CEL.176	476	CEL.233	1016	CEL.295	482	CEL.351	355
CEL.177	689	CEL.234	119	CEL.296	369	CEL.352	392
CEL.179	1015	CEL.235	44	CEL.297	663	CEL.353	393
CEL.180	1078	CEL.236	201	CEL.298	826	CEL.354	394
CEL.181	871	CEL.237	455	CEL.299	670	CEL.355	609
CEL.182	900	CEL.238	348	CEL.300	636	CEL.356	459
CEL.185	823	CEL.239	456	CEL.301	637	CEL.357	686
CEL.186	1029	CEL.240	508	CEL.302	483	CEL.358	395
CEL.189	124	CEL.242	330	CEL.303	484	CEL.360	610
CEL.190	301	CEL.243	368	CEL.304	418	CEL.362	396
CEL.191	783	CEL.246	749	CEL.305	510	CEL.365	611
CEL.192	63	CEL.247	552	CEL.306	700	CEL.366	397
CEL.193	64	CEL.248	941	CEL.307	575	CEL.367	398
CEL.194	477	CEL.249	816	CEL.309	1042	CEL.368	747
CEL.195	832	CEL.252a&b	479	CEL.311	734	CEL.369	718
CEL.196	183	CEL.253	178	CEL.312	638	CEL.370	399
CEL.198	377	CEL.254	331	CEL.313	298	CEL.372	719
CEL.199	118	CEL.255	512	CEL.314	370	CEL.373	400
CEL.201	243	CEL.256	332	CEL.315	680	CEL.374	547
CEL.202	276	CEL.257	245	CEL.316	599	CEL.375a&b	401
CEL.203	244	CEL.258	246	CEL.317	600	CEL.376	699
CEL.205	202	CEL.259	1055	CEL.318	681	CEL.377	935
CEL.206	710	CEL.261	1017	CEL.319	777	CEL.378	548
CEL.207	776	CEL.263	729	CEL.321	601	CEL.379	468
CEL.208	676	CEL.264	797	CEL.322	563	CEL.381	945
CEL.209	667	CEL.266	120	CEL.323	682	CEL.384	186
CEL.210	677	CEL.267	176	CEL.326	989	CEL.387	204
CEL.211	530	CEL.268	349	CEL.327	744	CEL.388	910
CEL.212	678	CEL.269	872	CEL.328	778	CEL.389	785
CEL.213	679	CEL.270	480	CEL.329	499	CEL.393	602
CEL.214	498	CEL.276	555	CEL.331	653	CEL.394	419
CEL.215	634	CEL.277	942	CEL.332	668	CEL.395	536
CEL.217	725	CEL.278	943	CEL.333	683	CEL.396	402
CEL.218	520	CEL.279	390	CEL.334	387	CEL.397	379
CEL.219	690	CEL.280	944	CEL.335	779	CEL.399	357
CEL.220	995	CEL.281	1000	CEL.337	990	CEL.400	469
CEL.221	478	CEL.282	333	CEL.338	513	CEL.401	460
CEL.222	635	CEL.286	833	CEL.339	564	CEL.402	485
CEL.223	916	CEL.287	1030	CEL.340	1018	CEL.403	486
CEL.224	132	CEL.288	274	CEL.342	354	CEL.404	487
CEL.225	5	CEL.289	417	CEL.344	464	CEL.406	684
CEL.228	346	CEL.290	996	CEL.346	356	CEL.407	500
CEL.229	347	CEL.291	481	CEL.347	391	CEL.408	698
CEL.230	378	CEL.292	658	CEL.348	465	CEL.410	537
CEL.231	524	CEL.293	509	CEL.349	466	CEL.411	531

Artifact Inventory Number	This Book Number	Artifact Inventory Number	This Book Number	Artifact Inventory Number	This Book Number	Artifact Inventory Number	This Book Number
CEL.412	565	CEL.486	829	CEL.556	553	CEL.624	511
CEL.414	691	CEL.487	409	CEL.557	715	CEL.626	730
CEL.416	358	CEL.488	371	CEL.558	873	CEL.628	798
CEL.418a&b	984	CEL.489	410	CEL.560	883	CEL.629	1043
CEL.421	403	CEL.490	579	CEL.561	753	CEL.630	446
CEL.424	404	CEL.491	422	CEL.562	766	CEL.631a-c	589
CEL.426	405	CEL.492	573	CEL.564	901	CEL.632	929
CEL.427	685	CEL.493	646	CEL.565	862	CEL.634	978
CEL.428	359	CEL.494	566	CEL.566	745	CEL.635	791
CEL.429	360	CEL.496	488	CEL.567	750	CEL.637	247
CEL.433	572	CEL.497	912	CEL.568	746	CEL.641	1034
CEL.435	538	CEL.499	580	CEL.569	830	CEL.843	447
CEL.442	501	CEL.500	411	CEL.570a&b	582	CEL.1836	931
CEL.443	612	CEL.501	423	CEL.571	840	CEL.1934	755
CEL.444	613	CEL.502a&b	654	CEL.572	841	CF.69	760
CEL.451	928	CEL.503	424	CEL.582	1031	CF.74	1044
CEL.453a&b	639	CEL.504	350	CEL.583	1001	CF.460	1041
CEL.454	388	CEL.505	461	CEL.584	946	CF.461	1014
CEL.455	614	CEL.506	618	CEL.585	255	CF.462	810
CEL.456	406	CEL.508	567	CEL.588	256	CF.463	884
CEL.458	615	CEL.509	502	CEL.589	302	CF.464	979
CEL.459	640	CEL.510	376	CEL.590	853	CF.465	834
CEL.460	407	CEL.512	581	CEL.591	1033	CF.468	855
CEL.461	641	CEL.514	425	CEL.593a&b	751	CF.469	835
CEL.462	361	CEL.515	372	CEL.594	334	CF.470	866
CEL.463	642	CEL.516	381	CEL.596	854	CF.471	952
CEL.464	786	CEL.517	568	CEL.597	583	CF.472	953
CEL.465	787	CEL.519	489	CEL.599	647	CF.473	874
CEL.467	643	CEL.520	373	CEL.599a	426	CF.475	846
CEL.468	576	CEL.521	351	CEL.601	443	CF.476	817
CEL.469	603	CEL.522	490	CEL.602	534	CF.644a-d	999
CEL.470	559	CEL.523	374	CEL.603	1020	CF.830	885
CEL.471	644	CEL.524	412	CEL.605	936	CF.831	761
CEL.472	616	CEL.529	711	CEL.607	780	CF.832	905
CEL.473	420	CEL.531	720	CEL.608	444	CF.834	863
CEL.474	645	CEL.533	726	CEL.609	754	CF.836	811
CEL.475	604	CEL.535	712	CEL.610	815	CF.838	886
CEL.476	577	CEL.543	713	CEL.611	781	CF.839	867
CEL.477	617	CEL.544	714	CEL.612	907	CF.840	954
CEL.479	380	CEL.546	881	CEL.613	660	CF.842	848
CEL.480	605	CEL.547	882	CEL.615	1032	CF.844	343
CEL.481	578	CEL.550	362	CEL.616	703	CF.846	470
CEL.482	521	CEL.551	606	CEL.617a&b	445	CF.847	125
CEL.483	788	CEL.553	569	CEL.618	218	CF.848	126
CEL.484	421	CEL.554	545	CEL.620	998	CF.1588	1003
CEL.485	408	CEL.555	619	CEL.621	661	CF.1589	127

Artifact Inventory Number	This Book Number	Artifact Inventory Number	This Book Number	Artifact Inventory Number	This Book Number	Artifact Inventory Number	This Book Number
C.F.1590	180	C.F.1953	1048	C.F.2123	1006	CG.304	1059
C.F.1624	203	C.F.1954	1049	C.F.2124	838	CG.315	805
C.F.1626	187	C.F.1958	1050	C.F.2125	257	CG.524	961
C.F.1628	363	C.F.1961	792	C.F.2127	898	CG.526	962
C.F.1630	818	C.F.1972	868	C.F.2128	1051	CG.527	806
C.F.1631	955	C.F.1973	448	C.F.2129	772	CG.529	918
C.F.1632	819	C.F.1974	890	C.F.2130	958	CG.533	1
C.F.1633	887	C.F.1976	1002	C.F.2131	959	CG.534	919
C.F.1635	849	C.F.1977	891	C.F.2143	662	CG.535	920
C.F.1638	875	C.F.1978	869	C.F.2145	316	CG.539	590
C.F.1639	820	C.F.1979	764	C.F.2146	803	CG.585	2
C.F.1642	789	C.F.1981	892	C.F.2148	877	CG.589	947
C.F.1644	757	C.F.2001	856	C.F.2150	205	CG.590	259
C.F.1645	799	C.F.2003	893	C.F.2151	322	CG.591	963
C.F.1646	930	C.F.2004	813	C.F.2152	151	CG.592	964
C.F.1647	758	C.F.2005	894	C.F.2153	258	CG.593	807
C.F.1648	850	C.F.2010	837	C.F.2272	858	CG.594	965
C.F.1649	888	C.F.2011	895	C.F.2273	821	CG.595	966
C.F.1659	1040	C.F.2012	842	C.F.2274	1091	CG.596	248
C.F.1660	756	C.F.2013	843	C.F.2276	822	CG.597	249
C.F.1661	889	C.F.2014	1065	C.F.2277	859	CG.598	250
C.F.1662	902	C.F.2015	269	C.F.2279a&b	1045	CG.599	344
C.F.1670	1005	C.F.2016	767	C.F.2282	1021	CG.600	967
C.F.1672	956	C.F.2017	982	C.F.2283	878	CG.601	299
C.F.1831	851	C.F.2018	896	C.F.2284	899	CG.602	300
C.F.1835	903	C.F.2019	768	C.F.2285	1022	CG.603	260
C.F.1838	836	C.F.2020	814	C.F.2287	960	CG.605	556
C.F.1839	852	C.F.2022	769	C.F.2288	801	CG.606	921
C.F.1840	957	C.F.2023	1052	C.F.2289	839	CG.607	921A
C.F.1918	980	C.F.2024	844	C.F.2290	860	C65.29	19
C.F.1919	981	C.F.2025	1035	C.F.2292	1038	C65.30	157
C.F.1921	268	C.F.2026	1036	C.F.2293	1023	C65.31	158
C.F.1923	794	C.F.2027	1037	C.F.2294	1056	C65.36	93
C.F.1924	762	C.F.2028	983	C.F.2295	1024	C65.37	188
C.F.1926	812	C.F.2029	1053	C.F.2296	879	C65.48	94
C.F.1927	906	C.F.2112	845	C.F.2297	861	C65.49	206
C.F.1928	763	C.F.2113	857	C.F.2298	802	C65.56	230
C.F.1930	932	C.F.2114	770	C.F.2299	804	C65.79	95
C.F.1935	1046	C.F.2115	864	C.F.2300	1039	C65.88	146
C.F.1936	904	C.F.2116	827	C.F.2301	1057	C65.89	280
C.F.1937	759	C.F.2117	865	CG.281	1007	C65.101	231
C.F.1938	800	C.F.2118	880	CG.282	1008	C65.105	20
C.F.1940	790	C.F.2119	765	CG.284	1066	C65.106	21
C.F.1941	876	C.F.2120a&b	771	CG.286	1079	C65.107	22
C.F.1951	648	C.F.2121	847	CG.287	1067	C65.108	207
C.F.1952	1047	C.F.2122	897	CG.291	1058	C65.109	139

Artifact Inventory Number	This Book Number	Artifact Inventory Number	This Book Number	Artifact Inventory Number	This Book Number	Artifact Inventory Number	This Book Number
C65.130	96	C66.216	9	C67.246	213	C68.432	923
C65.136	231A	C66.226	86	C67.247	141	C68.433	924
C65.159	1092	C66.227	281	C67.257	111	C68.470	809
C65.168	304	C66.251	270	C67.292	40	C68.471	727
C65.170	97	C66.313	221	C67.293	196	C68.510	223
C65.184	159	C66.314	222	C67.298	184	C68.520	453
C65.185	98	C66.319	216	C67.313	197	C68.525	541
C65.186	232	C66.349	87	C67.314	147	C68.530	286
C65.193	99	C66.359	211	C67.315	112	C68.531	925
C65.209	100	C66.410	282	C67.332	168	C68.539	926
C65.228	233	C66.411	283	C67.349	142	C68.554	650
C65.237	208	C66.469	284	C67.350	185	C68.560	687
C65.247	101	C66.482	106	C67.452	1025	C68.589	471
C65.248	102	C66.483	107	C67.483	731	C68.591	11
C65.255	103	C66.862	557	C67.535a&b	704	C68.592	88
C65.256	23	C66.875	293	C67.537	41	C68.603	175
C65.290	24	C66.876bis	321	C67.592	199	C68.627	273
C65.291	104	C66.877	285	C67.595	169	C68.633	45
C65.295	209	C66.878	324	C67.596	305	C68.646	219
C65.313	25	C66.882	10	C68.106	909	C68.674	1088
C65.319	234	C66.883	200	C68.107	1060	C68.675	1061
C65.331	140	C67.3	1004	C68.108	1080	C68.676	1062
C65.332	26	C67.7	163	C68.109	1081	C68.677	1063
C65.333	27	C67.9	164	C68.110	1082	C68.678	1027
C65.334	105	C67.10	968	C68.111	1068	C68.680	1028
C65.351	28	C67.15	34	C68.112	1069	C68.681	1089
C65.352	160	C67.16	165	C68.113	1070	C68.682	1077
C65.353	29	C67.69	189	C68.116	1071	C68.708	89
C65.377	235	C67.71	190	C68.122	1072	C68.714	224
C65.402	30	C67.73	279	C68.123	1083	C68.715	225
C65.403	31	C67.74	35	C68.124	1084	C68.719	144
C65.404	193	C67.91	166	C68.125	1073	C68.720	47
C65.405	272	C67.102	277	C68.126	1064	C68.721	48
C65.423	210	C67.136	36	C68.127	1074	C68.722	49
C65.429	32	C67.137	37	C68.128	1085	C68.723	3
C65.430	33	C67.138	108	C68.129	1086	C68.728	145
C65.432	161	C67.145	109	C68.130	1075	C68.729	4
C65.671	162	C67.146	194	C68.131	1076	C68.735	50
C66.1	174	C67.165	167	C68.154	1087	C68.740	1009
C66.16	6	C67.166	110	C68.270	735	C69.34	262
C66.133	181	C67.167	212	C68.273	46	C69.50	115
C66.142	220	C67.193	38	C68.376bis	705	C69.100	278
C66.167	85	C67.194	195	C68.401	732	C69.108	113
C66.169	133	C67.216	39	C68.413	922	C69.122	263
C66.190	7	C67.241	191	C68.416	808	C69.139	116
C66.205	8	C67.243	236	C68.419	261	C69.149	143

Artifact Inventory Number	This Book Number	Artifact Inventory Number	This Book Number
C69.172	42	C71.123	451
C69.246	693	C71.140	335
C69.264	649	C71.141	435
C69.265	491	C71.142	436
C69.303	976	C71.153	620
C69.310	252	C71.218	84
C69.318	128	C71.225	265
C69.355	413	C71.227	266
C69.358	977	C71.228	267
C69.363	251	C71.229a&b	336
C69.440	303	C71.230	337
C69.456	449	C71.231a&b	437
C69.457	450	C72.8	182
C70.6	117	C72.70	68
C70.57	148	C72.71	69
C70.83	948	C72.83	287
C70.133	969	C72.135a	70
C70.180	43	C72.136a	71
C70.244	970	C72.140	593
C70.245	591	C72.141	594
C70.314	493	C72.142	595
C70.318	592	C72.143	596
C70.319	971	C72.144	597
C70.324	427	C72.145	598
C70.336	428	C72.146	1026
C70.355	659	C73.1	170
C70.358	972		
C70.396	306		
C70.484	651		
C70.496	652		
C70.498	973		
C70.527	264		
C70.666	429		
C70.667	430		
C70.668	431		
C70.669	721		
C70.671	584		
C70.672a&b	432		
C70.674	375		
C70.675	992		
C70.677	433		
C70.678	782		
C70.679a&b	434		
C71.36	275		
C71.53	82		
C71.92	83		

GLOSSARY

Acanthus leaf The spreading leaf of the acanthus plant common in Greece and Italy, a favorite decorative motif since the fifth century B.C.; often used on the triangular heat shield of lamps.

Air hole A tiny punched hole near the juncture between the discus and the nozzle. Whether it was designed to admit air, however, has never been determined. Broneer discusses the possibilities of its purpose (Broneer 1930, 9–12).

Archetype See Patrix.

Arretine ware Fine pottery of the late Republican and early Imperial period, originally from the area of Arezzo, characterized by a coral color and exterior decoration in low relief.

Base The bottom of the lamp, flat or raised on a ring. If the potter signed his lamp, the signature, a name, device, or monogram, was usually within the circle of the base, either incuse or in relief.

Bead molding Narrow convex molding. Usually a part of the encircling molds around the discus at the outer edge of the lamp top.

Biscuit, Bisque Ware once fired, ready for application of a slip or glaze.

Carination The angle on the body of a biconical oil reservoir formed by the joint of the two halves of the lamp.

Clay Certain kinds of earth combined with water to form a cohesive mass that can be shaped into objects that, fired in a kiln, become pottery or ceramic ware. The different colors are usually the result of metal oxides or other colorants in the clay; for example, iron oxide produces red clay.

Clay body A combination of several kinds of clay prepared for use in pottery, composed of clays with properties that prevent warping and reduce shrinkage. A body could also be prepared with grog to increase tensile strength.

Colorant A metal oxide, carbonate, or other material added to give color to a clay body, a slip, or a glaze.

Cone The clay thermometer, named for its shape, used in the firing chamber of the kiln to indicate the temperature. Cones are made of different kinds of clay, which melt at different temperatures. The potter uses several cones, placed where they can be viewed through a peephole, to know when to stop firing. In kilns with modern temperature gauges, cones are unnecessary.

Crosshatch and slurry The potter's method of joining two surfaces by scoring them and pressing them together using slurry (clay slaked with water) as the adhesive. The halves of moldmade lamps were probably joined by this method.

Dimensions Length, width, and height of the lamp. All dimensions of lamps and lamp fragments are given in meters. When the lamp is whole, the dimensions, Length, Width, and Height, are spelled out in full. Otherwise the abbreviations P.L. (Preserved Length), P.W. (Preserved Width), and P.H. (Preserved Height) are used.

Discus The area, usually round, covering the oil reservoir partially or completely. It may be large or small, flat, concave, or recessed, plain or decorated. The concave surface on wide discus lamps was usually embellished with the discus relief.

Discus relief The figural relief or device on the discus. It could depict any image from an enormous repertoire available to an imaginative potter; material for the discus relief was often drawn from other sources.

Domestic and Coarse Ware Unglazed ceramic ware for kitchen and daily table use; a catalogue of Cosan utilitarian vessels has been published by Dyson (Dyson 1976).

Ear A small decorative element like a tiny handle added on one or both sides of the oil reservoir. Ears vary in shape and decoration.

Fabric The wall of the lamp, used in reference to the thickness or quality of the clay.

Filling hole A hole on the top of the lamp through which oil was poured to fill the reservoir.

Fluting A ribbed effect achieved by the potter running his fingers, a tool, or a template over a surface to make indentations or ribs. Handles are often fluted by the potter simply running his fingers along a strip of clay.

Glaze A glossy or matte coating on ceramic ware obtained in the firing by covering the clay surface with material high in silicates. In the firing these materials go through a melting and running process that produces a glossy surface that is impervious. Only one Cosan lamp has a true vitreous glaze.

Grog Sand or crushed refractory material (fired pottery or brick) ground fine that is added to the clay body to increase tensile strength.

Handle The vertical or horizontal attachment, usually placed opposite the nozzle, by which a lamp can be grasped. Except for the wall lamps, Cosan lamps have only vertical handles.

Heat shield A decorative device above the handle on certain ornate lamps. The most common shields were triangular or crescent-shaped, inclined at about a 30° to 45° angle from the horizontal plane of the oil reservoir to which they were attached by a stem. Heat shields were imitations of similar devices on bronze lamps, which may have shielded the hand from the heat when the lamp was carried. On clay lamps the heat shield might act as a handle and would protect the hand from the flame if the lamp were held by the thickened projection below the heat shield.

Hump A large mass of clay centered on the potter's wheel from which lamps could be thrown and cut, allowing the potter multiple production from a single centering; throwing "off the hump" is especially desirable when small objects, such as lamps, are to be made in quantity.

Imbrication Overlapping leaf or scale pattern, like fish scales.

Infundibulum *See* Oil reservoir.

Italo-Megarian Ware Delicate hemispherical bowls with fine relief decoration, usually without a foot, copied from metal prototypes. They were first manufactured in Athens in the third century B.C., and then copied in Rome, beginning about the beginning of the second century B.C. See M. T. M. Moevs, "Italo-Megarian Ware at Cosa," *MAAR* 34 (1980) 161–227.

Kiln The oven in which pottery is fired to make it hard and durable. In antiquity, kilns were usually fired with the readiest available fuel—wood, charcoal, straw, or dung.

Levigate To refine clay making it suitable for manufacture; to separate the fine particles from coarser material by suspending the clay in a liquid.

Ligature The joining of two or more letters in an inscription into a single sign.

Lug A small projecting earlike device sometimes pierced to allow attachment of a cord or chain. It could also be used for grasping or carrying. With three lugs on the top, a lamp could be suspended from a lampstand. On ceramic ware, such as Factory Lamps, lugs were usually decorative, not functional.

Luting, Luted The attaching of one surface of partially hardened clay to another by scoring or crosshatching the edges to be joined and then painting them with slurry as an adhesive. They are then pressed together; sometimes a thin coil of clay is applied and smoothed into the joint. *See also* Crosshatch and slurry.

Matrix The two-part mold (or negative) made by a two-phase process of encasing or enveloping a patrix in plaster or clay and dividing this casing, the matrix, along the widest dimension of the patrix. Probably oil was applied to the patrix as a separator to allow easy removal of the matrix. A matrix could also be carved directly in soft limestone.

Micaceous Containing mica, any of various silicates crystallized in thin sheets that break into particles and glisten in light. Clay may contain varying amounts of mica naturally, and the amount helps to pin down the location of the clay beds.

Mold *See* Matrix.

Moldmade lamps Lamps usually made in a two-piece mold (matrix), although more pieces might be used for complex shapes. All Cosan molded lamps were probably made in two-piece molds. The handles were included in the molds after the early Claudian period.

Nozzle The projection of a lamp to hold the wick, which extended down into the oil reservoir. A lamp may have a single nozzle (*monolychnos*), two nozzles (*dilychnos*), or multiple nozzles arranged in a line, an arc, a ring, or other shape.

Oil reservoir The central body of the lamp into which oil was poured, also in modern sources called the *infundibulum*.

Palmette A stylized design like the fanning tip of a palm branch, a common decorative motif; it often decorates the triangular heat shield of a lamp.

Patrix The original model for a lamp, from which matrices or molds could be made. The model was carved from soft stone or wood, or it was modeled in clay and then fired very hard with filling and wick holes indicated. The patrix is also called the archetype.

Plastic So-called "Plastic Lamps" are those in the shape of body parts, animals, pinecones, etc.

Provenance, provenience The findspot or source of a lamp, where it was made, found, or acquired.

Register The two halves of the mold or matrix were registered by scoring on the outside or by means of mortises and tenons on the contact surfaces in order to ensure an exact fit of the two halves of the lamp within the mold.

Relief The decoration or scene on the discus (*see* Discus relief), executed in low relief. Lamps with such decoration are sometimes called Relief Lamps.

Rim The outer band of the top surface of Triangular Nozzle, Pouter Pigeon, and Long Voluted Nozzle Lamps framing the discus. This was usually set off from the discus and composed of combinations of rings and moldings. It might be flat or convex, wide or narrow.

Rim profile The cross section of the rim showing the variety and spacing of moldings and decoration. Loeschcke (Loeschcke 1919, 5) made the first classification of these, which he referred to as Shoulder Forms, with drawings. Broneer in his catalogue of the lamps from Corinth (Broneer 1930) used Loeschcke's classification and made several additions, referring to the patterns as Rim Profiles. The Rim Profiles of the Cosan lamps cover a longer period of time than either of the earlier classifications and provide many additions.

Ring A very narrow convex ridge.

Scroll A roll or spiral, especially that finishing a volute.

Self-slip A slip made from the same clay as the vessel without the addition of a colorant (*see* Slip).

Sgraffito Scratching through a top surface to cut into or reveal the surface or clay beneath.

Shoulder The sloping edge of the rims of certain lamps.

Slip, or slurry Clay diluted with water used, (1) as adhesive when parts of a lamp are joined together, and (2) as a coating for a lamp, giving a smooth, semiimpervious surface and color, if a colorant is added to the mixture of clay and water. Most Cosan lamps have been coated with a colored slip. The finish on lamps described as *vernice nera* is not a vitreous glaze, but in this catalogue the term Black Glaze Ware has been accepted, since it has become standard.

Spatulate A shovel form. The outer edge slightly convex or straight. The ends of the edge form points.

Stem The connection between the heat shield and the oil reservoir.

Thin Walled Ware Unglazed ceramic ware of very fine quality and extremely thin fabric. *See* Moevs 1973.

Throw To shape a piece of pottery on the wheel. Because the first step in making a vessel is to throw a ball of clay on the wheel with force to make it adhere before it is centered, the entire process of creating a wheelmade vessel is called "throwing."

Tooling The use of an instrument to carve or shave a leather-hard ceramic object while it turns on the wheel; also the marks made by the instrument.

Volute A decorative device on each side of the nozzle with scrolls at one or both ends (one-scroll volutes and two-scroll volutes). The volutes form a visual and physical connection between the nozzle and the oil reservoir. Often a volute ends in a scroll that is flattened on top and extends down the side of the nozzle or oil reservoir in a small, neat cone.

Wheelmade lamps Lamps made by being thrown on a wheel, probably from a hump, which would save the potter having to center a small amount of clay each time he made a lamp. The throwing was only of the body or oil reservoir. To this were added the nozzle and handle, formed separately and attached before firing.

Wick A twist or braid of any material that brings the oil by capillary action from the oil reservoir to the nozzle. Wicks in antiquity were made of flax, hemp, oakum, and cotton.

Wick hole The hole in the nozzle to accommodate the wick.

ABBREVIATIONS AND SELECTED BIBLIOGRAPHY

This bibliography is limited to works that are relevant to the Cosan lamps treated in this catalogue. Abbreviations of the titles of periodicals and standard reference works are in general those accepted by the *American Journal of Archaeology* 95 (1991) 1–16.

AA *Archäologischer Anzeiger.*
AdI *Annali dell'Istituto di Correspondenzu Archeologica.*
AJA *American Journal of Archaeology.*
AJP *American Journal of Philology.*
Alarcão/DaPonte A. M. Alarcão and S. DaPonte, "Les Lampes," *Fouilles de Conimbriga* 6 (Paris, 1976) 93–114.
Alföldi A. Alföldi, "Die Kontorniaten und das Neujahrsfest," *Die Kontorniaten* 38 (1943) 37–48.
Alicu/Nemeş D. Alicu and E. Nemeş, *Roman Lamps from Ulpia Traiana Sarmizegetusa*, British Archaeological Reports, Supplement Series 18 (1977).
Almagro/Lamboglia M. Almagro and N. Lamboglia, "La estratigrafia del decumano A de Ampurias," *Ampurias* 21 (1959) 1–24.
Alram-Stern E. Alram-Stern, *Die römischen Lampen aus Carnuntum* (Vienna, 1989).
Alvarez Ossorio F. Alvarez Ossorio, "Lucernas o lamparas antiguas, de barro cocido, del Museo Arqueologico Nacional," *Archivo español de arqueologia* 15 (1942) 271–87.
Amaré Tafalla M. T. Amaré Tafalla, *Lucernas romanas de Bilbilis* (Zaragoza, 1984).
Andreae B. Andreae, et al., *Pompeji, Leben und Kunst in den Vesuvstädten* (Recklinghausen, 1973).
Andrén A. Andrén, "Scavi e scoperti sull'acropoli di Ardea," *Opuscula romana* 3, Skrifter utgivna av Svenska Institutet i Rom 4:21 (1961) 1–68.
Anselmino L. Anselmino, "Lucerne," *Studi miscellanei* 23 (1972–76, *Ostia IV*) 86–100.
AntCl *L'Antiquité classique.*
Anti C. Anti, "Le lucerne romane di terra cotta conservate nel Museo Civico di Verona," *Madonna Verona* 6 (1912) fasc. 24, 181–94; 7 (1913) fasc. 25, 6–24; 8 (1914) fasc. 30–31, 99–116, fasc. 32, 207–15.
Antichità d'Ercolano *Le lucerne ed i candelabri d'Ercolano e contorni*, *Le antichità d'Ercolano* 8 (Naples, 1792).
Antico Gallina M. Antico Gallina, *Le lucerne fittili di Dertona* (Tortona, 1985).
AntJ *The Antiquaries Journal. The Journal of the Society of Antiquaries of London.*
ArchEph *Archaiologike Ephemeris.*
AthMitt *Mitteilungen des Deutschen Archäologischen Instituts, Athenische Abteilung.*
BABesch *Bulletin antieke Beschaving. Annual Papers on Classical Archaeology.*
Bachofen J. J. Bachofen, *Römische Grablampen nebst einigen andern Grabdenkmälern* (Gesammelte Werke, vol. 7, Basel/Stuttgart, 1958).
Bailey 1965 D. M. Bailey, "Lamps in the Victoria and Albert Museum," *Opuscula atheniensia* 6 (1965) 1–83.
Bailey 1972 D. M. Bailey, *Greek and Roman Pottery Lamps* (British Museum, London, 1963, 2nd ed. 1972).

Bailey 1975   D. M. Bailey, *A Catalogue of the Lamps in the British Museum* 1. *Greek, Hellenistic, and Early Roman Lamps* (London, 1975).

Bailey 1976   D. M. Bailey, "Pottery Lamps," in D. Strong and D. Brown (eds.), *Roman Crafts* (London, 1976) 93–103.

Bailey 1978   D. M. Bailey, "Common Italian Lamps: A Brief Guide," *British Archaeological Reports, British Series* 41 (1978) (The Lancaster Seminar, Papers in Archaeology 1) 243–301.

Bailey 1980   D. M. Bailey, *A Catalogue of the Lamps in the British Museum.* 2. *Roman Lamps Made in Italy* (London, 1980).

Bailey 1985   D. M. Bailey, supplement to *Libya Antiqua* 5; 3.2 *The Lamps* (Tripoli, 1985).

Bailey 1988   D. M. Bailey, *A Catalogue of the Lamps in the British Museum.* 3. *Roman Provincial Lamps* (London, 1988).

Bailey 1991   D. M. Bailey, "Lamps Metal, Lamps Clay: A Decade of Publication," *Journal of Roman Archaeology* 4 (1991) 51–62.

Bailly   R. Bailly, "Essai de classification des marques de potiers sur lampes en argile dans la Narbonnaise," *Cahiers ligures de préhistoire et d'archéologie* 11 (1962) 79–127.

Bairrao Oleiro   J. M. Bairrao Oleiro, *Museu Machado de Castro. Catalogo de lucernas romanas* (Coimbra, 1952).

Balil Illana 1968a   A. Balil Illana, "Marcas de ceramista en lucernas romanas halladas en España," *Archivo español de arqueologia* 41 (1968) 158–78.

Balil Illana 1968b   A. Balil Illana, *Lucernae singulares*, Latomus 93 (Brussels, 1968).

Balil Illana 1969a   A. Balil Illana, *Estudios sobre lucernas romanas 1* (Seminario de Arqueologia, Facultad de Filosofia y Letros, Universidad Santiago de Campostela, 1969).

Balil Illana 1969b   A. Balil Illana, "Bolli e segnature di figulini in lucerne romane del tardo impero," *Rivista di archeologia cristiana* 45 (1969) 7–13.

Baluţa 1961   C. L. Baluţa, *Opaitele romane de la Apulum 1*, Acta Musei Regionalis Apulensis, Studi si communicari, Arheologie-Istorie-Etnografie 4 (Bucharest, 1961) 189–220.

Baluţa 1975   C. L. Baluţa, "Lucernae singulares apulenses," *Arheoloski vestnik* 26 (1975) 111–14.

BAR   *British Archaeological Reports*.

Baradez   J. Baradez, "Nouvelles fouilles à Tipasa," *Libyca* 5 (1957) 227–33.

Bartoli/Bellori   P. S. Bartoli and G. P. Bellori, *Le antiche lucerne sepolcrali figurate* (Rome, 1691).

Bass/Van Doorninck   G. F. Bass and F. H. Van Doorninck, "A Fourth-Century Shipwreck at Yassi Ada," *American Journal of Archaeology* 75 (1971) 27–37.

Baur   P. V. C. Baur, *The Lamps. Excavations at Dura-Europos, Final Report 4. Part 3* (New Haven/London, 1947).

BCH   *Bulletin de correspondance hellénique*.

Belchior   C. Belchior, *Lucernas romanas de Conimbriga* (Conimbriga, 1969).

Beltran   L. Beltran, "Lucernas romanas del Museo Arqueologico de Zaragoza," *Caesaraugusta* 27–28 (1966) 77–88.

Benoit 1958   F. Benoit, "Nouvelles épaves de Provence," *Gallia* 16:1 (1958) 5–39.

Benoit 1961   F. Benoit, "Fouilles sous-marines: l'épave du Grand Congloué à Marseilles," *Gallia*, suppl. 14 (Paris, 1961).

Bergès   G. Bergès, *Les Lampes de Montans (Tarn)* (Paris, 1989).

Bernabo Brea 1947   L. Bernabo Brea, "Lipari," in *Notizie degli scavi di antichità* 1947, 215–16.

Bernabo Brea/Cavalier   L. Bernabo Brea and M. Cavalier, *Meligunìs-Lipára* 2 (Palermo, 1965).

Bernhard   M. L. Bernhard, *Lampki Starozytne,* Muzcum Narodowe w Warzawie (Warsaw, 1955).

Bisi Ingrassia   A. M. Bisi Ingrassia, "Le lucerne fittili dei nuovi scavi di Ercolano," in A. Carandini (ed.), *L'instrumentum domesticum di Ercolano e Pompei nella prima età imperiale*, Quaderni di cultura materiale 1 (Rome, 1977) 73–104.

Bonghi Jovino   M. Bonghi Jovino, "Lucerne," in A. Frova (ed.), *Scavi di Luni 2. Relazione preliminare delle campagne di scavo 1972–74* (Rome, 1977) 557–67.

Bonnet   J. Bonnet, *Lampes céramiques signées*, Documents d'archéologie française 13 (Paris, 1988).

Bovon   A. Bovon, *Lampes d'Argos*, École française d'Athénes, Études péloponnésiennes 5 (Paris, 1966).

Brants   J. Brants, *Antieke Terra-Cotta Lampen uit het Rijksmuseum van Oudheden te Leiden* (Leiden, 1913).

Breccia   E. Breccia, "Les Lampes 'Africaines' du Musée Gréco-Romain," *Le Musée Gréco-Romain au cours de l'année 1922–1923* (Alexandria, 1923) 25–31.

Broneer 1930   O. Broneer, *Terracotta Lamps,* Corinth, Results of Excavations Conducted by the American School of Classical Studies at Athens, 4 Part 2 (Cambridge, 1930).

Broneer 1977   O. Broneer, *Isthmia 3. Terracotta Lamps* (Princeton, 1977).

Brown 1980   F. E. Brown, *Cosa: The Making of a Roman Town* (Ann Arbor, Michigan, 1980).

Brugnoli/De Carolis   G. Brugnoli and E. De Carolis, *Lucerne greche e romane* (Rome: Gruppo Archeologico Romano, Quaderni 3, 1977).

de Brun/Gagnière   P. de Brun and S. Gagnière, *Les Lampes antiques en argile et en bronze du Musée Calvet d'Avignon* (Carpentras, 1937).

Bruneau   P. Bruneau, *Les Lampes*, Exploration archéologique de Délos faite par l'École française d'Athènes 26 (Paris, 1965).

Bruno 1970   V. J. Bruno, "A Town House at Cosa," *Archaeology* 23 (1970) 232–41.

Buchi   E. Buchi, *Lucerne del museo di Aquileia 1. Lucerne romane con marchio di fabbrica* (Aquileia, 1975).

Bucic   V. Bucic, *Svetila: oblike in Namen*, Katalog Vesna Bucic in Ferdinand Tancik Ljubljana and Narodni Mujej (1969).

Buttrey   T. V. Buttrey, *Cosa: The Coins*, Memoirs of the American Academy in Rome 34 (Rome, 1980).

Cahn-Klaiber   E.-M. Cahn-Klaiber, *Die antiken Tonlampen des Archäologischen Instituts der Universität Tübingen* (Tübingen, 1977).

Carandini 1969   A. Carandini, "Produzione agricola e produzione ceramica nell'Africa di età imperiale," *Studi miscellanei* 15 (1969–70) 95–122.

Carandini 1973   A. Carandini, et al., "Le terme del nuotatore," *Studi miscellanei* 21 (1973, *Ostia III*) 395–404 (C. Salone).

Carandini 1977   A. Carandini (ed.), *L'instrumentum domesticum di Ercolano e Pompei nella prima età imperiale*, Quaderni di cultura materiale 1 (Rome, 1977).

Carandini 1985   A. Carandini, et al., *Settefinestre: una villa schiavistica nell'Etruria romana*, 3 vols. (Modena, 1985).

de Cardaillac 1891   F. de Cardaillac, *Histoire de la lampe antique en Afrique* (Paris, 1891).

de Cardaillac 1922   F. de Cardaillac, *De Quelques lampes antiques découvertes dans l'Afrique du nord* (Tarbes-Lesbordes, 1922).

Carettoni   G. Carettoni, "Roma, Palatino. Saggi nell'interno della Casa di Livia," *Notizie degli scavi di antichità* 1957, 72–119.

Cerulli Irelli 1974   G. Cerulli Irelli. *La casa "del colonnato tuscanico" ad Ercolano*, Memorie della Accademia di Archeologia Lettere e Belle Arti di Napoli 7 (1974).

Cerulli Irelli 1977   G. Cerulli Irelli, "Una officina di lucerne fittili a Pompei," in A. Carandini (ed.), *L'instrumentum domesticum di Ercolano e Pompei nella prima età imperiale*, Quaderni di cultura materiale 1 (Rome, 1977) 53–72.

Chiesi   G. S. Chiesi, "Lucerne," in A. Frova (ed.), *Scavi di Luni* 1 (Rome, 1973) 727–32, 786–95.

Čičikova   M. Čičikova, "'Firmalampen' du limes danubien en Bulgarie," *Actes du IXe congrès international d'études sur les frontières romaines* (Bucharest/Cologne/Vienna, 1974), 155–65.

CIL   *Corpus inscriptionum latinarum.*

Clark   E. Clark, *Records of the Past* (n.p.) 170–86.

Colini   A. M. Colini, "Lucerne di spedizione?," *Colloqui del sodalizio tra studiosi dell'arte*, ser. 2, vol. 1, 1966–68 (1969) 62–69.

Collins-Clinton   J. Collins-Clinton, *A Late Antique Shrine of Liber Pater* (Études préliminaires aux religions orientales dans l'empire romain, edited by M. J. Vermaseren, vol. 64) (Leiden, 1977).

Cosa I   F. E. Brown, *Cosa I: History and Topography*, Memoirs of the American Academy in Rome 20 (Rome, 1951) 7–113.

Cosa II   F. E. Brown, E. H. Richardson, and L. Richardson, jr, *Cosa II: The Temples of the Arx*, Memoirs of the American Academy in Rome 26 (Rome, 1960).

Cosa III   F. E. Brown, E. H. Richardson, and L. Richardson, jr, *Cosa III: The Buildings of the Forum*, Memoirs of the American Academy in Rome 37 (University Park, Pennsylvania, 1993).

Cosa IV   V. J. Bruno and R. T. Scott, *Cosa IV: The Houses*, Memoirs of the American Academy in Rome 38 (University Park, Pennsylvania, 1993).

Cuomo di Caprio/Bianchi   N. Cuomo di Caprio and S. Santoro Bianchi, *Lucerne fittili e bronzee del Museo Civico di Lodi* (Lodi, 1983).

D'Arms   J. H. D'Arms, "Senators' Involvement in Commerce in the Late Republic: Some Ciceronian Evidence," *The Seaborne Commerce of Ancient Rome*, Memoirs of the American Academy in Rome 36 (Rome, 1980) 77–89.

DarSag   C. Daremberg and E. Saglio, *Dictionnaire des antiquités grecques et romaines* (Paris, 1877–1919) 3 (1904) 1320–39 s.v. "Lucerna, lychnus," (J. Toutain).

Darsy   F. M. D. Darsy, *Recherches archéologiques à Sainte-Sabine sur l'Aventin*, Monumenti di antichità cristiana, ser. 9 vol. 2 (Vatican City, 1968).

David-Weill   J. David-Weill, "Note sur deux lampes

égyptiennes en terre cuite," *Syria* 28 (1951) 265–68.

De Caro   S. De Caro, "Le lucerne dell'officina LVC," *Rendiconti della Accademia di Archeologia, Lettere e Belle Arti di Napoli* 49 (Naples, 1974) 107–34.

De Carolis/de'Spagnolis   E. De Carolis and M. C. de'Spagnolis, *Le lucerne di bronzo* (Vatican City, 1986).

de Franciscis   A. de Franciscis, "Scoperte subacquée a Pozzuoli," *Fasti archaeologici* 22 (1967) 317 no. 4603.

Delattre 1890–93   P. (A.L.) Delattre, "Lampes chrétiennes de Carthage," *Revue de l'art chrétien* 4.1 (1890) 134–39; 4.2 (1891) 39–51, 296–309; 4.3 (1892) 133–40, 224–29; 4.4 (1893) 34–40.

Delattre 1899   R. P. (A.L.) Delattre, *Lampes du Musée Lavigerie de St.-Louis de Carthage,* Musées et collections archéologiques de l'Algérie et de la Tunisie, ser. 3, vol. 8, part 3 (Paris, 1899) 32–48.

Delplace   C. Delplace, et al., "Présentation de l'ensemble des lampes découvertes de 1962 à 1971," *Ordona* 4 (Brussels/Rome, 1974) 7–101.

Deneauve   J. Deneauve, *Lampes de Carthage* (Paris, 1969).

Deonna 1908   W. Deonna, "Les Lampes antiques trouvées à Délos," *Bulletin de correspondance hellénique* 32 (1908) 133–76.

Deonna 1927   W. Deonna, "L'Ornamentation des lampes romaines," *Revue archéologique* ser. 5, vol. 26 (1927) 233–63.

Deringer   H. Deringer, *Römische Lampen aus Lauriacum* (Linz, 1965).

DialArch   *Dialoghi di archeologia.*

Dobbins   J. J. Dobbins, *The terracotta lamps of Tell Anafa*, University of Michigan, forthcoming.

Dobbins 1977   J. J. Dobbins, "The terracotta lamps from the Roman province of Syria," vols. 1 & 2, University of Michigan, 1977. Dissertation.

Domergue   C. Domergue, "Un Envoi de lampes du potier Caius Clodius," *Mélanges de la Casa de Velasquez* 2 (1966) 5–40.

Dressel 1880   H. Dressel, "La suppellettile dell'antichissima necropoli esquilino," Part 2, *Annali dell'Istituto di Corrispondenza Archeologica* 52.1 (1880) 265–342.

Dressel 1899   H. Dressel, *Corpus inscriptionum latinarum* 15.2 *Instrumentum domesticum* (Berlin, 1899) 782–870.

Dressel/Lamboglia   H. Dressel and N. Lamboglia, *Tipologia e cronologia delle lucerne romane, classificazione Dressel, Apuntes sobre cronologia ceramica,* Publicaciones del Seminario del Arqueologia y Numismatica Aragonesa (1952).

Duncan   G. C. Duncan, "Roman Republican Pottery from the Vicinity of Sutri," *Papers of the British School at Rome* 33 (1965) 134–76.

Dyson   S. L. Dyson, *Cosa: The Utilitarian Pottery*, Memoirs of the American Academy in Rome 33 (Rome, 1976).

EAA   *Enciclopedia dell'arte antica, classica e orientale*, 4 (Rome, 1961) 707–18 s.v. "Lucerna" (H. Menzel and J. Elgavish).

Ennabli 1973   A. Ennabli, et al., *La Nécropole romaine de Raqqada* (Tunis, 1973).

Ennabli 1976   A. Ennabli, *Lampes chrétiennes de Tunisie, Musées du Bardo et de Carthage*, Études d'antiquités africaines (Paris, 1976).

Evelein   M. A. Evelein, *De romeinische Lampen, Beschrijving van de Verzameling van het Museum G. M. Kam te Nijmagen* (The Hague, 1928).

FA   *Fasti archaeologici.*

Fabbricotti 1969a   E. Fabbricotti, *Le lucerne antiche dell'Antiquarium della Badia di Grottaferrata*, Bollettino della Badia Greca di Grottaferrata, n.s. 23 (1969).

Fabbricotti 1969b   E. Fabbricotti, *Ritrovamenti archeologici sotto la chiesa della Visitazione di Santa Maria in Comuccia*, Res tudertine 10 (Todi, 1969).

Fabbricotti 1974a   E. Fabbricotti, "Osservazioni sulle lucerne a perline," *Cenacolo* 4 (1974).

Fabbricotti 1974b   E. Fabbricotti, "Lucerne della Basilicata settentrionale," *Atti della Accademia Nazionale dei Lincei. Rendiconti* ser. 8, 29 (1974) 521–30.

Farka 1977   C. Walkenstorfer Farka, *Die römischen Lampen vom Magdalensberg,* Kärtner Museumsschriften 61 (Klagenfurt, 1977).

Ferraresi 1973   A. Ferraresi, *Le lucerne del museo civico "Antonio Parazzi" di Viadana*, Contributi dell'Istituto di Archeologia (Università Cattolica del Sacro Cuore di Milano) 4 (1973) 31–131.

Ferraresi 1980   A. Ferraresi, "Due lucerne di forma particolare dal territorio mantovano," *Studi in onore di F. Rittatore Vonwiller* 2 (Como, 1980) 169–82.

Ferreira   J. A. Ferreira de Almeida, "Introducão ao estudo das lucernas romanas em Portugal," *O arqueólogo portugùes*, n.s. 2 (1953) pp. 5–208.

Fink   J. A. Fink, "Formen und Stempel römischer Thonlampen," *K. Bayerische Akademie der Wissenschaften, München, Philosophisch-historische Klasse. Sitzungsberichte* 5 (1901) 685–703.

Fischbach   O. Fischbach, *Römische Lampen aus Poetovio*, Mitteilungen des historischen Vereines für Steiermark 44 (Graz, 1896).

Fitch   Cleo Rickman Fitch, "The Lamps of Cosa." *Scientific American*, 247.6 December 1982, pp. 148–60.

Flinders Petrie   W. M. Flinders Petrie, *Roman Ehnasya* (London, 1905).

Floca   O. Floca, "Collectia arheologica a muzeului de arheologie si etnografie a palatului cultural din Tîrgu Mureş, Buletinul 1," *Gazeta Illustrata* 6–7 (1937).

Forbes   R. J. Forbes, *Studies in Ancient Technology* 6 (Leiden, 1966), 122–96.

Fremersdorf   F. Fremersdorf, *Römische Bildlampen* (Bonn/Leipzig, 1922).

Giovagnetti   C. Giovagnetti, ed., *Lucerne romane nel Museo di Rimini* (Rimini, 1984).

Goethert-Polaschek   K. Goethert-Polaschek, *Römische Lampen: Katalog der römischen Lampen des Rheinischen Landesmuseums Trier: Bildlampen und Sonderformen* (Mainz, 1985).

Goldman/Jones   H. Goldman and F. F. Jones, *Tarsus, Excavations at Gozlu Kule*, 1.*The Hellenistic and Roman Periods*, (Princeton, 1950) 84–134 ("The Lamps").

Gostar   N. Gostar, "Inscriptiile de pe lucernele din Dacia Romana," *Arheologia moldovei* 1 (1960) 149–209.

Graham   J. W. Graham, "Lamps from Olynthus, 1931," in D. M. Robinson, ed., *Excavations at Olynthus* 5 (Baltimore/London, 1933) 265–84.

Grandjouan   C. Grandjouan, *Terracottas and Plastic Lamps of the Roman Period, The Athenian Agora, Results of Excavations Conducted by the American School of Classical Studies at Athens*, vol. 6 (Princeton, 1961).

Graziani Abbiani   M. Graziani Abbiani, *Lucerne fittili paleocristiane nell'Italia settentrionale*, Studi di antichità cristiana 6 (Bologna, 1969).

Grella   C. Grella, "Le lucerne di Aeclanum, Museo Irpino di Avellino," *Economia Irpina* 1 (1984).

Grose 1975   D. D. F. Grose, "Roman Glass of the First Century A.D., A Dated Deposit of Glassware from Cosa, Italy," *Annales du VIe congrès de l'Association Internationale pour l'Histoire du Verre* (Liège, 1975) 31–52.

Grose 1977   D. D. F. Grose, "The Glass from the Roman 'Colonia' of Cosa," *Bulletin de l'Association Internationale pour l'Histoire du Verre* 7 (1973–76, publ. 1977) 175–82.

Gualandi Genito 1973   M. C. Gualandi Genito, "Una fabbrica di fittili nella Bononia Augustea: l'officina di Hilario," *Atti e memorie. Deputazione di storia patria per le province di Romagna* 24 (1973) 265–315.

Gualandi Genito 1977   M. C. Gualandi Genito, *Lucerne fittili delle collezioni del Museo Civico di Archeologia di Bologna* (Bologna, 1977).

Gualandi Genito 1979   M. C. Gualandi Genito, "Cultura materiale, Emilia: lucerne dell'antica Laterna," *Il Carrobbio* 5 (Bologna, 1979) 262–71.

Gualandi Genito 1986   M. C. Gualandi Genito, *Le lucerne antiche del Trentino* (Trento, 1986).

Guzzo   P. G. Guzzo, *Le scoperte archeologiche nell'attuale provincia di Cosenza*, 3d ed. (Sibari, Jonica, 1980).

Haken   R. Haken, "Roman Lamps in the Prague National Museum and in Other Czechoslovak Collections," *Acta Musei Nationalis Pragae* 12, nos. 1–2 (Prague, 1958).

Haley   E. W. Haley, "The Lamp Manufacturer Gaius Iunius Draco," *Münsterische Beiträge z. antiken Handelsgeschichte* 9.2 (1990) 1–13.

Hanoune   R. Hanoune, "Lampes de *Graviscae*," *Mélanges d'archéologie et d'histoire de l'École française de Rome* 82 (1970) 237–62.

Harrington   H. Harrington, "The Prototypes of the Designs on Some Lamps," Harvard University, 1935 Ph.D. Dissertation.

Harris   W. V. Harris, "Roman Terracotta Lamps: The Organization of an Industry," *Journal of Roman Studies* 70 (1980) 126–45.

Hatt   J.-J. Hatt, "Les Fouilles de Strasbourg en 1953–1954: Découverte d'un dépotoir de céramique," *Gallia* 12 (1954) 323–39.

Hayes 1972   J. W. Hayes, *Late Roman Pottery* (London, 1972).

Hayes 1980   J. W. Hayes, *Ancient Lamps in the Royal Ontario Museum. 1. Greek and Roman Clay Lamps* (Toronto, 1980).

Hellmann 1985   M.-C. Hellmann, *Lampes antiques de la Bibliothèque Nationale. 1. Collection Froehner* (Paris, 1985).

Hellmann 1987   M.-C. Hellmann, *Lampes antiques de la Bibliothèque Nationale. 2. Fonds général: Lampes préromaines et romaines* (Paris, 1987).

Hellström   P. Hellström, *Labraunda. 2.1: Pottery of Classical and Late Date, Terracotta Lamps and Glass* (Skrifter utgivna av Svenska Institutet i Athen 4.5.2.1, Lund, 1965), 49–52.

Heres 1968   G. Heres, "Die Werkstatt des Lampentopfers Romanesis," *Staatliche Museen zu Berlin: Forschungen und Berichte* 10 (1968) 185–211.

Heres 1969   G. Heres, *Die punischen und griechischen Tonlampen der Staatliche Museen zu Berlin* (Berlin/Amsterdam, 1969).

Heres 1972a   G. Heres, *Die römischen Bildlampen der Berliner Antiken-Sammlung* (Berlin, 1972).

Heres 1972b   G. Heres, "Römische Neujahrsgeschenken," *Staatliche Museen zu Berlin: Forschungen und Berichte* 14 (1972) 182–93.

Herondevillefosse   A. Herondevillefosse, *Lampes romaines avec legende explicative* (n.p., 1894).

Howland   R. H. Howland, *Greek Lamps and Their Survivals*, The Athenian Agora, Results of Excavations Conducted by the American School of Classical Studies in Athens vol. 4 (Princeton, 1958).

Hug   Hug, "Lucerna" in Pauly-Wissowa, *Real-Encyclopädie der klassischen Altertumswissenschaft* 13.2 (1927) 1566–1613.

Iconomu   C. Iconomu, *Opaite greco-romane*, Muzeul regional de arheologie Dobrogea (Constanza, 1967).

Ivanyi   D. Ivanyi, *Die pannonischen Lampen, eine typologisch-chronologische Übersicht*, Dissertationes Pannonicae, ser. 2, no. 2 (Budapest, 1935).

JdI   *Jahrbuch des Deutschen Archäologischen Instituts.*

JÖAI   *Jahreshefte des Österreichischen Archäologischen Instituts.*

Joly 1968   E. Joly, "Nuove lucerne con vedute di porto nell'antiquarium di Sabratha," *Libya antiqua* 5 (1968) 45–54 and pls. 40–42.

Joly 1974   E. Joly, *Lucerne del museo di Sabratha* (Rome, 1974).

JRS   *The Journal of Roman Studies.*

Jurlaro   R. Jurlaro, *Ricerche e studi, Museo Francesco Ribezzo*, no. 3 (Brindisi, 1967).

Kennedy   C. A. Kennedy, "The Development of the Lamp in Palestine," *Berytus* 14 (1963) 67–115.

el Kilani   Abu-Bakr el Kilani and M. S. Ayoub, *Clay Lamps Found at Different Sites in Germa*, Ministry of Tourism and Antiquities (n.p., n.d.).

Knez   T. Knez, "Neue römischen Gräber in Dolensko (Unterukrain)," *Razprava* 6 (Ljubljana, 1969).

Labrousse/Mesplé   M. Labrousse and P. Mesplé, "L'Atelier de potier gallo-romain de Galane," *Gallia* 24 (1966) 161–87.

Lamboglia 1950   N. Lamboglia, *Gli scavi di Albintimilium e la cronologia della ceramica romana* (Bordighera, 1950).

Lamboglia 1952   N. Lamboglia, "Per una classificazione preliminare della ceramica campana," *Atti del Io congresso internazionale di studi liguri, 1950* (Bordighera, 1952) 139–206.

Lamboglia 1961   N. Lamboglia, "Problemi tecnici e cronologici dello scavo sottomarino al Grand Congloué," *Rivista di studi liguri* 27 (1961) 138–54.

Larese   A. Larese, *Le lucerne fittili e bronzee del Museo Concordiese di Portogruaro* (Rome, 1983).

Leibundgut 1963   A. Leibundgut, "Antike Lampen im Bernischen Historischen Museum," *Jahrbuch des Bernischen Historischen Museum in Bern* 43–44 (1963–64) 408–60.

Leibundgut 1977   A. Leibundgut, *Die römischen Lampen in der Schweiz* (Bern, 1977).

Lerat   L. Lerat, *Les Lampes antiques*, Catalogue des collections archéologiques de Besançon 1.1, *Annales littéraires de l'Université de Besançon*, ser. 2 (Paris, 1954).

Libertini 1930   G. Libertini, *Il Museo Biscari* (Milan/Rome, 1930).

Liceti   F. Liceti, *De lucernis antiquorum reconditis* (Venice, 1621).

Loeschcke 1909a   S. Loeschcke, "Keramische Funde in Haltern," *Mitteilungen des Altertumscommission für Westfalen* 5 (Münster, 1909) 103–322.

Loeschcke 1909b   S. Loeschcke, "Antike Lanternen und Lichthäuschen," *Bonner Jahrbücher des Vereines von Altertumsfreunden in Rheinlande,* Heft 118 (1909) 370–430.

Loeschcke 1919   S. Loeschcke, *Lampen aus Vindonissa, Ein Beitrag zur Geschichte von Vindonissa und des antiken Beleuchtungswesens* (Zürich, 1919).

Loeschcke/Niessen   S. Loeschcke and K. A. Niessen, *Beschreibung römischer Altertümer gesammelt von Karl Anton Niessen* 1 (Cologne, 1911; Zürich, 1919).

MonAnt   *Monumenti antichi pubblicati a cura della Accademia Nazionale dei Lincei.*

MAAR   *Memoirs of the American Academy in Rome.*

Maccario   L. Maccario, *Lucerne del Museo di Alba*, Civico Museo F. Eusebio (Alba, 1980).

Manière   G. Manière, "Un Puits funéraire de Cazères," *Gallia* 24 (1966) 101–46.

Marsa   J. Marsa, *Roman Lamps in the Prague National Museum and in Other Czechoslovak Collections*, Acta Musei Nationalis Pragae 26 (Prague, 1972).

McCann   A. M. McCann, et al., *The Roman Port and Fishery of Cosa* (Princeton, 1987).

MEFRA   *Mélanges de l'École française de Rome.*

Antiquité.
Menzel   H. Menzel, *Antike Lampen im römisch-germanischen Zentral Museum zu Mainz*, 2d ed. (Mainz, 1969).
Menzel/Elgavish   H. Menzel and J. Elgavish, "Lucerna" in *Enciclopedia dell'arte antica, classica e orientale* 4 (Rome, 1961) 707–18.
Mercando 1962   L. Mercando, *Lucerne greche e romane dell'Antiquarium Comunale* (Rome, 1962).
Mercando 1973   L. Mercando, "Lucerna" in *Enciclopedia dell'arte antica, classica e orientale,* suppl. 1 (Rome, 1973) 419–42.
Mercando 1978   L. Mercando, "Museo civico di Fano: lucerne romane," *Rivista di studi marchegiani* 1.1 (1978) 39–70.
Mikulčić   I. Mikulčić, "The West Cemetery: Excavations in 1965," in J. Wiseman (ed.) *Studies in the Antiquities of Stobi* 1 (Belgrade, 1973) 61–92.
Miltner 1929   F. Miltner, "Die antiken Lampen in Eisenstadt," *Jahreshefte des Österreichischen Archäologischen Institutes in Wien* 24 (1929) Beiblatt 144–79.
Miltner 1930   F. Miltner, "Die antiken Lampen im Klagenfurter Landesmuseum," *Jahreshefte des Österreichischen Archäologischen Institutes in Wien* 26 (1930) Beiblatt 67–114.
Miltner 1939   F. Miltner, *Forschungen in Ephesos* 4.2. *Das Cömeterium der Sieben Schläfer* (Baden/Vienna, 1937), 96–200.
Moevs 1972   M. T. Marabini Moevs, *The Roman Thin Walled Pottery from Cosa 1948–1954,* Memoirs of the American Academy in Rome 32 (Rome, 1973).
Moevs 1980   M. T. Marabini Moevs, "Italo-Megarian Ware at Cosa," "Aco in Northern Etruria: The Workshop of Cusonius at Cosa," *Memoirs of the American Academy in Rome* 34 (1980) 161–280.
Möhring   A. Möhring, "Sonderformen römischer Lampen im römisch-germanischen Museum, Köln," *Kölner Jahrbuch für Vor- und Frühgeschichte* 22 (1989) 803–73.
Montfaucon   B. de Montfaucon, *L'Antiquité expliquée et representée en figures* 5.2 (Paris, 1719).
Morel 1963   J.-P. Morel, "Notes sur la céramique étrusco-campanienne," *Mélanges d'archéologie et d'histoire del'École française de Rome* 75 (1963) 7–58.
Morel 1965   J.-P. Morel, *Céramique à vernis noir du Forum Romain et du Palatin*, Mélanges d'archéologie et d'histoire de l'École française de Rome, suppl. 3, 2 vols. (Paris, 1965).

Negev 1974   A. Negev, *The Nabataean Potter's Workshop at Oboda* (Bonn, 1974).
Negev 1986   A. Negev, *The Late Hellenistic and Early Roman Pottery of Nabataean Oboda,* Qedem (Monographs of the Institute of Archaeology, Hebrew University of Jerusalem) 22 (Jerusalem, 1986) 126–39.
Neumann   A. Neumann, *Lampen und andere Beleuchtungsgeräte aus Vindobona,* Der römische Limes in Österreich 22 (Vienna, 1967).
Nicolaou   K. Nicolaou, *The Historical Topography of Kition,* Studies in Mediterranean Archaeology 43 (Göteborg, 1976).
Noll 1937a   R. Noll, "Eine neue oberitalische Lampentöpferei," *Jahreshefte des Österreichischen Archäologischen Institutes in Wien* 30 (1937) Beiblatt 109–19.
Noll 1937b   R. Noll, "Die antiken Lampen im Landesmuseum zu Innsbruck," *Jahreshefte des Österreichischen Archäologischen Institutes in Wien* 30 (1937) Beiblatt 219–51.
NSc   *Notizie degli scavi di antichità.*
Orsi 1916   P. Orsi, "Lucania: Nocera tirenese," *Notizie degli scavi di antichità* 1916, 335–62.
Orsi 1929   P. Orsi, "Sicilia: Lipari," *Notizie degli scavi di antichità* 1929, 61–101.
Osborne 1924   A. Osborne, *Lychnos et lucerna, catalogue raisonné d'une collection des lampes en terrecuite trouvées en Egypte* (Alexandria, 1924).
Oswald 1931   F. Oswald, *Index of Potters' Stamps on Terra Sigillata "Samian Ware,"* (East Bridgford, 1931).
Oswald 1937   F. Oswald, *Index of Figure-Types on Terra Sigillata ("Samian Ware")* (Liverpool, 1936/37).
Oxé/Comfort   A. Oxé and H. Comfort, *Corpus vasorum arretinorum* (Bonn, 1968).
Oziol 1969   T.-J. Oziol, *Les Lampes* (Paris, 1969).
Oziol 1977   T.-J. Oziol, *Salamine de Chypre 7. Les Lampes du musée de Chypre* (Paris, 1977).
Oziol/Pouilloux   T.-J. Oziol and J. Pouilloux, *Salamine de Chypre 1. Les Lampes* (Paris, 1969).
Oziol/Rebuffat   T.-J. Oziol and R. Rebuffat, *Les Lampes de terre cuite en Mediterranée* (Lyon, 1987).
Paleani/Liverani   M. T. Paleani and A. R. Liverani, *Lucerne paleocristiane conservate nel Museo Oliveriano di Pesaro* I (Rome, 1984).
Panizza   P. Panizza, *Le lucerne romane della Valcomonica* (Brescia, 1984).
Passeri   G. B. Passeri, *Lucernae fictiles Musei Passerii,* 3 vols. (Pesaro, 1739–51).

PBSR   Papers of the British School at Rome.
Pavolini 1977a   C. Pavolini, "Le lucerne fittili romane del Museo Nazionale di Napoli," in A. Carandini (ed.) *L'instrumentum domesticum di Ercolano e Pompei*, Quaderni di cultura materiale 1 (Rome, 1977).
Pavolini 1977b   C. Pavolini, "Una produzione italica di lucerne: le Vogelkopflampen ad ansa traversale," *Bullettino della Commissione Archeologica Comunale di Roma* 85 (1976–77) 45–134.
Perlzweig 1961   J. Perlzweig, *Lamps of the Roman Period*, The Athenian Agora, Results of Excavations Conducted by the American School of Classical Studies in Athens vol. 7 (Princeton, 1961).
Perlzweig 1963   J. Perlzweig, *Lamps from the Athenian Agora* (Excavations of the Athenian Agora. Picture Books no. 9) (Princeton, 1963).
Piroli   T. Piroli, *Antiquités d'Herculanum* 6 (Paris, 1804–5).
Pisani Sartorio   G. Pisani Sartorio, "'Vogelkopflampen' e lucerne 'da spedizione,'" *Atti della Pontificia Accademia Romana di Archeologia. Rendiconti* 42 (1969–70) 81–93.
Pohl   G. Pohl, *Die frühchristliche Lampen vom Lorenzberg bei Epfach, Landkreis Schongau,* Schriftenreihe zur bayerischen Landesgeschichte 62 (Munich, 1962).
Polia   M. Polia, "Lucerne," *Studi miscellanei* 13 (1968, Ostia I) 81–85.
Pompéi   *Pompéi*, Catalogue of an exhibition at the Petit Palais in Paris (Paris, 1973).
Ponsich 1961   M. Ponsich, *Les Lampes romaines en terre cuite de la Maurétanie Tingitane,* Publications du Service des Antiquités du Maroc, fasc. 15 (Rabat, 1961).
Ponsich 1963   M. Ponsich, "Les Lampes romaines de la collection Ingres (Musée de Montauban)," *Revue archéologique du Centre consacrée aux antiquités nationales* 2, fasc. 5 (Jan.–Mar. 1963) 100–132.
Pontiroli   G. Pontiroli, *Lucerne antiche dei musei di Cremona* (Milan, 1980).
Provoost 1970   A. Provoost, "Les Lampes à récipient allongé trouvées dans les catacombes romaines. Essai de classification typologique," *Bulletin de l'Institut Historique Belge de Rome* 41 (1970) 14–55.
Provoost 1976a   A. Provoost, "Les Lampes en terre cuite. Introduction et essai de typologie général avec des détails concernant les lampes trouvées en Italie," *Antiquité classique* 45, no. 34 (1976) 5–39.
Provoost 1976b   A. Provoost, "Les Lampes antiques en terre cuite. Les Lampes-medaillon à réservoir circulaire," *Antiquité classique* 45, no. 34 (1976) 550–86.
Pucci   G. Pucci, "La produzione della ceramica arretina. Note sull'"industria" nella prima età imperiale romana," *Dialoghi di archeologia* 7 (1973) 255–93.
RA   *Revue archéologique.*
Radt   W. Radt, "Lampen und Beleuchtung in der Antike," *Antike Welt* 17.1 (1986) 40–58.
RAEst   *Revue archéologique de l'Est et du Centre-Est.*
RE   Pauly-Wissowa, *Real-Encyclopädie der klassischen Altertumswissenschaft* 13.2 (1927) 1566–1613 s.v. "Lucerna" (Hug).
RendPontAcc   *Atti della Pontificia Accademia Romana di Archeologia. Rendiconti.*
Richardson 1957   L. Richardson, jr, "Cosa and Rome, Comitium and Curia," *Archaeology* 10 (1957) 49–55.
Righini   V. Righini, "Le lucerne ellenistiche e romane di Faenza e del territorio faentino," *Studi faentini in memoria di Mons. Giuseppe Rossini* (Faenza, 1966), 165–90.
Robins   F. W. Robins, *The Story of the Lamp (and the Candle)* (London/New York, 1939, repr. 1970).
Robinson, D. M.   D. M. Robinson, "Terracottas, Lamps, and Coins," *Excavations at Olynthus* 14 (Baltimore, 1952) 330–402.
Robinson, H. S.   H. S. Robinson, *Pottery of the Roman Period: Chronology*, The Athenian Agora, Results of Excavations Conducted by the American School of Classical Studies at Athens vol. 5 (Princeton, 1959).
Rolland 1956a   H. Rolland, *Fouilles de Glanum 1947–1956* (Paris, 1956).
Rolland 1956b   H. Rolland, *Fouilles de St. Blaise (Bouches-du-Rhône) 1951–1956* (Paris, 1956).
RömMitt   *Mitteilungen des Deutschen Archäologischen Instituts, Römische Abteilung.*
Rosenthal-Heginbottom   R. Rosenthal-Heginbottom, *Römische Bildlampen aus östlichen Werkstätten* (Wiesbaden, 1981).
Rosenthal/Sivan   R. Rosenthal and R. Sivan, *Ancient Lamps in the Schloessinger Collection*, Qedem (Monographs of the Institute of Archaeology, Hebrew University of Jerusalem) 8 (Jerusalem, 1978).
Roux/Barré   H. Roux and L. Barré, *Herculanum et Pompéi,* vol. 7 (Paris, 1840).
Salomonson 1968   J. W. Salomonson, "Études sur la céramique romaine d'Afrique: Sigillée claire et céramique commune de Henchir el Ouiba (Raqqada) en Tunisie centrale," *Bulletin antieke Beschav-*

ing. Annual Papers on Classical Archaeology 43 (1968) 80–145.
Salomonson 1969   J. W. Salomonson, "Spätrömische rote Tonware mit Reliefverzierung aus nordafrikanischen Werkstätten," *Bulletin antieke Beschaving. Annual Papers on Classical Archaeology* 44 (1969) 4–109.
Salone   C. Salone, "Lucerne," *Studi miscellanei* 21 (1973, *Ostia III*) 395–404.
Santangeli Valenzani   R. Santangeli Valenzani, "Suppellettile da illuminazione: Lucerne," *Settefinistre. Una villa schiavistica nell'Etruria romana* 3, ed. A. Ricci (Modena, 1985), 212–15.
Sapelli   M. Sapelli, *Lucerne fittili delle civiche raccolte archeologiche,* Rassegna di studi del civico museo archeologico e del civico gabinetto numismatico di Milano, suppl. 2 (Milan, 1979).
Scheibler   I. Scheibler, *Griechische Lampen*, Kerameikos, Ergebnis der Ausgrabungen 11 (Berlin, 1976).
Scott 1969   R. T. Scott, "The Arx of Cosa, 1965–1968," *American Journal of Archaeology* 73 (1969), 245.
Scott 1971   R. T. Scott, Excavations at Cosa, 1969–1970: The Houses," *American Journal of Archaeology* 75 (1971), 213.
Scrofani   G. Scrofani, "Nuove testimonianze archeologiche dal territorio di S. Croce Camerina," *Sicilia archeologica* nos. 18–20 (June–December 1972), 101–110.
Shepard   A. O. Shepard, *Ceramics for the Archaeologist* (Washington, D.C., 1956, rev. ed. 1963).
Shier   L. A. Shier, *Terracotta Lamps from Karanis, Egypt: Excavations of the University of Michigan* (Ann Arbor, Michigan, 1978).
Sidebotham   S. Sidebotham, "Lamps from Carthage in the Kelsey Museum," in *Excavations at Carthage Conducted by the University of Michigan 1975*, 2 (Ann Arbor, Michigan, 1978), 217–38.
Siebert   G. Siebert, *Lampes corinthiennes et imitations au Musée Nationale d'Athènes* (Athens, 1966).
Skinkel-Taupin   C. Skinkel-Taupin, *Les Lampes en terre cuite de la Mediterranée grecque et romaine* (Brussels, 1980).
Smith   R. H. Smith, "The Household Lamps of Palestine," *The Biblical Archaeologist* 27–28 (1964–65) 2–31, 101–24; 29 (1966) 2–27.
Sotgiu   G. Sotgiu, *Iscrizioni latine della Sardegna* 2.1 "Lucerne," (Padua, 1968).
Stone   S. C. Stone, "Roman Pottery from Morgantina in Sicily," 2 vols. (Princeton, 1981), Dissertation. University Microfilms, Ann Arbor, Michigan.
Sussman   V. Sussman, *Ornamental Jewish Oil Lamps* (Jerusalem, 1972).
Szentléleky   T. Szentléleky, trans. Arpád Debreceni and D. M. Bailey, *Ancient Lamps*, (Amsterdam/Budapest, 1969).
Taylor   D. M. Taylor, "Cosa: Black Glaze Pottery," *Memoirs of the American Academy in Rome* 25 (Rome, 1957) 65–193.
Thompson   H. A. Thompson, "Terracotta Lamps," *Hesperia* 2 (1933) 195–215.
Thouvenot   R. Thouvenot, "Lampes en terre cuite," *Publications du service des antiquités du Maroc* 2 (1954) 113–25.
Toutain   J. Toutain, "Lucerna, lychnus," in C. Daremberg and E. Saglio (eds.), *Dictionnaire des antiquités grecques et romaines* 3 (Paris, 1904) 1320–39.
Travagli Visser   A. Travagli Visser, "Le lucerne del Museo Schifanoia," *Bollettino annuale dei musei ferraresi* 2 (1972) 115–36.
Vegas 1966   M. Vegas, "Die römischen Lampen von Neuss," *Novaesium* 2, Limesforschungen: Studien zur Organisation der römischen Reichsgrenze an Rhein und Donau, Band 7 (Berlin, 1966) 63–127.
Vegas 1968   M. Vegas, "Römische Keramik von Gabii (Latium)," *Bonner Jahrbücher des Rheinischen Landesmuseums in Bonn* 168 (1968) 13–55.
Vermaseren/van Essen   M. J. Vermaseren and C. C. van Essen, *The Excavations in the Mithraeum of the Church of Santa Prisca in Rome* (Leiden, 1965).
Vertet   H. Vertet, *Recherches sur les techniques de fabrication de lampes en terre cuite du centre de la Gaule* (Avignon, 1983).
Vessberg   O. Vessberg, "Hellenistic and Roman Lamps in Cyprus," *Opuscula atheniensia* 1 (Lund, 1953) 115–29.
Vikić-Belančić 1971   B. Vikić-Belančić, "Antike Lampensammlung in archäologischen Museum zu Zagreb," *Vjesnik* 3, 3rd ser., vol. 5 (Zagreb, 1971) 97–182.
Vikić-Belančić 1972–73   B. Vikić-Belančić, "Beitrag zur Erforschung 1972–73 des antiken Ansiedlungs Komplexes in Varazdinske Toplice," *Vjesnik* 3, 3rd ser., vols. 6–7 (Zagreb, 1972–73) 127–32.
Waagé 1934   F. O. Waagé, "Lamps," in G. W. Elderkin (ed.), *Antioch-on-the-Orontes* 1 (Princeton, 1934) 58–67.
Waagé 1941   F. O. Waagé, "Lamps," in R. Stillwell (ed.), *Antioch-on-the-Orontes* 3 (Princeton, 1941) 55–82.

Waldhauer   O. F. Waldhauer, *Die antiken Tonlampen, Kaiserliche Ermitage* (St. Petersburg, 1914, repr. 1976).

Wallis   G. H. Wallis, Nottingham (England) Museum and Art Gallery, *Illustrated Catalogue of Classical Antiquities from the Site of the Temple of Diana, Nemi, Italy* (Nottingham, 1893).

Walters   H. B. Walters, *Catalogue of the Greek and Roman Lamps in the British Museum* (London, 1914).

Webster   T. B. L. Webster, "Monuments Illustrating New Comedy," 2d ed., *Bulletin of the University of London Institute of Classical Studies,* suppl. 24 (1969).

Will 1956   E. L. Will, "Les Amphores de Sestius," *Revue archéologique de l'Est et du Centre-Est* 7 (1956) 224–44.

Will 1979   E. L. Will, "The Sestius Amphoras: A Reappraisal," *Journal of Field Archaeology* 6 (1979) 339–50.

Williams   H. Williams, *Kenchreai, Eastern Port of Corinth 5. The Lamps* (Leiden, 1981).

Wollmann 1917   H. Wollmann, "Retiarier-Darstellungen auf römischen Tonlampen," *Mitteilungen des Deutschen Archäologischen Instituts, Römische Abteilung* 32 (1917) 147–67.

Wollmann 1929   H. Wollmann, "Antike römische taschenspieler Lampen," *Mitteilungen des Deutschen Archäologischen Instituts, Römische Abteilung* 44 (1929) 87–90.

Wollmann 1930a   H. Wollmann, "Eine suditalische Tonlampe mit dem Abdruck eines geschnittenes Steines," *Mitteilungen des Deutschen Archäologischen Instituts, Römische Abteilung* 45 (1930) 29–32.

Wollmann 1930b   H. Wollmann, "Defixus in morsus ursorum et spongias retiariorum," *Mitteilungen des Deutschen Archäologischen Instituts, Römische Abteilung* 45 (1930) 227–33.

Zaccaria Ruggiu 1973   A. Zaccaria Ruggiu, "Lucerne," in A. Frova (ed.), *Scavi di Luni* 1 (Rome, 1973), 482–502.

Zaccaria Ruggiu 1977   A. Zaccaria Ruggiu, "Lucerne," in A. Frova (ed.), *Scavi di Luni* 2 (Rome, 1977), 290–304.

Zaccaria Ruggiu 1980   A. Zaccaria Ruggiu, *Le lucerne fittili del Museo Civico di Treviso* (Rome, 1980).

THE AMERICAN ACADEMY IN ROME is a center for the study and practice of the fine arts and for advanced research in the humanities. Founded in 1894, the Academy was chartered by an act of Congress as a private institution in 1905 in recognition of its singular contribution to America's cultural and intellectual life. The Academy's central purpose is its fellowship program. Each year, through a national competition, the Academy awards approximately thirty Rome Prize Fellowships in architecture, design arts, landscape architecture, literature, musical composition, painting, sculpture, visual arts, classical studies, archaeology, history of art, modern Italian studies, and postclassical humanistic studies. These fellowships provide the Rome Prize winners with a stipend, travel funds, room and board, and a study or studio in which to pursue independent work for six months to two years at the Academy's eleven-acre site on the Janiculum Hill. Distinguished professionals are also invited to live and work at the Academy as Residents. Since its founding, the Academy has awarded approximately one thousand fellowships and residencies. The Academy also maintains a research library with 110,000 volumes, representing one of the city's principal scholarly resources in classical archaeology and Roman topography. Exhibitions, concerts, lectures, and symposia given by Fellows, Residents, and invited guests draw international audiences to the Academy, strengthening ties between the American, Italian, and other European cultural and scholarly communities. The Academy is supported by gifts and grants from individuals, colleges and universities, foundations, corporations, and the National Endowments for the Arts and the Humanities. The Academy sponsors two series of publications: the *Memoirs* and *Papers and Monographs.*